C000064199

The Anwar-I-Suhaili: Or Lights Of Canopus, Commonly Known As Kalilah And Damnah

Arthur N. Wollaston

In the interest of creating a more extensive selection of rare historical book reprints, we have chosen to reproduce this title even though it may possibly have occasional imperfections such as missing and blurred pages, missing text, poor pictures, markings, dark backgrounds and other reproduction issues beyond our control. Because this work is culturally important, we have made it available as a part of our commitment to protecting, preserving and promoting the world's literature. Thank you for your understanding.

THE
ANWÁR-I-SUHAILÍ

OR

LIGHTS OF CANOPUS

COMMONLY KNOWN AS KALÍLAH AND DAMNAH

BEING AN ADAPTATION BY

MULLÁ HUSAIN BIN 'ALÍ AL WÁÏ'Z-AL-KÁSHIFÍ

OF

THE FABLES OF BÍDPÁÍ

TRANSLATED FROM THE PERSIAN

BY

ARTHUR N. WOLLASTON, M.R.A.S.

H.M. INDIAN (HOME) SERVICE

اگر گوش دارد خداوند هوش   ازینسان سخنها خوش آید بگوش

LONDON:
WM. H. ALLEN & CO., 13 WATERLOO PLACE, S.W.
Publishers to the India Office.
MDCCCLXXVII.

All rights reserved.

THE

ANWÁR-I-SUHAILÍ.

TO

MAJOR-GENERAL SIR HENRY CRESWICKE RAWLINSON,

K.C.B., D.C.L.

MEMBER OF THE COUNCIL OF THE SECRETARY OF STATE FOR
INDIA, AND LATE ENVOY EXTRAORDINARY AND MINISTER
PLENIPOTENTIARY AT THE COURT OF PERSIA ;

SIR JOHN WILLIAM KAYE,

K.C.S.I., F.R.S.

LATE SECRETARY POLITICAL AND SECRET
DEPARTMENT, INDIA OFFICE ;

AND

MAJOR-GENERAL SIR FREDERIC JOHN GOLDSMID,

K.C.S.I., C.B.

FOR MANY YEARS PUBLICLY EMPLOYED IN PERSIA
AND ADJACENT COUNTRIES ;

Is Dedicated a Work

WHICH OWES ITS EXISTENCE TO THE

KIND ENCOURAGEMENT RECEIVED AT THEIR HANDS

BY THEIR HUMBLE SERVANT

THE TRANSLATOR.

CONTENTS.

BOOK II.

BOOK III.

BOOK IV.

BOOK IX.

BOOK X.

BOOK XI.

BOOK XII.

BOOK XIII.

BOOK XIV.

TRANSLATOR'S PREFACE.

HE collection of Fables known throughout India under the name of the Anwár-i-Suhailí is generally supposed to take its origin from the Sanskrit, in which language tales of a similar description have been handed down from the remote ages of antiquity. Like most works of such a nature, its history cannot be traced with certainty; even when we come to the comparatively later times of Bídpáí or Pílpáí, the reputed author of the Fables which bear his name, who is supposed to have flourished about 300 years B.C., the mist of obscurity is not removed, and indeed it is matter of conjecture whether such an individual ever existed. Be this as it may, the tradition as handed down in the East is thus given by M. Silvestre de Sacy in his preface to 'Calila et Dimna, ou Fables de Bidpai en Arabe':

"Alexander, after having subdued the Kings of the West, turned his armies towards the East. He triumphed over all the sovereigns of Persia, and other countries, who dared to oppose him. In his march to enter the empire of China, he summoned the Prince, who then reigned over India, named Four, or, according to some manuscripts, Fourek, to recognise his authority and render him homage. Four, instead of obeying him, prepared for war, and took every fitting measure to assure his independence. Alexander, who had hitherto met with but feeble resistance, instituted formidable preparations against the King of India, fearing to receive on this occasion any check which would tarnish the glory of his arms; the Indian elephants especially filled him with great dread. He accordingly resolved to have recourse to stratagem. After having consulted the astrologers as to the choice of a day most favourable to the execution of his designs, he caused the most skilful workmen who followed his army to make some hollow bronze figures of horses and cavaliers : filling the interior of them with naphtha and sulphur, he ordered that they should be clothed with harness and trappings and placed in the first rank of his army, and that at the moment of engaging in fight the inflammable materials which they contained should be lighted. The day chosen for this proceeding having arrived, Alexander sent a fresh summons to the Indian chief, who obeyed it no more than at first, and the two armies advanced against one another. Four had placed his elephants in the first line, while Alexander's people, on their part, caused the figures of bronze, which had been ignited, to be advanced. The elephants had no sooner seized these with their trunks, than feeling themselves burnt, they cast to the ground those who rode them, and took to flight, treading under foot and crushing all those whom they met. Alexander in loud tones summoned Four to single combat. The Indian monarch accepted the challenge, and at once presented himself on the field of battle. The two champions fought the greater part of the day, without victory declaring for either one or other. Alexander commenced to despair of success, when his army, under his orders, raised a loud cry. The Indian king, thinking that his troops were suddenly attacked by the forces of the enemy issuing from an ambuscade, turned round to see what it was, while Alexander, profiting by the moment, dealt him a blow which knocked him off his horse,—with a second blow he stretched him dead. The Indian army then recommenced the fight, fully determined to perish ; however, again defeated, they yielded to the promises of Alexander. The victor, after having set the affairs of the country in order, and made over the government to one of his officers, whom he made king in the place of Four, quitted India to carry out the execution of his projects. Scarce had he departed when the Indians shook off the yoke which he had imposed upon them, and chose as their sovereign a person of the royal race, named Dabschélim.

"When Dabschélim found himself established on the throne, fortune having favoured him in all his undertakings, he abandoned himself to his passions, and displayed boundless tyranny towards his subjects. There was at that time in the states of Dabschélim, a Brahman named Bídpáí, who enjoyed a great reputation for wisdom, and whom every one consulted on important occasions. This philosopher, desirous of bringing back to sentiments of justice and humanity the Prince, whom the pride of dominion had led astray, assembled his disciples in order to deliberate with them as to the means fitting to be adopted to gain the end which he proposed. He represented to them that it was their duty and their interest to open the King's eyes to the vices of his administration, and to convince him that weakness, aided by clever stratagem, could succeed where force and violence would fail. He cited to them the fable of the Frogs who managed by aid of the Birds to exact vengeance from the Elephant who trampled them under foot.

"Bídpáí's disciples all excused themselves from giving their advice, and also represented to the philosopher the dangers to which the execution of his rash enterprise would expose him. Bídpáí declared to them that he would not desist, for any reason whatever, from his design, but that he would go and find the King, and represent matters to him, and he recommended them to join him again when they should learn that he was returned from Court : after that he dismissed them.

"Bídpái then presented himself to the King. Admitted to an audience, he saluted him, and remained silent. Dabschélim astonished at this silence, did not doubt but that the philosopher had some important affair to communicate to him. Addressing him first, he invited him to disclose the subject for which he had come, but did not leave him in ignorance, that if he interfered in affairs which kings ought to reserve to themselves, his bold temerity would not fail to be punished. The philosopher, after having demanded and obtained the King's permission to speak with openness, commenced by pointing out to him the qualities which distinguish man from other animals,—such as wisdom, temperance, reason, and justice,—qualities which include every virtue, and which elevate those in whom they are united, above all the ill chances of fortune. He then said that if he had hesitated to open his lips, it was in fact owing to the respectful fear with which the King's presence inspired him, seeing that sages recommended nothing so much as silence, but nevertheless he was about to make use of the liberty which the King had allowed him. Then, entering upon the subject, he reproached Dabschélim with not imitating the virtues of his ancestors, whose power he had inherited, and with imposing upon his subjects, on the contrary, the yoke of tyranny ; he then exhorted him to change his conduct. Dabschélim, mad with rage, warmly reproached him for his rashness, and ordered him to be crucified ; but no sooner had they seized the philosopher to execute the King's order, than the latter changing his plan, revoked his decree and contented himself with casting Bídpái into a dungeon. On this news the disciples of the Brahman dispersed, and sought safety in far countries. A long space of time elapsed ere Dabschélim called Bídpái to mind, or any one dared mention, in the King's presence, the name of the philosopher. One night, however, when the Prince could get no sleep, he reflected on the celestial motions, and the system of the universe. When he sought in vain to solve some problem relative to the revolution of the stars, he remembered Bídpái, and repented of the injustice he had committed in regard to him. Immediately he sent to seek him, and ordered him to repeat all he had said on the former occasion. Bídpái, after protesting as to the purity of his intentions, obeyed ; while Dabschélim, having listened to him with attention and signs of repentance, caused his bonds to be taken off him, and declared that he would intrust to him the administration of the empire. Bídpái accepted this charge with reluctance. The news of his elevation was no sooner spread abroad than his disciples hastened to return from their voluntary banishment to Dabschélim's kingdom, and established there a perpetual *fête* in memory of the happy change which had taken place in the King's conduct.

"Bídpái's administration produced most happy results for the kingdom and the sovereign, and the virtues of Dabschélim caused the whole of the Kings of India to submit to him, all anxious to recognise his supremacy. As regards Bídpái, having assembled his disciples, he informed them of the motives which had induced him to risk his life in the interest of the kingdom, and the care of his own reputation; and also communicated to them that the King had charged him to compose a book, which should contain the most important precepts of wisdom. He solicited each of them to write on any subject they might choose, and to submit to him their labours. This they promised to do. ·

"Now Dabschélim, when he found himself established on his throne, and when his good conduct had caused all his enemies to submit to him, aspired to a different kind of glory. The kings who had gone before him had all of them attached their names to some works composed by the sages and philosophers of their time: desirous of leaving a like monument of his reign, he found no one save Bídpáí who could fulfil his wish. Summoning the latter to his presence, he communicated to him his own intentions, and begged him to busy himself without delay in the composition of a work which, while appearing solely destined to form the manners of individuals, should be nevertheless designed to teach kings how they ought to govern, in order to assure the obedience and fidelity of their subjects. He at the same time explained to the Brahman his wish that in this composition, the grave precepts of morality, and the austere lessons of wisdom, might be mingled with amusing stories, and entertaining anecdotes. At the request of the Brahman the King allowed him a period of one year to carry this work into execution, and guaranteed him the necessary funds for the undertaking.

"Bídpáí first thought to assemble his disciples and deliberate with them as to the way which should be adopted to carry out, to the satisfaction of the King, the plan which his Majesty had conceived: but he was not long in recognising that he should abandon all extraneous assistance, and himself undertake the work, selecting one of his disciples as his secretary. Having then laid in a supply of paper, and of food sufficient for the subsistence of himself and his secretary for a year, he shut himself up with the latter in a room, the access to which was forbidden to any one else. There the philosopher, occupying himself without relaxation on the work which he had undertaken, dictated to his disciple, and then read over what the latter had written. The work was executed in this manner, and composed of fourteen books, each of which contained a question and an answer to the same. All the books were then collected into a single work, to which Bídpáí gave the name of 'Calila and Dimna.' Bídpáí introduced in this volume domestic and wild animals, and birds, so that the majority of readers should find thereby amusement and agreeable diversion, while men of sense might deduce therefrom matter of mature reflection. He wished to collect therein all that could be useful to mankind, in regard to the regulation of their conduct, the administration of their affairs, and the ordering of their family,—in a word, all that concerns their happiness in this world and the next; and that they should learn therefrom to obey their sovereigns, and to protect themselves from all which it concerned their welfare to avoid.

"Bídpáí in the first book represented what happened to two friends when a spreader of false reports introduced himself into their society: he was desirous that his disciple should carry on the discourse in this book after the fashion adopted by the King, so that precepts of wisdom should be mingled therein with amusing tales. Bídpái, however, reflected that wisdom would lose all its value when associated with frivolous discourses. Nothing could be so difficult, as it appeared to him and his disciple, as to carry out the King's wish; when all at once it occurred to them to employ animals as the medium of conversation. Thereby, while the choice of personages introduced would afford subject of amusement, wisdom would be disclosed in the discourses allotted to them. This plan, accordingly, would satisfy the frivolous tastes of the ignorant and vulgar, at the same time that it would attract the attention of men of learning.

"A year passed in this manner, ere Bídpái and his disciple interrupted their work, and issued forth from their retreat. At the time fixed, the King demanded of Bídpái if he had carried out his engagement. On the Brahman replying in the affirmative, the King summoned a numerous assembly of great men and *savants* of his empire. Bídpái attended accompanied by his disciple, and there, in presence of the King and all his Court, read over his whole work, and explained to his Majesty the subject of each chapter. Dabschélim, overwhelmed with joy, told Bídpái to demand of him whatever recompense he wished. The philosopher contented himself with asking that the volume might be transcribed, as had been done in the case of the productions of the King's ancestors, and guarded with care, for fear lest it should be transported out of India, and should fall into the hands of the Persians. The King then loaded Bídpái's disciples with presents.

"Nouschiréwan,[1] having heard talk of this work 'Calila,' had no rest till he sent the physician, Barzouyéh, to India to obtain it. The latter having by dint of great skill procured it, brought it away with him on his return from India, and deposited it amongst the treasures of the Kings of Persia."

The fables of Bídpái were introduced into Persia during the reign of Núshírwán, in the middle of the sixth century, at the request of that monarch, by the physician Barzúiyah, who made a translation into Pahlawí, the dialect of the country at that period. They were subsequently turned into Arabic about the middle of the eighth century; and again rendered into Persian in the early part of the twelfth century, by Abúl Ma'áli Nasrullah of Ghuzní, whose work is generally known as 'Kalílah and Damnah.' This last formed the basis of the version which was produced at the end of the fifteenth century, by the celebrated scholar Mullá Husain bin 'Alí al Wái'z-al-Káshiff, who resided at the Court of Sháh Abúl Ghází Sultán Husain, Sovereign of Khurásán, and who named it after his patron Amír Suhailí, the generalissimo of the last-mentioned monarch.

---

[1] King of Persia, A.D. 531 to 579.

Few works of Oriental literature are held in such exceptional estimation as the Anwár-i-Suhailí, which, according to that distinguished scholar,
Sir William Jones, comprises "all the wisdom of the Eastern nations."
As an entertaining story-book, no less than an instructive classical composition, it has an interest for many Eastern peoples, which we in this
country, accustomed to the sober language of the West, cannot perhaps
altogether realise. In spite of this, however, it has appeared in no less
than twenty different languages. Apart from its inherent merit, it is a
text-book both in India and in this country, for candidates who wish to
be examined in the Persian language. Though not as a whole a difficult
work, it contains passages beyond the powers of a beginner. Help from
a Munshí, at any rate in England, is rarely obtainable ; nor are natives, as
a rule, clever in the art of explanation. On the other hand, there are not
even in London, and certainly not elsewhere in the British Isles, many
proficient European teachers to whom to refer ; while, too, some persons
may wish to pursue their studies unassisted. Recourse can, it is true,
be had to Eastwick's admirable translation, but this does not altogether
meet the requirements of the case, since his verses, beautifully as in most
instances they embody the spirit of the Persian, are too free renderings
of the original text to be of much assistance to a learner ; moreover, the
book is out of print, and not easy to procure. A want, therefore, appears
to exist, which it is hoped the present translation may supply. Designed for the use of students, not for advanced and proficient scholars,
critical remarks have been sparingly introduced, as tending rather to
embarrass than assist the beginner. A few notes will be found mostly
of an explanatory nature, where it was thought additional information,
or more elaborated description, might tend to throw light on the meaning
of the author. The remainder consist in some cases of corrections of
typographical errors in the Persian text, of a nature to mislead the
student—at other times, of confessions of ignorance on the part of the
Translator—and lastly, of acknowledgments due by him for suggestions
borrowed from Eastwick's work, to which he feels he is indebted for
many valuable hints, though in not a few instances he has not hesitated
to deviate from that scholar's renderings of passages.

Elegance of style has throughout been sacrificed to closeness of translation. Doubtless certain pages would read more agreeably to English
ears, curtailed of the many lengthy and entangled sentences, which are
characteristic of the Oriental school of thought, but in view of the idea
with which the work was undertaken, none of these could be expunged.

In order, however, to make the work as attractive as possible to the ordinary public, an illuminated edition has been prepared, which may, it is hoped, draw more general attention to a composition not less instructive or entertaining than the Fables of Æsop. Should such be the case, and any person take up the present translation merely seeking amusement, he is advised to skip the preface by Mullá Husain, a composition as dull and insipid as can well be imagined.

No attempt has been made to achieve the impossible task of conveying an idea of the beautifully - balanced and rhythmical sentences of the original Persian, or of preserving the endless *équivoques* scattered throughout its pages ; hence many passages, especially proverbs, which in the Persian are sparkling and brilliant, appear tame and heavy in English. Many of our own proverbs literally translated into a foreign language would be equally bald and meaningless.

The poetry throughout appears as prose, though for the sake of facility of reference all the stanzas are printed in a distinctive form. A metrical version, even had the Translator been qualified to attempt one, would have left the student in difficulties just when he most needed aid.

The translation having been compiled at spare moments extending over a series of years, will doubtless be found to contain mistakes which might have been avoided had a less desultory mode of work been possible. Nor can the Translator expect to have altogether escaped erroneous renderings, which are wellnigh unavoidable when, in addition to the inherent difficulties of translation, the very letters themselves give occasion to mistakes, owing to the numerous insignificant-looking dots which are scattered in every direction, and on the precise number and location of which, the meaning of the various words in a vast number of instances entirely depends. Moreover, as remarked by Keene, " it requires a more thorough knowledge than any foreigner can hope to acquire, to seize the exact meaning of all those idioms, refined similes, and distant allusions, in which the Persian language abounds,"—a remark the force of which is intensified when, as in the present instance, the " foreigner," has never enjoyed the advantage of studying the language in the country where it is spoken. But no difficulties have been intentionally shirked ; and, indeed, some renderings are so hazardous, that if any critics are prone to dispute their accuracy, the Translator can only plead that he has done his best, and say in the words of Mullá Husain, " Do not wound my soul with reproaches."

The Persian text is that edited by Colonel Ousely, edition 1851. The

Arabic quotations are in part taken from Keene's and Stewart's publications; but for by far the greater portion the Translator is indebted to the courtesy of Mírzá Nasrullah Fidai, a native gentleman at present on a visit to this country, who has been good enough to turn them into Persian. For the accuracy of the English renderings the Translator himself is responsible; but they have been subjected to a careful scrutiny on the part of Sir Frederic Goldsmid, a scholar to whom the Translator's most cordial acknowledgments are tendered for this and much other valuable aid.

Lieut.-Colonel Ross, her Majesty's Political Resident in the Persian Gulf, now on leave, has in some instances favoured the Translator with suggestions as to the renderings of difficult and obscure passages, a kindness for which the latter begs to express his warmest thanks. To Major - General Sir Henry Rawlinson, Sir John Kaye, and Dr Rost, the Librarian at the India Office, the Translator is indebted for kind encouragement in the completion of a task, which otherwise would most probably have been laid aside; while his grateful acknowledgments are due to the Secretary of State for India in Council, for liberal assistance, which has enabled him to lay the work before the public.

WESTFIELD, SURBITON, *July* 1876.

ANWÁR-I-SUHAILÍ

COMPOSED BY

MULLÁ HUSAIN BIN 'ALÍ AL WÁI'Z-AL-KÁSHIFÍ

———•———

IN THE NAME OF THE MERCIFUL AND COMPASSIONATE GOD.
MAY GOD PROSPER IT, AND BRING IT TO
A SUCCESSFUL CONCLUSION.

ANWÁR-I-SUHAILÍ.

MULLÁ HUSAIN'S PREFACE.

HE LORD, the All-wise (may His wisdom be magnified) whose joyful portion of praise and thanksgiving, according to the command, "*And there is nothing but what proclaims His praise*," flows and proceeds from the tongue of all His creatures, both high and low, and the benefits of the tables of whose endless bounty, in conformity with the firm decree, "*And bestow on each thing its existence and then guidance*," permeate and spread amongst all sections of created beings, both in heaven and earth,

O teacher of the mysteries of subtle wisdom!
Enlightener of the wise soul!
Bestower of the pearls of penetrating intelligence!
Who deckest with day the darkness of night—

in the ancient benign writings, and in the book worthy of all precedence and honour, in this manner commanded the illustrious, the prophetic asylum, the sovereign of the royal residence "*To me with God*," the reader of secrets, "*And he taught thee something thou didst not know*," the resplendent orator, "*I am the most eloquent of Arabs and Persians*,"

Muhammad! by whom everything that exists, throughout all eternity,
Is bedecked with the splendour of his name;
A lamp, the light of whose eyes is resplendent,
All mankind being illumined by his radiance.

"*May the benedictions and blessings of God be on him, and on his posterity, and on his near friends, and on such persons as follow him, and on those who end in him*," with the view of directing the students of the designs of intention, and of affording assistance to those who aim at obtaining benefit. In the following manner also he displayed to that teacher of knowledge—"*He who is firm in his knowledge*"—the way of instruction for those preparing at the school of manners, and the road of information and understanding for the pupils at the college of enterprise and search: "*Summon to the way of thy Lord with wisdom and good advice."* The purport of these auspicious words was this: "O thou who invitest people to the tables of the favours of righteousness and sincerity, and O thou who showest mankind the way to the path of the affairs of both this life and the next, summon my servants by the road of wisdom to the right direction, and by means of sound admonition turn to the garden of happiness, from following after lust, those who worship me; for rebellious spirits cannot be rendered obedient, save with the thongs of wisdom, nor can self-satisfied dispositions be corrected except by the admonitions of probity: *' If thou hadst been harsh and cruel-hearted, assuredly they would have been scattered.'*

Every tamer of horses, who renders his wild steed obedient,
Uses with discretion the unaccustomed girth;
When measures are too violent, the steed becomes ungovernable,
And if want of energy be displayed, the colt is rendered void of spirit.

"Just as it is impossible to render untamed colts obedient without paying regard to the minutiæ of kindness, so also will it be impracticable, without the aid of the arrangements of wisdom, to bring into submission the sensual feelings of mankind at large, who, the powers of evil and ferocity being predominant in their dispositions, without let or hindrance have grazed in the pasture, *' Let them be that they may eat and become happy,'* and have paid no heed to the bridle of the prohibition against what is wrong, or to the thong of the injunction to act rightly."

By wisdom every difficulty can be solved,
By wisdom the heart can accomplish its object.

"He who has obtained wisdom, without doubt has obtained a great good."

Seek wisdom, and learn magnanimity,
That men may see you improve from day to day.

Now the good advice treated of in this invitation is termed a discourse, of such a nature that it is not concealed from the hearer, that it is sincere admonition, and pure kindness and consideration. It has been said that good advice is an universal discourse, from which each listener can derive benefit, according to his ability and power: witness the teaching of the Kurán and the precepts of that sacred book, which is a compilation relating to all matters, both external and internal, comprehending the mysteries of this world and the next, every reader and hearer thereof sharing, in his own degree, its language and purport: *"To that the speaker alludes."*

The spring season of its excellence keeps the heart and soul verdant:
Through its colour (it appeals to) the men of the world: with its perfume (it touches) the votaries of religion.

Now this kind of discourse was neither prevalent nor customary amongst any of the greatest prophets before our prophet (may the highest blessing and salutation be upon him); nay, more, it is peculiar to Muhammad, *as in allusion to this he (may the blessing and peace of God be upon him) said,* "I have found all the *words which were to be found;"* and by reason that true obedience is the heir of perfect intimacy (with God), and the source of the attestation of kinship (with Him), assuredly the natures of the select throng of His illustrious people, who are distinguished with the mark, " *Ye were the best people that have proceeded from mankind,*" have become the receptacles of the light of the resplendent beams of

His universality, the borrowing of which may proceed from the illumined corner of that illustrious Being's boundless gift of prophecy; for which reason they deem such to be the perfect discourse, wherein the eyes of superficial observers derive benefit from the contemplation of the beauty of its mystical meanings, and are enlightened by its language and speech, while the nostrils also of the inner man are perfumed with the sweet odours of the truths and subtilties, which become manifest from beneath the plain signification; so that every one, according to his capacity, partakes of the tables of its boundless excellence.

No searcher leaves that door without obtaining his object.

Now, from the scope of these prefatory remarks, it will be understood that the more the face of every word is adorned with the down and mole of wisdom, and the cheek of every exhortation with the ruddiness of universality, the more will the heart of its sincere admirers possess a liking for the enchantments of its splendour.

> Whoever is fairest amongst the lovely,
> On her will the affections be placed.

Now, amongst all the works, the edifice of whose composition, and of all the books, the foundation of whose construction is fixed upon the propositions of wisdom, and includes the benedictions of advice, there is the compilation "Kalílah and Damnah," which the wise men of Hind have completed in a peculiar manner, and the general arrangements of which the Brahmans, distinguished for wisdom, have accomplished in a certain method, mingling together admonition, wisdom, amusement, and humour.

By reason of the tendency of most natures thereto, the composition of the discourses is formed of anecdotes, the tales and narratives being uttered by the mouths of animals, beasts, and birds, and a variety of advantageous maxims and auspicious exhortations being mingled together in the contents thereof, so that the wise may derive profit from perusing it, while the ignorant may read it for amusement and relaxation. Its lessons also are easy for the instructor, no less than the student to retain. In pure truth, that book, abounding in wisdom, is a garden, the trees of whose mysteries are illumined with the flowers, "*And therein there is for you something which your souls shall desire and your eyes shall revel in,*" and the sides of whose rose-beds are perfumed and scented with the breezes, "*A thing which neither eye hath seen nor ear heard.*"

> Every saying therein is the blossom in a garden,
> More brilliant than a fire-fly.
> Its language resembles the freshness of youth;
> Its mysteries are indicative of the water of life.

The spring of that fountain of truth and mystical meaning is of such a nature that, from its first appearance till the present time, in every tongue, it has afforded benefit to students in the court of desire, and to intelligent persons in the assembly of prosperity. The robe of the following beautiful verses is a lovely and worthy dress of honour upon the exalted stature of this book:

> In appearance like a glorious robe, the fringe of happiness,
> Its contents the seal of auspiciousness, the signet of fortune:
> The rosy cheeks of its verses are full of amorous glances and blandishments,
> The musky ringlets of its language entwine and encircle one another:
> From its perfect speeches, the light of resplendent knowledge
> Appears clear, like the mysteries of divine science in the bosom of the pious.

The enlightened sage Bídpáí, the Brahman, compiled this book in the Hindí tongue, in the name of the world-adorning king, Dábishlím of Hind, who was ruler of several of the kingdoms of Hindústán: may be, for this reason, in the commencement of the preface somewhat is inscribed with the pen of explanation. The aforesaid sage has placed the edifice of his words upon the basis of exhortation, which should be of service to kings in punishing their subjects, in spreading the carpet of justice and commiseration, in fostering and assisting the chiefs of the state, and in restraining and repressing the enemies of the kingdom.˙ Dábishlím having made this book the high altar of his desires, and the pillar of his wishes, with the key of the perusal thereof invariably opened the doors of the solution of difficulties, and the unravelling of intricacies. Now this precious gem in his time was concealed from the sight of every one, like a royal pearl in the recess of its shell; or like a ruby of Badakhshán, which does not show its face from the bottom of the mine save after a thousand agonies. After him, too, all his descendants and offspring, who sat on the throne of sovereignty in his stead, followed that same line of conduct, and strove to conceal it. In spite of all their efforts the breeze of the virtues of that book rendered the quarters of the world fragrant, like the outskirts of a garden, and the musk-scattering bag of its excellencies scented with amber the nostrils of the seekers after the odours of its annals and traditions.

> Merit is like musk, which although remaining concealed,
> Through the diffusion of its perfume, the nostrils are apprised thereof.
> The face of the sun cannot be besmeared with clay;
> From time to time the effect of its light increases.

Till in the time of Kasra Núshírwán this tradition was prevalent, that in the treasuries of the kings of Hindústán was a book, containing a collection of conversations between beasts, animals, birds, reptiles, and wild creatures, whatever concerns monarchs in regard to government and caution, and is of service to rulers of the land, relative to the observance of the regulations of sovereignty, being recounted in the folds of its pages; it might be considered the capital stock of all admonition and the medium of every benefit. Núshírwán, from the rain of whose beneficence the shrubs on the brink of justice became verdant, and from the drops of the showers of whose benevolence the freshness of the rose-garden of the expanse of equity was áugmented,

> The world was adorned with his equity,
> Which removed away the dust of injustice—

conceived a violent desire and an irrepressible inclination to peruse this work. The physician Barzúiyah, who was foremost of the doctors of Fárs, at the request of Núshírwán, set out for Hindústán and remained there a long time. With a variety of contrivances and devices having got fast hold of that book, he took possession thereof. After translating the Hindí words into the Pahlawí dialect, which in that day was the language of the kings of Persia, he placed it at the service of Núshírwán. Having at the region of acceptance obtained the honour of approbation, it reached the highest round of the ladder of perfect dignity in the sight of the king, the edifice of whose affairs as regards the manifest traces of justice and kindness, the conquering of cities, and the subjugation of the hearts of mankind, was based on the perusal of that work. After Núshírwán the kings of Persia also[1] used their utmost endeavours to honour and protect it, till the

---

[1] نیز in the Persian text is a misprint for نیر.

time that the Second Khalífah of the 'Abbásís Abú Ja'far Mansúr bin Muhammad bin 'Alí bin 'Abdullah bin 'Abbás (may the peace of God be upon him),
hearing tidings of that book, displayed the most ardent inward desire to
become possessed thereof. Having, with arts of finesse, acquired a Pahlawí copy,
he commanded Imám Abúl Hasan 'Abdullah bin Mukanna', who was the most
learned of his race, to translate the whole of it from the Pahlawí into Arabic.
Constantly perusing it, he laid the basis of his state orders, and the structure of
the decrees of justice and clemency, upon the advice and precepts therein. On
another occasion he commanded Abúl Hasan Nasr bin Ahmad Sámání, one of
the learned men of his time, to transcribe the said copy from the Arabic tongue
into the Persian dialect, and Rúdagí the poet, according to the orders of the
king, strung it in verse. Once more Abúl Muzaffar Bahrám Sháh bin Sultán
Masa'úd, a descendant of Sultán Mahmúd Ghází Ghaznawí, who is praised by
the learned Sanáí, issued an edict to the most eloquent of the eloquent, and the
most perfect of orators, Abúl Ma'áli Nasrullah bin Muhammad bin Al Hamíd
(may God rest his soul and increase his triumph in the abodes of Paradise),
that he should make a translation from the copy of Ibn Mukanna'; and this
book, now known as "Kalílah and Damnah," is the translation of our aforesaid
lord. In truth, its expressions are beautiful, like sweet life, and fresh as it
were tinted coral, while its enchanting words resemble the glances of honey-
lipped, lust-exciting beauties, and its soul-exhilarating mystic meanings are like
the waists of smooth-faced charmers.

Its letters, like the ringlets of the idols of Chigil,[1]
Are altogether the abode of the soul, and the dwelling of the heart :
Its mysticisms, from beneath the letters in black,
Shine forth like the sun, and glitter like the moon.

Its blackness, of which the collyrium of the pearls of meaning is a symbol,
might be given a place upon the whiteness of the pages of sight; while upon its
paper, of which the morning dawn of joy is an emblem, might be placed the
blackness of the world-seeing eye.

It is fit that the writer in the palace of eternity should inscribe
The black type of his composition upon the paper of the eyes of the Húrí.

Notwithstanding that those who sit on the throne at the court of style, are
unanimous in praising the excellence of its language, and commending the eloquence of its composition,

"Assuredly the speech is that which Hazám spoke ; "

yet, by reason of the adoption of strange idioms, and of language immoderately
overlaid with the beauties of Arabic expressions, coupled with excessive use of
metaphors and allegories of various kinds, added to glowing language and pro-
lixity in words and obscurity in expression, the mind of the hearer is unable to
derive any pleasure from the aim of the book, or to comprehend the object of its
design : the judgment, also, of the reader cannot discriminate between the commencement of the tales and the conclusion, nor distinguish the introduction of the
speeches from the end thereof. Now this state of things must assuredly be the
cause of irksomeness, and the occasion of weariness to the reader or listener, particularly in the present easy-going days, when the disposition of its sons is luxurious to such a degree, that they desire to understand the meaning, without its

---

[1] A city in Turkistán famous for its beauties.

being arrayed with the marriage-decoration of language; how much more so
when, as regards some of the words, they are in need of examining works on
dialect, and of investigating treatises containing the explanation of meanings? On
this account it seemed probable that a book so precious would become neglected
and abandoned, and the inhabitants of the world remain deprived and bereft
of any share in its benefits; accordingly, at this time his Majesty, the seat
of authority, whose pure-minded soul includes all perfections, and whose exalted
nature has risen from the horizon of excellence and mystical meanings, the mighty
Lord who, notwithstanding his intimacy with his Majesty the Sultán of the age,
and the Emperor of the period, the spreader of the carpet of security and safety,
the diffuser of the signs of tenderness and compassion, the sun of the summits of
imperial dignity and monarchy, the Jupiter of the constellation of sovereignty
and rule,

> The lustre of the eyes to sovereigns, monarch of both horizons!
> Sháh Abúl Ghází Sultán Husain, (may distinction and piety be your share).

" May the High God perpetuate his kingdom and monarchy," and in spite of his
gaining approbation in the sight of the affection of his Majesty, who is the
elixir of life, shook off the dust of the worldly pomps, *" But existence in the
world is only a deceitful chattel,"* from the skirt of his exalted ambition. On the
pages of his guileless heart,

> The mystery of this five-days' fancy,
> Which the ignorant call possessions and wealth,

was not inscribed; and the purport of this auspicious speech, that

> The mole of piety looks best on the face of majesty:
> The robe of modesty appears most fitting on the stature of royalty,

he made the desire of his eyes as regards his affairs. Accordingly, he considered
that aiding the demands of the oppressed, and prospering the necessities of the
disappointed, are the means of obtaining a store for eternity; and, with reference
to the purport of this excellent saying:

> Fortune's ten days' friendship is fickle and deceitful;
> Seize the opportunity, O friend! to benefit your comrades,

he did not render himself conspicuous by slighting it. *And he is the great
Amír, the place of the collection of high excellencies, through the loftiness of his
ambition, the happy recipient of the gifts of the sole King, the regulator of the
government and religion, the Amír Shaikh Ahmad, generally known as Suhailí
(may God bestow on him, as an especial distinction, the peace of Salmán,
and the perfection of Kumail),* who, in all sincerity, is Canopus, shining from the
right hand of Yaman, and a Sun resplendent from the horizon of affection and
fidelity.

> O thou Canopus! how far do thy rays extend, where is thy horizon?
> Thy light, where'er it shines, is indicative of prosperity.

Keeping in view universal benefit to mankind, and widespread advantage to
individuals, both high and low, he issued his exalted command that this humble
servant without capacity, and this contemptible atom of but small intellectual
store, Husain bin 'Alí al Wái'z, surnamed Al Káshifí (may the High God assist
him with His hidden kindness), should be bold enough to clothe the aforesaid

work in new garments, and array in the theatre of clear expression, and in the chamber of pleasant metaphors, the beauty of its mystic tales, which were obscured and overlaid with a veil of deep words and a curtain of difficult phrases, in such a way that the eyes of every spectator should share the beauties of the bridal-chamber nymphs of its narrative, without the glance of penetration, or the penetration of sight; and that the heart of every learned person should be able to enjoy the society of those charmers of the recess of the soul, without the trouble of imagination, or the imagination of trouble.

> Thus spoke an eloquent man to me:
> " O gardener in the parterres of speech !
> In this pure heaven-like expanse,
> Display the tree of meaning in such a manner,
> That whoever eats the fruit thereof
> May say to him who exhibits it, ' O fortunate man,
> In this beautiful garden are fresh fruits,
> Each one more lovely than the other !' "

Since there was no help but to obey the edict of that incomparable being, and the saying " *Wisdom is from Yaman!* " displayed itself in the horizon of the light of Canopus,

> Since wisdom is from Yaman, according to the saying of the Arab chief,
> What wonder if it should be visible in the light of Canopus?

after praying for success and asking permission, I busied myself in this matter, and that which proceeded from the invisible world on the language of the pen, and the pen of language, was indelibly inscribed. Now it should be known that the basis of the work " Kalílah and Damnah " is laid upon practical wisdom, and this latter is indicative of a knowledge of the workings of the will, and the natural actions of the human race, in such a manner as to conduce to the settlement of their affairs both in this world and the next, and to lead them to arrive at the perfection towards which they are tending. This sort of wisdom is, in the first place, divided into two kinds, one relating to the individual alone, the second in regard to the world at large : the former concerning every person singly, intimacy with another not being admissible, is termed the " correction of manners ;" while the latter, relating to the general mass of society, is again subdivided into two sorts : —First, Domestic and home companionship, which is termed " social economy ;" the next, the intermingling in the city and country—nay, more, in the kingdom and empire—this is designated " political economy." The aforesaid book comprises the three above-mentioned divisions, with several advantages relating to the latter kind, and that which concerns the correction of manners is not mentioned therein, save cursorily ; accordingly, although it were possible to recite some of the virtues of morals, we were unwilling that any radical change in the plan of the work should be introduced ; consequently, opposing any addition of chapters which are not therein, we have adhered to the same arrangement that the Sage of Hind adopted, and omitting the two first chapters of the work, from which not much benefit could be imagined, and which were not included in the original of the book, we have written the fourteen remaining chapters in a clear and easy style. We have also confined the volume to tales composed of questions and answers between the King and the Brahman, as was in the afore-mentioned original. Before reciting the opening chapters, we deemed a story necessary to serve as a prelude to the narrative itself. Considering that overstrained language is used in the style of the aforesaid book, if, in the composition of this volume, the reins of grandiloquence should incline from the road of the manner of letter-writers, and the highway of the productions of authors, towards common-place phraseology, the excuse will be clear.

> I, who have pierced these pearls of composition,
> Have spoken what I have been told to say.

Again, in the midst of the tales, having kept within bounds, as regards the varieties of Arabic words, in quoting some verses of the Kurán, and traditions needful to be mentioned, as well as memorable sayings and well-known proverbs, *ennui* is not occasioned by the use of Arabic verses; the pages, too, of its language are ornamented with the pearls of Persian poetry, as it were gold and gems worked up together.

> Language, according to the example of the wise,
> Should mingle together verse and prose.
> For at one time the mind derives pleasure from the former,
> At another period it finds gratification from the latter.

In the place where the chapters are written, wherever the recital of an anec-dote, or the introduction of a proverb may seem expedient, in accordance with the consideration that

> A nosegay of roses is bound round with grass,

with bold step I shall proceed on the way, using my own discretion. This con-temptible mortal, though in attempting this composition he deems himself the target for the arrows of reproach, yet, with [1] the tongue of supplication in the court of apology, he would convey the proverb, " *He who is commanded will be excused,*" to the place of representation amongst the learned arrayed in eloquence, and the orators attired in wisdom; and in opposition to the threat, " *He who com-posed made himself a target,*" he murmurs forth this plain apologetic saying, " *He who dispensed justice displayed something new.*"

> Though the eye of justice is clear-sighted,
> It deems that to be a pearl which is really but a glass bead.
> I am ashamed of my imperfect production,
> Therefore do not wound my soul with reproaches.
> On the road amongst the high-minded populace
> It is not allowable to taunt the fallen.
> The merit-discerning eye is free from guile,
> If the worthless eye finds fault, what matter?

> " *The eye of favour is dim to all faults.*"

" *May God guide us to that which He approves, and be pleased with and seal our condition, our desires, and our destinies, well and beneficially.*"

This composition, which is called 'The Lights of Canopus,' has fourteen books, in the manner now detailed :

BOOK I. On avoiding the speech of calumniators and slanderers.

BOOK II. On the punishment experienced by evil-doers, and the misery of their end.

---

[1] أَ should be inserted in the Persian text before زبان

BOOK III. On the intercourse of friends, and the advantages of assisting one another.

BOOK IV. Explanatory of observing the circumstances of one's enemies, and not being secure from their treachery.

BOOK V. On the evils of negligence, and allowing one's object to slip from one's hand, and being careless as to the same.

BOOK VI. On the misfortune of precipitancy, and the evil of hastiness in matters.

BOOK VII. On caution and deliberation, and finding escape by means of stratagem from the wiles and treachery of foes.

BOOK VIII. On avoiding the malevolent and envious, and not trusting their flattery.

BOOK IX. On the excellence of pardon, which is the best attribute of kings.

BOOK X. Explanatory of requiting deeds by way of retaliation.

BOOK XI. On the misery of seeking too much, and being disappointed in one's affairs.

BOOK XII. On the excellence of clemency, serenity, quietness, and firmness, particularly as regards kings.

BOOK XIII. Explanatory how kings should avoid the speech of the treacherous and malignant.

BOOK XIV. On the want of kindness in the revolutions of time, and on basing one's affairs on Fate and Destiny.

After an index to the chapters of the stories, which will be indicative of the speeches themselves, the commencement opens—

Success is from the one God.

BOOK I.

INTRODUCTION.

ON AVOIDING THE SPEECH OF CALUMNIATORS AND SLANDERERS.

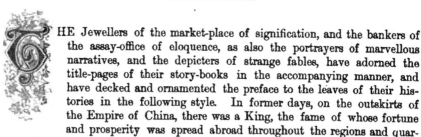 HE Jewellers of the market-place of signification, and the bankers of the assay-office of eloquence, as also the portrayers of marvellous narratives, and the depicters of strange fables, have adorned the title-pages of their story-books in the accompanying manner, and have decked and ornamented the preface to the leaves of their histories in the following style. In former days, on the outskirts of the Empire of China, there was a King, the fame of whose fortune and prosperity was spread abroad throughout the regions and quarters of the world, and the renown of whose greatness and dignity was resplendent like the noonday sun; famous monarchs placed the ring of obedience towards him in the ear of their soul, and sovereigns of exalted power threw the mantle of submission over the shoulders of their mind.

> In pomp like Farídún,[1] in dignity like Jamshíd,[1]
> In majesty like Sikandar,[1] in power like Darius;[1]
> By reason of his justice, like as on the cheeks of moon-like damsels,
> Fire and water were collected together in one spot.[2]

On the edge of the carpet of his daily increasing fortune, world-subduing chiefs, and ministers of sound deliberation, constantly bound the girdle of service on the loins of their soul, and at the foot of his heaven-rivalling throne powerful grandees and wise councillors perpetually sat on the chair of affection for him. His treasury was filled with various gems and manifold coins; his numerous and famous army passed all limit of reckoning or computation; his magnanimity was joined with generosity, while his majesty was mingled with retributive justice.

---

[1] Ancient kings of Persia, famous for their justice, their conquests, and the magnificence of their reign.
[2] As we should say, the lion and the lamb lie down together.

> He wounded the faces of the rebels,
> And struck down with the sword the heads of warriors.
> His justice overpowered the blood-stained miscreants ;
> His clemency consoled the helpless.

This Monarch was called Hamáiyún Fál,[1] since from his universal justice the fate of the subjects was prosperous; while by reason of his perfect kindness the condition of the helpless and poor was made happy and tranquil. If the officer of justice does not take care to guard the possessions of the people, the thief of rebellion, by the aid of tyranny, will bring destruction upon the fortunes of high and low; and if the light of the taper of justice does not throw a reflection on the gloomy cell of the unfortunate, the blackness of oppression will render the sides and quarters of the kingdom dark like the hearts of tyrants.

> Good accrues to a monarch from his justice:
> The protection of God is the security of his house.
> Should the sovereign repent himself of his equity,
> The country would be ruined by his injustice.

This Monarch had a Minister, who cherished the people and dispensed clemency. His world-adorning wisdom was the taper of the kingdom's chamber, while his right-thinking penetration solved a thousand difficulties with a single reflection. The ponderous weight of his kindness kept the ship of the sea of rebellion firm in the whirlpool of adversity; while the severe wind of his retribution tore up, root and branch, the skirt-clinging trees of the thorny places of injustice.

> When his acute understanding set about a matter,
> A hundred armies were overthrown by one solitary device ;
> When he administered the affairs of the state,
> He overturned kingdoms with a mere epistle.

Since, by reason of his auspicious intellect, the affairs of that kingdom obtained great lustre, he was called Khujistah Rái.[2] Now Hamáiyún Fál never embarked on any matter except after consulting Khujistah Rái, without whose advice he did not commence anything either great or small. Without the Minister's permission he neither bound the loins of combat in the plain of war, nor did he, unless with such consent, sit in the banquet-room on the throne of ease and repose. Assuredly it behoveth famous kings and mighty monarchs, in accordance with the command, "*And take counsel with them in your business,*" not to undertake the affairs of the state without the assistance of the counsel of acute-minded ministers. They should also govern all their proceedings and orders by the counsel of perfect ministers and skilful senators, so that, according to the purport of the precept, "*No tribe take counsel, save God guides them towards the soundest matters,*" whatever proceeds from them may be in conformity with what is right, and may comprise the desire of the world, and the repose of mankind.

> In every case counsel is necessary,
> Nothing good comes to pass without deliberation.

By chance one day Hamáiyún Fál went out hunting, and Khujistah Rái, like fortune, attended on the royal stirrup. The expanse of the covert became the envy of the heavenly sphere, by reason of the feet of the august Monarch, and the Eagle

---

[1] Good omen. [2] Auspicious intellect.

of the skies, in anxiety lest it should become the food of the royal falcon, departed towards the centre of the earth. The animals of the chase, having broken their bonds, and leapt from confinement and imprisonment, set out in search of game. The leopard-skinned panther turned its body into eyes to see the beauty of the dark-eyed antelope. The dog, with lion-like claws, learned an hundred foxish tricks in its anxiety to approach the hare. The high-flying hawk, like a flashing arrow from the bow-string of an archer, set its face towards the summit of the skies; while the captive-making falcon with the wounds of its blood-spilling claws rent open the artery veins in the throat of the birds.

> The swift-flying hawks coming forth,
> Sharpened their claws in the blood of their prey.
> The talons of the royal falcon joined the spoil.
> Not a parrot remained on high, nor a partridge.
> On every side panthers laying snares,
> Blocked the way of escape for the deer.
> From the galloping of swift Arab horses,
> The expanse of the desert became unbearable to the goats.

When the King had finished the pleasures of the chase, and cleared the desert of animals and the air of birds, his cavalcade obtained permission to return, and the Sovereign and his Minister set out towards the capital; but at this time, from the rays of the sun, their steel helmets became soft like wax, while from heat of the horse armour, which boasted itself equal to a flame of fire, the swift-going charger was withered up on the spot.

> Both mountain and mine became temples of fire,
> Earth and sky also waxed hot.
> The birds of heaven concealed themselves amongst the boughs,
> While animals also crept into holes.

Hamáiyún Fál said to Khujistah Rái, "To move about in such a hot atmosphere is not wise, nor will the shade of the tent afford a protection from the heat. From the violence of the warmth the terrestrial globe is scorched like a blacksmith's forge, and the centre of the earth, like the globe of the sun, is become a mine of fire. What kind of device do you suggest, that we may for a while obtain the shade of repose, and that, when the Phœnix of the sun is disposed to retire to the nest of the west, we also may descend to the abode of honour?" Khujistah Rái loosened the tongue of praise, saying:

> O sun of dominion! O shadow of God!
> Thy canopy is more prosperous than the shade of the Phœnix.[1]

"Your servants, who seek protection under the shade of the phœnix-like banner of your sovereignty, have no fear of the flame of the sun's world-consuming torch.

> Why should we be sad from the heat of the sun of calamity,
> Since the canopy of thy kindness is our protection?

"But for the exalted person of the King, the shadow of God, under the shade of whose fortune mankind finds repose, to be careful respecting the heat of the air, from which various pains and headaches arise, appears to be the very essence of wisdom.

---

[1] There is an evident error here. The word in the text is ھای, which is absurd. Probably ھمای, "Phœnix," is meant.

The welfare of the whole horizon depends on thy safety.

" In this neighbourhood I observe a hill, lofty, like the ambition of the brave, and high, like the dignity of the pious. A short time ago I arrived there; from head to foot the slopes thereof were covered with verdure, and a thousand sweet fountains sprang forth from its pure heart. Its odoriferous herbs and flowers glittered like the stars of the firmament, and its fountain-supplying brooks sparkled as the rivulets[1] of the garden of Paradise. The best course is to turn the reins of desire in that direction, so that for a while we may rest at ease, like verdure under the shade of the willow, and for a time may be refreshed and joyous, as it were jessamine upon the brink of a river, or the border of a pasture."

Behold us sitting and passing life on the edge of a stream,
Which itself is a sufficient indication to us how the world is fleeting.

Hamáiyún Fál, in accordance with the words of Khujistah Rái, set his face in that direction, and having in a little time traversed the interval, with the dust of the hoof of his splendid dun-coloured horse, made the skirt of the mountain like the sleeve of the prosperous, the kissing-place for the fortunate. He saw a mountain which pushed its mighty head beyond the height of the sphere, and extended its summit like a fresh sword to the gold-spangled shield of the sun; or like a shaikh, who according to the saying, " *And the mountains are stakes*," drew the foot of stability within the border of majesty, while from his weeping eyes a torrent of tears flowing reached his skirt. The king, having ascended the top of the mountain, bound his garments round his loins like a cloud, and wandered about in every direction. All of a sudden an expanse came into view, in extent and capacity like the plain of Hope, and an open space appeared of extreme magnitude, resembling the region of Expectation. As regards verdure it was like the rose-garden of the skies, and its brooks and breezes were as it were the fields of Paradise. All around it violets raised their heads, intermixed with roses, like the ringlets of entrancing beauties, and verdant hyacinths, together with self-sown tulips, like perfumed moles of sweet-lipped beauties, sprang up charmingly. The willow of Tabaristán was clad in its vermilion satin garment, and the erect cypress raised aloft its verdant silken top. The language of the musk-laden breeze scattered abroad to the four quarters of the world the secrets of the plants of this rose-garden; while from the nightingale's discourse the tale of the rose's colour and perfume ascended to the ears of the inhabitants in the palace of the universe.

Its streams and climate were pleasant and heart entrancing—
A blessed abode was it, a glorious spot—
Sweet flowers growing on the banks of the rivulets,
Bathed their hands and faces in hoar-frost.
Trees, like idols, raised aloft their figures,
Each excelling the other in beauty.
On the boughs sweet-songed birds,
With organ-notes, poured forth their strains.
The cypress-tree, which outstript heaven,
Upon every leaf had the inscription, " Beautiful Túba." [2]

---

[1] حرباى in the Persian text is a misprint for جريباى. [2] Name of a tree in Paradise.

In the midst of this meadow was a pool, the water of which was soul-refreshing, like the fountain of life, and the very essence of delight and purity, as the stream of Paradise.

> There swam therein fish like silver,
> As it were the new moon in the round sphere.

The Minister ordered that the brink of the pool should be decked with the regal couch, and Hamáiyún Fál took his seat on the throne of repose ; and the attendants of the fortune-resembling stirrup severally sought their ease on the bank of the stream, and under the shade of the trees. After that infernal atmosphere, they considered that Paradise-resembling halting-place a rare treat, and each of them recited this verse, as applicable to his case :

> O God ! I am quit of the desert of grief and misery,
> And am sitting bedecked in the rose-garden of Paradise.

The King and his Minister alighted, in a corner of the space, from their horses and elephants, and without playing, by checking the queen of their frivolous imagination, severed the connection of their aspiring souls from the follies of the chess-board of worldly concerns, and reflected on the wonders of divine creation and the marvels of His endless works. They recited a hymn in praise of the Most High Monarch, the painter of whose decrees, with omnipotent brush, had drawn such a beautiful picture on the surface of the mountain's stony tablet, and[1] the magic of whose power had produced all these varied-coloured plants from its flinty heart. At one time they recited this verse from the pages of the Gulistán :[2]

> Not alone the nightingale on the rose, warbles songs of his bounty,
> But every thorn recites his praises.

At another time they contemplated this picture on the pages of the Nigáristán:[3]—

> Sometimes he makes of the playful breeze a chariot for the rose-leaf,
> At another he girds a chain of pure water round the feet of the wind.[4]

From the enchained letter which the divine pen drew across the face of the page of the water, they read the inscription, "*And we caused springs to flow therein;*" and from the emerald-coloured tablets of the herbage, which were decorated with the characters of the omnipotent pen, they perused the verse, "*And we made gardens therein.*" In the midst of all this, Hamáiyún Fál's glance lighted on a tree stript of its leaves, and hapless, like a bough which had experienced autumn, and very old, like aged men left without life or growth. The sickle of the rustic, Time, was determined to cut and prune its limbs, and the saw of the carpenter, Fortune, had sharpened the teeth of avidity in tearing to pieces its woof and warp.

> The young tree is the delight of the garden ;
> When it is old, it is cut down by the gardener.

The midst of this tree was hollow, like the soul of an empty-hearted darwísh ; and a troop of bees had taken refuge in that castle, with a view of storing up honey as food for their support. When he observed the buzzing of the bees, he inquired of his experienced Minister, "What is the cause of this collection of swift-flying birds[5] around this tree, and by whose command do these workers go up and down this meadow ?"

---

[1] ‌ـ should be inserted before نیر‌ک .　　　[2] A famous Persian composition.　　　[3] Ibid.
[4] Ripples on the water.　　　[5] So called because they have wings.

> What is the object of their going to fro? and
> Upon what are they intent in this field of battle?

Khujistah Rái opened his lips, saying, "O mighty monarch! they are a flock of great use, and doing no harm; by reason of the cleanliness and comeliness which characterise their nature, they have obtained the honour of divine revelation, as exemplified by the saying, '*Thy Lord sent a message by revelation to the bee;*' and by aid of the favour of the royal command, '*Find houses in the mountains,*' they have bound the girdle of obedience on the loins of their heart. They have a king called Ya'súb,[1] in size bigger than the rest; all of them, by reason of his majesty and pomp, placing the head upon the line of obedience. He himself takes his seat upon a square throne composed of wax, while ministers, chamberlains, warders, porters, beadles, and deputies have their allotted duties. The ingenuity of his subjects is so great that each of them makes for himself an hexagonal house of wax, such that there is no difference in the sides thereof, nor could abstruse geometricians accomplish the like without compasses, rulers, and other instruments. When the houses are finished, by command of the sovereign they issue forth. The chief of the bees then, in their language, extracts from them a promise that they will not change their delicacy for burliness, nor contaminate the skirt of their purity with the foulness of uncleanness. In observance of their pledge, they sit only on the stems of sweet-smelling roses and delicate flowers. So what they carry away from those lovely leaves in a little while becomes mingled in their interiors into a kind of fresh pleasant-flavoured mucus, and issues forth as a sweet drink, such that in the medicine-house of wisdom the description '*Therein is a cure for men,*' rightly applies to its nature. When they return to their own homes the watchmen sniff them: if they have been true to their promise—that is to say, if they have avoided whatever is not pronounced clean—it is allowable for them to enter their hexagonal cells, and the abodes prepared for them; but if (God forbid!) the purport of this verse:

> Stretch forth the hand of fidelity towards the zone of integrity:
> Strive that you violate not your pledge,

has been overlooked by them, and an odour, which may be the cause of disgust and detestation, is found with them, they are at once severed in twain; if the porters are negligent, and let them pass, and the king should smell this disagreeable odour, having personally inquired into the matter, he causes that unfortunate bee to be brought to the place of punishment: first of all, he orders the porters to be killed, and afterwards slays the unmannerly bee, so that others of like kind may not act the same. If it should happen that a strange bee from another hive wishes to enter their home, the porters restrain him: should he not desist, they kill him. It has been asserted that Jamshíd, the Sovereign of the world, copied from them the institution of doorkeepers and beadles, together with the plan of porters and watchmen, and the arrangement of a throne and seat of royalty, and in the course of time reached great perfection." When Hamáiyún Fál heard these words, his joyful heart conceived a desire to see their arrangements; he rose up, and coming to the foot of the tree, was for a while delighted with their throne and court, their habit of coming and going, and rules of serving and waiting: he observed a troop who had bound on their loins the divine command, Sulaimán-like sitting on the steed of the air,[2] and selecting pure food and

---

[1] That is, Prince or Chief.
[2] "Muhammadans," says Eastwick, "believe that Sulaimán or Solomon possessed a throne on which he could transport himself through the air."

B

cleanly spots: no one having any business with another's profit or loss, and
none injuring or molesting those of his own condition.

> Glad news! the mighty restrain their hands,
> The great are wise, the lofty humble.

He said: "O Khujistah Rái! the wonder is, that notwithstanding the inherent
cruelty which is embodied in their nature, they do not endeavour to injure one
another, and in spite of possessing a sting, they give nought but honey: also,
though ferocity is planted in their disposition, they are yet kind and gentle; for
we see the contrary amongst men, masses of whom injure their own kith and kin,
and desire to overthrow the fabric of existence of those like themselves."

> Look around, how by reason of want of manliness,
> Man is fearful of his fellow-creature.

The Minister replied: "These animals which you behold are all created with a
similar disposition, while men are born with various natures: seeing that soul
and body, stolidity and merriness, light and darkness, are mingled together in
their composition, and the coin of dominion and empire, and the dues of loftiness
and meanness have been poured into their mould, consequently every one's disposition appears different, and his nature distinct. *'In truth all men knew their
own drinking-places.'* A share of angelic reason has been given them, while,
on the other hand, a portion of the nature of devils has been allotted them: so
that every one with the hand of acceptance may catch the skirt of wisdom, and
advance with the feet of honour to the dignity—*'And assuredly we have revered
the children of Men;'* but every one who places the head of obedience upon the
line of the command of sensuality, from excess of meanness also will remain
ensnared in the lowest depths of—*'Nay, more, they are most in error as to the
way:'* as it has been beautifully said:

> You are partly angelical, partly demoniacal,—
> Abandon Satan, and surpass angels in excellence.

"Most men, by reason of pursuing after evil-producing sensual lusts, display
mean inclinations—such as greed, avarice, envy, hatred, oppression, pride, hypocrisy, folly, slander, suspicion, calumny, and the like thereof."

> Many ignorant persons, not knowing themselves,
> Approve of error, to the exclusion of merit.
> They are smoke reaching the brain,
> Or wind blowing on a lamp.

The King said: "According to what you have explained, and the truth of the
case as regards the sensual, which you have indicated, the real interest of mankind
at large is for all persons to draw the foot of retirement under the skirt of repose:
and having shut upon themselves the door of other people's society, to busy
themselves in private devotion: perchance there may arise a way of escape from
the blood-stained whirlpool of wickedness, the origin of this blamable disposition.

> It were better if they could reach the shore from that midst.

" I have heard that there is rest in solitude, and repose in retirement: and I am
this day sure that the society of most men is more deadly than an adder's poison,
and intimacy with them more burdensome than the dangers of giving up life.

Now some wise men have for a long while passed their existence in the corner of a cave, or the depths of a pit, fixing their gaze on this precept—

> Whoever is wise indeed chooses the lowest depths,
> Since his heart finds contentment in retirement;
> Seclusion verily is better than the dark deeds of mankind:
> The wise man avoids the tumult of his fellow-creatures.

" Again, perfect, pure-minded darwíshes seek to withdraw even from their own selves; how then, such being the case, can they associate with others ? "

> I wish for solitude, so that, if like a whirlwind the revolution of the spheres
> Should strike this paltry world, it would not touch me.

Khujistah Ráí said : " What has flowed from the divine lips of His Majesty, the world-protecting Monarch, is the very essence of truth, and the germ of accuracy; since society is the means of unsettling the mind, and retirement the cause of repose, both inwardly and outwardly, as has been said :

> Would you know who, night and day, is at rest ?
> It is the recluse who does not join the throng.
> The heart of the tender rose, when in the bud, remains tranquil:
> When it is mingled in the mass it withers.

" But some wise religious men and learned doctors, on the ground of expediency have preferred the state of companionship and the condition of society to retirement, and have said that intimacy with an honest comrade is better than seclusion, but that, at a period when a pleasant friend cannot be found, solitude is better than society.

> One should withdraw from one's rivals but not from friends ;
> Fur garments are for winter, not spring.

" In fact society is the means of obtaining advantage and benefit, and a bond of union in the way of the lofty and good.

> Do not withdraw the hand of search from the skirt of society.
> Be not a recluse, for there is danger of insanity.

" According to the purport of the tradition, ' *There is no monastic life in Islám,*' it is understood that the benefits of society are greater than the advantages of seclusion; how then is it possible for a man to throw himself in the way of retirement, and not seek the companionship of his fellow-creatures ? As the authority of the divine power has made the bulk of men adapted for mutual intimacy, each one being in need of another, they are for this reason of an urbane disposition, that is, seek to be sociable, which may be described as living in cities, and the object of which is mutual aid and assistance amongst members of the human species ; indeed the life of individuals as well as of the general body of mankind is not conceivable without such mutual help. If, for example, any one requires to obtain for himself food, raiment, or habitation, first of all he must get ready to hand the carpenter's and smith's tools, without which preparations, implements for sowing and reaping, and all connected therewith, cannot be procured. During this period his life could not be supported without food. After arranging this apparatus, if all his time were thus spent in one employment, some things he would not be able to carry out and accomplish ; how much less when he has to busy himself in doing a mass of things? Accordingly it is a necessity that all should assist one another, each one attending to business even beyond the measure of his wants, and giving to another who needs it, whatever remains over and above, and taking wages in exchange according to the degree of his labour, so that by means of such social intercourse the affairs of the community may be settled. Now from these prefatory remarks it is clear that men stand in need of each other's assistance, which, however, is not possible without assembling together; therefore for the bulk of mankind to seclude themselves is amongst the number of impossibilities, and the saying, ' *The concourse of men one with another is a mercy,*' is also in allusion to this state of things."

> Seize the skirt of sociality, and perform thy work,
> Since no matter is accomplished in solitude.

The King replied: "What the Minister has explained is the purest wisdom, and the choicest knowledge, yet so it appears to my mind that, seeing that they are in need of mingling together, assuredly the diversity of their dispositions will be the cause of disagreement, because some may be stronger than others, according as their form and vigour may be greater, while some others may surpass their fellows in wealth and station; amongst numbers, too, greed and avidity may be predominant: they who, as regards strength and riches, surpass their neighbours, will display in their temperament tyranny and oppression; and assuredly this overweening power will drag most men in the chains of its servitude. Again, the covetous person will hanker to bring within the grasp of his possession the greater part of other men's property; such a state of things may be the cause of disagreement, and ultimately lead to wickedness."

> Contention raises such a fire
> As to consume, with its heat, everything existing.

The Minister replied: "O mighty Monarch, the protector of wisdom! a device has been arranged to avert such strife, whereby each person, being made content with his own possessions, the hand of his violence is restrained from the property of others. This device is called punishment, the basis of which is fixed on the rule of justice, by which is meant the observance of moderation, that being the centre of the circle of excellence, which according to the command, ' *The best things are means,*' includes this, ' extremes are indications of baseness;' as has been said:

> Know that the nature of mean and extreme
> Is as far apart as the Sun and the Lesser Bear;
> Therefore the choice of moderation is in all matters advisable.
> For this reason, that ' Virtue consists in moderation.'"

The King said: "Whence can this moderation, by the recognition of which the face of things assumes an aspect of justice, be ascertained?" The Minister replied: "The designer thereof is a most consummately perfect person ' *Aided by God,*' sent by the Divine Majesty to his creatures. Wise men call him Námús-i-Akbar,[1] while the leaders in religion designate him 'messenger' or 'prophet.' Assuredly his commands and prohibitions will be in accordance with men's welfare in this world and the next. When that prophet (' *upon whom be the blessing and peace of God* '), who founded his rules of justice, turns towards the realms of

---

[1] "The Great Secretary," an epithet generally applied to the angel Gabriel, but in this instance the allusion is probably to Muhammad.

eternity, there will be no remedy, save governing by a ruler, for carrying out the articles of religion fixed by him. Since most creatures are indifferent as to their welfare, and are overcome by the pursuit of avarice and sensuality, therefore, as a matter of course, there is a necessity for the existence amongst them of a strong governor, who, having observed the prophet's rules of command and prohibition, that is to say, his code of law, shall put in force regulations for the administration of justice, that the head of religion may be exalted to the crown of fortune, and also the garments of the kingdom ornamented with the fringe of the magnificence of faith, since ' *Government and Religion are twins.*'

> Amongst men of wisdom, king and prophet
> Are like two rings on the same finger.

" In a similar sense it has been said :

> The Law derives majesty from the King,
> And the King dignity from the Law."

Hamáiyún Fál said : " Of what kind should be that powerful ruler, whose existence, after the Prophet ('*may the blessing and peace of God be with him,*') is a necessity amongst mankind, and what his disposition for settling the affairs of the kingdom and faith ? " Khujistah Rái replied: " This ruler must be skilled in the regulations of punishment and the minutiæ of justice, since, if he be not so, the kingdom is nigh to decline, and the government on the brink of destruction.

> Your kingdom becomes established through justice,
> Your affairs are rendered sure by means of your own integrity.

" Again, he must take care to foster the pillars of the state, and be aware what set of persons he is to befriend and keep up an intimacy with, and what class he should maintain in subjection and avoid their society; since amongst the attendants of the threshold of royalty there are but a small number who entirely bind upon the loins of sincerity the girdle of devotion to the king's interests, and strive for the sovereign's good reputation in this world, and deliverance in the next; nay, more, the greater part of them follow the way of attendance with the view of obtaining their own advantage, or warding off misfortune from themselves.

> Boasters who are beloved by you,
> Strugglers who are much to you.

" Since the basis of their affairs is greed, assuredly hatred of any one to whom they cannot discharge their obligations will take possession of their hearts, and they will bear envy towards other persons, the benefits of whose services with the king are greater than the advantages of their own class : now when hatred and envy exhibit themselves in such people, having instigated various deceptions, they will represent unfounded circumstances. If the king should be devoid of the cloak of caution, and should listen with the ear of approval to the words of slanderers, not taking any pains in investigating and examining the facts of the case, many evils and miseries will be produced thereby, and varied wickedness and crime will consequently arise.

> Lend no ear to the words of a slanderer,
> Since his bosom is diseased with malignity :
> In a moment he sets the world at variance,
> In an instant he brings injury on the globe.

"But when the watchful and clever-minded sovereign looks into affairs, and himself examines details and trifles, discriminating between the splendour of rectitude and the darkness of falsehood, the basis of his sovereignty, both as regards this world will be free from adversity, and also in the world to come he will reach the fortune of deliverance, and the eminence of a place in Paradise.

> He who in this house for one night acts justly,
> To-morrow his home will be the abode of plenty.
> Justice is obligatory upon sovereignty;
> Prosperity becomes lasting through freedom from oppression.

"Every prudent king who, having placed the basis of his proceedings upon wisdom, makes the admonitions of the learned his rule of action, will both render his kingdom populous and his subjects happy and joyous, like the illustrious monarch of Hind, Dábishlím, who based his sovereignty upon the code of the discourse of the sage Bídpáí, the Brahman; from the latter he inquired as to what was befitting kings, consequently for a long while he spent his time in prosperity, and though he passed from this transitory abode to the palace of eternity, his good name and virtuous reputation still remain upon the pages of time."

> Whenever I reflect as to all in the world,
> A good name is the sum of life to mankind.

Hamáiyún Fál, when he heard mention of Dábishlím and Bídpáí, like a newly-opened rosebud upon the delicate lips of which, at the time of dawn, the movements of the morning breeze brings a smile, flourished in the expanse of joy and the plain of gladness; and blandly he replied, "O Khujistah Ráí! it is a considerable time since a longing after the story of this king and the Brahman has been fixed in my innermost heart, and the idea of their conversation and interviews taken possession of the cloister of my mind's abode."

> For a lifetime we have been coveting the tip of thy ringlets.

"Although I have performed the obligations of search, and made inquiry respecting the circumstances of their case from every one, yet I have not obtained the truth as to their story, nor is a letter from the register of news concerning them become known."

> I have not from any one observed a trace of that ravisher of hearts;
> Either I get no news of her, or she has left no vestiges behind.

"Perpetually, too, have I opened the ear of intelligence, (thinking to myself,) from whose mouth should I hear their name, and constantly have I turned the eyes of hope towards the highway of expectation, (wondering) where the beauty of these circumstances would show its face."

> I lend an ear to report: where are there tidings of that lip?
> My sight is towards the highway, O Lord! where is the light of her presence?

"Since I perceive that my Minister is informed of their story, I discharge the dues of thanks to Almighty God, saying:

> At length my soul has accomplished its object,
> And what I sought from God has befallen me.

"I am in hopes that as quickly as possible you will impart to me the words of the King and the Brahman, for by detailing these discourses, the advantage of discharging the dues of gratitude towards me will accrue to you, while, as regards myself, by reason of hearing those exhortations, a variety of benefits will reach both peasant and noble; now words, by the narration of which a debt of gratitude is discharged, and from the blessing of listening to which, universal good befalls both high and low, will be extremely beneficial."

> The discourse of sages of enlightened mind
> Is a key to the door of wisdom's storehouse;
> Open the door of the hoard and bring forth coin,
> It will be the true metal of probity.
> Give advice of this nature to kings,
> For in them lies the welfare of the subjects.

COMMENCEMENT OF THE STORY OF KING DÁBISHLÍM AND BÍDPÁÍ THE BRAHMAN.

The Minister of enlightened mind and accurate judgment opened the tongue of explanation, and with eloquence of words gave forth a stream of oratory, saying:

> O blest-footed King of kings, who producest
> Good fortune to the stars of heaven by thy face!

From the parrots of the sweet abode of eloquence, and the luscious-tongued nightingales of the garden of genius, I have heard that in one of the large cities of Hind, which is the mole [1] on the face of monarchies, was a King of wakeful fortune and victorious days, and a world-adorning, peasant-cherishing, tyrant-consuming Sovereign. The regal throne was beautified with the golden fringe of his boundless justice, while the royal couch was adorned with the ornament of his commands and prohibitions. The hue of oppression and injustice was swept away from the pages of the world, and the face of equity exhibited itself to all mankind in the mirror of kindness.

> The regions of the world were illuminated with the splendour of his justice,
> Indeed, the government of the world was enlightened by his equity.

This King was called Rái Dábishlím, the meaning of which epithet, in the dialect of the country, is "a great king." By reason of his extreme majesty he did not throw the lasso-ring of his ambition save on the parapet of the ethereal palace, while from excessive independence he did not cast his eyes save on high matters and great undertakings. In his army were ten thousand herd of mighty elephants, and the number of his warriors and heroes did not come within the bounds of computation. He had full treasuries, and territories well peopled.

> You alone possess as much as all kings together combined.

In spite of all this greatness, he thoroughly investigated the affairs of his subjects, and personally inquired the history of each of his suppliants.

> Withhold not the hand of kindness from your subjects;
> Treat with consideration the affairs of your people.

When he had established the portions of his kingdom with administrative

---

[1] A mole is considered by the Persians a sign of beauty.

measures, and had swept away the enemies of the country from the expanse of his territories, constantly, in peace of mind, he used to grace the banquet of repose, and gratify the desire of his heart with prosperity. At his court there were always present confidants clad with wisdom, and sages clothed with excellence, who adorned the assembly with pleasant speeches and fine discourses. One day he was sitting on the throne of ease, and gracing the regal banquet.

> He arranged according to wont the banquet-chamber,
> He opened the door of merriment and joy.

After enjoying the songs of the melody-making, sweet-voiced musicians, he conceived a desire to hear an edifying story of wisdom, and after he was satiated with the spectacle of the cheeks of moon-faced and delicate-templed beauties, he became anxious to witness the splendour of instruction-affording conversation. Making inquiry of the sages, and various companions of laudable disposition and generous nature, he adorned the ear of his understanding with the gem of their discourse, which resembled a royal pearl.

> Speech is a pearl, which appertains to the ear of the king.

Accordingly, each one of them set forth a description of praiseworthy qualities, and an account of acceptable dispositions, so that the swift charger of speech moved along the plain of beneficence and benevolence. All the sages were unanimous that generosity is the highest of qualities, and most perfect of dispositions: consequently they have narrated as regards the First Master, that the most excellent of the attributes of the Most High God is that He is termed beneficent, since His benevolence permeates amongst all His people, while His generosity descends on all His creatures. Now the Great Prophet (may the blessing of God rest upon him) has stated that beneficence is a plant growing in the garden of Eden, and finding nourishment and sustenance on the banks of the stream of Paradise— since " *Generosity is a tree in Paradise.*"

> To act benevolently is the source of happiness;
> True wealth consists in abandoning money.
> Do you seek a sign of ever-flowing riches ?
> It is nought but generosity of soul.

After the King was apprised as to the matter, his original natural benevolence was aroused, and he commanded that the door of boundless wealth should be opened, and a proclamation issued of generosity towards high and low: strangers and citizens were made content with gigantic portions, and small and great were enriched with a full share above their fellows.

> From the cloud of his palm flowed rain-drops of benevolence.
> He washed the inscription of want from off the leaves of fortune.

All day, like the shining sun, he was occupied in distributing gold, and, like resplendent Fortune, in producing delight, till the time that the golden-winged Phœnix of the sun inclined towards its nest in the west, and the Raven of black-faced night drew the pinion of darkness over the region of the earth.

> When Day had concealed its mysteries within a veil,
> Veiling Night disclosed its secrets;
> The Súfí [1] of the Sun sat in retirement;
> The Skies took in their hands the rosary of the Pleiades.

---

[1] A religious order acknowledging no spiritual head.

The King placed the head of repose upon the pillow of rest, and the horsemen of Sleep overran the courtyard of the area of his brain. The painter of his imagination pictured to him a serene-faced old man, on whose forehead were visible the traces of probity, and the evidences of benevolence on his temples : he entered and saluted the King, saying, " You have to-day expended treasure in the way of God, and have given a vast sum as alms, with the view of conciliating the divine Majesty: in the morning put your foot in the stirrup of fortune, and set out towards the east of your capital, for an immense hoard and a gratuitous treasure have been intrusted to you : by the discovery of such a collection you will place the foot of honour upon the top of the Lesser Bear, and pass the head of glory beyond the pinnacle of the exalted Sphere." The King, when he heard this good news, jumped up from his sleep, and was rejoiced at the idea of the treasure, and at the oracular old man's glad tidings. He performed his necessary ablutions, and attended to the discharge of his duties of worship, till the time that the divine treasurer opened the door of the storehouse of the horizon, and the hand of the gold-scattering sun drew the pearls of the stars from the repository of the heavens under the skirt of its garment.

> In the morning, when the silvery break of day
> Drew the golden bolt from the door of its treasures.

The King commanded that a steed, quick-paced as the wind, should be adorned with a golden saddle, and a bridle jewelled with pearls ; having with auspicious omen and happy presages mounted, he turned his face towards the region of the east :

> Fortune and prosperity went with him, stirrup to stirrup ;
> Victory and power accompanied him rein to rein.

When, beyond the limits of habitation, he arrived at the expanse of the desert, he cast his glance on every side, seeking some tidings of the object of his search. In the midst of this his eyes alighted upon a hill, with head lofty like the ambition of generous men of piety, and stable-footed like the fortune of just monarchs. At the skirt of that hill a dark cave appeared, with a man of enlightened mind sitting at the door thereof, and like the " Companion [1] of the Cave," freed from the vexation of rivals :

> Informed of and indifferent to all that goes on—
> Interested [2] in, and concerned with, all existing beings.

When the King's eyes alighted upon that Devotee, his soul became desirous of the latter's society, and his heart conceived an attachment for his companionship. The old man, reading on the pages of the King's enlightened mind a delineation of his desire, opened the tongue of supplication.

> O thou, to whom God has given sovereignty over the kingdom of the soul !
> Your abode is the heart and the eyes,—alight and enter.

" O King ! though the sorrowful cell of the afflicted is contemptible in comparison with the gilded palace, and the corner of the abode of the unfortunate is of no avail like the jewelled mansion, yet

> It is an old custom, and a regular habit,

---

[1] Abúbakr, who, together with Muhammad, for a time remained concealed in a cave.
[2] Lit., "consumed."

that kings should cast a glance of universal kindness on the state of the poor, and gratify recluses with their society and footsteps : such is reckoned the summit of perfect qualities and noble dispositions."

> To regard the poor increases greatness.
> Sulaimán, in spite of all his dignity, observed [1] the ants.

Dábishlím approved the speech of the Devotee : having alighted from his horse and become familiarised with the saint's blessed words, he sought a supply of grace.

> When the grace of the darwísh accompanies,
> Its possessor acquires intelligence of the inmost secrets.
> He who gains information respecting spiritual matters,
> Obtains it from the favour of the wise.

After that the King had expressed his intention of departing, the darwísh loosened the tongue of apology :

> From the hands of a beggar like myself there flows not
> Hospitality for a monarch such as yourself.

" But I have an off-hand present which descended to me from my father; I will place it as an offering in the King's way—it is a treatise on wealth, the purport of it being, that in the corner of this cavern there is an immense treasure, as well as endless pearls, coins, and gems; now, since I have found the wealth of contentment—' *Contentment is a treasure which does not perish*'—I have not sought after it, and, by reason of improving my own time, I also have made my capital of the riches of resignation, than which there is not, in the market of reliance on God, any coin more current.

> He who has not seen the face of reliance on God has seen nought;
> He who has not experienced the glories of contentment has experienced nought.

" If the great Monarch, the conqueror of kingdoms, will deign to reflect the light of condescension thereon, and order his servants to occupy themselves searching for it, and, conveying the proceeds to the royal treasury, to disburse it in any such expenditure as may be right and proper, it is not far distant." Dábishlím, after hearing these words, narrated to the darwísh the circumstances of the preceding night, and informed his friend in the cave of the state of the matter. The darwísh said, " Although this trifle is not worthy the consideration of the King's exalted condescension, yet since it is consigned from the invisible world it must obtain the honour of acceptance."

> Since what comes from the unseen world is without blemish.

The King commanded that all should busy themselves searching the regions and sides of the cave. In a short time, having discovered the direction of the treasure, they brought the whole hoard to Hamáiyún's gaze.

> Many ornaments composed of royal pearls,
> Many seals, bracelets, and ear-rings :
> Many caskets, and boxes with gold locks,
> Full of rubies, sapphires, pearls, and gems :
> Some utensils of gold, and vases of silver,
> And every kind of choice rarity.

---

[1] نظرها in the Persian text is a misprint for نظرها .

The King commanded them to break the locks off the boxes and caskets. He saw delicate pearls and rare niceties; and in the midst of all observed a box set with jewels, the top and sides being bound with strong bands, and fastened with a steel lock of Turkish design, inlaid with gold. The strength of that lock was such that neither the teeth of any key could undo the fastening thereof, nor could the genius of any solver of difficulties, by any contrivance, find the mode by which it was fastened. Much as they searched they found no trace of the key, and no signs of opening the box appeared. The King conceived an earnest desire to undo that lock, and displayed a great wish to see what could be within the box. He said to himself, " It appears to me that more costly rarities than valuable pearls may be placed in this cabinet, otherwise what can be the cause of all this fastening ? " Accordingly he commanded clever-handed smiths to perfect their skill in breaking the lock. When the box was opened a casket fell out therefrom, decked with pearls like the stars of heaven, and within that casket was a jewel-box, arrayed like the orb of the moon with exceeding brightness. The King, ordering the cabinet to be brought to him, opened with blessed hand the top thereof, and saw a piece of white silk, upon which several letters were written in the Syriac character. The King was astonished, wondering what this could be. Some said it was the name of the owner of the treasure, while others suggested that it might be a talisman written with a view of protecting the hoard. When the discussion of the pillars of the state on this matter ended in tumult, Dábishlím said, " Uncertainty will not be removed till this is deciphered." But no one of the attendants was acquainted with that style of writing. Of necessity they hastened in search of some one who could discover the purport thereof, till at length they got tidings of a philosopher who was very clever in reading and writing strange letters. By the exalted command they shortly brought him to the foot of the imperial throne. Dábishlím, after the dues of homage, said, " O sage, the object of my anxiety is that you should explain in clear language the meaning of this writing, and describe plainly and accurately the purport of these lines."

It may be that from this writing I shall gather somewhat of my desire.

The philosopher took that writing and brought every word, letter by letter, before the glance of his inquiry. After much reflection he said, " This is a writing embracing many advantages, and is assuredly of itself a scroll of wealth. The purport of the language is this : ' I, King Húshang, have put aside this treasure on behalf of a great monarch and a mighty sovereign called Dábishlím : by the inspiration of God, being conscious that this store will become his portion, I have placed this testament in the midst of the gold and gems, so that when he carries off this wealth, and peruses these precepts, he may consider to himself that to be deceived with gold and pearls is not the part of wise men, since they are but borrowed possessions which every day will be passing through the hands of others, and with no one will they ever remain constant.

> Who wishes for this world's riches ?
> To whom have they been constant that they should be so to me ?
> There is not the marrow of fidelity in these bones ;
> There is not the perfume of security in this rubbishy world.

' This testament is a manual of practice which kings cannot neglect, therefore it becomes the wise monarch, the companion of fortune, to act according to these precepts, and to recognise that every sovereign, whoever he may be, unless he views with acceptance these fourteen rules which I now explain, the edifices of his prosperity will be overturned, and the foundation of his monarchy will not be consolidated.

'The first precept is this: Whomsoever of his attendants he exalts by near approach to himself, as regards the ruin of such individual, he must not allow the words of any other person to be honoured with acceptance, seeing that whoever is nigh the king assuredly will be envied by every one; when they discover that the basis of the sovereign's favour is fixed on him, they will strive with pleasing deceit to ruin and injure him, and making a show of well-wishing and advice, they will speak flowery and treacherous words, till at length the feelings of the king become ill-disposed towards him, and, under the guise of such conduct, they achieve their object.

> Do not listen to the talk of every one, but attend to my speech;
> Men of malignity have a word for every affair.

'The second precept is this: He must not admit calumniators and slanderers into his society, for they seek to raise strife and war, and their end is very disastrous; nay, more, when this disposition is observable in any persons, as quickly as possible he should quench the fire of their calumny with the water of the sword of punishment, so that the smoke thereof should not darken the expanse of the world.

> The fire by which mankind is consumed
> Cannot be cured except by being extinguished.

'The third precept is this: He must observe the way of kindness and benevolence towards the chiefs and pillars of the state, since by the help of united friends, and the assistance of harmonious companions, matters will be completely carried out.

> Truly by unanimity the world may be overcome.

'The fourth precept is this: He must not be deceived by the kindness and flattery of enemies; much as they may fawn and humble themselves, he should, by way of caution, pay no regard to them, since in no case will friendship proceed from an enemy.

> Avoid an enemy under the guise of a friend,
> Like as it were a bundle of sticks and a piercing fire:
> When his object cannot be effected with open enmity,
> Blandly he will open the door of stratagem.

'The fifth precept is this: When the gem of desire comes within his grasp, he must not be negligent and destroy it through carelessness, since a remedy will not again appear, and repentant though he be, it will avail nothing.

> The arrow shot from the stall will not return to your palm,
> Though you bite with your teeth the back of your hand.[1]

'The sixth precept is this: He must not display levity or haste in matters; nay, more, he should lean towards reflection and deliberation, since the evils of rashness are great, while the advantages of patience and tranquillity are beyond calculation.

---

[1] An expression indicative of remorse.

In any matter wherein you are engaged, be not hasty;
Turn not your reins from the way of deliberation:
For what is not done can soon be performed;
When carried out, then, of what avail is regret?

'The seventh precept is this: He should not by any means let the reins of deliberation slip from his hand; if a body of his enemies are banded together for his destruction, and he sees it advisable to conciliate one of them, so that by such means escape may be possible, let him at once take such a step. In accordance with the saying, " *War is stratagem,*" he should overturn the edifice of their deceit by the hatchet of treachery, for sages have said:

The snare of one's enemy can be avoided by treachery.
" *It has been truly said, ' The reply to what is harsh is harsh.'* "

'The eighth preceipt is this: He should avoid malicious and envious persons, nor must he be deceived by their smiling words; since when the tree of hatred is planted in the soil of the heart, it cannot be imagined but that the fruit thereof will be injury and oppression.

In whatever bosom hatred takes up its abode
The heart becomes hardened with wickedness.
When looking at you he speaks pleasantly,
When he is gone, he secretly plots your destruction.

'The ninth precept is this: Having clothed and arrayed himself with pardon, he must not rebuke or chide his attendants for slight offences, since nobles, by the water of pardon and clemency, always efface the representation of crime from the scroll of their inferior's affairs, drawing over their errors and crimes, by means of kindness, the skirt of indulgence.

From the period of Adam till the King's time
Pardon is the part of the great, crime that of the lower ranks.

'If wrong-doing and treachery should become apparent on the part of any of the personal attendants, and they receive pardon from the king, they should be again overwhelmed with the water of kindness, so that they may not be ruined and dejected in the desert of disappointment.

Those who have received consideration at thy hands,
Treat kindly, and do not all at once overthrow them on the ground.

'The tenth precept is this: He should not behave oppressively towards any person, so that, by way of retribution, " *And the requital of evil is an evil like thereto,*" misery may not recoil upon himself. Nay, more, he should drop the rain of kindness upon the heads of mankind, so that in the garden " *If ye do well ye do well to your own souls,*" the rose of desire may come into blossom.

If you do good, men will in return behave rightly towards you;
But if you do wrong, men will act even worse towards you.
At present you are unacquainted with either good or bad;
A day will come when men will apprise you of both good and bad.[1]

---

[1] That is, at present you are unaware of the results of your actions, but a day will come when the effects of your deeds will overtake you; then you will learn whether your conduct has been good or bad.

'The eleventh precept is this : Display no inclination for an action which may be unsuited to the case and unworthy of the occasion, since many persons neglecting their own affairs step forward towards matters unbefitting them, and not being successful, leave also their own business unfinished.

> A crow learned the walk of a lovely partridge ;
> It did not avail him, and he lost his own style.

'The twelfth precept is this : He should adorn his own condition with the jewel of mildness and sedateness, since a gentle disposition is pleasing, and the proverb, *" It is wellnigh that the meek man is a prophet,"* is a true saying.

> The sword of mercy is sharper than the scimitar of iron ;
> Indeed it is more victorious than an hundred armies.

'The thirteenth precept is this : Having selected true and trustworthy servants, he should avoid malignant and treacherous men, since when the attendants on the threshold of royalty are endowed with an honest disposition, both the secrets of the kingdom are kept, and also people remain secure from harm at their hands. Now if, God forbid, the countenance of their affairs is blackened with the stain of perfidy, and their words reach the degree of the king's confidence, it may be that they will cast the innocent into the region of destruction, from which bad results will arise both in the present world, and also in that to come.

> The servant of the King should be faithful,
> So that in this kingdom there may be an increase of splendour.
> But if he turn his face towards treachery,
> The country is ruined by his villany.

'The fourteenth precept is this : Vexation must not rest upon the skirt of his ambition, owing to the troubles of the world and the vicissitudes of fortune, since wise men always are ensnared in the mesh of misfortune, while the careless pass their lives in peace and quiet.

> The lion has a chain on his neck, while the fox all night,
> At freedom, wanders over ruins and hills.
> The prudent do not put their feet beyond the cell of grief ;
> The negligent, in excess of joy, stray through the world.

'For he well knows that without the assistance of Divine kindness and never-changing grace, the arrow of happiness will not reach the target of desire, and in spite of abundance of skill and merit, no matter can be accomplished without the aid of Fate and Destiny.

> Prosperity does not come by means of acquiring knowledge and skill ;
> It depends upon the decrees of Fate and Destiny.

'To each of these fourteen before-mentioned precepts is a story attached, and a trustworthy narrative. Now if the King is anxious to gain information as to the particulars of those histories and tales, he must start towards the mountain of Sarándíp, which is the resort of the father of mankind, where this knot will be unfastened, and the object of search will, in that garden of peace, perfectly display itself, *" And God is the aider to the acquirement of the wish and the attainment of the wished-for object." ' "*

When the sage conveyed in its integrity this interlude to the ears of the Sovereign, and offered to the King's high magnanimity this casket of jewels, wherein was contained the pearl of spiritual matters, Dábishlím caressed him, and kissing those pages, with the greatest respect, made them an amulet for the royal arm, saying, "The wealth which has been indicated to me is a store of secrets, not a purse of money and coin—a treasury of spiritual matters, not a collection of jewels and pearls. Since, thank God ! I possess such an amount of worldly goods that I have no need of this more, and can with magnanimity consider this trifle just discovered as if it had never been found, it behoves me, in gratitude for this code of morals, which is indeed true wealth, to devote as alms amongst the deserving, such of this hidden treasure as has come to my possession, so that the offering of this spiritual reward may be procured by the victorious spirit of King Húshang ; and we also, in accordance with the decree, '*He who points to a good action is like him who does it*,' will obtain a share of benefits in return." The king's ministers, by royal command, gave to the deserving all that treasure, both money and pearls, by way of eternal consolation.

> Money is bestowed especially for purposes of benevolence—
> Look indeed at the word benevolence [1] from a poetical point of view.

When he had finished all these arrangements, he set out towards the capital of his kingdom, and adorned the royal throne of sovereignty with his majesty. All night long he was contemplating starting for Sarándíp, so that his desire might be completed and his object brought to an issue, and that, having become duly apprised as to the details of the precepts, he might make them the support of his monarchy and the foundation of the edifice of his sovereignty and dominion. Next day, when the newly-risen sun, like a pomegranate-coloured ruby, displayed itself from the corner of Mount Sarándíp, and the diamond-like heavens scattered scraps of arrow-headed pearls upon the region of the world,

> The gold-scattering Sun displayed itself,
> The jewelled night-illuminating Stars dwindled away.

Dábishlím commanded that two of his Majesty's attendants, who, on account of the sincerity of their advice, were constituted counsellors, and who, by reason of the value of their judgment and aid, were the pivots of the state, should be summoned to the foot of the royal throne. After honouring them, he disclosed to them with regal condescension the circumstances of the night's illusion, and said, " A desire to journey to Sarándíp has taken possession of my mind, and the intention of starting and setting off to that locality has snatched the reins of choice from the grasp of my power ; in these circumstances what do you deem advisable, and what seems to you the proper course in this case ? For a long time I have loosened the knot of difficulties with the tip of the finger of your deliberation, and have placed the basis of the affairs of my kingdom and possessions upon your right-minded judgment. Now also convey to the place of representation that which is required of your true counsel, and is befitting your penetrating thought, so that I, on my part, having scanned the ins and outs thereof, may make whatever plan may find the inscription of unanimity, the basis of my proceedings."

> Affairs should be based upon deliberation,
> Since without forethought matters come to nought.

The ministers said, " It is not right to give an answer to this speech off-hand, for

---

[1] " Diram," money, rhymes with " Karam," benevolence.

as regards designs and affairs of kings, due reflection is befitting, since words not pondered are like gold not weighed. •

> Reflect on your words, then speak.

"During this day and night we will think over this matter, and will test the coin of every suggestion upon the touchstone of proof. Whatever ideas happen to prove sound, to-morrow we will honour them by representation." Dábishlím approved of this arrangement. Next day at early dawn they came before his Majesty the King, and each one having taken his place at his appointed spot, opened the ears of intelligence to listen to the Sovereign's commands. Permission to speak being given, the elder minister, dutifully dropping on his knees, performed the dues of praise and adoration, saying :

> O conqueror of the world and bestower of kingdoms ! to whom by the decree of Fate
> Sovereignty is established till the day of eternity.

"It has occurred to your servant that though but little advantage can be imagined from this journey, yet great difficulties will have to be attempted, and ease, repose, rest, and delight, being put on one side, the heart must be set on struggles and abstinence. It is not concealed from the enlightened mind of the King, the Conqueror of the World, that ' *The spark of travel is a portion of hell*,' is a flame which consumes the heart, and an arrow which pierces the soul ; and that, ' *Exile is the greatest of calamities*,' is a dart which penetrates the vitals. Men of experience consequently deduce therefrom, not to place the foot beyond the cell of their own home, for drops of tears are trampled under foot, because they find no place on the corner of their own abode.

> In a journey are difficulties, abasements, and misery ;
> If there be happiness and delight, they arise from remaining at home.

"A wise man should not exchange ease for toil, nor give from his palm the hard cash of pleasure for gains on credit ; neither should he willingly prefer the wretchedness of exile to the delights of repose, lest that befalls him which happened to the Pigeon." The King inquired, "What was that ? "

STORY I.

The Minister replied : I have heard that two Pigeons lived together in one nest and were confidants in the same abode. No dust of rivals settled on their minds, nor were their hearts vexed with the adversities of the world. Content with grain and water like darwíshes, secluded, they intrusted themselves to the road of confidence in God. One was named Bázindah,[1] the other Nawázindah.[1] Morning and evening they together sang sweet melodies, and at all times with heart-enchanting tongue, cooed with varied strains.

> In remembering the face of our idol, we reckon retirement a treasure,
> In love of which we withdraw from all the world.

Fortune became envious of the concord of these two intimate friends, and the time-wounding eye darted down upon those two noble companions.

---

[1] Each of these words means a " player or singer."

> The heavens have no object but this,
> To separate friend from friend.

Bázindah conceiving a desire to travel, said to his friend, "How long shall we remain in one nest and pass our time in one abode? My desire is to wander for two or three days over the world, putting into practice the exalted order, '*Say, travel the earth*,' for in travel many wonders are seen, and countless experience is obtained. Sages have said, '*Travel is the cause of victory*.' Till a sword is drawn from its sheath on the battle-field of heroes, it will not become honourable; until the pen moves at the tip, the representation of beautiful expressions will find no place on the page of existence. The heavens, which are always moving, are higher than anything; while the earth, which is stationary, is trampled under foot and trodden upon by every one both high and low."

> One must observe the globe of the Earth, and the Heavens,
> What the former is from rest, and the latter from motion.
> Travel educates a man, and is the threshold of dignity,
> Travel is a store of wealth, and the master of skill.
> A tree if it be moved from place to place
> Neither undergoes the danger of the saw, nor the misery of the axe.

Nawázindah replied: "O friend and companion! you have not undergone the toil of travel, nor have you experienced the vexations of exile. The saying, '*Travelling is affliction*,' has not reached the ears of your soul, and the blast, '*Separation is burning*,' has not blown upon the rose-garden of your heart. Travel is a tree from which comes no other fruit than the burden of separation, and exile is a cloud from which nought but the drops of humiliation rain down."

> At evening prayer of the wretched, the poor and helpless
> Sit at the roadside, their heart rent in a hundred pieces.

Bázindah rejoined: "Although the toil of exile is heartrending, yet the pleasures of town and the sight of the world's wonders are productive of happiness: again, when the temperament is accustomed to the fatigue of travel, it is no longer troubled thereby, while the mind, through being occupied with the wonders of the country, is not so much affected by the dangers of the road."

> If in exile there is the thorn of distress, what matter?
> Together with the thorn always grows the rose of desire.

Nawázindah said: "O dear friend! the pleasures of the world and the delights of the garden of Paradise in company with familiar friends and intimate companions are delightful. Now when any one is deprived of the happiness of seeing his comrades, it is clear to what extent his woes will experience relief by that enjoyment, and what amount of benefit his anguish will receive from such sights. Now I am conscious that the pain of separation from friends, and the misery of parting from companions, are the most severe of all ills, and the most intense of all sorrows.

> Separation from seeing one's friends is typical of the infernal regions.
> Heaven defend me, I said wrong, since Hell is indicative of it.

"Now since, thanks to the Most High God, we have lodging and provision, draw the foot of repose within the skirt of security, and do not give the collar of desire to the hand of lust."

> Snatch the skirt of tranquillity, and be at ease,
> For change holds in its sleeve the stone of separation.

Bázindah said: "O solacer of this world! do not say another word respecting separation and parting, since there is no lack of intimate friends in the world, and
whoever quits one companion, when he takes up with another, no longer grieves.
If I am here deprived of the converse of one comrade, in a little while I shall
betake myself to the society of another confidant. You have yourself heard that
it has been said:

> Neither set your mind on any one friend, nor on any particular abode,
> Since the land and sea are wide, and men numerous.

"I am in hopes that after this you will not read to me the book of the difficulties
of travel, since the flame of the dangers of journeying renders a man experienced,
and no crude pampered person ever gallops the steed of Hope along the plain of
Desire."

> Many journeys must be undertaken before the simpleton becomes experienced.

Nawázindah said: "O dear friend! at the time when you take away your heart
from the society of your comrades, having severed the cord of your former intimacy, you may join yourself to new companions, but the purport of the sage's
speech—

> 'Do not by any means let an ancient friend slip from your hand
> On account of every new ally, who may not be good,'

"may be neglected by you; what effect will my words have upon you? but

> 'He will sufficiently satisfy the desire of his enemies' hearts,
> Who does not listen to the words of well-meaning friends.'"

The conversation having ended here, they bade adieu to one another. Bázindah
having torn his heart away from the society of his comrade, set off flying,

> Like a captive bird flies from its cage.

With sincere anxiety and earnest desire he traversed the expanse of the air, and
enjoyed the delights of high hills and Paradise-like gardens. Suddenly at the
skirt of a mountain which, as regards height, boasted an equality with the
dignity of the loftiest heavens, and from immensity of size considered the whole
terrestrial globe as a mound of earth at its feet, he saw a meadow, the circuit
of which, decked in green, was more heart-enchanting than the garden of Paradise, while its scent-laden north wind was more perfumed than a bladder of
musk from Tartary.

> A hundred thousand roses blossomed there,
> The verdure therein was luxuriant,[1] and the water silent;
> Roses of every kind of colour,
> The perfume of each extending a league.

Bázindah was charmed with this pleasant abode and delightful expanse. Since
it was late in the day, he deposited there the encumbrances of his journey. He
had scarce rested from the fatigues of the way, nor for a moment enjoyed rest or
repose, when all at once the swift-pacing chamberlain, the Wind, drew a cloud as

---

[1] Literally, "awake."

a canopy across the expanse of the air, and the slumbering world, with the noise of soul-deafening thunder, and the fear of heartrending lightning, became like the tumult of the last day.   On one side thunderbolts consumed the hearts of the spotted tulips; on the other, darts of hail transfixed the eye of the wakeful narcissus on the target of the earth.

> The bosom of the hill was rent in pieces by the lightning's dart,
> While the terrestrial globe trembled at the shocks of thunder.

All this time Bázindah had no shelter where he might be secure from the darts of the rain-clouds, and was unable to procure an abode where he might remain protected from the severity of the intense cold.   At one time he concealed himself under a bough, at another made the leaves of the trees his shelter.   Every moment the fury of the hail and rain became greater, and every instant the horror of the thunder and lightning increased.

> Dark night, terrible thunder, and rain so pitiless as this,
> What care for us have they who are satiated at banquets?

In short, after great tribulation, he passed the night till day, and dejected, patiently bore that ill-timed calamity: every moment he thought about his abode in the nest, and the company of his wise friend, and with a hundred regrets and griefs heaved a cold sigh from his distressed bosom, saying:

> If I had known that separation from you
> Would have been so disagreeable and heartrending,
> I would not have quitted you for an instant,
> Nor would I have been absent from you for a single day.

When the scout of early Dawn had displayed its traces, the same moment the dark writing of the clouds was effaced from the pages of the world, and the expanse of the land and the regions of the globe were illuminated by the brilliancy of the earth-enlightening sun.

> The Sun drew a streak [1] of gold from the east,
> The Sun enlightened the entire inhabitable world.

Bázindah again took to wing, undecided as to whether he should return to his own home, or, since he had formed the intention, should entirely, for two or three days, wander over the regions of the world.   In the midst of this a Royal Falcon, swift-winged and cruel-clawed, who in search of game descended to the earth quicker than the rays of the sun, and when flying aloft reached the heavens more rapidly than the light of the eyes,

> At one time attacking like fire-spreading lightning,
> At another flying about like flame-quenching [2] wind,

planned Bázindah's destruction.   When the helpless Pigeon's eyes alighted upon the merciless Royal Falcon his heart began to palpitate, and all the power and motion in his limbs and body vanished.

> When a royal falcon darts on a pigeon,
> It must needs be overthrown.

When Bázindah again saw himself caught in the snare of misfortune, he called to

---

[1] Literally, "dagger."   [2] *i.e.*, by blowing it out.

mind the advice of his faithful friend, and discovered the full extent of his own imperfect ideas and improper imaginations.

He made vows and promises,

that if he should escape in safety from that dangerous place and extricate himself in security from that whirlpool, he would never again allow the idea of travel to pass through his mind, and that holding in the highest esteem the society of his intimate companion, which like the philosopher's stone only leaves traces in the regions of non-existence, for the rest of his life the name of travel should not escape his lips.

> If again I get in my palm the skirt of your society,
> As long as I live no one shall drive you from my grasp.

By the blessing of so excellent an intention, which comprehended additional repose, the door was opened to him. At the very moment when the claw of the Falcon was about to bring him within his grasp, in another direction a hungry Eagle, from the danger of whose clutch the Eagle of the Skies was not secure in its heavenly nest, and who, when hungry, carried off Aries and Capricorn from the meadow of the Spheres,

> Aries from fear thereof could no longer pasture in the Heavens,
> But blood-tinged Mars every day was on the alert,

had soared aloft in scent of food: when he saw how matters stood between the Falcon and the Pigeon, he said to himself, "Though this Pigeon is a trifling morsel, and a contemptible atom, yet, on the whole, I can breakfast on him, and afford my impatient soul some little consolation." He planned to snatch away the Pigeon from the Royal Falcon, who, since the ferocious strength inherent in his nature could not be placed in the balance with that of the Eagle, did not sufficiently weigh his attack, but placing himself in the scales with the latter, entered upon war and combat:

> Bird with bird joined combat,
> He with a hundred stratagems escaped from the midst.

They both being occupied battling with one another, Bázindah, thinking it a fine opportunity, rushed under a stone, and located himself in a crevice wherein a sparrow, were he to try, could not possibly enter: miserable, he passed another night under the stone. In the morning, when the white-pinioned Dove of dawn commenced to fly from its nest in the Heavens, and the blackish, Phœnix-like Crow of night became concealed from sight,

> When the Peacock of the Sun with good omen
> Strutted forth in the garden of the Spheres,

though Bázindah, from hunger, had no power to fly, he commenced, at all hazards, to move his pinions, in fear and trembling darting his glance right and left, and scanning everything before and behind him. Suddenly he saw a Pigeon with several grains strewed in front of him, a thousand devices and schemes of like kind being adopted. The army of hunger overran the kingdom of Bázindah's body; and when he saw one of his own kind, without reflecting he advanced, and ere he had scarce got a grain in his maw, his feet were caught in the snare of calamity.

The world is Satan's net, self-indulgence the bait,
Greed after gain quickly entices the bird of the soul into the snare.

Bázindah began to reproach that Pigeon, saying, "O brother! we are both of a sort, and this event has come to pass by reason of my consanguinity with you: why did you not give me notice of the state of affairs, and perform the dues of generosity and hospitality, so that I might have taken warning, and not, in this manner, have fallen into the snare?" The Pigeon replied, "Cease this talk, for caution avails nought with Fate, and exertion has no effect on Destiny."[1]

When the arrow of Destiny[1] is shot from the string of Fate,
The shield of deliberation can never avert it.

Bázindah said, "Can you in any way show me the road of escape from this terrible calamity, and till the last day, place round my throat the necklace of obligation?" The Pigeon replied, "O simple-hearted! if I knew such a device I would free my own self from the snare, and would no longer, in the manner you see, be a cruel catcher of birds. Your case is very like that of the young Camel who, after going a long way, became tired; lamenting and interceding, he said to his mother, 'O unkind person! pray halt a while that I may recover my senses, and may for an instant[2] rest my from fatigue.' His mother rejoined, 'O inexperienced child! do you not see that the end of the guiding-string is in the hands of another? Had I entire power, I would relieve my own back from its load, and your feet from travelling.'"

The young Camel said to his mother,
"We have journeyed enough, at length rest a while."
She replied, "If the rope were in my hands,
No one would see me burthened in this line."

Bázindah, when he gave up all hope, began to tremble, and with a great effort attempted to fly; the cord of his hope being strong, the thread of the snare, which by lapse of time had become worn, was snapped, and his own throat being loosed from the noose of the net, with free wings he flew away and set out towards his own country. From delight at finding a light escape from such a heavy snare, the pangs of hunger passed from his mind. In the midst of his flight he arrived at a retired village, and alighted on the corner of a wall near a corn-field. A young Rustic who was watching the corn-field, while going his rounds, passed in the locality of that secluded spot: when his eyes alighted on the Pigeon, the flame of a desire after roast food, drawing smoke from his heart, he manœuvred to put a small shell in a sling and discharged it. Bázindah all the while paid no heed to this sport, and turned towards the corn-field and the region of that secluded spot and meadows. All of a sudden, from the jugglery of the deceitful Heavens, the baneful effect of that shell reached the pinion of that broken-winged bird: in excess of fear and dread dropping his head, he fell to the bottom of a well, which was at the foot of that very wall. Now this well was so deep that the dome of the skies appeared at the top thereof like an orb, and were the black and white threads of night and day to be woven together they would not have reached the bottom thereof.

It was not a well, but such a pit, that its depth

---

[1] لـمـا in the Persian text is a misprint for لـمـا.
[2] لـحـظـة in the Persian text is a misprint for لـحـظـة.

> Extended from thence to the seventh World;
> If the Spheres wished to know its circuit,
> They would be disappointed, and have failed to encircle its expanse.

When the young Rustic saw that his object was at the bottom of the well, and the thread of deliberation too short to reach it, he became hopeless and left that half-dead Pigeon in the prison of torture. In short, Bázindah, sad-hearted and broken-winged, passed another night and day at the bottom of the well; in language of his own experience, his thoughts wandering to Nawázindah, he recounted his state of weakness and wretchedness, and condition of impotence and helplessness, and exclaimed:

> Let me call to mind when the end of your street was my abode,
> My eyes obtained brightness from the dust at your door.
> It was in my thoughts that I should never be without a friend.
> What can I do since my endeavours and desires have come to nought?

Next day Bázindah, in the best way he could, by means of every device he knew, conveyed himself to the top of the well; crying and lamenting, at breakfast-time he arrived in the neighbourhood of his own nest. Nawázindah, when she heard the noise of her companion's pinions, flew from her nest to meet him, saying:

> "It is I who again fix my eyes in contemplating my companion,
> How shall I return thanks to thee, O clever and dear friend?"

When Nawázindah had embraced him, discovering his extreme weakness and thinness, she exclaimed, "O dear friend! where have you been, and what are the circumstances of your case?" Bázindah replied:

> I have undergone the pangs of love, do not ask what.
> I have tasted the poison of separation, do not ask me how.

"As regards the toils, the miseries, the difficulties, and distresses, which I have undergone,

> "I need a night of rest, and pleasant moonlight,
> To tell you an account of all that has happened.

"Briefly what I have to say is this: I have heard that much experience is acquired by travel; to me, at any rate, this wisdom is apparent, that so long as I live I will never again go a journey, nor unless necessity compels, leave the corner of my nest; nor will I, of my own free will, exchange the happiness of seeing my friends for the toil of the struggles of exile."

> I have no desire again to engage in the contest of travel,
> For I am perpetually happy in the society of my friends.

"Now I have adduced this story that His Majesty the King, the protector of the world, may not exchange the pleasures of a settled abode for the anguish of travel, nor willingly elect separation from friends and acquaintances, of which the result is nought but lamentation and tearful eyes."

> When the love of friends and acquaintances crosses my mind,
> My home is inundated with the water of my tears.

Dábishlím said: "O honest Minister! though the toils of travel are great, yet the benefits thereof are countless. When any one during his journey falls into the whirlpool of distress, he gains instruction and improvement, and acquires experience which will be useful to him all his life. Without doubt great advancement is obtained by travel, both as regards external and also as concerns spiritual matters. Do you not see that the Pawn, after journeying six stages, by its skill, acquires the dignity of a Queen; while the bright-faced Moon, by journeying fourteen nights, advances from the crescent to the degree of a full orb?

> From travel your servant becometh a great Monarch.
> Without journeying, how could the Moon become beautiful?

"Now, if any one droops his head in the corner of the habitation he possesses, and does not place his feet beyond the abode of trouble of his native soil, he will remain deprived of the sight of the wonders of town, and have no share in the service of great individuals. Hawks take their place upon the wrists of monarchs because they do not droop their heads in their nests, while owls remain behind the wall of meanness, for the reason that they never raise their souls from desolate abodes.

> Like a royal hawk swoop down and pounce.
> How long will you, like an owl, be behind a wall?

"Indeed, one of the great saints, with these verses, incited the body of his disciples to travel:

> He who travels is praiseworthy;
> With perfect excellence he will become the light of every eye.
> Nought is purer than water,
> But when once it remains in one spot it stagnates.

"Now, if that Hunting Hawk which grew up with the young ones of the Kite had remained in the nest of the latter, and had not flown in the atmosphere of travel, assuredly he would not have attained the honour of being nurtured by the sovereign."

The Minister besought, saying, "What are the circumstances of the case?"

STORY II.

King Dábishlím said: I have heard a tradition, that once upon a time two swift-flying Hawks lived as companions together: their nest was situate upon the pinnacle of a hill, such that the Eagle of the Spheres could not, by the power of his flight, reach the neighbourhood thereof; nor could the Vulture of the Sky, in spite of his lofty soaring, attain anywhere near it:

> It was a mountain such that nothing similar was on the face of the earth;
> It was a heaven, you would say, above the skies.

With freedom of wing they passed their time in that abode, and lived happy and joyous in the presence of one another.

> Do thou, O nightingale! when you approach the rose,
> Consider yourself fortunate, for the Fates are propitious.

After a while the High God bestowed an offspring on them. By reason of their inmost pangs at the sight of their son, both of them used to go about in search of food, and on account of their feelings of affection collected provisions from every quarter, till in a little time his strength began to increase. One day, having left him alone, they had both gone somewhere, and a delay occurred in their return. The young Hawk's pangs of hunger being aroused, he began to seek around, and, fidgeting about in every direction, reached the edge of the nest: suddenly tumbling out, he fell with his face on the slope of the mountain. By chance, in that spot a Kite had come forth from his nest, with the object of procuring food for his young ones. While he sat watching in the midst of the mountain, his eyes alighted upon the young Hawk, who was setting out from the top to the foot: the Kite thought to himself that it was a Mouse which had escaped from the claws of a Kite.

> In the pan, in every thought, I see your face.

Without reflection he pounced down, and ere ever he reached the ground snatched up the young Hawk in the air, and carried him to his own nest. Now, when he came to look closely, he perceived by the appearance of the claws and beak that it was one of a species of hunting birds. Through kinship, feelings of affection overspread his heart, and he thought to himself, "Divine consideration may be traced in this circumstance, in that He has made me become the means of his salvation, since, if I had not been present at that spot, and this little bird had fallen from the top of the mountain on the earth, assuredly all his limbs and members would have been scattered asunder, and his bones, having been ground to pieces by the injuries of the stone of calamity, would have gone like dust to the wind of annihilation. Now, since the divine decree has so ordained that I should be the means of preserving his life, it is right that he should become a companion of my children in their education; nay, more, I will take him in the place of a son, and he shall be treated like the rest of my children." Accordingly, that Kite, by way of kindness, took upon himself the fledgling's education, and just as he conducted himself towards his own little ones, in the same manner did he treat him, till the young Hawk grew up, and his natural disposition—since "*Mankind are mines, like mines of gold and silver*"—began to develop and exhibit itself. Though he imagined himself to be one of that Kite's own offspring, yet he discerned that his form, his aspirations, and his dignity were different from theirs. For a long while he wondered to himself, "If I am not one of them, why am I in this nest? and if I belong to this family, why am I different to them in appearance and disposition?"

> I neither consider myself within this circuit,
> Nor do I deem myself excluded from this throng.
> It is best that, whether I be so or not,
> I should pass my time happily, and not worry myself.

One day the Kite said to the Hawk: "O dear son! I observe you are much distressed, and the cause of dejection is concealed from me. If you have some anxiety on your mind, tell me, so that I may be in the way of settling it for you; and if some idea is passing through your mind, without delay make it known, so that, to the extent of my power, I may strive to put it in execution." The Hawk replied: "I, too, observe in myself traces of melancholy, nor do I know the cause thereof; and if I knew, I could not say.

> Look at this wonderful rose which has blossomed for me;
> You can neither trace the colour, nor conceal the perfume.

" Now it seems to me expedient that you should be pleased to grant me permission to go about the world for two or three days; it may be, by the blessing of travel, the dust of grief will be swept from the page of my heart, for when the mind is occupied with the wonders and marvels of cities and lands, maybe the representation of joy will appear in the mirror of the heart." When the Kite heard mention of separation, the smoke of grief arose in his soul, and he said:

> ' Speak not a word of bitter separation;
> Do what you will, but do not this.'

In tones of lamentation, he cried out, "O son! what idea is this you have conceived, and what device is this you have concocted? Say not a word about travel, for it is a sea ruinous to mankind, and a dragon destructive to the human race.

> Travel is a place of torment to the inhabitants of this world;
> For which reason, " sakar," hell, is similar in form to " safar," travel.

" Most men who make choice of travel do so with the view of obtaining the means of support, or because it is impossible to remain in their own country; but neither of these two has happened to you. Thank God! there is a cell of repose, and provisions are procurable wherewith life may be spent. You, too, are exalted above my other children, all having bowed their neck to your greatness. In spite of all this, to elect the pains of travel, and to abandon the repose of remainng at home, appears removed from the road of wisdom. Long ago it was said:

> ' To let slip good days is not the part of the wise.' "

The Hawk replied: " What you have spoken proceeds from kindness and consideration; but whenever I reflect with myself, this food and lodging do not appear in accordance with my condition, and things pass through my mind to which I cannot give expression." The Kite, perceiving that the proverb " *All things revert to their original* " was verified, abandoned this line of conversation, and said: " What I am telling you is based on contentment, while what you speak is of the nature of greed. Now the covetous are always disappointed, and till a person becomes satisfied he will find no rest. Since you are not filled with gratitude for the favour of contentment, and are not aware of the value of the wealth of repose, I fear that the same will befall you as happened to that greedy Cat." The Hawk inquired, " What was that ? "

STORY III.

The Kite replied: In former days there was a very decrepit old woman, who had a cell narrower than the hearts of the ignorant, and darker than the graves of the miserly: a Cat, too, lived with her, who never in the mirror of imagination had seen the face of bread, and who never had heard either from stranger or acquaintance the name of meat. She was, in fact, content if now and then she sniffed the smell of a mouse in its hole, or ever saw its footmarks on the surface of the ground. If sometimes, by aid of fortune and the assistance of good-luck, a mouse came into her clutches,

> Like a beggar finding a hoard of gold.

her face was brightened with joy, and past grief consumed with the flame of her internal warmth; and for a whole week, more or less, she lived on that amount of food, saying:

> What do I see? is it when awake, O God! or in my dreams?
> Myself so favoured after [1] such torment.

Seeing that the old woman's home was the abode of famine to that Cat she was invariably weak and thin, and from afar seemed like the apparition of thought. One day, in excess of feebleness, she came out on the roof with the greatest anxiety, and saw a Cat who strutted on the wall of a neighbouring house, and like a furious lion walked with measured tread, moving his feet slowly from excess of fatness. When the old woman's Cat saw one of her own kith and kin so sleek and fat she was astonished, and uttered a cry:

> At any rate, you arrive strutting; will you not say whence?

"Whence get you so sleek, for it seems to me that you have come from the banquet-house of a chief of Khatá? Whence is this your sprightliness, and whence this your dignity and pomp?" The neighbouring Cat replied, "I eat the crumbs from the sovereign's table; every morning I am present at the king's court, and when the banquet-tables are spread I display boldness and intrepidity, and always snatching some morsels of fat meat or fine bread, till next day pass my time in comfort." The old woman's Cat inquired, "What sort of a thing is fat meat, and what kind of taste has fine bread, for in the whole course of my life I have never seen nor eaten aught but the old woman's broth and the flesh of mice?" The neighbouring Cat smiled, and said, "It is for this reason you cannot be distinguished from a spider. Now this appearance and form which you possess is a reproach to our race, and I consider this look and condition which you have brought from the house to the desert a disgrace:

> You have indeed the ears and tail of a cat,
> All the rest appertains to a spider.

"Now, were you to see the king's court, and smell the perfume of that delicious food and agreeable diet, assuredly the proverb, '*He shall restore bones to life when they are rotten,*' would come from the veil of secrecy to the expanse of manifestation, and you would experience new life."

> When the perfume of a loved one passes over the grave of a dear friend,
> What wonder if it gives life to these decayed bones?

The old woman's Cat, in tones of the greatest supplication said, "O brother! the dues of neighbourship, and the bonds of consanguinity, are strong between you and me; why should you not perform the rights of generosity and fraternity, and this time, when you go, take me with you? It may be, by your good fortune, I shall find sustenance, and by the blessing of your society attain some place."

> Withdraw not your head from the society of the pious,
> Restrain not your hand from the girdle of the prosperous.

The neighbouring Cat's heart being consumed with her lamentations and cries, he arranged that this time he himself would not be present at the head of the banquet without her. The old woman's Cat getting fresh life at the good news of

---

[1] ‏ سب ‏ in the Persian text is a misprint for ‏ سپ ‏.

this promise, came down from the roof, and told the state of the case to the old woman, who commenced to give advice, saying, "O dear friend ! be not deceived by the words of men of the world, and do not abandon the nook of contentment, since the vase of greed is never filled, save with the dust of the grave, and the eyes of desire are never sewn up but with the needle of eternity and the thread of destruction."

> Contentment enriches a man.
> Proclaim to the world-encompassing greedy person
> That he knows not God, nor worships him,
> Since he is not satisfied with his daily lot.

The ideas respecting the tables of the king's bounty which entered the Cat's head were not such that the medicine of advice had any effect upon her.

> Advice all the world over is like wind in a cage—
> In the case of lovers, like water in a sieve.

In short, next day, together with the neighbouring Cat, crouching and jumping along, she betook herself to the king's court, and ere ever that helpless wretch arrived, the true proverb, " *The greedy are disappointed*," was curiously exemplified, and bad fortune poured the water of disappointment upon the fire of her crude desires.   Now, the cause thereof was this : the day previous, the Cats, having overran the top of the tables, had made a noise and tumult past all limit, and with their cries and screams had annoyed both guests and host.   On this very day the king had issued an order that a body of archers with fleet notched bows should stand watching in ambush, so that every cat which, having drawn the shield of impudence before its face, should enter the plain of audacity, should eat as its first delicate morsel a heart-piercing dart.   The old woman's Cat, unaware of this state of things, when she inhaled the perfume of food, inconsiderately, like a falcon, turned her face towards the hunting-ground of the tables : scarce had the balance of the scales of appetite been weighed down with heavy morsels, when a heartrending arrow transfixed her bosom.

> Blood flowed trickling from her bones.
> In fear of life she ran away, exclaiming,
> ' If I could escape from the hand of this archer,
> Both myself and the mouse would remain in the old woman's solitary abode.
> The honey of my life is not equivalent to the wound of the sting.
> 'Tis better to be content with the syrup of what one has.' "

"Now I have adduced this story that you also may appreciate the corner of my nest, and may esteem the amount of food and eatables which, without any effort on your part, accrues to you ; and being content with a little, may not seek more, lest you fail to reach that dignity, and this station also slips from your hands."   The Hawk replied : "What you say is honest advice and pure kindness ; yet to droop the head over trifles is the part of the helpless, and to be content with mere meat and drink is the nature of animals.   Every one who would sit upon the cushion of eminence must rise to great things, and whoever would place the diadem of honour upon his brows must bind the girdle of enterprise on his loins ; great ambition is not satisfied with mean matters, and exalted wisdom does not approve of low stations."

No one will find the road of eminence
Till he has trodden the way of lofty ambition.
Seek rank that you may reach the moon.
No one, in a well, can drink the nectar of rain.

The Kite replied: "The fancy that is in your head will not be realised by mere thought, nor will this pot of desire boil by impracticable wishes. No affair is accomplished unless the arrangements are settled, and no result is brought about unless preparatory plans are executed."

You cannot by boasting recline in the place of the illustrious,
Unless you make ready all the paraphernalia of greatness.

The Hawk replied: "The strength of my talons is the best means of acquiring the favours of fortune, and the onslaughts of my beak are the truest way of obtaining the rank of exalted position. Maybe you have not heard the story of that Warrior who, by aid of his warlike arm, made pretensions to sovereignty and monarchy, and ultimately the robe of his ambition was ornamented with the fringe of dominion?" The Kite inquired, "In what way was that?"

STORY IV.

The Hawk replied: In former days there was a poor Mechanic, overwhelmed with maintaining his family, and who, from excess of poverty, had never read a letter from the page of joy; while the profits of his handiwork did not suffice for more than the expenses of his family, and the produce of his occupation did not go beyond procuring bread and raiment. The favour of God (may His Majesty be glorified!) bestowed upon him a dear son, upon whose forehead[1] were manifest the traces of dignity, and upon whose temples were evident the signs of fortune.

Of good fortune and happy omen,
A beautiful plant in the garden of joy.

By the blessing of his footsteps the father's circumstances became easier, and by the favour of his existence the produce of the latter's trade began to gain upon his expenditure. The father, perceiving the auspiciousness of his son's footsteps, gave him an education to such degree as opportunity allowed; while the son, during his childhood, was always conversing about bows and arrows, and sporting with shield and sword. Though they sent him off to school, he turned up in the midst of the plain; and though they instructed him in his letters, he showed an inclination for the straight spear. Perpetually, from the inscription of the sword, he was reading an account of the subjugation of the world; and constantly, in the picture of the shield, he was witnessing the sketch of exaltation.

When his instructor wrote the letters "ha" and "mím,"
Shields and helmets were in his mind.
He so formed the alphabet, "alif, be,"[2]
That "be" was shaped like a bow, "alif" like an arrow.

---

[1] ﺤﭙﻪ in the Persian text is a misprint for ﺤﻴﻪ .
[2] Alluding to the shape of the letters in Persian.

When he passed from the condition of childhood to the verge of manhood, his father one day said, "O son! my mind is much concerned as regards your condition; now the time of youth has no connection with the period of infancy. The traces of audacity and boldness are prominently evident on the pages of your circumstances; and I am anxious that, before evil lusts cast you in the desert of wantonness, I may make the strong citadel—'*Whoever takes a wife in truth he perfects half his religion*'—your abode. Even so I have arranged the hand of negotiation, according to your condition, so that from the tribe which is akin to ourselves I may lead a lady to the path of marriage with you: as regards this, what seems advisable to you?" The son replied, "O illustrious father! I have settled the hand of promise with her whom I wished, and have laid down the amount of her dowry. I will not trouble you in the matter, nor do I expect from you assistance or aid." The father rejoined, "O son! I am perfectly aware of your circumstances; you have not means whereby to carry out your promise. Whence is that which you say you have prepared? and who is the bride which you have selected?" The son went to the house, and brought thence a sword, a hundred times more fatal than the glances of beauties, and a thousand times more precious than the teeth of red-lipped damsels; he then said, "O father! know that I will betroth the bride of Dominion, and wed the virgin of Sovereignty: nor is there a surer betrothal for this than a sharp sword, nor a better dowry than a blood-shedding dagger."

No one engages in strife with men of good fortune.
The marriage portion of the bride of Empire is nought but the sword.

So, since that young man's ambition was confined to obtaining Sovereignty, in a little time he overran the whole country, and with the force of his world-subduing sword conquered most of the kingdoms of the universe: hence it has been said:

The bride of Dominion will not contract marriage, except
There first be given her a dowry from the jewels of the sword.

"Now I have adduced this story that you may know that, whatever may be the appurtenance of fortune is prepared for me; and the grace of God has opened the doors of happiness upon the face of my circumstances. I also am in hopes that soon I shall obtain my object, and place the hand of desire upon the neck of my ambition. Now I will not, through the treachery and deceit of any one, deviate from my arrangement, nor abandon this design."

We will not through reproach quit the end of this street.

The Kite, perceiving that this bird of exalted ambition would not fall into the snare by means of the thread of stratagem, nor be trapped with the grain of treachery and deceit, from necessity gave him permission to travel, and placed the scar of separation upon his own distracted bosom. The Hawk, having bid adieu to the Kite and his young ones, flew from the nest, and soared aloft. After he was tired he alighted upon the top of a hill, and scanned every direction with the eye of pleasure. Suddenly he observed a beautiful - plumed Partridge commencing to strut along in the very fulness of majesty, from the noise of whose cry a clamour resounded in every part of the hill. The Hawk finding a natural desire to make the Partridge his prey, with one swoop filled his own stomach with the flesh of his breast, which was agreeable to his disposition: he found the meat such that its delightful taste was like that of the water of life, and its charming flavour equal to the pleasures of enchanting delicacies—"*And the flesh of birds such as they desire.*"   Now since, during the whole course of his life, he had never tasted flesh so delicious, he said :

> From head to foot you are quite acceptable to my feelings ;
> One would say you had been created on my behalf.

He thereupon thought to himself, "It is a sufficient advantage of travel that ready at hand I have found escape from disagreeable food, and have got a taste of flesh, which is acceptable to my soul—having been exalted from a dark and narrow nest, and from low and unaspiring companions to dignified spots and lofty abodes.

Now this as yet is the first world-illuminating result.

So, after this, what delight as yet will come from the cell of secrecy to the expanse of manifestation ? "

What will Omnipotent Power itself bring forth from the screen ?

Accordingly, for several days the swift-flying Hawk winged about in ease of mind, and with joyous pinion hunted the partridge and quail ; till one day he was sitting on the top of the hill, at the skirt of which he saw a troop of horsemen arranged in ranks for hunting, with birds of prey, fluttering to capture their feathered victims.

> From dread of the sound of the drum,
> All the hunting birds stretched out their wings :
> On one side the male hawks, quick in flight,
> Sharpened their claws in the blood of the prey ;
> While on another side the royal falcon, as plunder
> Carried off the coin of life from partridge and quail.

Now it was the Monarch of that kingdom who had come out hunting with his attendants, and their domain happened to adjoin the foot of that very hill.   In the midst of this, the Hawk which was on the King's wrist flew up in pursuit of a prey, while this other lofty-minded Hawk, having determined to chase the same, suddenly carried it away from before him.   The King, whose glance alighted upon this rapid flight and capture, conceived an affection in his heart for him, and the illustrious order was issued that clever-handed hunters should, with pleasant stratagem, cast the noose of the snare around his throat ; and by the guidance of fortune he arrived at the honour of serving the King.   The benign glance of the Sovereign having become assured regarding his personal ability and natural skill, in a short time, by the aid of prosperity, he was allotted a seat on the royal wrist ; and by means of exalted ambition he reached from the abyss of meanness and contempt to the summit of dignity and prosperity.   Now, if he had been content with the abode where first he took his place in the society of crows and kites, and had not through travelling crossed the expanse of the desert and the tracts of the waste, his acquirement of such rank, and his advancement to such dignity, would have been amongst the number of impossibilities.

"Now I have adduced this story that it may be known that by travel great advancement is obtained, and men are raised from the lowest depths of obscurity and abasement to the highest degree of approbation and grandeur."

Travel is the heart's spring season, by which
The rose of mankind's desire comes into blossom.
Travel so that you may obtain your wishes,
For God has said, "*Then go your way through the tracks thereof.*"

When Dábishlím finished speaking, another Minister advancing performed the dues of praise, and said, "What his Majesty, the shadow of God, has spoken relative to travel and its advantages, is not of a nature that the suspicion of doubt can surround it; but, as it appears to the mind of your servants, for the royal person of the Sovereign, in whose wellbeing is bound the repose of mankind, to make choice of the toils of travel, and to turn from the heart-enchanting garden of happiness towards the soul-entrapping desert of grief and distress, seems far from the path of wisdom." Dábishlím replied: "To undergo vexation is the part of men of valour and the business of lions in the forest of war. Now, without doubt, till the skirt of the ease of kings is transfixed with the thorn of toil, as regards their weak subjects, the rose of delight will not blossom in the garden of repose; and so long as the foot of ambition of sovereigns does not tread the desert of fatigue, the head of the destitute poor will not reach the pillow of rest."

No one will rest within your kingdom
When you yourself seek nought but your own repose.

"Know that the servants of God are of two kinds,—one kings, to whom is given the pleasure of ruling countries and issuing commands; the other subjects, to whom is granted the advantage of security and repose: these two classes do not meet together in the same place, either quiet must be elected, and the reins of government be abandoned, or else that very regal grandeur must suffice, and the hand be withdrawn from delight and tranquillity:

Him who stamps his foot upon the head of pleasure and affluence,
Fortune will make a chief and ruler in the world.
The rose is assigned sovereignty in the garden because,
Notwithstanding its delicacy, it makes its bed of thorns.

"Sages have said, '*Labour is the cause of riches;*' to strive and labour will cause the toiler to reach the pinnacle of the abode of fortune; and to travel with the foot of fidelity the desert of peril, will bring the beauty of what is desired within the sight of observation. The acquirement of wealth is dependent upon attempting dangers:

The girdle of sovereignty can never be bound
On him who is disposed to self-indulgence.

"Whoever raises the standard of toil in the plain of ambition, and in undertaking dangers abandons the habit of ease and repose, will very quickly attain his object, and see the face of his wish with the eye of desire, just as with that Leopard who conceived a hankering to rule over a joy-producing forest, by the blessing of the labour and toil which he evinced, and by the good results of the patience, under severe sufferings and hardships, which he possessed, in a short time the veil of restraint having fallen from the face of his desire, he stretched the hand of hope to the skirt of his object." The Minister inquired, "How did this happen?"

STORY V.

King Dábishlím replied: In the regions of Busrah was an island with an extremely delightful climate, and a very pleasant and charming forest: pure fountains flowed on all sides, and life-giving breezes blew in every direction:

> There were trees their heads intertwining;
> In that delightful spot was beautiful and juicy fruit,
> Its shrubs were more enchanting than the tree of Paradise,
> Its herbage sharper-tongued than the lily.

From its extreme beauty it was called " the joy-increasing forest." A Leopard was master of that wood, by reason of whose majesty fierce lions could not set their foot in that retreat, while owing to his grandeur beasts and animals were not able to let the thought of that wood encompass their minds:

> When in rage he lashed his tail upon the stones,
> The Lion of the Spheres, through fear, loosened his talons;
> On the highway where he sat but for a moment,
> He blocked the passage of mankind for a year.

For a long time he had passed his life in that forest according to his heart's desire, and had not seen the appearance of disappointment in the mirror of fortune. He possessed a child by whose face the world seemed resplendent, and in meeting the lustre of whose eyes radiance was added to his sight. He had a plan that when this child increased in years, and dipped his teeth and claws in the blood of lions, he would make over charge of that forest to his possession, and, at leisure, pass the rest of his own life in the nook of contentment. Scarce had the bud of desire blossomed on the plant of design, when the autumn of death scattered the fruit of his life's garden to the wind of annihilation:

> O ! the many intentions which are scattered in the dust !

When this Leopard was seized in the clutch of the Lion of death, several animals, who in former days had coveted that wood, all at once began stirring and planning possession thereof. The young Leopard, seeing that he had no power to oppose them, elected to migrate. A great contention having arisen amongst the beasts, a blood-spilling, fear-exciting Lion was victorious over all of them, and brought that joy-increasing, Paradise-like spot by force into the region of his possession. Now the young Leopard, having for several days undergone hardships in the mountain and desert, betook himself to another wood, and explaining to the animals of that locality his own distress of mind, sought their assistance in remedying his troubles. They having been apprised of the victory of this prey-seeking Lion, and of the ardour of this oppressing, mighty[1] beast, refused to afford aid or assistance, and said, " O helpless wretch ! at present your home is in possession of a Lion, from whose fury not a bird will fly across that wood, nor an elephant, from dread of him, wander around that desert. We are not able to fight him, nor to endure his teeth and claws, while you, too, cannot contend or strive with him. Our opinion demands that you should return to his court, and with pure sincerity enter his service."

---

[1] Literally, " Lion."

> When a person cannot be overthrown by you,
> The foot must not be fixed in combat with him.
> It is better for you to be civil to him,
> Displaying regret, and apologising.

This speech proved reasonable to the young Leopard; and it seemed to him advisable to make choice of attendance on the Lion, and according to his power to perform the dues of servitude. Accordingly he put in execution the proverb, " *To return is most laudable;* " and through the medium of one of the pillars of the state attained the honour of waiting on the Lion, and having been received with royal favour, he was appointed to a station suitable to his ambition. The Leopard, having fixed the skirt of servitude on the girdle of affection, evidenced such traces of ability and industry as from hour to hour became the cause of extension of intimacy and increase of consideration, to a degree that he became the envy of the pillars of the state and the chiefs of the Sovereign. Notwithstanding this, every moment he laboured and toiled more and more in his service, and every instant strove still further in looking after the interests of the state.

> He who strives and labours the most,
> His circumstances will advance beyond the rest.

Once an urgent matter in a far wood pressed upon the Lion; and at that time the oven of the Ethereal Sky was very hot, and the expanse of the desert and mountain was burning like a furnace of molten precious glass : from the excessive heat of the air, the marrow of the animals boiled in their bones, and crabs in the midst of the water were like fish roasting upon a gridiron.

> Were a cloud all at once to be laden with drops,
> Owing to the heat of the atmosphere the drops would become sparks ;
> Were a bird to pass through the air,
> It would be consumed, wings and feather, like a moth ;
> From the virulence with which the sun poured down through the air,
> A heart of stone would have been consumed with its rays.

The Lion reflected within himself, " At such a time, when the shell at the depths of the sea is roasted like a bird upon a spit, and the salamander, through fear of the heat of the sun, will not put its foot on shore, from the midst of the fire, such an affair has occurred : amongst my attendants who may there be who, not being disturbed at undergoing difficulties, and not dreading the heat of the air, will set out on this errand ? " In the midst of this soliloquy the Leopard entered amongst the ranks of attendants, and observed the King distressed; as he was extremely generous and exceedingly sharp, having approached the royal throne, he was bold enough to inquire as to the cause of such deep thought. After ascertaining the account of what had happened, he undertook effectually to carry out the business. He obtained the royal permission, and set out with a band of attendants. Arriving there mid-day, he set about bringing the affair to a termination; and immediately that, through his eagerness, the case was settled, he gathered up the reins of return. The attendants and companions, who waited on the stirrup of his fortune, with one voice represented : " In this heat we have traversed all the way with the foot of diligence ; now, when the arrangements are finished, and there is no anxiety of any kind, while it is clear that your favour in the exalted presence is without limit, if you rest for a while under the shade of a tree, and, with the potion of cold water, quench the flame of the fire of thirst, certainly it will not be far wrong."

Be at ease, and no longer bear the burden of toil ;
Ungird thy loins, since the world's anxieties have no limit.

The Leopard, smiling, said : " My greatness and intimacy with his Majesty the King are a flag which with toil and labour I have raised : it would not be commendable to debase it through negligence and idleness, nor would it be well, through personal gratification and self-indulgence, to level with the ground an edifice which has been reared with great labour. Without enduring[1] grief the load of wealth cannot be obtained, and without partaking of the heartrending thorn, the pleasures of the rose-garden will not be procured."

Any one may entwine his hands round the neck of his object,
Who is able to place a shield against the darts of misfortune.
This result will not accrue from desire or wish,
But is obtained by tears from the eyes and blood from the heart.

News-bearers conveyed this intelligence to the King, and read from beginning to end the pages of this affair. The Lion nodded his head with approbation, and said : " Such a person is worthy of exaltation and position, for he can lift his head from the collar of difficulties ; and subjects may rest quiet during the just time of an exalted man, who does not lay his brow upon the pillow of repose."

Peace will accrue from that king,
Who can deprive himself of his own ease.
Happy is he, by whom the comfort of mankind[2]
Is elected, in preference to his own repose.

Accordingly he sent after the Leopard, and having distinguished him with the greatest consideration, confided the government of that forest to him, and made over to him his father's place, giving him in addition, also, the position of heir-apparent.

" Now the moral of this story is, that you may know, that to no one, without earnest and laborious endeavour, will the sun of Desire rise from the east of Hope, nor without due diligence will the prelude of Expectation result in the acquisition of what is coveted."

He who has not undergone grief will not obtain wealth ;
He reaps the reward, O dear brother, who performs the work.

" Now, since in this journey my object is to acquire knowledge, I have made a fixed purpose ; and. having brought the foot of Endeavour within the stirrup of Intention, the page of my departure shall not, through the mere thought of trouble, which may happen during my journey to and fro, find the inscription of violation ; nor shall the champion of exalted Ambition turn the reins from the direction, ' *In truth this is certainly a most necessary affair.*' "

When the king, with good object, puts his foot into the stirrup,
It is no wonder if the reins slip from the hands of the Skies.

When the Ministers perceived that the prohibitions of advice would not hinder his intention, having agreed in opinion with the King, they busied themselves in preparing the necessaries for travelling, and performed the dues of intercessions

---

[1] خمل in the Persian text is a misprint for تحمّل .
[2] Literally, " men and women."

for a happy journey; reciting this verse they raised a clamour beyond the revolving dome:

> You have planned a pleasant journey, may God befriend you!
> May the grace of the clear-sighted be the leader of your caravan!

Accordingly King Dábishlím intrusted the reins of state affairs to the able hands of one of the pillars of the kingdom, who was in a position of confidence; and as regards the repose of the subjects and the protection of the people, whispered in the ears of his intelligence several precepts which might serve as fringe to the robes of monarchy amongst the members these:

> The kingdom is Alexander's mirror,[1]
> In which you may see your own face:
> Your countenance will not appear handsome, unless
> You remove therefrom the rust[2] of tyranny.
> Take on yourself to enlighten the country as the dawn (does):
> Be fearful of the early morning breaths.[3]
> The life-destroying arrows of a hundred archers
> Are not so potent as the sighs of one old woman.

When his mind found leisure from the toils of his kingdom, together with a body of his intimate companions he set out towards Sarándíp: like the Moon, he traversed from stage to stage, and like the Sun, he moved from city to city.[4] At every halting-place he acquired experience, and especial advantages from every caravan; till, after traversing stages by land and sea, and undergoing the severities of warmth and cold, the coasts of Sarándíp came into his sight, and the perfumed gales of that region reached the King's nostrils.

> He who from the morning breezes inhales thy pleasant perfume,
> Gets precious news from a dear friend.

After he had for two or three days rested from the toils of his journey, at the City of Sarándíp, having left there his unnecessary impediments and baggage, he set out with two or three companions towards the mountain: when he had come to the top thereof, he saw a peak the shadow of whose skirt reached the Sun, and the gleams of whose summit added brilliance to the rays[5] of the planet Mars.

> In height it stretched aloft like the crystalline sphere,
> With its rocks it tinged the skies.
> When placed side by side with the celestial orb,
> Its pinnacle was the more lofty.
> The Heavens, compared with its iron-like peak,
> Appeared but mere verdure at its skirt.

On every side were meadows decked with various sweet-scented plants, and in all directions were flower-gardens indicative of the beautiful delights of the garden of Paradise.

> On the borders of the meadows were emerald fruits,
> Its mountains were girdled with jewelled zones;

---

[1] Alexander, says Eastwick, is said to have had a mirror in which he could see the whole world.
[2] It must be remembered that mirrors used to be made of polished metal.
[3] That is, the malediction of unhappy persons who rise betimes to pray.
[4] The word in Persian means both "month" and "city"—hence the point of the comparison.
[5] Literally, "dagger."

Amongst the plants on its rivulets, was the tree of Paradise,
And from the breeze of its parterres the Garden of Eden was perfumed.

Dábishlím wandered in every direction, and strayed through the blessed spots. In the midst of his perambulations his glance lighted on a cave, the darkness of which was like the pupil of the eye,[1] and the precept, " *There is light in darkness*," was made evident by its shade. On strict inquiry from the inhabitants of those regions, he ascertained that it was the dwelling of a sage called Bídpáí, that is to say, " a generous physician:" amongst some of the notables of Hind it has been rumoured that his name was Pílpáí, whom in Hindí they call " Hastí-Pát." He was a man advanced in ,the degrees of knowledge, the pearl of reason being ornamented with the decoration of excellence : at that time having abandoned the society of mankind, and being contented with but little subsistence, he had sewn up his eyes from worldly concerns, and had burnt up, with the flame of the fire of abstinence, the rubbish of impure dispositions. His wakeful eyes, from excess of his vigils, had not seen the countenance of sleep, nor, owing to his extreme self-mortification, had the ears of his understanding heard ought but the cry, " *God inviteth towards the dwelling of safety.*"

His breath was a store-house, from which truths poured forth,
His forehead a sun to morning risers ;
In each affair he was purse-holder to the spheres ;
In every matter he was the confidant of the secrets of Fate.

Dábishlím, desirous of meeting him, for a while stood outside the cave, and, representing his circumstances, sought from that perfect man's magnanimity permission to visit him. The Saint of enlightened mind having, by secret inspiration and indubitable indication, gained intelligence as to the intention of the world-subduing King, gave forth a cry, " *Enter therein, safe in peace.*"

The King was in that cave the mirror of wisdom,
The cavern became thereby the picture-gallery of China ;
He girded his loins in the service of the Saint ;
He bound on his soul the zone of attendance.

Looking round, he saw a Brahman, who had placed the foot of retirement in the world of solitude, and displayed the long flag of truth in the plain of attention to minute details. Angelic temperament was evident in his human appearance, and his bodily cleanliness was a manifest indication of the purity of his soul. The King with sagacity perceived that he himself would attain his own object at his hands, and by the blessing of his spirit would attain his own desires.[2] With the greatest respect he advanced ; when he came near the Brahman, having discharged the dues of salutation, he performed the necessary obeisance. The Brahman, after returning the greeting, and repeating the customary welcome, enjoined him to sit down, and asked him respecting the toils of the way, and inquired regarding his choosing the fatigues of travel, and abandoning the repose of his home. Dábishlím repeated from beginning to end the account of the dream,[3] the treasure, the scroll of precepts, and how, when complete, it was deposited at Sarándíp : the Brahman smiled, and said, " All praise to the ambition of the King, who in search of knowledge undergoes all this toil, and who, on account of the repose of his oppressed subjects, and the ease of his wretched creatures, chooses various kinds of troubles and misery."

---

[1] Dark eyes are a type of beauty amongst the Persians.

[2] نمراد in the Persian text is a misprint for بمراد .　　　[3] So خوات should be خواب .

O ! is it pleasant to you to have charge of the world ?
You may in such way preserve your kingdom.
The root of the plant which you water
Will on its boughs bear nought but good fruit.

Then the Brahman, having opened the lid of the casket of secrets, filled the shell of the King's ear with the pearls of wisdom: and having, for some days, laid aside his own affairs, busied himself in instructing the Monarch. In the midst of their discourse allusion was made to Húshang's Book of Precepts. The King recited them one by one to the Sage, and the Brahman addressed his words to the great King relative thereto, while Dábishlím engrossed the same, with the pen of imagination, upon the tablets of retention. Now the Book Kalílah and Damnah comprises the questions and answers of the King and the Brahman: and we have designed it in fourteen books, in the manner stated in the index of the volume, and "*Aid is from God, from whom aid is asked. He is sufficient for us, and in Him is our trust.*"

BOOK I.

ON AVOIDING THE SPEECH OF CALUMNIATORS AND SLANDERERS.

THE great king Dábishlím said to Pílpáí the sage: "The intent of the first precept was this—Whenever a person is honoured by being admitted to the presence of kings, assuredly he will be envied by his equals; and the jealous, having laboured to damage the basis of his reputation by words mingled with deceit, will alter the disposition of the king towards him: consequently, it becometh the monarch to deliberate well concerning the speech of the selfish, and when it is evident that it is not free from alloy and impurity, he should not convey it within the limits of acceptance:

> Give not place before you to a calumniator,
> Since he mixes together honey and the sting:
> To appearance, he presents honey, and feigns friendship,
> In reality he darts his sting, and produces misery.

"Now I request the Brahman to recount a story in illustration of this state of affairs, and to give a narrative of some one who, having been allowed to approach a monarch, by reason of the calumniatory speech of the jealous found the edifice of his dignity ruined, friendship ending in enmity, and concord in opposition."

The Brahman replied: "The centre of the foundation of monarchy rests upon this precept; and if a king does not restrain slanderers from doing harm and mischief, they will injure and frustrate the greater part of the nobles of the state, and by such means utter ruin will both find its way to the kingdom, and will also reach the sovereign: and when a wicked mischief-maker finds a means of interposing between two persons, assuredly the end of their business will incline towards sadness and vexation, just as it was between the Lion and the Ox."

The king inquired, "How was that?"

STORY I.

The Brahman said: It has been related that there was a merchant who had traversed many stages over land and sea, and had crossed the countries of the East and West—having experienced the ups [1] and downs of fortune, and tasted largely of the sweets and bitters of life—

> Wise, trustworthy, and sagacious,
> Exceedingly clever by reason of his experience.

When the van of the army of death, of which infirm old age is an indication, began to overrun the regions of his constitution, and the advanced-guard of the army of fate, of which white hairs are the intimation, seized the environs of the castle of his existence—

> In the watch of old age, when the drum of pain is sounded,
> The heart becomes cold to happiness and delight,
> White hairs bring a message from fate,
> A crooked-back conveys a salutation from death—

the merchant knew that at any moment the drum of departure might be sounded, and the capital of life, being but chattels placed in the dwelling of the body, be demanded back. Accordingly, he collected together his children, who were three intelligent, noble young men, but who, through pride of riches, and the rashness of youth, having deviated from the path of moderation, had stretched out the hand of prodigality towards their father's property, and shunning business and employment, spent their precious [2] time in idleness and sloth. The indulgent father, from excess of kindness and consideration, which are the necessary accompaniments of paternity, began to counsel his children, and opened upon them the doors of disinterested advice founded on the aggregate of fear and hope, saying: " O young men ! if you do not know the worth of wealth, to procure which you have taken no pains, by the canon of wisdom you will stand excused ; but it behoveth you to know, that property may be the capital stock of happiness in this world and in eternity, and whatever is sought of the dignities of both worlds may be acquired by means of wealth. Mankind seek for one of three advantages. Firstly, Abundance of sources of support, and comfort in the means thereof—this is the object of the mass whose ambition is confined to drinking and clothing, and striving for complete self-gratification. Secondly, Promotion in station, and advancement in dignity—and the classes of persons whose object is this are men of rank and position : now these two degrees cannot be attained except by wealth. Thirdly, Finding an eternal reward, and reaching the mansions of excellence—and the mass who are intent on this object are men of salvation and religious rank : and this eminence can be attained by means of lawful wealth. ' *The blessing of wealth is pure to a man that is pure,*' like as the spiritual elder said in the book ' Masnawí ' [3]—

> ' If thou devotest thy wealth on behalf of religion,
> The advantage of such wealth is pure,' the Prophet saith of it.

---

[1] Literally, " cold and warmth."

[2] ضرر in the Persian text is a misprint for عزیز .

[3] A famous Persian composition.

"Therefore, it is evident that by the blessing of wealth most objects can be attained; but to acquire property without occupation and search appears impossible; and if, perchance, any one should gain riches without labour, since in the acquisition thereof he has not undergone toil, assuredly, not knowing the value and worth of the same, he will quickly let them slip from his grasp. Consequently, having turned away your face from sloth, set your inclinations in the direction of industry, and occupy yourselves in the same trade of merchandise which you have, for a long time, observed on my part."

The eldest son said : " O father, you urge upon us an occupation—now this is opposed to confidence in God : and I am fully persuaded that whatever is fixed by Divine decree will come to me, although I make no labour or effort to acquire it, while as regards whatever is not befated me, though in search thereafter I use every endeavour, it will avail nought :

> Whatever is fated will arrive in due time,
> And whatever is not to be, without doubt will not come to pass—
> Therefore, in pursuit of that which will not happen,
> Why is it necessary to labour in fruitless toil ?

" And I have heard that it has been said by a wise man, that 'whatever was my destiny clung to me however much I fled from it, and whatever was not appointed for me avoided me though I clung to it:' therefore, whether or not we follow an employment, in any way,

> One cannot put away from one's self the destined lot.

" In corroboration thereof is the story of those two sons of a king, to one of whom, without any trouble on his part, the wealth of his father alighted, while the other, in expectation of that treasure, allowed the kingdom and monarchy to slip from his grasp."

The father inquired, " How was that ? "

STORY II.

The son replied : In the kingdom of Aleppo there was a prosperous Monarch and a powerful Sovereign, who had experienced many vicissitudes of fortune, and witnessed many changes of night and day. He had two sons who were engulfed in the whirlpool of the pride of youth, and intoxicated by the fragrance of the wine of prosperity. They were always addicted to playing and toying, and occupied in frolic and merriment; and they listened to the melody of this song from the voice of the lute and bells :

> Strive for pleasure, since in the twinkling of an eye
> Autumn arrives and fresh spring is past.

The King, who was a man of wisdom and experience, and possessed abundance of pearls and endless wealth, when he had witnessed the proceedings of his children, became alarmed lest, after his departure, having dissipated in waste those hoards, they should, as necessity required, scatter them to the wind of ruin. Now in the outskirts of that city there was a Devotee who had turned his back upon the possessions of the world, and had set his face towards making a provision for eternity :

> He was consumed with the radiance of Divine splendour,
> Enamoured with the Presence of God.

The King was intimate with, and had great faith in, him. Having collected together all his property in such a manner that no one gathered any inkling thereof, the Monarch buried the same in the Devotee's cell, and enjoined him: "When inconstant fortune and ephemeral dignity turn away their faces from my children, and the fount of prosperity—which, like a vapour, possesses no more than a semblance of form—is filled with the dust of misfortune, and my children become impoverished and necessitous, inform them of this property. Perhaps, after experiencing affliction and undergoing trouble, having recovered their senses, they will spend it in a proper manner; and having turned aside from prodigality and extravagance, they will follow the direction of moderation." The Devotee accepted the charge of the King, who, with a view to further his object, prepared a pit in his palace, and making things seem as if he had buried his treasure there, caused his sons to be apprised to the effect, that when the appearance of necessity presented itself, there would be hoarded there a complete store, which might be the support of life. Now a short time after these events both the King and the Devotee, having accepted the Divine invitation, fell senseless from the cup. "*Every soul shall taste of death.*"

> Every hapless human being must drink
> From the cup of fortune the wine "*All earthly things decay.*"

The property which was buried in the Devotee's cell remained hidden and concealed, no one having gained any knowledge of the circumstance. After the death of the father, the brothers fell contending and fighting over the division of the kingdom and property, and the elder brother, by reason of his strength and power, having gained the victory, took all the possessions to his own share, and left the younger brother afflicted and disappointed. Helpless he remained without a share of the dignity of sovereignty, and without a portion of his hereditary property. He thought to himself, "Since the sun of benefit and glory has lowered its face towards the west, and the cruel spheres have displayed the countenance of instability and unkindness, what result can accrue from again turning my face towards seeking after worldly possessions, or from trying again what has already been attempted before?

> All the things of this world, both old and new,
> When they are past are not worth a grain of barley.
> Prepare a better kingdom than this;
> Open the door of a better cell than this.

"Nought is better than this: Since the collar of fortune is gone from the grasp of my power, I will clutch the skirt of reliance on God and contentment, and not allow the rank of a darwísh, which is a never-lessening monarchy, to slip from my hands."

> The darwísh to whom is consigned the nook of contentment
> Is poor in name, but in reality is monarch of the world.

Accordingly, with this view he came forth from the city, saying to himself, "Such and such a Devotee was a friend of my father; it is right that I should set my face towards his cell, and at his feet follow the road of worship by the path of abstinence." When he reached the dwelling of the Devotee, he discov-

ered that the Parrot of his holy spirit had flown from the cage of the body
towards the gardens of "*In a lofty garden,*" and the cell of that holy man of
exalted mind remained empty. For an hour or so he was overpowered by grief
and misery. At length, having agreed to make that locality his place of abode,
he paid his devotions by way of discipleship in that same spot. Now in the
proximity to the cell there was a channel, and inside the cell a well having been
dug, and a way made into the channel, there was always a supply of water
flowing from the latter to the well; and the occupants of the cell had made use
thereof, washing and performing their ablutions therein. The Prince one day let
a bucket down into the well, but there came no sound of water; he made a careful examination; there was no water at the bottom of the well. He thought
to himself, "What has happened that the water does not flow into the well?
Now, if complete destruction has happened to the well and the channel, and
they have been entirely obliterated, it will be impossible any longer to remain in
this locality." Accordingly, with a view of finding out the true state of affairs,
he went down into the well and examined minutely the sides and surroundings
of the well, the water, and the channel. All at once a hole came into his sight,
whence a slight mass had fallen in the way of the water, the flow whereof
into the well being thereby prevented. He said to himself, "Whereto does this
pit lead? and whence does this orifice spring?" Accordingly he enlarged the
crevice. As soon as he placed his foot therein, he reached the treasure of his
father. The Prince, when he saw this countless riches and excessive treasure,
returned thanks to God, saying, "Although the wealth is great and the gems are
innumerable, yet I must not turn away from the road of reliance on God or the
highway of contentment, and I must spend it in proportion to my necessities,"

> Till we see what comes to light from the Invisible World.

On the other hand, the elder brother having become confirmed in his sovereignty,
had no regard for his subjects or army; and in the expectation of the fancied
wealth, which he imagined to be in his father's palace, spent whatever came to
his hands; and from excess of pride and grandeur he made no search for his
brother, and blushed at his acquaintance. All at once an enemy made his
appearance against him, and with a numerous destructive army attacked his
kingdom. The Prince, finding his treasury empty, and his troops without
equipments and miserable, repaired to that spot which his father had pointed
out as containing the treasure, with the intention of recruiting his army by
means of that boundless wealth, since "*There is no kingdom without men, and
no men without money.*" The more diligent were his efforts, the less did he discover any trace of the treasure; and the more he laboured and strove, the more
disappointed was he in obtaining his object.

> Listen to this advice, so that you may free yourself from grief—
> "You will be sorrowful[1] if you seek after that which Fortune has not ordained."

Now when he abandoned all hope of finding the property, having by a variety
of devices contrived to hold his own, he put his army in order, and having set
his face towards repelling the enemy, came forth from the city. After that
on both sides the ranks of battle had been arranged, and the flame of strife
kindled, an arrow from the rows of the enemy's army wounded the Prince
mortally, and he instantly expired; while from the same direction also they shot

---

[1] Literally, "drink blood."

an arrow, and the foreign king was slain, and both armies remained harassed and without a leader. It wellnigh happened that the fire of sedition began to rage, and that the inhabitants of both kingdoms were consumed with the flame of anarchy. At length the leaders of both armies collected together, and by mutual consent sought from the royal race and the sovereign family a king of benevolent nature and good disposition to whom they might confide the task of governing, and the affairs of the state. They unanimously agreed that the fortunate monarch, the head of whose prosperity was worthy of the diadem of exaltation, and the finger of whose happiness was deserving of the signet of empire, was that very God-fearing prince. The ministers of the country went to the door of his cell, and with the greatest respect and reverence bore him from the corner of obscurity to the court of approbation, and from the nook of retirement to the exalted throne of prosperity. So, by means of the blessing of confidence in God, both the wealth of his father came to him, and also the kingdom of his parent was confirmed to him.

"Now I have adduced this story that it may be evident that the acquirement of position in no way depends upon labour and occupation, it being better to rely upon godly trust than to place any confidence in employment."

> Employment is not better than trust in God.
> What is more desirable than resignation itself?
> Cultivate that very confidence, trembling neither hand nor foot.
> Your fortune is more constant to you than you are to yourself.
> Were you endowed with patience, Fortune would reach you,
> And cast herself round you like a lover.

When the son had finished this story, his father rejoined: "What you have said is quite right and correct, but this world is one of means and causes, and the Divine command has been issued to the effect, that the occurrence of most affairs in this world is dependent on causes. Now the benefits of occupation are greater than those of reliance on God; since the advantages of such reliance reaches only the person who reposes the confidence, while the gain of employment extends from the man who labours to other people; and to cause advantage to accrue is a proof of benevolence, since '*The best of men is he who benefits mankind.*' And if any one possesses the power to benefit others, it were a shame were he to be indolent, and to receive assistance from others. Perhaps you have not heard the story of the man who, after seeing the condition of the Hawk and the Crow, laid aside the doctrine of causes, for which reason Divine anger befell him?" The son inquired, "How was that?"

STORY III.

The father said: It has been related that a Darwísh was wandering in a desert, contemplating the effects of Divine mercy, and the ways of Providence. Suddenly he saw a Royal, Swift-flying Hawk, who had got a small piece of flesh in his claws, and was flying around a tree, and with great agitation hovering near a nest. The man was astonished at this state of affairs: for a while he stood watching, and saw that a Crow without either feathers or pinions had fallen into the nest, while the Hawk tearing the flesh into pieces according to the capacity of the unfledged Crow, placed it in his mouth: the man exclaimed, "Praise to God! Behold this royal favour and unlimited mercy, in that a Crow without feathers or pinions, possessing neither power to fly nor strength to move, is not left in the corner of this nest without means of support."

The surface of the earth is His universal board :
At this table of spoils what if it be enemy, what if it be friend ?
So wide is the table of His benevolence spread,
That the Phœnix eats its portion in the Mountain Káf.[1]

" Therefore since in search of my daily food I am never off my feet, and having set my head in the desert of greed, by a variety of contrivances obtain my bread, it must assuredly be owing to the weakness of my faith and the dulness of my belief."

The Giver of food being my surety for support,
How long shall I run in every direction like the mean ?
Content of heart, I draw my breath,
Since whatever reaches me is my all-sufficient allotted portion.

" It is best that hereafter I should place the head of repose upon the knee of retirement, and draw the line of indolence across the page of occupation and employment."

" Our daily sustenance is with God, He is blessed and high."

Thereupon, having washed his hands from the things of the world, he retired into solitude, and fixed his guileless heart on the causeless kindness of the Causer of causes.

Do not set your heart on the cause, and discard the Causer thereof.

For three days and nights he remained in the cell of retirement, but from no source did any gratuitous food make its appearance, and every hour he became thinner and more feeble. At length weakness overpowered his strength, and the Devotee became exceedingly emaciated, and incapacitated from performing his accustomary devotion and worship. The Most High God despatched the Prophet of that day to him, and sent a message of severe reproof, saying, " O my servant ! I have rested the centre of the World on causes and effects ; for although my power can produce results without cause, yet my wisdom has required that most things should be accomplished and brought to pass by means of causes, and in this manner the rule of giving and receiving benefits is brought about : therefore if you can become the source of advantage to others, it is better than that you should receive assistance at the hands of other people."

May you be like the Hawk, that you may strike the prey, and give up the delicious morsel ;
Be not a tuft-hunter after food, like the Crow without feather or pinions.

" Now I have adduced this story, that you may know that it is not feasible for every person to remove the veil of causes : and commendable reliance on God is such that, whilst the doctrine of causes is kept in view, there is firm confidence in the Almighty, so that there may be a participation in the benefits of ' *The industrious man is the friend of God :*' and a wise man has said, ' Labour lest you become indolent, and recognise that your daily food is from God, lest you become an infidel.' "

---

[1] A fabulous mountain, anciently imagined by the Asiatics to surround the world.

Be not negligent of causes, through reliance on God;
Listen to the proverb, " The industrious man is beloved of God."
If you have confidence in the Almighty, work diligently;
Perform your duties, then rest upon the Omnipotent Deity.

Another son commenced, saying: " O father! we do not possess power completely to rely upon God; consequently there is no remedy but to pursue an occupation: now, when we are busy in our avocations, and the Most High God, from the treasure of His benevolence, allots us our portion of wealth and affluence, what are we to do with it?" The father replied: " To collect property is easy; but to look after it, and derive benefit therefrom, is difficult; and when any one acquires money, two conditions must necessarily be observed:—1. It must be guarded in such a manner as that it may be secure from prodigality and plunder, the hand of the thief, the highwayman, and the pickpocket being restrained from it,—since money has many friends, and the possessor of wealth countless enemies.

Heaven strikes not the helpless,
It assails the caravan of the great.

" 2. From the profit thereof advantage must be derived, and the capital must not be squandered; since if all is taken from capital, and the interest is not deemed sufficient, after a little while the dust of annihilation will arise from such a course."

Whatever ocean is not supplied with water,
In a little while, will become dried up:
If you scrape away at a hill, and put nothing in place thereof,
In the end the hill will be overturned.

" Whenever a man has no income, and is perpetually spending money, or whenever a person's expenses are more than his receipts, in the end he will fall into the vortex of necessity: and maybe his affairs will terminate in perdition, like that prodigal Mouse who killed himself from grief." The son inquired, " How was that?"

STORY IV.

The father replied: It has been related that a Rustic had by way of store placed a quantity of corn in a granary, and shut the doors of expenditure thereon; so that when the day of extreme need and great necessity should arrive, he might reap benefit therefrom. By chance a Mouse, who from excessive gluttony was desirous of stealing a grain from the storehouse of the Moon, and of snatching, with the claw of greed, a cluster of the Pleiades from the field of the Sky, had taken his abode in the neighbourhood of that locality, and had made his nest in the environs of that granary: continually he used to make holes underground, on every side, and with his adamantine teeth carry on excavations in all directions. All at once the end of his burrow came out into the midst of the corn, and from the roof of his house grains of wheat, like bright stars from Heaven, poured down. The Mouse saw that the promise, " *In the heavens is your food*," had been realised; and that the proverb, " *Seek your food in the bowels of the earth*," was made clear. On beholding these benefits, he performed the dues of gratitude; but by the acquisition of these priceless gems, having obtained great riches, he began to display the arrogance of Kárún,[1] and the pretensions of Pharaoh. In a little while the mice of the neighbourhood, having become apprised of that state of things, girded the loins of attendance in his service.

> Those pretended friends whom you see,
> Are flies around the sweetmeats.

Parasites[2] and boon-companions collected around him; and, as is their custom, adopting the mode of flattery, said nought but what was in accordance with the wish of his heart and the desire of his nature, and never loosed their tongue except in his praise and eulogy, and in blessing and thanking him. He also mad-like opened his mouth in boasting and exaggeration, and his hand in prodigality; in the idea that the corn in that house would have no end, and the wheat from that hole would perpetually fall and drop, every day he squandered a large quantity on his companions, and not contemplating the end thereof in the designs of to-day, took no thought for the morrow.

> O cup-bearer ! we will drink wine to-day, for who has seen the morrow ?

During the time that these mice were busy enjoying themselves in that retired corner, an attack of famine and scarcity had overwhelmed the people, and the fire of hunger had been kindled in the bosoms of the anguished portionless wretches. In every direction they would have given their lives for bread, but no one paid any attention; and on all sides they would have sold their household furniture for victuals, but no one purchased them.

> Every one who desired even to catch a glimpse of bread,
> Saw nought but the orb of the sun in the sky :
> The world became emaciated from such distress,
> The hungry lamenting, and the satiated hard-hearted.

The proud Mouse, having spread the carpet of delicacy and luxury, was not aware of the year of dearth, and was uninformed as to the time of scarcity. When several days had elapsed, the Rustic became in great straits :[3] he opened the door of the house, and seeing that utter ruin had overtaken that corn, he heaved a cold sigh from the depths of his flushed heart, and bewailed bitterly the loss thereof, saying to himself, " It is not the manner of a wise man to lament an event the remedy of which is beyond the region of possibility ; now it appears best to collect the residue of the corn which is in the house, and to carry it to another place ;" accordingly, the Rustic occupied himself in bringing out that portion which remained. Now in that locality the Mouse, who deemed himself Master of the house, and Lord of the abode, was asleep; and the other mice, from excess of greed and covetousness did not hear the noise of the Rustic's feet, and the sound of his moving about above their heads. Amongst them, however, a quick-witted Mouse, having comprehended the state of affairs, with the view of ascertaining the truth, climbed up to the top of the roof, and through a window witnessed the real state of affairs. Having at once come down and told the purport of his story to his friends, he flung himself from that hole : and they also went forth, each one to a corner, and left their benefactor alone.

---

[1] A person proverbial for his wealth and avarice.
[2] Literally, " friends of the dish, and companions of the cup."
[3] Literally, " the business reached his soul, and the knife his bones."

Every one, in expectation of the parings, is your friend,
They are intimate with you in pursuit of some morsel.
When your property is diminished, their affection for you will decline;
They are willing that you should be ruined to benefit themselves.
From this company of hypocritical comrades,
It is better to sever yourself than to keep up an acquaintance.

Next day, when the Mouse lifted up his head from the pillow of repose, although he looked carefully right and left, he saw none of his friends, and the more he searched before and behind, the less trace did he find of his companions. He began to groan, saying;

I do not know where are those who were my friends:
What has occurred, that they are separated from me?

Then with the view of endeavouring to ascertain the truth relative to their affairs, after a lengthened time, during which he had chosen to be in retirement, he issued forth from the corner of his abode, and gained news of the misery arising from the scarcity, and the distress from the famine and dearth. In great trouble he went towards his own home, so that he might use every effort to protect the store which he possessed. When he reached the house, he saw no trace of the corn, and having come from that hole unto the storehouse, there was not remaining sufficient food for one night's meal. His power of endurance being exhausted,[1] he began to rend the collar of his life with the hand of misery, and repeatedly struck the head of melancholy upon the ground, so that his brains became scattered, and through the misfortune of prodigality he fell into the vortex of death and destruction.

"Now the moral of this story is this: A man's expenditure should be in proportion to his income; and he should derive benefit from the interest of the capital which he possesses, guarding it in such manner that the principal should not suffer diminution."

Every moment keep an eye on your expenditure and receipts;
When your income ceases, spend your money more slowly.

When the father had finished this story, the youngest son arose and adorned the preface of his speech with the gems of praise and eulogy of his father, saying, "O father! after any one has guarded his own property according to rule, and has derived full interest therefrom, how should he spend that income?" The father replied, "The road of moderation in every case is commendable, particularly as regards the means of support. Therefore it behoveth a man of property, after obtaining the interest, to keep in view two other rules: 1. He must avoid improper extravagance and prodigality, so that regret be not brought forth, and men loose not the tongue of reproach against him; and, in truth, waste of property and immoderate expenditure are suggestions of Satan. *'Truly the extravagant are the brothers of devils.'*

Amongst men of exalted nature
Stinginess is more commendable than prodigality;
Although everywhere liberality captivates men's hearts,
Yet he who acts according to rule is acceptable.

"2. It is necessary to avoid the opprobrium of stinginess and the reproach of

---

[1] Literally, "folded up."

parsimony, since a miser, both in matters of religion and the world, has an evil name; and an avaricious worldly man is at all times execrated and miserable. The property also of a miser becomes ultimately a target for the arrow of plunder and dissipation. Like for example, a large reservoir, into which water perpetually flows from several springs, and having no egress in proportion to its ingress, necessarily seeks in every direction an outlet, and runs out from every corner till, fissures appearing in the sides, it finally happens that the reservoir is in a moment swept away and demolished, and the waters thereof are dispersed in every quarter and direction. *'Threaten the miser with misfortune or an heir.'*"

> The wealth from which the miser derived no benefit,
> Has been scattered to the winds by a prodigal hand,
> Or has reached some heir, who never,
> Except with aversion, calls him to mind.

When the children heard their father's admonitions, and well understood the advantages of his words, they each of them made choice of a trade, and set their hands to the task. The eldest brother of them embarked in merchandise and undertook a distant journey. With him were two Oxen of burden, such that the Taurus of the skies had not power to oppose their strength; and the Lion of the heavens, owing to their vigour and majesty, like a fasting Cat, concealed the claw of fear in the fist of helplessness.

> In bulk like an elephant, in impetuosity like a lion,
> Bold in appearance, resolute in pace.

One was named Shanzabah and the other Mandabah. The master merchant used always to look after them and attend to their wants himself; but when their journey was prolonged and they traversed distant parts, languor found its way to their condition, and symptoms of weakness became evident in the aspect of their affairs, and by chance a large mire appeared across their path and Shanzabah stuck therein. At the master's orders, with the utmost contrivance they extricated him: but since he had no power to move, the merchant appointed a person, whom he had enticed by reward, to look after the Ox, and arranged that when the latter recovered his strength, the man should send him after the caravan. The hireling having remained for one or two days in the desert became weary of his loneliness, and forsaking Shanzabah conveyed the news of his death to his master. Mandabah also, at that stage, from excess of weariness and separation from Shanzabah, expired. But in a little while the power of motion returned to Shanzabah, who in search of pasture wandered in every direction, till he arrived at a meadow adorned with various kinds of sweet herbs, and decked with different species of plants. The gardener of Paradise, from envy of that garden, bit the finger of jealousy; and the skies, in contemplation thereof, opened the eyes of astonishment.

> From the roses, the newly-sprouted herbage, and flowing water therein,
> (May the malevolent eye be averted), you would have said that it was a second
> Paradise.

To Shanzabah such a spot was very acceptable, and he deposited the chattels of residence in the region of that meadow. When he had for a while grazed therein, without any bond of constraint or check of control, and had passed his time according to his mind's content in that soul-exhilarating atmosphere and heart-entrancing plain, he became extremely strong in body and corpulent. The delight of repose, and the pleasure of rest, impelled him, from excess of joy, to bellow loudly. Now in the neighbourhood of that meadow was a majestic and extremely mighty Lion, in whose service many wild beasts had girded their loins, while innumerable animals had placed the head of obedience upon the line of his commands. This Lion, by reason of the pride of youth, the pomp of majesty and prosperity, the number of his dependents, and the magnitude of his suite, imagined that no one was greater than himself, and took no notice of the fierce-assaulting tiger and the strong-bodied elephant; but he had never seen an ox, nor heard him bellow. When the roar of Shanzabah reached him, he was much frightened; and from dread lest the animals should know that fear had found its way to him, he did not stir in any direction, but remained in one spot.

In his retinue were two crafty Jackals — one named Kalilah, the other Damnah; and both were renowned for their quickness and penetration, but Damnah was the most arrogant, and the most eager in search after rank and fame. Damnah having with penetration discovered from the Lion that he was overcome by fear, and that he was occupied with what was passing in his mind, said to Kalilah : " What say you concerning the state of the King that he has abandoned the pleasure of travelling about, and remains fixed in one spot ? "

> The traces of anxiety on his temples
> Are indicative of his melancholy heart.

Kalilah answered : " What has such a question to do with you, and what does it concern you to talk like this ? "

> Whence art thou, and whence this conversation about state secrets ?

" We obtain our livelihood at the court of this Sovereign, and pass our time in ease under the shadow of his government. Be content therewith, and abandon investigating the secrets of kings, or examining their affairs; for we are not of such a degree that we can be honoured with the confidence of monarchs, nor that any words of ours can reach the ear of rulers. Therefore, to mention them is giving ourselves unnecessary trouble; and whoever interferes in a business which does not concern him, will meet with that which befell the Monkey."

Damnah inquired, " What was that ? "

STORY V.

Kalilah replied : It has been related that a Monkey saw a Carpenter sitting on a plank and cutting it; and he had two wedges, one of which he drove down into the crevice of the board, so that it might be more easy to cut it, and the slit for the stroke of the saw might be opened. When the crevice widened beyond a certain extent, he hammered in another wedge and drew out the former one; and in this manner carried on his work. The Monkey was delighted. Suddenly the Carpenter, in the midst of his labour, on an emergency, rose up. The Monkey, when he saw the place vacant, at once sat down on the wood, and his tail slipped down into the crevice of the wood in that part which had been cut. The Monkey drew out from the cleft in the wood the foremost wedge before he hammered in the other one. When the wedge was drawn out both sides of the board sprang together, and the Monkey's tail remained firmly fixed therein. The poor Monkey, being ill with pain, groaned, saying :

E

It is best that every one in the world should mind his own business :
Whoever does not keep to his own affairs acts very wrongly.

" My business is to gather fruit, not to drive a saw; and my occupation is to
disport myself in the woods, not to strike the hatchet or axe."

Whoever acts thus, such will befall him.

The Monkey was talking thus to himself when the Carpenter returned, and beat
him as he deserved: and the affairs of the Monkey, through his meddlesomeness
ended in his ruin.   Hence it has been said :

" Carpentering is not the business of an ape."

" Now I have adduced this story that you may know that every one should
attend to his own affairs, and not place his feet beyond his sphere, since, ' *For
every business there are men ;* ' and how beautifully it has been said—

I remember a proverb from a friend,
' For every man a business, and for every business a man ' !

" Abandon this which is not your business, and consider as good fortune the
little food and provision which accrue to us."   Damnah said : " Whoever seeks
to be near to kings must not do so to procure food and provisions, since the
stomach can be filled anywhere and with anything ; nay, rather, the advantage
of attendance on monarchs is the finding of an exalted station, wherein one may
with kindness do good for one's friends, and deal severely with one's enemies ;
and he whose ambition demeans itself after food is to be reckoned amongst the
brutes—like a hungry dog, who is delighted with a bone, or an ignoble-natured
cat, who is contented with scraps of bread ; and I have noticed that the Lion,
when hunting a hare, should he see a wild ass, having drawn back his hand,
sets his face towards pursuing the latter.

Be of lofty ambition, since before God and man
According to the degree of your aspirations will be your esteem.

" And whoever gains high dignity, though like a rose his life should be short, yet
the wise, by reason of his good reputation, deem his existence to have been
lengthy; and whoever demeans himself to paltriness and grovelling ideas, though,
like the leaf of a pine-tree, he may remain for a while, yet amongst men of
excellence he will not be esteemed, and they will consider him as nought."

O Sa'di ! the man of good reputation never dies,
He who perishes is the man whose name is not held in estimation.

Kalílah replied : " It well becometh that class of persons to seek after dignity
and station who, by honourable lineage, superior manners, and high birth, are
fitted for, and deserving of them.   Now we are not of such an order as to be
worthy of high honours, and we cannot, in search thereafter, raise the foot of
endeavour."

I conceive ideas boundless as the ocean—alas!
What is there in the head of this vain-scheming drop ?

Damnah said : " The source of greatness is wisdom and good manners, not
birth and family.   Whoever possesses sound intelligence and perfect knowledge
will raise himself from a mean position to exalted station, and whoever has a

weak intellect and feeble understanding will demean himself from high dignity to inferior rank—

> With the assistance of exalted wisdom and acute penetration,
> The noose of power can be cast over the heavens ;
> If the eyes of the soul are not opened by ambition,
> They cannot set their glance on things of eminence.

" And it has been said by the wise, that advancement to high rank is acquired by much labour, while the descent from a lofty position is obtained with but little trouble—just as a heavy stone is lifted up from the ground on the shoulders only with much toil, but can be thrown down again with the slightest movement : for this reason is it that no one, except the man of lofty ambition who can endure vexation, can have any desire for exalted employment—

> My soul, trials of love do not befit the delicate ;
> It is the lion-hearted and afflicted who should place their feet in such a contest.

"Whoever seeks the repose '*Obscurity is ease*,' having washed his hands of reputation, will remain constantly a recluse, in the cell of misery and disappointment ; and whoever has no anxiety about the thorny place ' *Notoriety is misfortune*,' in a short time, having plucked the rose of his desires, will, in the expanse of honour, sit on the throne of delight.

> Till a person suffers grief and pain, his worth will not increase.
> Till a ruby bleeds[1] from its heart, it is of no value.
> On the scroll of happiness, never did a traveller himself
> Find the inscription of fortune free from the blemish of labour.

" Perhaps you have not heard the story of the two Travellers, of whom one, by means of undergoing grief and labour, reached the pinnacle of monarchy, while the other, by reason of indolence and self-indulgence, remained in the abyss of need and distress ? "   Kalílah inquired, " How was that ? "

STORY VI.

Damnah said : Two Travellers, of whom one was named Sálim[2] and the other Ghánim,[3] were journeying together, and in society of one another traversed stages and distances.   Their path lay at the foot of a hill, the summit of which kept rein by rein with the bay horse of the sky, while its middle was girt stirrup to stirrup with the vault of the celestial girdle.   At the foot of that mountain was a spring of water, in purity like the fresh-faced and rosy-cheeked, and in sweetness like the words of the honey-lipped and sweet in speech.   In front of the spring a large reservoir was constructed, and around it shade-giving trees interlapped one another top to top.

> On one side grew branches of odoriferous shrubs ;
> On the other, trees shot out their tops.
> The hyacinth fell at the foot of the cypress ;
> The violet bowed its head before the lily.

---

[1] Literally, " turns its heart into blood."   [2] Safe.   [3] Laden with spoil.

In short, the two Companions arrived from the dreadful desert at this nice resting-place, and when they found that the spot was pleasant and the abode agreeable, they halted therein for their usual rest; and after reposing walked round the sides and edges of the reservoir and the fountain, casting their glance in every direction. Suddenly, on the brink of the reservoir, in the part where the water flowed in, they saw a white stone, whereon was written in dark characters, the like of which could not have been inscribed except by the divine pen upon the pages of wisdom—"O traveller! you have honoured this place by alighting. Know that we have provided, in the best manner possible, refreshment for our guests, and have supplied the tables of advantage in the nicest style. But the conditions of the agreement are, that abandoning reflection, you should put your feet in this spring, and not dreading the danger of the whirlpool nor the terrors of the vortex, should scramble to shore in any way you can. At the foot of the mountain has been placed a lion cut out of stone; put it on your shoulders, and, without reflection or deliberation, in one run, reach the top of the mountain, neither desisting from your undertaking through fear of deadly beasts which come in your path, nor by reason of the scratches of the heart-rending thorns which seize your skirt, since, when the journey is accomplished, the tree of your desire will bear fruit."

> So long as a person does not journey along the road he will never reach his
>   destination:
> Unless he risks his life, he cannot reach the goal of his wishes.
> Though the whole world attain the glory of prosperity,
> Not one beam of its radiance would reach the idle man.

After he had become apprised of the purport of the writing, Ghánim turned towards Sálim (saying), "O brother! come let us with the foot of labour traverse this dangerous plain, and, as far as may be possible, use our efforts to ascertain the precise state of affairs as regards this talisman."

> We will either successful place our feet on the very summit of the heavens,
> Or else, rejected, offer our head in the path of ambition.

Sálim replied: "O dear friend! on the ground of a mere inscription, the writer of which is unknown, and the purport thereof unintelligible, to undertake a great danger, and by reason of imaginary advantages which are but conjectural, and benefits which are but supposititious, to cast one's self into considerable danger, is a proof of folly. No wise man would take a poison which is certain, when the antidote is but doubtful; nor would any prudent person agree to undergo labour in cash, for repose on credit."

> Amongst men of wisdom, there is no comparison
> Between one moment of grief and a thousand years of ease.

Ghánim replied: "O dear comrade! the desire of repose is a prelude to ignominy and disgrace, and the undergoing of danger a token of prosperity and glory.

> Whoever seeks ease and tranquillity
> Will not gladden his heart with prosperity;
> And whoever fears the anguish of intoxication
> Will not drink wine from the cup of desire.

"The aim of a man of high ambition does not descend to food and lodging, nor does he rest the foot of search till he has attained an exalted dignity. The rose of delight cannot be plucked without the thorn of trouble, nor can the door of the storehouse of desire be opened except by the key of toil; and in my case ambition, having seized the reins, will drag me to the top of the mountain, and I shall not fear the whirlpool of misery, nor the burden of the load of affliction."

Should affliction overtake us in pursuit thereof, perchance,
When we are longing for the temple of Makkah, even deserts will seem easy.

Sálim answered: "Admitted that for the odour of the spring of prosperity one can undergo the tumult of the autumn of affliction, yet to set out on a road which has no end, and to travel on an ocean of which the shore is not visible, appears far removed from the path of wisdom. Whoever commences an undertaking, it behoves him, like as he is aware of the beginning, also to regard the finale; and on the initiation of an affair, having cast a glance at the termination thereof, to weigh the advantages and disadvantages with the scales of wisdom, so that profitless vexations may not be undergone, nor the coin of precious life be scattered to the winds of destruction.

While you have not firmly fixed your feet
Do not move your steps in search of anything.
In every affair wherein you embark, first
Make sure of a loophole for you to emerge.

"It may be that this inscription has been penned in derision, and this writing executed in joke and fun. So this spring may be a whirlpool wherein by swimming one cannot reach the shore, and, if deliverance therefrom should become feasible, perchance the weight of the Lion of Stone may be such that it cannot be lifted on the shoulders; if that too were brought to pass, it is possible that the top of the mountain cannot be reached in one run; and even if all this were accomplished, it is not at all known what the result will be. At any rate I will not be an associate in this affair, and I would restrain you also from proceeding further in this business." Ghánim replied: "Abandon such language, for I will not by the words of any one be turned from my intentions, nor by the temptation of '*The imps of men or genii*' break the oath that I made; I know that you have not firmness to join me, nor will agree to accompany me, but at any rate contemplate the sight, and with prayer and supplication lend me your assistance."

I know that you have not the power to drink wine,
But at any rate come to the revels of the intoxicated.

Sálim, perceiving that his comrade was determined in the matter, said: "O brother! I see that you will not desist by reason of any words of mine, nor will you abandon this impracticable business. Now I have not the power to witness your proceedings, nor can I make a diversion of a matter which is neither in conformity with my disposition nor agreeable to my inclination. I have thought it right that

I must withdraw my chattels from this vortex."

Accordingly, having placed his traps upon a dromedary, he said farewell to his comrade and set out towards the highway. Ghánim having washed his heart of life, came to the brink of the spring, and said:

I will plunge into the boundless Ocean,
Either to be drowned or gain the pearl.

Accordingly, having firmly bound the skirt of resolution round his loins, he placed his feet in the spring.

> That was not a spring, nay, more, it was a sea,
> Which there showed itself under the guise of a spring.

Ghánim perceived that the spring was a dangerous whirlpool, but having a stout heart, by swimming steadily, he reached the shore of deliverance, and having come to the brink of the water and collected his senses, lifted on his back, with power and might, the Lion of Stone; and having willingly undergone a thousand kinds of trouble, in one run he reached the top of the mountain, on the side of which he saw a large city, the atmosphere being delightful and the country heart-ravishing.

> A city, from its beauty resembling Paradise,
> . From the freshness of its appearance, like the Garden of Eden.

Ghánim, having halted on the top of the mountain, cast his glance towards the city, when suddenly a violent sound issued from that Lion of Stone, so that trembling fell on the mountain and plain, and the echo thereof reaching the city, a concourse of men came out from right and left, and turning their faces in the direction of the mountain, set out towards Ghánim, who looked on with eyes of astonishment, amazed at the mass of people. All at once a body of nobles and grandees having arrived, performed the ceremony of prayer and the dues of praise, and with the utmost consideration mounting him upon a quick-going horse, bore him towards the city, and anointing his head and body with rose-water and camphor, arrayed him in regal robes, and with the greatest respect and veneration consigned the reins of the sovereignty of that region to his able hands. Ghánim having inquired as to the meaning of this proceeding, heard a reply to the following effect: "Sages have placed in this spring which you behold, a talisman, and that Lion of Stone has been constructed after varied thought and deliberation, and after contemplating the rising of the constellations, and beholding the stars and planets. Now whenever it enters the mind of a worthy man to pass by the spring, and carrying off the Lion, to ascend to the top of the mountain, assuredly that state of affairs will arise at a time when Fate has reached the king of this city. The Lion accordingly begins to roar, and the noise thereof reaching the city, the inhabitants come out, and making such person king, pass their time in rest, under the shadow of his justice, till the period when his turn also comes to an end.

> When one departs, another takes his place.

And when by Divine Decree, the Sun of this country's Ruler sets in the horizon of death, as a concomitant circumstance, the star of the glory of that possessor of Fortune arises from the summit of that mountain. A long time has elapsed since the custom has been practised in the manner above narrated. Now you to-day are King of this city and Monarch of this world."

> This country is yours—issue whatever commands you will.

Ghánim perceived that the undergoing of all these troubles was at the dictates of Fortune.

> When Fortune comes to the aid,
> She accomplishes every business in a proper manner.

"Now I have adduced this story that you may know that there is no honeyed potion of happiness and favour without the sting of misery and anxiety; and whoever is ambitious to become exalted, will never be trampled under foot by every base person, nor be content with an inferior position or menial station. And till I procure the dignity of access to the Lion, and enter amongst the number of the attendants of his Majesty, I will not lay my head on the pillow of repose, nor stretch out my feet on the bed of ease." Kalílah said: "Whence have you procured the key of such a door? and how have you devised a means to enter upon such a matter?" Damnah replied: "I am desirous that, on the present occasion, when astonishment and irresolution have found their way to the Lion, I should offer myself to him; it may be that by reason of the potion of the medicine of my advice, gladness will accrue to him, and by this means my intimacy and dignity in his presence increase." Kalílah rejoined: "How will you obtain access and approach to the Lion? and even if you did, since you have never been in the service of kings, and are ignorant of the customs and habits of attendance, in a short space, it may be, you would lose what you have gained; now for this you could not again provide a remedy." Damnah said: "When a man is wise and able, he is not at a loss to manage great affairs; and whoever has confidence in his own skill, in every matter which he undertakes, will in a proper manner completely perform his obligations. Again, if Fortune manifest herself, she shows the way which is proper, like as it has been reported, that the sun of the prosperity of a certain artisan being exalted, he found the dignity of monarchy, and the tradition and rumour of him became spread abroad in the world. One of the ancient kings wrote an epistle to him, 'Your trade is carpentering and you are well skilled in that art; from whom have you learnt the arrangements of monarchy, and wisdom in the discharge of duty?' He wrote in reply, 'He who bestowed the government upon me did not omit any item of instruction relative to the management of the world.'"

> When wisdom opens the book of instruction,
> There proceeds from me what is right.
> When the candle of any person is illumined by Fortune,
> He will unite all the characteristics of goodness.

Kalílah rejoined: "Kings do not by their favours bring all men of excellence into prominence—nay, more, they distinguish by regal kindness their own kith and kin, who by inheritance and their own endeavours, have found access in the royal service. Since you have no hereditary rights as regards the Lion, nor yet any acquired merit, it may be that you will remain excluded from his favours, and such may be fatal to your wishes." Damnah replied: "Whoever acquires a lofty rank in the service of a monarch, advances on the road by degrees, nor does such dignity manifest itself without personal effort and labour, in addition to what accrues from the royal patronage. Now I am seeking that very thing, and am searching for the same, and have brought myself to think it right to undergo much trouble, and to taste disagreeable mixtures; and I am aware that whoever selects attendance on kings needs make choice of five things: 1st, He must subdue the flame of anger with the water of long-suffering; 2d, He must avoid the temptation of the demon of lust; 3d, He must not allow deceitful greed or strife-exciting avarice to overpower reason, his guide; 4th, He must place the edifice of his actions upon rectitude and moderation; 5th, He must with courtesy and civility encounter events and trifling matters which arise.

Whoever is endowed with such qualifications, assuredly his wishes will be completely successful."

Kalílah said : " It has occurred to me, that supposing you were to gain access to the King, by what means would you be accepted by him, and by what device would you acquire station and dignity." Damnah rejoined : " If I should obtain access to His Majesty, I would keep in view five considerations : 1st, I would serve him with complete sincerity ; 2d, I would confine my ambition to conforming myself to his wishes ; 3d, I would recount his deeds and words with accuracy ; 4th, When a matter arises which may be in conformity with what is right, and I see therein advantage to the kingdom, I would deck it out before his eyes and mind, and bring before his sight the advantages and benefits thereof, so that his joy may increase by reason of the accuracy of his understanding, and the correctness of his judgment ; 5th, If he should enter on a business, whereof the end may be destructive and the conclusion injurious, so that misfortune may accrue therefrom to the kingdom, with sweet explanation and great gentleness I would point out to him the evil thereof, and warn him of its termination. Now, whenever the King shall perceive my merits, he will distinguish me by his kindness and favour, and always be disposed for my society, and inclined to my advice, since no talent ever rests concealed, neither does any man of merit remain without a share of patronage and assistance."

Merit is like musk—when does it remain concealed ?
From the perfume thereof the world, in a moment, becomes full of odour :
Go ! strive to acquire merit, so that from your worth
The expanse of the earth may all at once become filled with the mention (of you.)

Kalílah said : " So it appears that your inclination is fixed upon this, and your intentions resolved to accomplish this plan ; at any rate be very cautious, since attendance on kings is full of danger, and an affair replete with difficulty, and wise men have said that none but an ignorant fellow, who has not inhaled the perfume of wisdom, sets about three things : 1st, The service of kings ; 2d, Tasting poison in a spirit of doubt ; 3d, Proclaiming one's secrets to women. Sages also have compared kings to a lofty mountain, wherein though there are mines of priceless pearls, still it is the habitation of tigers, snakes, and other noxious creatures—it is both difficult to travel across it, and also hard to take up one's abode thereon. It has also been said, that intimacy with kings is like a sea—since the trader who makes choice of crossing an ocean either will acquire much gain, or be caught in the whirlpool of death."

In the sea are innumerable advantages,
But if you wish for safety, it is on shore.

Damnah responded : " What you have spoken is from the best intentions ; and I am conscious that a king is like a consuming fire, whoever is nearest thereto is in most danger.

Avoid the society of sovereigns,
Just as a bundle of dry sticks a fierce fire.

" But whoever dreads danger will never attain high rank.

From danger greatness arises—since four hundred per cent [1]
Is never gained if the merchant dreads danger.

---

[1] Literally, " ten forty,"—*i.e.*, ten becomes forty, or at the rate of four hundred per cent.

"And three things cannot be undertaken except by men of high ambition—the service of a king, a journey by sea, and contending with an enemy. Now I do not reckon myself of mean ambition, therefore why should I fear the service of the King?"

> When the arm of my ambition is such,
> Whatever I seek is in my sleeve:
> Do you desire dignity and grandeur?
> Strive according to the ambition which you possess.
> In short, as regards whatever you take in hand,
> While your ambition is strong, you will perform it.

Kalilah said: "Although I am opposed to this idea, and regret such a design, yet since your mind is bent upon this matter, and your desire fixed on this enterprise—may all be well."

> Behold the end of thy path—go, be happy and prosperous.

Damnah departed, and made his obeisance to the Lion, who inquired, "What person is this?" They replied: "The son of such a one who, for a long while, was a servant of the exalted threshold." The Lion said, "Yes, I know." Accordingly he summoned him to the royal presence, and said, "Where do you live?" Damnah replied: "According to the custom of my father, I am at present a servant in your heaven-resembling court, and have made it the high altar of my needs, and the temple of my desires; and I am in expectation that if something has occurred, and the august order be issued, by my wisdom I may settle the point, and with enlightened intelligence may deliberate thereon: as, too, the pillars of the state and the great men of your presence, in the arranging of some affairs have need of assistance, it may be that, in the court of kings, some event may occur, which can be settled by the aid of inferiors.

> In such a direction a fly becomes of service like it were a peacock.

"A matter which is brought about by an insignificant needle, a mighty spear is powerless to settle; and in an affair which a tiny penknife accomplishes, a flashing sword is inadequate. No servant, however powerless and contemptible he may be, is devoid of means to avert misfortune or bring about advantage, since that dry stick which falls despised upon the footpath may possibly one day be of service, and although it is of no value, it may be that a toothpick will be made thereof, or by its means the wax may be extracted from the ear."

> Though a nosegay does not proceed from me,
> Yet I may be sticks for the pots.

When the Lion heard the speech of Damnah, he was astonished at his eloquence and oratory, and turning round to those around him, said: "As regards a man of intelligence, though he may be of no repute, yet his wisdom and knowledge, unwittingly on his part, will cause his excellence to become apparent amongst people: just as when he who raises the splendour of a fire, wishes that it should burn low, assuredly it lifts its head aloft."

> He, in whom there are signs of loving a friend,
> Will exhibit them in his countenance.

Damnah was delighted at these words; and perceiving that his treachery had taken effect on the Lion, and that his deceit had been very efficacious, loosened the tongue of advice, and said : " It is incumbent upon all servants and attendants, according to the extent of their understanding and knowledge, to think over that which happens to the King, and each one should represent whatever occurs to his mind, and not abandon the path of sincere advice, so that the King may thoroughly understand his dependants and followers, and becoming apprised of the measure of the intellect, judgment, sincerity, and discretion of each of them, may both derive benefit from their service, and also reward each one according to his merit. Since, so long as a grain is concealed in the womb of the earth no one attempts to rear it, but when it draws the veil of the ground from its face, and, clothed in an emerald dress, raises its head from the collar of the soil, it becomes apparent that it is a tree which bears fruit, or a plant from which profit is derived—then, without doubt, it is cultivated, and the produce thereof turned to account. Now, in all matters, the root of everything is the patronage of kings. Amongst men of worth, whomsoever they distinguish by kind looks, according to the degree of favour will be the benefit they will derive from such persons."

> I am as it were a thorn and earth, while you are the sun and cloud :
> I would produce roses and tulips were you to nurture me.

The Lion replied : " How ought wise men to be fostered, and by what means can advantage be gathered from them ? "

Damnah rejoined: " The root of the matter is this : the king should look upon reputation, not birth ; and if a body of persons without worth, should make merit of the service of their progenitors and ancestors, he should show no regard thereto. Since it behoves a man to confirm his lineage by merit, not by his forefathers."

> Be proud of your own merit,
> Do not make capital of your ancient descent ;
> O foolish man ! live not with the dead,
> By your reputation make the dead themselves to come to life ;
> Boast not, O young man ! of your departed father,
> Otherwise, you are a dog rejoicing over a bone.

" Mice, although they live in the same house with men, yet by reason of the worry and annoyance they occasion, it is deemed necessary to attempt to destroy them ; while hawks, which are wild and untamed, since benefit can be anticipated from them, are enticed with the utmost care, and gladly nourished with honour upon the wrist of indulgence. Therefore it behoveth a king not to scrutinise whether it be friend or stranger ; nay, more, he must seek men of wisdom and skill, and whenever a person may be negligent in matters, and wanting in merit, he must not allow him to take the priority of men of excellence or worth ; since to give to senseless persons the dignities belonging to wise men, is like binding on the feet the jewel appertaining to the head, and fastening on the brow the ornament for the feet. And wherever men of merit remain unappreciated, and ignorant foolish persons get into their hands the reins of power, complete ruin will find its way into the affairs of such a country ; and the misery of such a state of things will reach the fortune of both king and subject."

> Tell the phœnix never to cast its noble shadow
> Upon the country where the parrot is less esteemed than the crow.

When Damnah had ceased speaking, the Lion, having treated him most kindly,

made him one of the number of his personal attendants; and having taken a
liking and affection for his conversation, based his own transactions upon his
advice and exhortation. Damnah also having selected the path of wisdom,
intelligence, and penetration, in a little while became the intimate confidant of the
royal sanctuary, and in ordering and arranging the affairs of the country and state,
became general referee and councillor. One day, having found a propitious
time, and a suitable opportunity, he sought a private interview, and said : " For
a long time the King has remained fixed in one place, and has abandoned the
pleasures of exercise, and the delights of the chase; I am anxious to know the
cause thereof, and to discuss this matter, to such extent as is in my power."
The Lion wished to conceal from Damnah his state of fear: in the meantime
Shanzabah made a horrible bellowing, and the noise thereof so upset the Lion
that the reins of self-possession fell from his hands; of necessity he disclosed
his secret to Damnah, and said : " The cause of my alarm is that noise which you
hear; now I am not aware from whom the sound arises, but I think his strength
and form must be in proportion to his voice: if such be the case, it is not
expedient for me to take up my abode in this place."

Damnah inquired, " Is there anything else besides this sound which occupies
the King's heart?" He answered, " No." Damnah said: " It is not then meet,
for such cause, to migrate from your hereditary possessions, and to abandon your
accustomary native soil; what importance is there in a sound, or weight in a
noise, that any one should by reason thereof leave the place? Moreover, it
becometh a king to be firm-footed, like a mountain, so as not to be shaken by
every wind, nor to jump from his seat at every cry."

> That you may not start at every breath,
> Draw your feet within your skirt, like a mountain.

" Wise men have said, that no consideration must be paid to loud sounds or
large form, since appearances are not in all cases indicative of facts, nor in
every instance does what is external resemble what is within; a reed though it
is stout is broken by a slender stick, and a crane though large-bodied remains in
the grasp of a weak-framed hawk. Whenever a person takes account of large
bulk, that will befall him which happened to that Fox." The Lion inquired,
" What was that?"

STORY VII.

Damnah said : It has been related that a Fox went into a forest, and, impelled by the desire of food, wandered in every direction: he arrived at the foot
of a tree, on the side of which a drum had been suspended, and whenever the
wind blew, the branches of the tree waved to and fro, and knocked against the
top of the drum, whence a terrible noise proceeded. The Fox saw a domestic
Fowl under the tree, digging her beak in the ground in search of food. Having
concealed himself in ambush, he was anxious to make her his prey; but suddenly
the noise of the drum reached his ears: he looked round and saw a very large
figure from which a tremendous noise fell on his ears. The appetite of the Fox
being aroused, he thought to himself, " Doubtless its flesh and skin will be in
proportion to the sound." Leaving his place of ambush for the Fowl, he looked
up into the tree: the Fowl, being put on her guard by this circumstance, hur-
ried away. The Fox, after a hundred toils, scrambled up the tree, and laboured

persistently, till at length he tore open the drum, but found nothing beyond parchment and pieces of wood. The fire of remorse entered his heart, and the tears of regret began to fall from his eyes: he exclaimed, " Alas! that on account of this mighty mass, that is nothing but wind, that lawful prey has slipped from my hands, and I have derived no benefit from this flimsy figure."

> The drum is indeed perpetually sounding,
> But what result is there, since nothing is within?
> If you are wise, seek the substance;
> Be not deceived with the appearance, for that is nought.

" I have narrated this story that the King may not abandon the pleasures of hunting and exercise on account of a formidable sound and imposing figure. If the matter be carefully investigated (it will be seen that) nothing arises from that sound and bulk; and if the King command it, I will go up to him, and make known to your Majesty the explanation of the affair, and the real truth as to his business." The speech of Damnah pleased the Lion, in accordance with whose orders he went in the direction of that sound: but when he was out of the Lion's sight, the latter began to reflect, and to regret that he had sent Damnah, saying to himself, " I have committed a great error and acted thoughtlessly: and sages have said that there are ten classes of men upon whom a king should place no reliance as regards intrusting them with secrets, and to whom he must not give a hint, relative to such of his private affairs as he is particularly desirous to keep undivulged: — 1st, He who, without having committed any crime or misdemeanour, has experienced at court injustice and reproach, and who has had for a long time to endure grief and vexation. 2d, He whose property and reputation have been lost in the service of the king, and whose means of livelihood have thereby become straitened. 3d, He who has been dismissed from his post, and has no hopes of regaining his situation. 4th, The mischievous wretch, who foments disturbance, and has no inclination for peace and repose. 5th, The criminal, whose friends have experienced the sweets of pardon, while he himself has tasted the bitterness of punishment. 6th, The culprit, whose comrades have been chastised, while, as regards himself, more severe measures have been adopted. 7th, He who does approved duty, for which he has been unrequited, while others, without past service, obtain more favours than himself. 8th, He, whose post an enemy has sought, and having at length superseded him, and gained his station, has become the associate of the king. 9th, He who deems his own advantage to be coupled with the ruin of the king. 10th, He who, not having found favour at the court of his monarch, makes himself welcome with the enemy of his king.

" To these ten classes of men kings must not intrust their secrets, on the principle that, until the rectitude, and honesty, and generosity, and worthiness of any one shall have been well tried, they should not make him become apprised of their secrets.

> Tell not your secret to every person; for in this globe of the earth
> We have travelled much, and found not one to whom a secret could be confided.

" Therefore, in accordance with these premises, it was not judicious to have been hasty until Damnah had been proved, and it seems removed from the path of wisdom and prudence to have sent him to an enemy. Now this Damnah appears to be a person of intelligence, and has for a long time experienced slights and disappointments at my court. If (God forbid!) the thorn of annoyance has pierced his heart, he will in such case intrigue and raise discord, or else, finding an enemy superior to me in power and pomp, and feeling an inclination for his service, will make him acquainted with what he has learnt of my secrets, and certainly the remedy thereof would be beyond the reach of deliberation. Why have I not practised the saying, ' *Circumspection is to have a bad opinion* '? and why have I deviated from the spirit of the sage's maxim?

> Be not evil-minded, but suspicious,
> And rest secure against treachery and deceit.

"If misfortune should arise from this mission, I should deserve a hundred times as much." Indulging in such reflections, in great perturbation of mind, he alternately rose up and sat down, and scanned the road with eager eyes. Suddenly Damnah appeared in sight. The Lion became somewhat tranquil, and remained in his place. When Damnah arrived, after performing the dues of obeisance, he said:

> "May our King endure as long as the sphere revolves!
> May the sun of his fortune shine on his servants!

"O Monarch of the world! he whose noise reached your august ears, is an Ox, busy grazing in the neighbourhood of this forest, who has no business beyond eating and sleeping, and whose ambition does not extend beyond his throat and stomach." The Lion inquired, "What is the extent of his power?" Damnah said, "I did not see in him any magnificence or majesty which would enable me to form an opinion as to his strength; and to my mind, I discovered no such grandeur as to lead me to consider him worthy of more than usual veneration." The Lion replied, "One must not impute to him weakness, nor should one be thereby deceived, since the violent gale, though it does not injure delicate grass, yet roots up mighty trees; and great and clever men do not display their strength and prowess till they discover an enemy on an equality with themselves."

> When will the hawk be eager to pursue the finch?
> The falcon does not open his talons to hunt a gnat.

Damnah said, "It is not right that the King should attach so great weight to the matter of the Ox, nor take so much account of his importance, since, with much discretion, I have discovered his designs and become acquainted with the true state of his affairs; and if your exalted mind demands it, and your illustrious injunctions obtain the honour of being issued, I will fetch him, so that having placed the face of attention on the line of obedience, he may cast the coverlet of service upon the shoulders of affection." The Lion was pleased with this speech, and commanded that the Ox should be brought to him. Damnah approached Shanzabah, and with stout heart, and without thought or hesitation, began the conversation.

> He first of all said to him, "Whence did you come?

"and when did you alight here? and for what reason have you visited this spot, and proposed to take up your abode herein?" Shanzabah began to explain the true state of affairs. Damnah, being apprised of his circumstances, said: "The Lion, who is king of beasts and monarch of these districts, has sent me with an order to bring you to him, and has given me a command to the effect, that if you make haste he will overlook any neglect which hitherto may have been observable relative to your doing homage; but if you delay, I am immediately to return, and report what has occurred." Shanzabah, who had heard the name of the Lion and the beasts, was afraid, and said, "If you give me courage, and protect me from his punishment, I will come with you, and, through your kindness, obtain the honour of doing service to him." Damnah entered into a compact with him, and made such promises and conditions that the mind of the Ox was relieved. Both turned their faces towards the direction of the Lion. Damnah went in advance, and informed the Lion of the approach of the Ox, who after a while arrived, and performed the dues of homage. The Lion warmly interrogated him, and said, "When did you arrive in this quarter? and what was the cause of your coming?" The Ox retold his story in its entirety. The Lion said, "Remain here, so that you may obtain a full share of our kindness, liberality, benevolence, and generosity; for we have opened the doors of favour upon the populace adjoining our territory, and have spread the bountiful tables of kindness before the attendants of our threshold."

> In this kingdom, though you travel much,
> You will not find any one complain of us;
> Foremost in every business that we undertake,
> We pay regard to the welfare of our subjects.

The Ox having discharged the allowance of devotion and praise, bound on his loins the girdle of service with eagerness and zeal. The Lion, on his part, having conceded the privilege of access to the royal presence, day by day admitted the Ox into a closer intimacy. Having honoured and dignified him to an unusual and undue degree, His Majesty in this way set about investigating matters and searching out the real truth, and discovered the measure of Shanzabah's intellect and wisdom, and the degree of his judgment and experience. He found him distinguished for great sagacity, and endowed with acuteness and ability; the more he examined into his qualities, the greater became his reliance on his abundant knowledge.

> He saw that he possessed a good disposition, and enlightened understanding,
> Weighing his words, and estimating the worth of men;
> Possessed of knowledge of the world, and endowed with learning,
> A traveller, and experienced in the ways of society.

The Lion, after reflection, deliberation, and due consultation, and after having prayed for the blessing of God, confided his secrets to the Ox, whose station in favour and prosperity every hour became more honourable, and his dignity with regard to the issuing of orders and commands more eminent, till at length he surpassed all the pillars of the state and nobles of the presence. Now when Damnah saw that the Lion honoured the Ox to the last degree of excess, and that, in granting him rewards and favours, he passed the bounds of moderation, neither paying any attention to his (Damnah's) advice, nor consulting him respecting matters of importance, the hand of envy drew the collyrium of dislike across the eyes of his mind, and the fire of enmity threw the flame of jealousy into the corner of his brain.

> Envy, wherever it creates a flame,
> First consumes the envious themselves.

Sleep and repose deserted him, and rest and quiet removed their chattels from the region of his bosom. He went complaining to Kalílah, and said, "O brother! behold the weakness of my intellect, and stupidness of my comprehension; for my chief desire has been confined to promoting the repose of the Lion, and I brought the Ox into his service. He, having obtained access and acquired authority, has surpassed all the attendants at court, while I have fallen from my position and dignity." Kalílah replied:

"My beloved, you did it yourself. What devices avail for what we have ourselves performed?"

"You have struck this axe on your own foot, and you have yourself stirred up this dust of strife in your own path, and to you has happened that which befell the Devotee." Damnah inquired, "What was that?"

STORY VIII.

Kalílah said:—It has been related that a certain King bestowed a valuable dress and a costly robe of honour upon a Devotee. A Thief having learned this fact, became covetous, and by way of discipleship repairing to the Devotee, elected his service, and evinced zeal in learning the customs of the sect; till by such means he was admitted into confidence. One night, having found an opportunity, he stole the clothes and fled. Next day, the Devotee could not see them, and finding that the new disciple had vanished, perceived that he had taken them. Setting out towards the city in search of the Thief, he saw on the road two animals fighting, and wounding one another's heads. Whilst these two sharp-clawed combatants, like lions, were contending with each other, and the blood was dripping from the limbs and members of each of them, a Fox had come up and was licking their blood. Suddenly, in the midst of their battle, Mr Reynard came between them, and on either side received the shock of their heads against his ribs, and was captured in the bonds of death. The Devotee, having derived additional experience from this scene, passed on. In the evening, when he arrived at the city, the gate being closed, he wandered about in every direction seeking a place to halt. By chance a woman was looking down into the street from the roof of her house: she discovered from the Devotee's bewildered manner that he was a stranger, and invited him to her home. The Devotee consented, loosed his shoes in her house, and occupied himself in reading the Kurán in a corner of her dwelling. This woman was notorious for her debauchery and improper conduct, and entertained several damsels for purposes of immorality and vice. One of them, the glance of whose beauty taught the secret of loveliness to the nymphs of Paradise, and at the splendour of whose cheek the world-illuminating Sun burned with the fire of jealousy; whose languishing eye, with the arrow of its glance, pierced the midst of the bosom like as it were the centre of a target; and whose life-giving lips, with the sweetness of her mouth, gave delight to the palate of the heart, like a bag of sugar—

> Walk majestic, moon-like, resembling the lofty cypress,
> Two tresses entwined like a musky noose;
> From her delicate chin a ball (of flesh) protruded,
> Upon which a necklace of double chin was suspended;
> As regards the necklace and ball, that adorable idol
> From the Moon borrowed the necklace, from the Sun the ball—

had[1] become enamoured of a youth of handsome appearance, dark-haired, witty, of cypress-like symmetry, with aspect like the moon, sweet-tongued, and slender-waisted, so that the lovely women of Khatá, on account of his curling locks, writhed (in despair) like a hyacinth, and the sweet-lipped beauties of Samarkand were, like the hearts of lovers, in distress because of their longing for his tumult-exciting sweetness.

> A face! what sort of a face? A face like the sun.
> Ringlets! what sort of ringlets? Each tress composed of curls.

And constantly, like the Sun and Moon, they abode together in one house, and, like Venus and Mercury, were united in one constellation. Moreover, this youth, on account of the jealousy of his love, would not allow any other companion to taste a draught from the cup of the society of that damsel, nor those thirsting in the desert of pursuit, after a thousand troubles, to reach the pure fountain of her (presence).

> My jealousy on your behalf is such that, were it possible,
> I would not permit you even to enter the thoughts of others.

The wicked old woman became straitened in circumstances owing to the damsel's proceedings, and powerless through loss of income. Not being able to triumph over the damsel, who had thrown off the veil of propriety, and had devoted herself heart and soul to love for her sweetheart, she of necessity planned the destruction of the young man. The very night that the Devotee arrived at her house, she had matured her schemes, and having watched her opportunity, measured out a deep draught of wine to the lover and his mistress. When the inmates of the house were retired, having put a little deadly poison, pounded, in a reed, she then extended it to the young man's nose, and seizing one end in her mouth, placed the other up his nostrils intending to give a blow, and thereby convey the deadly effects of the poison to the young man's brain; but suddenly he sneezed, and from the force of the moisture which came from his brain, the whole of the poison went into the throat and gullet of the old woman, who became at once a corpse.

> You also will meet with that fate which you have planned for others.

[2] The Devotee saw these proceedings. At length the night, which in duration resembled that of the Day of Judgment, was, after much anxiety, succeeded by the dawn, till the hour when the devotee, Morn, having been liberated from the womb of the darkness of night, had spread the carpet of adoration before the high altar of the horizon; and the meaning of the exalted maxim was made known to men—" *And he will send them forth from darkness into light.*"

> The mirror-like dome (of the sky) was bright,
> The mirror of polished metal lost its rust.[3]

The Devotee, having withdrawn himself from the dark house of wickedness and sin amongst those people, sought another abode. A Shoemaker, who considered himself one of his disciples, by way of receiving a blessing, brought the

---

[1] In the Persian text this part of the sentence is separated from the other portion by an interval of four or five lines.

[2] I have somewhat deviated from the exact translation of this passage, which should be " The Devotee, *when* he saw these proceedings, ... the Devotee withdrew himself from the dark house," &c.; but the rendering as above seems more agreeable to English ears.

[3] See Note 2, p. 51.

religious man to his house, and instructed the inmates to look after him, while he himself went to a banquet with some friends. His wife had a lover of good disposition, with handsome face and luxuriant curls—

> Witty, gallant, roguish-eyed, and amorous,
> Whoever may be so handsome would cause ruin to the soul.

Their accomplice was the wife of a Barber, who by her enchantments made fire and water blend together, and, by her mellifluous speech, melted hard stone like wax—

> Mischief-making, who, deceitfully reciting a verse,
> Made the gnat to have an affection for the phœnix;
> Making use of a crystal rosary;
> In the place of a cord, she took a Brahminical thread;
> Her lips moved in prayer—her prayers were full of deceit and perfidy;
> Outwardly spotless garments, inwardly the stain of fraud.

The wife of the Barber, when she found the house empty, sent a person to her accomplice, desiring her to tell her lover, "To-night there is sugar without the annoyance of flies, and companionship without interruption from the police and patrol;"

> Arise! and come here: you and I know (for) what!

Her lover, in the evening, having come to her house, was awaiting the "*Opening of the door*," when suddenly the Shoemaker, like an unexpected calamity, made his appearance, and saw the man at the door of the house. The truth was that previous to this the Shoemaker had some suspicions, and there was a doubt in his mind as to the relations between his wife and this young man. On the present occasion, when he found him at the door of the house, the side of conviction prevailed, and entering the building in a great rage, he began to beat his wife. After chastising her severely, he tied her firmly to a post, and placed his own head upon the pillow of repose. The Devotee was arguing within himself: "To strike this woman without apparent cause, and without visible offence, is contrary to manly behaviour; and it is my duty to make intercession for her, and not acquiesce in this inconsiderate behaviour,"—when, suddenly, the Barber's wife arrived, and said, "O sister! why do you keep this young man waiting so long? Step forth quickly, and prize the opportunity for love."

> If the lover purposes asking for the grief-sick one,
> Say "Welcome, for there still remains a breath."

The wife of the Shoemaker, in tones of melancholy, called to her side the Barber's spouse, and said:

> O tranquil mind! what do you know of the vexed heart?
> What do you understand of the torments of deeply-afflicted lovers?
> O Ringdoves, fluttering on the top of the cypress!
> What do you know of the grief of mind of birds who are snared?

"O dear friend! listen to my miserable lamentation, and become acquainted with my wretched condition. This harsh, unkind husband, perhaps has seen him at the door, since he rushed into the house like a madman, and, after violently beating me, with cruel severity tied me to this post. If you have compassion on me, and are disposed to extend pity towards my friend, quickly loosen me, and

F

help me to tie you to this pillar in my place. After as soon as possible I have made an apology to my companion, I will return and release you. By doing this, you will both place me under an obligation to you, and will also confer a favour on my friend." The wife of the Barber, from excess of kindness, having agreed to loose the Shoemaker's spouse, and be bound herself in her place, sent her away. The Devotee, hearing this conversation, became possessed of a thread regarding the quarrel between the husband and his wife. In the meanwhile the Shoemaker, being awakened, called to his wife. The Barber's wife, fearing that, not recognising her voice, he would learn the whole matter, had not courage to answer. Much as the Shoemaker cried out, yet not a breath proceeded from the Barber's wife. The fire of his wrath being kindled, he snatched up a cobbler's knife, and going to the post cut off the nose of the Barber's wife, and placing it in her hand, (exclaimed,) "Behold a present you may send your lover!" The Barber's wife, through fear, did not breathe a sigh, and said to herself, "What a strange affair!

One has tasted the pleasure, another has experienced the pain!"

When the Shoemaker's wife returned and saw her adopted sister with her nose cut off, she was extremely grieved, and, with many apologies, untied her and bound herself to the pillar; while the Barber's wife, with her nose in her hand, set out for her own house.

From astonishment, sometimes she smiled, and sometimes wept.

The Devotee saw and heard all these proceedings, and was more and more astonished at these marvels, which became manifest from behind the curtain of obscurity. The wife of the Shoemaker, resting awhile, then in prayer extended the hand of deceit and guile, saying, "O Lord! O King! Thou knowest that my husband has cruelly treated me, and has bound on my neck by calumny and falsehood a crime which I have never committed. By Thy mercy show pity, and give me back my nose, which is the ornament of the face of beauty." During the time that the wife was making this intercession, the husband awoke, and hearing her deceitful lamentation and mischief-making prayer, cried out, "O bad and corrupt woman! what prayer is this you are making? and for what are you asking? The petition of the wicked avails but little at this court, and the supplications of the impious are not current in this quarter."

Should you desire a matter from the invisible world to be unravelled,
You must have both a pure tongue and a clean heart.

Suddenly the woman cried aloud, "O tyrant and oppressor, arise! that you may see the Divine power and Infinite goodness, since in that my skirt was undefiled from the disgrace of this accusation, Almighty God has restored my mutilated nose, and freed me, amongst mankind, from ignominy and dishonour." The simple-minded man arose, and having lighted the lamp, advanced and saw his wife uninjured, with her nose in its place, nor could he anywhere find any trace of wound or injury; in short, having confessed his fault, he busied himself apologising, and, with the utmost kindness, asked her pardon. He then unfastened the bands from her hands and feet, and made a vow that, without positive evidence and clear proof, he would not again proceed to such extremities, nor, on account of the tattle of every mischief-making tale-bearer, vex his innocent wife and virtuous spouse; and that for the rest of his life he would not disobey the commands of this chaste matron, whose prayers assuredly had no screen (of deceit) before them.

On the other hand, the Barber's wife, with her mutilated nose in her hand, came to her own house, overpowered with anxiety as to what stratagem she should devise, and how explain this affair to her husband, and what excuses she should make in the matter to her friends and neighbours; also what answer she should give to the inquiries of her family and acquaintances. In the meantime the Barber awoke, and called to his wife, "Give me my implements, for I am going to the house of a certain gentleman." The wife delayed replying, and deferred giving him his implements, but at length handed her lord a solitary razor. The Barber, in a rage, in the darkness of the night, threw the razor towards his wife, and began to abuse her. She threw herself down, and screamed out, "My nose! my nose!" The Barber was amazed; and the friends and neighbours, having entered, saw the wife with her garments stained with blood, and her nose cut off. They reproached the husband, who, helpless, remained in a state of bewilderment, possessing neither power to confess nor tongue to deny. But when the world-illuminating morn drew aside the curtain of darkness, and the earth-revealing mirror of the sun was shining like the cup of Jamshíd [1]—

> The Commander of the East hoisted his standard;
> The Monarch of the West was immersed in a sea of blood—

the friends of the woman, being collected together, brought the Barber before the Magistrate. By chance, the Devotee had also come out from the Shoemaker's house, and, by reason of the bonds of friendship which existed between himself and the Magistrate, was present at the court of justice. The usual inquiries were made, after which the friends of the Barber's wife gave their account of the affair. The Magistrate then asked, "O sir! why did you think proper, without apparent crime and legitimate cause, to mutilate this woman?" The Barber, being perplexed, was unable to make any excuse; and the Magistrate, in accordance with the peremptory command, "And for wounds retaliation," gave orders for retaliation and punishment. The Devotee arose, and said, "O Judge! respecting this matter, some reflection is necessary, and the eyes of penetration must be opened—since the Thief did not carry off my garments, nor have the wild animals killed the Fox, nor did the poison kill the wicked woman, nor has the Shoemaker cut off the nose of the Barber's wife; nay, more, we ourselves have produced all this mischief." The Magistrate withdrew his hand from the Barber, and turned his face towards the Devotee, (saying,) "Give us an interpretation of this pithy saying, and an explanation on this point." The Devotee narrated all he had heard and seen, from beginning to end, and said, "If I had not had the desire to get a disciple, and had not been deceived by the foolish talk of the Thief, that artful knave would not have found his opportunity, and would not have carried off my garments; while, if the Fox had not displayed great greed and cupidity, and had refrained from bloodthirstiness, the accident from the wild beasts would not have befallen him. If, too, the profligate woman had not planned the death of the imprudent young man, she would not have given her sweet life to the winds; and if the Barber's wife had not aided in that unlawful act, she would not have been mutilated and disgraced. Whoever does wrong must not expect good, and whoever seeks for sugar-cane must not plant the seeds of the wild gourd.

[1] Jamshíd is said to have possessed a cup in which were depicted future events.

Thus spoke a wise and experienced sage—
'Do not wrong, lest you suffer ill from the world.'"

"I have related this story that you may know that you have shown yourself this path of trouble, and opened the door of this grief and misery upon yourself."

Anyhow, of whom shall we complain, since all that has happened to us is the result of our own actions?

Damnah said, "You speak truly, and I myself have done this. Nevertheless, what means of liberating myself do you propose, and what method of undoing this knot do you suggest?" Kalílah replied, "From the first I was opposed to you respecting this matter, and did not agree with you relative to the commencement of this affair; now, also, I find it expedient to keep myself aloof from this business, and see no cause for interfering. Perhaps, however, you will devise something on your own behalf, for it has been said,

'Every one knows his own affairs best.'"

Damnah replied: "It has occurred to me to compass this matter with arts of finesse, and to try every possible means to eject this Ox from this position—nay, more, to have him expelled from this country, since I cannot permit any delay or sloth, when it becomes a question of self-defence; and if I be negligent, I shall not be excused by men of wisdom and courage. Moreover, I do not seek any new post, nor am I soliciting any more than that which pertains to my service; and wise men have observed that there are five contingencies in which men of intelligence may be pardoned for taking action: 1st, In the search for a dignity and station which they formerly held; 2d, In avoiding an evil of which they have already had experience; 3d, In protecting the gains they possess; 4th, In extracting their souls from the whirlpool of calamity which may have encircled them; 5th, In contemplating the means of obtaining gain, and averting evil as regards future times. And I am striving to recover my own position, and that the splendour of my state may be renewed: and this is the way; with craft I will pursue the Ox till he shall bid farewell to the earth's expanse, or, at any rate, shall pack up his traps from this abode; for I am not less powerful than that weak Sparrow who became revenged on the Hawk." Kalílah inquired, "How was that?"

STORY IX.

Damnah answered: I have heard that two Sparrows had built their nest on the branch of a tree, and as regards this world's goods, were satisfied with water and grain. On the summit of a hill, at the foot of which that tree happened to be, a Hawk had his abode, who at the hour for seeking his prey used to dart forth from his nook like lightning, and as a thunderbolt clean consume the harvest of life of tender-winged birds.

Were he at any time to strike his talons upon the birds,
Were there fifty[1] such, he would bear them all away.

Whenever the Sparrows hatched their young, and the time was nearly come

---

[1] There is a play upon words in the Persian text, which cannot be retained in the translation.

that they should fly, the Hawk would dart out from his hiding-place, and seizing their little ones, make them food for his own offspring. Now, in accordance with the command, "*Love of home is a part of faith,*" those Sparrows were unable to remove from that abode; while, owing to the cruelty of the tyrannical Hawk, it was also impossible to remain.

Neither bent on travelling, nor desirous of remaining.

Once upon a time their brood, having become strong and fledged, used to move about; and the father and mother, rejoicing at the sight of their offspring, were delighted with their attempts to fly. All at once the thought of the Hawk crossed their minds, and in a moment, rolling up the carpet of delight, they began with perturbation and impatience to lament and complain. One of the young Sparrows, on whose brow the marks of discretion and maturity were manifest, having inquired into the cause of that circumstance, and the reason of their change from mirth to sadness, they replied, " O son !

Do not ask us as to what degree is this anguish of heart;
Inquire from the tears in our eyes, since they are our interpreters."

They then related all the particulars respecting the cruelty of the Hawk and the carrying off of the young ones. That son replied : " To turn one's neck from the commands of Fate and the will of Providence is not becoming to creatures. But the '*Causer of causes*' has appointed a remedy for every ailment, and sent a cure for every woe; assuredly if you use your best efforts to avert this calamity, and take steps to untie this knot, both the misfortune may be warded off from us, and the burden also be removed from your minds." The Sparrows approved of this speech, and one of them remained to look after the little ones, while the other flew away in search of a remedy. When he had proceeded a short distance he fell into this train of thought, " Where shall I go, and to whom shall I tell the grief of my heart ?"

I am seized with sadness of heart, and do not know the remedy for anguish of
mind;
The cure for heart-ache is difficult enough—am I not aware of it ?

At length it occurred to his mind that he would narrate his story to whatever animal might first come in view, and would ask from him a remedy for his affliction. By chance a Salamander, having appeared from out of a mine of fire, was strolling about in the expanse of the desert; the eyes of the Sparrow alighted upon him, as his strange shape and peculiar aspect came into sight. He said to himself, "'*I have fallen upon good.*' Come ! I will disclose my internal grief to this strange bird; perhaps he may undo the knot of my business, and show me the way towards a remedy." He then, with great respect, approached the Salamander, and after the usual salutations, observed the customs of offering service; and the Salamander also, with considerate words, discharged the dues of kindness towards travellers, and said, " Signs of fatigue are visible in your countenance; if it is from weariness of travelling, remain a few days in these parts, so that repose may take its place; and if things are otherwise, explain matters, so that, to the extent of my power, I may strive to remedy them." The Sparrow opened his mouth and represented to the Salamander his state of misery, in a manner that, if he had told it to a flinty stone, it would have crumbled in pieces from distress of mind.

> To whomsoever I recount my tale,
> I open a hundred fresh sores in the heart of that helpless one.

On hearing this story the fire of the Salamander's pity was kindled, and he said, " Be not sad, for I will avert this calamity from your head, and will this night arrange to burn the Hawk's home and nest, with all that therein is: do you show me where you live, and return to your offspring till I come to you." The Sparrow pointed out the situation of his dwelling in such a manner that the Salamander remained in no uncertainty thereon; and with glad heart, and a mind free from the burden of grief, turned his face towards his own nest. When evening was arrived, the Salamander, with a number of his own kith and kin, each of them carrying a quantity of naphtha and sulphur, set out towards that abode; and, under the guidance of the Sparrow, betook themselves to the neighbourhood of the Hawk's nest. The Hawk, together with his off-spring, unprepared for any calamity, had eaten to repletion, and fallen asleep. The Salamanders, having thrown on the nest the naphtha and sulphur which they had brought, turned back; and the wind of Divine justice having blown, the flame of vengeance burst upon the nest of that Tyrant. He and his brood woke up from the sleep of carelessness at a time when the hand of pre-vention was helpless to extinguish that fire, and all were in a moment, together with home and nest, burnt to ashes.

> The tyrant raised a conflagration by oppression;
> When the flames arose, they consumed him first of all.

" I have narrated this story, that you may know that every one who labours to repel an enemy, notwithstanding that he himself may be small and weak, and his rival great and powerful, may hope for victory and triumph." Kalílah said: " Now that the Lion has distinguished the Ox from among the rest, and hoisted the standard of his fortune, it would appear extremely difficult to divert the affection of the King's heart from him, or to cause the Monarch to alter his feelings towards him: for sovereigns, when they patronise any one, do not, without good reason, disgrace him, nor, unless some great event happens, do they cast out of their sight him whom they have exalted."

> Water does not draw wood below—what is the reason?
> It is ashamed to bear to its depths that which it has itself nourished.

Damnah rejoined: " What grounds can be more complete than these, that the King has in an undue measure patronised the Ox, and has allowed the other Ministers to fall into contempt, till, necessarily, they have become disgusted with his service, and the advantages of their labours and the fruit of their advice are lost on him? From such a state of affairs great calamities must be anti-cipated. Wise men have said that danger may arise to a king and misfor-tune to a country from any one of six things: 1st, Mortification — that is, causing the well-wishers to become disappointed in him, and leaving men of wisdom and experience in disgrace. 2d, Strife—which is such that unreason-able war and inconsiderate undertakings arise, and the swords of antagonists become unsheathed. 3d, Lust—that is, having a passion for the fair sex, and excessive love of the chase; being addicted to wine, and having an inclina-tion for trivial pursuits. 4th, Adverse fortune—that is, such occurrences as happen in the world, like plague, famine, earthquake, fire, flood, and the such-like. 5th, Hastiness of temper—that is, readiness to quarrel, and an eagerness to inflict torture and punishment. 6th, Ignorant stupidity—which is this, having in time of peace an inclination for war, and during warfare being disposed for peace; at a period of conciliation entering into disputation, and where the barriers of harshness should be drawn across, opening the door of kindness.

> Peace and war out of season are of no service;
> Let a rose keep its place as a rose, and a thorn as a thorn."

Kalîlah said: "I perceive that you have girded your loins for revenge, and are lying in ambush for Shanzabah, and wish that through your own agency some harm may befall him. Now I know that the infliction of injury produces no good effect, and that, as a retribution, the evil of every person will revert to himself.

> He who did wrong experienced nought but evil;
> Misfortune quickly recoiled upon him.

And whoever opens the eye of warning and observes [1] the retribution of bad and good, doubtless will be disposed towards mercy and compassion, and will restrain his hand and his tongue from oppression and inflicting pain: in such sense a Monarch, the dispenser of Justice, spoke." Damnah inquired, "How was that?"

STORY X.

Kalîlah replied: I have heard that in former times there was a certain King who opened the hand of despotism and oppression, and placed the foot of perverseness beyond the path of justice and kindness.

> World-consuming, merciless, and tyrannical,
> From his bitterness the face of the earth itself became soured.

Men day and night, by reason of his injustice, lifted up their hands in prayer and loosened the tongue of imprecation. One day this Monarch went hunting, and on his return issued a proclamation saying, "O men! till to-day the eyes of my heart have been veiled from beholding the countenance of rectitude, and the hand of my misdeeds has drawn the sword of tyranny across the faces of the abject oppressed and the sorrowful injured; now I am become honestly resolved to protect my subjects, and firmly determined to dispense justice. This is my hope, that after to-day the hand of any oppressor will not strike the knocker of annoyance upon the door of my subjects' houses, nor the foot of any tyrant touch the threshold of the abode of any poor person."

> Do not look for plenty in those regions and lands
> Where you see the peasant distressed by the King.

On this good news fresh life appeared to his subjects, and owing to this happy intelligence the Rose of delight of the poor blossomed in the Garden of Hope.

> From this blessed news that has suddenly come,
> Rejoicing has reached the heart, and glad tidings the soul.

In short, the felicity of his justice reached such a climax that lambs drank milk

---

[1] ـلـ in the Persian text is a misprint for ـلـ.

from the breasts of fierce lions, and the pheasant also by way of recreation played with the hawk. On this account they gave him the name of the "Justice-dispensing King."

> So surely did he lay the foundation of justice,
> That fire became the protector of sulphur.

One of the Privy Councillors of the State, at an opportune time, asked the particulars of the case, and made inquiry regarding the change from the bitterness of violence and oppression to the sweetness of kindness and confidence. The King replied: "The day that I went hunting, I was galloping in every direction, when suddenly I saw a Dog running after a Fox, the bones of whose leg he crunched with his teeth. The hapless Fox, maimed in his leg, crept into a hole, and the Dog returned. All at once a Man on foot threw a stone and broke the Dog's leg; he had not gone many steps when a Horse kicked the Man on foot and broke his leg, and that Horse also had not proceeded far on the road when his foot slipped into a hole and it was broken. I came to my senses and said to myself, 'Do you observe what they have done and what they have seen? Whoever does that which is not right will experience that which is not agreeable.'"

> Take care that you seek after good, and do not wrong,
> Since you will experience both the bad and good.
> If on all occasions you desire to do what is right,
> You will see yourself exalted;
> And if you travel the road of evil, you yourself,
> Ruined, will suffer poverty.

"I have narrated this story that you may reflect as to retribution, and abandon cherishing wicked thoughts, lest misfortune therefrom come upon you, and the saying, '*Whoever dug a well for his brother, why, truly, he fell into it,*' should be manifested. A wise man has said, 'Do not wrong lest evil betide thee, and dig not a pit lest thou fall into it thyself.'" Damnah said, "I am the oppressed in this matter, not the oppressor, and suffer wrong instead of inflicting injury; and if the oppressed purpose to be revenged on his oppressor, what retribution will follow thereon? and if misery come upon the tyrant by the hand of him who is aggrieved, what injury will thereupon arise?" Kalílah replied, "I grant that in this matter ruin may not overtake your affairs; but how will you encompass the death of the Ox, since his strength is greater than that of yours, and his friends and allies more numerous than your comrades and well-wishers?" Damnah answered, "The edifice of my arrangements must not be reared on great strength and countless allies, but preference must rather be given to intelligence and deliberation; for it often happens that a matter is accomplished by stratagem and device, which could not be effected by means of force and violence. Has it not reached you how a Crow by stratagem encompassed the death of the Snake?" Kalílah said, "How was that?"

STORY XL

Damnah replied: It has been related that a Crow had taken up her abode in the middle of a hill, and had made her nest in the cleft of a rock; and near to that crevice there lived a Snake, the water of whose mouth was a deadly and fatal poison, and the saliva of whose gums was the destroyer of the essence of life and existence. Whenever the Crow had young ones, the Snake used to devour them, and consume the Crow's heart with grief for the loss of her offspring. When the tyranny of the Snake had passed all bounds, the Crow, being in despair, made known her troubles to a Jackal who was a friend of hers, saying, "I am pondering over a means of escape from the misery which the Snake causes me, and from the anxieties occasioned by this life-pursuing oppressor." The Jackal inquired, "In what way will you proceed in this matter? and by what stratagem will you avert his mischief?" The Crow said, "I intend, when the Snake is asleep, with my bloodthirsty beak to peck out his earth-seeing eyes, so that he may not be able again to hurt those who are the light of my vision, and that my children, who gladden my sight, may rest secure from the violence of his malevolent glance." The Jackal replied, "This scheme is a deviation from the road of propriety, since it behoves wise men to plot against their enemies in such a manner that their own lives may not be imperilled. Take care and abandon this design, lest you ruin yourself like the Heron, who endeavoured to destroy the Crab, and gave his own precious soul to the winds." The Crow inquired, "How was that?"

STORY XII.

The Jackal replied: There was a certain Heron who took up his abode on the borders of a lake. The principal object of his life was to search for fish, which he used to catch according to his needs, and passed his existence in ease. When the weakness of old age overtook him, and his bodily strength began to give way, he became incapacitated from hunting fish, and was entangled in the net of grief. He said to himself:

Alas, the caravan of life! that it should have so passed away,
That not even its dust has reached the atmosphere of our country.

"Alas! that for trifles I should have given my precious life to the winds, and not have hoarded anything which might be of service or assistance to me in the time of my old age! Nowadays I have no strength left, and one cannot dispense with food[1]; my best course is to base my plans upon stratagem, and spread the net of deceit and fraud."

Perhaps by this pretence my days may pass.

Thereupon he sat on the margin of the lake, like one uttering lamentations, heaving sighs, and moaning. A Crab from afar beheld him, and coming near, in pert tones thus addressed him: "O beloved friend! I see you are dejected: what is the cause of it?" He replied, "How can I be otherwise than melan-

---

[1] This might also be rendered "strength."

choly, for you know that my means of livelihood and sources of support were, that every day I used to catch one or two fish, and in such manner procured a bare subsistence, and food just sufficient to keep body and soul together? No very great harm thereby befell the fish, and my time also was adorned with the ornament of contentment and gladness. To-day two Fishermen, passing by, said, ' There are many fish in this lake; we must take counsel respecting them.' One answered, ' In such and such a lake there are more fish than there are here; first let us settle their business, and then turn our faces again to this spot.' Now if things turn out in this fashion, I must sever my affections from sweet life, and connect them with the bitterness of death." The Crab, when he heard this news, immediately turned back, and went to the fish and related to them the sad intelligence just as he had heard it. Agitation and distress of mind having fallen upon them, together with the Crab, they set out towards the Heron, and said, " This news has reached us from you, and the reins of deliberation have been snatched from our hands.

> The more we look at this matter from head to foot,
> Compass-like,[1] from helplessness, the more we are bewildered.

Now we wish to deliberate with you, since ' *He who is consulted is trustworthy.*' It behoves a wise man, even though he be an enemy, when he is consulted, not to neglect the dues of advice—especially in a matter wherein his own advantage lies. Now you yourself say that the permanence of your being is linked with ours, and your life dependent on our existence: therefore, as regards our business, what seems right in your eyes?" The Heron replied, " I myself overheard this conversation from the mouths of the Fishermen; there appears no means of resisting them, and nothing occurs to my mind beyond this device: I know near to this a pool, of which the water, as regards purity, resembles the true dawn, and in power of reflection surpasses the world-displaying mirror: you can count the grains of sand on its bottom, and see the eggs of the fish in its depths: and in spite of all this, the diver, Understanding, cannot reach its bottom, nor the traveller, Sense, see its shore; and no fisherman has ever cast a net in that pool, nor have the fish of that lake been enslaved by any other bonds save the chain [2] of the waves.

> It is a Lake like the sea;
> But a sea which is illimitable.

" If you can remove there, you may pass the rest of your life in security, tranquillity, repose, and delight." They said, " This is a good idea, but without your assistance and aid our removal is not possible." The Heron replied, " I will not withhold from you anything within my power and ability; but the opportunity is short—at any hour the fishermen may arrive, and the chance will be lost." The fish entreated him, and, after much solicitation, it was agreed, that every day having fetched several fish, he should convey them to that lake. Then the Heron every morning brought several, and ate them on the top of a little hill in that vicinity; and when he returned, the others hastened to move and change their abode, each one seeking to be in advance of the other. Wisdom, with the eye of warning, contemplated their error and want of caution, and Fortune, with a thousand eyes, wept over their miserable plight: and assuredly, whoever is

---

[1] Those who make no progress are said to " move in a circle," such as would be described by a pair of compasses.

[2] *I.e.*, the ripple of the waves.

deceived by the flattery of an enemy, and thinks proper to rely upon a contemptible, badly-disposed person, will incur a like punishment. When some days had elapsed, the idea of this lake entered the Crab's head, and he became anxious to remove there. He communicated his intention to the Heron, who thought to himself, " There is not any one more inimical to me than him; it is best that I should also carry him to his friends." He therefore advanced, and having taken round his neck the Crab, set out towards the resting-place of the fish. The Crab, who had from afar seen their bones, discovered what was the state of affairs, and said to himself, " A wise man, when he sees that his enemy is compassing his death, if he omits to exert himself to the utmost, will have assisted in his own ruin; while, if he uses his endeavours, one of two things will result,—if he be victorious, he will leave a name for bravery upon the page of time, or, if unsuccessful, he will not, at any rate, be reproached for want of zeal and honour."

When an enemy purposes to kill you, to avert the calamity
Strive with might and main, if you have the reputation of being wise;
Since, if successful, you will have obtained your end,
And, if you fail, then you will be exonerated from blame.

The Crab then threw himself on the Heron's neck, and began firmly to throttle him. The Heron, who was old and weak, after little pressure on the throat, became senseless, and falling through the air, lay prostrate in the dust. The Crab let go his hold from the Heron's neck, and, taking his own path, bent his steps in the direction of the remaining fish. Having added to the condolence for absent friends congratulations for the safety of those present, he gave an account of the circumstances which had happened. All were delighted, and considered the death of the Heron as new life and perpetual existence.

A single breath of life, after the death of such an enemy,
I deem better than a hundred years of ordinary existence.
I do not rejoice at the decease of an adversary, but
One moment of separation from an enemy is better than aught you can tell me.

" I have narrated this story that you may know that many persons, through deceit and fraud, encompass their own death, and also meet with ruin from their own plots, according to the tradition, ' *Base fraud does not take effect except upon its author.*' However, I will show you a method, the adoption of which will be the cause of your own preservation and the destruction of your enemy." The Crow said, " One must not neglect the caution of friends, nor act contrary to the opinion of men of discernment."

O Cup-bearer! you direct me to the wine-shop:
To act contrary to your advice is not the way of friendship.

The Jackal replied, " The proper plan is this: You must fly aloft and cast your eye over the roofs of the houses and over the plains. Whenever you see an ornament which can be carried off, alight and bear it away; and in the face of Heaven fly along, in such a manner that you may not be hidden from the eyes of mankind. Beyond doubt, some men will follow after you in search of the ornament. When you arrive near the Snake, drop the decoration upon him, so that those persons may see him: first of all, they will release the Snake from the cage of life, and then bear off the ornament. So your mind, without any effort on your part to injure him, will obtain repose." The Crow, according to the advice of the Jackal, setting out to a populous place, saw a woman, who, depositing a trinket [1] on the roof of a house, occupied herself with her ablutions. The Crow carried it off, and, in the manner suggested by the Jackal, threw it down near the Snake. Some men, who were following the Crow, at once crushed the Viper's head, and the Crow obtained deliverance.

An enemy departed from amongst us, and tears also from our bosom.

Damnah said, " I have narrated this story that you may know that what can be accomplished by treachery cannot be effected by mere strength." Kalílah rejoined, " The Ox possesses strength, dignity, intelligence, and deliberation. You cannot by treachery prevail against such a person, since in whatever direction you, with stratagem, make a breach, he with thought will repair it : perhaps before you can make a supper from him, he may breakfast upon you. But maybe the tale has not reached your ears of the Hare who planned the capture of the Fox, and was herself entrapped ? " Damnah said, " How was that ? "

STORY XIII.

Kalílah answered : I have heard that a hungry Wolf was traversing a forest in search of food. He saw a Hare sleeping under the shade of some sprigs of grass—the slumber of negligence having overpowered all her limbs. The Wolf deemed her a rare prey, and began slowly to advance towards her. The Hare, in alarm at the Wolf's breath, and fear of his step, having awakened from sleep, jumped up anxious to flee. The Wolf, occupying the middle of the road, said :

" Come, come ! for I cannot bear your being so far away ;
Do not flee, do not flee, since I am in despair at your absence."

The Hare, from dread of him, was rooted to the spot, and, commencing to use entreaties, rubbed the face of supplication on the ground, saying, " I am aware that the fire of hunger of the chief of beasts is raging strongly, and that inordinate appetite is aroused by your search after food. Now, with my insignificant body and delicate form, I am not more than a solitary mouthful for the King : of what value shall I be ? and from eating me, what result [2] will accrue ? Now, near to this there is a Fox, who from excessive fatness cannot move along, and from his immense obesity is unable to stir : it appears to me that his flesh, owing to its juiciness and freshness, is like the water of life, and his blood, owing to its sweetness and delicacy, resembles luscious sharbat. If your Excellency will give yourself the trouble to go, by means of such stratagem as I can devise, I will entrap him, and your Majesty may breakfast upon him. If this pleasure be procured, well and good ; if not, then am I still your captive and prisoner."

Bring others into your snares, since we ourselves are enslaved.

The Wolf was deceived by her artful stories and deceitful tales, and took the road to Reynard's house. Now in that neighbourhood there really was a Fox, who could have taught even Satan treachery, and have given a lesson in deception and cunning to Understanding and the Imagination.

---

[1] پيـاپه in the Persian text is a misprint for سيـراپه .
[2] Literally, " What will be bound ? what will be loosened ?"

A young Fox, active and artful was he;
Rather shall we say he was the lord of that district;
He was the frolicking trickster of the plain and village;
He took the precedence of all wild animals in gambols;
The beasts of the plain, also, were in lamentation on account of him,
And the village dogs howled because of him;
The moment he sprang forth, he was lost to sight,
Sweeping the surface of the firmament with the brush of his tail.

The Hare had a long-standing enmity with him; and at this time, having found
an opportunity, she purposed to be revenged. Having left the Wolf at the
entrance of the cavern, she stepped into the abode of the Fox, and performed
the customary salutations and welcome. The Fox also, with great respect,
returned the courtesy, and said:

" You are welcome: whence have you arrived ?—come and sit down:
  Come in, for I will give you a place near my two eyes: sit down."

The Hare replied: " I have for a long time been desirous of obtaining the pleasure of meeting you; but on account of the impediments of fickle Fortune, and
the accidents of perfidious and inconstant Time, I have been deprived of that
happiness. Nowadays a holy man, who in Egypt, by the king's condescension,
has been exalted to dignity, and who, throughout the kingdom of piety, cherishes
his disciples, having come from the holy sepulchre, has honoured this place with
a visit. Having heard, through fame, of the seclusion and retirement of your
Excellency, he has made your humble servant his medium, in order that the
eyes of his heart may be illumined by your world-adorning beauty, and the
nostrils of his soul perfumed by the odours of your musk-like words. If you
permit such a visit, well and good; but if the time is not propitious, another
occasion may occur."

Either let him return from this door, like a sudden calamity,
Or let him alight, like an answered petition.

The Fox read on the page of this speech the appearance of treachery, and in the
mirror of these words beheld the semblance of deceit. He said to himself, " It
is right that I should treat them in their own fashion, and pour some of their
own drink down their own throats."

Against throwers of clods, stones are cast in return.

The Fox thereupon warmly welcomed the Hare, and said: " We have already
girded our loins with the desire to assist travellers, and opened the door of our
cell upon the face of the pious, with the view of being benefited by the beauty
of their state and the perfection of their conversation, particularly in the case
of such a holy man as you describe. What shortcomings in hospitality could
there be on my part towards a being of such perfect description as you have
been mentioning ? or in waiting upon him, what trifle could I omit ?—' For
the guest, when he alights, alights to his own appointed food ;' and sages have
said:

In the world you find that every person eateth his own allowance,
Whether his loaf be on your table or on his own board;
Therefore, you should accept as a favour your guest, seeing that
He consumes bread which is his own, though it be at your hospitable table.

Nevertheless, I hope that you will delay a while, so that I may sweep out the corner of my small abode, and spread for my guest of blessed foot a carpet which may be worthy of the occasion." The Hare imagined that her speech had deceived the Fox, who would at once honour himself by waiting on the Wolf. She accordingly replied : "The person in question is one indifferent to ceremony, and of disposition befitting a darwísh, and cares not for adornment of place or garments ; but since your honourable mind wishes that ceremony should be observed, it is of no consequence." Saying this, she retired, and laid before the Wolf all that had transpired, and conveyed the good news relative to the Fox being deceived ; and since, "*In every novelty there is pleasure,*" he again began afresh to describe the flesh and fat, and juiciness and freshness, of the Fox. The teeth of appetite being sharpened, the Wolf's mouth watered at the deliciousness of the Fox's flesh ; and the Hare, on account of this good service, bethought herself to obtain her release. But the Fox, by reason of caution and foresight, had a long time previously dug a deep pit in the middle of his abode, . and by degrees carried away the earth, and concealed the top with a few sticks and straws ; and had also a secret way by which he could, in case of need, make his exit. When he dismissed the Hare, he came to the edge of the pit, and arranged the rubbish upon it in such a manner that, on the slightest occasion, it would give way; then having gone to the entrance of the secret passage, he cried aloud, " Oh dear guest ! will you give yourself the trouble of stepping this way ?" and at the same time that they came in, he made his exit from the cavern. The Hare [1] with great lightness of heart, and the Wolf with excessive greed, came into that dark cell. The instant that they placed their feet upon the rubbish, they fell to the bottom of the pit. The Wolf imagined that this device was the act of the Hare, whom he instantly tore to pieces, and delivered the world from the disgrace of her existence.

" I have narrated this story that you may perceive that stratagem is of no avail against men of wisdom, and that he who is endowed with a share of caution and foresight will not be deceived by the trickery of any one." Damnah replied : " It is as you say ; but the Ox is proud of himself, and is not on his guard against my enmity. I may be able to overthrow him by means of this want of caution, since the arrow of deceit, which is shot from the bow of friendship, is the more efficacious : and perhaps you have not heard how the cunning of a Hare prevailed against the Lion, and since he was unsuspicious of treachery on the part of the former, he fell into the whirlpool of death, notwithstanding his wisdom and intelligence ? " Kalílah said, " How was that ? "

STORY XIV.

Damnah said : It has been related that in the neighbourhood of Baghdád there was a meadow, the breezes of which added perfume to the fragrance of Paradise, and the lustre of its odoriferous plants illumined the eyes of the firmament ; from each one of its rosy-cheeked branches shone a thousand stars, at the beauty of every one of which stars the nine Spheres were astonished.

> The running stream in the verdure tarries in its course,
> Like quicksilver in a mould of lapis lazuli ;

---

[1] خرگوش in the Persian text is a misprint for خرگوش.

Sweet-scented herbs blossom on the banks of the rivulet;
The zephyr scatters perfume, and the air is scented with musk.

And in that meadow were many wild animals, who, on account of the agreeable climate and the delightful plains, coupled with the abundance of water and profusion of good things, used to pass their time in pleasure and repose. But in the neighbourhood there lived a fierce-natured mischief-seeking Lion, who every day showed his evil-disposed face to those helpless creatures, and rendered their life and existence disagreeable. One day they went in a body to the Lion, and, having performed obeisance and submission, said: " O King ! we are come as your subjects and servants ; and you, every day, after much trouble and endless toil, may either hunt down one of us or not, while we, from dread of you, are always in the distraction of misery, and you, also, are wearied with the fatigue of pursuing us. Now we have devised a scheme which may be productive of ease to yourself, and the cause of security and quietude to us. If you will not trouble us in that manner, nor every day make our time miserable, we will send some game at breakfast-time as an allowance for the King's kitchen, and will not suffer any negligence in the performance of this." The Lion gave his consent thereto, and they every day cast lots, and according to the name of whomsoever of them was drawn, they sent him as the allowance for the King. In this way a considerable period passed. One day the name of the Hare came forth, and Fortune made her the target for the arrow of calamity. She said to her friends, " If you use some leniency as regards sending me, I will deliver you from the tyranny of this oppressor." They replied, " In this matter there is no difficulty." The Hare waited an hour, till breakfast-time was passed ; and the ferocious nature of the Lion being aroused, he ground his teeth with rage and anger. The Hare gently approached him, and found that he was very distressed, the fire of hunger having upset him,[1] and the fierceness of his anger being manifest in his movements and posture.

To heat the oven of the stomach continually
Will cause agony in the day when nothing is to be found.

The Hare saw that the Lion, from excess of rage, lashed the tail of revenge upon the ground, and sought in his heart to violate the engagement ; slowly she went before him, and greeted him. The Lion inquired, " Whence did you come ? and what is the case with the beasts ? " She replied, " According as it was arranged, they sent a Hare in company with me, and we intended to pay our respects together ; but a fierce Lion met us by the way, and seized her. Though I [2] used my best endeavours, representing ' these are the repast for the monarch of beasts, and the allowance of the King,' he paid no attention to my words, but said, ' This is my hunting-ground, and the game therein belongs to me.

Perhaps you have not heard that " Every lion has his forest ! " '

" O King ! he so boasted and bragged, in describing his strength and magnificence, that I lost all control, and having escaped from him, hastened to convey to your enlightened mind a narrative of the case." A foolish sense of honour being aroused in the breast of the hungry Lion, he said :

" I am such a person that, in the art of piercing and striking,
I can instruct even lions in the mode of fighting.

---

[1] Literally, "having seated him on the wind."
[2] " I " seems more suitable to the context than the literal translation " we."

> Which of the lions will be bold enough
> To place his claws upon my prey ? "

Whereupon he said, " O Hare ! can you show him to me, so[1] that I may pluck from him the justice which your heart demands, and may also wreak my own vengeance ? " The Hare said, " Why should I not be able ?　He has spoken of the King various disrespectful words; and if I had been able I would have made the goblet of his skull a drinking-cup for the beasts of the plain."

> But I hope in God that I may see him
> In your clutches, according to my heart's desire.

Thus she spoke, and went in advance.　The innocent-minded Lion, being deceived by her treachery, followed in the rear.　The Hare brought the Lion to the top of a large well, the water of which, from its purity, like a polished mirror[2] reflected objects with distinctness, and showed without blemish the nature of the external form and appearance of every person looking down into it.

> No one could look therein but that as regards his own image
> He scanned it in its glittering surface.

She said, " O King ! your worthless enemy is in this well, and I am alarmed in dread of him.　If your Majesty will take me in your bosom, I will show you your enemy."　The Lion, having caught her up in his breast, looked down into the well, and saw in the water the reflection of himself and the Hare: he thought that it was the very Lion, with the Hare that was destined as his own allowance in his clasp.　Dropping her, he threw himself into the well, and after two or three plunges consigned his bloodthirsty soul to the flames of Hell. The Hare, returning in safety, apprised the animals of the circumstances of the case.　Having discharged the dues of thanks to Almighty God, they grazed in repose in the gardens of security and safety, repeating this verse,

> One quaff of water after the malevolent (are departed)
> Is more enjoyable than a life of seventy years.

" By citing this story it may be gathered, that however strong an enemy may be, it is possible in a period of careless indifference to gain the victory over him." Kalílah said, " If you encompass the death of the Ox in such a manner that the Lion may not be grieved, it is well, and you may be in a measure excused; but if his death cannot be effected without vexation in the King, beware that you mix not yourself up with this business—for no wise man, in order to promote his own personal comfort, will elect to cause his master pain."　With these words the discourse terminated; and Damnah, having abandoned attendance, withdrew into the nook of retirement: till one day, having found an opportunity, he burst upon the Lion privately, and stood like a person afflicted with melancholy, and grieved, with sore mind and drooping head.　The Lion said, " It is days since I have seen you.　Is all well ? "　Damnah replied, " May God grant that the end may be well ! "　The Lion jumped up and exclaimed, " Has anything happened ? "　" Yes," he answered.　The King ordered him to repeat it. Damnah then said, " For that, privacy and leisure are necessary."　The Lion observed, " This very hour is opportune.　Repeat it as quickly as possible, since important matters do not admit of delay; and if the business of to-day be postponed till to-morrow, a thousand calamities will ensue."

---

[1] ﺗﺎ in the Persian text is a misprint for ﺗﺎ .　　　　[2] See Note 2, page 51.

Do not delay, but bring forward the chief matter,
Since in procrastination there is much misery.

Damnah began: " It is not expedient to be rash in the utterance of any speech which may meet with the disapprobation of the auditor; and nothing should be spoken without considerable deliberation and much reflection, unless there be complete reliance upon the wisdom and discernment of the hearer; also it is incumbent that the listener should regard the circumstances of the speaker, whether or not he is likely to offer good advice in a friendly spirit. When he is assured that the speaker has no motive beyond discharging the obligations of gratitude for benefits received, it becomes him to lend a willing ear to what is spoken, particularly when advantages and benefits may accrue to him therefrom." The Lion responded: "You are aware that in acuteness of penetration and fulness of wisdom I have become an exception to the rule, and that in hearing what any one has to say I make kingly discretion the habit of my mind ; so without ceremony say what you wish, and without hesitation do not conceal whatever has occurred to your mind." Damnah answered: " I, too, have found permission to be courageous, seeing that my confidence in the wisdom and knowledge of the King is beyond all bounds ; further, it is not disguised that I speak from mere kindness and pure sincerity, and that I do not defile myself with doubts and suspicions, with machinations and evil designs. However, nothing but the touchstone of the royal mind will ascertain the genuineness of the coin of (my) words."

Praised be God ! that the mouth of the King is a touchstone,
Which distinguishes between our base coin and pure metal.

The Lion said: " The completeness of your fidelity is evident, and the traces thereof are manifest on the face of your affairs; and, altogether, your words are fraught with kindness and friendly advice. Suspicion and doubt find no means of obtaining an entrance about them." Damnah replied: " The existence of the race of animals is bound up with the duration of the life of the King; therefore, every subject who is distinguished by, and celebrated for, the marks of an honest disposition and pure descent should not, in the performance of what is right, and in relating the truth, withhold his advice from the King; for wise men have said, ' Whoever conceals the truth from the King, or keeps his ailment secret from the Physician, or does not think proper to proclaim his poverty and want to his friends, will have been dishonest towards himself.'" The Lion observed: " Your affection and friendship have, before this, been apparent to me, and I have perceived your honesty and integrity; so now, say what has happened, so that after learning all the particulars of the case, I may devote myself to deliberating thereon." Damnah, when with treachery and fraud he beguiled and deceived the Lion, opened his mouth and spoke:

" O King ! may wisdom be thy guide,
May victory be thy friend, and foes thy scorn.

"Shanzabah has held private meetings with the chiefs of the army, and has treated with the nobles of the state, saying, 'I have tried the Lion, and have learned the measure of his force, strength, intelligence, and penetration ; and in each of these have beheld many flaws and numerous infirmities.'

He was not such an one as we imagined,
Nor was he such as we had pictured him.

G

"I am astonished that your Majesty has gone to such an excess in honouring this ungrateful traitor, and with reference to dominion and authority has made him one with yourself: in return for these kindnesses, such conduct has proceeded from him, and as a requital for so great favours, he has put forward such pretensions. Certainly, in accordance with the saying, '*Verily man is rebellious if his will be independent,*' whoever sees his hand supreme as regards commands and prohibitions, and finds the reins of controlling[1] the affairs of state in the grasp of his power, the demon of mischief will place eggs in the nest of his brain, and the lust of disobedience will break out from the blackness of his heart."

> Whosoever fortune uplifts from the well of obscurity,
> Him she places on the summit of approbation;
> Strange would it then be, were he not to make pretensions to royalty,
> And not to throw his snares around the head of the rebellious.

The Lion said: "O Damnah! think well what words are these you are saying. How have you ascertained the truth of these rumours? and, if things are such as is understood from your assertions, what plans can be devised respecting this business?" Damnah replied: "The eminence of Shanzabah's dignity and the greatness of his rank are known to the King; and when a Monarch sees one of his servants rivalling him in height of station, in wealth, and in honour, he must speedily remove him out of his way, otherwise the matter will get beyond his reach, and the King will be overthrown. As to remedying this business in such a manner as the enlightened mind of the protector of Sovereignty demands, how can my weak imagination and defective understanding rise to such a pitch? But I perceive that any remedial measures in this matter of the Ox must be carried out with speed; for if you procrastinate, affairs, without doubt, will arrive at a pitch that the foot of deliberation will be powerless to measure the extent thereof.

> Your adversary was an ant, it became a snake.
> Bring vengeance on the head of this ant, which is grown to a viper;
> Do not give him longer to live, nor throw away the opportunity,
> Since the snake will, if it find occasion, become a dragon.

"It has been said that men are of two kinds—the cautious and the helpless: the helpless is he who, at the time of the birth of an affair and the occurrence of an event, is stupefied, distracted, hesitating, and amazed; while the cautious is he who, making use of foresight, always contemplates the end of matters. Again, men of caution are of two kinds: 1st, He who, before the appearance of danger, makes himself acquainted with the nature thereof, and at the outset sees, with the eye of wisdom, that which others arrive at only after the termination of affairs, and at the very first stage of a business takes counsel respecting its conclusion.

Consideration first, action last.

"Such a person can convey himself to the shore of deliverance before he falls into the whirlpool of misfortune; and he is termed most prudent. The second is he who, on the advent of a calamity, maintains his courage, and does not give way to wonder and astonishment: doubtless the road of rectitude and the means

---

[1] Literally, "loosening and fastening."

of deliberation will not remain hidden from such a person, who is called prudent. As bearing upon the circumstances of these three kinds of individuals, of whom one is 'very wise,' and another 'partially wise,' and the third 'a negligent fool,' there is a story of three Fish who happened to be in a pond together." The Lion inquired, "What was that?"

STORY XV.

Damnah said: It has been related that there was a pond at a distance from the highway, and concealed from the view of passers-by; and its hidden waters were pure like the faith of the pious, and the contemplation thereof was all-sufficient to those seeking after the fountain of life. This pool was connected with a stream of running water, and in it there abode three beautiful Fish, such that *Pisces*, from envy of them, was broiled on the frying-pan of jealousy, like Aries from the heat of the Sun. One of these Fish was "very prudent," the second "prudent," and the other "helpless." Once upon a time, in days of spring, when the world, beautified by parterres of roses, became like the Garden of Paradise, and the Earth's surface, with its bright, sweet-scented herbs, resembled the azure vault full of stars; when the Chamberlain, the Zephyr, had adorned the surface of the earth with carpets of various colours, and the incomparable Gardener of Creation had decked the plain of the world with Roses of different hues—

> The garden, from the gentle breeze, was heavy with musk,
> The jessamine, in its delicacy, was like the cheek of a beloved one;
> At the breath of the dawn the rose expands its lips,
> Like a smiling beauty caressing her lover—

suddenly two or three fishermen happened to pass by that pool, and by the Divine Decree discovered for a certainty the precise facts how these three Fish abode in that lake. Having mutually agreed upon a rendezvous, they hastened to fetch their nets. The Fish having learned this, though immersed in water, became the associates of the fire of sorrow; and when night arrived, the one who was endowed with perfect wisdom and possessed the greatest prudence—since often he had suffered violence from Fortune, and the capriciousness of the tyrannical Heavens, and since his foot was firmly fixed on the carpet of experience—turned in his mind the idea of escape from the net of the fishermen, and the thought of deliverance from their bonds.

> Recognise that person as wise and learned
> Who firmly establishes the basis of his proceedings;
> He whose prudence is not sound,
> The edifice of his affairs is very insecure.

He therefore quickly set about his task; and without waiting to consult his friends, went out at that place which adjoined the running stream. In the morning the Fishermen, having arrived, securely blocked up both ends of the pool. The partially wise Fish, who was adorned with the ornament of wisdom, but had not a share of the store of experience, when he saw what had happened, was filled with much remorse, and said: "I have been neglectful, and this is the termination of the business of the incautious. Like that other Fish, I should, previous to the advent of a calamity, have been filled with anxiety on my own account, and before the attack of misfortune have devised a plan of escape.

> The remedy for an occurrence should be taken before it happens;
> Regret avails nought when the matter has got beyond your reach.

"Now when the season of flight is lost, it is a time for cunning and stratagem; and although it has been said that at the time of affliction deliberation no longer avails, and that in the period of misfortune no further advantage can be derived from the fruit of wisdom, yet, in spite of this, it behoveth a man of understanding not in any way to be in despair respecting the beneficial results of knowledge, nor, in repelling the devices of an enemy, to admit of any delay or procrastination."[1] Therefore, having feigned himself to be dead, he lay drifting upon the surface of the water. A Fisherman took him up, and fancying he was lifeless, threw him down on the edge of the bank. The Fish, with subtlety, cast himself into the running stream and escaped safe and sound.

> Die, O friend! if thou desirest freedom,
> Since without dying you will not find a friend.

The other Fish, in whose affairs negligence was predominant, and in whose actions incapacity was apparent, bewildered and stupefied, confounded and irresolute, went from right to left, and darted up and down, till at last he was captured.

"The King from the recital of this story should be satisfied that in the matter of Shanzabah despatch is needed; and that before the means and opportunity slip away, he should with a sharp sword strike the fire of regret into the soul of that base wretch, and having scattered to the winds of destruction the harvest of his life, should cause the anguish of his family to reach the Heavens."

> When you are superior in power to a treacherous enemy,
> With the stone of misfortune dash out his brains.

The Lion replied: "What you have narrated is understood by me; but I do not imagine that Shanzabah contemplates perfidy, or will allow himself to recompense my former favours by subsequent treachery—for up to this time I have not allowed myself (to display) ought but goodness and benevolence towards him." Damnah said, "So it is; for, by these favours of the King, he has attained his present position.

> Whenever you choose you may produce a scar;
> But as you can apply a salve, it matters not.

"An ignoble, badly-disposed person will be sincere and honest so long as he has not reached the position at which he is aiming; but when his object is gained, the desire to obtain other stations for which he is unfitted will arise from the repository of his imagination: and wise men have said that the edifice of service amongst the mean and unprincipled is (reared) on the rule of fear and hope—when he becomes secure against the anxieties of terror, he makes turbid the fountain of his goodwill; and when, by the acquirement of property, he becomes rich, the fire of ingratitude and rebellion breaks out." The Lion responded, "Then as regards servants of a mean disposition and contemptible mind, what kind of treatment must be pursued, in order that the traces of their ingratitude may become evident?" Damnah answered, "They must not be

---

[1] I fancy توقـع should be نوقف .

deprived of favour in such a manner that, having suddenly lost hope and resigned service, they should turn towards the enemy; nor, on the other hand, must such wealth and fortune be bestowed upon them that, having attained great riches, presumptuous thoughts should arise with them. Rather is it expedient that they should pass their time between fear and hope, and that their affairs should be constantly balanced between promises and threats, between hopes and fears,—since wealth and security make them puffed up with themselves, thereby causing rebellion and tumult, while despair and poverty make servants bold, thereby occasioning loss of power to Kings."

> The man without hope becomes bold and free-spoken;
> O friend, do not act in such a manner that I shall become desperate!

The Lion said: "It occurs to my mind that the mirror of the condition of Shanzabah is free from the rust [1] of this description, and the page of his heart clean and pure from the inscription of such a design. I have always befriended him, and invariably shown him unremitting kindness. Considering that at all times he has received favour and courtesy at my hands, how can he, in return for that, plot evil and mischief?"

> Since my heart, in affection for him, makes itself conspicuous,
> Why should he hoist the banner in enmity to me?

Damnah said: "The King should know that nothing straight ever proceeds from a crooked-minded person; and that a badly-disposed individual, of mean origin, by trouble and painstaking, will never become a man of amiable disposition and pure nature. '*Every vessel leaks with what is in it.*'

> From the bottle that which is within will trickle out.

"Perhaps the story of the Scorpion and the Tortoise has not reached the King's illustrious ears?" The Lion inquired, "What was that?"

STORY XVI.

Damnah replied: A Tortoise was friends with a Scorpion, and they constantly lived in friendship with one another, and in the display of affection—

> From dawn till twilight they were friends and companions,
> From evening till morn they were associates and allies.

Once it so happened that, by force of circumstances, it was necessary that they should emigrate from their native land. In company together they set out for another place of security. By chance their way lay in the direction of a great river, and a large running stream appeared in their path. Since it was impossible for the Scorpion to cross the water, he remained bewildered. The Tortoise said, "O dear friend! what is the matter with you, that you have given the collar of the garments of life to the hand of lamentation, and have gathered up the skirt of your heart from joy and cheerfulness?" The Scorpion replied, "O brother! the thought as to how I am to ford this water has plunged me into the whirlpool of trepidation, since it is not feasible for me to cross the stream, and the power to separate from my friends is not possible."

---

[1] See Note 2, page 51.

You are going on, while I, broken-hearted, will remain;
It is strange that without thee I exist—strange indeed that I exist at all.

The Tortoise answered: " Be not in any way dejected, for, bearing you across the water without difficulty, I will bring you to shore, and having made a boat of my back, I will make my bosom a shield against your calamities; since it would be wrong after acquiring a friend with difficulty to part with him with ease."

O companion! go, with all you possess,
Purchase a friend, but do not part with him for any consideration.

The Tortoise having then taken the Scorpion on his back, cast himself into the stream and moved onwards. Whilst swimming across a sound reached his ears, and he felt a tapping on the part of the Scorpion. The Tortoise inquired, " What noise is that which I hear, and what action is it you seem busy performing?" The Scorpion replied, " I am trying the point of my sting against the coat of mail of your body." The Tortoise was excited and said: " O unmanly fellow! on your account I have thrown myself into the whirlpool of danger, and with the protection of the boat of my back, you are crossing this water; if you are not sensible of the kindness and attach no weight to the dues of former intimacy, at any rate what is the cause of your stinging me? especially since it is certain that no injury will reach me from this proceeding, and that your heart-irritating sting will take no effect on my stone-like back."

It is probable that the hand and heart of that person will themselves be wounded,
Who in the way of altercation strikes his fist against a wall.

The Scorpion replied: " God forbid that such ideas as these should ever, in the whole period of my life, enter or have entered my mind! It is no more than this: my nature leads me to sting whether the wound be upon the back of my friend, or the bosom of my enemy."

Whoever possesses a contemptible disposition,
It will, unwittingly, show itself on his part;
The scorpion stings a stone,
Though he can produce no effect thereon.

The Tortoise thought to himself, that wise men have rightly said, " To cherish a man of mean disposition, is to give one's own reputation to the winds, and to lose the clue of one's own affairs."

There is no disinclination to pour on the earth gold and ornaments,
But there is an aversion to show kindness and manliness to the grovelling.

" It is a saying of the wise, that ' Whoever has no lineage in his origin, hope has no share in him, since it is out of the order of things for a base-born person to take leave of the world without doing evil to all who may have befriended him.'"

How is it possible to nourish a person of bad origin?
Why should any one cherish a snake within his own house?
The wild-gourd will not by cultivation produce the flavour of the sugar-cane.
Roses are not gathered by him who only nurtures thorns.

" From the narration of this story it may have crossed the enlightened mind of the King, that regarding the inconstancy and mean disposition of Shanzabah, he should be filled with alarm, and ought to listen with ears of judgment to the counsel of his devoted servants. Whoever pays no attention to the advice of counsellors, though they may speak with brusqueness and freedom, the conclusion of his affairs and the termination of his business will not be devoid of regret and reproach : as when a sick person regards with contempt the doctor's commands, and partakes of food and drink according to his own inclination, certainly every moment weakness and want of strength will gain more ascendancy over him.

> " If a counsellor speaks with an air of severity, what matters it ?
> Patience is bitter, but it bears sweet fruit.

" And it must be known that the weakest of kings is he who is negligent regarding the termination of affairs, and who holds in contempt the important matters of state, and who, whenever an event of magnitude occurs, lays aside caution and foresight ; and after that the opportunity is lost, and the enemy is victorious, suspects those around him, and imputes the state of affairs to each one of them."

> The attention that you ought to bestow upon your own affairs,
> Why should it be left to another ?
> And when, by so doing, you have committed an error,
> Why should it be placed round the neck of another ?

The Lion replied : " You have spoken with much assurance, and deviated from the limits of politeness ; however, the speech of a counsellor must not be rejected on account of its roughness. As regards Shanzabah, on the supposition that he is an enemy, it is clear what action will proceed from him ; and, as a matter of fact, he is my food, since the essence of his existence derives support from herbs ; whereas flesh is the source of my strength, and invariably herb-eating bodies are subservient to brute creatures. I do not deem him of such consequence as to think that the idea of opposing me would enter his mind, or that the desire of destroying me would find a place in his innermost heart.

> When will it occur to an adversary to boast of fighting with such an one as
>   I am ?
> When can gnats contend with raging elephants ?

" And if Shanzabah, like the Moon, should dare to oppose the Sun of my prosperity, which shines from the horizon of Omnipotent favour, he will be ruined and overwhelmed : and if, like the Sun, he should draw the sword against the orb of the august Phœnix-like crown of my head, which resembles the firmament of Heaven, in the end he will fail."

> The empty-handed, if he profess to be rich,
> Is like a lame horse, who tries to amble.
> I have exalted the head of that animal,
> I will again bring the lasso round his neck.

Damnah replied : " Let not the King be deceived, in that he says, ' He is my food ;' or, ' I can overpower him ;' since if by his own self he cannot oppose you, he will gain his end by means of the united assistance of his friends ; or else by deceit and perfidy, or stratagem and cunning, he may create impressions ; and I fear lest having incited the beasts to opposition against the King, they may league with him : and one person, however strong-bodied and powerful he may be, cannot overcome a multitude."

> Gnats, when in a mass, will attack an elephant,
> Strong and robust though he be.
> Ants, when working together,
> Will drag off the skin of a fierce lion.

The Lion said : " Your words have taken effect in my mind, and I am conscious of the integrity of your advice : but this idea has seized me,—I have exalted him and raised his standard of power and advancement, and in public meetings and gatherings, have recited his praises, and loosened my tongue in laudation of his wisdom, intelligence, sincerity, and integrity : if I allow myself to act in a contrary manner, I shall be charged with changeability of word, levity of disposition, and imbecility of understanding, and my words will be rejected in the minds of men, and my promise become of no value in their hearts."

> When you yourself have exalted the head of any person,
> So long as it is in your power, refrain from overthrowing him.

Damnah rejoined : " Good counsel, and a correct determination, are this : when there are indications of hostility on the part of a friend, and dependants give themselves the airs of lords, one must at once close accounts with them, and snatch one's skirt from their company and society : and before an enemy finds an opportunity for breakfast, one must prepare his supper for him. Notwithstanding that the teeth may be a man's old comrades, from whom various benefits and advantages accrue to him, yet when they are diseased, no cure can be found for their pain except extraction : and when food, which compensates for the wear and tear of the body and nourishes the springs of life, becomes corrupt in the stomach, there is no relief from the injury it occasions, except by voiding it."

> Him, who brings no consolation to thy afflicted heart,
> Forsake, even though he has been to thee like thine own soul.

The fraud of Damnah produced its effect on the Lion, who said, " I abhor the society of Shanzabah, and for me again to meet him is of the number of impossibilities : my best course is to send some one to him, and making clear to him the state of affairs, give him permission to go wherever he wishes." Damnah fearing that, if this speech should reach Shanzabah, he would in such case lay before the Lion his warrants of protection, and that his own deceit and treachery would come out from the secret abode of concealment into the courtyard of disclosure, said, " O King ! this arrangement is far from prudent ; for so long as words are not spoken the power of choice remains, but after they are uttered, the remedy is beyond the region of one's capability.

> A word not spoken, you have power to say ;
> But when uttered it cannot again be kept secret.

" When a word escapes from the mouth, or an arrow flies from the bow, the former cannot return to the speaker, nor the latter to the thumb-stall : and it has passed into a proverb, that 'Whatever comes to the tongue comes to ruin ;' it has been said, too, by a wise man, that 'The tongue is the interpreter of the mind, the mind the lord over the region of the body, and the words of a speaker pearls from the treasury of existence; so long as the door of the casket of conversation is fastened with the nail of silence, and the seal of reserve placed on the top of the jewel-box of speech, all the odoriferous herbs grow in safety in the garden of life, and all the young plants of existence produce the fruits of security and repose: but when the rose-bush of eloquence begins to smile, and the nightingale of oratory commences to sing, there cannot be security, since the fragrance of the rose-garden of speech will be either the cause of recreation to the heart, and the strengthening of the brain, or else will occasion the manifestation of defluxion and be the source of headache: since when language is reserved, many difficult knots will be untied by one felicitous expression, whereas, when speech is mischief-making, by one sentence out of place the neck of the speaker will be enchained with heavy bands.' "

If, with the eye of wisdom, you reflect as to speech,
It is a capital which brings both profit and loss;
The proof thereof is this—that a witty saying hitherto unspoken,
Will either render a person miserable with anguish of heart or bring him to life.
Yes, it frequently occurs, that the snare of pleasantry
Consigns the speaker to destruction, the moment the word escapes his lips.

" O King! if this speech reaches Shanzabah, and he perceives how he is situated, and sees [1] his disgrace, maybe he will proceed to contend with you, and commence battle, or else raise sedition. Men of caution do not visit an open fault with a secret punishment, nor do they inflict a public chastisement for a hidden crime: the true course is, for you to meet his clandestine offence with a secret retribution." The Lion said, " To repel and reject one's attendants on mere suspicion, and to labour to deprive them of their privileges without positive evidence, is like striking an axe on one's own foot, and suddenly deviating from the road of manliness and the path of integrity."

It is not acceptable, according to law and wisdom,
For a King to issue decrees without certain evidence;
Since his commands, like the shafts of Heaven,
At one time take away life, at another restore it.

Damnah answered : " Men of authority cannot have better evidence than their own intelligence: so, when this treacherous rascal arrives, the King must scan him with a careful eye, then the worthlessness of his fidelity will be evident in his malevolent countenance, and the baseness of his designs in his revolting face. Now the tokens of his inward deception are these: he will come before you changing colours and perplexed, and will look carefully about on the right and on the left, and before and behind, and prepare for strife and collect himself for opposition." The Lion said, " You speak well; and if I observe any of these indications, assuredly the dust of doubt being removed from the road of truth, the timidity of suspicion will be exchanged for the degree of true knowledge." Damnah, when he perceived that, by means of his mischief-making language, the fire of misfortune had raised aloft in that quarter, was anxious to see the Ox, and kindle on his part the flame of ruin.

Strife between two people is like fire:
The wretched interloper supplies the fuel.

---

[1] مهابنة in the Persian text is a misprint for مهاينة.

He bethought himself that the interview with Shanzabah must come to pass at the direction and counsel of the King, so that he might be removed from all suspicion. He said, "O Monarch! if your exalted orders should attain the honour of being issued, I will see Shanzabah, and having become acquainted with some of the secrets of his heart and the treasures of his mind, will narrate them to you." The Lion gave him permission. Damnah, like one overwhelmed with grief and misfortune, approached Shanzabah, and observed the custom of salutation and greeting. The Ox, having exhibited reverence befitting, began in kindly and considerate tones to say, "O Damnah!

> Call to mind if ever you remember me.

"For many days you have not gladdened the eyes of friends with the light of your beauty, nor made the cell of your companions a rose-garden with the flowers of the plants of society and courtesy."

> During your life, not one moment do you remember your friend;
> While not for an instant could he possibly not think of you.

Damnah replied: "If by necessity I have been precluded from the honour of meeting you, surely, body and soul, I have constantly, in imagination, been in the society of your heart-ravishing beauty, and perpetually sown the seed of friendship and affection in the soil of my mind.

> I have made windows from my heart towards thee, my life.
> Unknown to thee, I have often toyed with thee.

"Both in the cell of retirement and the corner of privacy I have been and will be occupied in the duties of prayer and praise, which are the means of the increase of prosperity and happiness." The Ox replied, "What is the cause of your retirement?" Damnah said: "When one cannot be master of one's own inclinations, but is the slave of the orders of another, scarce drawing a breath through fear and danger, never for a moment passing one's life and existence save in dread and trembling, and not a word issuing from one's lips without nervousness and terror, how should one not select the corner of one's abode, and close the door in privacy against both stranger and friend?"

> From the strife of this mischief-making age,
> Arise and fly wherever you can;
> And if your foot has not power to run away, at least
> Put out your hand and cling to the skirt of retirement.

The Ox replied: "O Damnah! speak more clearly than this, and be good enough to enter more fully into particulars; so that the advantages of your advice may be more complete, and the benefits of your discourse more perfect." Damnah said: "There are six things in this world, which are not possible without six others,—worldly possessions, without pride; the pursuit after trifles, without labour; an assembly of women, without misfortune; partiality for the society of base people, without disgrace; association with the wicked, without repentance; attendance on the king, without calamity. To no one is it given to quaff from the wine-vault of this world without becoming intoxicated and insolent, and lifting up the hand of rebellion from the collar of haughtiness and presumption; nor does any one follow a single step after vanity without meeting with destruction; nor does any man sit with women without becoming entangled in various plots; nor can a person associate with wicked and seditious men without in the end repenting it; no one places reliance upon a mean and contemptible wretch without becoming miserable and dejected; nor can any individual elect to associate with kings and come safe out of such a destructive whirlpool.

> The society of kings, by the light of analogy,
> Recognise as a boundless ocean:
> To such a sea, pregnant with fears and dangers,
> Whoever is nighest is most miserable.

"In this matter it has been said:

> 'In the sea are innumerable advantages;
> But if you desire safety, it is on shore.'"

Shanzabah replied: "Your speech tends to show that something distasteful has overtaken you, at the hands of the Lion, and that in dread of him you are overwhelmed with fear and alarm." Damnah said: "I do not speak these words regarding my own self, nor am I sad on my own account; but rather, in this matter, I consider my friends before myself, and the anguish and despondency which have overpowered me are on your behalf. You know in what way there have been past bonds of intimacy and former ties of friendship between you and me, and that the pledges and engagements which we from the first contracted with each other have up till now, for the greater part, been faithfully discharged; therefore I have no alternative left but to communicate to you all that has occurred, whether good or bad, advantageous or detrimental." Shanzabah trembled within himself, and said: "O dear friend and agreeable comrade! quickly inform me of what has happened, and do not withhold any of the particulars demanded by the delicacies of affection and sincerity." Damnah said: "I have heard from a trustworthy person that the Lion has uttered from his august lips, 'Shanzabah has become very fat, and at this court there is no need of him, and his absence or presence is a matter of indifference. With his flesh I will make a banquet to the beasts, and one day I will make my own particular repast, as well as give a feast to the public, off his body.' Having heard this speech, and knowing him to be headstrong and haughty, I have come here to apprise you, and thus to confirm by proof the fidelity of my engagement, and discharge that which is imposed upon me by the rules of manliness and the custom of honour and generosity.

> I will tell you all that due diligence requires of me,
> Whether you take advice from my speech, or whether you become vexed.

"Now the right course at the present time appears to me this, that you should prepare a plan, and with the utmost promptitude set about devising a remedy, and arranging matters. Perhaps by stratagem you will find liberation from this whirlpool, and by some bright idea gain deliverance from this predicament." When Shanzabah heard the speech of Damnah, and reviewed in his mind the agreements and compacts of the Lion, he said: "O Damnah! it is not possible that the Lion should deal treacherously with me. The state of the case is this: no perfidy has been displayed on my part, and my firm foot has not slipped from the path of conscientious service, while, as regards your words, I am convinced of your rectitude, and am persuaded of your sincerity; the inference is that numerous falsehoods have been imputed to me, and that, by treachery and deceit, the Lion has been rendered furious. Now in his service are a crowd of worthless people, all of whom are illustrious masters in concocting tales, and fearless adepts in perfidy and oppression; these he has often tested, and has observed a number of misdeeds and depraved acts on their part: therefore, whatever they say of others in this respect, he believes, and makes his own deductions accordingly: undoubtedly, from the foulness of the society of the wicked, suspicion falls upon the good, and by such erroneous ideas the path of rectitude becomes concealed. The story of the Goose, and the falsity of its experience, is a clear proof on this point, and an ample illustration of such a state of affairs." Damnah inquired, "How was that?"

STORY XVII.

Shanzabah said: "A certain Goose saw the light of the moon[1] in some water; thinking it was a fish, he endeavoured to seize it, but found nothing. Several times he made an attempt in like manner, but when he discovered that the only result of such pursuit was identical with that which a thirsty man would experience from the contemplation of a vapour resembling the sea, or with that which poor deluded creatures might derive by observing desolate houses, he entirely gave up hunting after fish, and suddenly abandoned his pursuit. On other nights, when he *did* see a fish he thought it was the light of the moon, and made no attempt to seize it, and paid not the least attention to it, saying:

' *Who attempts what has been tried, confusion will surround him.*'

Now the fruit of his experience was this, that he was continually hungry, and passed his life without provisions and food.

"Now, if the Lion, as regards me, has been made to hear anything, and if, according to the proverb ' *He who listens is alienated,*' aversion has filled his heart, and he has believed the same, the cause of it is his having had similar experience of others; while the truth is, there is between myself and others the same difference that there is between clear day and dark night, and between the lofty vault and the debased centre."

Do not judge the actions of the virtuous by yourself,
Since, when you write the word "shír" (lion), it may also mean "shír" (milk).
Two kinds of bees feed on the same spot—
From one proceeds a sting, from the other, honey;
Two kinds of deer live on grass and water—
From one flows blood, from the other exquisite musk.

Damnah said: "Perchance the aversion is not on that account; nay, more, it may be owing to the custom of kings, who give high rank to a person unworthy of the distinction, and, without any apparent cause, make others who are deserving, objects of plunder and destruction."

The king of Hurmúz never saw me; yet, without a word, showed me a hundred kindnesses.
The king of Yazd saw me, and I sang his praises, but he never gave me anything.

---

[1] It must be remembered that "moon" and "fish" are expressed in Persian by the same word.

Such is the action of kings!   Thou, O Háfiz![1] must not grieve.

O God! the giver of daily bread, may thy peace and help be poured upon them!

Shanzabah said: "If this aversion which you have intimated to me, on the part of the Lion, is without cause, by no offerings can the foot of Repose measure the road of integrity, nor can the eye of Hope see the face of its desire, since, if there be a cause for enmity, it can be averted by efforts to please, and apologies.   But if (God forbid!) there be no ground for it, and either by deceit or calumny his mind has been perverted, the hand of remedy will be powerless, and the means of cure hopeless; for there is no clear standard regarding falsehood and slander, and no settled boundary to treachery and fraud.   Now, as regards what has occurred between me and the Lion, I am conscious of having committed no offence beyond this—I have, for his own good, taken the opposite side to him in judgment and deliberation, and sometimes, in arranging and planning matters of state, I have expressed ideas such as may be expedient, rather than such as would accord with his good pleasure: possibly he may have imputed this to boldness and want of respect, and regarded it as audacity and impudence.   Neither has ought which has proceeded from me been without great advantage; and in spite of all this, I have observed respect and attention with regard to his majesty and grandeur, and, to crown all, have never shown want of courtesy, and have to the fullest extent discharged the dues of honour and reverence.   How can he entertain the thought that kindly advice should become the cause of fear, or sincere service give rise to enmity?

> Medicine has caused the disease, then here what hope is there
> Of the ailment vanishing and the sick man recovering?

"If this also is not the case, it is possible that pride of sovereignty and the independence of empire may be the reason why he is angry with me; since it is a characteristic of pride and a feature in greatness to be by nature averse to sincere friends, and to put confidence and regard in traitors and flatterers, on which account wise men have said, 'To dive to the depths of the sea with a crocodile, or to suck drops of poison from the lips of a snake whose tail has been cut off, is more akin to safety than waiting upon kings, and is more peaceful and productive of repose than to be near to monarchs.'   I knew that great were the dangers of serving sovereigns, and boundless the misery of managing their affairs; hence some men of wisdom have compared kings to fire, since, although the light of favour illumines the dark cell of the hopeful, yet with the flame of punishment a servant's harvest of past dues is consumed; and true wisdom is agreed upon this, that whoever is nearest to fire is most miserable.   But the multitude who from afar behold the brilliancy of the light of fire are ignorant of its consuming properties, so they imagine that there is pleasure, and think that there is advantage, in being near to kings; but in truth this is not the case, for if they were aware of the punishments of a monarch, and the dread and majesty of a king, it would be manifest to them that a thousand years of favour are not equal to one hour of torture.   The story of the dispute between the Hawk and the Domestic Fowl confirms this."   Damnah inquired, "What was that?"

---

[1] A celebrated Persian poet.

STORY XVIII.

Shanzabah said : Once upon a time a Hunting Hawk was engaged in a dispute with a Domestic Fowl, and beginning to contend, said, " You are a most faithless and treacherous bird : yet in fact trustworthiness is the frontispiece of the page of acceptable manners ; and in addition, according to the tenor of the saying, ' *Verily the perfection of a promise is a part of faith,*' fidelity is a perfect proof of religion ; generosity and manliness, also, require that no one should inscribe the pages of his affairs with the mark of treachery."

> A Dog who is grateful for roast meat,
> Is better than that person who is unthankful.

The Domestic Fowl replied : " What ingratitude on my part have you seen, and what treachery have you observed ? " The Hawk answered : " The signs of your ingratitude are these,—that, in spite of all the kindnesses which men show to you, without trouble or exertion on your part, apportioning you water and grain, from which the springs of life derive their existence ; while day and night, being apprised of your circumstances, they strenuously guard and watch you ; and owing to their felicity you possess food and lodging—yet whenever they wish to catch you, you flee before and behind them, and fly from roof to roof, and run from corner to corner.

> Thou knowest not the requirements of salt,[1]
> And thou fearest thine own benefactor.

" While I, who am a wild animal, after having associated with them for two or three days only, and eaten food from their hands, keep in sight what is their due for this : hunting the game, I give it to them ; and however far I may have gone, yet on merely hearing a call, flying, I come back."

> A trained bird, however far any one may cast it,
> Yet flies back with joyful wing when he says, " Come."

The Fowl replied, saying : " You speak truly. Your return and my flight are owing to this, that you have never seen a Hawk cooking on a spit, while I have beheld many Domestic Fowls roasting in a frying-pan. Were you ever to see such a sight, you would never come near them ; and if I flee from roof to roof, you would hasten from hill to hill."

" I have narrated this story that you may know that the mass of people who court the friendship of kings are unaware of their punishments ; and he who has seen the effects of their severity is not familiar with repose, nor can tranquillity be discerned in him."

> Affliction is more severe to those who are nearest,
> Since they are aware of the violence of kings.

Damnah rejoined : " It is not surely that the Lion cherishes these thoughts towards you on account of the greatness of his royalty and the pomp of his prosperity, since you possess much excellence and countless virtues, and monarchs are not, at any time, independent of men of worth." Shanzabah replied :

---

[1] A person dependent on another is said to "eat his salt."

" Maybe my worth has been the cause of his aversion, since, in the case of a swift horse, that very virtue is the cause of his captivity ; and the fruit-bearing tree, by reason of its produce, has its top and branches lopped ; the nightingale, also, on account of its merit, is imprisoned in a cage ; while the peacock, for the elegance and beauty of its feathers, is plucked and put to shame.

> All my knowledge becomes my punishment,
> Like the brush to a fox, or feathers to a peacock :
> Merit is my fault, otherwise, on my head
> Would be a crown of jewels, not of earth.

" And assuredly, since worthless persons are more numerous than meritorious men, and since between them there is perpetual natural animosity, the former being more victorious by reason of their numbers, use their victory so violently to degrade the condition of men of excellence, as to exhibit their movements and attitude in the garment of sin, making confidence appear in the shape of treachery, and rectitude in the robe of wickedness, and the very worth, which is the cause of prosperity and the means of happiness, they render the origin of malignity and the source of adversity.

> When the eye is malevolent (may it be plucked out),
> A vice in its sight appears a virtue.

" And a wise man has said relative to this :

> ' If a virtue raises its head from our midst,
> A person without merit strikes it with his hand.
> The efforts of an excellent man are frustrated,
> In order that his merit may be injured.'

" And also in describing the injustice of those who seek for faults, they have said :

> 'Though the eye of justice is clear-sighted,
> It deems that to be a pearl which is but really a glass bead.
> The custom of wise men is to be just in their actions,
> The deeds of the base are nought but scratching to pieces ;
> They who have not a heart endowed with compassion,
> Allege those to be woollen garments which are silk.' "

Damnah said : " Perhaps the malevolent have concocted such a scheme ; on that supposition, how would the matter end ? " Shanzabah rejoined : " If such be not the will of Destiny, no evil will accrue[1] therefrom ; while if Divine Fate and the Omnipotent Decree shall be in accord with their treachery and deceit, by no contrivance will it be possible or practicable to avert the effects thereof."

> When Fate takes the lead, of what avail is deliberation ?

Damnah answered : " It becometh a man of wisdom in every case to make prudent forethought a preliminary to all his actions, since no one bases his conduct on wisdom without being successful in his aims." Shanzabah rejoined : " Wisdom only accomplishes her designs at a time when Fate is not contrary, and stratagem is of avail at that season only when Destiny does not flow in opposition thereto. Against the Decrees of Providence there is no remedy, nor

---

[1] Literally, "will come therefrom to the regions of existence."

does any device avail. Deliverance from the bonds of Fate and the chains of Destiny is not, by any contrivance or deliberation, imaginable for any one.

"Every fire, which the hand of Fate kindles,
Burns up all thoughts and deliberations.

"And when the Creator, God, the most Holy and the most High, shall send forth His decrees, He makes dark and cloudy with the bodkin of negligence, the cautious eyes of those possessing sight, so that the way of escape from those Decrees becomes concealed from them—' *When Fate arrives the sight is blinded.*'

"When the decree of Fate arrives,
All the prudent become blind and deaf.

"Perhaps you have not heard the story of the Rustic and the Nightingale, and their disputation may not have reached your ears." Damnah inquired, "What was that?"

STORY XIX.

Shanzabah replied: It has been related that a certain Rustic possessed a charming and delightful garden, and pleasure-grounds sweeter than the Rose-bower of Paradise. Its atmosphere gave salubrity to the breeze of spring, and the perfume of its spirit-refreshing plants conveyed fragrance to the brain of the soul.

A Rose-garden like the flower-garden of youth,
Its roses were washed by the water of Life ;
· The song of the nightingale therein produced delight,
Its fragrant breeze was mingled with repose.

In one nook of this garden was a Rose-bush, fresher than the tender plant of happiness, and more exalted than the branch of the young tree of delight. Every morn upon it there blossomed Roses of various hues, like the cheeks of heart-ravishing tender maids, or the face of silver-bosomed jessamine-scented damsels ; and the Gardener began to be enamoured of those lovely Roses, saying,

"I know not what the rose speaks from beneath its lips,
That it should again bring the songless[1] nightingales into lamentation."

One day the Gardener, according to his usual custom, having come to see the show of Roses, beheld a Nightingale uttering her lamentation, and rubbing her head on the front of a Rose, and separating from one another, with her sharp pecks, the binding of its gold-worked volume.

The nightingale, which contemplates the rose, becomes enamoured :
The end of the thread of its power slips from its hand.

The Gardener, seeing the scattered leaves of the Rose, with the hand of perturbation tore the collar of patience, and hung the skirt of his heart on the penetrating thorn of restlessness. Another day the self-same state of affairs occurred, and the flame of the loss of his Rose,

Inflicted a fresh wound upon the top of that scar.

---

[1] That is, "silent."

The third day, also, by means of the peckings of the Nightingale,

> The Rose was broken to pieces, and the thorn remained.

Disquietude having reached the heart of the Rustic on account of the Nightingale, he placed the snare of treachery in her path, and entrapped her with the bait of deceit, and put her in confinement in a cage. The dejected Nightingale, parrot-like, broke into speech, saying: "O friend! for what cause have you imprisoned me, and for what reason are you disposed to torture me? If you have acted in this manner so as to hear my melody, is not my own nest in your Rose-garden, and the joy of my home, every morning, within the limits of your grounds? But if another purpose has crossed your mind with regard to me, give me notice of what is in your mind." The old Rustic said:

> How long will thou afflict me, O God? O Rival, mayest thou not remain!
> Till when wilt thou conceal her cheek, O God? Vanish away, O veil!

"Are you entirely ignorant of what you have done regarding my fortune, and how you have several times grieved me by depriving me of my beloved friends? A retributive punishment for such conduct would be just this, that you should be cut off from the society of your friends and country, and, deprived of joy and pleasure, should pine away in the corner of your prison; while I, distressed at the loss of my friends, should lament in the retirement of sorrow."

> Lament, O Nightingale! if you are to be friends with me,
> Since we are two lovers weeping, and our occupation is to lament.

The Nightingale replied: "Abandon such ideas, and consider that, if I be confined for such a degree of offence as injuring a rose, you who have tortured the heart itself, how will you fare?"

> The revolving Spheres, it may be imagined,
> Know the truth as to good and bad;
> He who does right it comes home to him,
> If he acts wrongly, it is to his own detriment.

This speech had its effect on the heart of the Rustic, who released the Nightingale. She, her mouth being opened by obtaining her freedom, said: "Since you have shown me kindness, assuredly—in conformity with the tradition, '*Is there any recompense for generosity except generosity?*'—I must make a return for such: know that beneath the very tree where you are standing there is a vessel full of gold, take it, and use it for your necessities." The Rustic examined the place and found the Nightingale's words true. He said: "O Nightingale! it is strange that you see a pot of gold under the earth, and did not perceive a net upon the surface of the ground. The Nightingale replied: "Do you not know that, '*When destiny descends, caution is in vain*'?

> With Fate it is impossible to contend.

"When the Divine Decree is issued, light no longer remains to the eyes of penetration, and neither deliberation nor wisdom is of any avail."

> Against the claws of the hand of Fate struggle not,
> Since your hand has no power whatever;
> Caution will not avail against the Omnipotent Decree;
> Accept whatever proceeds from the hand of Fate.

H

"I have recited this story that it may be evident that I am no match for the hand of Fate and Destiny, and have no alternative but to place the head of submission upon the line of the Divine Decree."

> The boundary of my desires is the threshold of my Lord and friend,
> Since whatever befalls me, proceeds from His will.

Damnah rejoined: "O Shanzabah! what I know for certain, and have clearly ascertained, is this, that what the Lion has contemplated respecting you does not proceed from the backbiting of enemies, or your superior worth, or the caprice of kings; nay, more, excess of perfidy and deceit leads him to such a course, since he is a mighty tyrant and an evil-disposed traitor and an impostor. The first-fruits of his society give sweetness to life, but the termination of his service possesses the bitterness of death. So it must be considered that he is a painted deadly snake, outwardly adorned with hues of various colours, inwardly filled with a fatal poison, against which no antidote is of avail."

> There abounds every stratagem, fraud, treachery, and cunning,
> But not rectitude and manliness, nor patience and submission.

Shanzabah replied: "I have tasted the food of the honey of his benevolence, now is the time of the sting of his oppression; for a while I passed my existence in gladness and repose, now is the period of distress and grief.

> O heart! thou hast tasted for a while the sweets of intimacy,
> Now you must experience the pain of separation.

"Of a certainty Fate, having caught me by the collar, has brought me to this marsh, otherwise how could I have been deserving the society of the Lion, a person who covets me, while I am a fit subject for his food? It is not right that he should be able to entice me towards him with a thousand snares, or with a hundred thousand stratagems and tricks should possess the power of casting me into the net of intercourse.

> I, what am I, that intimacy with him should be my ambition?
> Is it not enough for me that I see him from a distance?

"But Divine Fate and your misleading representations, O Damnah! have drawn me into this whirlpool of destruction, and now the hand of deliberation falls short of the skirt of prevention, and the issue of matters, by reason of my want of caution and foresight, is not in harmony with my wishes; and I myself, on account of inexperienced desires and depraved ambition, have raised up a fire that will consume me with the flame of affliction and the heat of anguish, ere the smoke reach me.

> How can I act? I have myself done this; what remedy is there for what we
> have done ourselves?

"And sages have said, 'Whoever is not contented with a sufficiency of this world's goods, and seeks for more, is like a person who arrives at a hill of diamonds; every moment his eye lights upon one of larger dimensions, and thinking over its higher value he keeps advancing, till he has reached a place where he finds the object of his search; but his return will then be impossible, since the particles of diamond will have lacerated and torn his feet. That imprudent person having been immersed in the thoughts of gain is not aware of the state of affairs; consequently, in deep distress, he is overtaken by death on the mountain's top, and finds his last resting-place in the stomach of the birds.'"

> Through undue eagerness your business is ruined;
> If you wish for profit do not search beyond the proper measure.

Damnah responded: "You have uttered most worthy words, for the source of every misfortune which befalls a person, is lust and covetousness.

> Abandon covetousness, for it is a calamity to heart and soul;
> The avaricious man is put to shame everywhere and by all mankind.

"The neck that is enchained by greed, will ultimately be severed by the sword of repentance, and the head in which the desire of cupidity has taken hold will eventually be dragged in the mire of disgrace. Many persons impelled by excess of greed and avarice, in the hope of acquiring wealth, have fallen into the whirlpool of affliction, and, attracted by the allurements of gain, have been caught in the desert of misfortune; like that Hunter who was filled with the desire of capturing the Fox, but the claws of the Leopard snatched the breath from his body." Shanzabah inquired, "How was that?"

STORY XX.

Damnah answered: A Hunter one day wandering over the plain, saw a Fox, very active and alert, crossing the expanse of that desert and sporting about, showing his beauty in every direction. The Hunter looked with delight upon his brush, thinking he might sell it for a great price. The intensity of his greed urging him on to follow after the Fox, he thereby discovered his hole, near to which he himself dug a pit, and covering it with rubbish and sticks, placed a dead carcass on the top thereof. Having concealed himself in ambush, he awaited the capture of the Fox, who by chance came out from his hole. Attracted by the odour of the carcass, Reynard gradually approached to the edge of the pit, saying to himself, "Although the brain of desire is perfumed with the fragrance of this carrion, yet the savour of misfortune also reaches the palate of caution, and wise men are averse to any business in which there is a probability of danger, and persons of intelligence do not commence an affair wherein it is possible to imagine there may be treachery.

> Wherever the line of difficulty is drawn;
> Strive to be beyond that boundary.

"And although it is possible that there may be here a dead animal, yet it may also be that a snare is placed underneath it, and in either case caution is best."

> When two matters come before you,
> And you do not know which to undertake,
> That one wherein is suspicion of danger,
> Is the one regarding which you should exercise caution;
> And that wherein there is no fear and no danger,
> You must diligently pursue.

The Fox, having thus deliberated, abandoned the carcass, and followed the road of safety. In the meanwhile a hungry Leopard came down from the mountain, and, attracted by the smell of the carcass, jumped down on the pit. The Hunter when he heard the sound of the trap, and the crash of the animal as he fell into the pit, imagined that it was the Fox; owing to excess of greed, without waiting to reflect, he cast himself to the bottom of the hole. The Leopard, thinking that the man would prevent him eating the carrion, jumped up and ripped open his stomach. The greedy Hunter, through the misfortune of avarice, fell into the net of destruction, whereas the contented Fox, by abandoning cupidity, found deliverance from the whirlpool of misfortune.

"This story is profitable as showing that the evil of greed, and the calamity of avarice, make a free man a slave and bring a slave to ruin."

> If you were to acquire a crown too large for your brow,
> By the dust of the saints' feet, it would give you headache.

Shanzabah answered: "I have acted wrongly, in that at the commencement I elected service with the Lion, and did not perceive that he does not recognise the worth of service; for it has been said, 'To associate with any one who is ignorant of the value thereof, or to serve any person who does not appreciate it, is like a man sowing seed in unfertile ground, in the expectation of raising a crop; or like whispering of grief and joy in the ears of a man born deaf; or like writing odes, tender and fresh, upon the surface of the running stream; or like sporting with images round a warm bath;[1] or like expecting drops of rain from a severe whirlwind.'"

> To seek fidelity from a Monarch is much the same as
> Searching for fruit from the boughs of an erect cypress.
> A willow-plant will not give you a sugar-cane,
> Though you water it a thousand times with the stream of Paradise.

Damnah answered: "Cease these traditions, and set about deliberating upon your business." Shanzabah said: "What remedy can I devise, and what stratagem can I concoct; for I know the qualities of the Lion, and my intelligence compels me to believe that he has no other intentions towards me than what are right and good; but those around him are plotting my destruction, and exerting themselves to ruin me. Now, if such be the case, the balance of the scale of my life leans more towards the basin of death than to that of existence, since treacherous tyrants and deceitful oppressors, when they are leagued[2] together, and joining hands, with united design plot against a person, in all circumstances gain the victory over him and overthrow him, as in the case of the Wolf, the Crow, and the Jackal, who plotted the destruction of the Camel, and being united overcame him, and thus gained their object and wishes." Damnah inquired, "How was that?"

STORY XXI.

Shanzabah replied: It has been related that a black-eyed Crow, a fierce-clawed Wolf, and a wily Jackal were in the service of a Lion of prey, and their locality was near the common highway. In the neighbourhood a trading Camel had been left behind; after a while, recovering his strength, he roamed in every quarter in search of forage; his path happened to lie in the direction of that forest, and when he arrived near the Lion he saw no other course than to be

---

[1] A paragraph is omitted, as being not altogether suitable to English ears.
[2] Literally, "have their backs together."

submissive and humble to him. The Lion also caressing him, inquired after the precise state of his affairs, and after being apprised thereof, questioned him respecting the circumstances of his stay and of his movements. The Camel replied:

If previous to this I had been a free agent as regards my own affairs,
Now that I have seen you, the reins of power have slipped from my hands.

"Whatever the King may command will assuredly include a provision for the safety of his servants."

You know better than ourselves regarding our wellbeing.

The Lion replied: "If you are so disposed, you may rest tranquil and secure in my society." The Camel was delighted, and passed his time in that forest till a considerable period had elapsed, and he had become very fat. One day the Lion went in search of game, and an infuriated Elephant struck him two or three times, and a mighty combat and great battle ensued between them, and the Lion having received several wounds, retired again to the forest; groaning and wounded, he slank to his lair. The Wolf, the Crow, and the Jackal, who, as parasites, partook of morsels from the table of his generosity, remained without food or victuals; and because the nature of the King was benevolent, and he possessed that pure kindness which monarchs feel towards their servants and dependants, when he saw them in that condition he was touched and said: "Your grief is more painful to me than my own trouble; if in this locality you ensnare a prey I will go out and finish the business for you, and having done so, will return." Having quitted their attendance on the Lion, they retired to a corner, and taking counsel with one another said: "What advantage is there to us from the existence of the Camel in this forest? To the King no benefit arises from his presence, nor have we any regard for him. Now we must persuade the Lion to kill him, and for two or three days the King will thus obtain repose from seeking after a delicate morsel of food, and we also shall according to our circumstances be benefited." The Jackal answered: "Do not indulge in such an idea, since the Lion has given him protection and brought him into his own service; and whoever urges the King to act with treachery and emboldens him to break his promise will have acted perfidiously; and a traitor in all cases is scorned, neither God nor man being pleased with him."

Whoever indulges in treachery,
His religion is severed from what is right and correct.
The true coin of mankind springs from honesty,
The base metal from perfidy.

The Crow suggested: "Can some stratagem be devised relative to this matter, and the Lion be relieved of this obligation? Remain here till I go and return." He then went and stood in the presence of the Lion, who inquired, "Have you tracked any game or brought intelligence of any prey?" The Crow replied: "O King! through hunger the eyes of none of us have performed their duties, nor is there left to us the strength to move about; but a means has crossed our minds by which, should your Majesty be agreeable thereto, we shall all obtain complete tranquillity and much delight." The Lion said: "Explain the meaning of your speech, so that I may be apprised of the state of affairs." The Crow replied: "This Camel is a stranger amongst us, and one cannot imagine that any advantage is to be gained from his company; as a make-shift here is game come to hand and a creature fallen into the net." The Lion was enraged, and retorted: "Dust upon the head of the companions of this age, who only practise arts of hypocrisy and habits of deceit, and who at once abandon the way of kindness, liberality, manliness, and courage!

> Seeing that fidelity is not the friend of the people of this age,
> Do not look for trustworthiness from them, since their occupation is nought
>   save iniquity.
> A dog is better than those stealthy cats, who with cunning
> Engage in no chase but around the domestic table.

"In what sect is it allowable to break a promise, and in what religion is it permissible to harbour designs against a person whom one has taken under one's own protection?"

> Any firm branch which has been raised up by thyself,
> Do not break with thine own hand, since so doing would injure thyself.

The Crow replied: "I am aware of these promises; but wise men have said that 'one soul may be made a sacrifice for the inmates of a house, and the inmates of a house for a tribe, and a tribe for a city, and the inhabitants of a city for the gracious person of a King, who may be in danger; since his safety may confer a benefit upon the subjects of his kingdom:' and further, for a violation of promise a means of exit may be devised, so that the person who pledged himself may be clear from the attribute of treachery, and his body secure from the pain of want and the dread of hunger." The Lion dropped his head; and the Crow returned, saying to his friends, "I recounted my narrative to the Lion: at first he was obstinate, but in the end he quieted down. Now the plan is this: we must all go to the Camel, and after representing to him the hunger which the Lion is enduring, and the anguish which has reached him, we will say, 'Under the protection of the majesty and the shadow of the glory of this fortunate Monarch, we have passed our days in gladness; to-day, when this event has occurred, manliness demands that we should give our life and soul as a sacrifice for him, otherwise we shall be recognised as ungrateful beings, and be precluded from the mark of generosity and manliness.' Our proper course will then be, to go in a body before the Lion, and again express to him our thanks for his benefits and favours, and confess that it is out of our means to do aught but make our lives and souls a sacrifice on his behalf. We will then each of us say, 'To-day let the King breakfast on me,' and the rest will object thereto: possibly the Camel may be the one doomed to destruction." Accordingly, they went in a body to the Camel, to whom they repeated the above details: by reason of the simplicity of his heart, he was deceived by their treachery and wiles. Having arranged things in the manner above described, they went to the Lion, and after they had finished expressing their thanks and gratitude, and presenting their praises and prayer, the Crow loosed his tongue, saying:

> O King! may prosperity in this world be thine,
> And thine be joy, at the banquet of gladness!

"Our repose is linked with the health of the King's own self: now that the occasion has arisen, and the King can obtain a bare subsistence from off my flesh, he must be kind enough to kill me, and make use of me." The others exclaimed, "What good will accrue from eating you, and what satiety will arise from your flesh?"

Who are you that you should at all enter into account?

The Crow, on hearing these words, hung down his head, and the Jackal commenced his speech, saying:

O King! from whose grasp in the day of wrath
The messenger Fate seizes the scroll of death.

"It is a long time since, under the shade of your august Government, I have passed my time, secure from the heat of the Sun of calamity. To-day, when the Moon of your Excellency's dignity is overwhelmed by the eclipse of misfortune, I am desirous that the Star of prosperity may rise from the horizon of my circumstances, and that the King, having made food of me, may be at ease as to anxiety about his breakfast." The others replied: "What you have spoken was from excessive affection, and the purest gratitude, but your flesh is rank, vile, and noxious, God forbid that by taking it the King's distress should be increased!" The Jackal was silent; and the Wolf, advancing, loosed his tongue, and said:

O King! may God be thy friend;
And thine enemy, in the day of battle, thy prey.

"I also am anxious that, having given myself as a sacrifice, your Majesty will graciously place my frame on your gums." His friends exclaimed: "You have spoken thus from pure sincerity and special regard; but your flesh would choke one, and its ill effects would be like deadly poison." The Wolf then withdrew his steps, and the Camel stretched out his long neck, snapping the guiding-rein, "*Every tall man is a fool,*" and commencing his speech, after the customary prayers, said:

O King! at whose threshold the azure Heavens
Have opened the door of conquest and victory.

"I have been exalted by your Excellency, and, fostered under your good fortune, should I be worthy of the King's kitchen, or be fit for rations for his table, my life is of no consequence."

I will not forsake the place of your abode while breath remains,
And if the matter touch my life, I will abandon even that.

The others, with one voice exclaimed: "This speech arises from excess of kindness, and sincerity of faith; and certainly your pleasant flesh agrees with the constitution of the King. May a Divine blessing attend your magnanimity, since on behalf of your benefactor, you have reckoned your life of no value, and by this means have left a good name as a memorial."

A magnanimous man is worth an hundred thousand diram;
When the matter becomes a question of life or death, then is his opportunity.

Then with one accord they set on the Camel, who, poor creature! scarce drew a breath before they tore his carcass to pieces.

"I have narrated this story that you may know that the treachery of designing persons, especially when they are leagued with one another, will not be devoid of effect." Damnah replied, "How do you propose to avert this?"

Shanzabah answered : " My thoughts now wander from the road of rectitude, and I know of no remedy beyond battle, contest, war, and slaughter : since, whoever is killed in defending his property, or guarding his person, enters into the circle of martyrdom, and the advantages referred to in the saying, ' *Whoever is slain, except on his own account, is a martyr,*' extend to him. Again, if my fate, at the hands of the Lion, be determined and fixed, at least I will be slain with honour, and destroyed with dignity and zeal.

> If I die with a good name, it is allowable ;
> I need a name, since the body must die.

Damnah said : " A wise man in the time of war does not take the lead, nor in the season of battle does he allow himself to go in advance : since ' *The first blow is the violence :*' and to incur great danger, by one's own choice, is not a proof of wisdom : nay, more, men of discretion with humility and kindness circumvent the designs of their enemies, and deem it best to avert quarrels by conciliation.

> Pleasant deceit is better than unacceptable rage ;
> It is better to sprinkle water than fire.
> When a plan can be executed with kindness,
> Why is it necessary to give the rein to violence ?

" And again, one must not spurn, or hold in contempt, a weak enemy ; since, if he be destitute of strength or force, possibly he may not be without power as regards treachery and deceit, and with fraud and cunning may raise the fire of strife, the flame of which cannot be quenched by the water of deliberation. And you yourself are acquainted with the sway of the Lion, and his authority needs not explanation or enlargement : therefore take good account of his enmity, and be not unmindful of the malignity of his warfare ; for whoever despises an enemy, and thinks not of the end of the battle, will rue it ; like the Spirit[1] of the Ocean, who scorned the Water-fowl." Shanzabah inquired, " How was that ? "

STORY XXII.

Damnah said : It has been related, that upon the shore of the Indian Ocean was a kind of bird which they called Títawa, a pair of which had their home on the margin of the sea, and had taken up their abode upon the brink of the water. When the breeding-time arrived, the Hen said : " I must seek a place wherein to lay my eggs, so that I may pass my time in ease of mind." The Male replied : " This is a pleasant place, and a delightful locality, and moreover it seems impossible to migrate from this spot ; so now you must deposit your eggs." The Hen answered : " Here is a point for reflection, for should the sea roll in its billows, and rob us of our offspring, and the toil of our time and days become fruitless, what will deliberation then avail ? " He replied : " I do not think the Spirit of the Ocean will act thus boldly, or exhibit such disregard of us ; and, even supposing that he should contemplate such a disgraceful proceeding, and allow our offspring to be drowned, justice can be demanded from him."

> I will smite the Heavens, if they revolve contrary to my desire ;
> I am not such an one as to be treated with contempt by the celestial Sphere.

---

[1] Literally, " envoy or agent."

The Hen replied : " To wander beyond the limits of one's own bounds is not becoming, and to exceed one's proper sphere in boasting is not acting like a wise man. By what means can you threaten the Spirit of the Ocean with your revenge, and by what grandeur can you reach the dignity of contending and fighting with him ? "

> You are making a plundering excursion to despoil yourself,
> Since you are but a sparrow and ape the hawk.

" Abandon this idea, and select a place of security, and a protected spot, for the eggs ; and do not turn your head from my advice, for whoever does not listen to honest words, nor pay any attention to the counsel of sincere friends, will meet with that which befell the Tortoise." The male Water-fowl inquired, " What was that ? "

STORY XXIII.

The Hen said : It has been related that in a lake the water of which, from the clearness of its nature, reflected things like a polished mirror, and from its purity and beauty was indicative of the Water of Life and the Spring of Paradise, there abode two Geese and a Tortoise. On account of their proximity to one another, the thread of their circumstances was drawn into intimacy, and neighbourship ended in their living under the same roof, and the sight of each other having brought pleasure, they passed their life in comfort.

> Happy is the life spent in the presence of friends ;
> Agreeable is the existence passed with affectionate companions.

Suddenly the hand of treacherous Fortune began to scratch the face of their affairs with the claw of calamity, and the mirror-like spheres of the Heavens began to give signs of separation, in the aspect of their affairs.

> *" What joy is there which fortune does not darken ? "*

> Delightful is wine when drunk from the cup of union with those we love,
> Yet there is the after-effect of the headache of separation :
> No one at this table eats a morsel of bread,
> But what a stone comes between his teeth.

In the water which was the source of their life and the support of their existence, there was a great diminution of quantity, and an enormous difference apparent. The Geese when they became aware of the state of affairs, removing their affection from their familiar home, formed the intention of migrating.

> Travel is better for him who, in his own locality,
> Has a heart dejected with grief for this or that :
> For although the troubles of travel are bad,
> Yet they are better than the afflictions of one's native soil.

So with hearts full of grief, and eyes moist with tears, they approached the Tortoise, and introducing words of farewell, said :

> " Time's malevolent eye has separated us from you ;
> How can we say what Time's evil eye may bring about ? "

The Tortoise uttered lamentations on account of the agony of separation, and with excess of grief was loud in his complaint, saying, "What speech is this? and how can I be supposed to exist without you, or how is it possible for me to live without my intimate friends?

> Alas! without you life is not endurable.
> What is existence itself in your absence?
> Life, altogether, apart from you,
> Is but death under the name of life.

"And, since I do not possess power to say farewell, how can I bear the burden of separation?"

> I am as yet the cypress, filled with life by your eyes not yet departed.
> My heart, at the thought of separation, quivers like the aspen.

The Geese replied : " Our hearts also are wounded with the anguish of separation, and our bosoms burning more and more with the heat of the flame of the fire of parting; but it is wellnigh that the distress arising from want of water will give the dust of our life to the winds of non-existence, therefore, by necessity, we are abandoning our friends and acquaintances, and making choice of the anguish of exile."

> A desponding lover never willingly went from the street of his mistress.
> No one, by choice, quitted the garden of Paradise.

The Tortoise said : " O friends! you are aware that the misery of want of water is greater in my case, and my existence without water would not be possible. At the present time, the obligations of a long-established friendship demand that you should take me with you, and not leave me solitary in the desolate home of separation."

> You are my very soul, and intend to take your departure.
> When the soul departs, what can this lifeless body do?

They replied : " O incomparable friend and noble comrade! the grief of quitting you is greater to us than that of leaving our native soil, and the sorrow of separation from you is the cause of excessive anxiety and affliction of heart; and wherever we go, although we may be in great comfort, and pass our time in perfect happiness, yet, without sight of you, the fountain of our existence will become muddy, and the eyes of our fortune cloudy. We also have no desire beyond intimacy and companionship with you; but for us to travel along the surface of the earth, or to pass over a far and long distance is impossible, and for you also to fly in the expanse of the air, and to accompany us, is out of the question. In such case, how can we go together, or in what manner can you join us?" The Tortoise answered : "Your genius can produce a remedy for this matter, and your minds may devise some plan for this affair; but, with my soul afflicted at the thought of separation, and my heart broken by the burden of estrangement, what can I suggest?"

> First of all, a (sound) heart is needful for every matter;
> Right deliberation cannot proceed from a broken spirit.

They said : " O dear friend! for a while we have found, on your part, a lightness of intellect, and have discovered a hastiness and frivolity of temper. Perchance, whatever we may advise in this matter you will not perform, nor will you adhere to what you have promised." The Tortoise replied : " How can it be that you should utter words for my welfare, and I should think otherwise ? or that, when a promise is made on my behalf, I should not cause it to be fulfilled ? "

I made a promise that I would never violate my vow ;
I made an agreement that I would not deviate from my obligations towards you.

The Geese replied : " The agreement then is this—that when, having lifted you up, we fly through the air, you must absolutely not say a syllable, since whoever may happen to cast his eyes upon us will throw in a word, and either openly or by allusion make some remark. It is therefore necessary that, notwithstanding anything you may hear spoken, whether plainly or by innuendo, or any movement you may observe, you should close the path of reply, and should not, for good or evil, loose your tongue." The Tortoise replied : " I agree to your conditions, and assuredly, having placed the seal of silence upon my lips, will not offer a reply to any creature."

> In remote Greece I fell in with an old man ;
> I said to him, " O sir ! than wisdom and intelligence,
> In all circumstances, what is better in a man ? " He replied,
> " If you inquire the truth, 'tis silence, silence ! "

They brought a stick, and the Tortoise seized the middle of it firmly with his teeth, while the Geese, having lifted up the two ends of it, bore him off. When they had reached a height in the sky, their flight lay over a village, and the rustics, being apprised thereof, were astonished at the sight, and having come out to see the fun, right and left raised a cry, " See how the Geese are carrying the Tortoise ! " Since the like of such a sight in those days had not appeared to that people, every moment their cry and clamour became louder and louder. For a while the Tortoise maintained silence ; at length the pot of his indignation began to boil, and his patience being exhausted, he exclaimed :

> " May every one become blind who cannot see ! "

At the same moment that he opened his mouth he fell from aloft. The Geese exclaimed, " ' *Nothing belongs to a messenger but to arrive.*' It is incumbent on friends to give advice, and the fortunate to listen thereto."

> Well-wishers give advice, whilst
> The fortunate are they who receive admonition.
> But when will my advice, though I am your well-wisher,
> Take effect upon you, who are perverse ?

" The moral of the story is this—that whoever does not listen with willing ear to the admonition of friends, will have exerted himself for his own destruction, and drawn down the mask of disgrace before his ignominious face."

> He who does not lend an ear to the words of the excellent,
> Bites to the quick the tip of the finger of regret.

The male Water-fowl said : " I have heard this story which you have narrated, and am aware of its signification, but be not afraid, and keep your place, since cowardly and nervous people never attain their ends ; and I still assert that the Spirit of the Ocean will consider it his duty to be kind towards us." The Female laid her eggs : when the young ones burst the white lining of the eggs, and raised their heads from the collar of life, the sea, rolling its billows, seized them under the skirt of death. The mother, on seeing this calamity, became dejected, and reiterated : "O ignoble wretch ! I knew that you could not trifle with the waves. Now you have given your children to the winds, and have raised a flame in my soul : so devise a plan whereby you may apply salve to my wounded heart." The Male replied : "You speak disrespectfully, since I will perform my promise, of which you are aware, and fulfil the conditions of my compact, and will snatch justice from the Spirit of the Ocean." In short, he went to the other birds, and having collected together in one spot all those of every species who were chiefs and leaders, he explained to them his condition, and requesting their help and assistance, in a tone of lamentation commenced singing this verse :

"The circumstances of my affliction of heart are without limit.
Now is the season of assistance, and the time of help.

"If, in this calamity, my friends are not all animated by one object and one desire, and do not in a body snatch justice for me from the Spirit of the Ocean, his boldness will increase, and by-and-by he will encompass the ruin of the offspring of other birds ; and when this habit shall become confirmed, and this custom perpetuated, we must dissever our minds from our children, and bid adieu to our country and home."

[1]We must either, with a hundred efforts, work his sorrow with disgrace,
Or else we must place our feet in the sad abode of non-existence.

The birds, at this intelligence, were dejected and broken-hearted ; interlacing their wings, they hastened to attend the court of the Phœnix, and caused an account of the above-mentioned events to reach the place of audience, and said : "If you are grieved on account of your subjects, you may still be their monarch ; but if you do not cherish the affliction of those who are oppressed, nor feel any sympathy for the injured, the inscription of monarchy amongst birds will be erased from the pages of your fortune, and the patent of being their protector will be intrusted to another."

Take care that you bear the griefs of the humble ;
Fear the oppression of fortune.

The Phœnix, having soothed them, started from his capital, with his servants and dependants, to avert that calamity ; and the birds becoming stout-hearted from his aid and support, set their faces towards the shore of the Indian Ocean. When the Phœnix, with an army the limit of whose ranks could not be contained in the capacity of the reckoning of any accountant, and the number of whose various rows and phalanxes could not possibly be weighed in the scales of thought and possibility,

All warriors, impetuous, bold, and bloodthirsty—
All courageous, warlike, and revengeful ;
With a feathery armour, and coat of mail thrown over their bosom,
Their claws and beaks protruding like javelins and daggers.

arrived in proximity to the Ocean, the morning breeze, which stirs into motion the chain of waves, conveyed that news to the Spirit of the Ocean, who, when he saw that in his own capacity there was no power of resisting the Phœnix and

---

[1] Eastwick and Keene differ in their translation of this line ; I have followed the rendering of the latter.

his army of birds, of necessity, being compelled to apologise, restored to the
Water-fowl his offspring.

" The object of reciting this tale is this, that one must not despise an enemy,
though he may be most contemptible, since by a tiny needle a matter is accomplished which a long spear is unequal to perform; and a firebrand, although
it may appear small to behold, yet burns whatever comes in contact with it; and
wise men have said that 'the friendship of a thousand individuals will not
prevail against the enmity of a single person.'"

> As friends, a thousand persons would be too few;
> As an enemy, one would be too many.

Shanzabah said: "I will not commence the struggle, lest I should acquire the evil
reputation of being ungrateful for kindness; but when the Lion plots my ruin,
I must necessarily consult my self-defence and preservation." Damnah replied:
" When you approach the Lion, and observe that, having made himself erect, he
strikes his tail on the ground, and when the flame of his wrath, blazing like the
fire of his eyes, meets your sight, then you may know that he has determined
your death." Shanzabah said: " If anything of this sort is manifest, assuredly,
the veil of doubt being drawn from the cheek of certainty, one will be apprised
as to the treachery and plots of the Lion." Damnah, delighted and merry-
hearted, set out towards Kalflah.

> When a foolish person derives pleasure from the griefs of others,
> In such an one do not look for sincerity and good faith, since he is apart from
> all such.

Kalflah said, "How has your business progressed? and how has the matter
ended?" Damnah replied:

> I am thankful to Fate, and also to Fortune.

" Praise be to God! this matter is completely set at rest, and this difficult business
has been satisfactorily and easily accomplished." At the time that Damnah was
thus speaking, Fortune, with the tongue of retribution, was muttering the purport of the following verse, in the Assembly of Prudence, into the ears of the
wise men:

> " With delight the companions seized the ringlets of the cup-bearer;
> May the heavens grant them power to retain their hold!"

They then both went towards the Lion, and by chance the Ox followed in their
footsteps. The eyes of the Lion alighted upon him, and Damnah's treachery
began to take effect. The Lion commenced to roar, striking the tail of authority
on the ground, and grinding his teeth from excess of rage. Shanzabah knew
of a certainty that the Lion was meditating his death, so he said to himself,
" The service of kings, by reason of fear and dread, and the attendance on
monarchs, through terror and fright, is like living in the same abode with a
snake, and being neighbour to a lion; although the former may be asleep, and
the latter concealed, yet, in the end, the one raises his head and the other
opens his mouth."

> Do not render service to the king, for I fear
> That it will be suddenly like the companionship of the stone and the ewer.

Thus he thought, and made ready for battle. On both sides were visible the signs which the barefaced Damnah had pointed out. The fray commenced, and cries and shrieks were spread through the expanse of the earth and the dome of heaven.

> From their tumult, the wild animals and beasts
> In that plain and desert were disturbed.
> Some withdrew to the caves of the mountains,
> Others were concealed beneath heaps of rubbish.

Kalílah, having witnessed the state of affairs, drew near to Damnah, and said:

> You have mixed together, in colour and smell, a hundred devices,
> And then have fled from the midst of the scene;
> The rain of two hundred years will not lay
> The dust of the calamity which you have raised.

"O ignorant fellow! do you observe the disastrous termination of your machinations, and are you aware or not of the lamentable conclusion of your arrangements?" Damnah rejoined: "What is this disgraceful termination?" The other replied: "In this business which you have done, seven misfortunes are evident: 1st, You have unnecessarily involved your benefactor in trouble, and grievously imbittered the Lion's existence; 2d, You have caused your own master to acquire the reputation of having violated his promise, and of having dealt treacherously, and you have allowed him to gain this bad name; 3d, You have, without cause, laboured to accomplish the destruction of the Ox, and have cast him into the whirlpool of death; 4th, You have taken on your own neck the blood of that stranger, who will be slain through your instrumentality; 5th, You have made every one suspicious of the King's probity, and it may be that, owing to fear of him, people will quit their native land and migrate to other homes, and being removed from their families will remain exiled in the distress of poverty and the misfortune of exile; 6th, You have exposed to the risk of death the commander-in-chief of the army of the beasts, and assuredly the knot of their concord will after this be disarranged; 7th, You have made manifest your own helplessness and weakness, and have not brought to pass your pretension that you would accomplish this matter with kindness and conciliation. Now the most foolish of men is he who arouses dormant strife, and wishes to bring about by war and severity an end which might be accomplished by peaceable and gentle means." Damnah retorted: "Perhaps you have not heard that it has been said:

> "When a matter cannot be accomplished by wisdom,
> It becomes necessary to adopt rash means."

Kalílah replied: "In this matter what item have you arranged by the rule of intelligence, and what method have you settled by the aid of the architect of deliberation, that failing[1] these you have of necessity had recourse to force and violence? Anyhow, do you not know that good judgment, and accurate cogitation, are preferable to boldness and courage?

> *"Judgment excels the bravery of the bold."*

A truly wise man with a single word successfully accomplishes a matter,
Which cannot be carried out by an hundred large armies.

---

[1] Literally, "not going to the front."

" Your self-satisfaction and conceit of your own opinions, as well as your infatu-
ation with the dignity of this deceitful world, which, like the illusions of a phantom,
leaves no trace behind, have always been known to me; however, I delayed proclaiming this to you, thinking that perhaps you might become circumspect, and
awaken from your dream of pride and negligence, and from the intoxication of
the wine of arrogance and ignorance, and be cautious; but now when you have
passed all bounds, and every moment are growing more bewildered and distracted in the desert of error and the gulf of folly, it is time that I should
mention somewhat of your excessive stupidity and craziness, and your inordinate
boldness and malevolence, and enumerate some of the blemishes of your sayings,
and the malignity of your deeds, though it will be but a drop in the ocean, and
an atom from the mountain."

> That you may be aware what things you have done,
> It is that you have acted wrongly in having designed frauds;
> Amongst all mankind you are held in no estimation,
> And if all others are something, you yourself are a nobody.

Damnah rejoined: "O brother! from the commencement of my life till the
present time I do not think that an improper word, or an unbecoming action,
has proceeded from me; and if you have seen any blemish on my part, assuredly
you should proclaim it." Kalîlah answered: "You have many faults. 1st, You
think that you are free from blame; and 2d, Your speech preponderates over your
actions; and it has been said that no danger to a king is so great as when the
words of his minister are superior to his deeds; and men of this world, with
regard to their actions and speech, are of four kinds. 1st, They who speak but
do not act; such is the nature of hypocrites and misers. 2d, They who do not
speak but act: such is the state of true [1] and manly men. 3d, They who speak
and act: such is the habit of those who are experienced in life. 4th, They who
neither speak nor act: such is the disposition of the mean and low-minded.
Now, of these classes, you are amongst those who speak, but who do not adorn
their speech with the ornament of action. I have always found your words to
excel your skill; and the Lion being deceived with your tales, this so dangerous
matter has befallen him; and if, God forbid, mischief should happen to him,
confusion would arise in this kingdom, and the rebellion and perturbation of the
subjects would pass all limits, and all persons and property remain in danger
of ruin and plunder. Now the crime of all this public scandal would be on
your neck."

> He who does wrong in thought or deed,
> Where again will he see the face of goodness?
> He who plants the bough of injury,
> Whence will he gather the fruit of advantage?

Damnah replied: "I have always been an upright minister to the King, and in
the rose-garden of his affairs have planted nought but the tree of good-advice."
Kalîlah said: "The tree, of which the circumstances now apparent are the fruit,
had better be rooted up, and the advice which produces such results as are now
come into view, had better have been unspoken and unheard. How can it be
thought that there is any benefit in your words, which, in reality, are not
adorned with the ornament of action? Theory without practice, like wax with-

---

[1] آدميان must be taken to mean "real true men."

out honey, gives no pleasure; and speech without action, like a tree without leaves or fruit, is only fit to be burned.

> Theory whereof there are no signs of practice,
> Is a body which possesses no soul:
> Theory is the tree, and practice the fruit thereof;
> The tree merely grows for its fruit:
> The bough which is without fruit is unpleasant,
> And is a supply for the cook's fire.

" Great men, with the pen of benevolence, have written upon the pages of their volumes that from six things no advantage can accrue: 1st, Words without action; 2d, Property without wisdom; 3d, Friendship without experience; 4th, Knowledge without probity; 5th, Almsgiving without purpose; 6th, Life without health. A king, though he may of himself be just and not tyrannical, yet a minister of bad nature and malevolent disposition will deprive his subjects of the advantages of the justice and kindness of their sovereign; and through fear of the minister's opposition, the tale of woe of the oppressed will not reach the honour of the region of royalty: like as when in pure, sweet water the form of a crocodile is apparent, no thirsty swimmer, though extremely faint, will either spread out his hands, or place his feet therein.

> With thirsty soul, I have arrived at a pure fountain,
> Of what avail is it, since I have not strength to drink the water?

Damnah said: " In this affair I had no intentions beyond the honour of serving the King." Kalílah answered: " True servants, skilful attendants, and experienced courtiers are the ornament and decoration of the Court of Monarchs; but you are anxious that others should be pushed aside from serving the Lion, and that you yourself should be the exalted confidant and privy councillor, and that access to the royal presence should be limited to you. Now this state of things is from excessive ignorance and extreme want of wisdom, since kings cannot be bound to any single thing nor any one person, and the dignity of the monarch resembles the grandeur of beauty and handsomeness; for just as a dearly-loved mistress, the more numerous her admirers, the more she displays to them the beauties of her charms—so kings, the greater the array of servants and dependants, the greater will be their wish for more attendants and retinue. This crude desire which possesses you is a clear proof of your extreme want of judgment, since wise men have said that five things are signs of folly: 1st, Seeking one's own advantage in the misfortunes of others; 2d, Expecting eternal reward without practising worship; 3d, Using harsh language and coarse manners when toying with women; 4th, Gaining a knowledge of the minutiæ of learning by sloth and indolence; 5th, Looking for friendship from mankind without fidelity and observance, on your part, of the dues of intimacy. Now from the excessive kindness I possess, I am uttering these words; but it is as clear as the Sun that the black night of your villany will not be illumined by the torch of my exhortation; nor will the darkness of ignorance and the obscurity of envy, which are mixed up in your nature, become removed by means of the light of my advice.

> One cannot, with the water of Hagar's[1] well or the Stream of Paradise, make white
> The garment of any one's fortune, when it happens to have been woven black.

---

[1] Name of a famous well at Makkah.

" And my language to you is similar to that which the Bird [1] spoke to another Bird, saying : ' Do not indulge in profitless grief, nor waste your words on a set who are not in a mood to listen ; ' but he paid no attention, and ultimately retribution for the same overtook him." Damnah inquired, " How was that ? "

STORY XXIV.

Kalilah replied : It has been related that a troop of Apes had their abode in a mountain, and supported themselves with the fruits and herbs thereon. By chance, one evening, blacker than the heart of sinners, and fouler than the tempers of those whose fortunes are spoilt, the army of winter began to assault them, and from the shock of the intensely cold blasts their blood began to congeal.

> By reason of the cold, the Lion of the Sphere was desirous
> To turn inside [2] out the skin on his body ;
> In the rose-garden the birds were restless,
> Thinking that it would be pleasant to be on the spit in front of the fire.

The hapless creatures being distressed by reason of the cold sought a place of refuge ; and girding themselves with activity in search thereof, ran into every nook. Suddenly on the side of the road they saw a piece of glittering cane thrown down. Thinking it was fire they collected some sticks and strewed them round it. They then blew with their breath. Over against them a Bird on a tree exclaimed, " That is not fire ; " but they paid no attention, nor did they desist from their profitless occupation. By chance another Bird arrived in the neighbourhood, and said to that Bird : " Do not trouble yourself, for they will not desist on account of what you say, and you will become vexed ;

> Him who is linked with misfortune from the commencement of an affair
> Abandon, for he will not by any effort become prosperous.

" And to endeavour to correct and put right such persons, is like trying a sword upon a stone, or seeking from deadly poison the elements of a potent antidote."

> Whoever by nature happens to be of a bad disposition,
> From him expect no good ;
> Since you can never by any endeavour make
> From a black crow a white hawk.

The Bird, when he perceived that they paid no attention to what he said, from warmth of kindness, came down from the tree in order that he might clearly convey his advice to their ears, and admonish them as regards their fruitless trouble. The Apes, having surrounded the Bird, separated his head from his body.

" Now my business with you is of a similar nature, and I am wasting my time, and speaking to no advantage ; and while you will derive no benefit, I also am in fear of injury."

> If a hearer do not approve of your advice,
> Why in vain should you lay burdens upon your tender heart ?

---

[1] The text reads man, which the sequel of the story clearly shows to be a mistake.
[2] That is, to put the shaggy side innermost, so as to keep the body warmer.

I

You said : " Be mounted on the steed of happiness,
That you may arrive at an abode, and be free from grief."
He heard not, and in like manner goes his own way :
Leave him, that he may lag on foot through his folly.

Damnah rejoined : " O brother ! great men, as regards lesser individuals, have
performed the obligations of sincerity by giving advice and admonition, and
avoiding bias and hypocrisy; and it is necessary that persons of excellence
should press the rights of exhortation and counsel whether any one will listen
or not."

Do not withhold your advice from any one, but speak ;
Though the fault be on the part of the hearer.
The clouds do not withhold the drops of rain from the mountain,
Though they make no effect on its stony heart.

Kalílah replied : " I have not closed against you the door of advice ; but I fear
that you have reared the edifice of your actions on hypocrisy and fraud, and
accustomed yourself to be self-opinioned and wilful. *' The worst characteristic is
obstinacy.'* You repent now that the time has passed for repentance to be of
any avail, and however much you may bite the back of your hand, and rend
the surface of your breast, it will be of no effect ; and the end of an affair based
upon treachery and deceit will be finished in evil, and the conclusion thereof
in disgrace. Like as it happened to that crafty Companion, the crime of whose
cunning, becoming the noose of the snare of misfortune, clung round his own
neck, while the incautious Comrade, through the blessing of rectitude and simple-
heartedness, attained his desires." Damnah inquired, " How was that ? "

STORY XXV.

Kalílah said : It has been related that there were two Companions — one
wise, the other imprudent : the one from his excess of intellect and cunning
played a thousand deceptions on the water, and him they called " Sharp-wit ; "
the other, from excess of folly and ignorance, made no distinction between gain
and loss, and him they named " Light-heart." They entertained the project of
trading ; and in company of one another set out on their journey, travelling
stages and marches. By chance they found a bag of gold in the road, and
esteeming it a rare prize, lingered a while. The wise Companion said : " O
brother ! there is in the world much wealth that is not utilised ; now it appears
best to be content with this bag of gold, and to end existence in repose in the
corner of our home."

How many times will you go round the world in search of gold ?
The more your wealth increases, the greater will be your anxiety.
The cup of the eye of the greedy will never be filled.
So long as the shell is not content[1] it will not become full of pearls.

They then returned, and having approached the city, halted at a resting-place.
The imprudent Companion said, " O brother ! come and let us divide this gold,
and divesting ourselves of fear, each of us spend our share in whatever

---

[1] There is a tradition that, during spring, when a drop of rain falls into the mouth of an oyster,
the latter at once closes itself and sinks to the bottom of the ocean, together with its precious
charge, which in process of time becomes a pearl].

manner we like." The wise Comrade replied, "To divide the gold is not judicious at the present time. The correct course would be to take that amount which is requisite for our expenses, and the remainder, with the utmost care, we will put in a place of deposit; and after the lapse of several days, having further taken sufficient for our wants, we will in like manner put back the remnant in a secure spot, so that it may become more removed from misfortune, and nearer to safety." The careless Companion, being deceived with this cunning, acquiesced in his proposal. In the manner above related, having taken out money for current expenses, they together buried the remainder under a tree, and set out towards the city, each one resting at his own abode.

> Another day the deceitful heavens
> Opened the top of the box of treachery.

The Comrade who claimed to be intelligent went to the foot of the tree, and having brought forth the gold from out of the ground, carried it off; while his imprudent partner, unaware of what had happened, busied himself in spending the money in his possession till none was left; he then went to his shrewd Comrade, and said, "Come, let us get somewhat of that hidden treasure, for I have been much in want." The cunning fellow played the simpleton, saying, "All right." They then both went together to the foot of the tree. The more they searched the less did they find. Sharp-wit laid his hand upon the collar of Light-heart, and exclaimed, "You carried off the money, and no one else is aware thereof." Helpless, though he took an oath and was much distressed, it was of no avail; in short, the matter between them progressed from strife to their appearing before the Judge, and from altercation ended in an appeal to justice. The shrewd Comrade brought the negligent one to the Magistrate's court, and set forth his charge, and recited to the Judge the particulars of the story and the drift of the case. After a denial on the part of Light-heart, the Judge questioned Sharp-wit as to the sufficiency of the proof of his claim. The latter replied, "*O Kází, may God Almighty preserve thee!*"

> Enjoy thy life, since at the throne of Fate
> The orders relative to a lengthened existence for thee are set with a seal.

"I have no witness save that tree under which the money was buried, and I am in hopes that God the Most Holy and the Most High, by His divine power, will cause that tree to break into speech, so that it may bear witness as to the theft of this unjust traitor, who has borne off all the money and made me disappointed." The Judge was astonished at this speech, and, after much conversation and endless discussion, they agreed that next day, the Judge being present at the foot of the tree, they should seek evidence therefrom; and if its testimony should agree with what had been alleged, he should issue orders in accordance with such evidence. The clever Companion went to his house, and narrating the whole story to his father, drew aside the veil from before the face of the matter, saying, "O my father! in reliance upon you, I formed the idea of adducing the tree as evidence, and, trusting to your assistance, I have planted this tree of stratagem in the court-house of Fate; and the whole affair is linked with your kindness. If you agree, we will carry off that money, and seize several other sums, and pass the rest of our life in happiness and repose." The father replied, "What concern can I have in the matter?" The son rejoined, "The interior of that tree is hollowed in such a manner that if two persons were to lie hidden therein, they could not be seen. To-night you must go and pass your time inside the tree, so that to-morrow when the Judge comes, and seeks evidence, then as is customary, you may bear witness." The father replied, "O son! abandon treachery and deceit, since if you succeed in deluding the creature you cannot deceive the Creator.

> The Ruler of the Spheres knows all your secrets,
> For he is acquainted with you hair by hair and vein by vein.
> I grant that by treachery you may deceive the people.
> How will you act with Him who knows the minutest particles one by one ?

O how many stratagems (there are) upon the originators of which punishment arrives ! and retribution also alighting upon them, they become disgraced and exposed. Now I fear lest your treachery may be like that of the Frog." The son inquired, "How was that ? "

STORY XXVI.

The father replied : It has been related that a Frog had fixed her residence in the neighbourhood of a Snake, and had taken up her abode in the region of that blood-thirsty tyrant. Whenever the Frog had young ones, the Snake used to devour them, and made the Frog's heart afflicted in consequence of the wound occasioned by the loss of her children. Now this Frog was on terms of friendship with a Crab, to whom she one day repaired, saying, "O dear friend ! devise for me some suitable plan, for I have a victorious enemy and a triumphant foe, near whom it is not possible to live, nor is it feasible to migrate or remove from this spot, since the place wherein I have made my abode is extremely pleasant, and my habitation is a delightful meadow, whereof the circuit, adorned with minarets,[1] like the garden of Paradise, produces delight, and the heart-enchanting breeze thereof, like the ringlets of the fair, spreads odours.

> A hundred thousand roses blossomed therein;
> The verdure was in motion, but the streams were sluggish ;
> There was every variety of rose with regard to colour,
> The perfume of each of which reached a league—
> The book of the rose opened its hundred pages.
> The tulip held in its palm the cup of wine.
> From the North Wind, laden with perfume,
> The quarters thereof became filled with fragrance.

" Now no one of his own choice would quit such an abode, nor bear his heart away from this kind of glorious Paradise."

> My abode is amongst the bowers of beautiful girls. What a lovely place it is!
> Not a wise man in the world would quit such a locality.

The Crab replied : " Be not dejected, since your powerful enemy can be captured in the bands of treachery, and your triumphant foe be cast into the net of deceit."

> If any one scatters the grains of deceit,
> He brings to his snare many birds of intelligence.

---

[1] Probably alluding to the yellow golden-cupped flowers, which are compared to minarets.

The Frog replied : " In this matter, what proposition from the book of treachery have you evolved, and what remedy have you discovered in repelling the affliction wrought by this evil-designing antagonist ? " The Crab answered : " In such a place is a Weasel, pugnacious and ferocious. Catch some fish and kill them, then carry them from the Weasel's hole to the abode of the Snake, so that he may eat them one by one, and go in search of others. Doubtless, when he arrives at the Snake's hiding-place, he will also turn him to account and free you from the affliction and misery of the Viper." The Frog, according to this plan, which was in conformity with Fate, encompassed the death of the Snake. And when two or three days had elapsed subsequent to this event, the Weasel entertained the design of bestirring himself in search of fish for food. Repeating the arrangement to which he had become accustomed, he once more went in search of fish, on that very road which he had previously traversed, with the foot of desire, and not finding any fish, devoured the Frog and all her little ones.

> You carried me off from the clutches of a wolf;
> When I came to look, in the end, you yourself were the wolf.

" I have narrated this story to show that the end of treachery is embarrassment, and the termination of fraud and deceit repentance and humility."

> Do not step in the desert of treachery and deceit,
> Since, in the end, you will fall into the net of misfortune.

The son replied : " O father ! moderate your language, and put a stop to your far-off and distant anticipations, since this matter is but little burdensome, and very advantageous." The greed of wealth and love of his offspring drew the hapless old man from the paths[1] of rectitude and religion into the desert of violence and treachery, and the saying, " *Verily your wealth and children are a temptation to you,*" was exemplified; leaving the road of manliness neglected, and entirely folding up the carpet of liberality, he allowed himself to undertake a course of action forbidden and disallowed alike by law and common usage, and on that black evening, with anxious heart, took his place in the hollow of the tree. In the morning, when the enlightened-minded Judge, the Sun, was manifest in the Court of the Sky, and the treachery of the black-faced Night had become to mankind like refulgent day, the Judge, with a troop of notables, arrived at the foot of the tree, near which large numbers of people were arrayed to view the sight. The Judge, turning towards the tree, after explaining the claim of the plaintiff, and the denial of the defendant, demanded of it the true merits of the case. A voice issued from the interior of the tree, " Light-heart has borne off the money, and oppressed Sharp-wit, who is his companion." The Judge was astonished, but perceived with penetration that some one was concealed within the tree, but that it was not feasible to bring him to light except by some fitting device.

> The secret of any design which is concealed from the eye of wisdom
> Will not become clear except in the mirror of deliberation.

He then commanded them to collect a heap of firewood, and to place it close to the tree, and set light thereto, so that grief[2] for that untutored and inexperienced individual sprang up in the bosom of his family. The greedy old man for a

---

[1] Literally, " halting-place."
[2] It is impossible to preserve the several *equivoques* of the original Persian ; the meaning is simply that the man's family would have been grieved at the treatment he received.

while kept his patience, but when he saw that the matter might become fatal, pleaded for quarter. The magistrate, having brought him out and pacified him, questioned him as to the true state of the case. The old man, half-burned, related precisely what had occurred. The Judge, having learned how matters stood, explained to the people the nature of the rectitude and forbearance of Light-heart, and the treachery and wickedness of Sharp-wit. Simultaneously with these events, the old man, through his deception, transported the trappings of life from this transitory World to the Palace of Eternity, and by means of the heat of the fire of this Sphere was brought into contact with the flames of Hell. While, as regards the son, after that he was severely chastised and had undergone rigorous punishment, he set out towards the city, with his dead father placed round his neck; whereas Light-heart, owing to the happy results of his integrity, trustworthiness, rectitude, and honesty, recovered his money, and occupied himself in carrying on his own business.

"Now the object of narrating this story is this, that it may be known to mankind that treachery in the end meets with no approval, and that misfortune and contempt are the finale of perfidy."

> Whoever places his foot in the straits of deceit
> Will ultimately give his head to destruction:
> Treachery is a viper, which has two heads,
> Each of which is dangerous in various ways:
> If one head vexes the enemy's heart,
> The other brings misery to its own author.

Damnah replied: "You have given the name of treachery to intelligence, and designated deliberation as fraud and perfidy. Now I have concocted this scheme with right forethought, and conducted this so great affair with true intelligence." Kalílah answered: "You are weak-minded and slow of deliberation, to a degree that language is powerless to describe; and you are steeped in malignity of mind and excess of greed, to such a pitch as explanation fails to recount. You have seen to what extent your treachery and deceit have advantaged your master and benefactor: so that at the last what will be the punishment and torture for yourself, since the disgrace of your two-faced and double-tongued conduct must produce a bad result?" Damnah replied: "What is the harm of my double-faced proceedings? since a beautiful rose, by reason of its two cheeks, is the ornament of the rose-garden; and what fear is there from my double-tongued conduct? since the pen of a writer, with its two nibs, is the guardian of property and the kingdom: it is the business of the sword, which is one-edged, to spill blood; while the comb, which has two sets of teeth, has its abode in the parting of the hair of lovely damsels."

> He drinks blood like a sword, in this age, who
> By reason of his natural integrity has but one face and one tongue:
> While to him who, like a comb, is double faced and tongued,
> They will give a seat of sovereignty, above their heads.

Kalílah said: "O Damnah, cease prating, since you are not such a two-cheeked rose that, in contemplation of your beauty, the eye becomes illumined; on the contrary, you are the heart-wounding thorn, from which nought but misery accrues to mankind: nor are you such a two-nibbed pen, as to afford news of the secrets of the country and empire, but rather a two-fanged viper, since the wound of your tongue is nought but pernicious poison: indeed the snake is preferable and superior to you, since from one of his forks poison issues, whereas from the other the antidote flows; while, as regards you, from both your tongues poison trickles, and leaves no trace nor sign of antidote. Now it behoveth every one to produce from their tongue every antidote on behalf of friends, though if, as regards one's enemies, poison appears it is fitting; like it has been spoken by a sage:

' I have upon the tip of my tongue both the antidote and the poison;
The former is for my friends, the latter for my enemies.' "

Damnah rejoined: " Cease reproaching me, for perhaps peace will take place between the Lion and Shanzabah, and the basis of friendship and confidence again be settled." Kalílah said: " This is another of the collection of your impracticable speches; but perhaps you are not aware that there are three things which remain undisturbed until three other things [1] have taken place; but afterwards repose is among the number of impossibilities, and stability may be said to be out of the question. 1st, Water of a fountain or canal, however pure it is, till it arrives at the sea, when it is merged in the ocean pureness and sweetness cannot again be anticipated from it. 2d, Concord exists among relations, so long as men of evil designs and contentious dispositions do not come amongst them; but after the entrance of such wicked and impious persons, harmony and union cannot be expected amongst an assembly of relatives and connections. 3d, The reservoir of society and affection is undefiled, so long as there is no opportunity of speech given to informers and inciters to strife; but when a double-faced and two-tongued traitor finds an opportunity of treachery between two friends, no reliance can again be placed upon their friendship. Now henceforth, if the Ox should escape from the clutches of the Lion, it is not possible that, by the courtesy and flattery of the latter, he should turn from his path; or that he should show a disposition for friendship and alliance with him; and even supposing that the doors of intercourse remain open, each one will be suspicious of the other."

When a cord is broken it can be mended,
But in the middle there remains a knot.

Damnah said : " If, having abandoned attendance on the Lion, I should become observant of religious duties in the recesses of my abode, and if, having seized with the hand of desire the skirt of your profitable society, I should place the head of retirement within the collar of privacy, how would it be ?" Kalílah rejoined : " God forbid that I should again be intimate with you, or be disposed to be friendly with you: for I always feared associating with you, and always in my mind disapproved of your society; since wise men have said, ' The society of the ignorant and base must be avoided, and the service of the wise and good must be embraced; for companionship with the low and mean is like nourishing a viper; the more a snake-catcher may foster it, the more grief will he experience, and ultimately he will give him a taste of poison from his fangs: whereas the service of the wise and good is like a perfumer's casket, since, though none of the contents thereof may be poured upon a person, yet the odours of its scents will perfume the nostrils.' "

May you be like a perfumer, by whose side
Garments become fragrant, by reason of his scents !

---

[1] خبر in the Persian is a misprint for خير .

How long will you, like a blacksmith's forge of fire,
Emit smoke and sparks on every side ?

" O Damnah ! how can one have any hope of fidelity and benevolence on your
part, since you have practised such conduct towards a King who has made you
beloved, respected, honoured, and famous, to so great a degree that, under the
shadow of his fortune you, Sunlike, boast of ˙your grandeur, and by reason of
service at his Heaven-like threshold, place the foot of self-glorification upon the
head of the Lesser Bear, and have thus treated his favours and kindnesses as if
they had never existed ?

You are neither ashamed with regard to God, nor yourself ;
Neither also do you blush with reference to the people.

" Now, were I to flee a thousand leagues away from such a person, generous
wisdom would hold me excused ; and were I to abandon intercourse with such
a worthless wretch, reason, which is my guide, would deem such a step
justifiable.[1]

'Twere best to abandon the society of apparent friends,
Since absence is better than the presence of those who are disagreeable ;
When from the companionship of a comrade gladness does not spring up in
· your heart,
'Twere more pleasant to be a hundred leagues away from such an associate.

" And whereas from the society of the good and just there is advantage beyond
measure, so the intimacy of the unworthy and base is utterly ruinous : and
companionship with the wicked quickly bears˙ fruit, and the misery thereof in
a short time becomes apparent.   Therefore it behoveth him who is extremely
prudent to make friends with discreet, worthy-living, right-speaking, and good-
natured persons, and to shun intimacy with liars, traitors, evil-disposed and base
men.

Since you cannot shut the door upon the face of mankind,
You must sit in the cell of retirement :
It is incumbent to acquire good associates,
Since every malevolent heart is not suitable for companionship.
I remember this speech of a wise man
(May there be pity upon his pure soul !)
That ' whoever was friends with the ignorant,
In the end was ensnared by their friendship.'

" Whoever forms an acquaintance with an unworthy man, or is aided by a
foolish friend, the same fate will betide him which befell the Gardener."   Damnah inquired, " What was that ? "

STORY XXVII.

Kalílah replied : It has been related that there was a certain Gardener, who had
been for a long time occupied in various kinds of horticulture, and passed a happy
life in the cultivation of pleasure-land and a Rose-garden.   He had a parterre,
the Eden-like appearance of which, from the beauty of its trees, threw the dust of

---

[1] Literally, " would connect me with rectitude."

envy into the eyes of the garden of Paradise, and from the freshness of its flowers and rivulets placed the blot of jealousy upon the bosom of the Rose-garden of Khawarnak.[1] Its various-tinted trees appeared resplendent like the peacock, and its gold-spangled roses resembled the magnificence of the crown of Káús.[2] The surface of the earth was decked like the cheek of a gaudily-attired mistress, and the breeze of its atmosphere was scented as it were the sanctum of an Ambergris - selling merchant: its young and luxuriant trees, from the amount of fruit thereon, were bent in back like old men : and its delicious fruits were like the sweetmeats of Paradise, ripened without the heat of fire ; the varieties of produce of spring and autumn were extremely juicy, and very pleasant : its innoxious apples, like the chin of beauties with bodies fair as silver, captivated the heart, and from their charming colours and repose-producing odours, enchained the world.

They have compared an Apple to the chin of a friend ;
Its colour is red, and its face radiates through the garden.
An Apple is like a lamp shining from a tree ;
In the splendour of day who has seen a lamp on the end of a branch ?[3]

Pears depended from every branch, like goblets of the Water of Life, mingled with bowls full of sweet Sharbat, and with the smokeless fire of their beauty stimulated the desires of the worthless and profitless idlers.

What shall I say in praise of the Pear ? since in sweetness and lusciousness
It is like so many flagons of sugar suspended in the air.

And the Quince, covered with down, like the sleepless-nighted [4] Súfís, raised its head, with yellow cheeks, from the womb of the sanctuary of nature, and its dust-stained face placed the grief-soiled hearts of lovers upon their guard, respecting the Sun of the affection of their Moon-faced beauties.

The yellow of the Quince is from the Sun,[5] and I from affection am yellow.
Its yellow is from the Moon and Sun, and mine from affection of my own
    Moon-like love.

The golden ball of the Orange, from the midst of its green leaves, was like the globe of the brilliant Sun shining in the Celestial Sphere ; and the golden censer of the Citron, with its heart-refreshing perfume, and soul-inspiring fragrance, was resplendent in the expanse of the garden.

The Pomegranates therein, like the lips of a smiling mistress,
Are the agreeable objects of competition for rivals.
To test them the Celestial Jeweller
Had cast ruby gems into the fire.[6]
When my speech sings the praises of the Peach,
My words regarding it seem fresh and sweet ;
Scarce ever does lip meet lip upon it,
But beautiful and pleasant juices trickle therefrom.

---

[1] The garden prepared in Babylonia for King Bahrám, and said to be of great beauty.
[2] A king of Persia.
[3] Meaning, I presume, that he who has seen it can judge of the beauty of the apple.
[4] Literally, "Night-rising."—See note, p. 24.
[5] It is impossible to do justice to this couplet, which is a play upon the word "mihr," meaning either "sun" or "affection."
[6] In allusion to the seeds of the Pomegranate, which are red.

In one direction an incomparable Fig, of the beauty of which the hand of Omnipotence, according to the saying "*And the Fig*," has proclaimed the praises, and given to it an excellent sweetmeat composed of poppies and sugar-candy. In another direction, glittering Grapes in explanation of the perfection of which the Pen of Wisdom has drawn across the honoured page, "*And in it we raised up grain and the grape*," were like a juicy blister, breaking out upon the surface of the green leaves. On the outskirts of the gardens, the golden ball of the Water-melon, with tender down and beautiful cheeks, shone resplendent like a full Moon, which showed its face upon the horizon of the azure Sphere.

> A Melon like a ball planted in a meadow
> Carried off the ball [1] amongst the fruits of Paradise.
> The tender down on its skin contained not a hair,
> Musk and musk-wine [2] did not equal it in perfume.

The worthy rustic was so wrapped up in all his trees, that he had not a thought of his father, nor anxiety about children, and passed his time in solitude in that garden. Ultimately, he became wearied of the loneliness of his seclusion, and exceedingly tired of the strangeness of his retirement and want of friends.

> The rose and the violet are all here, but since there are no friends, what advantage is there?

In short, by reason of the misery of his solitude, troubled in his mind, he came forth to wander in the plain: and at the skirt of a hill, the extent of the bounds of which, like the long road of Hope, was not visible, he commenced to wander. By chance a Bear, of savage disposition and disagreeable appearance, of revolting aspect and brutal temperament, had also, by reason of his melancholy feelings, turned his face from the top of the mountain downward. Of a sudden when they met, on both sides, in consequence of mutual sympathy, the chain of affection was put in motion, and the heart of the Rustic conceived a desire for intimacy and companionship with the Bear.

> Every atom that is in the Earth and Heaven
> (Gravitates) towards its own kind, like straw and amber;
> Fire is attracted to fire,
> Light also seeks after light;
> The sincere, also, are inclined to the sincere,
> The sad, too, are attracted towards the ailing;
> What seizes hold of the vain, 'tis vanity;
> And what is agreeable to the wise, wisdom.
> Men of folly attract the foolish;
> The remnant, too, are pleased with those who are left.

The inexperienced Bear, having observed the Rustic's demonstration of regard, became entirely devoted to his society, and on a mere hint laid his head at his feet, and made his entrance into that Paradise-resembling garden; and by gifts and *douceurs* of those pleasant fruits, friendship was confirmed between them, and the root of the tree of affection became firmly fixed in the ground of the heart of each of them.

---

[1] There is a celebrated oriental game called "chaugán" played with club and ball.
[2] Musk is here taken to be the blood of the musk-deer.

> In a corner of the garden they remained for a while
> Perpetually content with each other's society.

Whenever the Gardener, by reason of excess of indolence, under the shade of repose used to place the head of ease upon the pillow of rest, the Bear, from affection and friendship, would sit at the head of the pillow and drive the flies away from the Rustic's face.

> I am unwilling also that a fly should throw a shade on that lip.

One day the Gardener, after his usual fashion, was asleep and dreaming, and many flies were collected together on his face. The Bear was busy in driving them away, but the more he did so, the more they returned, and when he kept them off one spot they renewed the attack in another quarter. The Bear became distracted, and lifting up a stone of twenty máns weight, with the intention of killing the flies, dashed it on the face of the hapless Rustic. The flies experienced no ill effects from the anguish occasioned by that stone, whereas the old Gardener was ground to dust. On this account sage men have said that in every case a wise enemy is better than a foolish friend.

> A wise enemy, from whom there arises grief to the soul,
> Is better than a friend who is foolish.

" I have recited this story to show that friendship with you will produce this very result, that one's head will be involved in ruin, and one's breast become a target for the arrow of misfortune."

> The society of the foolish is like an empty pot,
> Which is hollow within and black without.

Damnah answered: " I am not such a blockhead as to be unable to distinguish between the advantages or disadvantages which may accrue to me from my friends, or not to discriminate between their good or bad qualities." Kalílah said: " I know that you are not such a fool as this; but the dust of selfishness has blinded and obscured the eyes of your heart, and very likely because of this selfishness you will desert your friend and offer in justification thereof a thousand unacceptable double-faced deceits; just as in the matter between the Lion and Shanzabah you have produced all this treachery, and yet you lay claim to being innocent-skirted and of a good disposition. The case of you and your friends is like that of the Merchant who said, " In a city where a Mouse eats an hundred máns of iron, what wonder is it that a Sparrow-hawk should carry off a child ? " Damnah inquired, " How was that ? "

STORY XXVIII.

Kalílah said: It has been related that a Merchant with but small capital went on a journey. As an act of foresight, he deposited an hundred máns of iron in the house of a friend, so that if necessity should arise, he could make it a store of support, and strengthen the bonds of life. After that the Merchant had finished his journey, and once more arrived at his destination, he needed that iron. The friend to whose care he had intrusted it, had sold it and spent the proceeds thereof. The Merchant one day went to him in search of the iron. The man in whose charge it had been placed, having brought him inside the house, said: "O sir, I securely placed that iron in a corner and became easy in my mind, ignorant of the fact that a Mouse's hole was there; before I became acquainted with this circumstance the Mouse found an opportunity of securing the prize, and ate up all the iron." The Merchant replied: "You speak truly, since mice have great affection for iron, and their teeth are very potent upon such a delicate and soft morsel."

> Iron is a delicate morsel for a mouse,
> And like syrup eases the throat.

The man to whom the property had been intrusted was, truth to tell, delighted at hearing these words, and said to himself, "This foolish merchant has been deceived by my speech, and has thought no more of the iron; nothing can be better than to show him hospitality and display the customary observances in feasting him, so that the present state of affairs may be confirmed." Accordingly he gave the Merchant an invitation, saying:

> If as a guest you place a foot in my cell,
> You will give me pleasure and are heartily welcome.[1]

The Merchant replied: "This day, as far as I am concerned, a matter of necessity has occurred; but I swear to you that I will return at dawn." He then went out from the house, and carrying away thence one of the man's sons, secreted him in a building. In the morning he went to the door of his entertainer's house, who, in great distress, loosed the tongue of apology, saying, "O beloved guest! excuse me, for since yesterday one of my sons has been missing, and two or three times a proclamation has been made in the city and suburbs, but I have obtained no clue respecting the lost child."

> Like Jacob, lamenting, I sigh,
> (Saying,) "Who has any news of Joseph who is lost?"

The Merchant said: "Yesterday when I left your house I saw a child of the appearance you describe whom a Sparrow-hawk had carried off, and flying along, bore him through the air." The man to whom the iron was confided, uttered a cry saying, "O senseless fellow! why do you narrate what is impossible, and why do you lay yourself open to the charge of telling me so great a falsehood? How can a sparrow-hawk, whose entire bulk is not half a mán, carry off and bear through the air a lad whose weight is ten máns?" The Merchant smiled and said, "Do not be astonished at this, since in a city where a mouse can eat an hundred máns of iron, a sparrow-hawk also can carry through the air a child of ten máns." The man in charge of the property perceived how matters were, and replied, "Be not dejected, since the Mouse has not devoured the iron." The Merchant rejoined, "Be not sad, for the Sparrow-hawk has not carried off your son; give me back my iron and take back your child."

"I have narrated this story that you may perceive that in a sect where treachery can be shown towards a benefactor, it is evident what can be devised towards other people. Now since you have acted thus towards the King, there will remain to others no confidence in your integrity, nor desire for your acknowledgment of favours, and it is clear to me that it is necessary for me to hold myself aloof from the blackness of your wrong-doing, and obligatory to avoid the darkness of your treachery and deceit."

[1] Literally, "will place your foot upon my eyes."

My fortune is bound up in severing myself from such as you,
My store of happiness in not seeing your face.

When the conversation between Kalílah and Damnah had reached this point,
the Lion had finished his business with the Ox, whom he had dragged in the
dust and blood. But when the Lion with the claw of punishment had settled
the matter of Shanzabah, and relieved of his existence the expanse of the desert,
the violence of the King's rage began to lessen, and the intensity of his fury to
abate. He fell into a train of reflection, saying to himself, "Alas for Shanzabah with so much wisdom, intelligence, judgment, and worth! I do not
know whether this action of my life has been consistent with true rectitude,[1]
or whether my feet have wandered in sin; and whether, in that which they
have conveyed to me concerning the Ox they have done what is right, or have
travelled the road of treachery. At any rate I myself, through being incited
to such an act, have become overwhelmed with misery, and with my own hand
caused my own faithful friend to taste the potion of death."

Is it thus a friend at length acts towards friend?
I am impious if any impious person would do thus.

The Lion having bowed the head of repentance, and loosened the tongue of
reproach, blamed the precipitancy and haste of his own proceedings, and the
thought of Shanzabah, in language of the occasion, brought home to his
Majesty's mind the meaning of this verse:

O friend! does any one destroy a friend without cause?
And then does any, like me, kill a faithful ally?
Do not call me a friend—treat me as your[2] enemy;
Would any one thus injure even his foe?

The constant smiling of the Lion, owing to the grief occasioned by this affair,
was changed to lamentation, and his ordinary hot temper, on account of the
excessive warmth of excitement arising from this event, became doubled.

The hand which has removed you has placed in my bosom the thorn of grief,
So that, by reason of this thorn of sorrow for you, how again can a rose
blossom?

Damnah, who had seen from afar the effects of repentance on the temples of the
Lion, and had observed upon his forehead the proofs of regret, having broken off
conversation with Kalílah, went to the royal presence and said:

O King! may the throne of prosperity be thy place!
May the couch of the Heavens be thy resting-place!
May thy radiant forehead be exalted by joy!
May the head of the enemy be cast under thy feet!

"What is the cause of your meditation, and what can be the reason of your
reflection? Where is there a time more pleasant or a day more auspicious than
this when the King is strutting in the region of victory and triumph, while
his enemies are wallowing in the mire of disgrace and the blood of disappointment?

Behold, the morn of Hope has drawn the sword of victory!
Behold the day when the enemy has reached the night of death!

[1] Literally, "whether in this business I have drawn my breath in rectitude."
[2] Or it may mean, "as my own enemy."

The Lion said : " Whenever I call to mind Shanzabah's humble service, the varieties and evidences of knowledge displayed by him during our intimacy, as well as his manifold good sense, pity overpowers me, and I am overwhelmed with grief and vexation ; and in truth he was the back and support of the army, and by his assistance the strength and prowess of my servants' arms were increased."

> He has departed from whom the business of the world possessed stability ;
> He has gone by whom the abode of the kingdom was secured.

Damnah replied : " There is no ground for pity on the King's part as regards that ungrateful traitor ; nay, more, it behoves you to return thanks to Almighty God for this victory which has occurred, and to open the doors of delight and pleasure in the court of the heart by reason of the conquest which has taken place.

> The morn of victory has risen in the east of Hope,
> The night of blackness has passed away for foul designers.

" This auspicious scroll of victory with which the calendar of prosperity is adorned, and this publication of fortunate conquest with which the register of happiness is ornamented, must be considered as an illustrious preface, and a remarkable frontispiece to the pages of time.

> To day good fortune has brought me glad tidings.
> Prosperity, with the note of hope, has many songs.
> This is the day which my heart has sought with a thousand prayers ;
> This is the time for which my soul longed with a thousand desires !

" O King ! protector of the world ! it is wrong to pardon any one from whom one cannot be secure as to life ; while it is the act of wise men to confine in the prison of the grave the enemy of the State. Now if a snake should wound the finger, which is the ornament of the hand and the instrument for grasping and holding, in order to save life the rest of the limb is amputated, and the pain of such wound is deemed the very essence of repose."

> What affair will your enemy do that you keep him in your memory ?
> It is better that you should gladden your heart at his death.

The Lion was in some measure pacified by these words, but Fortune snatched justice for the Ox, and ultimately Damnah's business resulted in disgrace and ignominy. The plant of his bad actions and the seed of his deceitful speech bore fruit, and he was killed in retribution for the Ox. The end of treachery and deceit has always been condemnable, and the termination of fraud and malevolence contemptible and unpropitious.

> The malevolent in their contrivances are slain,
> Like scorpions, who seldom return to their homes.
> If you act wrongly do not expect good,
> Since the wild gourd will not bear grapes.
> Do not expect, O you who have sown barley in autumn,
> That in time of harvest you will reap wheat.
> Similar to this spoke a man of the world,
> " Do not wrong lest you experience evil from the world ;
> He will find good in both worlds
> Who does good to the people of God."

BOOK II.

INTRODUCTION.

ON THE PUNISHMENT EXPERIENCED BY EVIL-DOERS, AND THE MISERY OF THEIR END.

HE King said: "I have heard the story of the calumniator and slanderer who, by excess of cunning, concealed the beauty of confidence with the appearance of suspicion, and having caused his benefactor to swerve from the road of manliness, made him celebrated for want of fidelity, and for not keeping his promise; how such person's words, mingled with deceit, having taken effect, he impelled the Lion to attempt the ruin of the pillars of the State, and the overthrow of his own majesty. At the present time, if the eloquent Philosopher thinks fit, let him narrate the termination of Damnah's affairs, and explain how the Lion, after the occurrence of that event, when he recovered his intelligence, became suspicious of Damnah; in what way he remedied the matter, and how he became apprised of the nature of the latter's treachery, and with what excuse Damnah continued his hold, and with what contrivance arranged his own security, and what was the termination of the matter." The Philosopher said:

O King! may the kingdom and religion be under your protection!
May the lamp of merit be a taper on your path!

"In truth, vigilance and foresight demand that kings should not be moved by merely hearing a speech, nor until manifest proof and clear evidence is obtained as to the truth of a matter, should they put their orders concerning it into execution.

Listen not to the words of a designing person,
Since if you take action you will repent it.

"And after that the speech of an interested person has happened to be acceptable, and disapproved actions or improper language have occurred, the remedy and amends should be that the slandering informer be punished in such a manner that it should be a warning to others, and from the dread of that chastisement no one should hereafter set his feet in such an affair; and all should be enjoined to avoid the same road.

> Cast away the root which produces a thorn,
> But cultivate the tree which yields fruit;
> The lamp of the tyrant is better extinguished,
> It is preferable that one should be burnt than that mankind should be blemished.

"Now the story of the Lion and Damnah is a verification of this speech, since, when the former was apprised of the treachery of the latter, and became aware of his deceit and fraud, he commanded that he should be punished in such manner that the eye of warning in other people was thereby enlightened, and they perpetually recited the verse, ' *Therefore take warning, O ye possessed of eyes.*' Now the nature of the story was in this wise."

--------o--------

When the Lion had finished the affair of the Ox he repented of the haste which he had exhibited in that business, and with the teeth of reproach bit the finger of regret, and placed the head of remorse upon the knee of anguish.

> He drew a cold sigh through regret and grief (saying),
> "Who in this world has acted as I have done?"

He was perpetually thinking, "Why did I in this matter act hastily?" and constantly considering, "Why did I not carry out this affair with reflection and deliberation?"

> I abandoned the reins of my soul to the hand of lust;
> I acted contrary to wisdom and intelligence, and did wrong.
> Now I know it, but the knowledge thereof is of no avail to me;
> What profit is it to say frequently, "Why did I act thus?"

The Lion passed a long time in this manner in anguish and grief; and by reason of his vexation of mind and despondency of heart the repose of the beasts was marred, and the condition of his subjects became straitened; and the idea, "*Men are of the same faith as their kings,*" having spread over the inhabitants of that forest, all were distressed and miserable.

> My heart, like a tulip, is burned up, and from the violence of my sighing
> Whomsoever you see is afflicted with the same evil.[1]

The greater part of his time he used to call to mind the good service and former attendance of Shanzabah; and his vexation having increased, anguish and sorrow overwhelmed him: it was a consolation to the Lion to speak of traditions concerning the latter, or hear him mentioned.

> I am not at any time unmindful of your memory;
> I either mention your name or listen thereto.

[1] Literally, " scar."

He had private interviews with each of the beasts, and demanded stories from them. One night he entered into conversation with a Leopard on this matter, and explained to him his distress of mind and anguish of heart. The Leopard replied : " O King ! to think much over a matter wherein the hand of deliberation fails to reach the skirt of remedy thereof is conducive to insanity, and to seek to rectify an affair which is within the limit of impossibility is out of the pale of wisdom and intelligence ; and wise men have said :

> To bring back to the thumb-stall an arrow which has been shot
> Is feasible, but not to bring you back.

" And whoever attempts to seek anything which it is impossible to obtain, may not improbably let slip from his hand that which he already possesses, without finding that for which he is searching : just as the Fox conceived a desire to obtain a fowl, and lost the piece of skin which he had despised." [1] The Lion inquired, " How was that ? "

STORY I.

The Leopard said : It has been related that a hungry Fox had come forth from his hole in search of food, and was wandering in every direction, and, in quest of a morsel, traversing the expanse of the plain with the foot of greed and gluttony. All at once an odour, such as to lend additional strength to his soul, reached his nostrils. Following the trail thereof, he saw a piece of fresh skin, which had been left by one of the beasts who had eaten the flesh thereof. When the eyes of the Fox alighted upon this piece of skin they sparkled, and by reason of the quantity of the food his frame became completely reinvigorated.

> I was dead, but the fragrance of a heart-enticing friend reaching me,
> Once again my departed soul returned to my body.

The Fox, having brought the piece of skin into the claw of his possession, turned his face towards his own abode.

> When a friend is obtained, retirement is best of all.

In the midst of his way his path happened to be on the outskirts of a village : he saw some fat fowls busy feeding on the edge of the plain, and the servant, by name Zírak,[2] had girded the loins of guardianship in watching them. The Fox's desire for the birds' flesh was aroused, and from delight at the idea of the brains in their heads, he forgot all about the piece of skin. In the midst of these circumstances a Jackal happened to pass by that village. He inquired, (saying,) " O brother ! I observe that you are extremely perplexed—what event has occurred, and what affair has happened ? " The Fox replied : " O dear friend ! do you see these fowls, every tongue of whose condition is perpetually repeating the saying, ' *And the flesh of birds such as they shall wish,*' and the purport of the verse, ' *And you shall have therein whatever your heart shall desire,*' pervades them from head to foot ?

> From head to foot all the soul is clothed with flesh :
> A soul so extremely pleasant and pure is rare.

---

[1] I am somewhat doubtful if this rendering be correct.   [2] Clever or sharp.

"And after that for a while I have been overwhelmed with the misery of starvation and the pain of hunger, the treasurer of the storehouse of provisions has given me a piece of skin; and now the allurement of desire demands that I should get one of those birds in my clutches, and that the palate of my wishes should be gratified with its luscious flesh, which has the flavour of life."

> My life is bitter, but if my love from her sugar-scattering lips
> Bestow sharbat upon me, the desire of my heart will be satisfied.

The Jackal replied: " Alas, alas ! a long time has elapsed since I have been in ambush for these fowls, and on the look-out to capture one of them; but that servant Zírak, who is in charge of them, watches the road of guardianship in such a manner that the hunter, Imagination, from dread of his protection, cannot throw their form into the snare of fancy, nor can the painter, Contemplation, from fear of his vigilance, draw their picture upon the tablet of thought. Now I pass my life in this idea, and consume day and night in the mere fancy thereof; do you then who have found a fresh piece of skin esteem it a prize, and abandon such extravagant notions."

> Fix your mind upon the sweetheart whom you possess,
> Avert your eyes from the rest of the world.

The Fox rejoined: " O brother! till on the summit of desire one can attain the wish of the heart, it would be a great shame to consign one's self to disappointment in the abyss of vileness and meanness; and so long as one can enjoy, in the garden of repose, the rose of delight, it would be a dreadful error to place a foot in the thorny ground of adversity and distress.

> So long as one can put one's foot on the throne of greatness,
> Why should one take a place in the mire of disgrace ?

"Now, ambition will not allow that my aspirations should be satisfied [1] with a piece of insipid skin, or that I should deprive my heart of the pleasure of fat juicy flesh." The Jackal said: "O vain, foolish person! you have given the name of exalted ambition to uncommendable greed, and applied the grand epithet of greatness to improper avarice, but you are heedless of the fact that 'Greatness is in humility,[2] and repose in contentment.'

> If in this market there is aught to be gained, it is by the contented darwísh :
> O God ! make me abound with humility and contentment !

"Nought is better than this, that you should be contented with the portion which has been fixed for you by the court—'*Sustenance is allotted (by God)*'—and that you should not commit the presumption of which the result, '*Whoever seeks a thing with which he has no concern verily abandons what does concern him,*' is decreed.

> Daily food is distributed, and the time thereof fixed.
> Sooner or later than that, it cannot be procured by any effort.

"Now I fear lest, by reason of this presumption in which you have indulged, that piece of skin also may slip from your hands, and you may all at once be over-

---

[1] Literally, " that I should drop my head."
[2] I have taken the word which signifies " poverty " as referring to a poor or humble state of mind.

thrown. Now, your case much resembles that of the Ass, who sought after a tail and gave his ears to the wind (of destruction)." The Fox inquired, "How was that?"

STORY II.

The Jackal replied :

> There was an Ass who had no tail ;[1]
> Day by day his grief for want of a tail grew greater.
> He set out in search of a tail—
> He sought a tail, and drew his breath.
> Suddenly, involuntarily on his part,
> He went in the midst of a field of ripe corn.
> A Rustic by chance spying him from a nook,
> Jumped up, and cut off his two ears.
> The hapless Ass desired a tail ;
> He did not find a tail, but lost both his ears.
> He who steps beyond his limits,
> Such is his punishment in the end.

The Fox, by reason of his excessive greed and covetousness, frowned, and said :

> I am thinking of my friend. Should any one imagine in his heart
> That I should omit to remember him, his idea is vain.

"Observe the sight, how, by a pleasing stratagem, I will bring a delightful fowl to my clutches, and with what contrivance I will entice into the net of my possession this worthy prey." Thus he spoke, and setting his steps towards the fowls, left there the skin. The Jackal, when he saw that his advice made no impression on the stony heart of the Fox, turned his face away from him, and hastened to his own abode. In the neighbourhood there was a Kite hovering about ; his glance lighted on the piece of skin, and thinking it a dead animal, with the greatest joy brought it within the region of his possession, and soared aloft in the air. On the other hand, the Fox had scarce got near the fowls, when Zírak jumped up from his hiding-place, and threw his stick at him. As soon as the Fox felt the effect thereof, the hapless creature, in fear of his life, abandoned all thought of the fowls' company, and with great haste scrambling along, set out towards the piece of skin. When he reached the destined spot, he saw no trace of the skin. In prayer he raised his eyes to heaven, desirous of representing in a supplicating manner the condition of his affairs. Just as he was weeping over his misfortune he saw the Kite, who, having seized in his talons the piece of skin, was carrying it away, saying :

> "You have gained at play, and the prize has fallen to your lot.
> Since you have played unfair, what shall any one do?"

The Fox, from vexation at not finding the fowl, and from regret at the piece of skin slipping from his hands, struck his head upon the ground till his brains were scattered.

"Now the object of reciting this story is this: the King has destroyed with

---

[1] It is impossible adequately to render in English this story, which is a play upon a word which means both "tail" and "breath."

his own hands one of the pillars of his kingdom, and does not trouble about the wellbeing of his remaining counsellors, and omits to look after the desires of the attendants at his court, or to show kindness to the chiefs and heads of his army. Shanzabah, being killed, cannot by any means be recalled; yet the residue of former servants remain apart from attendance." The Lion, after much deliberation, said: "This speech is the very essence of kindness and well-wishing; but, as regards Shanzabah, I have committed an error, and my perturbation is chiefly with a view of making amends for the same." The Leopard replied: "The remedy and cure thereof will not be procurable in anxiety; nay, more, will come to pass by right deliberation and correct judgment.

> When an ant falls into a glittering cup,
> His deliverer must use remedial measures, not force.

"The proper course is this: the King of the beasts, having cast aside impatience and folly, should place the edifice of his affairs upon deliberation; and as regards the matter of Shanzabah, and the investigation of the real truth as to his condition, should enter upon the case in such a manner that the ins and outs thereof may become clear to his intelligent mind; and if that which has been communicated to the King's ears relative to Shanzabah really occurred, the latter met with the punishment of treachery and the retribution of perfidy; while, if they have invented a calumny regarding him, and repeated words which were never uttered, it is incumbent that the tale-bearer and scandal-monger should be made the target of the arrow of revenge."

> It is right to thrust away him who is bad.

The Lion said: "You are the Minister of the kingdom, and for a long time I have been much benefited by your right judgment, and have made your foresight, in procuring advantages and repelling misfortunes, my guide and leader. Remove this affair in such way as is required by enlightened reason and bright intelligence, and bring me out of the whirlpool of misery by the assistance of your deliberation." The Leopard promised, "In a short time I will display to the King's radiant notice the truth of this affair, and not leave a particle of the minutiæ of investigation under the screen of secrecy or the veil of delay."

> Everything, with enlightened intelligence,
> I will unravel, like hair from dough.

The Lion found comfort at this promise, and as it was evening, the Leopard, having asked permission, set out towards his own home. By chance his path lay near the dwelling of Kalílah and Damnah. He saw that a dispute was taking place between them, and high words were uttered on both sides. The Leopard had been from the very first suspicious of Damnah. At this time, when the sound of speaking and expostulation reached his ears from their abode, his fears were increased. He came forward, and, standing behind a wall, opened the ears of attention to listen to their conversation. Kalílah was saying, "O Damnah! you have performed a great act, and perpetrated a stupendous deed, and have caused the King to break his promise, linking him with the deepest treachery; you have, moreover, raised the fire of strife and confusion amongst the animals and beasts, and I am not sure but that, any hour, the punishment thereof may reach you, and you may be overtaken with trouble and chastisement therefrom.

Whoever unsheathes the sword of oppression,
The sky, too, will rain down blood upon that person.

"And I know that when the inhabitants of this plain are apprised of your deed, no one will excuse you, or assist to liberate you; nay, more, they will all with one voice agree in killing and torturing you. For me, after this, to live in the same house with you is not right, for it has been said:

Sit not for a while with the bad, since the society of the wicked,
Though you yourself may be pure, will contaminate you.
The sun in all its majesty
Is obscured by an atom of a cloud.

"Arise! and be intimate with some other companion, and henceforth cease acquaintance and intercourse with me, since you shall not again be friendly or associate with me." Damnah replied: "O dear friend!

If I remove my heart from you and take away my friendship,
Upon whom shall I cast that love, where shall I bear that heart?

"Do not separate from me, nor deprive me of your society, and do not reproach me any more relative to the affair of Shanzabah, since to call to mind a matter which has been done is a source of misery, and to deliberate over an affair which does not come within the province of prevention is amongst the category of impossible imaginations: drive out of your head perverse melancholy, and turn your face towards joy and repose, since an enemy has travelled to the world of non-existence, and the atmosphere of Desire has become clear of the dust of suspicion; the cup-bearer of Inclination has poured the draught of repose into the cup of delight, and the doors of Hope are opened on the face of prosperity, while the rosebud of Expectation has bloomed in the garden of glad tidings."

O cupbearer! give wine, and be not sad at foe or friend,
Since the former has passed away, according to the wish of our heart, while the
latter has arrived.

Kalîlah said: "Notwithstanding you have deviated from the path of manliness, and with the axe of treachery have destroyed the foundation of generosity, yet you claim repose, and expect your time to be passed in security and happiness."

You have concocted a vain scheme, you have devised an absurd plan.

Damnah responded: "It is not that I was unaware of the disgrace of treachery, and the punishment of deceit and guile, or that the baseness of calumny and the abomination of malevolence were concealed from me; but the desire of dignity, the greed after wealth, and the promptings of envy, instigated me to such an action; and in the present circumstances I know no remedy for this matter, and cannot devise any cure for it."

The remedy of this business is beyond the region of possibility: what can I do?

The Leopard having heard this portion of their discourse, and found out the exact state of affairs, went to the Lion's Mother, and said: "I will disclose a secret, on this condition, that the Queen promises not to permit it to be revealed without absolute necessity." After a profusion of oaths, promises, and protestations, he repeated in its entirety what had occurred between Kalîlah and Damnah, and related in detail the reproaches of Kalîlah and the confession of

Damnah. The Lion's Mother was astonished at the account of this affair. Next day, according to her usual custom, she came to see the Lion, whom she found extremely sad and dejected. She inquired, " O Son ! what is the cause of your pensiveness, and the reason of your vexation ? "

> Why has your full moon become dejected ?
> Why has your waving cypress become a mere spindle ?
> On what account are all these your sighs,
> And to whose violence are all these lamentations due ?

The Lion replied : " My sadness is due to nought but the destruction of Shanzabah, and the reminiscence of his virtues and qualities ; and, much as I try, the memory of him will not quit my mind, nor the recollection of him be forgotten in my heart."

> By your soul, you are not forgotten for a moment !
> And though you were so, now you exist not—what shall I do ?
> Do not say in irony, " Khusrau,[1] forget me."
> I would do so if you could be forgotten ; since you cannot, what shall I do ?

" Whenever there is a consultation respecting the affairs of the country, and I am in need of a kind friend and generous adviser, a trustworthy companion, or a faithful servant, the thought of Shanzabah rises before me, saying :

> ' In manner of service, and in point of fidelity,
> You may seek far, you will not find such an one as I am.' "

The Lion's Mother said : " As regards the victory of the light of certainty over the darkness of doubt and conjecture, the testimony of no one is equal to the evidence of a pure heart. Now from the King's words it is understood that his heart is witness to the innocency of Shanzabah ; and assuredly, since his destruction was not after conclusive proof and clear evidence, and since a slanderer, under the guise of rectitude, represented his circumstances contrary to what was true, every moment fresh regret and endless repentance will arise. Now if, as regards what had been represented to the King, he had exercised reflection, and with the bridle of patience had restrained in its violence the steed of rage, and removed the darkness of that doubt with the brilliancy of clear wisdom, he need not at this moment have fallen into the net of repentance, nor must he have placed the volume of pleasure and joy upon the shelf of non-existence."

> Conduct the affairs of the world with deliberation,
> Since, in any matters, haste will not be of any avail :
> Were the lamp not to blaze with such brilliancy,
> It would neither consume itself nor the moth :
> Patience affords a key to every lock ;
> No one ever saw a patient man overwhelmed with regret.

The Lion replied : " O Mother ! as you have said, in this matter my natural feelings were superior to my reason, and the fire of rage consumed the edifice of understanding, and now there is no course but indifference, to remedy a matter which is included in the category [2] of impossibility ; but the worst of the case may be this,—my subjects have made me the target for the arrow of reproach,

---

[1] A celebrated king of Persia ; but the allusion is probably to a poet of that name.
[2] I have borrowed this rendering from Eastwick, not being able to improve it, nor, indeed, to suggest another.

and cast upon my name the lot of faithlessness and oppression: and however much diligence I display to connect the Ox with open treachery, and fix a patent offence upon him, so that perchance I may be excused by others for slaying him, and be exempt from the jeers of my acquaintances and the taunts of strangers, I cannot in any way arrange or settle this. The more I reflect, the better does my opinion of him become, and the more do I regret and repent his death. The hapless Shanzabah, too, had a clear intellect and a praiseworthy disposition, and with all these qualities, one cannot ascribe to him the charge of malevolence; neither was he a person of that class in whose brain vain desires and impossible schemes have their abode, so that it should have passed through his mind to kill or contend with me; also, as regards him, there has proceeded no such neglect of the various degrees of kindness, and different sorts of favours, as could be a bond of enmity and aversion, and the cause of antagonism and contention. Now I am anxious to use every effort to investigate this matter, and to prosecute this inquiry to the limits of excess: and though it may be that this regret is without avail, and that sorrow will not find a remedy by this narration, yet it may be that consolation will accrue to my spirit therefrom, and the strife-exciting slanderer be punished, and my apology be accepted amongst mankind. Now if you have become acquainted with anything in this matter, or have heard any tidings, inform me and give me advice." The Lion's Mother said:

> I have a mind full of gems of secrets;
> But there is a seal[1] on my mouth.

"I have heard some talk, but it is not allowable to divulge it, and I have discovered some particulars, but it is not permissible to reveal them, since some of those around you have imposed upon me to keep this secret, and have used their utmost efforts to conceal matters—'*The hearts of the noble are the graves of secrets.*'

> I inquired of an old toper, 'Wherein is the road of security?'
> He demanded a glass of wine, and replied, 'In the keeping of secrets.'

"Now the King is aware that it is a great fault to divulge secrets, and an unutterable crime to disclose a person's confidences: were it not that wise men have insisted upon avoiding that habit, I would otherwise have repeated everything, and swept away the mire of lamentation from the expanse of the heart of my beloved and prosperous son." The Lion replied: "The proverbs of the learned and the sayings of the wise are numerous; though many of them have enjoined refraining from disclosing secrets, it was in view of the wellbeing and safety of the speaker: some there are, too, which, with regard to universal interest (since general advantage may be conceivable therefrom) have commanded the declaration of such secrets; now, if any one should unjustly design the destruction of a Mussulmán, and impart the secret to a third party, and under severe and harsh obligations disclose it to him, and enjoin him strictly not to reveal it; and if that friend, with the view of protecting that Mussulmán, should unfold the secret, and inform him thereof, so that he might guard his interests,—assuredly such person would not, at law, be punished, neither would he become blameable before God: and to conceal a secret in such circumstances as these, would appear like being partners with wicked men. Now it may be that he who has communicated this intelligence has wished that by divulging this secret to you he may withdraw his feet from the midst thereof, and intrust it to the care of

---

[1] Literally, "nail."

your keeping, or he may have had dread of me, and made you the medium of disclosing this secret. I am in hopes that you will inform me thereof, and relate whatever is befitting your counsel and kindness."

> Disclose your secret, for we are to be intrusted with confidences ;
> Abandon consequential airs, for we are suppliants.

The Lion's Mother said : " This observation which you have made is much to be commended, and this line of argument which you have adduced is greatly to be praised ; but the disclosing of secrets has two clear evils : 1st, The enmity of that individual, who having reliance on a certain person, has made him acquainted with his secrets. 2d, The suspicion of others ; for when a person becomes known as betraying the confidences[1] and revealing the secrets of mankind, not a soul will again repeat a word to him, nor will any intrust him with a secret : he will both be driven from the sight of his friends and also overwhelmed by the taunts of his enemies.

> Much as my heart is wasted from concealing my secret,
> Yet, from dread of my enemies, I ever place a seal on my lips.

" Also in the sayings of the wise I have observed that, ' *He whose secret is not dead, his ruin is not dead.*' Whoever does not conceal the gem of his secret in the casket of non - existence, assuredly that secret will hoist the standard of destruction over his head ; and it has passed into a proverb that ' whoever lets a secret escape from his hands, lays down his life in return.'

> Do you wish to keep your head in its place, preserve your secret.

" Perhaps you have not heard the story of that Attendant who dared to disclose the King's secret, and ultimately gave his head in exchange for the same?" The Lion inquired, " How was that ? "

STORY III.

The Lion's Mother said : In days past there was a King, the throne of whose sovereignty received lustre and glory from the ornament of his justice and the splendour of whose unsparing kindness shone through the regions of his kingdom.

> In pomp like Farídún, in dignity like Jamshíd,
> In majesty like Sikandar, in power like Darius.[2]

One day he had gone out hunting at a spot where a tent was nigh at hand. When every one was busy in settling the affairs which pertained to his post, he said to his own Attendant, " I wish to race horses with you, since I have for a long time been anxious to know whether the pace of this black horse on which I am mounted, is better than that of the piebald which you are riding." The Attendant, in accordance with the command of his Monarch, began to gallop his horse, and the King also gave the rein to his quick-going courser. As soon as they were a long way from the hunting-ground, the King, dropping his stirrups and pulling up the reins of his horse, exclaimed,—" O Attendant ! my object in journeying thus far was this : At the present moment something entered my

---

[1] Literally, " rending the veils."　　　　　　　[2] See note 1, page 12.

mind, and a thought overpowered my imagination, and amongst all my courtiers none being worthy to be intrusted with this secret, I wished to secure privacy to tell it you in such a manner that no one should have any suspicions." The Attendant performed the oath of devotion, and said:

O Khusrau![1] may the sun of the firmament be thy servant!
May Fortune be resplendent, and shine on thee!

" Though this contemptible atom does not value himself so highly, yet since the light of the sun of favour has intrusted me with the shadow of Fortune, I am in hopes that the morning breeze, which is the confidant of the secrets of the truths of spring, will not inhale an odour from this expanse, neither the heart, in spite of its becoming the treasury of this coin, extend its feet to the limits of this news."

In like manner as the soul is concealed in the body,
So will I keep your secret hidden in my heart.

The King having praised him said: " I am in great dread of my own brother; and nowadays I read on the page of his actions and attitude the representation of my destruction and ruin, and I behold that he has bound himself with the girdle of hatred to encompass my death. Now I, also, am purposing and desirous to remove the stone of his existence from my path, and free the expanse of the country from the thorn of his malevolence before that ruin shall befall me at his hands.

A weak fox! Whose dog is he,
That he should occasion injury to a strong lion?

" You must always be on the alert as to his affairs, and observe the obligations of caution as regards my protection and preservation." The Attendant made obeisance, and having charged himself with the matter of preserving and concealing the circumstance, ratified it with various assurances; but he had scarce arrived at his own home, ere he drew the writing of perfidy across the volume of his affairs, and having wandered from the road of affection and confidence, placed his feet in the desert of treachery and ingratitude.

Moderate your soul's affection for your companions, since in the rose-garden of
  Fortune
The perfume of friendship and sincerity is never found in any comrade.
I intrusted a secret to a person, and suffered much torture therefrom.
Would to God I had first of all known that one cannot find a confidant!

The Attendant, having sought an opportunity, betook himself to the service of the Sultán's brother and apprised him of the case just as he himself had heard it. The King's brother at once, for a sum, received the favour from him, and befriended him with numerous promises and countless largesses, and with right deliberation also guarded himself from the machinations of his brother. In a short time, as is the wont of the vicissitudes of Time, and the instability of the actions of Fortune, the Spring of that brother's prosperity became changed to the Autumn of adversity, and the blossom of success fell down from the tree of his existence.

What Spring breeze blows in the Heavens,
That in its rear there is not the adversity of Autumn?

[1] A celebrated king of Persia.

To be perpetually nurtured in the bosom of Mother Fortune
Do not expect, since there is not therein the perfume of hospitality.

Now when the royal throne and the regal couch remained void of the glorious majesty of the elder brother, the younger brother placed his foot upon the pedestal of the throne of monarchy, and exalted the diadem of royalty to the pinnacle of prosperity.

In the parterres of the kingdom of Fortune there blossomed the rosebud of joy;
The rose-garden of monarchy was verdant with the heads of the shrubs.

The first commands which issued from the lips of the King, and the earliest orders for the execution of which the exalted signal was given, were as to the destruction of the Attendant. Helpless he loosened the tongue of supplication (saying)

O Khusrau![1] may thy dominion be prosperous!
May thy star be resplendent and auspicious!

"What is my fault but sincerity and affection for thee?"

The retribution for what I have done is not this.

The King said: "The worst of crimes is to disclose a secret, and as regards you this fault has been perpetrated; and after that you have failed to guard the secret of my brother, who selected you as the confidant thereof from amongst all his attendants, what reliance can I have in you?"

It is better to separate from a faithless friend.

Though the Attendant exhibited perturbation, it was of no avail, and he was overtaken with the King's punishment, and lost his head through the disclosure of a secret.

If your tongue keeps its secret,
What concern has the sword with your head?

"Now the advantage to the King from the recital of this story is this: The disclosure of secrets produces no good result, and it will not procure the fruit of happiness to become a babbler of men's confidences." The Lion replied: "O dear Mother! he who reveals his own secret, his object is to disclose it—and if not, it behoveth him to become the confidant of his own secret; but after that a person has divulged the secret of his own mind to another, if the latter in turn repeats it to a third party there will be no room for vexation. Since it is no wonder if, when a person cannot endure his own load, another should have no power to bear the same.

When you yourself are not (a fit) confidant of your own secrets,
How could any other person be intrusted therewith?

"Again, when, as regards the disclosing of a secret, a person reveals what is proper, though betraying the confidence is considered a fault, yet the evidence of such good intentions may be a screen in front of the offence. I am in hopes that, having done me the favour of revealing what is right, you will remove the load of grief from my heart; but if you cannot do so clearly, give a hint thereof, and if you cannot make use of plain sentences, at any rate do not refuse to

[1] See note, page 153.

adopt metaphors." The Lion's Mother said : "On the condition that you cause punishment and retribution to reach that infamous rascal who has raised the dust of this strife, and that you conceal the beauty of pardon from his fearless eyes, which were blind to behold the path of rectitude and right dealing. Though the learned in religion and the skilled in the knowledge of the true God have laboured to show the excellence of pardon and the glory of kindness, and have stimulated and encouraged the practice of that custom and the adoption of that habit, yet as regards crimes the effects of which may bring ruin to the world, and the misery therefrom be diffused throughout the human race, punishment is better than pardon. If as a set-off for this crime from which vexation has accrued to the King's soul, and the skirt of his rectitude and confidence has become stained with the disgrace of perfidy and treachery, retribution does not follow, it will be a source of courage to other wretches, and the pretexts of evil-doers will thereby gain additional strength, and every one will consider it a reliable example and a true model for oppression and wickedness. Consequently here there must be no place for pardon and connivance ; and according to the peremptory precept, '*And in this retaliation you have life,*' remedial measures must be recognised as imperative.

> Every person who commands the people to be oppressed
> Is the enemy of the kingdom—give orders for his destruction.

"The object of this exordium is this : The traitor Damnah, who has impelled the Monarch of the world to this course, is a tale-bearer, a sycophant, a worthless scoundrel, and a villain." The Lion rejoined : "I know it ; you must return till I have reflected as to his punishment." The Lion's Mother went back to her home, while the Lion, after much thought, commanded the army to be paraded before him, and having summoned to his presence the chiefs and nobles, the ministers and counsellors, requested his mother to be present ; and after that all, both high dignitaries as well as subjects, were assembled together, he issued his august mandate that they should bring Damnah to the foot of the royal couch : having turned away from him, the King occupied himself in deep and profound reflection. Damnah observed it, and found the door of misfortune opened, and the road of deliverance closed : turning his face towards one of the King's attendants he softly said to him : "What is the reason of this meeting together of the assembly, and what has happened that the King is absorbed in thought and reflection ?" The Lion's Mother heard this, and exclaimed : "The King is deliberating about your life ; and since your treachery is known, and the villany of your depravity is evident, while the falsehood which you spoke concerning his dear friend has been unravelled, and the screen removed from before the face of your rascality and baseness, it is not right that you should be allowed to live, even for the twinkling of an eye, or that a man displaying such wickedness should be kept in the firmament of '*This existence is pure good.*'" Damnah replied : "The sages of old have not left any wisdom untold, but have made the way clear for the repose of people of modern times. Now one of their wise sayings is that, 'Whoever in the service of a king is resolute will quickly attain the honour of access, and whoever is in proximity to the sovereign, all the king's friends and enemies will become the foes of such a person '—the former by reason of their envying his dignity and station, the latter on account of his sincere advice as regards the interests of the kingdom and people.

> Whoever is nearest in the service of the king,
> His danger is greatest.

" ' *And those persons who are friends are in great danger* ': hence it arises that persons of sincerity have placed their backs against the wall of security and repose, and having turned their faces from the world, which is unstable, treacherous, and unreliable, have made choice of the worship of the Creator in place of the service of the creature—since in His exalted presence negligence and omission are not permissible, while oppression and tyranny are not allowable, and the requital of good with evil, or the recompense of obedience with punishment, is not conceivable : as regards, too, the orders of the King of kings there is never, in the least degree, any deviation from the direction of justice.

That justice is Divine which is uniform ;
As for the rest there is invariably at one time satisfaction, at another discontent :
There there is no oppression, though here there is tyranny ;
There there is nothing wrong, though here there are mistakes.

" Most of the arrangements of mankind, in contradistinction to the ways of the Creator, are marred with various contradictions and inconsistencies ; and deviating from connection with, and observance of, what is right, sometimes they bestow on criminals, who are worthy of punishment, the recompense due to the dealings of the sincere, while sometimes they rebuke righteous men, who merit encouragement, with the reproaches due to the sins of the base : since lust is predominant in their arrangements, and error evident in their deeds ; spite is manifest in their words, and hypocrisy visible in their actions ; good or evil are to them alike, and advantage or misfortune akin in their sight. May be that a person intrusts all the wealth on the earth's surface to the treasurer of the king, who will not, on his part, consider it in the least degree a favour, while he will raise to the summit of greatness the exalted head of another man who may abuse him.

Behold their indifference, observe their nonchalance,
As to whether you be the musician or become the mourner.

" I should not, from the commencement, have approached the outskirts of the King's service, nor have set my feet beyond the cell of retirement, or the corner of privacy. I should not have accepted the service of the Monarch, which is like a consuming fire, since whoever does not recognise the value of repose, and chooses the service of the creature rather than obedience to the Creator, will meet with that which befell the Recluse." The Lion's Mother inquired, " What was that ?"

STORY IV.

Damnah said : It has been related that a pious man, having abandoned worldly concerns, made choice of the corner of retirement, and, not considering food and raiment, was content with barley-bread and woollen clothes.

He was melancholy from grief, pulling at his collar ;
He girded himself, and went to the foot of a mountain ;
He turned his body from affluence to penury ;
He contented his heart with mere herbage in lieu of luxuries.[1]

The fame of that holy man's probity and rectitude in a short time reached the

---

[1] Literally, " he turned his heart from contentment to grass."

outskirts and borders of that region, and men from far and near, by way of invoking a blessing and benediction, began to repair to him. When they saw the effects of the light of worship beaming and radiant on his illustrious temples, having become more earnest in matters of religion, they displayed greater zeal. In this district was a King, just, liberal, and a friend to the Darwísh, and who gave precedence to the search after Divine favour in place of following after kingly lusts, and took for his example nought but the habits of the prophets, and the disposition of the saints.

A pure disposition, good nature, and straightforward conduct,
Are pleasant on the part of a poor man, but more excellent on that of a rich person.

When the news of the saintly Recluse reached him, having put in practice the saying, "*Happy is the chief, and happy the Fakír,*" he waited on the holy man, and having sought a supply of his blessed words, begged for some advice suitable for kings. The pious Recluse replied: "O Monarch! God has two palaces—one temporal, which is called the World, the other everlasting, which is named Eternity. Exalted ambition demands that you should not set your desires upon the temporal abode, but should fix your sight upon the kingdom of the everlasting world."

Seek the kingdom of Eternity, since that is pleasant—
An atom from that region is worth a hundred Worlds !
Strive that while in the midst of this present abode
You secure your portion in that realm.

The King inquired: "By what means can the conquest of that kingdom be obtained ?" The Devotee replied: "By assisting the oppressed and aiding the unfortunate: and it becomes every King, who wishes for everlasting rest, to strive for the comfort of his people."

That person sleeps at rest under the clay,
At whose hands men repose in ease of heart ;
Men enjoy the fruit of youth and prosperity,
Who do not inflict cruelty on their inferiors :
Such monarchs as nurture religion,
In the game of faith will bear off the ball [1] of good fortune.

When the Devotee had finished his advice, and filled the treasury of the King's mind with the pearls of exhortation, the holy, pure-minded man's counsels and homilies touched the Monarch, who, having placed the hand of inclination upon the skirt of his favour, perpetually used to seek the honour of his society, and by the blessing of obeying his heart-entrancing words turned his own head aside from the pursuit of sensuality and lust. One day the King was attending on the Darwísh, and conversing on every subject: all at once a crowd of petitioners for justice raised their complaints and cries to the ethereal globe. The Devotee sought them out, and inquired of each one separately as to the matter, and informed his majesty the King as to the order necessary and suitable to each case. In these circumstances the King became extremely obliged, and begged that sometimes the court of justice might be held in the Saint's blessed presence. The Devotee, in order that the suits of the petitioners might be speedily and properly settled, and that he himself, by reason of well-

[1] See note 1, p. 138.

arranging matters, might procure an everlasting reward, agreed : and in every case there issued from the lips of the Devotee whatever the circumstances of the time demanded. The King, too, with readiness and willingness showed a sincere regard thereto, till at length the matter reached such a pitch that most of the affairs of the kingdom were linked to the skirts of that exalted Saint's care; and he became daily more occupied in matters of state and property. By pleasing degrees, a hankering love of dignity, having placed its chattels in the core of the Saint's heart, made a breach in the wall of his inclination and time; and the desire to become possessed of greatness and renown, having turned aside the Darwísh's head from the pillow of repose, made him long for a crown of pomp.

Who is there that this bewitching enchantress does not turn aside from his path? Who is there but from her deceitful cup drinks the draught of imprudence?

The World is a bewitching damsel, who has made many lion-hearted men captive in the snare of her affection ; or a treacherous old woman, who has cast many a bold, herculean warrior into the pit of misfortune.

> Rustam[1] himself is in misery at the hands of Zál;[2]
> The giant himself is at the bottom of the well of pain ;
> Egypt is overwhelmed by the Nile of ruin ;
> Joseph stained by the blood of his shirt :
> Unity itself is found at the top of the road of separation ;
> Faithfulness itself is at the end of the street of hypocrisy :
> Nobility is found composed of the crowns of every monarch ;
> An ocean formed from the blood of every Isfandiyár.[3]

When in the place of the bitter draught of abstinence the Devotee had tasted of bodily ease, and quaffed the wine of lustful pleasure, the joys of devotion became forgotten in his heart, and he placed through his ear the ring " *Love of the world is the head of all sins.*"

> When the recluse hears the drum of prosperity,
> He experiences no further pleasure in the corner of seclusion.

The King also, when he saw that the proceedings and arrangements of the Recluse accorded with the advantage of the country, at once placed the reins of power in his able hands. The Darwísh formerly had to think about his bread, now the troubles of the world presented themselves, and the thought of procuring a blanket was changed for that of governing a kingdom.

> In that expanse which you beheld, not a rose remains in blossom.
> Autumn arrived, and the vernal covering of spring departs.

One day one of the holy men who now and then used to wait on the Devotee, and pass from night till morn in supplication and lamentation, arrived on a visit to him, and having observed the circumstances and state of affairs, the fire of jealousy was kindled in the regions of his heart.

The water of life has become turbid—where is auspicious-footed Khizr?[4]
Blood trickles from the stem of the rose—what has become of the spring-breeze?

---

[1] One of the the twelve champions of Persia.　　　　　　[2] Mother of Rustam.
[3] Killed by Rustam after a combat which lasted two days.
[4] A prophet who, according to oriental tradition, discovered and drank of the fountain of immortality, and in consequence will never die.

When evening arrived, and the noise of the people was entirely hushed, he said to the Devotee: " O Shaikh! what state of affairs is this which I see, and what appearance is it which I behold?"

> The day of hope used to be the sum of thy fortune;
> Where is that happy day, where that fortune?

The Devotee, though he employed the tongue of apology, could not speak a word which would prove genuine upon the touchstone of intelligence. His guest replied: " This speech is a personal pretext: the purport of this bombast, and inference from this language, is that your blessed heart has become inclined towards worldly possessions, and your illustrious mind ensnared in the bonds of dignity and wealth.

Of what avail are bones for a phœnix[1] like yourself of exalted worth and ambition?
Alas for the shadow of dignity which you cast over a carcase!

" Come and shake out the dust of your rivals from the skirt of solitude, and draw the head of retirement within the collar of trust in God, and do not bring the poison-stained viands of the World to the palate of desire."

> Do not stretch out the hand of desire towards the table of fortune,
> Since the viands thereof are defiled with poison.

The Devotee rejoined: " O dear friend! as regards conversation with mankind, and intercourse with human beings, no great change has occurred in my condition, and in my heart I am desirous of the very thing you mention." The guest replied: "Now you are ignorant (of your condition), because self-gratification has concealed the eye of prudence, and at the time that you come to be aware thereof, repentance will not be of any avail.

> Thus have you acted, and ultimately,
> When you become repentant, it will be of no avail.

" And your case resembles that of the blind man, who did not distinguish between a Whip and a Snake, and by reason thereof fell into the whirlpool of destruction." The Devotee inquired, "How was that?"

STORY V.

The Traveller said: Once upon a time, a blind man and one having sight alighted at a stage in one of the deserts. When early dawn appeared, and they were anxious to start, the blind man sought for his Whip. By chance a Snake happened to lie there, stiffened by the cold: the blind man, imagining it to be a Whip, took it up; when he passed his hand over it, he discovered that it was softer and better than his own Whip. Being on that account delighted, he mounted his horse, and forgot all about the Whip which was lost. But when daylight appeared, the other man, who could see, looking, and observing a Snake in the hand of the blind man, cried out: "O comrade! what you imagined to be a Whip is a venomous Snake: throw it from your hand

---

[1] The phœnix is said to feed upon bones: every head it overshades, according to tradition, will wear a crown.

before it can bite you." The blind man, fancying that his companion coveted the Whip, replied: "O friend!

What shall I do? The matter depends on fortune and luck.

"As I have lost my own Whip, the Creator has bestowed on me a better one. You also, if destiny befriends you, will find a nice Whip, but I am not one of those from whose hands treachery and deceit can take my Whip. The man who could see smiled, and said: "O brother! the dues of companionship demand that I should apprise you of this danger; listen to what I say, and throw that Snake from your hand." The blind man frowned, and said:

O plaintiff! why do you exert yourself beyond limit?
Lend your ear to this saying, 'Our daily food is fixed by divine decree.'

"You have planned to get my Whip, and are using every effort to induce me to throw it down, in the expectation that, after I have cast it aside, you will carry it off. Do not imagine such absurd ideas, and abandon such fruitless devices, since this is a Whip come to my hands from the Invisible World."

One must not desist through the wiles which an enemy plots.

Though the man who could see exerted himself to the utmost, and asseverated with deep and binding oaths, it was of no avail, and the blind man paid no attention to his words. Now when the air became warm, and the Snake lost its stiffness, it coiled itself about, and, in the midst of its writhings, inflicted a wound upon the hand of the blind man, who dropped down dead.

"Now I have adduced this story that you may not put confidence in the World, and neither be deceived by its appearance, which, like the figure of the Snake, is of various hues, nor take delight in its blandishments and caresses, since its wound is deadly and its poison fatal."

Do not expect sweet drink from the World,
Since therein honey is mixed with poison;
You imagine that to be honey
Which is, however, not so, but the potion of death.

The Devotee, having listened to this speech, reflected over the period of his seclusion and retirement, and contemplated the debasement of his attachments, which had kept the skirt of his heart from its original purity. He perceived that the language of that friend was dictated by the purest kindness and the sincerest affection; the tears of repentance began to trickle from his eyes, and he commenced heaving a plaintive sigh from his breast, which was consumed with the fire of regret.

I possess a soul consumed with grief—Why should I not heave a sigh?
Fortune is drowsy—Why should I not weep and lament?

All night, like a lighted candle, with burning heart the tears trickled down, and, like a moth, he was distressed in his desire after the flame of holy love; till the time when the white-clad devotee of true Morn spread the carpet of the Sun before the High Altar—"*The time when the morn breathed forth prayer,*" and the black attired Súfí of Night [1] was fixed in the womb, "*The time when the night draws in.*"

[1] See note, p. 24.

> When morn over heaven's bosom draws the robe of light,
> The earth lifts from its face the veil of dark night.

Men again entered the door of the Devotee's cell, and the tempest of pride beginning to rage, gave the harvest of nightly repentance to the wind of independence.

> Every night I say that to-morrow I will abandon such desires;
> But my inclination thereafter becomes renewed every fresh morn.

In short, the Devotee, having taken in hand the affairs of the state, and dismissed the chiefs and ministers from their posts, began also to swerve from the path of justice, as regards the settlement of matters. One day he ordered to death a certain subject, whom, according to law, it was not legal to kill: after the punishment he became repentant, and set about to avert and make amends for the same. The heirs of the murdered man, in the presence of the King, demanded justice from the Devotee: the state of the case having become known, the matter was referred to the tribunal of justice. At once the order of the judge was issued, to the effect that the Devotee should be slain by way of retribution. Though the Devotee produced intercessors, and promised wealth and riches, it was of no avail; and through the misfortune of sacrificing the service of the Creator to the companionship of the creature, having become engulfed in the whirlpool of destruction, he passed by the benefits of this world, and failed to attain an everlasting reward.

"Now I have recited this story on this account—since, having turned my face from the altar of divine obedience, I have hastened towards the King's Court, and having drawn my head from the line of the commands of my Providential Protector, I have placed it on the threshold of the monarch's service,

> I am worthy of any punishment which you can devise."

When Damnah had finished this interlude, the attendants on the royal throne remained astonished at his eloquence; the Lion, also, having in like manner dropped his head in reflection, did not know how to enter upon this matter, nor in what manner to answer Damnah. A certain Lynx, who was distinguished above all the courtiers as regarded royal access, when he discovered the bewilderment of those present in the assembly, turned his face towards Damnah, and said: "All this abuse which you have uttered respecting the service of kings, whose head, reaching to the stars, is exalted with the precious crown— '*A just king is the shadow of God upon earth*'—is not within your province. Perhaps you are not aware that one hour of the King's life, spent in dispensing justice and fostering his subjects, has been deemed equal to sixty years of obedience and worship; and many of the worshippers at the High Altar of piety and devotion, and the monarchs of the kingdom of revelation and miracles, have elected the service of Sultáns, since ' *The service of kings is half the road*,' with the view of helping the oppressed, and relieving the burden of the afflicted. Amongst such stories, that of the Enlightened-minded Saint is a·sound verification of this fact." Damnah inquired, "What was that?"

STORY VL

The Lynx replied: It has been related that in the city of Fárs there was a Shaikh, who had carried off the palm of excellence amongst the horsemen of the plain of sanctity,[1] and the summit of the crown of whose retirement had reached the top of the celestial Sphere.

> He, in the kingdom, having become a monarch and protector,
> Obtained a crown, by reason of his forsaking both worlds;
> Having galloped his horse through the plains of Eternity,
> He played the ball of everlasting 'chaugán.'[2]

They called him the Enlightened-minded Saint. The renown of his virtues was spread abroad throughout the regions of Rúm and the countries of the west, and the fame of his religious assemblies current amongst the inhabitants of Egypt, Damascus, the Hiiáz, and Yaman. The wits of 'Irák and the beauties of Kharásán alike placed their heads upon the line of affection for him, and the saints of Turkistán, no less than the lovers of Hindústán, extended the hand of friendship towards the skirt of veneration for him. One day, a Darwísh from Trans-Oxiana having conceived the idea of visiting the Shaikh's sacred precincts, after great hardships travelled from the region of Samarkand to the capital, Fárs. Assuredly, till the foot of search becomes wounded by the thorny ground of trouble, no person will, with the hand of attainment, reach the collar of the rose of Desire.

> When the nightingale cannot bear the burden of the thorn, it is better
> That it should never speak a word to the rose.

The wandering Darwísh, after crossing the desert of Mortification, alighted at the haven of peace and safety, and having with the lip of salutation kissed the ground of the Shaikh's threshold, raised the knocker of Desire. The servant of the monastery, after inquiring as to his case, and being informed as to the difficulties of the road, replied: "O Darwísh! stay here a bit, for his Excellency the Shaikh has gone awhile to wait on the Sultán, after which it will be his time to return." The Darwísh, when he heard mention of attending on the King, exclaimed: "Alas for the trouble of my journey, and the waste of time! What can I derive from a Shaikh, who enters the society of the Sovereign, and courts his conversation and discourse? and how can he show me the way of righteousness?"

> I had hoped, like a dog, to have expired at his feet.
> Alas! all such hopes have been in a moment scattered in the dust.

Accordingly, having quitted the monastery, he set his face towards the market. From the impurity of his own deceitful heart, which had not been tempered in the furnace of austerity, he struck a base impress upon the coin of the Shaikh's affairs, and, not being aware of the state of matters, gave utterance to inconsiderate reproaches.

> O thou! who complainest, while walking at the brink of the water,
> What knowest thou concerning the condition of us who plunge therein?

---

[1] This is Eastwick's suggestion.   [2] See note 1, page 138.

All at once, the eye of the city police officer lighted upon him. By chance, a thief, similar in appearance to him, had that night escaped from prison, and the King had severely rebuked the officer and patrol on account of their negligence, and caused them to use their best endeavours to discover the thief and cut off his hand. The officer saw the Darwísh, and, fancying that he was the escaped thief, at once caused him to be conveyed to the place of punishment. Though the Darwísh produced his credentials, and properly explained the state of the case, it produced no effect, and there appeared no help, but that he should have his hand cut off. At the time when the pitiless executioner had laid the sharp knife upon the hand of the Darwísh, and was about to amputate it, the cry of the Enlightened-minded Saint arose, and the Shaikh, in the midst of a magnificent detachment, arrived at that knot of people, and having inquired concerning the state of the case, was informed how the matter stood with the Darwísh. He said to the officer, " This is one of the holy men of my threshold; and the suspicion which you attach to him is unfounded : withdraw your hand from him." The officer, having kissed the hoof of the Shaikh's horse and returned his sincere obligations, apologised to the Darwísh, and went about his business. The hapless Darwísh, being delivered from the snares of death and the relentless hand of the executioner, proceeded along as one of the Shaikh's attendants. In the midst of their journey, the Exalted Saint laid his hand upon the Darwísh's shoulder, and whispered, " O brother! it is not seemly to reproach holy men, since, if we do not wait on the King, the afflicted like you would not be delivered from the hand of the oppressors." The Darwísh perceived that his own reproaches arose from ignorance and want of knowledge. Whatever proceeds from a man of excellence will be free from detriment. Since the desire of a perfect Shaikh mingles [1] in harmony with the will of God, therefore nothing will issue from him that is not in accordance with the designs of the Deity ; and no action of such person, though to appearance it may seem contrary to wisdom and intelligence, will be inexpedient.

> That son whose throat has been cut by the prophet Khizr [2]
> Will not recover his head by means of the common people.
> If his vessel be wrecked on the ocean,
> There would be hundreds of anxieties concerning the fate of Khizr.
> When his hands repair the damage,
> Assuredly the mischief will be mended :
> Should a person's head be severed from his body,
> He would produce a hundred thousand from the ground :
> Were a perfect man to touch the earth, it would become gold ;
> Were an ignorant fellow to handle money, it would turn to dust.

" The purport of reciting this story is this : great men in religion have made choice of serving the King, and have not been ashamed to attend the Court of Monarchs."

You, who are you, that you should in any way be held in estimation?

Damnah said: " What you have stated as to the great seeking admission to the service of kings is correct; but such proceeding has been with a view to some great advantage ; and they have not commenced without Divine inspiration, nor have they in any way allowed worldly or sensual objects to mingle therein : now, whoever is in such case, whatever he may do or say, no one will be bold

---

[1] Literally, "fades."　　　　　　[2] See note 4, page 158.

enough to reproach him. However, how should persons like ourselves attain such dignity, or how show ourselves entitled to covet such distinction? Again, as to what you have said, that the King is the Shadow of the Almighty, that also I grant; but it is one of the attributes of a monarch, that his actions should be nigh the road of rectitude, and far distant from the path of frivolity: he should neither foster any one with an ulterior object, nor inconsiderately order punishment: but the most meritorious of all the qualities of kings is to esteem attendants who possess good dispositions, while spurning those servants who are faithless and treacherous."

> The rose-bush of good men's affairs,
> He keeps verdant with the water of his condescension;
> While him who, thorn-like, is tyrannical towards people,
> He tears up root and trunk by his severity.

The Lion's Mother replied: "These words you are saying are true; but your case appears quite different, since all those present in this assembly agree that Shanzabah was a praiseworthy and laudable-natured attendant on the King: and it is on men's lips that the harvest of his hopes was consumed by the fire of your calumny, and the foundation of the King's confidence undermined by the baseness of your malignity."

> A flame was kindled by envy,
> The world was consumed by malevolence.

Damnah said: "It is not concealed from the King's enlightened mind, and all the Courtiers also are aware, that there did not exist between me and the Ox any sort of ill-feeling or enmity; how, then, can it be imagined that there was a long-existing feud? He himself, also, notwithstanding that he had the means to slay me, the opportunity to do me evil, and the power to ruin me, yet never pursued aught but the path of kindness and benevolence as regards me. Again, I was by no means so contemptible, and insignificant in the King's sight, as to busy myself injuring Shanzabah through malignity and hatred; but I advised the King, and communicated to the ears of my Sovereign, without any sinister motive, whatever utterances I heard, and saw the effects thereof. Now it was incumbent on me to recognise my obligations to the King for his kindness, and to narrate truly the appearance of treachery and evil designs on the part of the Ox. What I said, also, was investigated by the King himself, who verified my assertions and proved my statements: moreover, the thing was done according to the dictates of his own judgment. Many people, who were comrades of Shanzabah, and companions of his treachery and enmity, are now dreading me, who have made it my custom to speak the truth: '*Truth is bitter*' are true and correct words.

> All of whom I spoke honestly, at once became my enemies;
> Silence is always best, when one cannot proclaim the truth.

"Assuredly, hypocrites will endeavour to accomplish my destruction; but I never thought that the recompense of my advice, and the result of my service would be, that my mere existence should render the King pensive and sorrowful."

When Damnah's speech had arrived at this point, and the day was nigh spent, the Lion replied: " He must be made over to the Judges, so that they may investigate the matter: since, in sentences of punishment and cases of justice and equity, without clear explanation and necessary proof,

"It is not right that a decree should be put in force."

Damnah said: "What Judge is more righteous-dealing than the wisdom of the Monarch, and what Magistrate is more equitable than the perfect justice of the august King? but, thank God! the enlightened mind of the Sultán is a pure mirror—nay, more, a world-depicting cup,[1] wherein the circumstances of every one of his servants become manifest and clear.

> Having said to the volume of secrets, ' Be,' and it was,
> Your good pleasure was all-powerful with the leaves of Fate.

"Now I well know that, as regards removing the veil of obscurity, and drawing aside the curtain of doubt and suspicion, nothing is equal to the intelligence and prudence of the King, and certainly, when the mirror of his decrees is free from the rust[2] of envy and bias, I am confident that, if proper investigation be made my warrant of security will be brought to light, and my sincerity of heart, like the break of the lights of true morn, will become patent to mankind."

No one's secret will remain concealed when there is the brilliance of thy wisdom.

The Lion rejoined: "O Damnah! the investigation of this matter shall be pushed to the utmost extreme, and the examination of this affair pressed to the furthest limits of imagination."

> In the investigation of this speech I will use efforts,
> So strenuous, as even to extract a hair from a mass of dough;
> You know well that the very hidden secrets of the spheres
> I can altogether unravel by the brilliancy of my enlightened mind.

Damnah said: "By reason of my innocence, I am most anxious for such efforts and endeavours: for I am conscious that by this further investigation my sincerity will become still more clear; now, if in this matter I had committed any offence, I should not have continued as an attendant at the King's Court, nor should I, ruined, have sat awaiting for misfortune; but, repeating to myself the purport of the saying, ' *Therefore, go through the earth*,' should have departed to another kingdom."

Since wide is the earth's expanse.

The Lion's Mother said: "O Damnah! your endeavours concerning this investigation do not seem free from mental fear: you prudently desire to come forth innocent, but to seek escape from this difficulty without any question being asked about this matter of yours, is an absurd idea and vain expectation."
Damnah rejoined: "I have many enemies, and detractors concerning me are countless: my expectation is that the affair of mine may be intrusted to a Judicial Officer, who shall be free from bias and suspicion, and who shall correctly convey to the august ears whatever he may discover to have been said or heard, and that the King should represent this to his world-adorning judgment, which is the mirror of victory and conquest, so that I shall not be slain on mere suspicion, nor, on the Judgment-day, shall the reproach of my innocent blood arise."

---

[1] See note, page 83,   [2] See note 2, page 51.

I do not myself fear death: but
God forbid that your skirt should be defiled with blood!

The Lion said: "As regards any of my commands, I have not deviated from the path of justice, and I could not possibly set my feet in other than the road of equity: but if you have committed this treachery, you will meet with the punishment due to you."

What you sow in the field of life, that you will reap.

Damnah replied: "For what reason should I devise this perfidy; and by what means should the hankering after mighty undertakings, and the lust of exalted dignities, enter my mind? But I know the probity of the King, and have observed the evidences of his equity: assuredly, therefore, I shall not be deprived of his world-adorning justice, nor my hope be dissevered from the auspiciousness of his impartiality."

God created you to dispense justice;
Oppression does not proceed from a righteous King. ·

One of the Courtiers said: "What Damnah has spoken is not respectful to the King, but he seeks with such words to ward off his misfortune." Damnah rejoined: "Who is more kind to me, or who, as a friend, more devoted to me, than myself? whoever deserts himself in the place of need, and takes no care for his own preservation, what hope in him will remain to others?

Since you cannot look after your own business,
How can you attend to the affairs of others?

"Your speech is a proof of your want of understanding and judgment, and of your exceeding ignorance and error: but do not imagine that what has happened will remain concealed from the penetration of the Sovereign—nay, more, after deep reflection and kingly discernment, he will discriminate between your honesty and dishonesty, since his enlightened mind reviews in a single night the actions of a lifetime, and by mere thought brings immense armies under subjection."

His far-seeing, world-subduing penetration, in one moment,
Accomplishes such things as cannot be performed in a lifetime.

The Lynx said: "I am not so much astonished at your former treachery and deceit, as at your eloquence on the present occasion, your elucidatory discourses, smart sayings, and proverbs." Damnah replied: "Yes, this is the place for exhortation, if it rests on the seat of acceptance, and the time for proverbs, if they are heard by the ear of wisdom." The Lion's Mother rejoined: "O traitor! do you still hope to obtain your liberation by treachery and fraud?" "Not unless," said Damnah, "people return evil for good, or permit rectitude to be requited with censure. But, at any rate, I have discharged my promises of fealty, and fully performed my obligation of giving advice. The King well knows that no traitor could have the boldness to argue in his presence: if, as regards me, he permits oppression, the evil thereof will, too, recoil on himself, and if, in connection with my case, he displays haste, and becomes heedless of the advantages of deliberation, and the blessings of certainty and care, he will ultimately be sorry; for it has been said,

'Whoever, in his proceedings, acts with haste,
Ruins the abode of his own reason.'

" Whoever, through hastiness, remains deprived of the benefits of patience, will
meet with that which befell the Woman, who, having in her affairs displayed
rashness, could not tell the difference between Friend and Slave." The Lion,
who was attending to the words of Damnah, when he heard this quaint speech,
inquired, " How was that ? "

STORY VII.

Damnah said : It has been related that, in the city of Kashmír, there was a
Merchant possessed of great wealth and property, as well as innumerable servants
and dependants. He had a wife, moon-faced, dark-haired, so that the eye of
Heaven had never seen such a Sun, nor had such an Idol ever come into the
hand of the world : her cheeks were resplendent and gorgeous, like the Day of
union, while her locks were black, and endless, like the Night of separation.

Her beauty rivalled the pearl of mid-day sun :
She darted glances from her languishing, narcissus-like eyes :
Her cheek was like a rose sprinkled with rose-water ;
Her waist was slender, her bosom raised :
She was sweeter than conserve of roses,
Softer to embrace than a delicate rose.

Nigh to the Merchant was a Painter, who, for his skill, was the pointing-stock
of the world, and by reason of his pictures was the delight of the populace.
From his face-depicting brush, the souls of the painters of China were bewildered in the valley of astonishment, and from the genius of his colouring the
hearts of the artists of Khatá were overwhelmed in the desert of perplexity.

With dexterity, that clever master,
Like the wind, drew pictures upon the water ;
Like as it were the ringlets and faces of heart-ravishing beauties,
He painted the representation of Night upon the panel of Day.
When he drew his brush on the tablet of Imagination,
Reason, like a vapour, instantly vanished away.

In short, between him and the Merchant's wife a feeling of affection arose, and
the Painter conceived an immoderate passion for that beautiful model : the Monarch of Love acquired dominion over the kingdom of the heart, which is the
capital of affection, and the army of Lust began to overrun the seven regions of
existence.

The Monarch of Love overpowered the kingdom of the heart and faith.

The eyes of the young lover, like the hearts of the religious, became wakeful, and
his restless eyelids, as April clouds, began to drop tears.

Every night, in my friend's quarter, like a candle, I bewail with anguish of heart ;
At one time raging with pain, at another lamenting through grief.

The Merchant's wife, also, having seen the young man, abandoned her heart to
him, and placed the volume of patience and forbearance upon the shelf of
oblivion.

My heart has now gone, and my breast, also, has lost its soul:
  Depart, O patience! since here is no place for you.

The charm of love coming into play on both sides, they managed to meet without the aid of a confidant, and the road of intercourse between them was free
from the dust of rivals.   One day the woman said to him: "On every occasion
that you honour me with your presence, and adorn and illuminate my cell with
your beauty, doubtless [1] time elapses while you are making a sound by casting a
stone.   If, by the aid of painting—in which you are the leader of the age and
the chief of the period—you could, after thinking over the matter, design a picture,
and produce something which should be a sign between you and me, it would
by no means be unwise, but on the contrary prudent."   The young Painter
replied: "I will draw a two-coloured mantle, the whiteness of which shall be
like the stars shining in water, and the blackness thereof like the hair of a
Moor glittering upon the lobe of beautiful women's ears.   When you see that
signal, walk out quickly."   While they were thus communicating this arrangement to each other, one of the Painter's Slaves, who was standing behind a wall,
overheard them.

Hast thou a favour? open not your lips,
For behind the wall are many ears.

Several days elapsed, and the mantle was finished: the arrangement about their
meeting was then put in force.   One day the Painter had gone about some
business, and remained till late.   The Slave borrowed that mantle from the
Painter's daughter, on the pretence that he wished to find out the way in which
the colours were blended: having put it on, he went to the house of the fair
mistress.   The woman, without reflecting, from excess of delight at meeting her
beloved, did not distinguish between friend and rival, nor recognise stranger
from acquaintance.[2]
  The Slave, by means of that garment, obtained his desire, and after a while
returned the cloak.   By chance at that very moment the Painter arrived, and from
anxiety to see his mistress, having torn to pieces the garment of patience, threw
the cloak over his shoulders, and turned his face towards the Merchant's house.
The woman, having run back to him, made great protestations of love, and said:
"O friend! is all well that you have come back again this same hour?"   The
young man perceived what was the state of the case.   Having made an excuse
for coming, he at once returned, and learned the details of the affair.   He then
severely reproved his Slave and daughter, and burning the cloak, quitted the
society of his mistress.   Now if that woman had not been so hasty in the
matter, she would not have been defiled with the disgrace of the society of a
Slave, nor have been deprived of the company of a dear friend, or the intimacy
of a vital companion.

When you plant the tree of haste,
It produces the fruit of remorse.

"I have adduced this story that the King may know that he must not display haste in my case.   Now the truth is, I do not say this from fear of punishment, or dread of the King.   Though death is a sleep not to be desired, and
a repose not to be coveted, yet assuredly come it will, and many great men,

---

[1] For ﺑﻼﺷﮏ, I would suggest ﺑﯽ ﺷﮏ.
[2] A couplet is omitted as being not altogether suitable for English ears.

being struck down by its hand, have learnt that no one can possibly escape from the circuit of annihilation and decay : whoever places his feet in the world of existence, beyond doubt must drink the potion of fate, and clothe himself with the robes of destruction.

> Whom has Heaven placed in the sun of prosperity
> But at length, like early morn, it bestowed upon him but little permanence ?
> The tailor Fortune never, on the stature of any person,
> ، Sewed a shirt, but ultimately she rent it.

" If I had a thousand lives, and I knew that to give them up would be advantageous to the King, in an instant I would abandon them all, considering so doing as happiness in both worlds.

> If dear life were accepted by a beauty, like yourself,
> How could one keep back one's soul from her who is dear as life ?

" But it is incumbent on the King to look to the end of this matter, since he cannot preserve his country without men to wear swords, nor must he, on vain suspicions, slay trustworthy servants.

> You will remain alone, if you slay many friends.

" And servants who can properly conduct affairs cannot at all times be found, nor can dependants worthy of trust and deserving of patronage, be always brought to hand."

> It takes years before what was originally a stone, owing to the sun's rays
> Becomes a ruby in Badakshán, or a cornelian in Yaman.

The Lion's Mother, when she saw that Damnah's speech found the honour of a hearing in the ear of the royal approbation, was overcome with fear, lest all at once the Lion should place confidence in this gilded alloy, this truth-resembling hypocrisy, and these plausible falsehoods, and lest the softness of his speech, and smoothness of his language, should render the Lion indifferent as to the investigation of this matter. She turned towards the Lion, saying : " Your silence would lead to the belief that Damnah's words are honest and those of others false. I was not aware that in spite of your ability, penetration, intelligence, and wisdom, you are not affected by genuine speech, while you are moved by deceitful, vain words."

> How can the strains of the nightingale be acceptable to you,
> When you lend the ear of your understanding to the empty prating of birds ?

She then jumped up in a rage, and set out for her own home. The Lion commanded that they should bind Damnah and keep him in prison till the Judges, having investigated his case, should make clear the real truth. The Court of inquisition was dispersed. The Lion's Mother came to the Lion privately and said : " O son ! I have always heard what a marvel is Damnah ; now I am convinced that he is the prodigy of the age and the phœnix of the period : indeed, how could he speak all these glaring falsehoods, or in what way string together these captivating hypocrisies and sweet words ? He seeks such subtle means of escape, that were the King to give him opportunity to speak, he would with a single sentence extricate himself from this whirlpool. Now the truth is, in killing him the King and all his army will find great repose : it is better to let your mind be at rest respecting his case, and not to give him an opportunity of speech, or time for reply."

Haste is not proper, except in a good cause.

The Lion replied: "Envy and contention are the occupation of the attendants on Kings, and malevolence and strife the avocation of the nobles of the state: day and night they pursue one another, and seek out one another's faults and merits. The greater a man's worth, the more eagerly do they endeavour to overthrow him; and men of excellence meet with the greatest envy and jealousy, while malice is never directed against those without merit. Now Damnah is endowed with varied excellent qualities, and is one of my nearest attendants: maybe the envious, having leagued together, will desire by treachery to ruin him." The Lion's Mother replied: "How can malice arrive at such a pitch as to cast any one into the region of destruction?" The Lion said: "Envy is a fire which, when it flares up, burns everything, whether moist or dry; and excessive jealousy so influences a man, that he cannot see even what is for his own good—like as happened in the story of the three Envious persons." The Lion's Mother inquired, "How was that?"

STORY VIII.

The Lion replied: It has been related that three persons were travelling together, and having joined hands in friendship, set out on their journey. The eldest of them said to his two other comrades, "Why have you left your city and dwelling, and what is the cause of your wandering, since you prefer the discomfort of travelling to the luxury of neighbourship?" One of them replied: "For this reason: in the village where I was, things occurred which, being unable to witness, envy overpowered me, and perpetually I was consumed with the fire of jealousy. I thought to myself that for two or three days I would quit my native soil, so haply I might no longer behold what was unfit to be witnessed." The other comrade added: "I also, having been stricken with the same grief, elected to quit my country." The elder companion said: "You both are fellow-sufferers with myself, since from a similar trouble I have set my face towards the desert."

I speak the truth: I cannot witness
My companions eating while I myself look on.

When they discovered that they were all three of an envious nature, owing to kinship they journeyed along mutually pleased. One day a purse of gold having fallen in the way, all three together stopped there, exclaiming, "Come, let us divide the money, and also return hence to our own country, and pass two or three days in ease." The jealous disposition of each of them being aroused, they none of them consented, and each remained in a state of alarm lest another should get a share — they neither had determination to pass by the money, and leave it where it had fallen in the middle of the road, nor power to divide it amongst themselves. They remained one whole day and night in the wilderness, hungry and thirsty. Depriving themselves of sleep and food, they began to quarrel; but the affair remained unsettled amongst them.

The affairs of this world, which are endless,
Are a sea, which is without bounds:

On that account men of low ambition have fallen
Beneath that calamity for which there is no remedy.

Next day, at morn, the King of that country came out hunting, and arriving, with a body of his nobles, at that very spot, saw those three individuals sitting in the midst of the desert. Having inquired concerning the matter, they correctly represented the state of the case, saying, "We three persons are endowed with an envious disposition, for which reason, having quitted our hearths and homes, we are wandering about: here, too, the same quality shows itself, and the matter having ended in vexation and helplessness, we are anxious for a Judge who shall issue orders respecting the division of the money amongst us."

Thank God! we have obtained what we require.

The King said: "Each of you explain the nature of your jealousy, so that I may see the extent of your several deserts, and divide the money amongst you accordingly." One replied: ".My jealousy is of a degree, that I never wish to favour or act kindly towards any one, lest that person should become happy and comfortable." The next said: "You are a good man, without an atom of envy : my jealousy is of a kind, that I cannot see any one act benevolently towards another, or help him with his own property." The third individual added: "You both have no part in this matter, and your pretensions are preposterous. I for my part am such an one, that I never wish that any person should either befriend me, or do me a turn; so what could I desire as regards another ? " [1] The King seized the finger of astonishment with the teeth of deliberation, and was amazed at the speeches of those badly-disposed persons, upon the tablet of whose nature was visible the wretched inscription, " *Do they bear envy against men ?* " He said: " Even by your own words this money is not due to you, and each one deserves a punishment according to his offence. In the case of him who is unwilling to do a kindness to another, the retribution is that he should remain deprived of the advantages of reward, and should suffer loss and disappointment in both worlds : as regards him who cannot suffer kindness on the part of one person towards another, it is best that he should be at once freed from the bonds of existence, and the burden of such misery be removed from his soul : as for the third person, who is envious of himself, and seeks no good in his own behalf, it is right that he should be punished with various tortures and chastisements, and being for a long while held in the clutch of reproach and retribution, should taste the food of punishment, till the bird of his soul is caught in the snare, ' *Say, the Angel of Death, receives you.*' " Accordingly, he ordered that the first person should be left in that desert bare-headed and bare-footed, without any food or provisions, and that whatever he possessed should be taken away from him; and said :

"Towards him who wishes no good to any one,
No consideration must be expected.
Every plant which does not yield fruit
Must be pruned with the knife."

He also commanded that the second envious person should be beheaded with a ruthless sword, and be freed from the grief of his jealousy : while, as regards the third person, being rubbed with pitch, he was driven out in the sun, till, after

[1] Literally, " what will arrive to another."

a while, in great distress, he died. Thus he punished and revenged the shame-less envy of those three persons; and the truly great have said:

> "That ill which has no remedy is envy;
> The habit of envy is the way of demons and wild beasts.
> It is said, ' A jealous man is the enemy of mankind,
> Since, if you observe closely, he is even his own foe.' "

No misery is greater than that of envy, since the jealous person is always melan-choly at the pleasures of mankind, and miserable at the joys of others.

> Poor mortal man passes life in this sorrow,
> As to what is the reason that such a one exists.

"Now the moral of this story is, that it may be known that envy may reach such a pitch, that a person will not seek even his own advantage; hence it may be inferred to what extent he will desire that of others. I suspect that the story about Damnah may be the creation of envious parties." The Lion's Mother said: "I have not understood that the attendants at this Court are of a jealous disposition, nor have I any suspicion of their possessing such a detest-able quality. The probability is, that all are agreed together respecting his death, in consideration of the King's welfare; but whether or not, his destruction does not stand in need of such preliminaries." The Lion replied: "I have some doubts about this matter, and, with the view of dispelling them, I will display no haste in this affair of Damnah, lest, in benefiting others, I seek my own ruin, and, in pleasing the creature, I bring down the anger of the Creator. Unless I investigate the matter to the utmost, I shall not hold myself excused for killing him; since as regards Shanzabah,[1] with reference to whom I acted precipitately, I am compelled to undergo all this regret. It is not right that, on mere suspicion, I should ruin men of merit or persons of ability, and till the beauty of certainty displays its countenance in front of the screen of doubt, I will not issue any retri-butory order: nor will I neglect the purport of this saying, which originated from the exalted mind, and flowed from the pure genius, of one of the greatest of men:

> ' When your eye alights upon any fault,
> Reflect well respecting the punishment;
> For the ruby of Badakshán is easily broken;
> Once damaged, it cannot again be made whole.
> He who, with precipitancy, puts his hand to the sword,
> With his teeth will gnaw the back of the hand of regret.' "

The conversation between the Lion and his Mother concluded, and they both retired to their own apartments. When Damnah was taken to prison, and heavy chains were placed on his feet and neck, brotherly affection and friendly com-panionship impelled Kalílah to go and see him. As soon as he entered the prison, his eyes alighted upon Damnah. Tear-drops beginning to trickle from the clouds of his eyes, he exclaimed: "O brother! how can I see you in this misery and affliction? and after this, what pleasure in life will there be to me?"

> Without you, O rest of my soul! how can I live?
> Since you are not in my embrace, how can I be joyful?

---

[1] شُنْزَنَه in the Persian text is a misprint for شُنْزِبه .

Do you say, 'Manage away from me and live without me'?
I have acted the king, how can I take the part of a shepherd?

Damnah, also, broke into lamentation, exclaiming:

In my case separation from beloved friends
Wounds my soul, and lacerates my heart.

"All this trouble and difficulty, this misfortune of imprisonment and heavy fetters, do not so much concern me, as that I must be content to be parted from you, and be consumed with the fire of separation."

There is not a night but what, through separation from the taper of thy face,
My heart is scorched by the fire of grief;
Not a moment passes, but what, from soul-consuming separation,
My pallid countenance is stained with tears of blood from my eyes.

Kalílah replied: "O Damnah! since the matter has reached this pitch, and the affair ended in this manner, if in my present conversation with you I am harsh, it is no matter; for from the commencement of the case I foresaw all this, and used my best endeavours to advise you; but you paid no attention thereto, and were helped along by a weak intellect and faulty judgment; now it has happened, at last, as I said.

I said, 'O dear friend! do not go there, lest you be entangled.'
You ultimately went, and what I spoke also befell you.

"If, at the first, I had failed to advise you, or had been negligent in admonishing you, to-day I should have been a partner with you in this perfidy, and I could not have spoken such words as these. O imprudent person! did I not repeat to you the warnings of the learned, in that they have said in this matter, that 'the slanderer dies before his fated time;' now, the fact is, not that there is severance from life and the destruction of the pleasures of existence, but rather that grief arises which renders life irksome, and death every moment desirable, just as has happened in your case: assuredly, death is better than such a life."

Your heart being so worn with grief,
Non-existence is a thousand times better than life.

Damnah said: "O brother! you always spoke what was proper, and carried out the obligations of advice;[1] but greediness of soul, avidity after wealth, and the desire of dignity, weakened my intellect, and made your admonition of none effect in my mind. Though I was aware that the misery of this matter was endless, and the danger thereof without bound or limit, yet I entered thereon with the utmost eagerness: just as a sick man, whom the desire of eating has overpowered, though he is conscious of the evil of so doing, yet he pays no heed thereto, and acts according to his inclination: and such a person as cannot abandon the pursuit of sensual lusts, must undergo whatever accrues of misery and distress, and, if he complains, must also complain of himself."

I do not complain of any stranger, since, as regards my heart,
Whatever grief has overtaken it, has arisen from my own self.

Kalílah rejoined: "A prudent man is he, who, at the commencement of every

---

[1] بميت in the Persian text is a misprint for نميت.

matter, casts a glance at the termination thereof, and, previous to planting a tree, regards its fruit, so that he may not regret his deeds, nor be vexed about what he has said; since such remorse and regret will avail nothing, but to rejoice one's enemies, and grieve one's friends."

> What avails regret at last, when at the outset you did wrong?

Damnah said: "O brother! to be without an enemy is the condition of men of mean aspirations, and to pass life in security and live in pleasure is the part of all paltry and senseless persons; wherever there is exalted ambition, the individual has no means of avoiding severe distress and great danger."

> When with the club [1] of ambition you can bear off the ball of your desire,
> Place your feet in this plain, but first of all you must abandon hopes of life.

Kalílah replied: "Transient prosperity, and unstable dignity, are not worth all this grief and labour.

> Do not seek the fruit of delight in the expanse of the garden of Fortune,
> The less on this account that the fruits from that garden are the vicissitudes
>   of the World.

"You should not have cast the light of your regards upon this world's wealth and dignity, so that you would not have fallen into the pit of grief and distress: nor should you have planted the tree of malevolence and envy, so that you would not to-day have plucked the fruit of sorrow and misfortune." Damnah said: "I know that I have scattered the seed of this calamity, and whoever sows anything will assuredly reap the same.

> Good from good you see, and bad from bad;
> From barley, barley springs, and wheat from wheat.

"Now, having sown a poisonous plant, I cannot expect a honey-yielding rose. In the present juncture the matter has passed out of my grasp, and my hand is incapacitated. The tip of the finger of deliberation cannot loosen the knot of Fate, nor will the countenance of rectitude display itself in the mirror of meditation. I have become aware of my own fault, and can see my own error, and have perceived that the royal gem of Fortune is not worth the danger of the whirlpool of anxiety."

> At first, through the attraction of gain, the toil of the sea appears easy enough,
> I was in error in speaking thus, since an hundred pearls are not equivalent to
>   one tempest.

Kalílah inquired: "In what way have you now planned your deliverance, and by what pass have you marked out the road of escape?" Damnah said:

> To seek the way of escape from the entanglements of thy love
> May be difficult, since the breaches of deliberation are closed.

"It appears as though the ship of Life will be engulfed in this whirlpool of destruction, and the sun of Existence will set in the west of annihilation and death; but I will not by any means give way to imbecility, and, so far as cunning and deceit will help matters, I will spare no effort to extricate myself. But

---

[1] See note 1, page 138.

my grief is the more on this account, that, God forbid, you may be suspected with me, and by reason of the intimacy, bordering on the utmost limits of friendship, which has existed between us, you may fall into the whirlpool of destruction; and if, God forbid! they importune you to disclose what you know of my secrets, then my distress will display itself in two ways: 1st, Grief for your own self, and shame because that, on my account, you have fallen into trouble. 2d, No hope of liberation will remain to me because the integrity of your speech is manifest to every one, and to rebut clear evidence from such an one as you, who have reared the edifice of your affairs on rectitude and uprightness, will be impossible. On this supposition, the meeting between you and me will not occur till the Day of Judgment, and we shall not see one another till the Last Day." Kalflah replied: "I have heard what you have said: you know that I cannot be patient under pain, nor can I undergo the agony of torture or the anguish of punishment: I can neither conceal what I know, nor, with the view of being affable, tell any falsehood or invention: or ever they inquire of me, I shall repeat what has happened. Your best course is to confess your fault, and acknowledge what has occurred on your part, and, by repentance and penitence, deliver yourself from everlasting perdition: since you know of a certainty that in this matter your end is destruction, at any rate let not the punishments of this world be added to the agonies and torments of eternity: if in this transitory kingdom you suffer the woes of misery, at least, in the regions of futurity do not taste the bitters of punishment." Damnah said: "I will reflect on these matters, and take counsel with you as to what occurs to my mind." Kalflah, sad and full of grief, returned, and, having relieved his heart with varied anguish and distress, placed his back upon the bed of agony, and all night long twisted about: when morning arrived, his excitement abated.

It went, and scattered such desires in the mire.

But during the time when these words passed between Damnah and Kalflah, a thief, who, too, was confined in that prison, being asleep near them, was awakened by their conversation, and heard all their talk: he bore it in mind, and reserved it till an opportunity presented itself.

Every word has its time, every speech its place.

Another day, when the golden-clawed Lion of the Sun moved into the blue-coloured region of the sky, and the black-faced profligate Jackal of Night became concealed in the prison of seclusion,

The World became enlightened with the justice of day;
Oppression-producing night folded up her skirt.

Once more the Court of Inquisition was prepared and arranged. The Lion's Mother, having commenced afresh the case of Damnah, said: "To leave the wicked alive is tantamount to killing the innocent, and to do good to the bad is equivalent to injuring the righteous.

To act kindly to the bad is the same
As doing wrong to the righteous.

"Whoever, notwithstanding he has the power, leaves the wicked alive, or befriends the oppressor, becomes a companion in their guilt and infamy, and the threat, ' *Whoever assists the tyrant, God will make the latter overcome him,*' will overtake him.

> Do not wrong, and be not friends with the wicked;
> Be not delighted and merry with any bad person.

The Lion commanded the Judges to use the greatest expedition in conducting Damnah's case, and every day to represent what had occurred respecting either his treachery or integrity: accordingly, the Judges, Nobles, Dignitaries, Senators, both great and low, were present in the Private Council room and Public Tribunal. The Judges' deputy turned his face towards the members of the assembly, and said : " The King once more is using the utmost endeavours to investigate the case of Damnah, and to inquire into the charges which have been imputed to him, and has enjoined that, until the countenance of his affairs shall be free from the dust of suspicion, no other case shall be taken in hand. It is incumbent that the order which shall be passed concerning him shall not be inconsistent with the demands of justice, and shall not deviate or swerve from the road of rectitude towards violence and oppression. You must severally state what is known to you, since amongst the objects of thus speaking three distinct benefits are included. 1st, To assist in what is right, or to hoist the standard of rectitude and probity—both avails much according to divine law, and also, by the rites of manliness and the code of honesty, is of unspeakable value. 2d, To overthrow the edifice of oppression, or to lay waste the foundation of iniquity, and punish the deceitful, is in accordance with the will of the Creator, and in harmony with the nature of the majority of his creatures. 3d, To escape from men of treachery and hypocrisy, or to be secure from the fraudulent and wicked, is advantageous, and brings repose to all concerned." When this discourse terminated all present were silent, and in no quarter did any reply appear —since in this matter of Damnah, not having ascertained anything accurately, they were unwilling to speak ought on mere suspicion, lest, owing to their language, a decree should be issued, and from words which they might utter in a spirit of uncertainty blood might be spilt. Now when Damnah observed this state of affairs his heart became invigorated and radiant, like the Garden of Paradise from the spring breeze. However, frowning like those overwhelmed with grief, he said : " O nobles of the faith and government ! O chiefs of the country and religion ! if I had been a criminal I should have been delighted at this silence ; but I am innocent, and whoever is free from crime has no one's hand against him, and if to the extent of his ability he uses his best efforts in his own behalf, he will stand excused. Now I enjoin you on your oath, each of you, if you know anything of my affairs, to divulge it truthfully, pursuing therein the path of justice. As retribution will follow every word, therefore it behoveth him whose speech, as regards revealing the truth or destroying a person, is equivalent to a decree, to represent matters without admixture of surmise or conjecture, but rather in accordance with accuracy and certainty. Whoever shall cast me into the region of destruction through doubt and suspicion, will meet with that which befell the Doctor who possessed neither knowledge nor experience." The Judges inquired, " What was that ? "

STORY IX.

Damnah replied : It has been related that a person, without the capital stock of knowledge, or the ornament of experience, laid claim to be a Physician. He possessed neither consummate skill nor sound judgment. As regards his knowledge of medicines, he was ignorant to such a degree, that he could not distinguish between a Cocoa-nut and Turkish Wormwood ; while in the diagnosis of diseases he was inexperienced to such a point, that he could not discriminate between Ophthalmia and the Gout. In his acquaintance with compounds he overlooked the nature and quantities of drugs, and in writing prescriptions he took no account as to the quality or quantity of food or drink.

> A worthless Doctor, whoever saw his countenance
> Never again beheld the face of life.

Now in the city where this person had opened the shop of ignorance, and issued his death-dealing proclamation, was another Physician, famous for the perfection of his skill, and renowned for the happiness of his remedies and the good fortune attendant on his footsteps. His breath was entrancing like the spirit of 'Ísa, and his footsteps soul-reviving like those of Khisr.[1]

> When he wished it, with one or two breaths, versatile misfortune
> Descended from its unstable revolving dome.
> Such was the blessedness of his step, that were he to have entered the garden,
> He would have cured the aspen of its tremblings.

As it is the wont of treacherous Fortune, that men of merit invariably find nought but the dish of vexation at the head of the board of adversity, while those without worth carry off from the table of her benefits the dainties of great honour and dignity,

> The times will not buy merit, therefore I am broken-hearted :
> Where shall I go to trade with such unsaleable wares ?

the affairs of this most learned man of the age, and phœnix of the time, declined, and the star of the light of his eyes became overwhelmed in the eclipse of weakness. Gradually the light of the world-beholding sight of that dear man, by whom the vision of men of wisdom was illuminated, and the contemplation of the garden of whose beauty was to the pupil of the eyes of those endowed with sight, more lovely than the spectacle of a parterre or rose-bed, began to drow dim, till at length there remained no traces of brilliancy therein. Helpless, he sat retired in the corner of his abode, while that public-deceiving ignoramus began to put forward claims beyond all reason.

> The Fairy conceals her face, while the Demon coquettes and toys,
> Reason is consumed with astonishment as to what is this marvel.

In a short space of time he became intrusted with medical cases in that region, and the fame of his cures was carried, by deceitful report, in men's mouths and tongues. The King of that city had a daughter, like to whom no Sun had displayed itself on the horizon of beauty, nor had the perfume-seller Morn displayed any musk like that of her sweet-scented curling ringlets.

---

[1] A celebrated prophet—see note 4, p. 158.

M

> Moon-faced, musk-scented, heart-enchanting,
> Life-refreshing, soul-enticing, and Moon-like.

He had given her to his own brother's son, and the marriage and nuptials were celebrated with regal grandeur and royal splendour.

> The Sun had become the guest of the Moon,
> Venus had conjoined with Jupiter.

From the conjunction of these two auspicious stars a royal pearl was formed in the shell of her womb. By chance, at the time of her delivery, an accident happened, and a grievous illness befell the King's daughter. Having summoned the skilful Physician, they informed him of the nature of the malady. The learned Doctor, having been apprised of the exact state of the case, made a diagnosis of the disease, and said: "The cure of this malady is procurable by a medicine which is called Mihrán. Let a fourth part of a dram thereof be taken, and being pounded and sifted, let it be mixed with a little pure musk and cinnamon, and sweetened with sugar-candy: let it then be given to the patient, when her ailment will at once mend." They exclaimed: "O Doctor! where is that drug, and from whom must it be sought?" He replied: "I have seen a bottle of that medicine in the Imperial wine-cellar, placed in a box made of virgin silver, and bound with a lock of pure gold thereon, but now, from weakness of sight, I am powerless to bring it forth. Just at this time the pretending Physician came in, and said: "It appertaineth to me to discover that medicine, for I well know the composition of that mixture." The King, having summoned him to his presence, commanded him to go to the wine-cellar, and bring out such medicines as were necessary, and prepare that potion which the Physician had ordered. The ignorant Doctor went into the wine-cellar, and sought for a box of the description mentioned by the Physician, but as there were many boxes of that same sort, he failed to discover the medicine mentioned, and having indiscriminately carried off one of them, he brought it away. It happened not to contain the medicine they called Mihrán; but a little deadly poison, which had been put aside for state occasions, was concealed in that casket. He opened the lid of the box, and mixed that poison with some other compound, and having made a potion, gave it to the girl. As soon as she tasted it, she gave up sweet life. The King having witnessed this circumstance, through warmth for the loss of his daughter, raised the flame of lamentation to the firmament of Heaven, and commanded that the remainder of the potion should be given to the ignorant Doctor, so that he also expired on the spot, and retribution for his improper conduct immediately overtook him.

> It is a good proverb, "Whoever does wrong
> Harms not others, but rather himself."

"Now I have adduced this story that it may be known that every action performed through ignorance will terminate unfortunately, and every matter prompted by doubt and suspicion will be entirely encompassed with dangers." One of the attendants exclaimed: "O Damnah! you are of that class of persons, the malignity of whose minds is evident to those of high estate, and the impurity of whose disposition is manifest to the ordinary populace; the crookedness too, of your character accords with your form, shape, and figure." The Judge inquired: "Whence do you utter these words, and what ground have you for such language? You must adduce proofs thereof, and explain the reasons of your statement." He replied: "Physiognomists have adduced as a distinguishing mark that whenever a person has wide eyebrows — the right eye being smaller than the left, both being perpetually addicted to blinking—the nose inclining towards the left, and the glance constantly being directed towards the ground, his detestable disposition will be a mass of wickedness and deceit, and a heap of villany and treachery : now these indications are to be found in him." Damnah replied : " In the Omnipotent Decrees there is no possibility of partiality nor hypocrisy, and in the actions of the Divine Majesty there is no suspicion of omission, neglect, error, or mistake.

> Error and negligence are allowable in you and me,
> But no mistakes proceed from the Creator of the world.

" If these indications, which you have mentioned, can be considered reliable proofs and sound evidence—whereby truth can be distinguished from falsehood, wrong from right, and honesty from deceit—then men are freed from giving evidence and taking oaths, and Judges remain quit of lawsuits and actions : hereafter, too, no one will think proper to praise goodness, or deem it befitting to reproach wickedness—since no creature can get rid of those indications which, at the time of the creation of his being, were incorporated with him : therefore, according to the point you have cited, the punishment of good men, and the retribution of the wicked, are effaced from the pages of the decrees of law and justice. Now, if I had done this thing (*Heaven defend us therefrom !*) which has been alleged, it was for the very reason that these indications compelled me to such a course, and since it was not within the pale of possibility to avoid so doing, it is not proper that I should be overtaken with the punishment thereof.

> In this garden do not reproach me for what is self-grown :
> As I am nurtured, so do I grow.

" Accordingly, by your own words, I am freed from the bonds of misfortune, while you have given clear proofs of your ignorance and imposture, and with unknown words and groundless representations, with worthless pretensions and unheeded talk, have made an unacceptable entrance to the assembly of the learned."

> The learned elders, from the style of your discourse,
> Discovered the extent of your ignorance.

When Damnah answered in this manner, all the attendants placed the seal of silence upon the casket of their speech, and no one was able to utter a breath more. The Judge ordered them to take him back to prison, and convey a description of what had occurred to the Lion. As Damnah entered the prison, a friend of Kalílah, whom they called Rúzbih,[1] passed by him. Damnah sent after him, saying : " Since yesterday I have had no tidings of Kalílah, and at the present time I am very anxious to inquire after him.

> He is a friend who grasps the hand of his companion
> In adversity and distress.

" What news have you of him, and what excuse do you bring for his not coming ?" Rúzbih, on hearing the name of Kalílah, heaved a deep sigh from his distressed heart, and dropping tears of blood from the clouds of his eyes, exclaimed :

---

[1] Fortunate day.

> "His life has departed, where shall I seek a friend?
> His speech has ceased, to whom shall I tell my circumstances?"

Damnah was impatient at Rúzbih's distress, and cried out, "Tell me quickly the state of affairs." Rúzbih replied, "O Damnah! what shall I say?

> My soul is consumed, through separation from my friend;
> My heart is wounded, and I possess no remedy.
> Like a taper, the thread of my life is consumed from anguish of soul;
> Through pain of heart I cannot draw my breath.

"O Damnah! that dear friend has removed his chattels from this transient abode to the realms of Eternity, and placed the scar of separation on the hearts of his companions and acquaintances."

> O comrades alas! for we are without friends—
> We remain captives in the hands of the pain of separation.

Damnah, as soon as he heard tidings of the death of Kalílah, fell down senseless. After a long while, having recovered his consciousness, he broke into lamentation, and in tones of grief cried out with tears in his eyes:

> "Alas that the root of the rose-bush of joy is severed!
> What a pity that the fruitful branch of gladness no longer remains!
> O heart! heave a sigh, for thy repose of soul is gone.
> Alas! rain tears of blood, for light no longer remains to the eyes."

After Damnah had grieved beyond all limit, tearing with the hand of sorrow the garments of patience, perpetually rubbing his face in the dust, and lamenting in such a manner that no one could bear to listen to him, Rúzbih commenced to give his advice, saying: "O Damnah! you yourself know that the eternal Penman has not inscribed the name of perpetual existence upon the scroll of any created being, nor has the Delineator of human forms drawn the picture of life upon the pages of possibility, save with the pen, '*Everything shall perish except the face (of God) Himself.*' Neither, again, has the Tailor of the eternal workshop sewn the garment of any creature's existence without the fringe of annihilation, nor has the Chamberlain of the palace of omnipotency lit the taper of genius without the blast of adversity.

> Ever since Heaven has been the Architect of this building, except accompanied
>   by the thorn of grief,
> No one has ever discovered in the Garden of Life the rose of happiness.
> Nor in the Rosary of Existence, in Fortune's pasture,
> Was fresh Spring ever found free from the after-blasts of Autumn.

"This is a potion for all to drink, and a toilsome burden for all to bear. There is no salve for this wound save patience, nor any remedy for this disease but necessary endurance."

> Patience is necessary; for this pain of heart
> Has no remedy save long-suffering.

Damnah found complete comfort with these words, and said: "O Rúzbih! in thus lamenting, right is on my side, since Kalílah was a dear friend of mine and a sincere brother, on whom, in contingencies, I used to rely for protection, and by whose intelligence, knowledge, kindness, and advice I used to be aided on important occasions. His mind was a treasury from which the World could not gain any intelligence of the coin of secrets placed therein, and the spy, Time, remained hopeless of acquiring any information thereof. Alas that such a dear friend should have removed his prosperous shade from my head, and left me in the nook of this world's abode without companion, associate, comrade, or confidant !

To whom shall I tell my secret, since my confidant no longer exists ?
How shall I apply a remedy, since my intimate friend no longer remains ?

"After this, what pleasure will there be in life, and what benefit will accrue from the capital stock of existence ? Now, were it not that just at present a variety of ideas might enter people's minds, I would kill myself with weeping and lamentation, and free myself from the grief of solitude and the affliction of friendlessness—since from this whirlpool, wherein I have fallen, there is no chance of escape without the aid of friends and the assistance of allies."

Now apart from the street of hope, desolation must reign ;
When the remedy is beyond one's hands, one must remain helpless.

Rúzbih replied: "If Kalílah has slipped away from the expanse of life to the thorny ground of destruction and death, the tree of affection amongst other friends is fresh and verdant with the dew of intimacy."

Be not sad, should the branch of the rose be withered in this garden ;
The face of the wild rose is verdant, and the curls of the hyacinth resplendent.

Damnah said: "You say truly; your existence may be made the remedy for every ill, and your life the cure for every evil. To-day you are to me that very same friend and brother which Kalílah was; extend your hand and accept me as your brother." Rúzbih with the greatest joy advanced and said: "By this kindness you have pledged me to gratitude, and raised the standard of my glory to the highest summit. In what way can my faithful heart quit itself of the return for this consideration, or how can my praise-scattering tongue requite this kindness ?" Having then taken one another's hands, they tied the knot of brotherly affection ; and, as is customary and usual when swearing oaths, they agreed upon the conditions of friendship and intimacy. Damnah said : " In such a place is some hidden treasure belonging to Kalílah and myself; if you will take the trouble to bring it here, your labour will not be without reward." Rúzbih, according to Damnah's directions, brought the treasure. Damnah having separated his portion, gave Kalílah's share to Rúzbih, and requested him always to be at the door of the King's court, and ascertaining anything which might occur respecting him, to apprise him thereof. Rúzbih carried out this arrangement till the day of Damnah's death.

It is obligatory to perform one's promise.

Next day at morn the Lion's Mother, being present, inquired as to what had passed at the last meeting. The Lion narrated the circumstances of the case just as the Judges had represented them to him. The Lion's Mother, being apprised of the purport thereof became dejected, and said : "If I use harsher language, it may not be in accordance with the King's ideas ; while if I wink at the affair, the direction of sincerity and kindness will be abandoned." The Lion replied : " In reciting the chapters of sincere advice, respect and humility are not allowable. Now your words, without doubt, being free from the suspicion of un-

certainty, will very speedily be received with approval; tell me what you know."
The Lion's Mother said: "The King makes no difference between truth and falsehood, nor does he distinguish between his own advantage and disadvantage.
Now Damnah, having found an opportunity, will raise sedition, to quell which
enlightened intellects will be powerless, and sharp swords will fail to remedy
it." The Lion said: "Do not be absent to-day; it may be Damnah's case
will be settled." Accordingly, the exalted mandate was issued that once again
the Judges should meet together, and in the common assembly investigate afresh
the matter respecting Damnah. Both high and low came together by reason of
this command. The Judge's deputy repeated the same speech as before, and
asked for evidence respecting the matter of Damnah from those present. No
one spoke a word concerning him, or uttered a syllable either good or bad.
The Chief Judge, turning towards Damnah, said: "Although those present
befriend you by their silence, yet the hearts of your companions are agreed
as to your villany, and inwardly consent to your death. Under these circumstances, what can life avail you in the midst of these people? Now it is most
befitting the wellbeing of your circumstances and end to confess your crime,
and with repentance and contrition free yourself from everlasting punishment.
From your death one of two pleasures will accrue—either you will cause others
to be freed, or you will yourself escape.

> The wise say that death comprises a kind of pleasure.
> In explanation of this they kindly vouchsafe the world this statement:
> They say that he who dies must be one of two sorts,—
> Either he is bad, mankind being wasted from his violence;
> Or he is an inoffensive good person, so that the inhabitants of the world
> Strive to love him, and give place to him in their hearts.
> If one who acts rightly, he is freed from this prison of trouble:
> If of a bad disposition, the populace is delivered from his wickedness.

"O Damnah! if you confess your crime, you will reap two advantages, the fame
of which will endure in the face of the world. 1st, The avowal of your perfidy,
with the view of attaining everlasting safety, and choosing the realms of eternity
and happiness, in the place of a transitory and calamitous kingdom. 2d, The
fame of your eloquence, your readiness of language and the renown of your
oratory and speech-making, as exemplified by these witty rejoinders which you
have made, and the clever excuses you have adduced, will be current in the
mouths of high and low. Your ability and boldness are known to the men of
this day, and every one constantly bears witness to your excellence and understanding. Appeal then to your intellect and be wise, in accordance with the truth
of this proverb, 'Death with a good name is better than life with a bad
reputation.'"

> For any one to die with a good end,
> Is better than to live with a bad reputation.

Damnah said: "The Judge ought not to issue an order through his own surmises
and the suspicions of others, without clear proof and evident reason; nor should
he neglect the meaning, '*In truth, a half opinion is a sin.*' Now, if such suspicion has befallen you, and your judgment is convinced of my crime, at any rate
I know my own business better; and to conceal my certainty by reason of the
doubts of others, is not in accordance with the proceedings of law, nor in harmony with the rules of religion. Notwithstanding that on the mere suspicion

that perhaps I laboured to destroy Shanzabah, you have indulged in all this talk, and have destroyed belief in me; yet if, without reason, I strive for my own destruction, and, without cause, consent to my own death, by what explanation can I be excused? or how shall I be quit of the saying, ' *And cast not yourselves with your own hands to destruction'* ? I well know that no person has such claims upon me as myself: accordingly, how could I allow in respect of myself that which I would not deem permissible as regards those beneath me, and to which, in manliness, I could not assent?

> If I exile myself I may;
> What have others to do with my affairs?

" O Judge! cease this language. If it is advice, it should be better than this; while, if it is to disgrace me, it is preferable that it should not proceed from the Judge,—since the words of magistrates are decrees wherein it is necessary to avoid error, negligence, jest, or folly. It is the more strange that you, who always used to speak wisely and be just, should in this contingency abandon the road of caution, owing to the decline of my fortune and my adverse circumstances, destroying, through your own doubts and the suspicions of malignant people, the eyes of rectitude with the ophthalmia of negligence.

> The palace of every heart is by you filled with joy;
> Why should you be the grief of my hopeful soul?
> Such a rose as yourself has not blossomed[1] in the Spring of this world:
> Is it allowable that you should torment me with endless thorns?

" The Judges of the Court of wisdom, by the signet of whose decrees the merit-cherishing deed is authenticated, have pronounced the following order—viz., that the coin of all evidence which is not adorned with the stamp of certainty is not accepted or deemed of full value in the mint of approbation; and whoever gives testimony in a matter of which he knows nothing, will meet with that which befell that Falconer." The Judge inquired, " What was that?"

STORY X.

Damnah replied: It has been related that there was a Landgrave well known for his grandeur, and renowned and celebrated for the dignity of his person and the excellence of his qualities.

> In manner heart-entrancing, in speech agreeable,
> Boundless in wisdom, in merit beyond compare.

Now this Landgrave had a wife of soul-ensnaring beauty, and so agreeable as to raise a tumult in the world: her lips were more life-giving than the waters of Immortality, and her mouth sweeter than a heap of sugar.

> Her face like fire, her cheeks like water,
> More radiant than the moon or sun;
> Her eyebrows formed a bow, her eyelids arrows—
> Such bow and arrows captivated a hundred hearts.

With perfect beauty and heart-ravishing charms were joined purity and chastity;

---

[1] ڪَشْت in the Persian text is a misprint for ڪُشْت:

and her tumult-exciting cheek was adorned with the mole[1] of devotion and abstinence.

> Her eyes having abandoned the affairs of the world,
> Were concealed behind the curtain of modesty :
> The mirror had not, from afar, seen her beauty,
> And was frightened to associate with her shadow.

The Landgrave also had a Slave from Balkh, extremely forward and fearless, who never restrained the pupil of his eyes from the contemplation of what was unlawful, nor did he cleanse the lust[2] of his breast from the dust of wickedness and vice. Now this slave was appointed to attend on the Landgrave as Falconer, and was allotted the duty of hunting birds. One day the glance of that servant lighted upon that chaste matron, and the bird of his heart became ensnared in the net of her love.

> The hawk of this sorrowing heart has tumbled into thy net,
> Many are the auspicious birds fallen by the arrow of thy glance.

The slave abandoned himself to despair : though he raised the knocker of approach, the door of intercourse was not opened ; and though he used treachery and fraud in the matter, it was of no avail.

> My blandishments and entreaties do not captivate my handsome friend ;
> Oh, happy they who enjoy fortune in the shape of fair damsels !

The Falconer, in his anxiety to hunt that peacock of the Garden of beauty, girded his loins with hope ; though he let fly the hawk of Deliberation in the atmosphere of Intimacy, it did not find its way to the nest of its desire.

> Go, place this net for some other bird,
> Since the nest of the phœnix is very high.

After becoming hopeless, as is the way of bad men, he sought to plot against her, and tried by means of treachery to disgrace her. Accordingly, he bought two Parrots from a hunter, and learnt one of them to say in the Balkhian tongue, " I saw the porter sleeping in the house with the mistress of the family ;" while he taught the other to say, " At any rate, I will tell nothing." After the space of a week, they committed those sentences to memory. One day the Landgrave had arranged a banquet, and was sitting negligently on the throne of ease. The Falconer came in, and by way of a gift brought in the birds : the Parrots began their sweet sugar-like discourse, and, according to their wont, repeated those above two sentences. The Landgrave was unacquainted with the language of Balkh, but, from their pleasant voice and apparent conversation, joy overspread his heart ; and being enchanted with those enrapturing, love-inspiring sounds, he made over the birds to his wife, so that, having attended to them, she should exert herself to mind them. The hapless woman, who was also ignorant of the birds' language, cherished them, and nourished enemies in the semblance of friends.

> I cherished a person, and at length was disgraced by him ;
> How could I know that I was fostering my own enemy ?

In short, the Landgrave became so familiarised with the Parrots, that he would not sit at the banquet without their pleasant notes and incomparable melodies ;

---

[1] See note, p. 23.   [2] There is a play upon a word meaning "atmosphere" and "lust."

and by reason of their exhilarating prattle, he closed his ears to the delightful melody of the lute, and the tumult-exciting murmurs of the harp. One day a number of persons from Balkh came as guests of the Landgrave, who caused the Parrots to be brought to the assembly which had been prepared for these people. The birds, as was their wont, began to repeat those two sentences. The guests, after hearing them, looked at one another, till at length, dropping the head of modesty, they remained astonished at what had occurred. The Landgrave observed that the fire of his friends' joy was quenched, and the sweet perfume of his guests' delight changed to astonishment and perplexity. He inquired respecting the circumstances of the case, and exerted himself to the utmost: though his guests made apologies, they did not reach the place of acceptance. One of them, who was bolder, said: " Maybe, O Landgrave ! you are not aware of what these birds say ?" He replied : " I cannot understand the meaning of those words ; but, by reason of their ravishing voice, joy and delight are visible in my heart. Pray apprise me of the purport of their words."

> Not for one night have I seen Sulaimán,[1]
> How can I know the language of birds ?

They narrated to the Landgrave the purport of the Parrots' words, and apprised him of the meaning of that speech. The Landgrave withdrew his hand from the bowl,[2] saying, " O dear friends ! pardon me, since I was not aware of their signification ; but now, after I am acquainted with the circumstances of the case, no further excuse remains. In our city it is not customary to eat anything in that house where the lady is immoral and unchaste." In the midst of this conversation the Falconer-slave exclaimed, " I often have seen this, and will give evidence." The Landgrave jumped up from his seat, and commanded his wife to be slain. She sent a certain person to him, and gave a message, saying, " O fortunate Lord !

> " Whether you approve my death, or grant me life,
> Whatever order you pass, your commands are absolute."

" But in this matter bethink yourself, and be not hasty.

> " Do not, inconsiderately, kill me, since I am in your hands."

" Men of wisdom deem it necessary to reflect over matters, especially before spilling blood—since, if death is requisite, the opportunity remains ; while if, God forbid ! an innocent person is rashly doomed to destruction, and afterwards it is found that he was not worthy of death, the remedy thereof would be beyond the pale of possibility, and the sin hang round the neck till all eternity."

> Be not eager to punish without reflection,
> So that ultimately you may not repent what you have done.

The Landgrave commanded that his wife should be brought near the assembly and put behind the curtain : he then repeated to her the circumstances of the case, and said : " Parrots are not of the order of men that their words are mingled with malignity—they tell what they have seen : the Falconer also bears witness in accordance with what they pretend. This is not an affair for which eloquence can demand an excuse."

> If the crime is such, it cannot be pardoned.

---

[1] Sulaimán or Solomon was supposed to be acquainted with the language of birds.
[2] Literally, " wine."

His wife replied : "The remedy for my case is an imperative duty : whenever my circumstances are accurately known, if I am worthy of death, in a moment your heart can obtain repose." The Landgrave inquired, "How can the truth of this matter be ascertained ? " The wife replied : "Inquire from the men of Balkh whether or not these birds know anything else in the Balkhian tongue beyond these two sentences ; and when it is found that they can say nought beyond these two speeches, it will occur to your mind that this barefaced, shameless wretch, who could not attain his desire with me, and whose base disposition and wicked malignity did not secure their object, has taught them that speech ; while if they can say anything else in that language, my death is allowable to you, and to live not permissible for me."

The Landgrave paid due heed, and for three days the guests carried on an investigation, but heard nothing from the Parrots beyond those two sentences. When it became settled that the wife was absolved, the Landgrave abandoned his intention of slaying her, and commanded that the Falconer should be brought. The latter, having taken a Hawk on his hand, came with beating heart, thinking that perhaps he might attain honour. The wife said, "O perfidious villain ! did you see me acting against the Lord's good pleasure ? " He replied, " Yes, I did." At the moment that he uttered these words, the Hawk which he had in his hand, having attacked his face, pecked his eyes, and tore them out. The wife exclaimed, "Assuredly such is the punishment of eyes which think they see that which was never visible ; and ' *The retaliation of evil should be an evil similar thereto.*' "

> That eye which is malignant had better be rooted out ;
> The evil eye everywhere is held in the utmost detestation.

"I have narrated this story that you may know that arrogantly to make accusations, or to bear witness to what has not been seen, is the cause of disgrace in this world and ignominy in the next." When Damnah had finished speaking, having written down all his words, they at once sent them to the Lion, who explained to his Mother what had happened. The Lion's Mother being apprised of the circumstances, said : "O King ! my endeavours in this matter have had no further advantage than that this cursed wretch is suspected ; now after a while his stratagems and treachery will be fixed upon encompassing the King's death, and he will bring the affairs of the Monarch and his subjects to ruin. He will practise towards all the pillars of the state even more than he deemed allowable in the case of Shanzabah, who was a sincere, kind, and esteemed minister, since from a wicked spirit nought but bad deeds proceed, and from an impure disposition nought but villany and audacity spring."

> Do not expect a blessed phœnix from an ominous eagle ;
> Do not anticipate that a sparrow will act the part of a hawk.
> When matters are such that the dignity of a villain is exalted, what wonder
> If the hand of rebellion be extended in every direction ?

This speech took great effect upon the Lion, who was overcome by severe and long meditation. He exclaimed : "O Mother ! tell me from whom did you hear the story about Damnah, so that I may have an excuse for destroying him ? " She replied : "O King ! to reveal the secret of any one who has confided in me is not allowable by the rules of politeness, and I must guard with the feelings of veneration any disclosure which may be intrusted to the storehouse of my keeping. I can go to this extent as to ask that person's permission ; and if he grants leave, I will reveal the matter to you." The Lion agreed. The Lion's Mother, having left his presence, and honoured her own court by alighting there, summoned the Leopard, and with manifold consideration and esteem, paid her respects to him, saying:

O thou, whose violence, like Fortune, tries mankind !
O thou, the Sun of whose fame spreads over the world !

"The varied courtesy which the King of the Beasts displays towards you is known, and the traces of royal preferment and assistance in your behalf are written upon the scroll of evidence : for this reason it is incumbent upon you to be grateful for his favours, so that according to the promise, '*If ye are grateful, assuredly I will increase my favour towards you,*' day by day the affection of the King may increase." The Leopard replied: "O Queen ! by the aid of what language can I express my thanks for the Regal consideration and Kingly favour which the Monarch of the world has bestowed and continues to pour upon this humble servant, and by what power can I represent one thousandth part, or one tittle of my gratitude ?

Even if you suppose that like a lily I represent all tongues,
How could I discharge the obligation of describing it ?

"With the foot of gratitude I have traversed to the utmost bounds the regions of the plain of veneration ; now also whatever illustrious orders the Queen of the world shall deign to issue, she will see nought but submission and obedience." The Lion's Mother replied :

You form a manly estimate of your duties ;
Carry them out with the utmost generosity.[1]

"*A favour is no favour till complete.*"

"The King from the very first narrated to you what was in his mind, and you were intrusted with the obligation, as regards retribution for Shanzabah, of trying with every effort possible to obtain aught from the treacherous enemy.

Now you must discharge that obligation.

"The right course is for you to make obeisance to the King, and truly repeat what you have seen and heard ; otherwise the deceit of Damnah has had such effect that the Lion will abandon the idea of killing him. In such case no other person at the Lion's court will be safe from his malignity ; and in a short time, with treacherous wickedness, he will bring ruin to the fortunes of chiefs and people of authority, and he may with calumny and treachery design to destroy any one who has taken an active part respecting his case, or who has strived to accomplish his death." The Leopard replied : "O Queen ! the carrying out of this matter has been in my charge to such extent that I have concealed my evidence. The reason of my having kept back my testimony was, that the King might learn somewhat of the true state of the case concerning Damnah, and become aware of the particulars of his cunning and treachery. Now if, previous to this, I had plunged into this matter, and commenced to under-take this affair, considering that the King had not been apprised of Damnah's villany, nor of his malignant disposition and malevolent nature, possibly he

---

[1] Literally—
You have laid a foundation like heroes,
Complete it with the utmost generosity.

would have imputed malice to me, and have had evil suspicions; but now that the matter has gone thus far, I will not neglect the King's welfare, and if I had a thousand lives, and were to make a sacrifice of them for one hour's peace of mind to the King, yet I should not discharge one tittle of the dues of gratitude for his favours, but should deem myself deficient in the requirements of affection."

> Though I value his hair at the price of both worlds,
> Yet in both worlds I should be abashed before him.

The Lion's Mother then went to the Lion and related the matter of Kalílah and Damnah just as she heard it, and adduced the same evidence before the assembly of the beasts. This speech having spread abroad, the thief[1] who when in prison had obtained a clue to their conversation, sent a person, saying, "I, too, will bear witness." The Lion gave the command that he should be summoned, and he gave evidence as to what passed between the above while in confinement. They inquired of him, "Why did you not represent matters on the very day?" He replied: "A decree could not be assured by the testimony of one person; I did not therefore think fit thus needlessly to torture an animal." The Lion approved his speech. By the testimony of these two the order for the death of Damnah became imperative, and the signature of the Judges being affixed thereto, all the animals were unanimous for his death in retaliation for the Ox.

> Every foolish person who sows the seed of wickedness,
> At harvest-time will reap the fruit of punishment.

The Lion commanded that, having bound him, they should carefully take him away, and depriving him of food, should torment him with various punishments and cruelties, till he should die in prison from hunger and thirst. So the baneful effects of treachery and deceit having befallen him, he passed from the torment of confinement to the prison of eternal annihilation. "*Therefore the utmost part of the people which had acted oppressively were cut off; praise be unto God, who is the Lord of all creatures,*"—so that it should be known that such is the end of the treacherous, and such the termination of the deceitful.

> Whoever places a snare in the way of mankind,
> Will in the end fall into the trap himself.
> A good branch will bring forth the fruit of happiness;
> No one can gather a rose who plants a thorn.
> Since the punishment of good and evil is certain,
> Act well, for uprightness is best.

---

[1] As دو دیگر in the text is evidently corrupt, I substitute دزد for دو, and omit the remaining word signifying "other," as being inapplicable, only one thief having been mentioned.

BOOK III.

ON THE ADVANTAGES OF INTERCOURSE WITH FRIENDS, AND THE BENEFIT OF THEIR ASSISTANCE.

INTRODUCTION.

HE King said to the Brahman: "I have heard the story of the friends whose affairs, through the efforts of a malicious tale-bearer, ended in enmity, and an innocent person reached destruction; and how the Most High God brought retaliation upon that mischief-making traitor. Now, if time demands, tell an account of the condition of intimate and harmonious companions, and how they ate of the tree of friendship and affection, and opposed one back and front in repelling the enemy, each preferring the other's pleasure before his own." The Brahman replied:

"O Khusrau[1] of the age! who, by means of thy justice,
Hast extended thy throne over the ethereal dome;
The piebald steed of the spheres is subservient to thee, since by thy victories
Thou hast placed an hundred scars upon the face of the moon and sun.

"Know that amongst the wise of perfect disposition, and the learned endowed with praiseworthy qualities, no coin is of more value than the existence of sincere friends, and no dignity more exalted than to obtain honest companions.

Since, in the world, whether young or old,
No one can dispense with having friends.

"Now assuredly, the body of people, the coin of whose friendship has been adorned in the mint of sincerity with the impress of fidelity, and the plant of whose affection has been nurtured in the garden of integrity with the dew of unanimity and efforts to please, are a pleasure to the soul, and a source of grace and favour. The advantages of having friends are manifold, and the benefits

[1] See note, page 153.

thereof innumerable. Amongst the number is this—in days of prosperity they are the source of the articles of friendship and intercourse, while in time of adversity they follow the road of assistance, coupling therewith the allowance of comradeship and support.

> Secure a friend, for he is thoroughly desolate
> Who has no companion in the world.
> Of all the prizes on this earth,
> None is better than a faithful comrade.

———o———

"Of all stories concerning sympathetic friends and intimate companions, which have been inscribed upon the pages of history, the tale of the Crow, the Mouse, the Pigeon, the Tortoise, and the Deer is the most enlightened fable and beautiful anecdote." The King inquired, "What was that?"

STORY I.

The Brahman said: It has been related that in the region of Kashmír was a pleasant spot and incomparable pasture, such that, from the abundance of flowers, the surface of the soil was decked like the Garden of the Skies, while from the reflection of its scent-scattering herbs the wing of a crow appeared like the tail of a peacock.

> On every side were fountains like the waters of Immortality.
> The lamp of the tulip glittering in each direction;
> The violet growing, and the verdure springing up;
> The morning breeze snatching the collar of the rose;
> The anemone standing on a single stalk,
> Like cups of wine upon an emerald stem.

On account of the abundance of game in that pasture, hunters used much to resort there, and constantly spread the net of stratagem for capturing animals and ensnaring birds. In the neighbourhood of that forest a Crow had made his nest upon a large tree, in the pages of the leaves of which he had perused the saying, "*Love of country appertains to religion.*" One day, sitting on the top of the tree, he was looking up and down, and casting his glance right and left. Suddenly he saw a Fowler with a net on his shoulders, a bag on his back, and a stick in his hand, coming with the greatest haste towards that tree. The Crow, trembling, said to himself:

> O Lord! what has happened to this person
> That he advances with such perturbation?
> It is by no means evident on what account
> He thus comes with haste.

"Maybe he has girded his loins to ensnare me, and has placed the arrow of deliberation on the bow of deception with the object of capturing me. Now caution demands that I should keep my place, and look about,

> Till I see what issues from the curtain."

The Crow, concealed behind a leaf of the tree, fixed the eye of expectation. The Fowler, having come to the foot of the tree, spread his snare, and scatter-ing several grains on the top thereof, sat in ambush. A while passed, and an army of Pigeons arrived, the leader of whom was a Pigeon called " Ring-dove," of clear intellect, great wisdom, perfect understanding, and strong imagination. These Pigeons gloried in submitting to him, and prided themselves in obeying and attending him, passing their days in nought save his service, which was their capital of peace, and their ornament of safety and happiness. As soon as the eyes of the Pigeons alighted on the corn, the flame of hunger being aroused, bore off the reins of control from the palms of their power. Ring-dove, out of that compassion which is necessary on the part of chiefs towards their infe-riors, directed them to reflect and hesitate, saying :

" Do not advance towards the corn by the path of greed ;
Be cautious, for under each grain is a snare."

They replied : " O chief ! our case has become a matter of necessity, and our business reached a serious point : to stomachs devoid of grain, and souls full of fear, there is no place for listening to advice, nor opportunity for reflecting on the issue. Wise men have said :

'The hungry are bold to misfortune,
Since they are satiated of their own life.' "

Ring-dove perceived that he could not ensnare those greedy grain-seekers in the net of Admonition, nor could he draw them with the cord of reproach from the well of Negligence and Ignorance.

Whoever falls under the dominion of greed,
Will with difficulty be freed from its yoke.

He was anxious to step aside from them, and retire into a corner ; but the monarch Fate, having bound his neck with the chain of destiny, drew him towards the snare.

O incautious man that I am ! I go, while he trails the fish-hook.

In short, the whole flock of those Pigeons, all at once laying aside caution, alighted. No sooner had they pecked up the corn than they were caught in the Fowler's snare. Ring-dove lamented (saying), " Did not I tell you that the end of hastiness is uncommendable, and that it is not laudable to enter upon affairs without reflection ? "

O soul ! the way of love is full of affliction and misery !
He stumbles who travels on this road with haste.[1]

Perplexity and shame overtaking the Pigeons, they held their breath. The Fowler came forth from his lurking-place, and, with the greatest delight, ran along, so as to secure and bind them in confinement, and return to his own home. The Pigeons, when their eyes alighted upon the Fowler, were overcome with perturbation, each one striving for his own escape, and flapping his wings and pinions. Ring-dove said : " O friends ! you are each of you struggling for your own freedom, neglectful of the escape of your other companions.

---

[1] شتات in the Persian text is unintelligible. I have altered it to شتاب

Such things are not within the conditions of friendship.

" Amongst the canons of friendship is a decree that the delivery of one's comrades should be considered more important than one's own escape : just as, once upon a time, two companions were sitting together in a ship, when suddenly, near the shore, the vessel broke to pieces, and both fell into the water. A sailor on the sea-shore cast himself into the water, intending to seize one of them, but which-ever he selected cried out :

' O venerable sir ! in the midst of this terrible whirlpool,
Leave me, and seize the hand of my friend.'

" Now, if you do not possess power to place the life of your friends before your own existence, nor to esteem their safety in preference to your own deliverance, at any rate all of you exert your powers by way of assistance and concord, so that, by the blessing of such confederacy and union, it may be that the net will be removed from its place, and we shall all find escape." The Pigeons, carrying out the command, joined all their strength together, and by this device, rooting up the net, went their way. The Fowler, notwithstanding this circumstance, ran after them, and hoping that ultimately they would tire and fall down, went along, his eyes fixed in the air. The Crow thought to himself : " It will be a long time before such an extraordinary affair will come from the covering of non-existence into the expanse of reality ; nor am I secure from the like of this occurrence. It is best that I should hasten after their track, and discover how their case will end, and, making this experience a store for my own case, should avail myself thereof in time of need."

In the day of worldly experience secure your portion,
So that you may make use thereof in warding off accident.

The Crow flew after them, while Ring-dove, with his tribe, having carried off the net, soared along ; and the rapacious Fowler, with impudent face, set his eyes upon them, and so proceeded. When Ring-dove saw that the Fowler still followed them, and that the powers of greed, being aroused, compelled the latter not to desist from pursuing them till he should get them in his grasp, he turned towards his friends, saying : " This cruel-faced person has, with the utmost diligence, girded his loins to capture us, and is watching for our destruction ; till we get out of his sight, he will not remove his thoughts from us. It is expedient for us to turn towards habitations, and fly towards gardens and trees, so that his sight may be cut off from us, and, hopeless, he may return abashed." The Pigeons, in accordance with his counsel, turned their course and hastened from the direction of the forest and desert towards the houses. The Fowler, when he no longer saw them, turned back with the utmost regret ; while the Crow proceeded in like manner so as to discover the circumstances of their escape, and store it up to ward off like accidents, and to remedy similar events, till he had turned to account the purport of the saying, " *Fortunate is he who takes counsel from (the experience of) others.*"

A prudent man is he who, as regards the experience of profit and loss,
Extracts from other companions a share for himself.
He adopts whatever he perceives productive of good,
And leaves whatever he understands will result in evil.

The Pigeons, being secure from fear of the Fowler, referred to Ring-dove regarding their own freedom. That wise, right-deliberating person, after reflecting and meditating, replied: " In my opinion, without the assistance of faithful friends, no deliverance from this dangerous place will appear.

Without companionship this road will never come to an end.

" In this neighbourhood is a Mouse, by name Zírak,[1] who takes the priority amongst my friends for excess of fidelity, and surpasses all my comrades and well-wishers in the custom of generosity.

A sincere companion and faithful comrade,
Who in matters of friendship acts in no other way than uprightly.

" Maybe by his assistance deliverance from this snare will appear, and escape arise from this danger." Accordingly they alighted at a ruin where was the dwelling of the Mouse, and going towards his hole, moved the knocker of the door of desire. The noise of Ring-dove reaching the ears of Zírak, he came out, and seeing his friend bound in the snare of calamity, he caused the blood-stained stream to flow from the fountain of his eyes on the pages of his cheek, and raised a grief-imbued sigh from his warm heart to the summit of the skies, saying:

What state of things is this which I behold, what condition of affairs is it?
In such circumstances restraint is impossible.
O friends! how can I remain at rest,
When I see my own companions in fetters?

" O dear friend! O agreeable companion! by what stratagem have you fallen into this snare, and by what means have you been overtaken with this calamity?" Ring-dove replied: " Varied good and evil, and manifold benefits and ills, are bound up with the decrees of Fate and Providence; whatever the writer of Divine Design has inscribed in the palace of Eternity with the pen of Fate upon the pages of the affairs of mankind, will of necessity come to light in the expanse of existence, and escape or delivery therefrom will avail nought.

The pen has flowed, O son! with sweets and bitters;
Though you sit cross, what does it grieve Fate?

" Divine Decree and Almighty Destiny have cast me into this deadly whirlpool, and displayed the grain before me and my companions. Although I warned them against hastiness and rashness, and reproached them for precipitancy and want of caution, the hand of Fate has, nevertheless, drawn the curtain of negligence over the eyes of my prudence, and kept my clear-minded wisdom and far-seeing intelligence behind the dark veil of ignorance and stupidity. We were all suddenly overtaken by the hand of misfortune and the grasp of sorrow." The Mouse rejoined: " Oh! strange that any one like you, possessing so much intelligence and foresight, should not be able to oppose the evils of Fate, nor to repel the arrow of destiny with the shield of stratagem and deliberation!" Ring-dove said: " O Zírak! cease such talk, for many persons stronger, braver, wiser, and more learned than myself, and of more dignity, wealth, excellence, and perfection, have been unable to contend with the decrees of Fate, or to withdraw

---

[1] Clever or sharp.

N

their heads from the ordinances of the Unchangeable, '*There is no one can ward off His Decree, and there is none can avert His Judgment.*' When Fate, the Ruler whose commands all obey, sets in motion the chain of his purpose, it brings the fish from the depths of the sea to the open air, and causes the birds on the summit of the clouds to alight upon the surface of the ground. Nought can avail any creature concerning the decrees of Fate and Providence, save submission and resignation.

> Were all the atoms of the world to twist and turn,
> 'Twould be nought against the decrees of God;
> When Fate raises its head from its collar,
> The wise become utterly blind and deaf:
> Fish fall out of the sea,
> The net ensnares the helpless birds as they fly:
> This Fate is a terrible and violent gale;
> Mankind is like straw, powerless before it.

"And you must know that with regard to the spread of the mandates of Fate, the wise man receives a like decree with the ignorant, and the contemptible subject is on an equality with the world-subduing monarch in the whirlpool of Divine Destiny."

> The decrees of Fate cannot be kept off either by force or gold;
> It does not become any one to inquire "why" and "wherefore" as regards Destiny.

Zírak said: "O Ring-dove! be of good cheer, since every garment which the Tailor of Divine intention sews on the body of any one of the attendants at the threshold of his worship, whether his collar be decked with the button of prosperity, or his skirt adorned with the fringe of adversity, without doubt is the purest kindness and the veriest benevolence; more especially since the individual is not aware of the state of the case, and does not see the kindness which is embraced within its scope. In this sense it has been said:

> 'Dregs or pure liquid, it matters not to thee, drink and be happy,
> Since whatever our cupbearer pours out is the essence of kindness.'

"What has befallen you, when you examine it closely, comprises what is advantageous for your case, and the wise have said, 'There is no pure honey without the cruel sting, nor does the rose of pleasure grow without the thorn of distress.'"

> Many are the desires which are within the folds of disappointment.

While Zírak was muttering these words, and was occupied in severing the cords with which Ring-dove was bound, the latter said: "O dear friend! first of all loose the bands of my comrades, and having eased your mind on their score, turn towards me." The Mouse, paying no heed to these words, busied himself in his own work. Ring-dove again, with renewed energy, exclaimed: "O Zírak! if you seek to gratify me, and would respect the dues of friendship, it is obligatory that first of all you release my companions from their bonds, and by such kindness place the collar of obligation upon the neck of my soul." The Mouse rejoined: "You have repeated this matter, and pushed your endeavours to the utmost excess; possibly you have no regard for your own soul, and do not recognise the dues imposed upon you relative thereto? Are you indifferent to the proverb, '*Commence with thyself'*?" Ring-dove said: "You should not reproach me, since the regal title of chiefship over these Pigeons has been inscribed against my name, and I have taken the management of their affairs under charge of my care. Seeing that they are my subjects, they have duties imposed upon them towards me, while, on the ground that I am their chief, I have a necessary obligation towards them. After they have discharged their duty towards me, and through their aid and assistance I have escaped from the hand of the Fowler, I, too, must perform my necessary obligations, and discharge the dues of sovereignty; for whenever a king seeks his own repose and leaves his subjects ensnared in the bonds of misfortune, no long time will elapse before the wine of his comfort will be fouled, and the eyes of his prosperity clouded."

> No one will rest within your kingdom,
> When you merely seek your own repose.

The Mouse replied: "A king in the midst of his subjects is like the soul within the frame, or, as it were, the heart in the body; therefore, attention must first be paid to his case, since if the heart is well, no great harm arises from the disorders of the limbs; but if, God forbid! the heart becomes diseased, the soundness of the members is of no avail."

> If servants be fewer, what matter?
> From the king's head not a hair may be lost.

Ring-dove replied: "I fear that if you commence to unloose my cords, you will become tired, and some of my friends will remain ensnared; whereas, if I am bound, however fatigued you may be, you will not desert me, nor permit any negligence, in setting me free, to enter your mind. In time of misfortune, too, we have been companions together, so in the period of escape and freedom, to act harmoniously will be the purest generosity."

> If you would consider any one a friend deem him such
> Who is your ally in grief and joy;
> From a friend who is not such in time of both pleasure and pain,
> How can you derive delight, since he himself is an anxiety to you?

The Mouse said: "The custom of men of benevolence is such, and such the fundamental article of faith of men of liberal feelings. By this praiseworthy disposition and laudable nature the reliance of people on your friendship will become more refined, and the trust of your subjects in your kindness and benevolence be increased."

> For a friend, such a person is needed
> As can solve intricacies.

Accordingly, Zírak, with the greatest assiduity, and with unspeakable eagerness, severed the cords of the friends, and last of all freed Ring-dove's neck from the collar of calamity. The Pigeons, bidding him adieu, returned in safety and security to their own nests, while the Mouse descended to his hole. When the Crow witnessed how the Mouse lent his aid, and severed the bonds, he conceived a desire for his friendship and intimacy, and viewed his society and company as a rare prize. He said to himself: "I cannot be secure from the accident which has befallen the Pigeons, consequently I cannot be independent of the friendship of such a person as in time of calamity will lend his assistance."

> East and west are full of companions,
> But of the kind required there are but few;
> Self-interested friends are numerous.
> He who bears your burden is a friend indeed.

Thereupon the Crow quietly came to the Mouse's hole, and made a noise. The latter inquired, "Who is there?" He replied: "It is I, a Crow, and I have an urgent matter with you." Zírak was a very wise Mouse, who had experienced the ups and downs [1] of Fortune, and witnessed the good and bad of life. He had prepared many holes in that spot as places of refuge, and scraped a way from one to the other. He considered the remedy for events before they occurred, and arranged every matter in accordance with what is wise, and in harmony with what is expedient. When he heard the sound of the Crow, he turned himself round, saying: "What is your business with me, and what have I to do with you?" The Crow related the state of the case from beginning to end, and repeated his information respecting the Mouse's good faith and extreme integrity in regard to the Pigeons, saying: "Your great generosity and affection, your excessive kindliness and gratitude, are known to me, and I am aware how the fruit of friendship and the result of affection have accrued to them, and how, by the blessing of your company and intimacy, they have obtained escape from that deadly whirlpool, and I have confined all my ambition to obtaining your society, and am come to discharge the obligation of opening the door of friendship."

> We many expectant souls look to thee,
> The state of our hearts we have told thee; thou knowest.

The Mouse replied: "The road of intimacy between you and me is closed, and the way of intercourse forbidden.

> At your market I see no profit, but rather destruction of soul;
> For on this road there is a distance between us as far as east from west.

"Go! do not strike cold iron, nor move your feet in search of something which cannot possibly by any means be obtained, since to seek after that which is not within the region of possibility is like driving a vessel upon the ground, or galloping a steed upon the surface of the sea. He who is persevering in his endeavours after what is impracticable will bring laughter upon himself, and his stupidity will become patent in the sight of the wise."

> Take away this snare, endeavour to entrap another,
> For this game which you see will not come into your net.

The Crow replied: "Cease such language, for the benevolent do not leave the necessitous disappointed, nor when any one turns his face towards the gates of the prosperous do they strike the back of their hands upon the face of his supplication. I have sought protection at this court from the occurrences of time, and have made this threshold my place of refuge and protection from the calamities of the world.

> Save thy threshold, there is no shelter for me in the world:
> Except at this door, there is nowhere for me to lay my head.

"Now, since I have taken up my attendance at the ground of this very street,

---

[1] Literally, "warmth and cold."

and considered it my lot to wait at this sanctuary, I will neither through roughness turn away my face, nor will I from rudeness hasten elsewhere."

> If you strike[1] me with the sword of punishment, you are ruler;
> And if you honour me as your slave, I am your servant.

The Mouse said: "O Crow! abandon your stratagem, nor throw the grain of deceit upon the face of the snare of hypocrisy, for I well know the nature of your race, and since you are not of my kind, I fear your society.

> The society of aliens is excruciating torture to a soul.

"In no case can I be secure of you; and whenever any one strives to be intimate with a person upon whom he cannot depend, that will befall him which happened to that Partridge." The Crow inquired, "What was that?"

STORY II.

The Mouse said: It has been related that a beautiful-voiced Partridge was strutting at the skirt of a hill, and the reverberation of the sound of his cry echoed in the dome of the spheres. By chance a Hawk of prey passed thereby through the air: when his eyes beheld the Partridge strutting along, and the noise of the latter's merry sound fell on his ears, the Hawk conceived in his heart a desire to be intimate with him, and began to draw upon the tablets of his imagination the design of companionship with him, thinking to himself: "No one in this world is independent of a suitable comrade, nor can one do without an harmonious friend or kind ally, and it has passed into a proverb, 'that he who is without a friend is invariably out of sorts.'[2]

> He who has no friend in the world,
> The tree of his delight will bear no fruit.

"Now this Partridge is a pleasant-looking, merry-faced, intelligent-minded, pretty-strutting friend; my soul, in the society of such a companion, will become fresh and joyous, and my bosom, in love with such a comrade, will be cheerful and free from grief."

> A friend is needed—what sort of friend is required?
> A friend who will unloose the knot of my affairs;
> Whenever he shows his beautiful self,
> He will remove the dust of grief from the mirror of my soul.

Accordingly he gently drew towards the Partridge, who, when his eyes rested upon him, trembling, betook himself within the fissure of a rock. The Hawk alighted from the air, and sitting before that hole, narrated the circumstances of the case, saying: "O Partridge! previous to this I have overlooked your merits and your excellences; your charms, too, were not apparent to me: this day, by reason of your cry, joy has overspread my soul, and your heart-enchanting strut having ensnared me, I am in hopes that after this you will no longer fear and dread me, but will be disposed to be friends and intimate with

---

[1] This is the obvious meaning, though the word here rendered "strike" is generally applied to represent the action of producing a sound from a musical instrument by percussion, and I do not remember having met with an instance, where it is used as referring to the blow of a sword.

[2] The point of this proverb is lost in translation, being dependent in great measure upon a jingle of sounds.

me, so that the prelude of affection may produce good results, and the shrub of love yield the fruit of desire."

> Pre-eminent stands friendship, since therefrom the more the fruit of desire
> Is plucked by any one, the more it grows.

The Partridge exclaimed: "O valiant and mighty warrior! withdraw thy hand from this helpless, grief-stricken one, and having eaten some other Partridge, consider:

> That I should have an interview with you! alas, what a dreadful thought!
> That I should approach you! God forgive me, what an impossible idea!

"Whenever water and fire mingle together, companionship between you and me may be conceivable; and at a time when shade and sun combine, intimacy between us may be imaginable."

> Abandon such an idea, since it will not come to pass.

The Hawk rejoined: "O beloved! think to yourself that what but kindness could impel me to speak soft words to such as yourself. My talons are not so deficient that I am unable to pursue such as you, nor have weakness and imbecility so overtaken my beak that I am helpless in hunting my food. It is nought but this, that the desire of your society and company, and a wish for your intimacy and friendship, impel me to set in motion the chain of affection for you. On your part, many benefits are to be imagined from friendship with me: first of all, when my fellow-birds see that I nourish you under the shadow of the wings of my protection, they will withdraw the hand of violence from your skirt, and regard you with eyes of consideration, while you, happy, may perambulate the hill and desert with ease of mind. Again, I will take you to my nest, so that having reached a lofty abode and inaccessible dwelling, you will be raised above your fellow-creatures in exalted rank. I will bring you also a nice, handsome mate from your own kith and kin, whom you may have a sincere inclination to marry, so that embracing her with the hand of affection, you may pass your time at your heart's desire."

> Neither suffering violence from the times, nor reproach from the spheres,
> Your hopes realised, and the cup of your desire filled to the brim.

The Partridge said: "You are chief of birds, and the reins of rule over the feathered tribe are in the grasp of your power, while I am one of your subjects, and of those who pay dues to you; such as we, are not free from wrong and error, and during the time when I am nurtured by your kindness, and am hopeful of your care, it may be that somewhat may occur, on my part, which may not be pleasing to your Majesty's feelings, and the clutches of your royal anger may dash the brains out of my head: it would be better that I should seize the corner of retirement, and not exalt the banner of attending on rulers, which includes great dangers."

> The sight of the face of the sun I do not consider within my range:
> It is bettter that, like a shadow, I should sit behind a wall.

The Hawk replied: "O brother! have you not heard, and do not you know, that the eyes of friendship are blind to see defects, and every blemish which occurs on the part of a comrade appears a great beauty?

Poison from thee, thy friend would deem sugar;
Defects on thy part, thy friend would consider merits.

"Now, since I contemplate your proceedings with the eye of friendship, and inscribe the writing of your words and circumstances in the volume of affection, how can I draw the line of error through your conversation, or how interpret erroneously your sayings and actions?"

The eye of friendship observes no faults.

However much the Partridge adduced acceptable apologies, the Hawk retorted with pleasant replies. At last, with promises and protestations, he brought the Partridge from his hole, and having embraced one another, they again confirmed with oaths the alliance of friendship. The Hawk having carried him off, brought him to his own nest; being delighted with one another, they passed their time in happiness and joy. When two or three days had elapsed in this way, and the Partridge became safe as regards the Hawk, having followed the path of impudence, he spoke bold words, and in the midst of conversation uttered his cry out of place. The Hawk, through high consideration, pretending not to hear it, refrained from exercising vengeance, but ill-feeling therefrom took possession of his breast, till one day a slight weakness suddenly overtook the Hawk, such that he was unable to move in search of food, and passed the whole day in his nest. When night arrived, and his crop was empty of the food which it had possessed, the fire of hunger having raised itself, brought his savage feelings into play, and hatred [1] of the Partridge, which had been pent up by lapse of time, filled the Hawk with rage. Notwithstanding the monitor, Wisdom, brought before his sight the circumstance of the promise and agreement, he did not look thereon with the corner of the eye of approbation, and sought an excuse to violate his oath and devour the Partridge, who, seeing traces of anger in his appearance, and by the look of his eyes observing that his own death was settled, drew forth a cold sigh from his heart full of grief, saying:

I was like a lover; I said I would carry off the pearl of my desire.
How could I know what infinite waves this sea possesses?

"Alas! that I did not, at first, glance my sight at the end of the business, but joined company with one of a different race to myself, and let the advice of the wise—

'Avoid associating with those of a different kind'—

"be forgotten, consequently to-day the ship of my life has fallen into a whirlpool from which the sailor, Deliberation, will be powerless to extricate it, and the thread of my existence is snapped in such a manner that the tip of the finger of Counsel will be puzzled to join it together again."

There is neither fidelity in my comrade, nor hope of life;
Neither glad tidings from the spheres, nor good news from the world.

Such words he spoke to himself, while the Hawk, having in like manner opened the talons of cruelty, and moistened his bloodthirsty beak with the poison of oppression, devoted himself to seek a pretext. Since the Partridge, taking the greatest care, observed the dues of good manners, the Hawk could find no excuse for killing him. At last becoming beyond all control filled with rage,

---

[1] كيهلى in the Persian text is a misprint for كينهاى.

he said to the Partridge : "Is it allowable that I should be in the sun, while you pass your time in the shade?" The Partridge replied : "O world-subduing chief! it is now night, and all the world is wrapped in the shade of darkness; by the glare of what sun are you annoyed, and under the shade of what do I obtain repose?" The Hawk replied: "O ill-mannered person! do you accuse me of speaking falsely, and do you bandy words with me? I will punish you!" He no sooner spoke than he tore him up.

"Now I have adduced this story that you may know, that whoever associates with those not of his own kith and kin, or passes his time in company with any one from whose violence he cannot be secure, like the sweet-voiced Partridge, having given up his precious soul to companionship, the day of his life will be spent. In like manner I am your food, and can never live secure as to your disposition; therefore, in what point of view can the way of intercourse between you and me be opened, and by what means can the arrangements of comradeship be settled?" The Crow said : "O Zírak! appeal to your own wisdom, and reflect well what good could I derive from injuring you, and what repletion would eating you bring; while from the continuance of your existence, and the acquirement of your society, a thousand advantages are assured, and a hundred thousand benefits may be imagined. It is not right that I should have traversed a far and long distance in search of you, while you turn your face from me, and place the hand of rejection upon the bosom of my hope. With the good nature and pure disposition which you possess, it is not becoming that my rights as a stranger should be discarded, and a humble individual turn away hopeless from your threshold.

> The care of the poor is the cause of a fair name ;
> Why is it that this custom is not observed in your city?

"From the laudable disposition which I have observed in you, I do not fancy that you will absolutely deprive me of your condescension, or that you will not perfume the nostril of my hopes with the soul-exhilarating odours of your kindness."

> With you, who are humble, when will there be a habit of caring for the poor?

The Mouse replied : "No enmity is so potent as personal dislike, since if accidental discord arises between two individuals by slight means it may be averted, and by degrees the causes thereof be removed; but if there should happen to be innate enmity, and the traces thereof are implanted in the minds of both sides, and if in that ancient hatred recent animosity be included, and former feuds be united with subsequent disputes, to avert the same will by no means come within the circle of possibility, and to repel it will, in all cases, be beyond the pale of human power, its eradication being bound up with the destruction of both parties.

> Till the head is lost, the thought of this will not quit the mind.

"Wise men have said that personal enmity is of two kinds,—one when the evil is not confined to one of the two antagonists, this one being sometimes injured by that one, and that one at other times hurt by this: like the enmity of the elephant and lion, who cannot possibly meet without a battle; but the victory is not confined to one side, nor the defeat to be anticipated on one part; nay, more, sometimes the fierce lion gets the victory, on other occasions superiority rests with the tusks of the raving elephant. This sort of feud is not so violent but that the wound therefrom can receive a salve, for the reason that whoever comes off triumphant assuredly his heart will become tranquil. The second kind is when the loss is always on one side, and the gain on the other, like the antipathy of the mouse and the cat, or the wolf and the sheep, and suchlike, where the evil is always comprised on one side, and the good necessarily on the other.   This enmity is so deep-rooted that the revolutions of the heavens could not alter it, nor the changes of time unloose the knot thereof; and where it is known that there is a design against life on one side, without there having been any such on the other in former times, and when in future no disagreement would arise, in such case in what way can peace be possible, or how can intercourse be obtained?"

> The moment that day and night join together,
> Or the cord of sun and shade is united,
> I will associate with you; but in that case, too,
> Men of wisdom would laugh me to scorn.

The Crow said: "Thank God! my enmity towards you was not implanted by nature, and if my kind happen to be opposed to you, at any rate the mirror of my soul is free from the dust of discord, and the glass of my heart ready for the reflection of the rays of affection and friendship; and certainly since the maxim, '*From heart to heart,*' is an assured means of access, I am in hopes that the guileless heart of that dear friend will bear witness to the sincerity of my friendship."

> Do not imagine that thy sweetheart knows not thy heart.

The Mouse said: "You push your efforts to an excess, and annoy me with your friendship. If I attempt this, and you, too, keep to your purpose, maybe that from some slight cause the thread of friendship being snapped, you will relapse to your innate habits and natural enmity, just as water, however long it remains in a place, the smell and taste thereof being changed, yet its original properties remain, and when it is poured upon fire it never fails to quench it.   Intimacy with an antagonist, like associating with deadly snakes, inspires no confidence; and companionship with enemies, like friendship with sharp-clawed tigers, is not worthy of trial: and wise men have said, that one must not be deceived with the speech of an enemy, though he makes profession of friendship; nor must one be beguiled with his words, though he strives his utmost to be intimate.

> To hope for new [1] friends from previous enemies,
> Is equivalent to seeking for a rose in an oven.

"Whoever, having placed reliance on his enemies, becomes puffed up with their conceits, and hears with the ear of satisfaction their treacheries and deceits, will meet with that which befell that Camel-Driver." The Crow inquired, "What was that?"

STORY III.

The Mouse said: It has been related that a Camel-Driver in the midst of his journey reached a certain spot, where the people of a caravan had lighted a fire; after they left, the fan of the wind, stirring up the flames, rekindled the fire, the sparks of which, flying out on all sides of the desert, fell on some sticks, and

---

[1] و in the Persian text is a misprint for نو .

every corner of the plain was lighted up like a tulip-bed. In the midst of that fire a huge Snake, a large Serpent, tired and wretched, could in no direction find a path, nor on any side make his escape; it wellnigh happened that he was scorched like a fish on a gridiron, or like a roasted partridge on the top of the fire. Blood began to trickle from his poison-shedding eyes; when he saw that Driver he called for help, and said:

> "What would happen if you were to kindly take compassion on me,
>   And undo the knot of my firm-tied situation?"

The Driver was a God-fearing and kind man; when he heard the complaint of the Snake, and witnessed his misery and helplessness, he thought to himself, "Though a Snake is the enemy of mankind, yet, now he is distressed and perplexed, nought can be more proper than that I should be kind to him, and sow in the soil of practice the seed of benevolence, which produces no fruit but happiness in this world, and favour in the next." Accordingly, having fixed upon the top of his spear the bag which he carried, he held it out there, while the Snake, availing himself of the opportunity, went into the bag, and the Driver thinking it well, drew him forth from the fire; he then opened the mouth of the bag, and said to the Snake: "Go where you will, and, thankful that you have escaped from this misfortune, retire to your corner, and hereafter no longer injure mankind, for he who does evil to people has a bad name in this world, and in that to come will be disappointed."

> Fear God, and molest no one—
> This, and nought else, is the road [1] of happiness.

The Snake said: "O young man, cease this language, for I will not depart till I have inflicted a wound upon both you and your camel." The Driver exclaimed: "Have I not acted kindly towards you, and brought you out of the midst of the fire? is such my recompense, and such my reward?"

> On my part, my conduct was upright;
> On your side, why do you practise tyranny?

The Snake replied: "True, you did well, but it was misplaced, and you acted with kindness, but it was occasioned by an unworthy object. You are aware that I am the promoter of evil, and no benefit to mankind can be conceived on my part; accordingly, since you laboured for my escape, and acted considerately towards one who should have been treated badly, assuredly, in return for this, misfortune must befall you, since to do good to the bad is the same as doing harm to the righteous.

> Just as, by the rules of equity and wisdom, it is forbidden
> To do evil towards the pure and good;
> So, as regards the mean-natured who injure mankind,
> Kindness can by no means be displayed to them.

"Again, according to the mandate, '*Some of you are enemies to some others,*' between you and me there is a long-standing enmity, and foresight demands that the head of one's enemy should be bruised; and in accordance with the decree, '*Kill the two black things,*' it is incumbent upon you to destroy us, for there is a command that we should not be allowed to escape in safety; you have in

---

[1] ز in the Persian text is a misprint for ره; I fancy, too, the final letter is corruptly inserted in place of the izáfat, or sign of the genitive case.

this matter abandoned what is proper and prudent, and have acted with kindness, and assuredly I will wound you, so that others may gain experience thereby." The Driver rejoined: "O Snake! bring justice to bear, since in what faith would it be allowable to do wrong in return for good, and in what religion would it be justifiable to requite the pureness of kindness with the foulness of injury?" The Snake replied: "Such is the custom of you men; and I, too, will put in practice your own decree, and sell you what I have bought from you in the market of retaliation."

Buy in one moment what you are a whole year selling.

In spite of all the young man's endeavours, they were of no avail. The Snake said: "Elect quickly whether I shall first of all sting you, or commence with the camel." The young man replied: "Abandon such ideas, for to requite good with bad is ill-omened." The Snake rejoined: "Such is the custom of men; and I, too, am following the way of mankind." The Driver denied this assertion, saying: "If you can with proof establish this, and bring evidence in accordance with your contention, that to make return in this manner is the custom of men, I will purchase your bite with my life, and consent to my own death." The Snake looked round and saw a buffalo from afar grazing in the desert. He said: "Come, I will ask him as to the truth of the case." Accordingly, the Snake and the Camel-Driver both advanced towards the buffalo; the Snake loosed its tongue saying: "O buffalo! what is the recompense for good?" He answered: "If you ask according to the creed of the world, the return for good is evil. Behold, I was for a time with one of them: every year I produced a young one, and filled his (the man's) house with milk and butter, and the fabric of his establishment and the foundation of his life were based on me. When I became old and ceased breeding, he left off minding me, and turning me out of his house, set my head towards the desert. After I had grazed a while in the waste, and, having no duties to perform, had gained my heart's desire, signs of fatness became evident in me. Yesterday my master passed by here, and as I appeared to his eyes plump, he brought a butcher and sold me to him, and this very day they will lead me to the slaughter-house with the design of killing me. See, such was the return of all that goodness which I have mentioned!"

My case is such, O friends! to whom shall I tell my circumstances?

The Snake said: "See, you have heard! be ready as quickly as possible for the sting." The Camel-Driver replied: "In law a decree is not passed when there is but one witness; bring another and do what you like." The Snake looking round, a tree came in his sight. He exclaimed: "Come, and I will inquire of that tree." Accordingly they came together to the foot thereof, and the Snake inquired from it, "What is the recompense for good?" It replied: "According to the creed of men, the requital for good is evil, and the return for favour is injury. The proof is this: I am a tree grown in this wild, standing on one leg at the service of every comer and goer. When a mortal overpowered with heat, and weary, comes forth from the desert, he rests awhile under my shade, and seeks repose for a time; then when he opens his eyes he exclaims: 'Such a branch is suitable for the handle of my axe, and such a portion is fit and proper for my shovel: from its trunk several good planks can be cut, and from some of them beautiful doors might be made.' If they have a saw or axe, they cut off from my boughs and trunk whatever pleases them and carry it off;

and notwithstanding they have derived pleasure from me, they approve of all this cruelty towards me."

> I am thinking how I can shade his head ;
> He is in this perplexity, how he can dig me up by the roots.

The Snake exclaimed: " See, two witnesses have been produced, make over your body that I may bite you!" The man rejoined: " Life is very precious, and so long as there is any chance, it is difficult to sever the heart from the trappings of existence. If another person gives evidence in this matter, I will ungrudgingly resign my body to this calamity, and be content with the decree of Fate." It strangely happened that a Fox was standing by witnessing the affair, and listening to their conversation with ears of intelligence. The Snake said: " See ! inquire of this Fox as to what reply he will give." Scarce had the Driver asked the question, ere the Fox addressed the man, " Do you not know that the return for good is evil ? what benefit have you conferred on this Snake that you are worthy of punishment in retaliation ?" The young man repeated the circumstances of the case. The Fox replied : " You seem a clever man, why do you speak falsely ? "

> How can it be allowable for a wise man to talk wrongly ?
> It does not become a clever man to speak contrary to what has happened.

The Snake said : " He speaks truly ; see, he has the bag, with which he brought me out of the fire, tied to his saddle-straps!" The Fox expressed astonishment as to how these words could be worthy of credence, and a Snake of so great size be contained in so small a bag. The Snake exclaimed : " If you do not believe it, I will again enter this bag, so that you may see an illustration thereof." The Fox said : " If I witness this proceeding with my own eyes, and gather proof of this assertion, then I will pass a decree between you which shall not deviate from what is right, and wherein hypocrisy and malignity shall not enter." The man opened the end of the bag, and the Snake, deceived by the Fox's words, entered therein. The Fox exclaimed : " O young man ! when you find your enemy captured, give him no quarter."

> When your enemy is in your power, and defeated by you,
> Wisdom decrees that you should give him no quarter.

The man tied up the end of the bag, and struck it on the ground till the Snake was killed, and the sparks of his villany being extinguished, mankind rested secure from his malignity.

> It is best that whatever when alive is bad should be slain.

" The moral of this story is, that a wise man should not abandon the road of caution, nor be deceived with the lamentation of foes ; in no case, either, should he confide in them, so that he may not be exposed to their wickedness."

> Whoever is deceived with the speech of a foe,
> The taper of his wisdom will be darkened and without light.
> Would you know at what time an enemy can become a friend ?
> It is when darkness disappears from night.

The Crow said : " I have heard these words, which you have pronounced out of pure wisdom, and have illumined the eyes of my mind with the glittering pearls which you have brought forth from the mine of intelligence ; but it would be more worthy of your benevolence, generosity, kindliness, and magnanimity, to cease these laborious and earnest efforts, and, trusting my word, to open the way of intimacy. Wise men have said, 'Fly towards the benevolent, and avoid the base; for the generous, after a single hour's companionship, deem various kindness and attentions incumbent, and laying aside the feelings of reserve, extend their friendship and kindness to the utmost pitch of affection; while the mean, not recognising the claims of former intimacy, efface a hundred years of friendship in the twinkling of an eye.' Hence it is that the high-minded quickly make friends with mankind, and with reluctance display enmity, like a golden goblet which is slow to break and easy to mend; while the low-minded are loath to be friends, and the edifice of their intercourse is quickly overturned, like a pitcher of clay which is soon broken, and then in no way can any remedy be applied. How beautifully has it been said:

> 'Friendship must be sought of that kind,
> Which will remain firm to all eternity;
> A house whose foundation is of unburnt bricks,
> Is utterly overturned after one or two showers'!

"I am of that body that my friendship is worthy of confidence; with all this I am in need of your society, and having attended at this court, I will on no account turn away, and assuredly will taste no food, nor take any rest, till you cause me to become your intimate companion."

> I will not readily let go from my palm the skirt of a dear one like yourself,
> For with many blood-stained[1] tears you have come to my possession.

The Mouse said: "I will purchase with my life your amity and respect: all this roughness was on account that if you should meditate treachery, I should be reasonably excused, and you should not say that you had found an easy-going, quiet-jogging ally; otherwise, on the first word I found the burden of your friendship in my heart, and observed in my mind a desire beyond limit for your company."

> Since in this heart the leaf of friendly affection has grown,
> Know that there is friendship within that soul;
> No lover would of himself seek a meeting,
> Did not his mistress yearn after him.

Thereupon he came out and stood in front of the hole. The Crow exclaimed: "What hinders you coming more forward and seeking to be friends with me face to face? do you yet find your mind agitated, and see your heart unsettled?" The Mouse replied: "Whenever any one hazards his life for a friend, and stakes his precious existence for a companion, he may be called a sincere comrade and affectionate brother; but if in the same way in the affairs of this world a person is kind and does not refrain from assisting with his own goods, he is a middling friend, with proclivities towards what is fairly just. It has been said: 'He who shares his property and dignity with a friend on account of the requirements of the time or the necessities of the world, is like a hunter who scatters grain for his own benefit, not with the view of filling birds; and since this friendship is mingled with self-consideration, maybe the termination thereof will lead to enmity.'"

---

[1] خون آبه in the Persian text is more generally, if not invariably, spelt خونابه .

> Every individual who is tainted with self-consideration,
> Mingles enmity with his friendship.

"But he who sacrifices his life in the way of friendship, and rises above his own existence, is a friend without an equal, and the rank of him who gives up his soul in the way of affection, is more exalted than that of him who stakes his property."

> *'The generosity of the soul is the extreme of generosity.'*

> There are hundreds of thousands generous of their money;
> When the matter affects the soul, then is the rub.

"It is not concealed that in accepting your amity, and opening the way of meeting with you, there is danger of life to me; in spite of this, the matter has reached such a pitch in the way of affection, that,

> If the matter affects my soul, I will rise above life.

"If suspicion had arisen, this inclination would never have occurred, and I should not have come forth from the corner of my abode. I have confided in your friendship, and your sincerity in seeking my society has passed the region of doubt and suspicion; on my part, too, affection and attachment have been doubled and increased a thousand-fold: but you have friends whose nature in opposing me is contrary to your disposition, and whose opinion, as regards affection for me, will not agree with your sentiments. I am fearful that some of them will see me, and plot my death." The Crow said: "Between me and my comrades is an agreement, that they should be friends with my allies, and treat my foes as enemies." The Mouse rejoined: "Assuredly as regards him who entertains affection for an enemy's companion, and joins with a friend's enemy, it would be more fit to esteem him amongst the number of one's foes.

> It is good to turn the face of one's soul from two kinds of persons:
> From an enemy's friends, and from a friend's enemies.

"Hence it is that wise men have said that friends are of three kinds—sincere friends, friends of a friend, and enemies of an enemy; and that foes, too, are of three varieties—open antagonists, enemies of a friend, and friends of an enemy."

> I do not fear so much from an enemy himself,
> As from foes of a friend, and friends of a foe.

The Crow said: "I know the purport of your language. To-day, thank God, the arrangements of friendship and the articles of affection between you and me are affirmed and corroborated, in such a manner that I esteem him my own friend who is a comrade of yours, and consider him my ally who strives to seek your welfare. Whoever join with you, my union with them is necessary also, were they all rivals; and whoever separate from you, it is incumbent upon me to tear myself away from them, even were they all relations and connections."

> He upon whose cheek there is not the scar of submission to my friend,
> Were he my father, he would be my enemy and rival.

"Now my ideas, with reference to our close intimacy, and my intentions concerning our sincere friendship, are such that if I were to find ought opposed to you in my eyes and tongue, which are the sentinels of the body, and the interpreters

of the soul, in a twinkling I would cast both from the shore of existence into
the whirlpool of annihilation."

If one of your limbs be friends with your enemy,
Consider your enemy as two-fold—draw your sword twice, and inflict two
    wounds.

The Mouse on hearing these words became reassured, and advancing, addressed
himself warmly to the Crow. Having embraced one another, they spread the
carpet of joy.

Gird your loins for conversation, since a friend is within your embrace.

When several days had elapsed in this manner, and the Mouse had discharged
to the utmost of his power the dues of entertainment and the rights of hospitality, he said: " O brother ! if you make ready to abide here, and transport
to this abode your wife and children, it will be extremely nice ; and the favour
which accrues to my soul from your kindness will be doubled, for this place
wherein my abode happens to be is a verdant spot, and an enchanting region."
The Crow replied : " Respecting the beauty of this locality, and the great charms
and softness of the air, not a word can be said ; but it is near to the common
road, and close to the highway; from the going to and fro of those passing along
misery is to be expected, and from the concourse of travellers anticipation of
misfortune will arise. In such a place is a meadow which, from its extreme
freshness, is full of light like the garden of Paradise, while from the purity of
the air it is the abode of joy and gladness, as it were the regions of Eden."

New-grown turf upon the brinks of a rivulet,
The morning breeze scented with blossoms ;
The ringlets of the hyacinth with captive bonds
Ensnaring the locks of the violet.

" One of my friends, a Tortoise, dwells here, while I myself get abundance of
food in the neighbourhood; and mishaps but little reach those parts. If you
feel disposed, I will go there with you, and we will pass the remainder of our
life in ease and comfort." The Mouse replied :

Till my burial-shroud is placed under the ground,
Do not imagine that I will withdraw my hand from thy skirt.

" I hold no desire equal to the honour of your intimacy, and deem no wish
better than the happiness of your company. Where you walk majestically like
the sun, I will follow after like a shadow, and on whatever spot you pass displaying your sleeve, I like a skirt will fall at your feet. Till the collar of life
shall fall into the grasp of death, the destroyer of pleasures, I will not restrain
the hand of desire from the skirt of your society.

The skirt of perpetual Fortune and the collar of Hope,
'Twere a shame to seize them, and let them go again.

" This abode, where I dwell, is not my original home—nay, more, I came here
without choice. Though my story is long, yet it comprises many strange events:
as soon as a halting-place is settled, if your noble heart wishes it,

" I will narrate a little out of a great deal."

Upon this the conversation ended ; and the Crow seizing the Mouse's tail, they set out towards their destination. By chance the Tortoise was wandering on the outskirts of a fountain which formed their abode: when from afar he saw the blackness of the Crow, he was overcome with fear, and went down into the water. The Crow gently placed the Mouse from the air on the ground, and cried out to the Tortoise, who, hearing the voice of an acquaintance, came up from the water, and catching sight of a dear friend, raised a cry of joy to heaven.

> My absent friend has arrived in safety,
> And my blighted fortune has redeemed its pledge.
> How long can you, at any rate, be afflicted with the thorn of grief ?
> For now is the time of joy, since that rose is smiling.

Accordingly, they warmly addressed each other; and the Tortoise inquired, "Where have you been this while, and how has it fared with you?" The Crow repeated his story in its entirety, from the time of the Pigeons falling into the net till the period of their escape; how he desired to be intimate with the Mouse, and strengthened the bonds of affection for him, till the time he arrived at his ordinary abode. The Tortoise, after becoming acquainted with all the details of the story, displayed the utmost joy at seeing the Mouse, and said :

> With good omen have you arrived at this auspicious spot ;
> You are welcome, and may blessings and peace be upon you.

"My good luck has drawn you to this place, and the power of my fortune has caused the star of your beauty to rise on the horizon of this locality." The Mouse replied: "How can I make apologies for the kindness which you display, or with what language express my thanks for the condescension you have shown ? I have sought protection from the heat of the sun of calamity under the shade of your favour, reckoning the procuring of the fortune of your intimacy as the extreme of my trust and hopes."

> It was by Divine Grace that I inquired the way,
> And it was by the direction of God that I saw your face.

When they had refreshed themselves from the fatigues of the journey, and rested in that abode, which was a secure dwelling, safe from the attacks of the army of misfortune, and free from the dust of the annoyance of rivals, the Crow, turning towards Zírak, requested: "If you think fit, repeat to the Tortoise those tales and stories which you promised me, so that the bonds of intercourse between you may be strengthened, and through your conversation the greatest comfort may arise."

> Open your lips, and with that sweet story
> Fill my desolate heart with gratitude.

The Mouse, commencing to speak, said to the Tortoise :

STORY OF THE MOUSE.

O brother! my birth and parentage were in a city in the country of Hind, called Nádút, in which I had taken my abode in the cell of a solitary Devotee, in a corner of whose cloister I had made myself a home. Several mice waited on me, who day by day waxed more diligent in serving and attending on me.

A true disciple every morning used to bring tables of food for the Devotee, who took a little therefrom by way of breakfast, keeping the remainder as a store for supper. I used to watch when he went out of the house, and then at once jumped upon the table, and, at my heart's desire, ate such morsels as were fitting, and presented the rest to the other mice. The Devotee originated plans [1] to keep me away, but they were of no avail, and he schemed many devices for my destruction, but to no effect, till one night a cherished Guest alighted at the Devotee's home. When they had finished the customary salutation, and the necessary meal, and the beneficial tables of conversation had been spread, the Devotee inquired from him news as to his parentage, his designs, and the cause of his journey, and object of his travels. The Guest was an experienced man, who had tasted the sweets and bitters of life;

> One who had journeyed on sea and land for years;
> One who was acquainted with many circumstances.

He answered the Devotee honestly, and recounted, with pleasant description, whatever he had witnessed relative to the wonders of cities, and the marvels of every country. The Devotee, in the midst of his conversation, each moment struck his hands together, the reason being that the mice might be terrified at the noise of his fists. The Guest was disturbed at this proceeding, which appeared to betoken want of respect, and angry at this action, which seemed like absence of manners, he exclaimed: " O Devotee! to strike the hands together in the midst of a sentence is making a fool of the speaker. I do not consider a habit of derision, or a tendency to ridicule becoming to your condition, nor do I deem it in accordance with your circumstances to turn from the path of good manners towards buffoonery and jest."

> Be not inclined for derision and jest,
> For they are not worthy of the high-minded;
> He who makes fun and sport his occupation,
> There are none more destitute of reputation in the world than himself.

The Devotee replied: " God forbid that ever the thorn of derision should cling to the skirt of my condition, or the dust of jest mingle with the pure atmosphere of my soul! This action which you witness is with the view of frightening an army of mice, who have overrun the kingdom of my tables and board, and extended the hand of plunder and rapine towards whatever I store away. Owing to their attacks, I find no bread on my table, nor, from their molestation, can any food be kept in the house."

> A hundred such as I could by no effort restrain them,
> The moment they extend their hand to plunder.

The Guest inquired: " Are they all impudent and daring, or do some display more boldness?" The Devotee replied: "One of them is venturesome to a degree, that before my face he will bear away anything from my table, and before my eyes will show his boldness in plundering my food." The Guest said: " His audacity must have a cause, and his history has the same appearance as that of the man who earnestly represented to the host's wife, 'there must be at any rate a reason why you sell shelled Sesame for the same amount as that unshelled.'" The Devotee said, " If it is expedient, tell me how was that."

---

[1] لطح in the Persian text is a misprint for حيله

STORY IV.

The Guest said: On the road by which I have come, I arrived at night at a certain village, and alighted at the house of an acquaintance. After eating supper, and when conversation was finished, they arranged for me the bed-clothes, and I placed a pillow on the top thereof, but did not go to sleep. The Host went to his wife. Between myself and them there was no more than a partition of reeds, by reason of which I heard their conversation, and listened to all the parlance which ensued. The man said: "O wife! I am anxious to-morrow to invite a number of great men of the village, and set them down in the presence of this dear Guest, who is an offering arrived from the Unseen World, and I will give a banquet in conformity to my state." The woman replied: "I am astonished, that when there are not in the house things sufficient for the expenses of your family, and you have not within reach coin wherewith to purchase vegetables and salt, with such great wealth and lavish capital it should enter your mind to entertain guests, and you should dream of a set banquet. At any rate to-day, when you have power to save, put it aside as a store for to-morrow, and leave a balance for your wife and children, so that after you they may not stand in need of any one." The man replied:

> He has not the eye of experience who amasses and does not enjoy;
> He carries off the ball[1] of happiness who spends and gives.

"If there should happen to be a means of doing good and the power of acting kindly, we must not repent thereof, because, in truth, such will be indeed a store for Eternity. Whoever lays up a hoard in this world, will in the next meet with ruin of soul; since to collect money and treasure for future use is not auspicious, and the end thereof is unacceptable, just as in the case of the Wolf." The woman inquired, "How was that?"

STORY V.

The man said: It has been related that a skilful Hunter, from dread of whose net the deer did not put forth his feet in the desert, nor the wild goat, from fear of his stratagem and deceit, draw his head from his den—

> Quick-sighted, full of wisdom, of cute intelligence,
> Cunning, austere, of hard disposition—

had laid a snare, and a Deer had fallen into the trap. After the Hunter had issued forth from his lurking-place, desirous to approach the net, the Deer, in fear of his life, made a violent effort, and tearing up the snare, set out towards the desert. The Hunter, abashed, placing an arrow in his bow, shot it in the direction of the Deer, who fell down on his feet; the Hunter coming up drew him on his back and set out towards his own home. On the way a Wild Boar, charging him two or three times,[2] attacked him. The Hunter shot an arrow at him, and by chance the heart-transfixing dart went right against the Boar, who, from the anguish of that wound, ran his death-dealing tusks against the Hunter's

---

[1] See note 1, page 188.   [2] Literally, "two four."

breast, and both fell down dead on the spot. In the midst of these occurrences, a hungry Wolf arrived there, and saw the Man, the Boar, and the Deer, all slain; delighted at witnessing this state of things, he obtained support from this large bounty and supply of food, and said to himself:

> Much luck is needed
> Ere such a boon comes to my hands.

"Now is the time for reflection and deliberation, and the period for amassing and laying up a store, since if I let things alone it will be far from caution and circumspection, while if I am extravagant I shall be considered as ignorant and careless; it seems to me expedient and more becoming the requirements of the case, that I should to-day put up with the bow-string, and not string the bow of extravagance and impropriety. I will put this juicy flesh in a corner, and day by day impel the arrow of Desire at the target of Gratification; and placing this hoard in a nook, I will make it a store for the troubles of time, and times of trouble: since wise men have said:

> 'Do not eat the whole; I fear you will have to stand waiting a long while (for
>   more):
> Want does not become the venerable head.
> Consume somewhat of your wealth and leave a portion;
> Do not part with all at once.'"

The Wolf, from excess of greed, hankering after the bow-string, commenced eating it, and with one grind of his teeth the cord broke; as soon as the bow-string snapped, the corner of the bow entered his heart, and he at once expired.

> He too expired, and all this was left uneaten.

"The moral of this story is, that to be greedy in collecting wealth, and to hoard under the impulse of far-seeing hope, have a baneful termination and an unacceptable conclusion.

> What you have, enjoy this day, and be not dejected at Fortune;
> Since, when you arrive at to-morrow, to-morrow's portion will come to hand.

"Alas! how ill-starred are the people who first of all amass wealth with great toil, and ultimately pass their lives in endless regret!"

> How long wilt thou, O Sir! amass wealth
> Which will remain behind thee on death?
> Wert thou to accumulate the riches of Kárún,[1]
> Thou wouldst still remain greedy and covetous.
> Do not raise a fire, by which
> You will be burnt and consumed.

When the Host's wife heard these wise-seeming words, and the inspiration of good-fortune had conveyed to the ears of her intelligence the glad tidings '*Daily food is with God*,' she commenced tenderly to say: "O beloved! I have stored in the house a little Rice and Sesame for the children: now it is evident that it is not auspicious to hoard up for the future. In the morning I will prepare some food sufficient for ten persons; do you summon whom you will, and make sit down whomsoever you need."

---

[1] See note 1, page 62.

> Next day, when the fount of the sun
> Washed the dust of sleep from off its eyes,

the woman having shelled that Sesame, placed it in the sun, and set her husband to be well on the alert till it should be dry, lest the birds should carry off any of it, she herself being occupied in another matter.　Sleep overpowering the man, a dog came and put his mouth amongst that Sesame : the wife seeing that proceeding, was loath to make food therefrom ; she took it away, and set out for the market, while I, too, having somewhat to do in the bázár, followed after her. I observed her come to the shop of a Sesame seller, and exchange it measure for measure for unshelled Sesame.　The man cried out : "O woman ! at any rate there is some hidden mystery in this, since you barter like for like, white Sesame for Sesame with the shell on."

"I have repeated this story, because it also enters my mind, that that daring Mouse possesses all this power, boldness, and impudence owing to his locality, and it is a most probable surmise, that he has some money in the house, backed up by which he displays all this hardihood ; if the shrub of his condition should experience the autumn of poverty, this freshness and vigour would not be manifest in the plantation of his conduct, since it has been said, 'He who is without money is like a bird without feathers or wings.'

> Remain not without gold, since money produces money ;
> The worth of gold is valued beyond everything.
> They say there is a better selection than that of gold :
> Listen not, for the choice of gold brings gold.

"I am certain that the power of this Mouse must be by virtue of gold.　Fetch an axe, so that, having turned his hole upside down, I may look where the matter ends."　The Devotee at once brought an axe.　I was at that time in another hole, and heard what passed between them.　In my abode, too, were a thousand golden dínár, in which I used to revel, and from the spectacle of which my nature derived ever-increasing joy : in short, my delight of mind and ease of soul were dependent on that gold.　Whenever I used to remember it, satisfaction became manifest in my bosom, and joy and gladness accrued to my soul.　The Guest tore up the ground till he reached the gold.　What did he see ?

> Several coins, their cheeks radiant like the sun,
> Glistening in purity like the cup of Jamshíd ; [1]
> Handsome, red-faced, with the impress of true coin ;
> Precious, fit for the assayer.
> At one time he took the best in the palm of his hand,
> Breathing his silvery breath on them, he remained transfixed.
> They give joy to the feelings of the afflicted,
> They are the key of the lock of the world's difficulties.

The Devotee said : "This was the capital of that Mouse's impudence, and the cradle of his power, since property is the furbisher [2] of wisdom, and the prop of vigour ; after this he will not display any impudence at your tables, nor will he interfere with the food and victuals."　I heard these words, and observed traces of weakness and despair, and proofs of perplexity and abasement in my own person.　I was of necessity compelled to remove from that hole.　At the very

---

[1] See note, p. 83.
[2] An allusion to the polished metal mirrors formerly in use in Persia.

time that this sudden calamity came upon me, and such a dreadful misfortune alighted on my abode, I observed that my dignity in the hearts of the other mice began to decline, and that as regards the respect and consideration which were customary, a glaring difference appeared. The fire of my friends' kindness became quenched, and the pure fountain of their obedience and submission became defiled with the dust of obstinacy and rebellion.

Affection and fidelity no longer exist in the hearts of any one,
In my garden no delicious fruit remains;
Gold was the source of a hundred varieties of food and provision;
The gold has vanished, while food and provision no longer remain.

The mice who used to live on the remnants of my food, devouring the scraps of the tables of my kindness, and gathering the grapes of the harvest of my bounty, had the same expectation of favours, and desire after banquets. When their wishes and object were not gratified by me, they turned aside from serving and waiting on me, and breaking off their respect and allegiance, loosed their tongues in finding fault and condemning. They then quitted my society and joined themselves to my enemies, and those opposed to me.

When blindness fell on me from Heaven,
I pictured in my eyes many rogues,
Who all used to be at my side,
Devouring my scraps, like dogs in my street.

There is a well-known proverb, " *He whose money becomes less, his power is lowered,*" or he who has no money has no friends; the empty-handed and poor man will never accomplish any matter he takes up, nor will any desire which emanates from his innermost heart be gratified. Just as rain-water collected in summer can never return to the sea, nor unite with the rivulets; and because it has no source of supply, becomes wasted in the desert, and reaches nowhere. Wise men have said, that whoever has no brother, wherever he may happen to be, will feel strange; the memory, too, of him who has no children will be effaced from the pages of time; and whoever is poor and destitute will find no favour from friends: nay, more, the impoverished will have no friend at all, since whenever any one is himself poor, the mass who, like the Pleiades, cluster in a knot round his society, will become scattered like the constellation of the Bear—because the friendship of the mean and low-minded is confined to self-interest and worldly advancement.

So long as they consume the food there is,
They will buzz about you like bees;
Again when your village is in ruins,
And your purse like the body of a guitar,
They forsake your society and intimacy.
There was no friendship—it was a mere conceit:
I speak truly—they are bázár dogs,
Who esteem their bone more highly than yourself.

It has been currently said, that inquiry was made of a wise man, " How many friends have you?" He replied: "I do not know; for as I am befriended by Fortune, and possess extreme wealth and riches, every one makes show of friendship, and boasts of intimacy and affection. If, God forbid! the dust of adversity should cloud the eyes of my prosperity, it would at that instant become known who are my friends and who my rivals. A friend can be recognised in the time of adversity, and allies distinguished from rivals in the season of distress."

> Whoever is deserted by Fortune
> Will be abandoned by wife, children, and friends.

Also in the pleasant pages of the wise it is written, that one of the learned men was asked the question : "What can be the point in this, that men are inclined for the friendship of any one who has riches ? " He replied : " Wealth is beloved by mankind : as regards any one who possesses it, men esteem him, and when it slips away from his hand, they no longer collect around him."

> When the rose exhibits in the garden its golden skirt,
> The nightingale chants its praises with a thousand songs and melodies.
> But when its leaves are scattered by the wind,
> No one ever hears the name of the rose on the lips of the nightingale.

At this juncture one of the mice, who used to glory in attending on me, considering one moment of my society the capital stock of perpetual happiness, and who, by way of friendship, was constantly describing his fidelity and integrity in the following manner,—

> " I am so sincere in my love, that were you to strike a sword upon my head,
> At the time of trial I should stand firm like a taper "—

passed by me like a stranger, and in no way paid me any respect. Seeking him, I exclaimed :

> Are you going ? Do you pay me no respect ?
> No cypress-tree was ever more independent.[1]

" What, in the name of wonder, has happened to you, and what has become of all that affection and kindness which you used to display ? " The Mouse, frowning, said, with the greatest insolence : " You have been a foolish person. Men do not wait on any one for mere trifles, nor gather round an individual for nought. So long as you had money and were benevolent, we heartily served you, but now you are in difficulties ; and the wise say, that just as the necessitous man has no share in the pleasures of this world, so it is possible he will be deprived of the dignities of the next. *'Poverty is nigh becoming infidelity.'* The reason of this is that, perhaps in difficulties for his own food, and the necessary expenses of his family, he seeks for sustenance in improper ways, the punishment thereof being a source of pain and torture in that world ; just as in this world he is distressed with the anguish of poverty, so in that to come he will be confined and encaged in the prison of eternal misery.

> Like an infidel darwísh, nought of the world, nought of faith.

" ' *The loss of this world and of the next, certainly is a clear loss.*' Accordingly, if men will not associate with such a person as has squandered his worldly property, and is not known to possess eternal wealth, and turn aside from being intimate with him, it is excusable." I replied : " Cease such talk, for the poor man is a king, upon the forehead of whose excellence is placed the throne, ' *Poverty is my boast*,' and upon the shoulders of the nobleness of whose mind is cast the garment, ' *The fakír needs nothing.*'

---

[1] The cypress is called " free " owing to its freedom from curvature, and its independence of all support.

The affairs of a darwísh are beyond thy understanding.
Look not with indifference at the darwísh.
Poverty is like an upper story,
Since the poor take precedency of all.

Poverty is essential, and except poverty all is accidental ;
Poverty is health, and except poverty all is disease.

" Why, then, do you reproach poverty, and on what ground do you dislike the
society of the darwísh ? " The Mouse replied : " Alas ! alas ! what relation has
this your penury and want of means with the poverty approved by the Prophets and
lauded by the Saints ? This latter implies that the wayfarer on the road of truth
will accept nought of the coin of this world, nor of the capital of that to come,[1]—
that is to say, he abandons everything so as to acquire everything. *'None arrives*
at the total save he who has severed himself from the total.' The darwísh
displays such poverty as this, while the other kind of pauper is a beggar. Beggary
is one thing, and holy poverty another. The darwísh is he who abandons the
world, while the beggar is he whom the world has abandoned.

A beggar of bread is like a fish on land.
There is the appearance of a fish, but it has fled from the sea.
He is a pauper after dainties, but is not anxious after God.
Place not trays before dead souls.

' *Poverty is a treasure from the treasures of God,*' is a mystery of the belief
in the one God, and the essence of true learning, and glorification of the Almighty.
It is the water of the fountain-head of self-mortification, which washes off the
dust of worldly consideration from the face of the pious soul, or a robe from
the treasury of solitude, with which the Divine hand has clad the pure heart.
Poverty is the alchemy of the Omnipotent Ruler, and the mystery thereof is
beyond the circle of description or writing.

The first proceeding of a fakír is to stake his head,
To turn his ideas from all rivals.
When the head (life) is lost, and all things set aside,
Headless he must pursue some other task.

" But the seeming and necessitous darwísh is the root of all evils, the occasion of
the enmity of mankind, the overthrow of modesty and shame, the ruin of the
edifice of manliness, the origin of sin and wickedness, the destruction of power
and magnanimity, and the cause of misery and disgrace. Whoever is entangled
in the circle of poverty cannot avoid removing the veil of shame ; since the inscription, '*Modesty appertains to faith,*' is erased from the leaves of his condition,
he becomes disgusted with his existence, and is overwhelmed with misery and
distress. The guest, too, of ease removes his chattels from the court of his bosom,
and the army of grief gains ascendancy over the kingdom of his disposition,
while the candle of his wisdom remains without light, and his understanding,
sagacity, caution, and intelligence decline. The benefits of right deliberation in
his case produce bad results. Notwithstanding his sincerity he may chance to
be accused of treachery, and the good opinion in which his friends held him
becomes removed. If another commit a fault the crime is imputed to him. All
he does or says is wrong, and every quality, which amongst the rich is lauded

---

[1] It is not clear what can be meant by this sentence, since wayfarers on the road of truth would
surely gladly accept the capital of the world to come.

and praised, in the case of a poor man is a source of taunt and reproach. For example, if a man in indigent circumstances exhibits bravery, it is attributed to rashness, while, if he is accustomed to be liberal, it is designated extravagance; if he strives to be meek, it is reckoned weakness and impotency; if he is disposed to be gentle, it is called laziness and sloth; if he exhibits eloquence and oratory, he is dubbed a babbler; if he takes refuge in silence, he is termed, as it were, a picture in a warm bath; if he selects the corner of retirement, it is imputed to idiosyncrasy; if he puts on a smiling face and is sociable, it is deemed by way of jest and joke; if he takes pains as regards his food and raiment, he is spoken of as self-indulgent; if he is satisfied with rags and morsels, he is thought to be miserable and poor; if he dwells in one abode, he is crude and inexperienced; if he is anxious to travel, he is a wanderer and a desperado; if he passes his life unmarried, it is unnatural; if he becomes the head of a family, he is said to be sensual, and a slave of his passions. All his life a necessitous man is reprobated and condemned by men of the world. If in these circumstances they observe him hankering for anything — Heaven defend us! — enmity towards him is implanted in their minds, and admitting none of his requirements, they are all offended with him. The source of every misery which befalls mankind is greed. *'Whoever is covetous becomes contemptible.'* "

Misery proceeds from greed, honour from contentment.

When my friend repeated this discourse, I replied: "You say truly, and I have heard that were any one to remain so ill, that all hope of his recovery is precluded, or to become overwhelmed at separation, when hope of meeting is impossible to be imagined, or to happen to be an exile, having no chance of return, and the wherewithal for a residence not being procurable—all this would be more bearable than poverty and need. Now I see that this language proceeded from the fountain of wisdom, and the speaker in this sense recited his own experience.

> There is no worse calamity in the world than poverty;
> For the poor man there is in no case any advantage.
> To him whose heart is overwhelmed with the grief of avarice,
> Say die, for there is no remedy for such an ailment.

"Amongst the evils of want this is enough, that one must seek for something from mankind, and request the means of existence from those like one's self. In any case death is better than poverty and beggary; since to put one's hand into the mouth of a snake, and draw out thence deadly poison for one's sustenance, or to snatch morsels from a hungry lion, or to be boon companions with an enraged tiger, is more endurable than to bear one's necessities before the mean, or to undergo the disgrace of beggary. It has been said that the pleasure of receiving is not equivalent to the pain of asking, nor do the joys of power pay for the miseries of dismissal. A wise man has enjoined:

> 'There are four things which are a source of advantage and benefit,
> But which are not ultimately to be compared with four others:
> Life with the bitternesss of death; power with the disgrace of dismissal;
> Sin with the shame of repentance; receiving with the pain of asking.'"

Thereupon I turned away from that Mouse, and hastening once more to the entrance of my hole, observed that the Devotee and the Guest were dividing the gold between them, and that the former, having put his portion in a purse, placed it under his pillow. An unlucky greed began to tempt me, that if I could get somewhat of that money, once again strength of mind and ease of soul would return, and friends and brothers would desire my service, while my assembly would be adorned, and my society embellished. In this idea, I exercised considerable patience till they were asleep; then slowly I went towards the Devotee's pillow; the experienced Guest was at this time awake, with his eyes intent on this proceeding, and expecting what I was about; he struck me with a stick such a blow on my foot, that I was bruised with the severity thereof, and dragging my leg along, went to my hole. I waited there awhile till the pain abated, when again I issued forth with the same hankering; the Guest this time laid the stick on my head, so that I became stupefied, and, after endless contrivance, cast myself into my hole, and fell down senseless. The pain of that wound disgusted me with worldly possessions, and I forgot all about poverty and want.

> Why should any one complain of poverty?
> Since health is infinite wealth.

Of a truth I perceived that greed is the precursor of every calamity, and the prelude to every misery. Till the bird covets the grain, his neck is not ensnared with the noose of the trap, and till a man girds his loins with greed, his dress of honour is not exchanged for the coarse cloth of disgrace. Whoever chooses to journey by sea, or else undergoes any unreasonable danger, has avarice before his eyes, and from the darkness of covetousness the dust of distress rests upon the frontispiece of the face of the excellent, and the light-weight of cupidity lessens the worth of the wise in the balance of esteem.

> O brother! be not covetous, for avarice
> Will render a man wretched and despised.
> Hear two words, if you are so disposed,
> So that you may enjoy life:
> ' Draw your feet within the skirt of contentment;
> Hanker not after the wealth of mankind.'

It is strange that persons should seek for happiness in the multitude of wealth, unaware that ease may be obtained with but little thereof; and should look for riches in worldly possessions, not recognising that, by abandoning them they will obtain high dignity.

> He obtains honour who tears his heart from love of the world;
> He finds ease, who restrains the hand of cupidity therefrom.

Now my affairs, owing to this event, came to such a pitch, that I tore up the tree of covetousness from the soil of my heart, and obtained the fruit of contentment in the plantation of acquiescence, and became submissive to the Divine Decree, placing my head upon the inscription of Fortune, and saying to myself, "The World has proclaimed its peculiarities and faults in the fold of these occurrences and accidents; the purport is that the eyes of wisdom, when overwhelmed by the disease of greed, are blind to its defects. There is no palace in which the traces of its treachery and deception are not manifest, nor any mansion over the portico of which the indication of its designs is not inscribed. Whom has it exalted that it has not overwhelmed? and where has it planted a tree that it has not torn it up again? Whom has it cherished that it has not drunk his blood? and to whom has it opened the door of fortune that it has not afterwards brought a thousand distresses upon him?

> This contemptible World is like a base[1] woman,
> From whom her husband never derives pleasure;
> Who is there who places his feet on the ladder of her throne,
> But finds a sword upon his head at her hands?

"It is not worth while being vexed about such faithlessness, or grieving at its existence or non-existence, or being sad at the loss or gain thereof."

> The world is not worth shedding tears over,
> Nor indulging in fruitless grief at the gain or loss thereof.

After these reflections I removed from the house of the Devotee to the desert. Now there was a Pigeon who was friends with me, and whose love and affection were the occasion of intimacy between me and the Crow. The latter has told me an account of your kindness and generosity. The breeze of your virtues has reached me from the garden of his conversation, and the mention of your excellent qualities and benevolent disposition, has given rise to a sincere and earnest desire, and I was anxious through his kindness by means of the happiness of meeting you, to seek your company. I recoil from the solitude of retirement, since loneliness is a severe matter, and the sadness of desolation a difficult business; there can be no joy in the world like the society of friends, nor any grief equivalent to separation from companions and absence from allies. But thanks to the most High God, the rose of prosperity has begun to blossom on the heart-rending thorn of adversity, and the dark-faced night of distress to give place to the clear-minded, world-adorning morn of repose.

> The day of separation and the night of absence from friends have terminated.
> I read my omen, the star is vanished, and the matter ended.
> This is the morn of hope, which retires behind the curtain of secrecy;[2]
> Bid it come forth, for dark night's work is done.

———o———

"Such are my adventures, which I have repeated in their entirety, and now I am come to your neighbourhood, and am hopeful of your friendship and affection."

> And it is becoming that by aid of the polisher, your kindness,
> You should burnish the rust[3] of grief from the mirror of my soul.

When the Tortoise heard this discourse, he spread the carpet of kindness and began to display courtesy, saying:

> In the home where such a guest alights,
> Heaven's phœnix will place its nest.

"What happiness can compare with the honour of your society, or what joy can

---

[1] لاطا in the Persian text is a misprint for لاطا.

[2] تفیذ in the Persian text is a misprint for فیب.

[3] See note 2, page 51.

be equivalent to the pleasure of your intimacy? Just as you are anxious for my aid and friendship, I too am benefited by and glory in your society and company, and so long as the lamp of life shall be illumined, moth-like, I will revel in the taper of your beauty.

> Like atoms we place ourselves in the sun-rays of your affection;
> Were you to smite us with a sword, we would not sever ourselves from you.

"In this discourse, as you have repeated it, various experiences and different admonitions are contained, according to which lessons it is clear, that a wise man should be content with but little of this world's trash, and be satisfied with such an amount as that the hand of want need not be extended before any one; for he who desires more than is necessary as regards home and food, places his feet beyond the region of justice, and this injustice will overwhelm him in the whirlpool of calamity, and the desert of danger, and that will befall him which happened to that greedy Cat." The Mouse inquired, "What was that?"

STORY VI.

He said: It has been related that a certain person had a Cat, to whom was allotted as her daily portion such an amount of food as would quench the fire of hunger; but, from the ferocious qualities which had overpowered that crude-natured creature, she was not content with her allowance.

> O my friend! live poor and contented,
> For misery springs from cupidity, and honour from contentment.

"One day she passed nigh to a pigeon-house. From the heart-enchanting cooing, and the upper and lower notes of the pigeons, the Cat's appetite being set in motion, she cast herself into that tower; but the keeper of that citadel, and the watchman of that abode, at once seized her, and conveyed her from the rose-garden of life to the furnace of death. Before even the Cat could perfume the brain of her appetite with the marrow in the heads of the pigeons, the man tore off her skin, and stuffing it with straw, fastened it on the entrance of the pigeon-house. By chance her master happened to pass that locality, and saw his Cat in that plight. He exclaimed: "O impudent-faced greedy one! if you had been content with the portion of food which fell to you, they would not have taken your skin from you."

> Be content, O soul! with but little,
> Since without doubt misery springs from greed.
> Wealth-adoring Kárún [1] did not know
> That the riches of happiness are comprised in a nook.
> Concupiscence makes a man miserable;
> If you are wise love it not.
> Wild beasts, deer, and birds of the air,
> Are cast in the net by nought save desire after food.
> The tiger who tyrannises over the wild animals,
> Falls into the snare, like a mouse, from avidity after food.

"The moral of this story is, that henceforth you should be satisfied with food

---

[1] See note 1, page 62.

that may be but a bare subsistence, and with a hole which may protect you from the evils of heat and cold, and not be sad on account of money which is lost.

> Be not sad, O my soul! if wealth and property vanish;
> Be joyous, for this corpse is not worth lamenting.

"Recognise that a man's honour is according to his perfections, not according to his wealth. Whoever is adorned with personal merit, though he possess but little riches, is always beloved and esteemed: like a lion who, though he be confined in chains, yet dread of him is not lessened A rich man without merit is always contemptible and worthless: like a dog who, though decked with collar and ring, is none the less despicable and without value.

> Whoever is debased in the prison of ignorance,
> Is a beggar, though his wealth might fill a hundred vessels.
> The man who is rich in knowledge,
> How can he fix his eyes on gold and gems?

"Again, banish from your mind the affliction of exile, and attach no weight to separation from your native country and abode: since a wise man, wherever he goes, derives aid from his knowledge, while an ignorant person is a wanderer and a stranger in his birthplace and native soil.

> The man of merit is nowhere a stranger.

"Be not grieved because you say 'I had a store and it has been dissipated'; for wealth and worldly possessions tend to slip away, and their retention or loss is beyond the pale of reliance. Wise men have said that there are six things from which stability and permanence cannot be expected: 1st, The shadow of a cloud, which vanishes while you look at it; 2d, Interested friendship, which in a little time comes to nought like a flash of lightning; 3d, Women's love, which for slight reasons becomes quenched; 4th, The beauty of handsome damsels, which ultimately is changed; 5th, The praise of liars, which has no splendour; 6th, Worldly riches, which ultimately come to the place of destruction, and in regard to their possessors, never convey them to the end of the road of fidelity.

> With the ornaments, the trappings, the wealth, and chattels of this contemptible world
> Be not puffed up, since they will remain faithful to no one.

"It is not fit that wise men should be delighted with much wealth, or be sad at having but little thereof—since amongst the high-minded the whole world, with its goods and chattels, is not worth a blade of grass. Accordingly, precious life's harvest must not be scattered to the winds in seeking to acquire the same, nor must a grain of vexation be consumed in the thought of the loss or want thereof. They who are apprised of the mystery, '*Lest you be sad on account of that which passes away from you, or rejoice for that which comes to you,*' gallop the steed of ambition in the expanse of the plain of contentment, and staking the coin of life in the acquirement of the appurtenances of solitude, and the abandonment of the requisites of life, neither, when in possession of worldly things, open the doors of joy before the face of their soul, nor display regret or reproach at the loss thereof.

If the world slip from your grasp,
Grieve not thereat, for it is nought;
If the universe comes within your palm,
Rejoice not thereat, for it is nought:
Since the ills and good of the world are transitory,
Abandon this world, for it is nought.

" In truth, wealth itself must be considered something sent in advance, and possessions be recognised as a store laid up for the next world. Good conduct and acceptable conversation are riches which cannot be taken from any one, and which the accidents of Fortune, and the revolutions of night and day, cannot squander. The value of worldly goods is to prepare a possession for Eternity, and to make ready the materials for travelling the path to the World to come; since according to the saying, ' *We seized them suddenly,*' the messenger of death comes suddenly, and the yielding up of the deposit of the soul occurs at no fixed time, or certain period.[1]

Awaken from soft sleep that beautiful narcissus, for life
Is flitting, like the duration of a rose, in the twinkling of an eye.

" Although you are not in need of my counsel, and well distinguish between your own advantage and disadvantage, yet I am anxious to discharge the dues of friendship, and to assist you as regards your laudable disposition and praiseworthy habits. You are this day our friend and brother—and as regards what can be possible in favouring you, and imaginable in being civil to you, such will in every way come to pass; and though, impossible as is the supposition, traces of unkindness on your part were to become evident, on my side nought but the blessings of sincerity, and the usages of consideration, would be displayed."

Though you desert me, I cannot abandon you;
Though you break my heart, I cannot violate my agreement with you.

When the Tortoise recited these words, and the Crow heard how kind he had been in the matter of the Mouse, his heart was refreshed, and his joy became boundless. He exclaimed: " O brother! you have rendered me delighted, and doubled the source of my pleasure and happiness, while manifesting a portion of your excellent qualities. The best of friends is he, the bulk of whose friends at all times pass their existence under the shade of his kindness and condescension, and under the protection of his care and guardianship, while he opens the doors of benevolence to them, and makes it an obligation on his heart to comply with their petitions and adjust their necessities. He who in friendship, owing to some matter remains apart from his friend, is not fit for a friend. It is a tradition, that a great man had a friend, who one evening came to the entrance of his house, and knocked at the door. The great man knew that it was his companion. He fell into a long and deep reverie as to what could be the cause of his coming at that unseasonable time. After abundant reflection, he snatched his purse full of money, and belting on his sword, commanded the servant to light a candle, and go on before him. When he had opened the door, and shaken hands and embraced his friend, he exclaimed: ' O brother! I fancied three reasons why you come here at this unseasonable time: 1st, A calamity may have occurred, and you are in need

---

[1] That is, at no fixed period, which can be predicted beforehand.

of money; 2d, An enemy may have arisen to kill you, and you need assistance and aid in repelling him; 3d, You may be distressed at your solitude, and need some one to settle your affairs. Now I have prepared the needful for all these cases, and am come forth. If you need money, behold here is a purse of diram; if you seek for aid, here I am with my sharp sword; and if you desire a servant! lo, here is a fitting damsel.'

> Whatever you decree, your command is potent.

"His friend asked his pardon. By this beautiful proceeding the bonds of his reliance on the other's friendship and affection were confirmed.

> When your proceedings spring from friendship, act in such a manner
> That your friend may, at your hands, accomplish his object.
> It is better to regard the desires of your friends,
> For indifference produces anxiety.

"None but the generous can aid the benevolent person who has fallen into the whirlpool of calamity: just as when an elephant tumbles into the mire, none but other elephants can extricate him. If in settling the Mouse's affairs trouble befall you, there is no occasion for despondency, and keeping in view your reputation and generosity, you need not be filled with distress thereat, for a wise man always strives to gain honour, and leaves a fair memory. Now, if to acquire a good name, for example, one's head must be risked, one should not abandon one's[1] efforts: because Eternal life will have been purchased with destruction, and little sold for much.

> When the world is at your feet,[2] gain a good name,
> For, except a good name, nought can be procured from the world.

"Whoever will not share his bounty with the necessitous will not be reckoned amongst the number of the rich, while the name of him who passes his life in infamy and disappointment will not be included in the company of the living."

> O Sa'dí![3] the man of good name never dies;
> He is dead, whose reputation is not associated with goodness.

The Crow was thus speaking, when a Deer appeared from afar, running with haste; they thought that some one in search of him was at his heels. The Tortoise jumped into the water, the Crow sat upon a tree, and the Mouse crept into a hole. The Deer, reaching the brink of the water, remained as it were stupefied. The Crow cast his eyes in every direction, to see whether any one was on the track or not; but, though he looked to right and left, he saw no one. He cried to the Tortoise to come out of the water; the Mouse, too, put in an appearance. The Tortoise observed that the Deer was trembling and looking in the water, but without drinking. He said: "If you are thirsty, drink and be not afraid, for there is no fear." The Deer advanced, and the Tortoise commenced in tones of welcome, saying:

> "O dear friend! whence comest thou?
> Be not a stranger, for you arrive as an acquaintance."

The Deer replied: "I was alone in this desert, not mingling with those of my

---

[1] Literally, "withdraw from that direction."
[2] Literally, "at your desire."
[3] A celebrated poet, author of the Gulistán.

own kind, and perpetually the archers, stringing the bow of destruction, used to drive me from corner to corner. This very day I saw an old man in an ambush for me, and watching my proceedings wherever I went. I imagined that he was a Hunter, the snare of whose treachery would suddenly bind my feet: fleeing, I arrived here." The Tortoise said: "Fear not, for hunters never reach the neighbourhood of this locality; and if you like, keep company with us, so that we may bring you within the pale of our own friendship, and the edifice of the society of us three persons become settled with the support of a fourth like yourself; for the wise have said, that the more numerous are friends, the fewer will be the attacks of misfortune against them.

> Wherever a habit of affection and fidelity predominates,
> Tranquillity, ease, and content will abound the more.

"It is established that if there be a thousand friends, they must be considered as one; while if there be a single enemy, he should be reckoned as many."

> A thousand persons are needed as friends,
> But one is sufficient for an enemy.

The Mouse also whispered some sentences, and the Crow spoke several soothing words. The Deer, perceiving that they were kindly-disposed [1] friends and honest-minded companions, joined with them, and heart and soul became disposed for their society.

> How delightful is intercourse with a suitable friend!

The Deer took up his abode in that meadow, and his friends charged him: "Do not put your feet beyond this pasture which is around us, nor wander far from the neighbourhood of this fountain-head, which is a castle of security and safety." The Deer agreed to follow their injunction. Accordingly, they passed their time with one another. Now there was a patch of reeds, wherein at all times they used to assemble together, and, sporting about, narrate what had occurred. One day the Crow, the Mouse, and the Tortoise came to the appointed spot and waited a while for the Deer, who did not appear. This circumstance was the cause of heart-rending, as is the way of those who are in expectation, and agitation of mind overpowered them. They requested the Crow: "Take the trouble to fly in the air, and bring us tidings of the state of the absentee."

> O Zephyr! pass by the abode of my mistress; do not refuse,
> Nor withhold from her disconsolate lover any tidings of her.

The Crow in a little time brought the tidings: "I have seen him, captured in the snare of misfortune." The Tortoise said to the Mouse: "In this dilemma there is no hope except from you, and the standard of the Deer's freedom cannot be raised save through your assistance."

> Hasten, for time for work is slipping away.

The Crow then led the way, while the Mouse, running along, came near the Deer and said: "O dear brother! how have you fallen into this whirlpool? and, with all your wisdom and intelligence, in what way came you to give your neck to the snare of treachery?" The Deer replied: "Of what use is penetration to oppose the Divine Decree? and of what advantage are genius and ability against

---

[1] ‏جمله‎ in the Persian text is a misprint for ‏جمله‎.

the Royal Mandate? From the desert of Deliberation to the abode of Fate is an endless road, and from the expanse of Stratagem to the regions of Destiny a boundless distance intervenes."

> Having stepped beyond the door, we are deluded with a hundred deceits
> As to what they are planning behind the screen.

The Mouse replied : "You say truly.

> ' Whenever Fate erects the tent of destiny,
> No one can make boast of deliberation.' "

Thereupon he busied himself severing the bonds of the Deer. In the midst of this, the Tortoise, having arrived, displayed his grief and melancholy at the capture of his friend. The Deer exclaimed : "O dear friend! your coming to this place is more dangerous than what has befallen me, since if a Hunter should arrive, provided the Mouse has severed my cords, I can in a bound save my life, while the Crow can fly, and the Mouse take refuge in the corner of a hole; but you have neither hand to oppose nor face to fight, neither head to resist nor foot to fly. What trouble is this you have taken, and wherefore have you displayed such rashness?" The Tortoise rejoined : "O kind companion! how could I not come, and on what pretence[1] could I stay behind, and think it right? Existence spent in separation from friends, what pleasure has it? and life passed in absence from comrades, of what value is it?

> Lifeless, I existed ; do not consider this very wonderful,
> Since on the day of separation who esteems his existence?

" I am to be excused coming, since the desire of your beauty involuntarily drew me to this spot, and the wish to see you deprived me of patience and quiet; and as regards this amount of distance and necessary length of journey which have occurred, the companion, Endurance, has placed its feet in the path of non-existence.

> God knows that I cannot endure to be without thee,
> I cannot undergo the day of separation, and the night of solitude.

"Do not be dejected, for this very moment you will be free, and these knots being loosed, with quiet mind you will hasten to your home. In any case, thanks to God are incumbent, and due praise is imperative, for neither has injury befallen your body, nor destruction occurred to your life. Were it otherwise, a remedy for such could not be imagined, and the cure thereof would be beyond the limit of possibility." They were thus talking, when a Hunter appeared from afar; the Mouse, too, had finished severing the cords. The Deer leapt up, the Crow flew away, and the Mouse crept into a hole, while the Tortoise remained where he was. The Hunter came up, and finding the bonds of the Deer severed, seized the finger of perplexity with the teeth[2] of deliberation, and began to look right and left, as to by whom this matter had occurred, and by whose hand this affair had been done. His glance lighting upon the Tortoise, he said to himself : "Though this contemptible piece of goods cannot make amends for the misfortune of the Deer having escaped and the net being broken, yet to return empty-handed is injurious to the reputation of a Hunter." He at once seized the Tortoise, and threw him into a bag, and, casting it over his back, set out

---

[1] Literally, "by what explanation."   [2] See note, p. 28.

towards the city. The friends, after the Hunter's departure, congregated together, and it became clear to them that the Tortoise had been captured in his net. A cry came forth from their souls, and raising lamentations and screams to the summit of the ethereal sphere, they said:

> The day on which our sight was deprived of thy beauty,
> As often as we used our eyes, they filled with tears.

" What distress can be equal to separation from friends, or what misery equivalent to absence from comrades? He who remains deprived of the sight of his companions, and is destitute of rosy-cheeked intimacy, knows that the wanderers in the desert of Separation have the feet of perplexity in the mire, and the recluses in the cell of Desire place the hand of regret on their hearts."

What difference does our state make to you, who never were in pain?
What do you, who sit on the bank of a stream, know of the power of thirst?

Each of the comrades separately whispered some sentences, and made use of melancholy and painful language suited to the case; the purport of their words related to the self-same subject.

> The heart has no pleasure apart from the sweet lips of dear ones.
> Without beloved ones, life has no value to a sweetheart.

At length the Deer said to the Crow: " O brother! though our language is very eloquent, and the melodious phrases [1] we recite are extremely oratorical, yet this is of no use to the Tortoise, and our lamentations, our cries, our weeping and perturbation, are of no benefit [2] to him. It is more in accordance with good faith to devise some stratagem, and hit upon some plan, which may comprise his escape, and insure his delivery. The wise have said, that four classes are tried at four times: the courage of the brave may be known in the day of battle; the integrity of the upright may be discovered in the time of lending or borrowing; the affection and fidelity of women and children may be made patent in the day of poverty; and the probity of friends may be verified in the time of adversity and difficulty."

> I need a friend in days of distress.
> There is no lack of friends to me in prosperity.

The Mouse said: " O Deer! a scheme has entered my mind. It is expedient for you to go in front of the Hunter, and show yourself to him as fainting and wounded, while the Crow, sitting on your back, must make it appear as though he were attacking you. Assuredly when the eyes of the Hunter alight upon you, his heart will be delighted at the idea of catching you, and placing the Tortoise, together with the trappings, on the ground, he will turn towards you. Whenever he comes near you, limping along, go farther from him, but not so that his greed after you may be severed. Keep him one good hour busy hunting about, and do not abandon the path of encouragement and moderation in your movements, it may be that, having released the Tortoise, I may bring about his escape." His friends congratulated him on his intelligence, while the Deer and the Crow disported themselves, in the manner arranged, before the Hunter, who,

---

[1] Literally, "verses."   [2] Literally, "do not sit in his stomach."

foolish-like, when he saw the Deer limping along, and the Crow hovering around him, intending to attack his eyes, made sure he could capture the Deer, and setting down his bag from his back, went after him. The Mouse at once severing the string of the bag, let loose the Tortoise. After a while the Hunter, becoming tired of pursuing the Deer, was very fatigued. Coming to the mouth of the bag, he did not see the Tortoise, and found the strings cut. Astonishment overpowered him, and he thought to himself: "No one would believe these strange circumstances which I behold. First of all the bonds of the Deer are cut, then the Deer makes himself ill, and the Crow sits on his back, a hole is made in the bag, and the Tortoise escapes. To what can these proceedings be attributable?" In the midst of these cogitations fear overcame him, and he said: "Probably this is the abode of fairies, and the resting-place of demons. I must quickly return and sever all hankering after the animals of this desert." Accordingly the Hunter carried off the shreds of his bag, and his broken net, and set out in flight, vowing that if he got safely out of that wood, he would not again, during the remainder of his life, allow the idea of that desert to pass through his mind, and would restrain other hunters also, by way of kindness, from frequenting that forest.

For there perpetually the wind is in the clutches of the net.

When the Hunter went away, the friends again congregated together, and passed their time in their own abode, in ease, safety, quiet, and repose. After this, neither did the hand of misfortune reach the skirt of their affairs, nor did the talon of adversity scratch the face of their circumstances and case. By the blessing of their concord, and the advantages of their union, the knot of repose was settled, and the thread of companionship strengthened.

Thread, when single, may be snapped by the force of an old man,
When doubled, Zál-zar [1] would be powerless to break it;
The perfume of the rose, when unmixed, will in the end dry up the brain;
And if sugar be eaten alone it inflames the liver;
From either of these, alone, no strength accrues to the soul or heart,
Together, as Conserve of Roses, they will give vigour to both heart and soul.

Such is the story of the intercourse of friends, and the tale of the society and unanimity of companions: of honest affection in both prosperity and adversity, and of the observance of devotedness in time of both pleasure and trouble, and the discharge of the dues of comradeship in periods of both good fortune and distress. In the occurrences of the day and the incidents of the world, in all sincerity they displayed the utmost firmness; consequently, by the blessing of unanimity and mutual assistance, they escaped from several deadly whirlpools, and turning their backs on affliction and misfortune, abode happy and at rest on the throne of repose, and the royal seat of delight.

The wise should deem it incumbent, with the light of wisdom and purity of thought, worthily to reflect on these tales. Seeing that the friendship of weak animals produced such acceptable fruit and excellent results, if the mass of the wise, who are the select of mankind and the best of people, were to practise sincere friendship in this way, and lay the foundation of their intercourse on such a basis, and carry it to an end with honest intent and inward integrity,

---

[1] Name of Rustam's father.

would not the light of benefit spread over high and low, and advantageous effects becoming manifest on the pages of the circumstances of every one, would not the blessings thereof accrue to small and great?

> He who recognises the rights of intercourse amongst friends,
> Runs no risk of life save together with them;
> When no friend is on the scene, grief will follow;
> Few matters are performed without an ally;
> The society of such a person as is sincere and straightforward,
> Must be caught by the skirt, for he is faithful;
> Select such an one as acts uprightly,
> His soul will form a shield for you against the arrow of calamity;
> The worth of such a friend as is stanch,
> Is that of the soul's friendship from its preciousness.

BOOK IV.

EXPLANATORY OF OBSERVING THE CIRCUMSTANCES OF ONE'S ENEMIES, AND NOT BEING SECURE FROM THEIR TREACHERY AND DECEIT.

INTRODUCTION.

HE King said to the Brahman: "I have heard a tale respecting dear friends and worthy sincere comrades, and learned the result of their concord and unanimity; and gathered that,

> 'Whoever has a faithful friend, is never sad;
> Whoever has not a friend, has no joy of heart.'

"Now, if you will be good enough, repeat an account of an enemy by whom one must not be deceived, nor be carried away by his humility and submission; for the purport of the fourth precept was, that wise men, by reason of foresight, should not place any confidence in their enemies, since in no case can a foe become a friend."

> To seek a friend amongst enemies is the same
> As to make fire and water unite.

Bídpáí said: "Certainly, a wise man pays no heed to the words of an enemy, and does not purchase his hypocritical chattels of deceit and fraud: since an able foe, for his own safety, will make a display of the utmost kindness, and adorn his exterior quite contrary to his inmost thoughts, availing himself of the minutiæ of hypocrisy, and the pleasantries of deceit, under cover of which he will arrange deep plans and marvellous designs. Accordingly, it behoves a far-seeing wise man, however much kindness and attention he observes on the part of an enemy, to increase his own suspicion and self-reserve; and the more an antagonist puts out the foot of courtesy, the more he himself should fold up the skirt of friendship: since, if he be negligent and leaves a breach open, his enemy, who is always on the look-out for such a contingency, will suddenly rush from his ambush, and shoot the arrow of Device against the target of Desire. In such a case, the opportunity of remedy being lost, regret and repentance will be of no avail, and 'if' and 'would to heaven' will be fruitless; and that will happen to him which befell the Owl at the hands of the Crow." Dábishlím inquired, "What was that?"

———o———

STORY I.

He said: It has been related that in one of the kingdoms of China was a mountain of such a height, that the sense of Sight would have rested at several places on the road before it reached the summit; and the guardian, Intelligence, save with the ladder of Imagination, never put its foot upon the plateau of its altitude.

> No one, save in the mind's eye, ever saw its heights;
> No one, save with the foot of fancy, ever descended its depths.

In that majestic mountain, from the extreme height and extensive expanse of which,

> Its entire top was in the summit of the heavens,
> Its breadth stretched over the whole surface of the earth,

the all-wise Gardener, by mere power, had caused a tree to grow, the branches of which passed the Pleiades in altitude, and its roots were fixed in the centre of the earth.

> A mighty tree, every branch of which
> Contended with the tree of Paradise;
> Among its qualities, its roots were immovable
> (So wisdom proclaimed), and its branches in heaven.

On that many-branched tree were a thousand Crows' nests. These Crows had a king named Pírúz,[1] all of them being under his sway, and obedient to his commands and prohibitions, as regards settling and arranging their affairs. One night the king of the Owls, named Shabáhang,[2] by reason of an ancient enmity which existed between the Crows and the Owls, made a night assault on the Crows, with a numerous army and a bloodthirsty band, and hurled destruction on the lives of many of them.

> With manly arm he raised his hand,
> And laid low the heads of his enemies like dust.

In that dark night he consumed, with the fire of battle, many Crows whose deeds were black, and fixed on the collar of the condition of those unfortunate wretches the inscription, "*Kill them wherever you find them;*" and returned from that overthrow victorious, triumphant, jubilant, and exulting. Next day, when the black-winged Raven of Night had turned its face towards the nest of

---

[1] Victorious.   [2] The morning star.

the west, and the horsemen of the Stars, like a flock of Owls, were concealed
in the corner of retirement,

> The world-enlightening planet drew its sword,
> The army of night became dispersed by day.

Pírúz, having collected his army, introduced the story of the attack by the hosts
of the Owls, and said: "You have seen the night assault of the Owls, and
have witnessed their bravery; and this very day several of you are slain,
stripped of feathers, wounded, and broken-winged; but worse than this is their
boldness and valour, and their eagerness to injure and molest the Crows, and to
gain intelligence of our abode and home, as well as to become apprised of our
resting-place and nests. Doubtless the victory and triumph which these people
have experienced will embolden them, and this time they will return more
quickly, and on the next opportunity will gain a more complete conquest than
at the first occasion, and will make those who are sick of the disease of
defeat taste also of the previous draught (of death). Maybe if once again
they make a night assault in this manner, they will not leave alive one of our
army. Reflect over this matter, and, devising some suitable means, arrange
amongst yourselves a plan for repelling them."

> As yet this is the first attack of the enemy,
> Next time will be the occasion of treachery and deceit;
> If no one stops the progress of this current,
> Endless miseries will spring therefrom.
> Firmly guard the way of strife this very day,
> For to-morrow no means of remedy will appear.

When Pírúz had finished his speech, five Crows from amongst the Chiefs of
the army came near the King, and performed the dues of praise, and rights
of homage. These were famous amongst the Crows for the excellence of their
wisdom, and the abundance of their knowledge, and celebrated for the soundness
of their deliberation, and their deepness of thought; whatever they suggested
contained the secrets of superiority and success,[1] and every opinion which they
expressed, displayed indications of weal and advantage.

> With clear intelligence and correct deliberation, they removed
> The rust [2] of defeat from the face of the mirror of the world.
> With perfect wisdom and true device, they arranged
> The solution of a thousand difficulties of the spheres in half an hour.

The Crows used to rely in matters upon their counsel, and in repelling calamities
set about according to their advice. The King esteemed their opinion as auspicious, and as regards the arrangements of his affairs, did not deviate from their
words and suggestions. When Pírúz's glance alighted upon them, he favoured
each of them with his royal condescension, and promised them robes of honour
and presents worthy of their condition, saying: "To-day is a day to try your
wisdom and learning; whatever pearls you have stored in the casket of your
minds must be strung on the thread of explanation, and placed on the platter
of representation, and whatever coin has been struck in the assay-house of your
honourable minds upon the touchstone of reliance, must be conveyed from the

---

[1] فضاح in the Persian text is a misprint for فصاح .   [2] See note 2, p. 51.

mint of trial to the market of manifestation." The Crows, loosening their tongues of praise-giving, exclaimed:

> O King! may the world be under thy protection!
> May the earth and time be thy well-wishers!
> May the key of the door of victory be in thy hand!
> May the heads of thy enemies be scattered at thy feet!

"In this matter your exalted opinion is the superior one, and what passes through your enlightened mind is best and most suitable; what can we slaves say, which is not a thousand-fold more clear to the mirror of the regal understanding, and what thing do we know, which is not doubly inscribed on the tablets of the royal comprehension? but in accordance with the saying, '*He who is commanded will be excused,*' as regards anything which may be asked, to the extent of our ability, and the power of the measure of our comprehension and capabilities, an attempt shall be made."

> What we shall speak is patent to the exalted mind.

The King inquired of one of them: "What say you in this matter, and in what way would you devise a remedy for averting this calamity?" He replied: "O King! the wise who have gone before us have shown us the plan for this kind of event, and have enjoined that when any one is helpless to resist a strong enemy, assuredly he must say farewell to property, possessions, native home and soil, and turn away his face from his accustomed country and ordinary abode; for to proclaim hostilities is very dangerous, and to put down the foot in the battle-field of war is sorely calamitous, especially when a rout has been experienced at the hands of the enemy, and it has been deemed a chance even to fly from them. Whoever, without reflection, proceeds to revenge, and undertakes to contend with foes such that he has seen the effects of their fighting and combat, might as well sleep in the channel of a torrent, or place bricks on the surface of running water; and to rely on one's own strength and be deceived with one's own power and courage, is far removed from caution, for a sword has two edges, and the wind of victory may possibly blow from both quarters."

> Avoid contending with an insignificant person,
> For I have seen many torrents from drops;
> Battle not with a warrior stronger than thyself:
> Thou canst [1] not strike thy finger against a lancet.

The King turned towards another, and said: "What think you, and what seems to you expedient in this matter?" He replied: "As regards what the previous Minister has suggested, that we should flee and leave our homes desolate, my opinion is not in accordance therewith; nay, more, such a plan is not worthy of men of wisdom, since on the first attack, and after a single battle, to accept this misery, and bid adieu to native soil and home, would be the cause of reproach, and the occasion of loss of honour.

> It does not become valiant men to retire at every wound.

"It is more expedient for us to get ready for battle, and with the greatest pomp and magnificence prepare for war.

---

[1] That is, without injury to thyself.

Unless we unsheathe the sword,
Our name will not be celebrated for bravery.
We shall point the way to our own disgrace,
When we display weakness in presence of our inferiors.
If the Creator of the world befriend us,
We will vent our rage on the enemy with the sword.

"The auspicious King can embrace with the hand of delight the bride of the kingdom, at the time when the water of the fiery sword shall wash out the name of his evil-designing enemies from the tablets of existence, and the august Sovereign may convey the cup of repose to the lip of his desire, at the period when he shall break, with the stone of victory, the goblet of his brazen-faced foes' wishes. It is at present desirable, that we should set guards, and protect ourselves in every direction where any danger can be imagined. If the enemy attack us, we shall advance ready and prepared, and display valour in battle, till the face of victory shall come into the sight of Hope from the dust of the plain, or else our blood be mingled with the earth of the battle-field in the expanse of Reputation and Renown.

If we are slain having a good name, it is proper.

"Kings in the day of battle, and at a time of fame and reputation, must pay no respect to the issue of matters, and at a period of war should reckon life and property as worthless and of no value."

Reckless place your feet in the plain; behold,
The ball [1] of gratification is in the hollow of the club of desire.
Would you wish fortune to display itself to your heart's content,
You must face your enemy in the battle-field.

The King turned the face of condescension towards another, and said : "What, in your opinion, is requisite, and what inscription does your deliberation fix on the board of representation?" He replied: "I have no concern with the speeches of the others; it seems to me that we should send spies, and make use of men of sense as scouts, and, investigating in a proper manner the condition of our enemies discover whether or no they are disposed for peace; if they will be content with tribute and taxes from us, and will meet our kindnesses with the excellence of acceptance, we, too, having based our affairs on peace, to the extent of our power and the limits of possibility, will bend our necks under taxation, and, secure from the misery of war and the distress of their night assaults, will remain at rest in our own country.

In any case, so long as a matter may be accomplished by deliberation,
Civility to an enemy is better than war.
When a foe cannot be overcome by strength,
The door of strife must be closed by conciliation.
If you do not wish any injury to accrue from an enemy,
Stop his mouth with the amulet of kindness.

"One of the correct ideas and sound devices for kings is, that when the majesty and power of a foe become apparent, and there is dread lest his treachery and ascendancy should spread throughout the kingdom, and the subjects fall into the region of destruction and the whirlpool of annihilation, he should introduce the

[1] See note 1, page 138.

lucky throw of treachery, and cast back with kindness the two dice of the enemy, and having rescued these persons from the checkmate of misery, should cause his property to be a shield for his kingdom and dominions. Since to hazard a throw on the carpet of pride and annoyance, when the cast of the enemy remains thereon, or to throw wildly the dice of opposition, notwithstanding the strength of the adversary is superior, is far from the decrees of wisdom, and removed from the cradle of experience."[1]

Times are not propitious to you, then accommodate yourself to the times.

The King summoned another Minister, and said: "Do you also make your suggestions, and repeat whatever occurs to your mind." He replied: "O King! in my opinion it is more praiseworthy to abandon one's country, and suffer the disgrace of separation and the anguish of exile, than to snap the thread of ancient reputation, and to submit to an enemy who has always been inferior to us.

How can a hawk become subservient to a timid quail?
How can a fierce lion become a prey to the deer?

"If we agree to pay tribute to the Owls, and submit to their molestation, they will not be satisfied therewith, and will endeavour, to the utmost of their power, to exterminate and extirpate us. It has been said that condescension to an enemy is necessary to such an extent, as to obtain your desires from him, but matters must not be pushed to such an excess that the soul becomes abject, or the enemy's boldness increases. Now they will never be content with moderate tribute from us; our remedy is patience and moderation, and, if necessity should arise, there is no objection to war, because the distress of battle is better than loss of name and reputation."

To be dead under a[2] stone
Is better than to live in disgrace.

The King summoned the fifth Minister, by name Kárshinás,[3] and said: "I have much faith in your intricacy-solving wisdom, and boundless confidence in your world-adorning intelligence.

In intricacies regarding the spheres, or faith, or country,
No one ever saw a solver of difficulties like your prudent mind.
Save through your auspicious deliberation, no one will[4] obtain his desire;
Save through the felicity of your grace, no one will ever see the glory of the phœnix.

"What opinion do you pronounce in this matter, and what choice do you make between war,[5] peace, or exile from home?" Kárshinás replied: "My idea is this, that, except by compulsion, we should not elect war with the Owls; and so long as we can find some other way to get out of this business, we should not engage in battle, because they are bold in fighting with us, and we are inferior to them in combat; they are both superior to us in power, and also surpass us in might. Now, to deem an enemy weak, is the cause of being elate, and whoever is puffed up is nigh meeting with destruction. Previous to this I have

<hr>

[1] The terms here used are in reference to the oriental game of "nard."
[2] That is, to be in the tomb.   [3] Experienced.
[4] In the original the verb is in the past tense.
[5] ﺲﻨﺟ in the Persian text is a misprint for ﺲﻨﺟ.

feared their attacks, and what I dreaded I have seen with my eyes. They will not at present oppose us, because there are amongst them men of caution; and a prudent person will not, in any case, rest secure of his enemy, since when he is near, it is possible that he will suddenly swoop down, and when the distance is great, maybe he will return: at the time of defeat, it may be imagined he will make ambuscades, and when alone, it can be fancied he will plot some treachery and deceit. By this showing, at present war on their part is in the knot of postponement; but if, by way of supposition, they entertain the design of declaring hostilities, it is not expedient for us to engage in battle, since the wisest of creatures is he who abstains from combat, for that which is lost in fighting is the coin of life, for which no substitute will appear."

> Though strong like an elephant, and fierce like a lion,
> In my opinion peace is better than war.

The King said: "If you hold war in detestation, then what do you devise?" He replied: "This matter needs reflection, and must be traversed from top to bottom with the foot of Deliberation, since kings, through sound reflection and right thought, attain those objects, which are not procurable with much treasure, or countless servants and retinue.

> One may slay with the sword from one to a hundred,
> But with skill you may break the back of a whole army.

"The chief point in this matter is the enlightened perception of the King, and counsel with sincere ministers may be the cause of adding to the light of his wisdom, and the perfection of his splendour; just as the water of the sea derives supply by means of springs. Whoever, therefore, does not seek aid from the intellect of trustworthy counsellors of approved speech in a little time, whatever may have accrued to him by the assistance of fortune, and the favour of happiness, will be wasted and lost, and whoever, having a share in the auspiciousness of wisdom, makes a regard for the words of his counsellors, as it were, his upper and under garment, his prosperity will be lasting and his fortune firm. Nowadays, thank God! the King is adorned with the perfection of wisdom, and decorated with the beauty of deliberation.

> O thou, under the protection of whose wisdom is the kingdom of merit!
> O thou, from whose intelligence the Eastern Sun derives light!
> Thy right reflection, coupled with sound deliberation,
> Has adjusted the basis of justice.
> What respect could be paid to my counsel in juxtaposition to thy intellect?[1]
> Of what value is a small shell compared with a pearl?

"But since the King has honoured me with the compliment of consulting me, and conferred on me the dignity of a counsellor, I am anxious to say in reply some things at a private interview, and to proclaim others in the public assembly. Just as I disapprove of war,[2] so, also, I am averse to submission and subservience, nor would I agree to place our necks under taxation, or to bear scorn, to which our fathers have not submitted.

---

[1] Literally, "before your intellect;" the sense might therefore be, "in the opinion of such as thou."

[2] کشمرا in the Persian text is a misprint for جنگرا.

I submit my neck to the enemy, it produces no confidence;
It is better to die, than to live untrusted.

" A man of exalted ambition desires his life to be prolonged with the view of obtaining a lasting fame and permanent name; and if, God forbid! disgrace should attach to him, he would prefer that his life should be shortened.

Reputation should be good and untarnished; to die is better than to be dishonoured.

" It does not seem to me expedient for the King to display weakness, since the doors of misfortune are opened on those who give themselves up to humiliation, and the way of devising a remedy becomes closed upon them.

Be high-minded and demean not yourself, for the Spheres
Are most cruel to him, who is most abased.

" The remaining portion must be in private, so that it may be represented to the world-adorning intellect of the King." One of the attendants in the assembly said: " O Kárshinás! the benefit of counsel is, that every one amongst men of wisdom should speak somewhat, so that the arrow of Deliberation, as regards one of them, may reach the target of Desire. Wise men have said, that a conference is a collection of wise men, and wherever a body of prudent men enter upon an affair, the ins and outs thereof will be examined by them in the best possible manner, and the termination of that matter will be allied to victory and success; just as a sage has said:

' Rely not upon wealth, nor sword, nor shield;
Seek the opinions and counsel of learned men.
Sound wisdom will stand you in need,
Where sword and arrow would be useless.'

" Accordingly, what can be the object of imparting your words in private?" Kárshinás replied: " Every counsellor may not be trustworthy, and State secrets are not such that, like matters of common notoriety, or affairs of ordinary life, they can be discussed with every one. It has been said that secrets are disclosed on the part of counsellors, or of ambassadors and envoys; and how do you know but that a spy is present in this place, who is listening to what is said, so as to convey tidings to the enemy of all he hears, while they, duly reflecting on the same from beginning to end, will close the breaches of error, and the arrow of our Deliberation will fall short of reaching the target of Desire; and if, such a supposition being impossible, an enemy be not here, perhaps every one of those present may have a friend or companion who, maybe, will inquire a description from them as to news of this assembly, and an account of the words which passed; and in a short time an exact statement of our deliberations having been spread abroad in all mouths and tongues, will reach the ears of both friends and enemies; hence it is that they have insisted on the concealment of secrets.

How beautifully spake that wise man,
' If you would save your head, keep your secret ' !

" Whoever imparts his secret to another who has no tendency to keep confidence, will ultimately be filled with regret, but repentance will avail nought; and no one ought to strive so much to keep a secret as Kings, since if any one, save he who is truly a confidant of the Sovereign, is apprised of the Royal deliberations, utter misery may be imagined therefrom.

> If any one save yourself knows what is your opinion,
> You needs must weep at such opinion and knowledge.

" Many there are who have lost kingdom, sovereignty, nay, more, life and existence, by reason of divulging their secrets. Just as the King of Kashmír, who, because he disclosed what was in his mind to a Minister, in a short time fell from the summit of sovereignty to the abyss of helplessness, and the sun of his life set in the horizon of annihilation." Píruz inquired, " How was that ? "

STORY II.

Kárshinás said : It has been related that in the city of Kashmír was a King, who placed the reins of submission over the head of the bay steed of the Sky, and threw the noose of his power round the neck of refractory Fortune. From fear of the fire of his lightning-like sword, the wind had no power to blow contrary to the right direction, and from dread of his life-ravishing, death-dealing spear, the waters did not have sufficient strength to flow to and fro on the surface of the earth.

> He gave the world such a robe of security,
> That the sword was free from the disgrace of being unsheathed ;
> By reason of his justice the hearts of the oppressed, at morn,
> Forgot to discharge the arrow of a sigh.[1]

This mighty King, in the sacred sanctuary of the women's apartments, and behind the screen of pleasure, had a beloved one whose black ringlets, in length, added to the longest night of winter, and whose life-giving face, in perfection of beauty, carried off the prize from the fourteen-day old moon. If the vigil-keeping devotee, Night, were to see in his sleep a vision of her beauty, like pure-skirted Morn, through love of her face, he would have torn the collar of the religious dress of abstinence.

> August in aspect, in stature lofty,
> Her eyebrows like a bow, her ringlets like lassoes.
> As it were a cypress, which finds in the meadow
> Violets for locks, jessamine for cheeks.

The King was so enamoured with that damsel, that he considered the contemplation of her beauty the sum of life, and reckoned the sight of her ringlets and moles[2] the capital of existence. Every moment the charm of love for his mistress drew the pearl of his soul towards her, and the heart-enchanting thief of her tresses snatched away the coin of patience from the purse of his soul.

> I do not follow after her of my own accord—
> Throwing her ringlets around like lassoes, she gradually leads me on.

That brazen-faced, mischief-making woman, when she saw that the bird of the King's heart was ensnared in the net of her heart-ravishing ringlets, drew the bow of her eyebrows to the lobe of the ear, and discharged the arrow of her

---

[1] A similar expression occurs at page 51, see note 3.   [2] See note, page 23.

glance against the target of his bosom, and from hour to hour with soft blandishments and sweet caresses, placed additional bonds on the feet of his soul.

> Her lover-captivating ways and tumult-raising looks,
> Were garments sewn on her body.

By reason of the arrogance of beauty, she was not content merely with the King's love, but made conquests, too, in other regions and parts, and cast her heart-entrancing snare round the neck of the unfortunates in the desert of Desire. At length with a beautiful-faced youth amongst the attendants of the King, a good-looking young man amongst the confidants of his Court, the tender down on whose cheeks had arrived like the verdure on the brinks of the waters of Life, and whose delicate beard appeared as it were a hyacinth of Paradise upon the bank of the rivulet Kausar [1]—

> Round his pearly lips delicate[2] down grew,
> Like rare fruit upon the brink of the waters of Immortality—

she commenced her proceedings. This young man, too, had fallen under the dominion of love, and there remained on the frontispiece of his condition no inscription from the volume of patience, nor an atom of the vestiges of existence on the pages of life.

> Whoever becomes acquainted with love, will never drive away vexation from his soul.
> Anguish[3] nourishes his affection, nor does medicine remove his burden.

Perpetually questions and answers used to pass between the lover and his mistress, by means of the eyes and eyebrows, and they carried on converse with tokens and signs. One day the King was sitting on the throne of ease, and his heart was fixed on the soul-enchanting society of his loved one: that young man was in attendance, and everything was prepared for conviviality. The King was contemplating the soul-adorning beauty of his friend, and perusing on the pages of her cheeks the inscription, "*In the most perfect symmetry,*" while the woman, oblivious that the King was looking at her, cast glances at the young man, and conveyed from her lips a kiss so sweet that the skirt of the world was sugared therewith.

> Give one smile, and fill the skirt of my life with sugar.

The young man, too, in like manner, darted from the corner of his magic-like eyes glances, which would have produced a thousand tumults in the world.

> · He was like the playful narcissus half open;
> One half darted glances, the other half used blandishments.

The King being apprised of these proceedings, the fire of jealousy began to raise a flame in his soul; and perceiving their affection for one another, he immediately tore his heart from the society of his mistress.

> Men of learning agree in this, that fruit must not be eaten
> From a tree, which casts its shade in another garden.

He then thought to himself: "To act hastily in this matter appears removed

---

[1] A river in Paradise.

[2] سرو in the Persian text is a misprint for سبز.

[3] I somewhat doubt if such is the meaning of this line, but I cannot improve the rendering.

from the path of wisdom, and to act precipitately in restraining these two persons, who in truth are my enemies, is not in accordance with caution and foresight."

> Patience is better for a man than anything else.

Thereupon he passed over that proceeding as unseen, and carried his intercourse to the end, in the same manner as was his wont, and passed the night till morning in the brilliancy of the taper of his mistress's beauty; but his heart, like a moth, was consumed in the flame of the fire of vexation.

> King, lover, intoxicated, and such a mistress,
> How could he see her dallying with another?

In short, next day, when the sun, like Jamshíd,[1] raised the standard of victory and triumph over the dome of the turquoise-coloured palace of the sky, and the King of the Planets tore aside the veil of darkness from before the portico of the resting-place of the azure spheres—

> When from the chilly breath of tell-tale morn
> In an instant the glittering orb descended from the sky,
> The lovely-cheeked bride of the sun,
> Showed her face from behind a dark cloud—

the King came to the state-throne, and making a proclamation of justice, himself decided the causes of the petitioners.

> The king who is accustomed to justice
> Is the shadow of God's mercy.

After he had finished settling their arrangements, and ordering their affairs, he had a private interview with a Minister, who was the pivot of the kingdom. The executioner, Rage, urged him strongly to narrate to the Minister the proceedings of the night, and in concert with him make them taste of the potion of punishment; while the ruler, Wisdom, whispered, "Conceal your secret from him, and carry out the decree which your heart desires." At length the tendency to rage being predominant, he related to the Minister some portion of the secrets of his mind, and sought advice from him relative thereto. The Minister recommended also their destruction, and agreed in opinion with the King. It was determined to put these two persons to death; and it was arranged that each one, having been made to taste the potion of the poison of destruction, should be cast from the plain of existence into the whirlpool of annihilation, and the matter be carried out in such a manner as to be known only to the King and his Minister, so that the veil of infamy[2] should not be torn, nor the thread of reputation severed.

> Matters, such as these, are best secret;
> If you reveal them, you will ultimately repent of it.

The Minister came from the King's presence to his own house, and found his daughter overwhelmed with grief, and in despair. Having inquired the reason thereof, he ascertained, that on that very day his daughter had been in the Sultán's private apartments, and met with various unkindnesses on the part

---

[1] See note 1, page 12.
[2] The text is apparently corrupt as regards the word rendered "infamy;" the "veil of honour" would be more suitable to the context.

of the King's lady, and in the midst of her equals and associates been treated with much contempt. The Minister was annoyed at this affair, and with the view of consoling his daughter's mind, said :

> The messenger, the morning-breeze, last night informed me,
> That the day of adversity and grief is declining.

"Be not sad, for in two or three days the lamp of her life will be quenched, and the rose of her existence withered." The girl, with the view of settling the case, inquired respecting the truth of the matter. The Minister repeated a portion of what passed between the King and himself, and urged her to the utmost to keep the secret. The girl, delighted at this good news, came forth from her father's presence. Simultaneous with these proceedings, one of the servants of the house, and attendants of the Harím, had come with apologies and reassurances. When the opening excuses had been pleaded, the Minister's daughter said : "Be not dejected; though the King's lady without cause was unkind to me, yet ultimately she will meet with punishment and retribution."

> 'Twill soon be, that my enemy will be removed from my sight.

The servant, too, manifesting joy and delight, asked, "Whence speak you these words, and when will it be that deliverance for me from her tyranny and violence will appear?" The Minister's daughter replied : "If you have power to keep my secret concealed, I will disclose the truth of the matter, and not hold back a particle from you." The servant took an oath, and the girl related to her the precise facts. The servant at once returning, informed the lady of what had happened, and she, taking the young man in private, apprised him of the entire matter. They together seduced a body of others, and before the King learned thereof, coming to the head of his pillow, cast the vessel of his life into the whirlpool of non-existence. Now, forasmuch as he revealed his secret to the Minister, he fell from the position of prosperity—nay, more, from the region of life, into the straits of death, and the prison of destruction.

"Now the moral of this tale is, that should Kings consult their ministers, and profit by their experience and ingenuity, yet it is incumbent not to apprise any one of the secrets of their heart—since, when they themselves, in spite of their divine dignity, and the assistance of heaven, coupled with their exalted ambition, and noble mind, cannot keep their own secrets, how can others, who are of lower rank than themselves, and inferior in wisdom and intellect, conceal the same?"

> If you cannot yourself keep your own secret,
> Then why grieve if another disclose it?

When Kárshinás had finished this story, and had pierced a gem of such beauty with the diamond of heart-enchanting style, another of the attendants in that assembly opened the lips of rebuke, saying : "According to the words you have spoken, the way of counsel must be laid aside, and we must act according to our own judgment and opinion; the fact is, the abandonment of counsel is not acceptable to reason and wisdom, and the saying: '*And take counsel with them in the business,*' is a proof, that affairs should not be commenced without consultation.

> If you do not base the edifice of your affairs on counsel,
> You neither perform the dues of the law, nor treat reason with justice.

"The mandate of the Divine word, which directed his own chosen Prophet to deliberate with the attendants at the threshold of prophecy, is a proof that counsel must be an indispensable duty, and assuredly a firm decree."

> Counsel was enjoined by the Prophet;
> Why do you deviate from this path?

Kárshinás rejoined : "The injunction of the Most High God to the Prophet— may the peace of God be upon him !—respecting counsel, was not with the view that his own judgment should be aided by the deliberations of others, since the brilliant mind of the possessor of prophecy—may blessings and peace be upon him !—who was befriended by Divine Revelation, and assisted by Omnipotent favour, is a world-adorning mirror, wherein the truth as to matters becomes evident and manifest ; nay, more, it was by way of making known the benefits of counsel, and describing its advantages, so that mankind should become adorned with that acceptable disposition, and turn away from self-opinion and self-approbation towards deliberation and reflection. Wise men add strength to their own weakness by the help of the wisdom of others, just as the light of a lamp, which is doubled by means of oil, and the brilliancy of fire, which is increased by the aid of sticks. It was not to be understood from my words that counsel should be abandoned ; nay, more, the purport thereof clearly showed, that the result of such counsel, and the opinion founded thereon, must be kept concealed— since, in guarding a secret, and concealing what is in the mind, two distinct advantages are comprised : 1st, As a matter of experience, every affair which is kept undisclosed is most quickly brought to a happy conclusion, and the intimation, '*Seek aid in your important affairs with secrecy,*' is in allusion to this point ; 2d, If that device is not in harmony with Fate, and what is in the mind cannot be put in practice, at any rate the exultation of enemies, and irritation from those seeking for defects, will not arise."

> It is not so much matter that I cannot gain access to you,
> As that my rivals loose the tongue by way of reproach.

Píruz said : "O honest Counsellor ! I have the fullest confidence in your excessive kindness and loyalty, and I recognise you as apart from all the ministers and statesmen who attend this court, as regards intelligence and knowledge ; do not permit any shortcomings on your part[1] in declaring whatever enters your mind by way of advice and well-wishing." Kárshinás paid his respects, saying :

> O thou ! under the protection of whose justice beasts and birds find repose !
> And O thou ! from the perfection of whose wisdom body and soul are at peace !

"It is incumbent upon every servant, when his Lord plans some scheme, to tell what seems to him more sound ; and if he finds such intention bordering upon what is wrong, he should make clear the error thereof, speaking with humility : nor should he hold back till his Lord's opinions and devices are entirely corrected. Every Counsellor, who, deserting his benefactor, neither pays heed to the dues of counsel, nor performs the obligations of fidelity and trustworthiness, must be considered an enemy, and the habit of seeking advice from him be abandoned. Whenever a King in this manner respects and conceals his own secrets, and finds a sincere minister and trustworthy and reliable counsellor, and also deems it incumbent, according to regal law, to compensate the good, and in conformity

---

[1] Literally, " be not content with any deficiency on your part."

with the rules of sovereignty to punish and correct those who do wrong, it will commonly come to pass that his kingdom will be lasting, and his government firm, nor will the hand of the calamities of Time quickly carry off the gifts of Fortune from him."

While you can, lean towards faith and justice,
So that your kingdom may become firmly established owing to these two.
Make the world live at ease by your bounty,
So that you may be happy, and God pleased.

The King inquired, "In what manner must secrets be concealed, and from whom should they?" Kárshinás replied: "The secrets of Kings are of different degrees. Some are such that the King must even keep them concealed from himself—that is to say, he must labour to such a degree to guard them that, as it were, he himself could not be a confidant of them, much less could he tell an inkling thereof to another. In this view a wise man has said:

'What is not to be spoken, in your inmost heart
Keep so secret, that your own soul,
Were it to seek a long time,
Could not find it.'

"Some, others are such, that two persons might be honoured with being intrusted therewith; while as regards others, three individuals might share them, and even four or five are allowable: but the secret which has passed through your mind, relative to the affair of the Owls, is not fit to be intrusted to more than four ears and two heads." The King, after hearing these words, retired to privacy, and summoning the Minister Kárshinás, commenced to speak, first of all inquiring, "What was the cause of the enmity, and the reason of hostility and prejudice between us and the Owls?" He said: "In former days a Crow spoke some words, and the Owls on that account, hatred having filled their breasts, followed the way of strife; nowadays that quarrel and dispute remain unabated." The King inquired, "How was that?"

STORY III.

He replied: It has been related that a flock of birds came together and agreed, "We want a chief and leader, to whom in contingencies we may refer, and by whose aid, should enemies proceed to war, we will strive to repel them and ward them off." Accordingly each one of them placed the mark of sovereignty against the name of one of the birds, and others strove by proofs and pretexts to render the same null and void, till the Owl's turn arrived; a mass were agreed to make him chief, and to give the reins of power into the palms of his ability. When they had plunged into this matter, and commenced to band together, some in rejecting, others in accepting him, the fire of strife sprang up in their midst, and words passed from the limits of moderation to enmity and altercation: some in loyalty to the Owl raised the standard of revolt, while others cast the stone of discord into the amphitheatre of unanimity. In short, it was arranged that they should make another, not included in that number, their umpire, and accepting on both sides whatever he decreed, lay aside contention. By chance a Crow from afar came into sight; they exclaimed: "See, here is a person not belonging to this assembly; we will consult him. Again, too, he is of our kith and kin; and so long as great men and grandees of every kind amongst the species of birds are not unanimous, harmony will not be procured, and without concord, this matter which we have in hand is not practicable." Therefore, when the Crow joined them, they told him the state of the case, and sought his advice in the matter. The Crow replied: "What absurd idea and impracticable fancy is this? What connection is there between the ominous Owl and the post of administrator and ruler, or what business has this ugly-looking creature with the dignity of power and authority?

O fly! the locality of the phœnix is no plain of battle for you;
You represent your own case, and cause us annoyance.

"What has happened to the high-flying Hawk, who, as regards loftiness, can boast of equality with the Eagle of the Skies? What has become of the beautiful-shaped, delicate-looking Peacock, by the magnificence of whose plumage the garden of ornament and decoration is adorned? Where is the happy-omened Phœnix, the shade of whose fortune has placed the crown of glory upon the brow of famous sovereigns? The splendid and mighty Eagle, from the sound of whose prosperous wings and triumphant pinions the summits of the mountains tremble, why does he not appear? Even if all the famous birds were to die, and the weak, broken-winged ones also were to disappear, it would be better that the birds should pass their lives without a king, and should not allow the disgrace of submitting to the Owl, and the humiliation of serving him, since, together with a hideous appearance, he is deficient in intellect, and though rage overpowers him, he does not abandon habits of arrogance. With all this, too, he remains deprived of the beauty of world-illuminating day, which, according to the tradition, '*And we appointed the day for gaining the means of support,*' is the capital of the bázár of life, and is cut off from the light of the globe-adorning Sun, which, like the ornament, '*And we placed a burning lamp,*' is the creation-enlightening lamp, and world-illuminating taper: worse still, passion and levity predominate in his disposition, and haste and absurdity are manifest in his deeds. Abandon this improper idea, and base the edifice of your affairs on wisdom and intelligence, and fixing your arrangements upon the rules of learning, deem it incumbent, too, to remedy every contingency in accordance with what is expedient, so that you may constantly pass your time in ease and repose. You should, first of all, appoint from amongst yourselves a chief on whose wisdom, learning, intelligence, and ability complete reliance and perfect confidence may be placed, so that he may be sufficient of his own clear judgment for every circumstance which may appear, and every matter and event which may arise,[1] like that Hare, who constituted herself an ambassador from the Moon, and by her sound devices warded off a great calamity from her own tribe." The birds inquired, "How was that?"

STORY IV.

He said: It has been related that one year in the country of the Elephants, in the island of Zírbád, no rain happened to fall, and the clouds, like a mother, caused no drops to trickle from the bosom of kindness on the thirsty-lipped palate of the cradle of the earth: the fire of drought made the fountains dry,

---

[1] واقه, in the Persian text is a misprint for واقع .

like the eyes of the austere, and the springs were parched up, as it were the palates of desire among the wretched. The Elephants, impatient from anguish of thirst, complained to their King, who issued an order that they should hasten in every direction after water, and search in such a manner that nothing further should be possible. The Elephants measured with the foot of quest the regions and tracts of that kingdom, and reached a spring called the fountain of the Moon, and by the Persians termed Chasmah-i-Máh; it was a deep well having abundance of water. The King of the Elephants, together with all his retinue and armies, with the view of drinking water, repaired to that spring, on the outskirts of which many Hares had located themselves. Obviously, the Hares were distressed with calamity owing to these Elephants; each of them, whenever an Elephant put his foot on her head, experienced such anguish, that she was obliged to remove her chattels from the abode of life, and was so bruised, that the result cannot be defined, except by a reference to the expanse of annihilation.

> Drive gently towards the plain, since there are
> Heads crushed beneath the hoof of thy dun steed.

By one visit of the Elephants, many of them were bruised and crushed.

> Who will live if you return in this manner two or three times?

Next day they went in a body before their King, and said: "A just King should be the protector of the oppressed, and aider of the destitute; every Monarch occupies his throne with the view of administering justice, not of living for pleasure.

> For this cause you have gained this throne,
> That you may assist the unfortunate.

"Dispense justice to us, and snatching retribution for us from the Elephants, remedy the anguish we suffer at their hands, since any hour they may return, and this time trample under their feet many abject ones who, half dead, have scrambled from under their hoofs."

> You once showed your face—my heart, my understanding, my sense all
>   vanished:
> This time carry off my soul, for no other chattels remain.

The King said: "This is no small matter, that it can be lightly entered upon; whoever is intelligent amongst you must present himself, so that we may consult him; for to put our intentions into execution before deliberation has taken place, is not the nature of wise, prosperous persons."

> Whoever is endowed with much knowledge,
> Does nought without consultation.

In the midst of the Hares was one sharp-witted, called Bihrúz,[1] in whose complete wisdom, perfect understanding, clear intellect, and sound deliberation, men used to place confidence: when she saw that the King took this matter to heart, advancing she said:

> O King! are you sad on account of your hapless subjects?
> Such is the way, such the habit of dispensers of justice.
> Restrain not the glance of kindness from the condition of the destitute,
> So that you may enjoy crown, throne, fortune, and prosperity.

---

[1] Good day.

"Should the King think proper, let him send me on a mission to the Elephants, and appoint an officer to accompany me, so that he may see and hear what I do and say." The King said: "I have not, and will not have, any suspicion as to your rectitude, integrity, straightforwardness, and honesty. I have frequently observed and heard of your conversation and conduct.

As regards the stamp of your proceedings, it is sufficient that I have many
    times tested it,
And, on the touchstone of proof, have found your coin without admixture.

"You must go in peace, and do whatever you consider will meet the necessities of the time, and the requirements of the case. You are aware that a King's Envoy is his tongue; and whoever wishes to know the title-page of the scroll of any one's mind, or the interpretation[1] of the secret of such person's heart, can ascertain it from the words and deeds of his ambassador—since, if merit and excellence on the part of this latter become manifest, and acceptable indications, and praiseworthy practices are visible, they may receive it as a proof of the King's excellent judgment and perfect experience; while, if indifference and negligence are apparent, the tongues of scorners come into play, and they will find opportunity for slander and disparagement. Wise men in this matter have insisted much, and given countless injunctions, that whoever sends a messenger to any place, it is incumbent that he should be the wisest of his race, and the most eloquent amongst them in language, as well as the most perfect in conduct; and Kings of old, for the most part, used to send sages on embassies; Iskandar Zú'lkarnain,[2] indeed, commonly used to change his clothes, and go himself on missions, saying:

'Lions who hunt lions,
    Convey their own message, with their own feet.'

"A wise man in regard to sending ambassadors has said:

'It is incumbent that he who is sent must be wise,
    Bold, and powerful in speech;
Replying to whatever is asked of him,
    In such a manner as may be in accordance with what is right.
Making his words clear,
    In such way as the assembly may demand.
Many persons there are who, with a single harsh speech,
    Have set the world by the ears, and slain the inhabitants:
Others, again, with a solitary acceptable word,
    Have caused friendship amongst two hundred.'"

Bihrúz said: "O King! although I am acquainted with a portion, according to my circumstances, of the rules appertaining to the art of diplomacy, yet if the King, the protector of the world, would be kind enough to arrange on the thread of favour, some precious pearls from the casket of wisdom, making such the ornament of my life, and recognising them as the beauty of my glory, and capital to assist me, I would not deviate from such precepts, in all I do or accomplish, and in accordance with such rule of practice would carry out all my business." The King said: "O Bihrúz! the best qualification for an envoy, and

---

[1] The text has "interpreter" instead of "interpretation."
[2] "Two-horned Alexander," an epithet applied to Alexander the Great.

the most fitting attribute for an ambassador, is that the sword of the tongue, like a sharp dagger, should be employed with keenness and severity; but the pearls of consideration, and condescension, must be evident and patent upon his pages, and the light of courtesy and civility manifest and clear on his part: every word, from the appearance of which roughness is understood, must in the end be withdrawn with kindness and politeness: if at the commencement of a speech, through zeal, he opens with fear-shedding words, at the termination of his address, by way of solace and consolation, he must conclude with friendly expression, and captivating sayings.

Kind words remove the seed of hatred from the breast,
Courteous language clears away the frown of rage from the eyebrows.

"To sum up, the language of an envoy must be based upon the rules of softness [1] and harshness, of anger and tenderness, of gentleness and violence, of justice and obstinacy, and the way of binding and loosing, of taking and giving, of tearing and mending, of making and consuming, must be observed, so that he may both pay regard to the royal reputation and regal majesty, and also discover the designs of the enemy, and the secrets of their mind. To a wise man, as regards going on a mission, the substance of all precepts is summed up in this:

'Therefore send a wise person, and make no suggestions.'"

Bihrúz having then performed the dues of homage, came forth from the King's Court, and waited patiently till evening, having clad itself in dusky [2] garments, lowered the curtain of darkness before the portico of the azure heavens, and after a while the table-decker of Omnipotent Power brought forth in splendour the silvery platter of the Moon at the head of the tables of the Sky.

When Evening loosed its murky ringlets,
The Moon, resplendent, came forth from the sky.

At the time when the centre of the Moon had nearly reached the circle of mid-heaven, and the rays of the lesser luminary spread over the sides of the dusty globe, and the face of the earth was enlightened with the world-adorning beauty of that taper of the cell of the destitute, Bihrúz set out towards the island of the Elephants, and reaching their abode thought to herself: "For me to be near to these tyrants there is danger of life and risk of death, and though they have no design against me, yet forethought demands, that I should not meet my tyrants and oppressors, because, by reason of their superiority and grandeur, they have no regard for the poor and desolate, and if a thousand miserable wretches were to be deprived of their heads under the foot of their tyranny, the dust of that accident would not rest on the face of their violence.

What grief have you for the condition of us miserable wretches?
Were the lamp to grow dim, what matter to the zephyr?

"It is expedient for me to go to a height, and deliver from afar the message I possess. If it happens to be acceptable, well and good; and if my spells are not efficacious, at any rate I shall secure my soul in safety." Accordingly ascending an eminence, she cried from afar to the King of the Elephants, saying: "I am

---

[1] It is impossible to preserve the beauty, such as it is, of these sentences, which is derived mainly from the jingle of sounds.
[2] Literally, "reddish."

sent by the Moon, and no crime should be imputed to an envoy, whatever he says or hears ; ' *And a person who is sent has nought to do but convey his message.* Though his speech appears wanting in respect, and harsh, it is incumbent that it should be heard, since whatever message the Moon has given, I cannot use my discretion in adding thereto, or diminishing therefrom. You know that the world-encircling Moon is the chief of the bázár of Night, and the deputy of the Monarch of Day ; now if any one plots against her, and does not attend to her message with the ear of his soul, he will have struck a hatchet on his own foot, and laboured with his hand for his own destruction." The King of the Elephants, at these words, jumped up from his seat, and inquired, " What is the purport of your message ?" Bihrúz replied : " The Moon says, whenever any one sees that he is himself stronger and more powerful than his inferiors, and becomes puffed up with his might, ardour, vigour, and pride, desiring to tread under foot violently and forcibly those beneath him, such a proceeding is indicative of his ignominy, and this disposition will cast him into the vortex of destruction.

> Scatter not the seed of pride in the breast,
> Give no place to hatred in your heart.
> How long will you saddle the steed of violence ?
> Drive not quick, for he will not remain like this,
> Soon will this water pass over your head.
> The arrow of the spheres will pierce your shield—
> The end of this business will be of a different kind,
> Your affairs will slip from your hand.

' Through this pride, by which you consider yourself superior to other animals, and through your power and majesty, which are in the way of decline and departure, and on which you plume yourself, the matter has reached such a pitch and the case ended in this, that you have laid designs against my fountain, and brought your armies to that spot, and in excess of malevolence rendered that water turbid. Do you not know that the swift-flying eagle, if he soars above my spring, would be consumed, wings and feathers, by my jealous thunderbolt ; and if the star, Bull's Eye, looks thereon from the meadow of the Skies, with the glance of possession, Arcturus would sew up its eyes with the needle of majesty ?

> The demon arriving here bows his head,
> The bird flying here folds his wings ;
> Save with a guide, the spheres never
> Issue forth from its atmosphere and soil.

" From excess of kindness I have deemed it necessary to arouse you with this message. If you follow your own business, and refrain from this kind of hardihood, well and good ; if not, I will come in my own person and slay you with anguish : if you doubt this message, come this very hour, when I am present in my fountain, so that you may see me with your own eyes, and afterwards do not remain in the neighbourhood of this spring." The King of the Elephants was astonished at this story, and going towards the fountain, saw the shape of the Moon in the water. Bihrúz said to him : " O King ! take away a little water, and washing your face, perform your adoration ; maybe the Moon, moved by compassion, may be content." The Elephant elongated his trunk ; when the shock thereof reached the water, and it was set in motion, it appeared to the

Elephant as though the Moon was jumping about. He exclaimed : " O Envoy from the Moon ! perhaps the Moon is agitated because I put my trunk in the water." Bihrúz said : " Yes ; perform your adorations as quickly as possible, so that she may become composed." The Elephant prostrating himself, made obeisance, and agreed that afterwards he would not come there, nor bring the Elephants in the region of that spring : Bihrúz brought the news to the King, and the Hares were safe. By such stratagem did she avert so great a calamity from them.

" I have narrated this story, inasmuch as a man of ability is necessary amongst you, who may take the lead in your affairs, and endeavour to repel your enemies. If, at this very time, a clever, prudent person had been consulted by you, how would he have allowed you to draw the inscription of monarchy against the name of the Owl ? and he would, too, have apprised you not to permit yourselves to bear the ominous disgrace of such an one, since together with all the unacceptable attributes which he possesses, treachery, fraud, deceit, and cunning, also, are mingled in his nature, and no defects in kings are like perfidy, evilspeaking, deception, and want of faith.

> Whoever is unacquainted with affection and fidelity,
> Has no perfume of friendship in his heart ;
> The bosom which is darkened by treachery,
> Has no light within it.
> Act not treacherously, for amongst mankind
> There is no fault like insincerity.

" Kings are the shadow of the Creator—may His glory be increased ! without the sun of their justice, the expanse of the world will not be illumined, and save under the shade of their kindness and justice, the repose of mankind will not exist in the cradle of security and safety ; nay, more, the pavilion of Heaven cannot be raised, save with the pillar of equity, for ' *The heavens stand firm through justice.*'

> Were justice not to be mathematically exact,
> The azure dome of the skies would not exist.

" Since amongst the inhabitants of the world the thread of security is bound up with the existence of a just monarch, and the ladder of the skies, without the aid of equity and beneficence, as displayed by the kings of the age, would become rent in pieces ; since also the orders of sovereigns relative to men's life and property are current, and their decrees, like the mandates of Fate, as regards the contingencies of loosening and fastening affairs, are spread abroad and prevalent, therefore it is incumbent that a monarch should be trustworthy, not tyrannical, treating his subjects with affection, not with violence ; he should keep the mirror of his heart free from the rust[1] of hatred, and not allow the inscription of treachery and deceit to rest upon the tablets of his soul, seeing that hapless ones, who are overwhelmed with the oppression of a perfidious king, and the cruelty of a traitorous lord, will meet with that which befell that Partridge and Quail, at the hands of the fasting Cat." The birds inquired, " What was that ? "

---

[1] See note 2, page 51.

STORY V.

The Crow said: At the skirt of a certain hill I had my nest on a tree; in proximity to me was a Partridge, and by reason of our being close neighbours, the bonds of friendship were firmly cemented between us, and the constant sight of him produced intimacy on my part, and at times of leisure, conversation used to pass between us. Suddenly he disappeared, and the time of his absence became lengthened, so I fancied he was dead. After a while a Quail arrived and took up his abode in the Partridge's house, and by reason that I had no certain news of the circumstances of the latter, I made no objection to such a proceeding, and said:

" When one goes, another comes in his place."

A time elapsed in this manner, and the wandering Heavens made several revolutions, ere the Partridge returned. When he saw another in his place, commencing to get enraged, he exclaimed: " Leave my locality, and vacate my abode." The Quail replied: " The house is at present in the grasp of my possession, and I am the occupier; if you have any claim thereto, you must strive to make good the same." The Partridge replied: " Your possession is through plunder and rapine, while I have proofs and deeds in this matter." In short, severe strife ensued between them, and every moment the fire of discord increased, and the standard of obstinacy and contention was raised higher and higher. Though I invented devices by way of reconciliation, it was of no effect, and it was determined they should refer to a just judge, who, after hearing the speeches of both sides, should pronounce a decree in accordance with equity, and put an end to their pretensions. The Partridge said: " Near to here is a Cat, religious, fasting, devout, and not cruel. Every day he keeps a fast, and passes the night-season in worship; and from the time that they sound the drum of golden-cushioned Jamshíd,[1] the Sun, in the portico of the palace, ' *The heaven we have built,*' till the hour they spread the dusky-clothed carpet of the Sovereign of Night in the plain, ' *And we have spread the earth,*' he melts his precious soul in the crucible of abstinence with the fire of hunger. From the period that the hosts of the Stars, and the army of the glittering Planets move into the plain of the Heavens, till the time that the Divine Chamberlains, by means of the taper of the world-adorning Morn, which shines from the face of the horizon, show traces of the scout of the globe-illuminating Sun to the inhabitants of the regions of the earth, like a candle he stands with foot of devotion, and from the fire of affection and the flame of love, melts into tears.

> With the water of his eyes he washes his hands of the world,
> Seeking in the corner of poverty a store of grace;
> Turning the back of his feet on both worlds,
> An alien to himself, he becomes acquainted with God.

" His breakfast is confined to water and grass, and it is far from his habit to cause pain to animals, or spill their blood. No judge can be more just than he is, nor will any arbitrator better than him be found, who can give a true decision between us. We must resort to him, so that he may settle our case." Both consenting, they set out towards the Judge's house, while I followed in

---

[1] See note 1, page 12.

their track, anxious to look at the fasting Cat—who must have been one of the wonders of the world—and to witness his justice, as regards a decree between the two rivals. As soon as the eyes of the continual Faster fell on them, standing on his right foot, he turned his face towards the High Altar, and putting on the garment of devotion, set about performing the dues of supplication, and joined in long and lengthy prayers, labouring with the utmost care to put his body in posture.[1]

> Is that prayer the key of the door of the infernal regions,
> Which you parade so long before the eyes of mankind?
> When in secret you are wicked and mean,
> What avails the water of reputation upon the face of your affairs?

The Quail was surprised at his conduct, while the Partridge marvelled at his proceedings. Stopping till he should cease his prayers, they performed respectful salutations, and requested him to be a Judge between them, and to settle the affair of the house according to the decrees of justice. The Cat, after much solicitation and pressing, said: "Repeat to me the circumstances of the case." The Partridge and Quail represented the state of their claims. The Cat replied: " O young men ! old age has had great effect upon me, and utter ruin has overtaken my external senses. The motion of the millstone of the revolving spheres has scattered the dust of weakness upon my brow, and the icy hand of the cruel autumn of time has snatched away the water of freshness, and the lustre of beauty, from the plant of the garden of life, and the night of youth, which is the entire source of strength and glory, is changed into the hoary morn, which is the aggregate of all that is bad.[2]

> Alas ! the days of youth are passed—
> Life, of the kind of which you know, is vanished ;
> Designs lessen, regrets increase,
> The breeze of relaxation has quitted my head.

" Come nearer, and, speaking louder, repeat afresh the account of your dispute, so that being apprised of the claim of the plaintiff, and the reply of his opponent, I may issue a decree. Before I pass sentence, I will favour you with some friendly advice, and give you some exhortation embodying what is expedient for you as regards religion and worldly concerns.

> If you do not this day listen to my words,
> God forbid that to-morrow you should regret it !

" If, with the ear of your souls you listen to my words, and accept them, the fruits thereof will accrue to you in this world and the next; but if you reject them, and deviate from their purport, at any rate I myself shall be excused by my own conscience and feelings of right.

> I have performed the duty of giving advice,
> Whether or not you will accept it, that you know.

" It is right that both of you, seeking the road of propriety, should not deviate from the path of rectitude, neither ought you to be puffed up with worldly wealth and goods, which are destined to perish and slip away, nor by reason

---

[1] Literally, "to adjust the pillars."
[2] Eastwick's explanation respecting this passage is very happy. " Youth is compared to night, and old age to dawn, on account of the black locks of the young, and the silver hair of the old."

that you have foolishly got possession of, and brought within your grasp, something of the trash of this transitory world, shall you deprive yourselves of
eternal reward and everlasting favour." The Partridge said: "O just Judge!
if men confined their ambition to the search after what is right, and every one
clad himself in a habit of probity and rectitude, there would be no need to
appear before a judge, nor to trouble magistrates; and the custom of action
and defence, and of oaths and proofs, would be removed from the face of the
book of time. But since the eyes of both plaintiff and defendant are overwhelmed with the disease of self-interest, the appearance of rectitude never
comes into their sight; consequently they are in need of some one, the eyes of
whose heart are enlightened with the pearl-ointment of sincerity, and around
the mirror of whose vision the dust of self-advantage does not rest, so that
having witnessed the beauty of uprightness, he may display it to the eye of
their heart. In this point of view one of the great in religion has, by way of
story, strung together some verses." The Cat inquired, "How was that?"

STORY VI.

The Partridge said:

They appointed a judge who wept.
One of them said to him: "Whence is this crying?
This is not a time for you to lament and wail,
It is a season for you to be joyous and merry."
He exclaimed: "Alas! how can an uninformed man issue a decree?
He is an ignoramus in the midst of the two parties:
The two antagonists are apprised of their own affairs,
The hapless Judge, what knows he of the tricks of the two?
He is ignorant of, and has no interest in, their proceedings;
How can he proceed in regard to their lives and property?"
The other said: "The antagonists are informed, but biassed,
While you are ignorant, yet the taper of religion
(Since you have no interest in the matter)
Will be a sure light to your eyes.
Personal interest will blind those two parties,
And bias will entomb their knowledge.
When self-advantage arises merit is concealed,
And a hundred veils are cast over the eyes from the heart;
So long as you do not receive a bribe you can see;
When you are avaricious, you are ensnared and enslaved.
When a judge sets his heart on a bribe,
How can he distinguish between the tyrant and the oppressed?"

"Thank God! the rust [1] of self-interest has not clouded the mirror of your pure
heart, nor have the eyes of your integrity become dazzled with the rays of the
flame of bribery. For which reason, it is very certain, that you will display to
our sight what is right, and consign to the prison-keeper of Eternity, whomsoever
has withdrawn his neck from the decrees of Equity."

Cut off the head of him, who withdraws his neck from thy decree.

---

[1] See note 2, page 51.

The Cat rejoined: " You have spoken well, for in truth you should, each of you too, tear up the tree of self-interest from the soil of your hearts, and consider that he who is right is in reality victor, although to appearance his claim may not be successful, while the unreasonable complainant, spiritually speaking, is disappointed and defeated, although, as it seems, a decree is issued in accordance with his desires, since, ' *Of a truth that which is false passes away.*' How beautifully has it been said:

> ' If to-day you urge your steed against me,
> How will you to-morrow break from my lasso?
> To appearance you are victorious—hold!
> Regard things from a spiritual point of view, for numerous are the afflicted ones.'[1]

" I say to you, lay up a store for Eternity by your righteous conduct, and place no reliance upon life, which, like a summer shower, or the gay appearance of a garden of roses, will quickly pass away; and considering high and low amongst the beings of the world, and far and near amongst mankind, as precious as your own soul, do not allow towards them, what you would not approve as regards yourself."

Do not approve for others what is not acceptable to yourself.

In this way he breathed forth treachery and deceit upon them, till they became friends with him, and secure and at ease advanced without hesitation or care. At one bound he seized both of them, and supplied the kitchen of his stomach with food and provisions from their delicious flesh. The effects of his devotion, fasting, piety, and purity, by reason of his base desires and impure nature, were thus at once evidenced.

" I have adduced this story, that it may be known that no confidence must be placed in an evil-natured traitor. Now the matter of the treacherous-disposed, hypocritical Owl has this very aspect. His blemishes are endless, and his vices excessive. The number of them which come within the pale of description, are as it were a drop in the vast ocean, or an atom in comparison with the nine revolving spheres.

> Were I to sing praises for a hundred thousand ages, beyond doubt
> But one thing out of a hundred thousand would be spoken.

" God forbid that you should make choice of this proceeding, and cause him to sit upon the throne of sovereignty, since whenever the royal crown reaches his inauspicious head, without doubt the tyrannical Heavens will strike the stone of destruction thereon, and the moment the pedestal of the throne of monarchy is touched with his odious feet, the thunderbolts of the skies, through rage, will pour forth on it the fire of adversity; and since his nature is impure, and his disposition unfitted, the effects of your consideration will be lost on him."

> A pure disposition is needed to be worthy of Divine favour,
> Since every stone and clod does not become pearl or coral.

The birds, after hearing these words, at once desisted from such a proceeding, and abandoned the idea of becoming subservient to the Owl, who, humbled and dis-

---

[1] This somewhat obscure passage presumably means, "Though you are, to all appearances, triumphant, yet the injuries you have inflicted on so many persons will, in a spiritual point of view, draw down vengeance on your head."

tressed, remained in the corner of adversity, sad and sorrowful. He said to the Crow: "O black-faced, shameless wretch! having torn away from before yourself the screen of shame, you have admitted all this contempt upon me, and, injuring me, consigned me to the region of hatred and strife. You have raised up a dust of discord, which the revolution of the world will not quell in a hundred thousand ages, and reared a fire of strife, the flame of which the waters encircling the Heavens cannot quench.

My heart may fade, but the trace of your violence will never quit my soul.

"I know not whether anything has passed on my part, that you should have displayed all this love and affection, or whether you have deemed so much courtesy and kindness necessary by way of commencement; but know, that if a tree be torn up, from its roots there will spring up a branch, which, increasing and growing, will regain its original stature: but when the plant of friendship is cut with the saw of violence, it cannot in any way be imagined that the branch of fidelity will sprout from the root; or if a gash proceed from a sword, it may be cured and healed by a salve, but the wound of a speech can never be remedied, nor the scar removed by any ointment.

' That which the tongue has wounded does not heal.'

The wound inflicted on a heart by the sword of the tongue,
Will not be properly cured by any salve.
Between you and the person whom you wounded with your tongue,
There can be no intimacy save that of the stone and the pitcher.

"The point of an arrow, which is fixed in the bosom, may possibly be extracted, but the dart of the tongue, which pierces the heart, cannot in any way be removed.

The point of the arrow with which the heart is wounded, cannot be extracted.

"And everything imaginable, which causes annoyance to a person, may be remedied by something else, except hatred, the removal of which never, by any means, comes within the pale of possibility; just as fire, although it burns up everything, yet its power may be quenched with water, but the flame of malignity cannot be extinguished with the water of the Seven Seas. Poison, although fatal, yet its ill effects may be removed from the body with an antidote; but the venom of rancour cannot be eradicated from the heart by any balm. Henceforth, between my race and your tribe the tree of enmity has been planted, of which the root will reach to the depths of the earth, and its branches pass the summit of the Pleiades."

Of the shrub of hatred which has been planted in the bosom,
It is certain and sure what the fruit will be.
The tree of rancour will yield produce of such a kind,
That its flavour will not suit the taste of any one's soul.

The Owl, muttering this speech, departed, vexed at heart, and with drooping pinions; while the Crow, regretting what he had spoken, fell into long and profound contemplation, saying to himself: "This is a strange matter which I have, without thinking, taken in hand, and I have raised up for my tribe tyrannical-faced enemies, and violence-seeking foes. What business had I to advise the birds, for I was no more worthy to speak in this manner than the general body, who are older and better than myself? At any rate, these clever birds recognised more than myself the Owl's defects, and studied the requirements of the case more accurately than I: but wisely they contemplated the issue of this event, and the results of these words, and carried out the purport of the saying, '*He who keeps silence is safe.*' The tongue has been created in the semblance of a sword, so that it may not be employed in play, since sporting with a dagger is a trick of public performers, while warriors never put their weapon to the test save in the ranks of battle. To bare unnecessarily the sword of the tongue from the sheath of the palate, is like cutting one's throat, or staking one's head.

> When the tongue is in the habit of speaking,
> What wonder if the soul trembles through fear?
> Since swords were made to destroy life,
> They rightly shaped them like a tongue.

"Worse than this, these words were spoken face to face, and doubtless hatred and rancour would be increased on that account, and rage added to rage on hearing every unbecoming sentence. It has been said that, though a wise man may have full confidence in his own strength and might, yet it is incumbent not to allow of any unkindness towards an enemy, or to commence a dispute, and while relying upon his own preparation and majesty, not to stir up enmity. Since, though a person may have in the region of his possession a proved antidote and various medicines, it is not right that, in reliance thereon, he should be eager to drink deadly poison.

> Though the antidote is in your possession,
> Beware that you drink not deadly poison.

"Wise men are agreed that the effects of deeds preponderate over that of words, and the superiority of action to talk is certain. Now, the result of good deeds becomes manifest in the termination of matters, connecting the conclusion of the affair with what is right; so he, whose words are greater than his deeds, and who decks his conduct with enchanting explanations, and adorns it before men's eyes with sweet language and eloquence, in a short time will end his business in reproach and scorn. The results of talk without practice will be nought but regret and repentance. I am that great talker and little doer, who have not used salutary reflection, nor sufficient deliberation as to the end of affairs. If the crown of wisdom had decked the brow of my condition, and I had possessed a portion of the boundless treasury of wisdom, I should first of all have consulted some one, and after that it was decided to speak, should have delivered a discourse innocent and without offence, wherein was no harm.

> I spoke unweighed, bitter words;
> It was an impenetrable pearl I perforated.

"Since, without consulting learned advisers, or deliberating with sound men of wisdom, I have entered upon this affair, and have inconsiderately spoken some angry, strife-exciting words, what wonder if I be numbered amongst the multitude of the wicked, and be proclaimed ignorant, foolish, and a vain speaker? It has passed into a proverb, '*The great talker is a babbler,*' a great speaker is a futile talker, and though in external appearance there may be a difference between men and animals as regards speech, wise men assign the inferior degree to an evil speaker, and consider dumb creatures better than babblers."

Animals are silent, men talk;
To be dumb is better than to speak evil.
When a person says aught, it should be with discretion;
Otherwise, he should be silent like a beast.
Avoid the ignorant man, who prates of the deceased by the ten;
Like a wise person talk of but one, and be a careful speaker.

In short, the Crow trembled somewhat, and condemning himself in this manner flew away.

"Such was the commencement of the enmity between us and the Owls, as I have described." The King said: "O Kárshinás! I have heard what you say, wherein much benefit is comprehended. To associate with wise men, and to make their words the guide of one's affairs and circumstances, is an indication of happiness and prosperity, and a proof of approach to the rank of perfection.

The society of the good is like musk,
By the scented breath of which the marrow of the soul is affected.
Their actions point the way to knowledge,
Their words are a guide to wisdom.

"Now that the house of my heart has been illumined with the lamp of your enlightened words, nought save which can be a taper in the cells of the recluses of the human oratories, explain in what manner you design to remedy the matter of our soldiers, who, moth-like, have been consumed with the fire of the Owl's violence, and in what way you purpose to secure repose of mind for my subjects, and quiet of soul for my troops."

Your deliberation, whenever it sets about a matter,
Accomplishes a hundred things in a single instant.

Kárshinás loosed the tongue of praise, saying:

O King! may the world obey, and the skies befriend you!
May rapid victory precede your army!

"As regards what the enlightened-minded Ministers have conveyed to the place of representation, relative to war, peace, maintaining our ground, flight, and agreeing to pay taxes and tribute, I do not approve of any one of them. I am in hopes that by means of some kind of device we shall find an opening and an opportunity, for many persons, through a habit of stratagem and dissimulation, have obtained their desires, and by treachery and deceit have carried out matters which could not be accomplished by haughtiness, and the like thereof; just as the Robbers of the kingdom of Gurgán, by means of cunning, snatched a Sheep from the hands of the Devotee." The King inquired, "How was that?"

STORY VII

He said: It has been related that an abstinent Devotee had purchased a fat Sheep with the view of making a sacrifice, and having placed a cord round its neck, was leading it towards his own cloister. On the way a body of thieves, seeing that Sheep, opened the eyes of greed, and girding the loins of treachery and deceit, stood in the Devotee's path. The fierce passions of the Gurgání knaves were aroused, but they were unable, Leopard-like, face to face to bring that prey within their clutch; consequently, making choice of the wiles of the Fox, they were anxious to make the Devotee sleep like a Hare.[1] After much reflection, they were unanimous in opinion as to one particular stratagem, and agreed that having deluded the simple-minded, pure-natured Devotee therewith, they would get possession of the Sheep. Accordingly, one individual went before him, and said: "O Shaikh! whence are you bringing this Dog?" Another passed by him, exclaiming: "Where are you taking this Dog?" A third appeared in like manner, and said: "O Shaikh! maybe you intend to go hunting, that you have a Dog by your side?" Another comrade arrived from the rear, and inquired: "O Shaikh! for how much did you buy this Dog?" In like manner, one by one, from various sides and quarters, presenting themselves to the Shaikh, they were unanimous in saying the same words. One exclaimed, "This is a Shepherd's Dog;" another cried out, "This is a Watch Dog;" another launched abuse, saying, "This man is in the dress of a man of piety; why does he soil his hands and clothes with this Dog?" and another forbade him, saying, "A Devotee is carrying off this Dog to rear and nourish it for God." Each of the rogues in this way repeated their rascally speeches, and in this manner addressed themselves.

> They closed his eyes with blandishments, while their lips proclaimed various wiles.
> They bore away the heart from the lovers, each with[2] a different device.

From the multitude of these speeches, doubt overspread the Devotee's heart, and he exclaimed: "God forefend! the seller of this animal was a magician, and by sorcery has made a Dog appear in my sight like a Sheep; nought is better than that I should keep my hands away from this Dog, and, following after the vendor, recover from him the money, which I gave him as the price of the Sheep." The poor wretch of a Devotee, from excess of innocence, left the Sheep, and departed after the seller. That band having taken it, bore it to their house, and losing no time, at once slaughtered it. By means of this stratagem, the poor Devotee let the Sheep slip from his hand, and did not recover his money.

"I have adduced this story so that we, too, should pursue the way of stratagem, since, save by treachery and deceit, we shall not prevail over them."

> When you are not, as regards strength, an antagonist for your enemy,
> Do not abandon treachery and deceit:
> Since by stratagem you may be able
> To snap the cord of the bow of might.

King Píruz said: "Declare what you have to suggest." Kárshinás replied: "I will sacrifice myself in this matter, since it has been allowed that the death of one person, when it comprises the life and existence of a numerous body, is in accordance with reason and tradition. It seems to me right, that the King in the common assembly and the tribunal comprised[3] of high and low, should be enraged with me, and order me to be stripped of feathers, and stained with blood, and to be cast wounded, under that very tree, on the branches of which are our nests, while the King with all his army should depart, and remaining in

---

[1] An oriental phrase meaning "to be off one's guard."

[2] يقانوني in the Persian text is a misprint for بهابوي .

[3] مشتمال in the Persian text is a misprint for مشتمل .

a certain place await my arrival, till after having laid the snare of stratagem in their path, and finished my treachery, I shall return, and explain what may be befitting the requirements of the time." Accordingly, the King came forth from the secret interview full of anger; all the dependants were expectant as to what tidings would proceed from the private meeting of the King and the Minister, and what results[1] would appear from their deliberations and counsel. When they found the King enraged, lowering their heads, they remained contemplative. King Píruz commanded that Kárshinás should be stripped of feathers and tail, and with his head and feet stained with blood, be cast under the tree, while he himself, with his army and retinue, set out for a place which had been fixed and arranged. While this matter was being done and carried out, the Sun had set, and the Divine Tire-woman had decked out the brides of the Stars in the arena of the pearl-studded sky.

> When the shining sun disappeared,
> Dark Night arrayed its armies in the sky.

Shabáhang, the King of the Owls, together with his ministers, was the whole day thinking, "Since we have gained information respecting the abode of the Crows, and have slain or broken the wings of most of them, if to-night we make another assault on them, their day of life will be exchanged for the night of death, and we shall pass two or three days in peace in the corner of our nests."

> After the death of our foes we can live happy.

But when night, which is the day of the bázár of majesty and pomp for Owls, putting on the dress of darkness and the robe of sable, had obtained dominion over the throne of the sovereignty of the world, and the Chief of the armies of Zangbár had raised the murky standard over the hosts and race of the Tatárs, with the design of a night attack,

> The surface of the earth was imbued with amber,
> The cloisters of Heaven were full of smoke—

the King of the Owls, with all his host and retinue, introduced the consideration of a night attack; the whole body, being unanimous in this design, set out towards the abode of the Crows.

> A battle-seeking, strife-exciting band,
> All full of hatred, intrepid, and bloodthirsty.
> They tightly girded their loins with malice;
> Their heart was arrayed for war like a stone.

When the army of Owls arrived at the abode of the Crows, no trace of them appeared, nor was any sign of them manifest. The Owls, confounded, wandered in every direction, while Kárshinás was writhing under the tree and softly wailing. An Owl heard the sound of him, and conveyed the news to the King. Shabáhang, together with several Owls, who were Privy Councillors, and confidants of the King's secrets, came near him and inquired: "Who are you, and what is the state of the case?" Kárshinás told his own name, and that of his father, and proclaimed his position as Minister, and the fact of his abilities. The King said: "I know and have heard much account of you; now tell me, where are the Crows?" He replied: "My condition is a proof that I cannot be

---

[1] Literally, " opening of the doors."

possessed of their secrets." Shabáhang inquired: "You were the Minister of the King of the Crows, and the confidant of his secrets, his counsellor and trusted friend; by what treachery has this debasement befallen you, and for what crime have you become deserving of this punishment?" Kárshinás said: "My master became suspicious in regard to me, while the envious found opportunity of slander, till what has overtaken me befell me, and former service and previous loyalty were all at once cast into the expanse of non-existence."

All the service I had performed was without reward or thanks.
God forbid that any one should have an inconsiderate master!

Shabáhang inquired, "What was the cause of this suspicion?" He said: "King Píruz, after your night attack, summoned his ministers and demanded from each of them some plan relative to this calamity which had happened. My turn having arrived, he commanded: 'Disclose a remedy for the affair which has come to pass, and propound some stratagem for warding off this misfortune.' I replied: 'We have no power to resist the army of the Owls, since their boldness in battle is greater than our courage, while their strength and pomp are superior to our majesty and valour. Again the reins of the steed of fortune are in the hands of the power of the King of the Owls, and the pedestal of the throne of prosperity is decked with the Star-rivalling feet of their Monarch. Now, to grasp the fist of battle with men of happy fortune, is indicative of ruin, and to boast of contending with the lords of increasing prosperity, typical of misery.

To fight with a man of prosperity
Will cause the overthrow of the combatant, as he were a tree.
When mountain deer are in a city amongst lions,
Their homes will become desolate by their own deaths.

"'It is best we should send a messenger, if they light the flame of battle, we, having consumed homes and property with the fire of separation, will become scattered like smoke in a corner of the world; while, if they enter at the door of peace, having agreed to such taxes and tribute as they may demand, we will rest thankful.'

Would you keep your head? Turn not your face from tribute,
Otherwise neither head nor crown will remain to you.

"Our King was confounded and said: 'What words are these you say, and on what ground do you display all this boldness? Would you make me fear battle with the Owls? and do you place no value on my army in comparison with his retinue?'

If the enemy oppress with the sword,
I, too, have a sharp-pointed spear.
When I am eager for war,
I will overthrow the soul of my enemies in anguish.

"Again I loosed the tongue of advice, and through my affection and loyalty, renewed the measure of admonition, saying: 'O King! swerve not from the path of right, nor in the vanity of your heart enter upon an affair without reflection or deliberation. Affect humility, for a powerful enemy may be rendered obedient by kindness and conciliation, and a violent prey brought into the snare with courtesy and civility.

R

> Bliss in both worlds is comprised in these two sentences,
> ' Be kind to friends, courteous to enemies.'

" ' Much the same is the case of a strong wind, from which the insignificant grass, by reason of its humility, escapes in safety, while the many-branched tree, on account of its might and disdain, is torn up by the roots.'

> Oppress not, for the Heavens by reason of their own violence,
> Will close the way of cruelty against tyrants.

"The Crows being enraged at my admonitions, suspected me, (saying): ' You are inclined towards the Owls and desert us who are of your own race.' The King, owing to the words of my enemies, refused to accept my advice, and enjoined them to punish me in the fashion now seen. I observed in their idea that they would make war, and prepare some stratagem to repel you." When the King of the Owls heard the words of Kárshinás, he inquired of one of the Ministers, "How view you the case of this Crow?" He replied: "The matter respecting him does not need any consideration. As quickly as possible the surface of the earth must be purified from the baseness of his tenets, and this must be deemed great kindness and general good, nor should the opportunity be lost of killing him, than which we shall not obtain a finer chance. In the midst of these half-quenched embers, I see a fire, to extinguish the flame of which appears impossible.

> God defend us ! if smoke should proceed from this fire.

"Whoever allows an opportunity to slip from his hands after the loss of the chance, will never again have the means, and most commonly his repentance will no more be of any avail. When a person finds his enemy weak and solitary, it is best to free himself from him, since if the foe escape from that vortex, gaining strength and finding means, he will prepare an ambuscade of revenge.

> When an enemy escapes from you, you will not be free from him,
> And when he breaks away from your snares, you will not be delivered from him.
> Do you wish to be secure from misfortune at his hands ?
> When he comes within your power, give him no quarter.

"Beware that the King pay no heed to his words, nor give ear to his heart-ensnaring treacheries ; since the wise have said, that to rely upon an unproved friend is far from wisdom, what, then, should befall a deceitful, malignant enemy ? "

> In these days, when no reliance is placed on a friend,
> How can one be deceived by the speech of an enemy ?

Kárshinás having heard somewhat of these words, cried out in anguish of heart saying :

> "I am myself pained at heart, and wounded ;
> Do not you, too, sting afresh my sore."

These words having effect on the King of the Owls, he turned his face from that Minister, and inquired of another, "What say you?" He replied: "I cannot counsel his death, since a generous man, when he sees his enemy weak and help-less, should endeavour, with compassion, to remedy his condition, and display his own benevolent qualities to mankind, by the show of pardon and kindness, and give quarter to one haunted by terror and a refugee, as well as take by the hand a ruined downcast.

> Clear the way for good men;
> When you yourself are standing take the fallen by the hand.

"Some things render men kind to an enemy, just as fear of the Thief caused the Merchant's wife to be complaisant to her husband." The King inquired, "How was that?"

STORY VIII.

He said: It has been related that a certain Merchant was very rich, but extremely bad-tempered and ill-looking, added to which he was old, proud, miserly, and inhospitable.

> Horrible-faced, like a demon from the infernal regions;
> Idle talking, like a tame raven.
> His stony heart and soul of steel,
> Were heart-consuming and life-destroying, like separation.

This disagreeable-faced man had a Wife of pure nature, and handsome appearance, such that the Moon of the fourteenth night, by means of borrowing the splendour of her cheeks, made the dark night more resplendent than brilliant day, and the world-illumining lamp of the Sun, which is a lantern before the dome of the Sky, in presence of the light of the taper of her heart-adorning face, shone not forth. The tongue of Time, in praise of that soul of the world, sang these words:

> "The moon is beautiful, yet your face is more charming than it;
> The cypress is heart-enchanting, yet your stature is more erect[1] than it."

The jewel-scattering pen inscribed upon the pages of Explanation some of her charms in the following manner:

> "Though imagination were to draw the pen across the pages of thought,
> Your comely appearance has been formed more handsome than that.
> Every grace that is concealed behind the curtain of obscurity,
> Is visible in your lovely form."

The Husband, with a hundred thousand eager endeavours,[2] sought to approach her, while she, with a hundred thousand flights[3] avoided intimacy with him, neither enamoured with his fascinations, nor deceived by his spells. Every moment, when she was violent, the man renewed his affection, and every instant when she was filled with animosity, he displayed fresh love.

> Affection will not increase, unless you are filled with hatred.

Save with anguish of heart the hand of his desire did not reach the snare of her locks, nor did the rose of his wishes blossom in the garden of her face, without the misery of the thorn of affliction.

---

[1] See note, page 214.
[2] Literally, "hearts:" or possibly the words in the text may be taken as of Arabic origin, and be construed "looking and speaking amorously."
[3] Literally, "stages."

> I am a slave of a face, which should not be seen,
> Enamoured of ringlets, which must not be pulled.

One night a Thief went to their house. By chance the Merchant was asleep, while the Woman was awake. Being apprised of the Thief's arrival, she was frightened, and firmly embraced her husband, who, awaking from his sleep, and finding his charmer in his arms, from excess of joy, cried aloud, saying:

> Surely my fortune is awake, since that face of which, even in my dreams,
> I had no hopes, comes before my open eyes.

"What kindness is this manifested from the curtain of obscurity, and by what service have I become worthy of this favour?"

> Whence arises this affection, which you used not to possess?

When he looked closely, seeing the Thief, he exclaimed: "O valiant man of auspicious footsteps! take away whatever you like of my property, and bear it off, for, by the blessing of your footsteps, this cruel, faithless one has become kind and loving towards me."

"The moral of this story is, that there are some circumstances, by the witnessing of which any one would consider nought but forgiveness and consideration suitable for an enemy; of these is the state of this Crow."

> Be merciful when you see my condition, for it is a case for pity.

The King inquired of a third Minister, "What decree does your opinion pass in this matter?" He said: "It is best that the King should not strip him of the garments of life; nay, more, he should clothe him in the robes of security, and not withhold the indications of patronage and favour, so that, in return for that, considering the service of the King as an invaluable prize, he should open the doors of counsel and sincerity. Again, wise men labour to draw aside a number of their enemies, and casting the stone of discord in their midst, by every stratagem they know, make two parties appear, since difference of opinion amongst foes is the cause of ease of heart, and settlement of affairs with friends: just as the dispute between the Thief and the Demon was the cause of comfort to the Devotee. The King inquired of him, "How was that?"

STORY IX.

He said: It has been related, that a Devotee of pure disposition, abstinent, and innocent-minded, had made his cell in one of the outskirts of Baghdád, and used to pass his morning and evening in worshipping the Omniscient King, "*May his name be magnified.*" Since his skirt was cleaned of the dust of worldly considerations, and he had read the inscription of insincerity and faithlessness on the face of the book of the world, and knew that the draught of joy is not possible without the sting of adversity, nor the coin of the storehouse of riches procurable without the grief of the burden of adversity—

> There is not in this garden a single rose without a thorn,
> Nor are its tulips without the mark of blemish.

The flashing sword strikes you, you say it is the sun ;
It pales your face, you say it is gold [1]—

he drew his head within the collar of repose, in the cell of contentment, and was satisfied with the allowance consigned to him from the Invisible World.

We practised [2] contentment and submission,
And were satisfied with whatever we received from friends.

In short, one of his sincere disciples, being apprised of the Devotee's poverty and want, brought to the holy man's cell, by way of a gift, and as a means of support, a young fat Buffalo, from the delicious milk of which the palate of Desire became moist and sweet. A Thief witnessing this proceeding, the cravings of his appetite were aroused, and he set out towards the Devotee's cell. A Demon, too, in the appearance of a man accompanied him : the Thief inquired, " Who are you, and where go you?" He replied : " I am a Demon, who have taken this form, and assumed this appearance, and am going to the cell of the Devotee ; since most men of this kingdom, by the blessing of his instruction, have pursued the way of repentance and conversion, while the market of my temptation has become dull, I am anxious to find an opportunity to bring him to destruction. My condition is such as you have heard ; now tell who are you, and what is your business?" The Thief replied : " I am by profession a knave, and night and day am thinking how I can seize some one's property, and place the scar of misery on his heart : I am now proceeding to rob the Devotee of a fat Buffalo which he possesses, and consume it by way of my subsistence." The Demon said :

O soul of the world ! you are our friend.

"Thank God! the thread of kinship is strengthened between us, and it is a sufficient bond of friendship that the object of both of us is to injure him." Accordingly they set out on the road. At night they arrived at the cell of the Devotee, who had finished his portion of worship, and sitting upon the edge of the prayer carpet, had so fallen asleep. The Thief thought, " If the Demon intends to kill him, it may be that, awakening, he will cry out, and other persons near to him will be aroused : on this supposition it would be impossible to carry off the Bull." The Demon, too, fell thinking, " If the Thief drives out the Bull from the house, certainly the door must be opened, it is possible that the Devotee, through the noise of the door, may awake from his sleep, and his destruction be deferred." Accordingly he said to the Thief : " Halt, and give me time to kill the Devotee ; do you then steal the Bull." The Thief exclaimed : "Hold, till I carry off the Bull, then you kill the man." This dispute continued between them, till at length the words of each led to strife. The Thief out of vexation cried out to the Devotee, "Here is a Demon anxious to kill you ;" the Demon, too, screamed aloud, "Here is a Thief desirous of carrying away your Bull." The Devotee, being awakened by their quarrel, raised a cry, and the neighbours coming in they both fled ; so the Devotee's life and property, by reason of the dispute of these rivals, remained safe and sound.

---

[1] It is impossible to render these lines satisfactorily, owing to the double meaning which in the original some of the words possess. The purport I take to be, that we are so enamoured of the world as to make plausible excuses for all the calamities which happen therein.

[2] طرع in the Persian text is a misprint for طرح.

When disputes occur in the enemy's army,
What need to unsheathe the sword?

When the third Minister had finished his speech, the first Minister was confounded, and said : " I see that this Crow has beguiled you with his deceits and treachery; beware ! wake from the sleep of neglect, and drawing the cotton of conceit from the ear of your understanding, deem it incumbent worthily to reflect on the termination of this matter, for wise men, particularly as regards protecting themselves from the wiles of an enemy, rear the edifice of their proceedings upon the rules of expediency, and do not turn aside, owing to the false speeches, or inconclusive words of such; while, on the other hand, the incautious, paying no heed to this point, after but little blandishment, become courteous, and forgetting former hatred, and hereditary animosity, are pleased to set their hearts on reconciliation, not perceiving that though an enemy appears in a thousand shapes, the rust [1] of animosity will still remain upon the tablets of his heart.

I said to thy black ringlets, they will not again enthrall :
Years went by in just the same manner and way as used to be.

" More strange it is that, through ignorance, an edging [2] of Basrah in your eyes appears a wonderful thing from Baghdád, and a glass bead in your sight seems a royal pearl. Your case is similar to that of that Carpenter, who was deceived with the speech of his wicked wife." The King said, " How was that ?"

STORY X.

He said : It has been related, that in the city of Sarándíp there was a Carpenter, foolish to the utmost degree, who had a most beautiful and elegant wife, with eyes like a deer, who with a glance captured the raging lion, and with her tricky, fox-like looks made the wits of the world sleep carelessly like [3] Hares.

In appearance heart-deceiving and soul-ensnaring,
A fairy-faced, lover-enchanting idol.
At her ringlets the hyacinths writhed,
Through envy of her cheeks roses melted to water.

The Carpenter was enamoured of her, and would not rest a moment without seeing her. The woman of necessity behaved kindly to him, but at the banquet of love she drank the cup of Desire with other companions. In their neighbourhood there was a young man, in stature like a cypress, growing in the expanse of the living Spirit, and in appearance resembling a fresh rose, with its cheeks washed in the water of Life.

Cheeks such as could not be made from the sun or moon,
Beard such as could not be formed from black musk.

The glance of the woman alighted on him, and his heart, too, was enchained with love and affection for her. The matter between them from correspondence ended in secret visits, and letters and messages led to constant delight, and meetings at both morn and eve. A body of envious persons, the idea of the intimacy of

---

[1] See note 2, page 51.
[2] I have adopted Eastwick's suggestion that طِرَاز should be طَرَاز.
[3] See note 1, page 255.

two friends turning the splendour of their day into the darkness of night, and the thought as to why these two persons should together light the taper of companionship, consuming their black hearts with the fire of envy and jealousy—

> I was never envious of his station or wealth,
> But only that he had the company of a sweetheart—

being apprised of these proceedings, informed the Carpenter. The unfortunate wretch, though he did not possess much jealousy, was anxious to ascertain the truth, and busy himself with a remedy. He said to his wife: "Prepare food, for I am going to the market-town, and though the distance there is not great, yet several days will elapse; I know not how I shall exist away from you, or how endure the crucible of heart-consuming separation."

> O thou! who depriveth me, against my wish, of thy cheeks,
> Who is there who, of his own free will, would elect to separate from thee?

The woman, too, by way of ceremony made profession of attachment, and with cries of joy rained several drops of water from her eyes, and at once preparing the provisions, started her husband on his journey. The Carpenter, at the time of his departure, insisted strongly: "The door must be firmly secured, and the goods well guarded, so that thieves may find no opportunity during my absence, and no loss of property or goods occur." The woman agreeing to his injunction pledged her oath thereon: immediately he had left, she informed her lover.

> Come to the garden, for the roses are in blossom and not a thorn remains.

The Lover engaged: "When a watch of the night has passed, expect the rising of the morn of approach." The woman was delighted with the promise, and made ready the materials for entertainment.

> O what happy fortune! if for one night that Moon
> Were to alight at my unfurnished cell.

The Carpenter unexpectedly returned to the house by a secret way. By chance it happened to be a time when Sun and Moon were in conjunction, and lover and mistress were delighted at seeing one another. At one moment the beautiful-faced young man, with heart-enrapturing glance, threw the brand of perplexity amongst the harvest of her patience; at another, the moon-faced woman, with soul-enchanting blandishments, plundered the chattels of the young man's wisdom and understanding.

> Two toying, wisdom-ensnaring idols.
> From head to foot entirely comely and beautiful.
> The cheek of this one was like a candle for the chamber:
> The lips of that one a dainty for the worshipper of wine.

The hapless Carpenter waited till they became disposed to retire to the bed-chamber. He then gently went under the couch, so as to observe what went on in private. Suddenly the woman's eyes alighted on his feet: perceiving that the departure of her husband was a ruse to discover the truth of the case, she softly addressed her lover, saying—"Ask me, in loud tones, 'Do you like me best or your husband?'" The young man raised his voice, and said: "O sweet one! I want to know whether affection for me is uppermost in your heart, or love for your husband." The woman inquired: "What is the drift of this question, and what is the use of such a request?" The young man, in fear of soul, importuned her, and took her hand. The woman said: "I am speaking truly. These kind of misfortunes happen to women, either through carelessness and negligence, or by reason of sport and desire, and they select every kind of friend, and pay no regard to their ancestry or lineage, nor consider their bad disposition and unacceptable manners, and when their sensual wants are gratified, and their carnal desires begin to lessen, they hold such persons as strangers in their estimation.

> They desert their companion and lover,
> Not a thought of their friendship remains.

"But the husbands are in the place of the souls in their breasts, and like the light of their eyes.

> There is escape from life, but no avoiding them.

"May she never enjoy being, youth, food, or existence who does not esteem her husband a thousand times more than her own precious soul, and who does not wish for the capital of life, with view of easing his condition, and procuring him peace in the next World, and throughout Eternity."

> May my hopes be ruined if I exist without you!
> May my life be blighted if it be not at your disposal!

When the Carpenter heard this discourse, pity and compassion overspread his heart, and tenderness and sympathy overpowered him. He said: "It wellnigh happened that I acted wrongly in the matter of this woman, and, in the sight of God, I should have been culpable and guilty; at any rate, what was this evil suspicion that I had in regard to her, while the poor woman herself is miserable through grieving after me, and overwhelmed with love for me? Now, in the practice of affection and the way of friendship, if with all the love and liking that she has for me, she commit a fault, no great weight must be attached thereto, nor must much importance be imputed to the like of those practices which she has followed, since no creature can be free from negligence or error.

> Where is the person whose skirt is not defiled?

"I have foolishly brought all this grief upon myself, and cast myself into so much misery. My best course is now not to make the burden of love irksome to them, nor scatter her reputation before strangers in the mire of disgrace, since she acts thus by way of sport and want of thought, not designedly and deliberately. I must regard her merits and shut my eyes to her faults."

> If you possess one virtue, coupled with seventy faults,
> A friend would see but that one virtue.

Accordingly, he remained silent under the bed, in the self-same spot, and did not draw a breath till they had finished their loves, and the ensign of dark Night had dropped its head.

> When the Devotee of Day jumped up from the shade of Night,
> The world-adorning Morn breathed forth from the skies.

The stranger retired, and the woman herself made as though she were asleep on the top of the bed. The Carpenter slowly crept from under the couch, and gently and humbly sat on the top thereof, and with the sleeve of Kindness clearing off the dust of vexation from the woman's face, gently pressed his hand upon her limbs, till the deceitful woman opened her eyes, and seeing her husband at the head of the pillow, jumped up and said:

"The morn of happiness appeared, for my friend has returned :
A thousand thanks, for this dear companion has come back."

She then inquired, "When did you arrive in safety?" He replied: "At the time when that strange man had the hand of Desire in the embrace of your society; but since I knew that necessity was the cause thereof, I preserved your honour, and did not disturb him; and since I recognise your kindness as concerns my affairs, and am aware of your friendliness as regards my case, confident that you desire life on account of my society, and seek sight with the object of contemplating my beauty, if you dissipate in this manner, assuredly it must be from inadventure. Accordingly, it was incumbent upon me to be kind towards your friend, and to preserve your reputation. Be of good cheer, nor give place to fear and dread; banish alarm and anxiety, and pardon me, inasmuch as I had doubts respecting you, and indulged in a hundred kinds of evil suspicions about you. Thank God! things did not turn out as I expected."

What we fancied was wrong.

The woman, too, uttered words mingled with deceit, and anger beginning to fade on both sides, the hand of Peace was brought round the neck of Delight. The Carpenter, loosing the tongue of apology, spoke to this effect:

"May your offence, in the sight of God, be nought!
I am pleased with you, and may the Almighty be so too."

"I have adduced this story that, like the Carpenter, who was deceived with the speech of the wicked woman, you may not accept the wiles of this treacherous Crow, nor turn aside, through his hypocrisy and jugglery, from which there is the perfume of blood.

One should not be deceived with the words of an evil-designing enemy.
Whoever acts thus will in the end regret it.

"Every enemy who, owing to length of distance, cannot carry out his design, will by stratagem bring himself nearer, and adopting a habit of advising, with hypocrisy and humility, will push himself into a position of confidence. When he is apprised of the secrets, seeking an opportunity, he will set about his business with the utmost caution. Every wound that he inflicts, like the fiery lightning, will never miss consuming the harvest of life; or, as it were, the dart of unerring Fate, will never fail to reach the target of Desire, and the butt of Intention." The Crow said: "O heart-rending friend! to what purpose is all this eloquence, and what is the result of all these meaningless prefatory remarks which you have strung together? At any rate, what connection has this cruelty which has befallen me, and such injury as has overtaken me with stratagem and deceit? No wise man, with the view of benefiting another, will seek his own detriment. I have not accepted of my own choice this humiliation and torture. Every one knows that this punishment was nought save retaliation on account of my dispute with the Crows." The Minister said: "This act which you have done is the indication of your treachery, and you have freely and of your own accord given over your body to this torture. The sweetness of revenge which possesses your heart has rendered pleasant-tasted on the palate of your hopes the bitter potion of this cruelty. Many persons there have been, who with the view of destroying their enemies, have agreed to sacrifice themselves, and who, to render a service to their benefactor, so that the name of gratitude and loyalty may be left on the scroll of fortune, have cast themselves into the vortex of annihilation, just as that Ape who gave himself up to be killed, so as to avenge his friends." The King of the Owls inquired, "How was that?"

STORY XI.

He said: It has been related that a troop of Apes had their abode in an island, wherein were many fruits, both fresh and dry, while the water and climate thereof suited their constitution completely. One day a body of the grandees of that tribe were sitting under the shade of a tree, and chattering on every subject. At one time, like a pistachio, with smiling lips, they told stories of the impervious filbert-nut; at another, their eyes, like a moist almond, would not open, save to contemplate the beauty of the dry fig. All at once a Bear passed by them, and was extremely troubled in his mind at their composure. He said to himself: "Is it right that I should perpetually live miserable in the midst of stony mountains, and with a hundred thousand troubles obtain the tip of a thorn, or the root of some grass, while these Apes in such delightful spots and pleasant abodes eat fresh and moist fruits, and pasture on the surface of turf softer than delicate silk?"

My rivals, like roses, blossom in the spring of her society,
Why should I, in the autumn of separation, remain without leaf or sustenance?

Thereupon he determined to go in the midst of that troop, and with the axe of oppression turn upside down the basis of their rest. The Apes joining in battle, upwards of a thousand of them collected together, and made an attack, and confounding the Bear with the blow, wounded him. As regards the poor crude-natured beast, ere ever he had tasted of the shrub of Desire, the fruit of his ambition, the tree of his Delight withered away, and ere the cell of his nature was radiated with the light of the taper of tranquillity, the lamp of his strength died out.

Not a draught from the cup of delight has reached my lips,
The hand of violence has dashed the goblet of my desire against a stone.

In short, the Bear with the utmost eagerness jumped up from midst the Apes, and betaking himself to the hills joined in cries and clamour. A great body of his race having come forth, saw him in that condition and inquired of him the particulars of his battle, and details of his rebuff and defeat. The Bear repeated what had occurred, saying: "O the disgrace! that a powerful Bear must undergo this shame at the hands of weak Apes; never in former days did such a state of things occur to our ancestors;[1] and this evil reputation will cleave to our race till the Day of Judgment. It is best for you to join hands and league together, so that with one night attack, we may turn the day of their life into the night of death, and with the dust of violence darken the eyes of their hope."

---

[1] Literally, "fathers and grandfathers."

If there be security from the revolution of the skies,
We will require our revenge from the evil-disposed one.
We will so wound their head in battle,
That our name will remain till the last day.

The spirit of pride being aroused amongst the Bears, they kindled the fire of violence, and loosed the tongue of arrogance and boasting, raising to the skies cries of opposition and strife.

Battle is like an ant, and we are dragons,
Where is there escape from our clutches?
'Tis ours to raise the standard of war,
The enemy will lose his head and throne.

They then arranged that they should, that very night, occupy themselves in kindling the fire of destruction, and in the heat of war and the flame of battle, cast fire amongst the harvest of the Apes' life. At the time when the golden-clawed Lion of the Sun inclined from the area of the Spheres to the fountain,[1] " *In a spring of black clay,*" and the Great and Little Bear began[2] to strut in the region of the North Pole—

When the shining sun turns its back,
The air darkens, and the ground becomes rough—

all of a sudden the Bears of that mountain turned their faces towards the island of the Apes, whose King, by chance, together with a body of his chiefs and nobles, had planned a hunting-party, and that very evening had remained in the plain, while the other Monkeys, careless of attack from an enemy, were all of them resting in their homes; when all at once,

An army rushed forth like ants and locusts,
And waged through the earth a world-desolating war.

Before the Apes were aware, many of them were slain, and some, broken down and wounded, bore their souls to shore from that blood-stained whirlpool. When the Bears saw that fertile waste, and populous island free from enemies, they drew there the foot of permanency within the skirt of residence, and made that Bear, who had experienced misfortune and undergone injury, their chief; stretching out the hand of violence they brought into the maw of their possession every delicacy which the Apes in lapse of time had stored up.

O God! O God! what was amassed has been squandered.[3]

Next day, when the black-hearted world became bright like the cheeks of beauties, and the sun like Jamshíd[4] came forth on the throne of the azure vault—

When the army of dawn raised the standard,
The world drew the pen through the letter of night—

the King of the Apes, unaware of this state of things, set out towards the island. On the way a body of vanquished, who had escaped to shore, half dead, from the midst of the whirlpool of misfortune, having arrived, began to demand justice. The King, being apprised of the circumstances of the case, commenced biting the finger of perplexity with the teeth of regret,[5] and said: " Alas that my hered-

---

[1] Literally, " to Chashmah-i-Sár" (a celebrated fountain in Kohistán).
[2] لَبَ in the Persian text is a misprint for لَبَ.
[3] This might also be rendered " who has squandered, who amassed ?"
[4] See note 1, page 12.   [5] See note, page 28.

itary kingdom should have slipped from the grasp of my possession, and alack that my well-filled store has fallen into the hands of the enemy! At length adverse Fate has poured down the dust of adversity upon my brow, and at this last, fickle unstable Fortune has turned her face."

No one ever saw plenty or riches in the Flower Garden of the World ;
No one ever beheld the face of Prosperity tinted with fidelity.
It is not wise to rely upon the World—the city of deceit—
Since no one ever saw a palace of adversity more full of trouble.

Others, too, who attended the King's army, beginning to be disturbed, each one laid his complaint respecting his property, possessions, wife and family; amongst them was one named Maimún,[1] adorned with excellent wisdom, and distinguished from the rest by abundant intelligence, for which reason they paid him the utmost respect, both King and subjects deriving aid from his auspicious counsel.

By his enlightened soul and pure mind,
With true deliberation, he subdued kingdoms.
Saturn was his pupil in penetration,
Mercury his apprentice in the use of the pen.

Maimún, when he saw the King perplexed and others overwhelmed, opened the tongue of advice saying :

In misfortune be not impatient, for hence
Arise two evils—give ear to what I say :
First of all, friends are saddened ;
Secondly, enemies are delighted.

"To be impatient in misfortunes deprives a person of eternal reward, and makes him celebrated for want of self - restraint and rashness : in the like of this calamity there are but two things, which are of any avail : 1st, To display patience and increased resignation and constancy, for the tree of restraint will bear the fruit of desire, and according to the saying, '*Patience is the key of joy,*' to be long-suffering is the key of the doors of escape.

Patience is the key of the door of the storehouse of desire,
The person who opens the closed door is resignation ;
As regards the mirror of the bosom of the hapless,
It is long-suffering which removes the dust of oppression.

"2d, To make use of sound judgment and accurate deliberation, since when the lightning of a man of wisdom's intelligent mind flashes in the night of calamity, it can completely efface the darkness of cruelty from the pages of the condition of the ill-treated oppressed, and in one night of thought accomplish the matters of a thousand years."

With the salve of sound deliberation and honest judgment,
The wound of a heart torn in a hundred pieces can be cured.

The King of the Apes was consoled at the words of Maimún, and inquired, "How can this matter be remedied?" Maimún, seeking a private interview, exclaimed : "O King! my children and relations have been slain at the hands of this tyrannical band, and without the sight of them there will be no pleasure in life to me, nor delight in existence.

---

[1] Fortunate.

Without your face I can indeed live, yet
Such existence is a thousand times worse than death.

" Since the end of the business will be that the chattels of life will fall into
the whirlpool of annihilation, I am anxious, as quickly as possible, to convey
myself from the straits of worldly appurtenances, to the delightful plain of the
Eternal regions; and staking my own life, to snatch revenge for my friends and
beloved ones from those inconsiderate tyrants." The King said: "O Maimún!
the pleasure of revenge may appear sweet on the palate of life, and the delight
of victory over an enemy may be necessary to cause happiness of existence; but
when you are no more, what matter whether all the world be populous or
desolate, or be the heart where it may, whether it be at rest or disquieted?"

When in this expanse you are not to be seen,
What matter whether the rose be fresh or withered?

Maimún said: "O King! in this case of mine, death must be put before life, and
annihilation be chosen in preference to existence—since the light of my eyes
was the sight of the beauty of my children, and they have laid their faces in the
womb of the earth, and the pleasure of my heart was bound up with the contemplation of my family and kinsmen, but the harvest of their repose has been
scattered with the tempest of Fate. The basis of my support was my property
and possessions, but the savings of all my life are dissipated by the plunder of the
enemy. I am now anxious to display gratitude for the King's favour, and assist
with the salve of repose my companions, who suffer anguish of heart and torture
of soul, and scattering the coin of life, to leave a name on the pages of time.

It is my ambition to die with a good name,
First amongst all the multitude of desires stands fair fame.

" Nor must the King grieve for my death; and when with friends he sits at
the banquet of enjoyment, he must call to mind my fidelity."

When in the midst of desire you bring the hand of hope,
Call to mind the time of our society.

The King said: "How will you follow out this matter, and by which door
amongst the entrances of stratagem will you enter?" Maimún replied: "I have
arranged a device by which I will consume them in the desert of Mardázmáí[1]
with the flame of the Samúm:[2] most probably my idea will not deviate from
the highway of what is right. It is expedient for you to decree, that they should
root out my ears with their teeth, and breaking my hand and feet respectively,
should at night cast me into a corner of the waste wherein was our abode, while
the King with his attendants, and his body of vanquished, should disperse
throughout the sides and regions of this desert, till two days have elapsed. On
the morning of the third day, let them come and remain at rest in their own
abode, since there will be no trace of enemies, nor after that will any calamity
arise from the like of them." The King, in accordance with the opinion of
Maimún, commanded them to tear out his ears, and break his ribs, and cast
him upon the edge of the forest, while scattering his own army, he sat watching
his opportunity. Maimún, all night long bewailed, in such a manner that a
heart of stone would have moistened at his distress, and the hills have broken
into lamentation from his pain-mingled cries. The King of the Bears, at early

---

[1] Man testing.   [2] Scorching blast.

morn, came forth for a roam, and heard that piteous noise. Following the sound, he saw Maimún in that plight: though he was himself hard-hearted, he pitied him, and notwithstanding his stony disposition, compassion filled his soul. Busying himself inquiring into Maimún's case, and investigating his predicament, he sought an explanation of the matter. Maimún, cleverly perceiving that he was the King of that race, commenced to praise him. After performing the rights of homage, which befits the condition of Kings, he said:

> My earthly frame, with eyes and heart, is in fire and water;[1]
> See with thine eyes, and pity me in your heart, for the case is desperate.

"O King! I am the Minister of the King of the Apes, with whom I went out hunting. On the night of the attack I was not in the battle-field. Next day the vanquished having arrived, I gathered tidings of the King's descent on this country. The Monarch of the Apes, through the confidence which he had in my deliberation, requested a remedy for this matter, while I, by reason of my loyalty, indicated to him your Majesty's service, and said: 'The true plan is for us to bind the loins of servitude, and pass the rest of our lives as servants in attending the King, under the shadow of whose prosperity, we can live at rest with home and provisions, free from the adversities of time.'

> Under the protection of the fortune of the pious.
> Whoever is wise seeks his way.
> When you come into a garden of roses, you bear off the rose;
> If you pass towards a flower-garden, you carry away the hyacinth.

"The King was amazed at my speech, and uttered a variety of improper words as regards the multitude who dwell in this forest, When a second time I tried to restrain him, he ordered them to inflict all this torture on me, and commanded, 'Since he is loyal to their King and army, it is best to cast him near that island of theirs, so that I may see what kind of protection they will afford him.' They brought me here, and have requited my previous service with heart-rending consequences." Thus he spoke, and wept so with pain, that drops of tears began to trickle from the King of the Bears' shameless eyes.

> If I lament, the stone would become a heart of blood;
> If I cry, the eyes would become like Jaihún.[2]

The King said, "Where are now the Apes?" He replied: "There is a desert called Mardázmáí, where they have sought refuge. On every side they are collecting an army, and any hour, with bloodthirsty troops and a pitiless victorious band, they may make an attack." The King of the Bears was startled, and said: "O Maimún! what is to be done? God forbid that any misfortune should occur at their hands to my host!" Maimún said: "The King must be composed in this respect; and had I feet I would unexpectedly lead a body against them, and bring destruction on the fortunes of those ungrateful traitors." The King replied: "I know you are well acquainted with their abode. Now, if you can lead us against them, you will place the necklace of obligation round the neck of the circumstances of this body; and since, too, they have injured you, by revenge you will obtain your own desire." Maimún said: "How can I do it, since it is impossible for me to journey, and impracticable to move with these hands and feet?" The King said: "I know a remedy for this plight,

---

[1] That is, my frame is overwhelmed with anguish.
[2] A river. The meaning is simply, the eyes would be filled with tears.

and by an arrangement I can take you along." Accordingly he cried out to the leaders of the army, and the chief councillors of the court, to come nigh; and having explained to them the state of the case, said : " Make ready, for to-night we will attack the enemy." They all agreed to the suggestion, and prepared the implements of war. Tying Maimún upon the back of a Bear, they set out on their road. Maimún by signs showed them the way, till they reached the edge of the desert Mardázmáí. Now this was a sultry, waterless waste, in the expanse of which the spring clouds, from excess of dryness, were burnt up; and the swift messenger of the Moon, from the dangers of that desolate spot, lost its way in the Heavens. World-traversing Intellect, too, was unable to emerge from the straits thereof, and globe-encircling Imagination did not know its way from the abodes therein. A Samúm used to blow in that desert, such that whoever was overtaken by its effects at once melted away, and it made the sand and soil burn like a blacksmith's forge. By reason of this Samúm, no creature took up its abode in that waste, nor did any grass grow in that brackish, fatal spot.

> An extensive desert, full of dangers,
> At every step therein were a hundred perils.
> Its atmosphere was fire, and flames were air;
> Its soil was stone, its stone a magnet.

Maimún said : " Make haste, and before the whiteness of morn draws aside the veil from the face of the affairs of the world, we will tear away the curtain of their entire body from the expanse of repose; and sooner than the Turkish[1] clad King shall raise his gold-decked flag, we will make the banners of the pomp of these unlucky ones hang listless." The Bears, with the utmost eagerness, set their steps in that desert, and with their own feet traversed the plain of Fate and the region of destruction. The sun arose, but not a trace of the Apes appeared. Maimún, however, hastened to proceed, and deluded them with falsehoods and frauds, till the sun was high, and scorched with the warmth of its rays the sides and regions of those districts. The flame of the taper of the sun was resplendent to a pitch, that whoever looked into the air was burnt up like a moth, while he who put his feet to the ground melted away like wax.

> The soul became so inflamed with heat,
> That the lips consumed away like a taper from the glare thereof;
> From the warmth of the wind you would have thought that Fate
> Had raised another Infernal region in the earth.

The heat of the sun coming forth, hurled destruction upon the Bears, while the fiery Samúm, beginning to blow, was visible from afar like smokeless fire. Their King turned towards Maimún, (saying): " What desert is this, through dread of which our hearts are burnt up, and our souls parched? What is this which, like a flame of fire, is rushing towards us, coming violently and quickly?" Maimún replied: " O heart-rending tyrant! this is the desert of Fate, and that which is coming is the messenger of death: be of good cheer, for had you a hundred thousand souls you would not save one; and now that the Samúm is coming, it will burn you all to ashes, and you will be consumed with the fire of injustice, which you inflicted on the frames of the Apes." They were thus talking when the flame of the Samúm arrived, and burnt up on the spot Maimún, with the

---

[1] That is, the Sun.

host of the King and his army, and not one of them came forth from that desert. The third day, as had been arranged, the King of the Apes, together with his army, having come to the island, found the forest deserted, and the kingdom freed from the annoyance of rivals.

The evening of adversity passed away, and the morn of victory appeared ;
The autumn of grief vanished, and the spring of joy arrived.

" I have adduced this story, that the King may know that the malignant, by way of revenge, renounce their lives, and place no value thereon, in order to bring pleasure to their friends. Now I recognise the designs of Kárshinás from these treacherous speeches, and perceive a similar case to that very one just mentioned. Previous to this I have tried the Crows, and perceived the measure of their foresight and intelligence, and the extent of their deceit and stratagem ; and when I saw Kárshinás in this condition, I was sure that their opinions and views were allied to what is right, and their wisdom and ability greater than was supposed.

I had heard as to your magnanimity,
When I saw you it was a thousand times greater.

" It is expedient, that before he gives us a supper, we should make him eat a breakfast, and ere he begins to spill our blood, we should give the order for his death." The King of the Owls, when he heard this discourse, frowned, and said : " What is this harshness and want of compassion ? through loyalty to us a variety of afflictions and tortures have befallen this poor man, and we, too, are about to punish and kill him, and once more to leave an afflicted mortal in the crucible of trial : have you not heard that it has been said—

' Gladden the hearts of the distressed,
And remember the night of affliction ' ? "

Accordingly he commanded that, having borne off that Crow with honour and respect, they should bring him along with himself. The Minister said : " O King ! since you have paid no heed to my words, and turned away the face of acceptance from my suggestions, which are the essence of wisdom, and the germ of expediency, at any rate pass your life [1] with him as it were amongst enemies, nor for an instant be secure from his treachery and deceit, for his arrival is for nought but the ruin of the affairs of the Owls, and the benefit of the condition of the Crows." The King refused to listen to this advice, and despised the words of that incomparable companion. The Crow lived in the King's service with the greatest honour, and omitted nothing of the dues of servitude, or the rights of attendance ; delighting in some way or other each of the King's counsellors and associates, he caused them to be united to him ; consequently every day his dignity waxed higher, and he found out more and more the way to the heart of the King and his servants, till he reached such a pitch as to become the object of trust, and the confidant of secrets ; and when the perfection of his sincerity, and the abundance of his integrity were manifest, he became the counsellor of the kingdom, and the pivot of the State. In the commencement of affairs they used to take counsel with him, and carried out various important matters according to his judgment and deliberation. One day in the public assembly, and in a full meeting, he said to high and low : " The King of the Crows injured me

---

[1] زندكانى, in the Persian text is a misprint for زندگانى.

without a cause and punished me, when innocent; until I vent my spite against him, and boldly show my superiority over him, in what way can I get ease and repose, or how be inclined for sleep and food? to obtain this wish, and carry out this intention, I have reflected much, and for a lengthened period passed my time in thought and deliberation: the upshot of the matter is, that I perceive of a certainty that so long as I am in appearance a Crow, and have that shape, I cannot obtain my desire, nor fulfil my object. Now I have heard from men of wisdom, that when a wretched persecuted person under-goes pain at the hands of an unjust tyrant, and experiencing anguish from a ruthless oppressor, sets his heart upon death, and consumes himself with fire, every prayer which he utters in that condition will meet with acceptance: should the judgment of the King see fit, let him command me to be burnt; perhaps at the moment that the heat of the flame reaches me, I will ask of God, may his name be glorified, to turn me into an Owl, may be that by such means I shall gain the ascendancy over that tyrant, and wreak my vengeance on him." Now there was present in the multitude that Owl, who had striven to bring death upon Kárshinás: he said:

'Are you not impudent like the narcissus, or black-hearted like the tulip?
At any rate be not like the lily, two-faced and ten-tongued.'

The King inquired, "What do you say relative to this speech?" The Minister replied: "This, too, is another deceit, which he has invented, and a fraud tainted with the colour of hypocrisy.

From head to foot he is a mass of hypocrisy and fraud,
And by his wiles the poor are confounded.

"If his impure person, and base frame were many times burnt, and the ashes thereof made into clay with the water of the fountain of Paradise, and the potion of purity, yet his foul disposition and detestable nature would not alter, and the malevolence of his mind, and the perverseness of his faith, would neither become cleansed with water, nor burnt out with fire.

Hope not for good from a bad disposition,
For rust will not become white through washing.

"Even on the impossible supposition that his ignoble person were to become a peacock, or, for example, were his base disposition to be clad in the garb of a phœnix, none the less would he yearn for the society and affection of the Crows. Just as that Mouse, notwithstanding it obtained the form of a human being, yet reverted to its original nature, and would not associate with the world-adorning Sun, the bountiful Clouds, the delicious Breeze, or the firm-fixed Mountain." The King inquired, "How was that?"

STORY XII.

He said: It has been related that a Devotee, whose prayers were answered, was sitting on the brink of a rivulet, and with the water of contentment had washed his hands of the contamination of worldly considerations. A Kite flying along arrived there, and a young Mouse dropped from his beak on the ground, in front of the Devotee, who had compassion on it, and carrying it off wrapped it in his mantle, desirous to take it with him to his home; again he thought "I must not do so, since the people of the house may be worried by it, and suffer injury." He prayed that the Most High God might be pleased to make it become a Girl. The arrow of the Devotee's supplication reached the target of acceptance, and the Tire-woman of Divine Power arrayed it as a Girl, beautiful in appearance, and upright in stature, bright-faced and with distracting hair: such that the sun of her cheeks kindled the flame of jealousy in the harvest of the moon, and her musky locks produced anguish from the heart of black night.

Such is she in stature that she could taunt the cypress,
And such she is that she would have drawn the inscription of ruin [1] against the moon.

The Devotee, looking, saw a form created by the mere grace (of God) and found a Girl nurtured by His simple favour; he made her over to one of his disciples to love her as his own children. The disciple respecting the wishes of the Devotee, looked after the Girl, with the utmost diligence. In a little time the Damsel reached years of discretion. The Devotee said: "O beloved one! you have grown up, and there is no help but to unite your pure nature with another pearl in the thread of matrimony; I have left this matter to your own good pleasure; whomsoever amongst men or fairies, nay, more, from the highest beings to the lowest creatures, you may select, I will bestow you on him." The Girl replied: "I desire a husband powerful and strong, endowed with manifold might and majesty, and standing alone in a lofty rank, and exalted station as regards his greatness." The Devotee said: "By the description which you state the Sun would be such an one." The Girl rejoined: "Yes, I know that he is conquered by none, and will overcome all that is under the firmament: plight me to him."

Next day when the Monarch of the West,
Issued forth through this azure dome,
Time once more opened the doors of brilliance,
Again the world commenced to sport.

At morn, when according to the decree of the '*Creator of the morning*' the Sun rose from the horizon of the east, the Devotee recounted to him the state of the case, saying: "This damsel is extremely beautiful and of acceptable disposition; I am anxious that she should be under your control, since she has desired of me a mighty and powerful husband." The Sun, on hearing these words, waxing warm, replied: "I will indicate to you a more powerful being than myself, that is a Cloud, which hides my light, and deprives the inhabitants of the world of the beauty of my radiance."

The Sun, in spite of its altitude,
Is hidden by an insignificant Cloud.

The Devotee came to the Cloud, and repeated the same story as before; the Cloud blushing from shame at this speech said: "If you select me on account of my power and might, the Wind is superior to me, for he draws me from whatever quarter he wishes, and bears me along with him in whatever direction he chooses." The Devotee keeping this point in view, went to the Wind, and repeated an account of what had occurred. The Wind writhed with shame, and said: "What power

---

[1] Literally, "a fine."

and might can I possess? absolute strength is contained in a Mountain, for he has drawn the foot of patience within the skirt of majesty, and like the North Star rests on his own axis, while I have no greater effect thereon than a gentle voice in the ears of one deaf from his birth, or than the tread of a tiny ant's feet on the surface of a solid rock."

> If the wind sets the Clouds in motion,
> Yet when they reach the Mountain they are dispersed.

The Devotee approached the Mountain, and recited the scroll of his affairs. The Mountain cried out: "O Devotee! the might or strength of a Mouse is more than that of mine, since he riddles my sides with holes, and makes his home in my soul; my bosom in a thousand places is torn with his heartrending wounds, nor do I in any way know a remedy to keep him off." The Damsel exclaimed: "He says truly a Mouse is superior to him, and therefore a fitting husband for me." The Devotee then offered her to a Mouse, who, by reason of the consanguinity in which the end of the thread of the girl's nature terminated, took a fancy in his heart for her. He replied: "I, too, have for a long time been desirous of a sweetheart, who should be the companion of my fortune, but it is necessary that my partner should be one of my own race." The Damsel said: "This is easy. Let the Devotee pray that I may become a Mouse, and I will embrace you with the hand of delight." The Devotee, perceiving that on both sides there was a genuine desire, raised his palms in supplication, and sought from the Most High God, that He would turn her into a Mouse. The Devotee's intercession was immediately honoured with acceptance, and the indication, '*Everything returns towards its own original,*' being evidenced, the Girl became a Mouse, while the Devotee gave her over to the other Mouse, and departed.

> My soul! everything will revert to its original condition;
> We ourselves, since we are dust, must at length return to earth.

"Now the moral of this story is, that whatever is prompted by a natural disposition, however much other events may have diverted it from such condition, ultimately will revert to that its original state. An eloquent sage, in strings of verse, has proclaimed this very point in these beautiful terms and sweet strains:

> 'The tree which is of a bitter nature,
> Were you to give it a place in the garden of Paradise,
> And if, at the time of watering it from the streams of Eternity,
> You were to sprinkle on its roots honey, and pure nectar,
> In the end its nature would come into play,
> And it would produce just the same bitter fruit.'"

The King of the Owls, as is the way of the unfortunate, paid no heed to these counsels, and, imputing the Minister's words to envy, did not regard the termination of the matter. Every day the Crow adduced to them some pleasant tale, and each night some incomparable fiction, reciting strange stories and wonderful proverbs, till, becoming a Privy Councillor, he gained complete acquaintance with the details of the secrets and mysteries of their condition. Suddenly, watching his opportunity, he turned his face from them, and went to the Crows whose King, seeing him, with joyous wing began these words:

> "O friends! we may now attain the desire of our hearts,
> Since ease of soul and repose of mind and spirit have been secured."

Then King Píráz inquired: "O Kárshinás! what have you done?" He replied: "By the King's fortune I have performed what is befitting, and accomplished my object. You must act, for it is the time for snatching revenge and for seeing our enemies (in a state) according to the wishes of our friends." The King said: "Repeat the substance of your advice, so that, pursuing the matter by the light of intelligence, whatever is needed in way of materials may be made ready." Kárshinás replied: "In such a mountain is a cave, wherein during the day the Owls revert and collect together, and in the neighbourhood, too, many dry sticks are to be found. Let the King command the Crows to remove a little thereof, and heap it at the door of the cave, while I will bring some fire from the abode of some shepherds who have their home in that locality, and will cast it on the sticks: then let the King issue an order to the Crows to set their wings in motion, and raise up the fire. Every Owl who issues forth from the cave will be burnt, and any who do not come out will die from smoke." The King was pleased with this device, and carrying out the affair in the manner which had seemed expedient to the Minister, they consumed all the Owls with treachery, while a great victory befell the Crows, who all returned pleased and delighted, and loosing the tongue of congratulation for such a grand triumph, raised a cry of joy to the stars[1] above.

> At length Fortune gratified the King's wish;
> Fortune has fulfilled its promise of prosperity.
> Every joy which was lost to us through strife,
> Fortune with one kind turn has decreed to us.

The King and army, under obligation to Kárshinás for his excellent efforts, and acceptable proceedings, displayed the most strenuous endeavours in strong marks of honour and respect, and deemed it necessary and incumbent to eulogise and praise him to the utmost excess, and with lavish profusion. He uttered prayers for the King's welfare, and praised others according to their condition. In the midst of all this, the following proceeded from the King's tongue: "The felicity of your device, and the excellence of your judgment in exterminating and overthrowing the enemy, and bringing joy and happiness to your friends, were peculiarly remarkable." Kárshinás replied: "Whatever has occurred in this respect, was owing to the splendour of the King's Fortune, and the auspiciousness of the Sovereign's Fate. I saw traces of this victory on the very day that those unfortunates displayed such designs, and allowed such kind of oppression towards the helpless and weak, coveting possession of our hereditary kingdom, and ancient country."

> That black-minded wretch inflamed his eyes after your kingdom,
> Till his face became pale, and the world darkened before him.

Once more the King inquired: "How did you have patience for so long a time in company with the Owls, and how did you manage to get along with those who were of a contrary nature to yourself? for I know that the pious have no power to associate with the wicked, while the benevolent emphatically quit the sight of the base. It has been said that it is better to live with a vile snake than unwillingly to look upon a malevolent friend."

> If through the bitterness of separation one should die with the poison of grief,
> It is better than to be compelled to eat honey with an alien.

---

[1] Literally, "to the star 'Ayyúk."

Kárshinás replied : " It is as the King has said, and no grief is worse to a person than associating with aliens.

> The sight of an unsuitable friend is infernal torture.

" But a wise man, in view of his Lord's pleasure and ease of mind, will not avoid troubles, and, meeting with the utmost joy every distress that arises, will be complaisant; nor will a high-minded man at every disappointment and difficulty cast himself into the region of grief, or the whirlpool of vexation. Since, as regards every matter, the termination of which is connected with victory and success, if in the commencement thereof grief is to be undergone, and disgrace borne, it will have no great effect, for no store can be found without trouble, nor any rose plucked without the anguish of a thorn."

> Complain not of affliction, for in the way of enterprise,
> He will not attain repose, who does not undergo trouble.

The King said : " Repeat somewhat of the sagacity and learning of the Owls." He replied : " I did not see amongst them any clever man, save that one individual, who suggested my death, while they considered his judgment weak, and refused to listen to his admonitions with the ear of acceptance; nor did they reflect to the extent of considering, that I alighted in their midst as a stranger, having an honoured position amongst my own tribe, and being celebrated for learning and wisdom; and that I might, God forbid ! be plotting treachery and watching my opportunity for deceit. They neither recognised this of their own understanding, nor paid any heed to the words of councillors. They did not conceal, too, their secrets from me : consequently, they saw what they saw, and met with what befell them. It has been said that it is incumbent on kings to guard their secrets with the utmost care, especially from friends who are without hope, and from enemies filled with fear."

> A friend who is without hope from you,
> Do not in any case make your confidant ;
> Nor as regards an enemy, who is in dread of you,
> Is it allowable to reveal to him your secrets.

The King said : " It seems to me, that the cause of the destruction of the Owls was oppression." Kárshinás replied : " That is just it. Every king who follows the way of tyranny, it will soon be that the basis of his government is overturned. Permanency of sovereignty coupled with impiety is possible, but with cruelty and injustice it is out of the question. '*Monarchy will remain with infidelity, but with oppression it will not remain.*'

> Banish oppression at a swoop,
> For loss of life will overtake the tyrant.
> When a sovereign follows wrong counsels,
> Know for a certainty, that he acts wickedly towards himself.

" It has been said, that whoever does four actions must expect four things : whoever displays cruelty must make certain of his own death ; whoever associates with greedy women should be prepared to be disgraced ; whoever, as regards eating food, exhibits excessive avidity must anticipate being ill; and whoever relies upon worthless ministers of weak understanding must bid adieu to his kingdom. It has passed into a saying amongst the wise, that six persons should sever their desire from six things, and abandon hope of procuring them. 1st, A tyrannical, cruel sovereign from stability of kingdom, and permanence of government; 2d, A proud despot from the praise of mankind, or being remembered for goodness; 3d, Ill-tempered persons from having many friends; 4th, Malignant-faced, mannerless individuals from the rank of greatness; 5th, The miser from benevolence; 6th, The covetous from freedom from crime, since avarice will drive a man to what is wrong, and wherever avidity and greediness pitch the tent of residence, fidelity and rectitude remove thence their chattels. Now, when the King of the Owls became very greedy and covetous to kill and exterminate the Crows, as a consequence he deviated from the road of moderation and equity, and was overwhelmed in the desert of disappointment, and the expanse of contempt, and fell at length into the pit, which he had dug for the overthrow of others."

> Devise not evil against mankind,
> For you will bring misfortune on your own head;
> Do you not see the endless grief undergone
> By a digger of holes who prepares a pit for me?
> In the end, who ever carries a pitfall to completion,
> Slips to the bottom thereof, not I.

The King said: "How can any one discharge the debt of gratitude for this favour, since you have undergone endless anxieties, and, contrary to your own feelings, have humbled yourself before the enemy, and accepted service with a person, whose society your heart abhorred. Had they listened to the speech of their own councillor, the greatest danger to your life might have been anticipated." Kárshinás replied: "He may be called a man, who, when his intention is fixed upon accomplishing an affair, first of all washes his hands of life, and severing his heart from existence, places his feet in the plain of heroes.

> They have abandoned life, and placed their feet in the plain,
> Who, men of spirit, have carried off the ball[1] of happiness.

"If he sees it expedient to set about attending on one inferior to himself, he follows out the same till he obtains his object, just as the Snake, seeing it to his interest, submitted to attend on the Frog." The King inquired, "How was that?"

STORY XIII.

Kárshinás said: "It has been related that the infirmity of old age had made impression on a Snake, and complete weakness overtaken him; by reason of the loss of strength he left off hunting, and was perplexed in his affairs how to obtain food. Life without sustenance did not appear practicable, nor was it possible without strength to pursue that which would afford support. He thought to himself, "Alas for the vigour of youth! and ho for the time of prosperity! To expect now the return of the days of youth, or to hope for the renewal of

---

[1] See note 1, page 138.

bodily powers, bears a similar complexion to raising water from fire, or desiring to quench thirst with flames; with all this, would that the season of old age were lasting, and this short opportunity, too, were to be relied upon."

The time of youth passed, and the period of old age arrived,
O alas, for the society of friends, and the days of vigour!
Deem the time of old age, too, a prize, since with precious life,
Every moment which passes you will never see again, save in your dreams.

The Snake knowing that he could not recall the past, busied himself with plans for the future, the most important item in his affairs. He said: "As an equivalent for the strength of youth I have a little experience, which I have acquired, and a portion of forethought, the thread of which during a long life, I have obtained; now I must base the edifice of my affairs on absence of oppression, and gratefully accepting any disgrace which may happen, must begin to think as to how that can be obtained, which may be the support of life during the remainder which is left to me of existence." Accordingly he went to the brink of a fountain wherein were many frogs, who had a famous king and a celebrated chief whom all obeyed. He cast himself in the dust of the road after the fashion of broken-hearted mourners and sorrowing unfortunates. A frog immediately came[1] up to him, and inquired, "I see you are extremely sad, what is the cause thereof?" The Snake replied: "Who is there, who should more fittingly be grieved than myself, since the support of my life was in hunting frogs, and this very day a circumstance has occurred which has precluded me from chasing them, and if designedly I wish to catch one of them I am unable?" That frog went and brought the news to the King. The Monarch of the Frogs, being agitated at this strange circumstance, came near the Snake and inquired, "By what means has this calamity alighted upon you, and by what deed has this misfortune overtaken you?" The Snake replied:

I heave this heartrending sigh for a heart, which has broken faith:
Why should I lament for others, when I have pain of my own?

"O King! brazen-faced greed has cast me into the net of misfortune, and strife-exciting covetousness has opened upon me the door of this trouble. So it was that one day I plotted the death of a Frog, who, fleeing from my presence, threw himself into the home of a Devotee; through cupidity I went after him into that house, which by chance was dark, the Devotee's son being asleep. Unfortunately his great toe reached me; thinking it was the Frog, through heat of covetousness I dug my teeth into him, and he expired on the spot. The Devotee being apprised thereof, in agony for his son tried to kill me, while I turned my face to the desert, and went along with haste, the Devotee running after me, cursing and saying: 'I ask of my God, that he will make you miserable and destitute, and cause you to become the steed of the King of the Frogs; assuredly you shall be powerless to eat frogs, unless their King by way of charity shall give you aught.' Now I am come here of necessity, so that the King may mount me; and content with the Divine Decree and Omnipotent Mandate,

'We have bent our necks to the violence of the times.'"

These words pleased the King of the Frogs, who fancied himself honoured and

---

[1] The word زدن seems wanting.

dignified thereby; and perpetually sitting on the Snake and displaying his own vainglory, he sought to be superior to his race. Some time elapsed in this manner, when the Snake said: "May the life of the King be prolonged! There is no help but for me to have food and provision whereon to live, and discharge these duties." The King said: "It is as you allege; I am helpless without my steed, who in turn has no strength without food." Accordingly every day he allotted him two frogs as a portion to make use of them as his allowance for breakfast and supper. The Snake passed his time with this supply, and because in that humility a benefit was comprised, he was not ashamed thereof.

> The hand the sight of which brings disgrace on you,
> In times of necessity should be kissed.
> Any business which is humiliating, and causes additional annoyance,
> In a state of need will not appear so bad.

"Now I have adduced this story that it may be known, that if I exhibited patience and underwent disgrace, in view that the death of my enemies, and the safety of my friends were embraced therein, no great aversion overspread my nature. One's enemies, too, can be more quickly extirpated by means of courtesy and humility, than by war and combat; just as fire attacks a tree with fury, but can consume only that portion which is above the surface of the ground, while water, with gentleness and insidiousness, so roots up the greatest and strongest trees, that no hope remains of their being replaced.

> Be gentle, for every mighty work
> Can be accomplished with kindness and humility.

"Hence it has been said that intelligence and deliberation are better than bravery, because a warrior, however bold and strong he may be, is equal to (say) ten persons in the ranks, or at the utmost twenty, and if one should exaggerate an hundred individuals, but a thousand are the limit of the case: while a wise man by a single sound device will overthrow a kingdom, and perchance by deliberation may destroy an immense army, and ruin a populous kingdom."

> That can be accomplished with a single sound device,
> Which cannot be achieved with a vast army.
> The soul may be borne away with a sword,
> A kingdom may be subdued with deliberation.

The King said: "You gained a remarkable victory over your enemies, and an extraordinary triumph befell you." Kárshinás replied: "This matter was not entirely due to sound judgment, and excellent deliberation; nay, more, the glory of the King's Fortune and the auspiciousness of his Happiness were of assistance therein. It has been said, that if a multitude determine upon some business, and a body of people set their feet in quest of any affair, that individual would gain his object, who is distinguished for the excellence of his generosity, since the peculiarity of generosity is that the business of its possessor is successful; and if all were on an equality as regards generosity, he would attain his desires, whose firmness of mind and sincerity of intention were superior. If in this respect, too, they are equal, that person would accomplish his end, who has most friends and companions: if here, again, there is no difference, whomsoever Fortune helps, and good luck aids, would gain the victory."

When the star of Fortune rises in the sphere of Desire,
Whatever is wished is quickly attained.
If the constellations do not befriend you, give yourself no trouble,
For if you turn your face towards the sea, it becomes land.

The King said : " They did not value us to such an extent, or think that we could purpose revenge, since they had viewed us as of no account, and reckoned us impotent." Kárshinás said : " There are four things a little of which though small must be deemed much : 1st, Fire, a little of which is equally potent to burn, as much ; 2d, Debt, since the ignominy of having persons demanding money is the same as regards one diram as a thousand dínár ; 3d, Sickness, which though the disarrangement of the system may be but trifling, yet it brings weakness and disquietude ; 4th, An enemy, who though he may be contemptible and powerless, at length will accomplish his purpose. I have heard that a Sparrow, in spite of his weak condition, attained revenge on the strong-framed Snake." The King inquired, " How was that ? "

STORY XIV.

Kárshinás said : It has been related that two Sparrows had made their nest on the roof of a house, and passed their existence content with grain. Once upon a time children were born[1] to them, and both father and mother went in search of food to nourish them : having made into a pulp[2] what they obtained, they poured it down their offspring's stomach. One day the male Sparrow went out in a certain direction, when he returned he saw the female Sparrow flying round the nest in the greatest perturbation, while heartrending lamentations proceeded from her. He said : " O dear Companion ! what proceeding is this, which is visible on your part ? " She replied :

A thorn is piercing my bosom, hence I drop tears ;
I am sad within my feverish heart, hence I heave a sigh.

" Why should I not lament, for I was absent but an instant, when I returned I saw a terrible Snake, who had arrived, with the intention of killing our young ones : though I cried out saying—

Though you are victorious, dread your weak enemy,
Since the arrow of a morning[3] sigh will reach the target—

" it was of no avail ; and he exclaimed, ' A sigh will have no effect on the dark mirror (of my heart).' I replied : ' Take care, for I and the father of those children will gird our loins for revenge, and endeavour, as far as we can, to encompass your death.' The Snake smiled, and said :

To a companion who pursues the lion,
What can occur from such impotent ones as you.

" Since I was in no way a match for him, I am lamenting, but no one arrives on my complaint.

---

[1] Literally, " appeared."
[2] I have hazarded this rendering : the dictionary gives the meaning, " a grain with which a bird feeds her young."
[3] See note 3, page 51.

I complain enough, but there is no redresser.

"Now this cruel Tyrant has eaten our children, and gone to sleep, too, in our nest." On hearing these words the male Sparrow's soul was filled with grief,[1] and from loss of his children the fire of regret overpowered his heart. At that very time the master of the house was busy lighting a lamp: rubbing the wick with oil, and igniting it, he took it up in his hand, desirous of putting it in the socket. The Sparrow flew in, and snatching the wick from his hand, cast it in the nest. The master of the house, fearful lest the fire should catch the roof, and utter ruin ensue, at once went to the top of the roof, and cleared away beneath the nest so as to quench the fire. The Snake from before saw the violence of the flames, and from above heard a sound of a pick: he thrust his head from his hole he had in the roof, and as soon as he put his head out of the entrance the pick struck it.

"The moral of this story is, that the Snake held his enemy in contempt, and took no account of him, till in the end the latter crushed his head with the stone of revenge."

> Though the enemy be small, yet by way of caution,
> Esteem him great, and be in alarm at his proceedings.

The King said: "The carrying out of this affair, and the overthrow of the enemy, were due to the blessing of your judgment, and the auspiciousness of your sincerity. In every matter wherein I relied upon your words the results thereof were clearly good and proper; and whenever any one intrusts the reins of State arrangements to an honest minister, the hand of disappointment will never reach the skirt of his fortune, nor the foot of calamity encompass the plain of his happiness: just as has happened to me from the excellence of your judgment and knowledge.

> Wherever I turn my face, or whatever I plan,
> I am powerful when you are my helper.

"Now of all your excellences this was the greatest, that during the time you abode in the house of our enemies nothing escaped your mouth, from which they were affronted, nor did any action proceed from you, which caused them aversion or suspicion." He replied, "O King!

> "This, too, was due to your auspicious fortune.

"Seeing that I had no example in all my undertakings save the King's excellent disposition and virtuous habits, and whatever, to the extent of my knowledge, I had acquired from the praiseworthy qualities of the Sovereign, I made the guide of my actions; and, thank God! the King has united good understanding and accurate deliberation with majesty, pomp, awe, and bravery: the details of matters of importance are not concealed from him, nor are the occasions for haste and hesitation, or the seasons for contentment and rage, hid from him; at the commencement of every matter, recognising what is expedient, both for to-day and to-morrow, and also the course of events and contingencies, he contemplates the means of repairing the termination thereof; at no time is he, through kindness, indifferent in the way of caution, or negligent as regards the fame of his sovereignty or the splendour of his govern-

---

[1] There is a play upon words which it is impossible to retain.

ment. Whoever elects war with such a King, brings death on himself with a thousand cords, and removes life a thousand stages from before him."

> Time with eagerness draws your enemy,
> From the expanse of existence to the region of annihilation.
> Whoever breathes enmity against such as you,
> 'Twould be hard for death to give him quarter for half an instant.

The King said: "During this period of separation, I found no pleasure in eating or drinking, nor experienced any delight in sleeping or resting; but now, praises to the Most High God,

> "That the sun of prosperity has appeared from the summit of perfection,
> The fate of the unfortunate foe has begun to decline."

Kárshinás replied: "Assuredly whoever is overwhelmed with a triumphant enemy and powerful foe, till he is freed of such, will not distinguish day from night, or light from darkness, nor discern between head and foot, or shoe and turban. Wise men have said, that till complete health returns to a sick man, there is no pleasure in eating; neither does a porter rest, till he has laid aside his heavy burden from off his back; nor a lover take his ease, till he has reached the good fortune of meeting his beloved: nor, again, does the toil of a traveller lessen, till he has alighted at an inn: so a man who is terrified will not draw his breath in peace, till he rests secure from his triumphant foe."

> When any one finds rest from his enemy,
> He turns his reins towards repose of mind.

The King said: "What did you see of the Sovereign's nature and peculiarity as regards fighting and banqueting?"[1] He replied: "The edifice of his actions was based on conceit, personal admiration, pride, and self-indulgence: he had not any share of right deliberation, nor did he discriminate between sound judgment and faulty perception. All his followers, too, were of the same kind as himself, save that one individual who strove for my destruction." The King said: "What proofs were there of this latter's knowledge and wisdom?" He replied: "That his determination was fixed on my death, and in truth that device was akin to what is right: again, that he did not keep back his advice from his master, though he knew that the latter would not hear, and in his admonitions he observed propriety of conduct." The King said: "What are the rules regarding advice to kings?" Kárshinás replied: "Persons must speak with courtesy and civility, and be disposed rather to gentleness and tenderness than rudeness and harshness, and observing the utmost respect for their master, must not display rudeness or impudence. Though they observe faults or errors in his actions and words, yet, in calling attention to them, they must make use of good expressions, and adduce sweet hints, and enchanting proverbs, narrating in the course of the story the mistakes of others. Now the minister of the King of the Owls possessed all these qualities, and omitted no particle in this respect: with my own ears I heard him say to the King, 'Sovereignty is an exalted station, and a lofty dignity, nor can any one by his own exertion place the foot of desire on such an eminence, for save with the aid of Fortune and the assistance of Fate that

---

[1] Possibly the text is corrupt, since there does not seem any connection between fighting and banqueting.

rank cannot be attained : when by good luck this condition is acquired, it must be appreciated, and the utmost endeavours used to guard its precepts and protect its laws with justice and equity.

> O thou who hast attained a kingdom,
> Do you seek Good Fortune ?　Strive less to injure any one.
> One hundred revenging swords do not so much harm,
> As one oppressed individual brings about.

" 'Now it would be more befitting what is right that in his affairs he should avoid negligence, and not regard matters with the eye of contempt; for the stability of a kingdom and the retention of fortune are not possible, save with four things : complete caution, which sees the face of to-morrow in the mirror of to-day ; sound resolution, in the designs of which languor and infirmity will not find their way ; true judgment, which will not turn aside from the road of moderation to the direction of error and wrong ; and a sharp sword, which, like world-consuming lightning, scatters fire in the midst of the harvest of the enemy's life.' "

> In the kingdom of dominion the plant of justice will not be verdant,
> If it does not get water and light from the fountain[1] of the sword.

" All this he spoke, but no one paid any heed to his words, nor did his advice obtain the dignity of acceptance.

> Till all their matters were overturned both right and left.

" They neither benefited by his wisdom and penetration, nor did he himself by his cuteness and ability find an opening from that calamity.　In this respect the adage, ' *There is no counsel for any one who does not obey,*' was clearly exemplified."

> How can the opinion of any one appear good,
> When his words are unheeded ?
> Thus spoke a wise man : " Sound counsel
> When not acceptable to a person, is a mistake."

Such is the story of being cautious as to the treacherous snares, and perfidious frauds of an enemy, who, though he may strive to the utmost to be humble and meek, yet to be deceived thereby is far from the road of wisdom, since the solitary Crow, in spite of his impotency and weakness, in the above manner crushed powerful enemies, and numerous foes.　This was owing to their imbecility of understanding, and poverty of intelligence ; otherwise, had the Owls possessed but an atom of forethought, that Crow would never have attained that object, nor seen the face of such a victory, even in his dreams.　It behoveth a wise man to contemplate this lesson with the eye of example, and to listen to this warning with the ear of wisdom, knowing of a certainty that no confidence should be placed in an enemy, nor should a foe, however weak he may appear, be despised ; and though one hears a rival boasting of affection, and sees preparations for confirming friendship, one must not be led astray thereby.

> If an enemy makes boast of affection,
> A man of wisdom will not reckon him a friend.

---

[1] See note 1, page 267.

> A snake is of the same nature,
> Though he comes forth in appearance without his skin.

Another moral of this story is, to acquire sincere friends and honest companions; for such will be the best of treasures and the most advantageous of wares, seeing that the friendship of Kárshinás, coupled with his efforts and aid, produced such a result on behalf of the Crows, that they passed from the desert of fear and discord to the abode of security and safety. But if any one acts agreeably to this, know that he may both possess dear comrades, and also fold up his skirt in aversion to treacherous rivals. He will arrive, too, at the perfection of his desires, and the utmost of his wishes. God is the possessor of grace.

> Sit happy with honest friends,
> And fold up from malicious enemies the skirt of intimacy.

BOOK V.

---◆---

ON THE EVILS OF ACTING NEGLIGENTLY, AND OF ALLOWING ONE'S OBJECT TO SLIP FROM ONE'S HAND.

INTRODUCTION.

 HE King said to the Brahman: "You have narrated a story respecting being on one's guard as to the treachery of enemies, and not being deceived with their talk, and how one should protect one's self from the evils of hypocrisy and fraud on the part of opponents, and from the disastrous results of treachery and deceit of foes, however much they may pretend to friendship. Now I request you to repeat an account of some one who was eager in the pursuit of a certain thing, and after gaining his object, becoming negligent, lost the same." The Brahman loosed the tongue of praise, and recited these ornate [1] verses from the pages of laudation :

O Monarch of blessed steps ! who producest,
By thy face, good fortune for the stars of heaven.
The region of prosperity comes, like the shade of the wings of the phœnix,[2]
Upon every country whereon thou spreadest thy auspicious shadow.
What shall I say respecting the perfection of thy might ?
Most excellent may it be ! most excellent, for it surpasses all I can say.

"It is not concealed from the illustrious mind of the King, which is the region of endless bounty, that it is easier to acquire anything than to keep it. Since many persons, by happy chance and the aid of Fortune, coupled with the assistance of good luck, can amass, without the trouble of labour or the vexation of diligence ; but to preserve the same is not imaginable, save with enlightened judgment and sound deliberation ; and whenever any one is destitute of the orna-

---

[1] Literally, "the picture of these verses."   [2] See note, page 159.

ment of caution and foresight, when walking[1] in the plain of wisdom and prudence, his gains will quickly pass into the region of dissipation and ruin, and there will remain in the grasp of his power nought save regret and remorse : just as without the toil of labour or exertion the Tortoise obtained a dear friend in the shape of an Ape, whom, by reason of want of wisdom and stupidity, he let slip from his hand, while the wound of his folly and indiscretion was not healed by any salve." The King inquired, "How was that ?"

———o———

STORY I.

The Brahman said : It has been related that in one of the islands of the Green Sea were many Apes, who had a King named Kárdán,[2] the edifice of whose sovereignty was exalted by profound majesty and perfect administration of justice, and the foundation of his prosperity established by potent authority and universal equity. His subjects, by reason of his auspicious kindness, placed the breast of repose upon the bed of security and ease, and the inhabitants of that country, in gratitude for his endless gifts, loosed the tongue of thanksgiving and contentment.

By him tyranny was banished and justice gained.
God was pleased with him, and mankind content.

For a lengthened period he spent his time in joy and prosperity, and passed from the spring of youth to the autumn of old age and imbecility. The traces of weakness having overspread the region of his body, joy packed up the trappings of departure from his heart, and light from his eyes. The plant, too, of strength, which bore the fruit of desire, began to wither, owing to the hot blast of helplessness and impotency ; while the lamp of happiness was quenched by the violent gale of calamity and trouble, and the carpet of delight folded up through the attacks of disease and anxiety.

Seek not the traces of youth in old people,
For flowing water will not return to the stream ;
Desire must be banished from your head,
For the period of lust has come to an end.
When the dust of old age rests upon the brow,
Do not again expect pure pleasure.

Now the custom of perfidious Fortune is to change the verdance of the rose-garden of youth into the sadness of the thorny brake of old age, and to thicken the sweet beverage of wealth with the rubbish of the disgrace of poverty. There is no tranquillity of day in her case without the adversity of dark night ; nor is there clear-looking atmosphere without the dust of misery and vexation.

Together with the joys of Time are countless griefs ;
In the cup of Fortune there is no pleasant wine.

---

[1] This passage is obscure : Eastwick suggests that a negative should be introduced ; the sentence would then read, " Whenever any one is destitute of the ornament of caution and foresight, and *does not walk* in the plain of wisdom," &c.

[2] Experienced.

> What single individual ever in the garden saw the water-lily
> But that, from the tears of blood on its face, there is a bed of tulips?

This old husband-slaying woman, called the World, represents herself to the inhabitants of the earth in the clothes of a young bride, and with transitory ornaments, and fickle decorations, casts the heart of the foolish deluded ones into the net of affection for her.

> This World's dross [1] is a child-deceiving sport;
> Foolish are the men who are enamoured thereof.

In spite of her making her external adornments the means of deluding the enamoured in the plain of negligence, and rendering her unreal appearance the capital of greed, for the insane in the market of cupidity and lust, whoever fasten her in the matrimonial knot will not reach the hand of desire after her to the embrace of gratification, and whoever bring themselves into the snare of her company will not enjoy themselves for one night, according to the wishes of their heart.

> The bride of the World is a beauty; yes, beware,
> For this matron never wedded any one.

The childlike ones of the end of the street, " *This world's life is nought but a play and a recreation,*" fall into the snare of the net of her misfortune, and bound with her heart-ensnaring appearance, remain ignorant of her internal malignity, her slowness to perform her promise, her meanness of disposition and impurity of nature.

> Truly this world's fortune is like a speckly serpent,
> Soft, and of brilliant hue, while within full of poison.
> Through her deceits both rich and poor
> Are joyous, like the mind of one contemplating a treasure.

A man of Wisdom, the eyes of whose heart are illumined with the collyrium of pearls, " *The World is a bridge, so cross it, but do not repair it,*" pays no heed to her transient allurements, nor sets his heart on searching after her worthless dignities or profitless possessions, and since he recognises the instability of the world and the untrustworthiness of its wares, he turns his face in quest of eternal Fortune.

> Plant a root which will yield the fruit of everlasting prosperity,
> Since in this Garden of Life it is sometimes spring, sometimes autumn.

In short, the mention of Kárdán's old age and weakness having spread among men's mouths, great ruin overtook his royal pomp and regal majesty, and complete and utter destruction came upon the pillars of the might of his sovereignty, and the power of his sway and fame.

> If your prosperity be that of Jamshíd [2]
> White hairs are a sign that there is no hope.

From amongst the relatives of the King, there arrived a young tender-aged youth, on whose forehead were manifest the traces of prosperity, and the signs of good fortune evident in his movements and posture. When the pillars of

---

[1] مناع in the Persian text is a misprint for متاع .   [2] See note 1, page 12.

the Government saw of a certain his merits for the dignity of monarchy, and his aptitude for the station of sovereignty, and perfectly witnessed his absolute power in performing the matters of administration, and overthrowing oppression, as well as his adjustment of the affairs of government, and the protection of the subjects—

O thou in whose cheeks is evident the light of sovereignty !—

they entertained an affection for him in their minds, and bringing their hearts within the chain of obedience, and submission to him, said to one another :

> When the zephyr blows o'er the rose-garden,
> It is fit that the young trees should wave.
> It is spring when the musk willow comes into bloom,
> And old trees drop their dry leaves.

"This blooming - faced young man, the plant of whose life has grown and flourished on the brink of the rivulet of courtesy, possesses capacity that the rose-garden of Empire should produce leaves and fruit through his auspiciousness."

Behold the stately cypress from which the world becomes a pleasure-garden.

He too, by the minutiæ of cunning, having conciliated the army, and gained the favour of the subjects, gave each one a robe of honour, and a present according to his condition, and bestowed on them the good news of benevolence and promises of kingdom, coupled with the glad tidings of appointments and dignities. All at once high and low joining together brought the decrepit old man from the midst of the affair, and intrusted the reins of dominion over the realm, without trouble or difficulty on his part, to the grasp of that young man's power.

> At this good news the throne raised its form above the Earth,
> At such glad tidings the crown extended its head beyond the Heavens.

The helpless Kárdán, when he was denuded of the garments of sovereignty, not being able to endure such destitution, of necessity elected to migrate from his native land. Betaking himself to the sea-shore, he settled in an island, which had numerous trees and much fruit, and contenting himself with the juicy and dry fruits which were in that deserted spot, he resigned himself, saying :

"Whoever is content with dry and fresh things is king over sea and land."

In this manner, while in that lonely place, he indulged in habits of contentment, and traversed with steps of abstinence the highway of worship and submission. Day and night he occupied himself in making amends for the time he had passed in the pride of sovereignty, laying up, through repentance and penitence, provisions for the road of eternity, and preparing with the daily exercise of worship and devotion, a store for the journey of futurity: by means, too, of the radiance of the morn of old age, he removed the rust [1] which had settled on the mirror of his bosom, owing to the darkness of the night of youth.

> The morn of old age at length breaks ; be alert !
> Sleep is not good at the time of dawn.   Awake !

[1] See note 2, page 51, and note 2, page 249.

T

One day, having come to a fig-tree, under which he used to pass most of his time, he plucked figs. Suddenly, one slipping from his grasp fell into the water, and the noise thereof reaching the ears of the Ape, delight overspread his feelings, and joy overpowered his heart. Repeatedly, with that intent, he threw another into the water, and was charmed with the sound thereof. By chance a Tortoise, having come by way of travel to this island from the regions of the ocean, had taken up his abode under that tree, desirious of resting himself there for two or three days, after which he would return to his wife and family. In short, in the spot where the Ape used to eat his figs, the Tortoise was in the water under the tree. Whenever a fig fell into the water, he used to eat it with the greatest avidity, thinking that it was thrown down for him by the Ape, who considered this kindness and consideration towards him a necessity. He reflected: " Some one without former acquaintance is displaying this courtesy towards me. If the bonds of affection and the ties of friendship be formed between us, it is clear what a degree of favour and generosity will come to pass thereby. Keeping out of sight worldly advantage, the company of such a person, in whose nature are combined benevolent qualities and excellent disposition, and upon the pages of whose condition the pen of magnanimity has inscribed the sign of manliness and generosity, is one of the prizes of fortune, and assuredly, by means of the polisher of his society, the dust of vexation can be removed from the mirror of the heart, and through the light of his excellence, the darkness of misfortune can be banished from the atmosphere of the bosom. Hence it has been said :

' The heart, which is the mirror of sovereignty, is covered with dust.
I seek from God the society of an enlightened-minded person.' "

Accordingly, having formed the design of being intimate with the Ape, he raised his voice, and having performed the ceremony of salutation, as is customary, he represented the idea which he had conceived in regard to intercourse and companionship. The Ape responded cordially, and treated him with the utmost respect, displaying the greatest anxiety to be intimate with him, saying : " To be eager for the company of friends, and to strive to get many comrades, is a praiseworthy quality and a laudable disposition, and whoever has a true ally and an honourable brother will be exalted and prosperous in both worlds."

Persons of piety, as friends, are to a man
An ornament as regards religion, and a decoration as concerns the world.
Though the favours of Fortune are many,
Where is there a better boon than a companion ?

The Tortoise replied : " I am desirous of friendship and also of intimacy, but I do not know whether or not I possess fitness for the same." The Ape replied : " Wise men have established a standard as regards friendship, and have enjoined that, although one must not be without allies, yet every one is not fit to be a companion ; also, that friendship with one of three classes is incumbent : 1st, Men of wisdom and piety, since, by the blessing of their society, happiness in this world and the next may be obtained ; 2d, Men of benevolent disposition, who conceal the faults of their friends, and withhold not advice from their companions ; 3d, The number who are without self-interest or greed, and who place the edifice of their friendship upon sincerity and integrity. It is an imperative duty also to avoid friendship with three kinds of persons : 1st, Scoundrels and wicked men, whose ambition is confined to carnal desires, and whose affection will neither be the cause of repose in this world, nor the occasion of compassion in that to come; 2d, False speakers and treacherous persons, whose company is infernal torment, and intimacy with whom a great misfortune—they are perpetually repeating to others, relative to yourself, words which never occurred, and representing to you, concerning others, strife-exciting, mischief-making rumours, contrary to what is really the case; 3d, Foolish idiots, on whom no reliance can be placed in procuring advantages, nor in warding off evils: it often happens that what is deemed by them to be the essence of what is good and beneficial, is, in fact, prejudicial and baneful.

What benefit can you derive from a person such
That he does not distinguish good from evil, nor advantage from disadvantage?

" A proverb thereon has been spoken : 'A wise enemy is better than a foolish friend.' It may be that a foe, when endowed with the jewel of wisdom, clothing himself with foresight, will not wound till he sees his opportunity, so that, observing in his movements and postures the traces of revenge, one can guard one's self. But a friend who is destitute of the fortune of wisdom, however much he may lend his aid in deliberating on important events and matters, it is of no avail. It most frequently happens that such a person, by the faulty desires and incorrect judgment of the other, is caught in the straits of danger—just as from the friendship of the Ape, who acted as sentinel, it wellnigh happened that the life bark of the King of Kashmír fell into the whirlpool of destruction, and if a Thief, who was a wise enemy, had not cried out, there would have been no possibility of such a case being remedied." The Tortoise inquired, "How was that?"

STORY II.

Kárdán said : I have heard that in the kingdom of Kashmír was a great King, who had a treasury, the burden of which weighed heavy upon the strong-faced mountains, and an army, the idea of reckoning which did not enter the mind of subtle understanding. The standard of monarchy and prosperity was raised above the arch of the azure Spheres, and signs of his dispensation of justice, and care for his subjects were inscribed upon the revolution of Night and Day.

The world was subservient to his all-pervading command ;
Monarchs kissed the dust of his threshold.
Making the custom of justice and integrity his basis,
Through his uprightness and honour he rendered the world flourishing.

This King had an Ape upon whom in times of danger he used to rely, and in the care of whom he omitted no particle of regal behevolence; from the excess of sincerity with which the Ape was endowed, he became the special object of the King's condescension: at night taking in his hand a spear, like a drop of water (in brightness), he kept watch by the King's pillow, and did not let go from his clutch the end of the thread of that service, till the magnificence of the dawn of the rising of the true morn aroused from the couch of drowsiness the careless ones in the bedchamber of conceit. By chance a clever Thief, from a far city, came to that kingdom, and one night meditated robbery and plunder : putting on the garments of knavery, he wandered the streets. A foolish and inexperienced Thief had also come out with the same design : by reason of kinship they leagued together. The Thief who was a stranger, by way of counsel inquired, " To what place must we go, and whose house must we undermine ? " The foolish Thief replied : " In the stable of the Chief of the city is a fat sleek Ass, of which he is very fond, and to protect which he has placed a strong chain upon his four feet,[1] two servants having been appointed to attend him : it is expedient that first of all we go and seize that Ass ; at the end of the square of the city is the shop of a glass-blower, into which we will break, and carrying off beautiful and valuable glasses, and burdening that Ass, return having accomplished our desires." The wise Thief remained astonished at his words, and was desirous of thoroughly investigating this matter, when all of a sudden the patrol appeared in front of them. The wise Thief adroitly cast himself behind the protection of a wall, while the fool was captured. The patrol inquired, " Where were you going ? " He replied : " I am a Thief, intending to steal the Chief's Ass, and after breaking into the shop of the glass-blower to bear off some glasses, and take them to my house." The patrol smiled, and said : " Bravo ! should a Thief thus put his soul into the catapult of misfortune, on account of an Ass, which has so many guards, and cast himself into danger by reason of glasses, ten of which are sold for a small grain ?

You have not bought your soul for money, hence you know not its value.

" If you attempted such dangers on account of the King's treasury, then reason would excuse you."

If any one bears the burden, at any rate let it be the burden of a beloved one.

Thus he spoke, and, binding the Thief's hands, led him towards the prison. The clever Thief by reason of the knowledge [2] gained from the foolish knave was on his guard, and gathering experience from the words of the patrol, said to himself : " This thief was a foolish friend to me, while the patrol was a wise enemy ; this friend through his folly cast me into the whirlpool of destruction, and if this foe had not been wise, the matter, going beyond my control, the termination of the affair would have ended in death. Now, as the patrol said, it is befitting to turn my face towards the King's treasury, may be that my original design and full purpose will be attained thereby." Accordingly, coming gently beneath the King's palace he began to undermine it, and all night in greed after gold cut stone with steel.

> With his iron he gave such warmth to the stones,
> That there proceeded both fire and lustre.[3]

The night-roaming knave, the Sun, had scarce dug under the walls of the horizon, when the trench of the Thief was finished. Putting out his head at the place where the King's bedchamber was, he saw the Monarch asleep on a golden couch, various articles of luxury being placed near the royal throne, and numerous pearls scattered on the margin of the regal carpet. Camphor-like candles, similar to the faces of wealthy men of dignity, were alight, and the poor moths were consumed with the flame of disappointment, as it were the hearts of the fasting darwíshes.

> Though the moth and I are consumed, yet
> My heart and entrails are burnt, while his feathers and wings are singed.

---

[1] Literally, " hands and feet."
[2] This is hazarded as an intelligible meaning of an otherwise obscure passage.
[3] That is, the iron got hot and polished.

The Thief looked, and saw an Ape, with a spear in his hand, standing at the King's pillow, and opening right and left the eye of caution. The Thief was astonished at witnessing this, and said: "How has a miserable being, whose highest degree of rank would be straddling across a candlestick, placed his foot upon the carpet of royalty? and how has it happened that a sharp sword, with which is bound up the welfare of kingdom and people, has come into the hands of this despicable creature?" The Thief, overwhelmed in the sea of such thoughts, and confounded in the vortex of astonishment, scanned around, when all of a sudden several ants from the roof of the palace fell on the King's bosom, which was a world-adorning mirror, and commencing to move about disturbed the King's mind. The King in the midst of his sleep, owing to the worry of the ants, struck his hand upon his bosom, while the Ape ran in that direction, and saw some ants hurrying along the surface of the King's bosom. The fire of rage overwhelmed the Ape's mind, and he said: "How happeneth it that in spite of such a sentinel as myself, the star of whose eyes, like the planets, never for a single night has seen the face of sleep, dark-coloured ants are so impudent as to place their feet upon the bosom of my Lord?" Accordingly, his ignorant folly came into play, and owing to the annoyance of the ants, he used his spear to strike the King's bosom, and kill the ants. The Thief cried out: "Oh, unmanly bold fellow! keep back your hand, else you will overthrow the world from its foundation." He jumped up, and clutched firmly the Ape's hand with the spear in it. The King awoke from his sleep at the cries of the Thief, and seeing the circumstances of the case, inquired of him, "Who are you?" The Thief replied: "I am a wise enemy of yours in search of your property, and am come here to gratify my desires: if, but an instant, I had neglected to watch you, this dear friend and kind companion of yours would have filled your bed with blood." The King, having ascertained the particulars of the case, poured forth his prayer of gratitude, and said: "Yes, when Eternal condescension lends its aid, a thief becomes a protector, an enemy a friend." Accordingly he caressed the Thief, and enrolled him amongst the body of his attendants, and placing the Ape in chains, sent him to the stables. As regards the Thief who, having girt his loins for a nocturnal adventure, in the hope of a hidden hoard, had pierced the wall of a treasury, by reason of his being clothed with the garment of wisdom, the crown of prosperity was placed on his brow; while as concerns the Ape, who considered himself an intimate and confidant of secrets, since the thorn of ignorance clung to his skirt, the garments of honour were torn off his body.

> A wise enemy, from whom ruin overtakes the soul,
> Is better than a friend who is foolish,
> Since all that the ignorant does brings misery,
> And if there be advantage therein, it is trifling.

"The moral of this story is, that it behoves a wise person to become friends with a man of understanding, and avoid, at a league's length, society with the foolish."

> Shun not prison in company with suitable associates,
> But keep away from a garden of roses when void of fellow-comrades.
> If your enemy be wise it is better,
> Than that you should be friendly and like a brother with a fool.

When the Tortoise heard this story, which contained countless benefits, he said:

" O Sea of learning ! you have decorated the ear of my heart with the royal pearl of wisdom, now explain how many kinds of friends there are." Kárdán replied: " The wise have said that amongst men of the world, the bulk of persons who lay claim to friendship are divided into three species. Some are, as it were, food, since there is no getting on without their existence ; and without the contemplation of the radiance of their beauty, the taper of society will afford no light.

> The face of a friend is a lamp in the house of the heart ;
> The heart becomes serviceable owing to such a face.

" A class, too, are like medicine, since sometimes there happens to be need of them ; and another mass resemble pain, since they are never at any time of use : such are men of hypocrisy and deceit, who are face and tongue [1] with you, but nevertheless do not abandon the way of companionship with your rivals.

> In your presence they are more affable than light itself,
> Behind your back more unreal than a shadow.
> Impressive ! yes, indeed, but colder than their own souls.
> Alive ! ay, but more dead than their own hearts.

"Accordingly, it behoves a wise man to avoid these kind of friendly-faced enemies, and flee for refuge to sincere companions and honest allies."

> Break off from enemies, and seize hold of friends.

The Tortoise said : " What course should any one pursue so as to perform all the dues of friendship ?" The Ape said : " He who is adorned with six qualifications has no blemish in his friendship : 1st, He who if he gains information of a fault, does not strive to proclaim it ; 2d, He who if he becomes apprised of a virtue, represents that one as ten ; 3d, He who if he does you a kindness, does not retain it in his mind's ear ; 4th, He who if he receives a favour from you, does not forget the same ; 5th, He who if he sees something wrong on your part, does not arrogate over you ; 6th, He who if you demand pardon, grants it. With every one who is not endowed with these qualities you must absolutely not be friends, and if you become intimate with them, in the end regret will arise—and most men of the time are of this nature : consequently, a sincere friend resembles the Philosopher's Stone, and disinterested affection is like a Phœnix with its face turned towards the nest of non-existence."

> Whoever cannot trace the inscription of friendship,
> No one can walk with such a person as a companion.
> Save as in a mirror you cannot regard the face of a friend,
> Even in that case, what is the benefit ? since you cannot breathe upon it. [2]

When the conversation reached this point, the Tortoise said : " I fancy that I will place my feet firmly in friendship, nor will I omit one particle of the customs of comradeship. If you honour me with the dignity of your society, and cast round the neck of my heart the chain of obligation, till the resurrection of the last day, it will not be inconsistent with your magnanimity." The Ape, with professions of attachment, came down from the tree, and the Tortoise went from the water under the tree ; embracing one another, they made protestations

---

[1] As we say, " Hand and glove with you."

[2] That is, there is no benefit to be derived from associating with a fickle friend, who will hide his face from you on the least provocation, just as the reflection in a mirror is obscured with the slightest breath.

of friendship; both the loneliness of exile was removed from the heart of the Ape, and also the Tortoise was benefited by his society. Every day the plant of concord between them grew and increased, and the rose-garden of intimacy and friendship gained additional splendour and freshness, so that the Ape forgot his kingdom and monarchy, while the Tortoise did not call to mind his family or abode.

> I have a friend, what need that I should seek more ?
> The good fortune of his society is a sufficient solace for my soul.

A time passed in this manner, and the period of the Tortoise's absence was prolonged. His consort becoming distressed, overwhelming grief and endless misery overtook her, and soul-rending separation consumed her heart with the fire of remorse.

> Separation is a scar which, if made in the heart of a mountain,
> It would strike stones upon its bosom, and break into lamentation.

At length she repeated to one of her own kith and kin the complaint of her separation, and the tale of her desire, saying :

> My friend departed, but the desire after his face remained in my heart.
> I am like the cypress, my feet embedded in the mire from hankering after his form.
> I wished by means of his beauty to set at ease my own anguish.
> He hid his face, and thus my own affair remained in straits.

" I do not know in what place my wanderer has been overwhelmed in the mud, nor in what mire the foot of his heart has stuck. O might it be that the evening of separation were removed by the rising of the morn of his approach ! and the thought of love, which tends to phrenzy, quenched by the display of the splendour of his beauty !"

> Would that this beautiful rose would come back to the garden,
> Perhaps this soul, which has quitted the body, would return thereto.

When her companion witnessed all this vexation, she said: "O sister ! if you will not take it amiss, nor have any suspicions about it, I will inform you of his state." The wife of the Tortoise said : " O dear friend and confidant of occult secrets ! how can your words seem to be open to suspicion and self-interest, or how can falsehood and wrong appear in your advice ? A long time ago I tested the coin of your affection upon the touchstone of proof, and found all sterling value."

> I am aware that what you say is without doubt correct.

She said : " I have heard that your husband has happened to become associated and acquainted with an Ape, to whose friendship he has dedicated his heart and soul, deeming no favour equal to his society, and reckoning no delight commensurate with his company. He quenches the fire of separation from you with the water of the Ape's presence, and makes his beauty the solacer of his time in lieu of thinking about you." When the wife of the Tortoise heard these words, the fire of jealousy entered her head, and she exclaimed :

> The ocean of my heart has turned to blood, he is beloved by other friends.
> My bosom is filled with tears, he is in the embrace of another.

"O cruel fortune! you have given the harvest of my repose to the wind of separation, and blasted the field of my hope with the tempest of care. You have made the friend, who was the companion of my sad heart, the comrade of others, and have cast into the hands of others the associate at joy from the sight of whom I drew the representation of desire upon the carpet of love; and that faithless one, you would think, had never read the inscription of love upon the pages of intimacy, nor had that wanderer, you would say, in all his life, inhaled the perfume of companionship in the garden of affection."

> That bold one who did not recognise the worth of hapless me,
> Became a wanderer, not considering his own welfare.

Her friend replied: "Now that what was to be has been, profitless grief is of no avail. Some device must be arranged which will embrace the acquisition of ease of mind." Accordingly, they occupied themselves perusing the book of stratagem, the arrangements of which are explained by the verse, "*In truth your deceit is great*," and no better plan than the death of the Ape occurred to them. They cogitated on this point, and the wife of the Tortoise, by the counsel of her adopted sister, feigned herself to be ill, and sending a person to the Tortoise, gave a message that—

> "If my friend has the desire to inquire after me, who am grief-sick,
> Say, 'Come, welcome, for there is still life in her.'"

The Tortoise, having gained news of his wife's weakness and illness, asked from the Ape leave to go to his own home, and discharge afresh the obligation of meeting his wife and children. The Ape said: "O dear friend! you must, as quickly as possible, again grant me the honour of your company, and not leave me desolate in the corner of this waste alone and solitary; but indeed the grief itself of separation from you will not leave me by myself, nor will the pain of your absence allow of my being without a companion."[1]

> The lonely nights I have no companion save grief for you;
> Alas for the state of him for whom grief has a feeling of sympathy!

The Tortoise said: "O dear friend! and O repose of my fleeting spirit! the necessity for a journey has arrived, and an event beyond my control occurred, otherwise willingly, and of my own inclination, I would never have removed from your society, nor would I for an instant, of my own heart's desire, have withdrawn from waiting on you."

> I am removed from sight of you, but the necessity arose; otherwise it could not be,
> Since no creature desires that his soul should be separated from his body.

Accordingly, having, *nolens volens*, bid adieu to the Ape, he set out towards his own home. When his accustomed native soil was adorned and graced with the steps of the Tortoise, his friends and relations coming to him, raised to the stars[2] a cry of esteem, and the Tortoise, with a crowd of attendants, came to his own house. He saw his wife stretched on a bed of death, and in the garden of her cheeks, in place of a nosegay of purple flowers, a saffron-coloured rose had bloomed.

---

[1] That is, grief will always be my companion.   [2] Literally, "the star 'Ayyúk."

From lamentation [1] she had become like a reed, from weeping like a hair.

Though he presented the offering of salutation, he was not honoured with the gift of a reply, and though he practised courtesy and consideration, he met with no respect thereto, neither flattery and supplication alighted in the region of approbation, nor did deceit and dissimulation produce any result.

O heart ! bear thy capital of grief and supplication from her street,
For such worthless wares will not find there a market day.

He inquired of the adopted sister, who had appointed herself to attend on her : " Why does not this invalid open her lips to speak, and repeat to me, who am internally agitated, what is in her mind ? " The adopted sister drew a cold sigh and said :

O doctor ! do not, after this, apply a remedy for the ailments of the head ;
The disease of love is an ill for which medicine is of no avail.

" How will a sick person, who is beyond cure, and an invalid for whom medicine can hold out no hope, get leave from the heart to draw a breath ? and by what power would she possess strength for conversation ? " The Tortoise, beginning to lament, was very grieved and said : " What medicine is there which cannot be found in this country, and which it is not possible by effort and contrivance to discover ? Say quickly, so that I may wander over sea and land in quest thereof, searching both far and near, and amongst acquaintances and strangers. If like a fish I must go to the bottom of the Ocean, head foremost I will descend ; while if, like the moon, I must hasten to the summit of the skies, with the bow of fancy I will convey myself to the pinnacle of the Heavens. Heart and soul I can present in search of this medicine, and sacrifice for this cure the essence of water and clay, which are indicative of the growth of life."

What is life that I should not sacrifice it for you ?
I can devote my soul to you ; why should I not do so ?

The invalid's attendant replied : " This is a kind of disease peculiar to women, which appears in their breast, and cannot be remedied with ought save the heart of an Ape." The Tortoise inquired : " Whence can this be procured, or how discovered ? " The adopted sister, who was the originator of this treachery, and had devised a remedy for this anguish of heart, replied : " We, too, are aware that it is difficult to procure this medicine, and the toil of obtaining this remedy, which is similar to the Philosopher's Stone, is great and countless. We have not summoned you for this cause ; nay, more, it was that you might take a last look at a faithful friend, and bid her a final adieu, since the invalid has no hope of speech, nor is the comfort of health attainable."

Save the draught of blood I see no other potion for my ailment.
Save grief, I know no other comfort in life.

The Tortoise was afflicted beyond measure, and overwhelmed with grief. Though he thought of remedial measures, he saw no help but to kill the Ape. Of necessity he girt himself with greed as regarded his friend. Clear-minded wisdom, loosing the tongue of admonition, said : " O unmanly person ! to overthrow with treachery the former basis of friendship and affection, which has been established between you and the Ape, is far apart from manliness and generosity."

[1] It is impossible to preserve the play upon words in this verse.

For shame, that on account of a woman
You should treacherously tear your skirt [1] to pieces.

And headstrong lusts reproaching began to tempt him (saying): "To quit a wife, to whom appertained the joy of your home, the support of your existence, the aim of your life, and the custody of your money and possessions, or to pay respect to the rights of honour for a friend, who has neither relationship to, nor connection with you, appears not in accordance with a regard to the affairs of life."

By the canon of friendly intercourse, the dust of a companion of long standing, Is a thousand times better than the blood of new allies.

Ultimately, love for his wife being predominant, he determined in his mind to break, with the stone of treachery, the lantern of fidelity, and to render the basin of the balance of affection light with deceit and deception. The simpleton was unaware that the mark of insincerity is the scar of disgrace, the traces of which are not evident save on the brows of the condition of the unfortunate, and that the habit of breaking faith is the inscription of contempt, which is not written save on the tablets of the foreheads of the wretched. As concerns any one who by fraud and perfidy attains a degree of renown, no men of piety will have any desire for his society, and whoever becomes known for breach of faith and insincerity will not, amongst any persons, attain the honour of approbation; nay, more, they will deem it necessary to avoid his company and conversation, and consider it incumbent to reject his deeds and proceedings.

My spiritual guide and boon companion—may his soul be happy! Said: "Avoid intimacy with those who break faith."

The Tortoise, after plotting the death of the Ape, knew that till he should bring the latter to his own home, it would be impossible to attain his object. With this purpose he went to the Ape, whose desire to see him was extremely great, and whose anxiety to behold him passed the bounds of restraint. As soon as his eyes alighted on his friend's beauty, from excess of joy, with heart-ravishing melodies, he began to sing this song:

"A thousand thanks to God, that such a dear friend as you
Has at last shown your face to me after such an interval."

Warmly questioning the Tortoise, he inquired concerning the condition of his children and family. The Tortoise replied: "The grief of separation from you did not have so much effect on my mind but that joy accrued from the warmth of their society, and companionship with my wife and family occasioned delight and pleasure. Yet every moment that I thought of the solitude and separation from your companions and dependants, which had happened, or reflected on the loneliness and deprivation which had taken place in your case as regards sovereignty and happiness, love was quenched in me, and the purity of the potion of delight rendered foul; I said to myself: 'O unmanly person! is it lawful for you to sit here in the expanse of the garden of repose, upon the throne of delight, while your faithful friend makes his bed of dark earth in the thorny spot of solitude?'

Is it right that you like a rose should blossom here,
While your companion is journeying with a thorn in his foot?

[1] The skirt of integrity.

"Therefore I have come with the design that you should deem it fitting to honour me, and grace and gladden my home and children with your presence, so that my relations may recognise my position as your friend, and my companions and dependants thereby acquire honour and glory,[1] both their hearts being at ease through your presence, and my abode also adorned with your beauty. My position will be increased by the fortune of your footsteps, while by accepting my invitation no loss will accrue to you.

> What loss would there be, O Moon! were you to cross my path;
> Were from your face a ray to fall on my window?

"Again, I desire to set a body of persons before you at the banqueting tables, may be that I can discharge somewhat of what is due to your laudable qualities." The Ape said: "Cease such ceremonies, since when the chain of friendship is firmly secured, and the knot of affection and companionship settled, there is no need for undergoing the trouble of hospitality, and the ceremony of the customs of conviviality, as is done by the formal and punctilious. Since it has been said, '*The worst of brothers is that person for whom ceremony must be undergone,*' the worst of friends and comrades is he in regard to whom etiquette must be observed, and for whom the burden of ceremony must be undergone.

> Though there be no ceremony, yet one may live happy.

"And as regards the friendship and affection which have arisen on my part towards you, should you consider the same in any way too demonstrative, be not distressed thereat, since my glory in your virtuous qualities is extremely great, and my need of your fidelity and friendship infinite; for I happen to be removed from my native soil, home, kindred, country, dependants, and retinue, and am overwhelmed with the anguish of exile, coupled with the misery of solitude and loneliness. If the Most High God had not, by the blessing of your society, favoured me afresh, and bestowed upon me the blessing of your intimacy, in this my affliction and exile, who would have brought me out of the clutches of miserable fortune, or who have snatched me from the hand of distress and separation?

> In this solitude, in the palace peopled with adversity,
> At the sight of you I am happy, and glad of heart.

"So, upon such grounds, I am under great obligations to you, and your kindness towards me is endless. On this supposition there is no need of this trouble and painful ceremony. In friendship purity of faith is respected, not the arrangement of social dainties; and the bestowal of internal benefits is to be sought, not the preparation of external feasts."

> An unceremonious friend is needed; where there is a friend of that description,
> Though there be not between us the forms of etiquette, say, "Let them pass."

The Tortoise said: "O dear friend and intimate companion! the object of inviting you is not so much regard for the dues of entertainment, or preparation of something to eat and drink; nay, more, my wish is that separation, removing its chattels from the midst, I should perpetually attain the honour of your presence.

---

[1] مفاخرتی in the Persian text should be مقاخرتی.

In the way of love there are no halting-places, neither near nor far.

" If between friends there should happen to be a distance like that of East from West, since consolation occurs to them from the remembrance of each other, and ease accrues to their hearts, on both sides, from the thought of one another's charms, accordingly physical separation will not become a veil in the way of mental intercourse, and perpetually with the eyes of fancy, and the fancy of the eyes, they will contemplate the exquisite beauty of one another.

> If there be mental intercourse between me and a friend,
> What difference will it make, if there be local separation?

" A wise man has spoken to this effect :

> 'Though we have not in our hands the coin of intercourse,
> Yet fancy is perpetually dwelling before the eyes.
> If externally there be not companionship in the body,
> No matter since there is mental converse.'"

The Tortoise once more placing the arrow of Intercession in the bow of Supplication, began to shoot it at the target of Desire, and the power of Fate lending its assistance, it reached the mark of Gratification. The Ape said : " To seek to gratify a friend, in the laws of manliness, is an imperative duty, so I will not remain at this distance from my comrade, but will consider it a privilege to visit your brethren and dependants; yet it is impossible for me to pass this water, and extremely difficult for me to cross this sea which intervenes between this desert and your island." The Tortoise said : " Be of good cheer, for having taken you on my back, I will bear you to that island, in which are both security and ease, and also plenty and repose." In short, from the persistence with which the Tortoise made use of kind language, the Ape abandoned his opposition, and being subdued with the thongs of flattery and humility, gave him the reins of power. The Tortoise taking him on his back, set out towards his own home; when he reached the midst of the sea, the bark of his mind fell into the whirlpool of reflection, and he thought to himself : " What proceeding is this which I have taken in hand, and what result will there be from this save disgrace ?

> Whenever any one turns his face from the rose-garden of fidelity,
> The thorn of violence will pierce his bosom.

" To act perfidiously towards truly wise friends on account of weak-minded women, is not the way of men of noble spirit, and to let slip the end of the thread of the merciful God's good favour, in order to gratify Satan, is the cause of ruin and loss."

> Proceed not, proceed not ! for persons of good disposition act not thus.

Halting in the midst of the water, in this manner he struggled with himself, and the signs of irresolution were visible in his actions and postures. Doubt fell upon the heart of the Ape, who inquired : " What is the cause of your hesitation ! Maybe the burden of carrying me has become arduous for you, on which account, being heavily laden, you are going along thoughtfully ?" The Tortoise said : " Whence do you speak these words, and on what ground do you make this deduction ?" The Ape replied : " The signs of a struggle on your part with your own spirit, and of the irresolution of purpose which you possess, are manifest : maybe if you were to communicate with me, and confer on me the honour of explanation, by means of the assistance of my counsel, which is worthy of confidence, you might reach the shore of safety from the whirlpool of perplexity." The Tortoise said : " You speak truly ; I have fallen into a train of thought, but the sum of my deliberation is this : You are for the first occasion granting me the felicity of alighting at my abode, and my wife is sick, consequently the affairs of the house will not be free from confusion, nor, as I had intended, will the requirements of entertainment and the dues of generosity be properly discharged ; this will be the cause of shame and mortification."

> Though my sin is pardoned, I am ashamed.

The Ape rejoined : " Seeing that the sincerity of your faith is assured, and your desire to insure my comfort established, if you defer ceremony, and omit the rights and customs of strangers in dispensing hospitality, assuredly it would seem more befitting the ways of friendship and intimacy."

> By the display of ceremony strangers are made friends,
> But where there is intimacy what need is there of punctiliousness ?

The Tortoise once more proceeded and then halted ; the same idea as at first cropping up, he said : " Women urge me to break my promise and compact ; but I am aware that they do not possess the virtue of good faith, and to expect from them fidelity and uprightness is removed from the mode of the wise.

> Let not any one expect affection from women,
> Since the rose will not grow in the brackish desert.

" Accordingly, to be deceived with their allurements and to hasten in the direction of want of faith and manliness, in the code of rectitude and integrity, what kind of business is it, and amongst men of faith and principle what sort of proceeding will it appear ? " The Tortoise relapsed into thought, and halted again on the same spot. The Ape's suspicions were increased, and he was perplexed, saying to himself : " When doubt respecting his friends enters any person's mind, he must take refuge in deliberation, and folding up his skirt, must protect himself with hypocrisy and humility ; and if that doubt amounts to certainty, he will have freed himself in safety from their malevolence and deceit, while if the suspicion is unfounded, he will not be stigmatised with crime through observing the way of care and caution.

> If he is your friend, you sit at ease in security ;
> If he plays false, you will be freed from his treachery.

He cried out to the Tortoise, saying : " What is the cause that every moment you gallop the steed of Fancy in the plain of thought, and plunge the diver of Intellect into the sea of perplexity ? " He exclaimed : " O brother ! excuse me, for the illness and sickness of my wife, and the distress which my children undergo on account of her indisposition, have distracted me." The Ape said : " I am aware that your anguish of heart is on account of the illness of your wife. Assuredly it has been truly said : ' It is more endurable to be attacked with disease, than to look upon illness.'

> Deem him not in health who undergoes anguish for a sick person.

" Now repeat what is this malady, and what the way of healing it ; since for every disease there is a cure appointed, and for every ailment a distinct and clear means of remedy. Reference must be made to physicians of blessed spirit, of auspicious breath, and august steps, and in whatever way they suggest, efforts must be made in pursuit of the remedy thereof." The Tortoise said : " The doctors have indicated a medicine as a means of healing the same, to which the hand cannot reach." The Ape said : " At any rate, what is that compound which is not to be found in the shops of chemists, nor the wallet of the vendors of drugs ! If you divulge it, perhaps I may be acquainted therewith, and may indicate how to get possession of it." The Tortoise in the innocence of his heart replied : " That rare medicine which has cast me into the whirlpool of perturbation is the heart of an Ape." As soon as these words fell on the Ape's ears, though in the midst of the water, fire entered his bosom, and the smoke of melancholy reached his head, while his eyes began to grow dim : but forcibly collecting his ideas, he exclaimed : " O my soul ! do you see how, through the misery of greed and lust you have alighted in this terrible whirlpool, being overtaken by reason of negligence and stupidity with this great danger ? I am not the first person who has been deceived with the hypocrisy of enemies, or has given place in his ears to the words of dissemblers, and received in his heart the arrow of misfortune from the bowstring of designing men.

Many are the persons consumed with the fire of this affliction.

" Now I know of no resource but treachery and fraud, and no help beyond discretion and deliberation : if, God forbid, I should alight on the island of the Tortoises, a knot will have been formed in the thread of my affairs, to unfasten which the hand of thought will be powerless. Unless I make over my heart to them, remaining confined, I shall die of hunger, while if I wish to escape, I must cast myself into the water, and such a circumstance would cause my death. In the secure waste of my own abode, without forethought, having given the reins of power into the hands of the Tortoise, I am desirous after the pleasures of his island, and am worthy of a thousand such punishments and retribution."

I was distracted when I quitted your ringlets,
Nothing would be more befitting me than a band of chains.

Accordingly he said to the Tortoise : " I know the means of curing that virtuous matron, and the remedy in my hands is easy; do not give place to any anxiety on your part, since this kind of ailment often happens to our women, and we give them our hearts, and no pain arises to us from so doing: for it is quite easy for us to draw out our hearts from inside our bosoms and replace them. Moreover, we can live without a heart, and I will make no difficulty with you about such a trifle, since the wise have said that there are four classes, to be niggardly to whom regarding four things is not good : 1st, Kings must not be denied anything which they seek from persons for the welfare of high and low ; 2d, Worthy Darwíshes, who seek anything with the view of performing good works, and laying up a store of precious deeds in the sight of God, nought must be kept back from them ; 3d, Necessitous students, who have acquired a capacity for obtaining knowledge, and have journeyed with sincere steps in quest thereof, must be put in the right path ; 4th, Honest friends, whatever may produce ease of mind to them, the same being within our power, must not be considered toilsome or laborious.

What is the heart, that it should not be cast at the feet of a loved one ?
What is the coin of the soul, that it should not be scattered upon friends ?

" Had you informed me in my abode, I would have brought my heart with me, and it would have been very delightful had your spouse obtained perfect health so soon as my footsteps appeared : and I am so worried with my heart, that no other desire save that of being separated from it, ever enters my mind ; and whereas grief and sorrow have taken possession of its sides and regions, and such distress overspreads its environs, nought is more intolerable for me than the company of my heart, and I am anxious to sever the cord of its connection, maybe I shall escape from the thought of separation from my wife and family, and the idea of quitting kingdom and possessions, and so obtain freedom of mind from these heart-consuming griefs, and soul-melting reflections."

O God ! this single drop of blood which is called the heart,
How long will it undergo oppression from the injustice of moon-faced beauties?

The Tortoise said, " Where is your heart, since you did not bring it with you ? " The Ape replied : " I left it in my house, since there is a custom amongst Apes, that when they go on a friendly visit, and desire to spend the day pleasantly, the hand of grief not reaching the skirt of their joy and delight, they do not bring with them their hearts, which are the centre of grief and affliction, and the source of pain and distress, and every hour give rise to thoughts, which defile the purity of pleasure, and render miserable the time of happiness and prosperity. The heart, by reason of its changes, has been given the name of ' Kalb;' [1] every hour it inclines to a different direction—from good to bad, from what is advantageous to what is hurtful.

Every moment it has a fresh heart-enticing desire ;
Every instant, by reason of fancy, it moves to another place.

" Since I was coming to your house, I was desirous perfectly and thoroughly to obtain my own repose by the sight of you, and the face of the loved ones which belong to you, so I left my heart there, and it is very unfortunate that I should hear the news of the means of curing the matron, and not have brought my heart with me. When you consider my circumstances, as being your friend, it is possible you will pardon me ; but the body of your relations and companions will suspect that, with such former intimacy, and such accompaniments of affection as are assured between you and me, I make a difficulty about this trifle, and as regards your repose, neglect what would not occasion misery to myself, while it would embrace benefits to your dependants. If you would go back, so that we may return prepared and ready, it would be better." The Tortoise at once went back, and in the utmost confidence of attaining his desire, and carrying out his hopes, deposited the Ape on the brink of the water. The Ape quickly ran up a tree, and having discharged the allowance of gratitude and praise, perched himself upon the end of a branch. The Tortoise having waited for a while cried out : " O dear friend ! the opportunity of going will be lost."

Take pity, for the affair has passed all limits ;
Show thy face, for expectation has gone beyond all bounds.

The Ape smiled and said :

Call to mind, that what you professed
As to fidelity, turned out to the contrary.

[1] Meaning change.

"I have passed my life amongst royalty, and have tasted much of the ups and downs[1] of life; whatever fortune had given me she seized back from me, and whatever the spheres had bestowed upon me they sought again. Now having come within the multitude of the afflicted, and fallen within the pale of the wretched, I am not such that, destitute of the advantages of experience, I do not know what occurs, and cannot distinguish a suitable place from a treacherous locality. Cease these words, and never again sit in the assembly of the generous; abandon boasting of your good faith, and breathe not a word of your fidelity and manliness.

> Mention not the name of fidelity at the banquet of the good,
> For you have no fragrance of integrity.

"If any one commences about all his excellences, and speaks of his manliness and generosity, at the time of trial his knavery may be discovered, and his coin tested upon the touchstone of trial."

> It would be well if the touchstone of experience were to be introduced,
> So that the face of him who is false should be blackened.

The Tortoise uttered a lamentation: "What suspicion is this which you entertain of me? and what is this disposition which you impute to me? God forbid that anything contrary to your happiness should have crossed my mind, or plots or treachery concerning you have entered my imagination: if you were to cast a hundred thousand stones of reproach against my face, I would not remove my head from the dust of your threshold; and were you to sever in pieces my bosom with a merciless sword, I would not turn away my heart from your society."

> Though at the hand of my beloved one, I undergo a hundred vexations of spirit,
> Yet do not think that I will betake myself to the shore.

The Ape said: "O ignorant person! do not fancy that I am such an one of whom the Fox said, 'That Ass has neither heart nor ears.'" The Tortoise said, "How was that?"

STORY III

He said: It has been related that a Lion was overwhelmed with the disease of mange; added to constant fever, he was wearied with the anguish of scratching; at length, on account of the itching of his body, the thorns of irritation reached his heart, and his strength failed; leaving off his wanderings, he abandoned the pleasure of the chase. In his service was a Fox who used to pick up the fragments from his table, and the scraps of his food, and who gathered strength and victuals in the blessing of the leavings of his repast. When the Lion abandoned the chase, the Fox's affairs became embarrassed. One day, from want of food, and the cravings of hunger, he reproached the Lion, saying: "O King of the beasts! the thought of your sickness has distressed the animals in this waste, and the weakness of your condition and the traces of your anguish have infected all your servants, nay, more, the whole of your subjects.

> A hundred thousand beings tremble for your soul,
> And from anxiety regarding your debility, the world quakes.

---

[1] Literally, " warmths and colds."

" Why do you not cure this disease, and why do you not pay regard to remedying this heart-irritating pain ? " The Lion in anguish lamented, saying :

I have a thorn in my heart, which cannot be extracted by a needle ;
My heart is turned to blood, and this thorn will not come forth from my soul.

" O Fox ! a long time has elapsed since I have been worried to death by this agony, while from this irritation day by day I get weaker, and my frame from lassitude has become like a hair, while not a hair remains on my body. I know not how to cure this disease, or with what medicine to lessen this annoyance. At this very time one of the physicians, in whose words I have the fullest confidence, has commanded that I must eat the ears and heart of an Ass, and that save this remedy nought will be efficacious. From that time I have been contemplating as to how this object can be effected, or by what device on the part of my friends this result can be attained." The Fox said : " If the King's commands should be graciously issued, I, who am the meanest of your servants, having girded the loins of search, will set my feet in the way of enterprise, and it is to be hoped that by the blessing of the royal fortune, and the glory of your perpetual prosperity, this object will be attained." The Lion said : " What kind of trickery have you devised, and what treachery have you read from the book of deception ? " The Fox replied : " O King ! it has occurred to my mind that it is impossible for you to come forth from the desert since, seeing that not a hair remains on your body, and the glory of your beauty and the majesty of your splendour have somewhat suffered diminution, to move and to exhibit yourself to your acquaintances and strangers will occasion loss of dignity to the King and his sovereign awe : therefore it seems desirable for me to bring your object to this waste, so that the Monarch of the Beasts may destroy him, and have meat and drink off him according to your heart's desire." The Lion said : " Whence will you bring him here ? " He replied : " Nigh to this waste there is a spring, the amount of whose water would surpass the Gulf[1] of 'Umán, while in sweetness and deliciousness it is indicative of the fountain of Immortality.

In purity it is like the cheek of a beloved one,
In delicacy like the precious soul.

" A bleacher comes there each day to wash clothes, and an Ass, who is his beast of burden, every day grazes in the neighbourhood of that spring ; maybe he can be drawn by stratagem to this waste : but the King must vow that, when he has eaten the Ass's heart and ears, he will make an offering of the remainder to the beasts." The Lion agreed and gave his promise, ratifying it with an oath. The Fox, placing his hopes upon a bountiful banquet, turned his face towards the fountain-head. When he saw the Ass from afar, having performed the dues of salutation, he began in tender tones, and commenced softly to open the way of conversation with him.

With soft, gentle, and pleasant language,
You can lead an elephant with a hair.

Accordingly he inquired of him : " What is the cause that I see you sick and thin ? " He replied : " This bleacher is always working me, and neglects to groom me ; I am wasted with grief for forage, while he does not care a grain : it has wellnigh come to pass that the harvest of my life has been scattered to the

---

[1] The Persian Gulf.

U

wind of destruction, and in his estimation it goes for not even a blade of grass."

> During my life I have never been groomed,
> I have just heard the name of grass and grain.
> Every day I groan under this burden,[1]
> Every night I lick the dust from the wall.
> Deem it not a defect if I am wretched and thin,
> Since save blood and dust I have nought to eat.

The Fox replied : " O easy-going soul ! you have feet and power of moving ; for what cause have you selected such misery, and been overwhelmed with this calamity ? " The Ass replied : " I am known as a beast of burden, wherever I go it is impossible for me to escape the load of distress : moreover, I am not alone in this peculiar misfortune ; all my race are overtaken with the same grief, and groan under this load.

> Every one, according to his capacity, is overtaken with distress,
> No one has been granted a free pass.

" After much reflection, I have convinced myself that, since everywhere I must drink the cup of toil, and be clad in the garments of unpleasantness and suffering, at any rate I must abide in a house somewhere ; and I will not in any case undergo the reproach of folly on account of such a life as is not passed to my taste."

> Since it is of no avail to turn from door to door.

The Fox replied : " You have done wrong.

> You cannot die from distress, since I am living here.

" ' *In truth God's earth is spacious :* ' the plain of the earth has been made extensive, and the royal mandate, ' *Wander through the earth,* ' was sent forth on account of the oppressed and stricken."

> Travel about since the spot is unpleasant to thee,
> For it is no disgrace to go from this locality ;
> If thy habitation be irksome to thee,
> With the God of the universe the earth is not limited.

The Ass rejoined : " Wherever any one goes he will acquire no more than what is appointed to him ; therefore it is not wise to be greedy, and in addition to one's own load of endurance to undergo the severities of travel."

> A portion comes to every one who seeks the same,
> The toil of your labour is owing to your own impatience.
> The Almighty Dispenser gives an allowance to all,
> Fate places somewhat before each.

The Fox said : " This speech is of the exalted nature of confidence in God, but every one does not arrive at this dignity. The divine Majesty, may His glory be spread abroad ! has decreed that in the world the necessaries of every person should be obtained by the medium of daily work ; and the Causer of causes for every creature He feeds, displays in a different way the means of sustenance.

---

[1] Literally, " drink blood."

Seek[1] your daily bread, for the industrious man is beloved of God.

"If you are willing, I will bring you to a meadow, the soil of which is adorned and arrayed with the splendour of various coloured pearls, like the jeweller's cell, and the climate of which, as it were a perfumer's bag, is scented and fragrant with its ambergris-tainted breeze, and the odour of pure musk.

> The climate pleasant, and the country spacious;
> Fruit-bearing trees, and tender branches.
> Breeze (perfumed with) roses, and the ring-doves lamenting,
> Like as when disappointed lovers are in distress.

"Previous to this occasion I have advised another Ass, and have brought him to that place, which is the mirror of Paradise; and nowadays he struts in the expanse of repose at complete ease, and grazes in the garden of security and safety in tranquillity and health." In short, the Fox, acting perfidiously, breathed such deceits, and recited such treacheries, that the bread of his guiles became cooked in the oven of dissimulation; and as regards the Ass, owing to his inexperienced nature, the pot of desire began to boil, and he said: "It is not admissible to turn one's head from your counsel, which is the purest friendship and kindness, nor is it allowable not to respect your commands, which are the essence of affection and consideration."

> Whatever you decree I will make incumbent on my soul.

The Fox located himself in advance and brought him near the Lion, who from excess of hunger having planned his death, struck him a blow, which by reason of his own weakness was not efficacious, and the Ass set out in flight. The Fox was astonished[2] at the Lion's want of strength, and reproached him saying: "At any rate, what was the advantage of uselessly torturing an animal, and what benefit was there in displaying haste in a matter the opportunity of carrying out which was not wanting? True wisdom demanded that you should restrain yourself, and steadfastness of purpose directed that you should not let go from your hand the reins of power, so that you should not regret the end of the affair."

> Of what avail is remorse, now that the matter has left your hand?

These words fell heavily on the Lion, and he thought to himself: "If I say I have allowed myself to be incautious, I shall be deemed irresolute and changeable; while if I adhere to the promptings of my natural instincts, I shall be termed greedy, gluttonous, hasty, and impetuous. If, again, I confess to loss of power, I must of necessity admit that I am weak and impotent, and many bad results will arise, which are inconsistent with the welfare of the kingdom. It is best that I should not reply to the Fox, except with severity and harshness, but forbid him to speak such words as these." Accordingly he said: "Whatever kings do, it is very discourteous for their subjects to seek to be apprised thereof, or to inquire the secrets of the same.

> Place your head in submission to this decree, what business have you with
>   this and that?
> What has a poor, inexperienced person to do with monarchy?

---

[1] كوش . in the Persian text is a misprint for گوش

[2] متعجب . in the Persian text is a misprint for متعجب

"Nor can the mind of any of their dependants become enlightened as to the real state of sovereigns, and the capacity of subjects cannot penetrate what the judgment of kings may demand. *'None but their beasts can carry their presents.'*

> The helpless quail has not the maw of a hawk.

"Cease such questions, and employ stratagem to bring back the Ass; by this service the sincerity of your faith and the abundance of your integrity will become evident to me, and on my part you will be honoured with patronage and consideration beyond your fellows and equals." The Fox again approached the Ass, and with the utmost deference performed the dues of salutation and welcome. The Ass turned his face from him, saying:

> 'Twere a shame to be vexed about such a friend as you,
> Since on the road of faithlessness you desire nought but ruin to the soul.

"O vagabond traitor! first of all you promised me freedom, and in the end you made me a prey in the Lion's clutches."

> From none save you would such an action proceed.

The Fox replied : "O simpleton! what are you imagining, and what idea passes through your mind? Would you at mere magic, which you beheld, be dismayed in the search after wealth, and as soon as you have witnessed the prick of the thorn have you stepped aside from the enjoyment of the garden of roses? You must know that what you saw was sorcery, which seers have prepared and arranged by way of caution, on account of the insects and reptiles which rest in this place; seeing that this meadow is adorned with a variety of pleasant foods, and numerous delightful fruits, if this necromancy did not exist, wherever in the world there is an animal, he would come here, and the affairs of the inhabitants of this waste would become embarrassed. But now by reason of this magic, the different creatures do not come to this desert, and whoever reaches here and sees that form and figure which you beheld, does not again approach near this meadow, while the inhabitants of this waste pass their time in repose and ease. We, too, explain to any one with whom we are friends the secret of this charm, and expound to him this enchantment, which is nought but an apparition, so that without fear or dread he may attain these immeasurable favours."

> The Fox said : "This is magic and enchantment,
> Which appeared to your eyes as the head of the Lion.
> Seeing that I, who am of weaker body than you,
> Graze here night and day,
> Were it not that this kind of sorcery is carried on,
> Every empty stomach would have invaded this spot."

"First of all I was anxious to apprise you that if you saw anything of such a kind you were not to be afraid, but from the excess of agitation which I experienced on meeting you, it escaped my mind. Now since you are thoroughly informed as to this illusory appearance, return, for the result of my guidance will be nought but honour." In this way he performed his spells, and deluded the helpless Ass till the latter once again retracing the road of folly, and being deceived with the other's frauds, set his face towards the waste. The Fox went in advance, and conveying to the Lion the good news of the Ass's approach, requested that of a certainty he should not jump up, nor put his feet beyond the pale of calmness and sedateness, and however much the Ass might come in proximity to him, he should not pay any regard till the time that, having found thorough strength and a good opportunity, he should accomplish his purpose. The Lion readily accepted the Fox's advice, which was based on affection, and stood on his legs like a lifeless apparition, in a corner of the waste. The Fox said to the Ass: "Come, so that you may see the truth of this magic, and may know that there is absolutely no motion, nor imaginable harm therein." The Ass boldly advanced, and though he grazed round about the Lion, saw no movement on his part. Merrily he grew intimate with him, and gently became familiar, and being thoroughly at ease respecting his proceedings, fell to eating the grass. The poor Ass having been for a long time overcome with insatiable hunger, now, when he saw the tables of invitation spread out, and found the banquet of bounty ready prepared, commencing to eat, did not pull the rein till he was full beyond measure. Being satisfied, he slept in front of the spectre in the midst of the pasturage. The Lion, finding him off his guard, crept forth and tore open his stomach, and then said to the Fox: "Watch till I go to the fountain-head and wash myself. I will then eat the Ass's ears and heart, since the physicians have enjoined the cure of this disease in such fashion." The Lion set out towards the fountain, and the Fox ate the ears and heart of the Ass, which were the nicest portion thereof. When the Lion had finished the necessary ablution and returned, though he made every search, he could not find a trace of the Ass's ears or heart. He said to the Fox: "Where are these two members, with which I am to be cured, and who has taken them away?" The Fox replied: "May the King live for ever! this Ass had neither ears nor heart: because, had he the latter, which is the abode of wisdom, he would not have been deceived by my treachery; while if he had possessed the former, which are the seat of hearing, after witnessing the violence of the King, he would have distinguished the speciousness of my falsehood from honest language, and would not with his own feet have come to his own grave."

"I have adduced this story that you may know I am not without heart or ears. You have not omitted any particle of treachery, but I have by my own judgment and wisdom discovered it, and striven much so that the affair, which had become difficult, should be rendered easy, and my soul, which had reached my lips, again cast the light of life upon the regions of my body.

> The destruction, by your sword, of this wounded one was not decreed,
> Though there was nothing wanting on the part of your pitiless heart.

"After this do not expect to be intimate with me, and abandon the idea of returning, which is beyond the multitude of possibilities, and know for a certainty that,

> Were you the moon, I would look less at the heavens;
> Were you a cypress, I would pass less frequently the garden;
> Were you the source of life, I would on no account purchase you;
> I will no longer remember you, nor mention your name."

The Tortoise said: "You say truly; my assertions and denials are all the same. A wound has been inflicted by me on your heart, for which during all your life salve will never appear, and the scar of wickedness and violence has left a trace on my face to remove which is not within the pale of possibility. I know that I must set my heart upon drinking the bitter potion of separation, and must make my body a shield against the glancing poisoned sword of parting."

It is right if I must needs sit in blood,
Since why have I thus let my friend slip from my hand?
Whoever ruined himself as I have done?
Who with his own hand did what I have performed?
Were my soul for ever to ask forgiveness,
Yet it would never demand pardon for this offence.

Thus he spoke, and ashamed and confused, turned back, and for the rest of his life, separated from such a friend, lamented saying:

" Violence overtook me, as was my Fate, otherwise my friend,
God forbid! would not have experienced cruel treatment nor oppressive behaviour."

Such is the story of him who having acquired property or gained a friend, afterwards from ignorance and negligence scattered the same to the winds, and was overcome with everlasting remorse, and though he struck his head upon a stone, and a stone upon his head, it was of no avail. It behoveth a wise man to make the moral of this story his guide, and to appreciate an object which is attained, whether as regards the things of the world, or as concerns inmost friends. Whatever slips from one's hands will not return for wishing, and remorse or regret will be unavailing.

When you gain your object, appreciate it,
And let it not slip your grasp, for repentance will follow.
Many there are who readily give their hoards of wealth to the winds,
And are then distressed for want of a diram:
For what is gone from the hand will not in any case return,
Though one laments and tears one's clothes.

BOOK VI.

ON THE MISFORTUNE OF HASTE, AND THE EVIL OF IMPETUOSITY.

INTRODUCTION.

HE world-subduing King having distinguished the enlightened-minded Brahman with the honour of an exalted discourse, said :

Bravo ! thy mind is apprised of the secrets of the Almighty ;
Bravo ! thy eloquence reveals mysteries to mankind.

"You have narrated a story of some one who was successful in his desires, but neglectful in protecting the same, till his object slipping from his hand, he was overtaken with repentance and became overwhelmed with the anguish of torture, and obtained nought but remorse and sorrow. Now repeat an account of some one, who in the accomplishment of his designs acted hastily, and was destitute of the advantages of deliberation and reflection, till at the end of the affair and the termination of his proceedings, what happened. And when the seed of precipitancy is sown in the field of practice, what product will it afford ?" The Brahman loosing the tongue in praise of the King, said :

O King ! may the laws of the world remain lasting in thy hands !
May the regions of the garden of the Universe be joyous with thee !

"When any one does not rear the fabric of his affairs on patience and firmness, and does not securely fix the foundation of his arrangements upon constancy and calmness, the end of his proceedings will incline to reproach, and the termination of his affairs will be passed in regret. The most praiseworthy quality with which the Most High God has adorned mankind, and by the blessing of which He has conferred on the human race an honoured position, is the ornament of gentleness and the virtue of sedateness.

Long-suffering is the treasury of wisdom ;
Whoever is void of clemency is, as it were, a demon or brute.

" A proverb has been spoken in this respect: ' When you invert " hilm "[1] (gentleness) it becomes " milh " (salt),—that is, it is the salt of the table of manners. It assuredly happens that if any one outstrips his peers in the ac- quirement of different virtues, and carries off the ball[2] of superiority from the men of his time, in the display of various excellences, when he unites therewith harsh disposition, precipitancy, haste, and levity, his other merits, like food with- out flavour, are acceptable to no natures, and from his levity of disposition and imbecility of understanding, disgust overspreads men's hearts. *'But if thou hadst been severe and hard-hearted they had surely become scattered from around thee!'* Notwithstanding all those perfections which were combined in his Excellency the Lord of the Universe, *'On Him be the best salutations and most perfect offerings,'* a gracious address from His Majesty the Lord of Lords reached him to this effect: ' O Muhammad! if you had been of a harsh disposition, hard- hearted, hot-tempered, and spiteful, assuredly the armies of Stars—" *My com- panions are like the stars* "—which now are collected around you, like the Pleiades, would be scattered as it were the constellation of the Bear.' Again, he praises the possessor of friendship and the lord of religion, Abraham, the friend of God—*'On our prophet and on him be the salutations of the All- Merciful '*—for this quality where he says, *' In truth Abraham was kind and merciful,'* seeing that the compassionate person is beloved of men's hearts, and the souls of high and low are all inclined towards him.

> Long-suffering is the pillar of reason,
> Precipitancy always tends to misery.

" Hastiness has no connection with men of wisdom, and the truly learned con- sider it amongst the devices of Satan, since *'Caution is from God, haste from the Devil,'* and the meaning of these words has been explained in this manner:

> Haste and precipitancy are wiles of Satan,
> Patience and restraint are charms of the Merciful God!
> By degrees there sprang into existence from the Almighty,
> During six days, this earth and sphere;
> Otherwise it was in His power, with Káf[3] and Nún,
> To have created hundreds of worlds in an instant.
> This tardiness is for your instruction:
> Act with patience in your affairs. What is done slowly is successful.

" Whenever any one, as regards his affairs, gives over the reins of power to the hands of precipitancy, assuredly, in the conclusion, his proceedings will end in repentance, and at the last his case will terminate in regret and sorrow.

> He who undertakes a matter without thought or deliberation,
> Will ultimately regret what has been done.

———o———

" In regard to this matter, many histories and countless anecdotes are described and mentioned in the pages of entertaining stories, and pleasant tales. From

---

[1] It must be borne in mind that the short vowel " i " is not written in Persian.
[2] See note 1, page 138.
[3] That is, the Almighty need only have said " Kun " (" let it be "), which word is composed of the two letters Káf and Nún.

amongst the number of these, the story of the Devotee, who, without reflection, placed his feet in the plain of frivolity, and having stained his hands with innocent blood, gave the hapless Weasel's life to the winds, is illustrative of this rashness." The King inquired, " How was that ? "

STORY I.

He said : It has been related that a Devotee, after living a long time alone, was anxious to carry out the religious duty—" *Matrimony is my regulation, therefore he who turns away from my regulation does not appertain to me* "—and put in practice the injunction, which must be obeyed—" *Marry and produce children.*" He took counsel with one of the Devotees of the time, and performed the rites of asking for a blessing and seeking permission. That Devotee said: "You have conceived a very praiseworthy idea, since marriage is befitting for existence, and thoroughly expedient, and a safeguard in the affairs of religion, as well as a protection for household goods. Again, numerous offspring, wherefrom permanence of reputation is derived, are procured thereby.

The face of fortune will never shine upon a man,
Till a wife lights upon him the lamp of domesticity.
Pass not life in the corner of solitude ; since
Founding a family is a city of delight in the garden of security and repose.

" But strive to obtain a gentle companion, and avoid an unacceptable spouse." The Devotee inquired, " With what woman must I elect to associate ? " He replied : " With a woman who shall be affectionate, prolific, and upright,—that is to say, who shall love her husband, produce numerous offspring, and be cautious of doing wrong. A modest wife, in whatever house she enters, adds light to light."

The society of a virtuous wife is advantageous in this world and the next :
O the happiness of the man who has such a wife !
From a sweet companion the wish of the heart will be gratified :
He whose star is in the ascendant must possess an associate.

He said, " What sort of woman's society must I avoid ? " The other replied : " There are three kinds of women from whom one must keep aloof—widows, heiresses, and those who are dissatisfied ; for the widow is a woman who, having had a husband before you, and separation between them having occurred either by death or divorce, will constantly desire his society. An heiress is one who possesses property and wealth, and by her riches she will place you under an obligation. A dissatisfied woman is one who, when she sees you, drops her voice, and makes herself ill, though not really sick. Now the society of such a wife is like dying afresh every hour."

A bad wife in a good man's home
Is hell even in this earth to him.
Beware of associating with a badly-disposed woman.
" *Save us, O God, from the torments of hell !* "

Once more he asked, " Of what age shall I select a wife ? " The Devotee said :

" It must be a young delicate [1] wife, since old women bear off freshness from the checks, and having ought to do with them produces weakness and languor.

> That woman whose back is like a bow,
> Her mind is straight [2] like an arrow.
> The society of a girl who entrances the soul,
> Is like deadly poison when she becomes old.

" Women from ten years old till twenty are regions of security and places of hope; from twenty till thirty they soothe the hearts of those who seek them, and are a delight to the souls of those who are disposed towards them; from thirty till forty they are the possessors of property and children, and persons of high ambition; and from forty till fifty they are in the meshes of name and reputation, and at the court of dissimulation and flattery. But after fifty is past, they are black misfortunes, ruinous to property and dignity, rose-gardens which have experienced autumn, fabrics drenched with rain, turbid fountains, uncultivated soil, worthless dragons, and mines of distress and grief."

> When woman after fifty treads that region,
> 'Twere better that a man should jump on one side;
> Since he who escapes from the clutches of fifty,
> Ultimately falls into the hands of sixty. [3]

The Devotee inquired, " What do you say as regards excellence and beauty?" He replied: " In the case of woman, the best thing is modesty and good disposition. If the good fortune of handsomeness is joined thereto, it resembles light upon light."

> Her face is beautiful, her merits perfect, and her skirt pure,
> Then the devout of both worlds are ambitious after her.

" If a beautiful, good-looking woman should be of an unpleasant disposition, she is calamitous to the soul, and a perpetual torment; while a good-tempered wife, though of ugly appearance, is a dear friend, and the splendour of the domestic circle.

> When a friend is affable, and a comrade sincere,
> Though there be no beauty of face, the eyes are enlightened.
> Avoid an unsuitable companion,
> Though by reason of her beauty, your house should become a garden of roses.

" In this regard, two or three verses from the results of the thoughts of that wise man must be kept in the receptacle of the mind:

> ' A good, obedient, chaste wife
> Renders a poor man a king.
> If you are melancholy all the day, be not dejected,
> Since at night [4] your loved one will be in your embrace.
> If she be modest and sweet-tongued,
> Regard not either her beauty or ugliness.

---

[1] بورسید in the Persian text is a misprint for نورسیده.

[2] That is, the disposition of a woman whose back is bent with age is harsh and unbending.

[3] Meaning, I presume, that if you escape the clutches of a woman fifty years old, you will be ensnared by one sixty years of age.

[4] شب in the Persian text is a misprint for شب.

An evil-disposed woman, though handsome,
Where will there be a place for her in the heart?
Her appearance is heart-enchanting like the Húrís of Paradise,
But she has another face, hideous like a demon.
It is better to be imprisoned by the judge,
Than that you should behold in your home knitted brows.
It is better to go barefooted than to have shoes too small,
The misfortune of travel is better than war in your house.
Close the door of joy upon that dwelling,
Whence the tones of woman issue high.
May the eye of woman be blind to strangers!
When it sallies forth from the house, may it be entombed!'"

In short, after boundless inquiry and endless search, by the aid of lofty fortune and the assistance of exalted ambition, the Devotee obtained from amongst a great tribe and distinguished family a wife, the representation of whose cheek lent brilliance to the scout of Morn, and the colour of whose glistening ringlets added darkness to the perfume-seller of Night. The eyes of the azure Spheres had never seen her equal, save in the mirror of the Sun; and the sharp-sighted portrayer, Imagination, had never beheld the like of her auspicious portrait, except in the world of dreams.

O sun! your face has captivated the world of beauty!
A full moon in the horizon of the Heaven of symmetry;
A cypress and rose superior to you in stature and appearance never grew
In the garden of beauty, or the parterre of comeliness.

In addition to charming appearance, she was adorned with a happy disposition, and the excellence of her nature was graced with a sweet temper. The Devotee returned thanks for such a boon, by the offering of his worship to God, and the edifice of his intimacy with that Húrí-faced friend being laid in this manner, he was anxious for children. No wise man makes mere sensual gratification the basis of a family; nor, save in quest of a good son, who in causing the blessings of faithful prayer to be obtained, is equivalent to constant almsgiving, does he give himself up to such matters.

The object of woman's anguish, and of the toil men undergo,
Is this very pleasure of beloved children.

When some time had elapsed, and this had not come to pass, the Devotee becoming hopeless, commenced to place the face of supplication upon the dust of intercession, and began to discharge the arrow of prayer from the bow of sincerity. Since he had entirely made himself nought in the road of prayer, according to the saying, "*Who answereth the weary when they call upon him?*" the arrow of his supplications reached the target of acceptance.

Whoever is pure in heart and just,
His entreaties will reach the All-glorious Being.
That prayer of irresponsible persons is the prayer of another:
That intercession is not made by him, it belongs to God.
God made the prayer, for man is but mortal:
Both the prayer and its acceptance are from the Almighty.

Accordingly, after loss of hope, the doors of favour were opened with the keys of compassion, and the Devotee's wife became pregnant. The Saint was greatly delighted, and anxious every day to keep talking of his offspring, save whose name, after the performance of his religious rites, he uttered nought. One day he said to his wife: " O companion of my time, and dear friend! may it soon happen that the royal pearl shall come from the shell of your womb to the arena of manifestation, and a beautiful-faced son strut forth from the secret recess of obscurity to the plain of evidence, and I will assign him a good name and a fitting designation; after which I will endeavour, to the limits of possibility, to educate and advance him, so that he may learn the ordinances of the law, and I will make a fair attempt to correct and train him, with the view of his being graced with the manners of his sect, and in a short time becoming a great man of exalted station in religion, and a shaikh, endued with miraculous powers and inspiration. Then I will bring him a noble lady into the compact of marriage, and from them children and grandchildren will spring, and our race by their blessing become perpetuated, and our name, by means of their offspring, be everlasting on the pages of Time."

> His name will remain throughout ages,
> Who leaves an offspring as his memorial.
> Hence the name of the shell remains in the ear,
> Because the royal pearl itself is seen therein.

The woman said: " O dear companion! O pious chief! these words are not worthy of one who performs adoration, nor fit for one who celebrates the praises of God. First of all, you resolved on the birth of a child, and it is possible that I may not have an offspring; and if I do, it may not be a son. Even if it were, it is conceivable that he may not attain the happiness of growing up and living. In short, the basis of this matter is not manifest, while you, foolish and wrapt in imagination, are sitting on the steed of desire, and, like ignorant idealists, are driving the courser of hope in the expanse of ambition, not aware of the extent of this plain.

> You cannot either with desire or ambition traverse the road;
> You cannot with boasting or bombast accomplish the business.
> Thousands of persons are consumed with vain desires,
> Not one of whom does Fortune favour with the wish of his heart.

" Your words resemble the proceedings of that Holy man who spilt honey and oil upon his face and hair." The Devotee inquired, " How was that?"

STORY II.

She said: It has been related that a Holy man had a house in the neighbourhood of a Merchant, in the blessing of whose friendly company he passed his time in repose. The Merchant used constantly to sell honey and oil, by which greasy and sweet transactions he acquired his gains. By reason that the Holy man passed his time in a praiseworthy manner, and perpetually sowed the seed of the love of the Almighty in the field of his guileless heart, the Merchant had placed confidence in him, and pledged his own reputation to supply his needs. The benefit of riches is just this: to get possession of the hearts of the poor, and acquire a store for Eternity from possessions which pass away.

> O rich man ! obtain the hearts of the poor,
> For hoards of gold, and stores of money will not abide.

The Merchant, also, welcoming the opportunity of doing good, every day sent the Devotee for his sustenance a little of the stock which he employed in his commercial transactions, and the Holy man, using somewhat thereof, placed the remainder in a corner. In a little time the vessel became full therewith. One day the Devotee looked into the pitcher, and thought to himself, "How much honey and oil are collected in this vessel?" Ultimately he made a guess at ten mans, saying: "If I can sell it for ten dirams I will part with it, and purchase with the same sum five strong sheep : these latter every six months will breed, and each produce two young ones : in a year they will amount to twenty-five, and in ten years herds will have resulted from them : having obtained by these means a thorough stock, I will sell some of them, and by such method adorn my possessions. Then I will seek a wife of good family, who, nine months after, will bear me a son, whom I will teach learning and manners ; but when the weakness of infancy is exchanged for the strength of maturity, and that delicate cypress stands erect in the expanse of youth, possibly he may deviate from my commands, and may commence to be rebellious : on this supposition it would be necessary to make him behave properly, and I would correct him with this very staff which I have in my hand." Accordingly he drew forth his stick, and so immersed was he in the sea of imagination, that, having pictured as present the head and neck of the mannerless son, he brought down his staff, and struck it upon the pitcher of honey and oil. By chance that vessel had been placed upon the top of a shelf, under which he himself was sitting, facing it. When the stick alighted upon the pitcher, it was at once broken to pieces, and all the honey and oil spilled on the Holy man's head, face, clothes, and hair.

> And all those fancies fled in an instant.

" I have adduced this story that you may know that, without clear certainty, you must not plunge into the like of these conversations, nor is it fitting to be deceived with ' be thou,' ' perhaps,' ' haply,' and ' it may be.' It has been said that when any one makes ' if ' and ' perhaps ' his consort, the children which spring from them will be ' Would to Heaven ! ' "

> When " If " and " Perhaps " are married,
> A child is born to them, named " Would to Heaven ! "

" It behoves a wise man not to base his affairs upon fancy, and not to give place in his heart to crude imaginations, which resemble the worthless wiles of a demon."

> For years we have fancied, that from the revolutions of the spheres
> Matters would terminate in this or that way.
> Either that in this manner we shall discover hoards of silver and gold,
> Or that in such a kingdom our decree will prevail.
> Ultimately it became clear that all this was no more than imagination.
> Whatever the Absolute Ruler wishes, that same will come to pass.

The Devotee, accepting this advice with the ear of his soul, woke from the sleep of vanity, and abandoning these words, did not again encompass himself with presumption. But when the period of his wife's confinement arrived, and the time of the child being in the prison of the flesh had ended, there was born an elegant-looking, pleasant-faced son, the signs of whose beauty ,and good qualities were evidenced in the perfection of his condition, and the marks of whose dignity were resplendent and radiant on the forehead of his circumstances. The Devotee's morn of hope commenced to smile from the horizon of desire, and the nightingale of his joy to chant forth on the rosebud of delight.

> A beautiful gem appeared from the circle of excellence :
> A radiant star arrived from the sphere of manifestation.

The Devotee, being in raptures at the child's beauty, fulfilled a variety of vows which he had made, and night and day, having girt his loins in attendance on the cradle, as regards other matters, drew in his mind the writing of oblivion, and constantly expended his ambition on the boy's growth, strength, majesty, freshness, and lustre.

> How long, like the zephyr, shall I give the breath of my ambition to you,
> So that you may come forth from the bud like a rose joyful and smiling ?

One day, his mother desiring a bath, carefully intrusted her son to the father, who besides that had no other business. A time elapsed, and a confidant from the King of that country came and summoned the Devotee; it being in no way possible to delay, he was compelled of necessity to quit the house. They had a Weasel to whose care they used to confide the house, and from whom in every way they acquired repose, and who, too, in repelling noxious creatures and vicious animals, used his best efforts. The Devotee went out, and left him with his own son. So soon as he was out of sight of the house, a large Snake approached the cradle. When the Weasel saw this dart-natured, armour-clad (creature), and this fierce-angered, hatred-seeking (reptile), like the letter alif, which at the time of its being still becomes transformed like the shape of a circle [1]—a rapid-going (viper), which sometimes like a bow which is bent, met tip to tip,

> Sometimes bent round like a shield, sometimes straight as a dart ;
> Sometimes its body coiled in lasso-like rings.
> Not a cloud, but two forks of lightning are concealed within ;
> Not an ocean, but mighty waves appear therein—

making for the cradle, anxious to kill the child, he himself jumped up, and taking the Snake by the throat, with the utmost contempt ensnared him in the noose of death; so by the blessing of the Weasel's protection the infant escaped from that whirlpool of destruction. After these proceedings the Devotee returned. The Weasel, wallowing in blood, ran up to him, full of anxiety, in that a good action had been achieved by him. The Devotee, thinking that his son had been killed, and this besmearment was with his blood, the flame of anger was kindled in the grate of his heart, and the smoke of rashness reached the window of his brain; while his reason, owing to the darkness of the smoke of precipitation, which, like the cloud of oppression, is the means of blackening the world, drew its face behind the veil of concealment. Before investigating the affair, or inquiring into the case, he struck the Weasel with a stick, and, breaking the bones in his back, pounded its head into the chest of its bosom. When he came to his house, he saw his son resting safely in the cradle, and the huge-framed Snake lying in pieces. The smoke of regret issued from his heart, and he began to strike the stone of remorse upon his bosom, lamenting, groaning, and saying :

---

[1] In allusion to the habits of a snake, which, when about to move, uncoils itself and becomes straight.

Henceforth grief and I (go together), and every one knows that
From this time forth a happy mind is an impossible state not to be expected.

" Alas that the fire of this heartrending calamity will not be quenched with the
water of apology, nor will the shield of excuse ward off the arrow of shame
for this soul-consuming proceeding ! What an improper action was this which
proceeded from me, and what an unworthy business is this which has occurred at
my hands !

If I drink blood from shame at this melancholy proceeding, it is right,
And proper were I to abandon my soul from misery at this affair.

" Would that this child had never come from non-existence into being, and that I
had not become intimate with or fond of him, so that by reason of him this innocent blood had not been spilled, and my steps not have alighted on this unworthy
affair. In that I have without cause occasioned the death of this my own companion, and have without reason sent to the region of destruction the defender
of my house, and the protector of my precious offspring, what reply shall I give
to my Creator ? and what apology shall I present to mankind ? Henceforth
the collar of scorn will not be removed from my neck, nor the inscription of
reproach be erased from the pages of my circumstances."

My name is a sign for reproach and scorn.
O ! would that my name had never existed, nor trace of me either !

The Devotee, with such thoughts, writhed within himself, and from such regret
and grief kept bewailing his distress. His wife returning, and witnessing these
proceedings, opened the tongue of reproach, saying :

I never knew you thus unkind.

"Anyhow, is this the way you discharge your gratitude for the favour of God, in
that, at the period of old age, He miraculously bestowed on you a son? And should
you so make return for the gift of the Almighty, in that He delivered the being
who fills the recesses of your heart from the soul-destroying wound of the Snake?"
The Devotee, lamenting, said : "O dear friend ! do not speak to me such kind of
language,

" Since I am distressed at the questions, and ashamed of my reply.

" I, too, am aware that I have been remiss in expressing my gratitude to God,
and in recognising the worth of His endless bounties, and that I have deviated
from the straight highway of patience, which, indeed, is the road of the travellers
on the paths, ' *You have no patience save from God.*' Now, by reason of my hastiness and ingratitude, I shall neither be mentioned in the scroll of the patient, nor
recorded in the pages of the grateful. Your reproach in these circumstances is
like stinging the top of a wound, or making a salve of salt for a sore."

To reproach the heart of a lover, torn in a hundred pieces, is like
When a wound is made with a sword, sewing it up with a needle.

The wife replied: " You speak truly. Now no benefit will accrue from reproach,
and from this matter which you have done experience is to be derived,—viz., that
the end of impetuosity is regret and shame. Hastiness and want of steadiness

are in all cases contemptible, and a man who acts rashly will be disappointed in obtaining his desire.

> Hastiness and evil are works of the Devil,
> Causing regret to the soul, and anguish to the body.

" But not you alone have fallen into this snare, and opened upon yourself the door of this misery, since ere this the like of this event has often occurred, and a similar accident countless times happened. I have heard that a King killed his own Hawk, which was innocent, and for years his heart was consumed with the fire of regret and his bosom burnt up with the flame of repentance." The Devotee inquired, " How was that ? "

STORY III.

She said: It has been related that in ancient times a certain King was fond of hunting, and used perpetually to gallop the steed of desire in search of prey, and continually to cast the noose of joy over the neck of the game. This King had a Hawk, who at one flight brought down the phœnix from the summit of Mount Káf,[1] and from fear of whose talons the Eagle of the skies remained concealed in the azure nest of the heavens.

> When he expanded his feathers and wings,
> The bosom of the spheres was lacerated with fear.
> And if he hastened towards the heavens,
> The Eagle of the skies drooped his feathers.

The King was very fond of this Hawk, and always attended to him with his own hand. By chance the King one day, having taken that Hawk in his hand, went out hunting. A Deer jumped up in front, and the King in his excess of anxiety galloped after him. He did not overtake the Deer, and happened to separate from his retinue and followers. Some of the attendants galloped after him, but the King rode so hastily that the zephyr, notwithstanding that in the twinkling of an eye it traverses the world, could not have encircled him, nor the north wind, notwithstanding its swift motion, have overtaken the dust of his steed.

> You went forth a distance beyond measure,
> The foot cannot tread where you have been.

In the midst of these proceedings, the fire of thirst was kindled, and the King's mouth became parched. He galloped his steed in every direction, and, seeking water, traversed the regions of the waste and desert, till he arrived at the skirt of a hill, and saw that from the top thereof pure water was trickling. The King brought out a cup which he had in his sash, and rode beneath the hill, and collected in the cup that water which trickled drop by drop, desirous of drinking it. The Hawk took to wing and upset the whole cup. The King having become vexed in his heart at this proceeding, once more placed the cup beneath the hill, till it was filled, with the intention of conveying it to his lips. Once more the Hawk began to fly, and spilt the vessel.

> They bring near their lips, and are not allowed to taste.

[1] See note, page 60.

The King being distracted with thirst, hurled the Hawk upon the ground and killed him. Concomitant with these proceedings, one of the King's attendants arrived, and seeing the Hawk dead, and finding the King thirsty, immediately pulled out a ewer from his saddle-straps, and washed the cup clean, intending to give the King some water. The King said: "I have a great longing for this pure liquid which trickles from the hill, but I cannot possibly collect it in a cup drop by drop. Go up the hill, and having filled the cup from the source of the water, come down again." The attendant, having ascended the hill, saw a spring, which, like the eyes of hard-hearted misers, gave forth drops of liquid with a hundred regrets. On the brink of that fountain there was a dead dragon, which being affected by the rays of the sun a poisonous slime was mingled with the water of that spring, as it trickled drop by drop from the hill. Alarm having overpowered the attendant, he hurriedly came down to the foot of the hill, and conveyed the circumstances of the case to the place of representation, and gave the King a cup of cold water from his ewer. The King placing the cup of liquid to his lips dropped tears.

> He drank some water, and quenched his anguish of heart;
> What he drank with his lips he shed from his eyelids.[1]

The attendant asked, "What can be the cause of your weeping?" The King heaving a cold sigh from his heart filled with grief, said:

> "I have a grief, which I cannot disclose;
> I have a tale, which I cannot hold secret."

He then repeated in its entirety the account of the Hawk, and the spilling of the cup of water, and said: "I am grieved at the death of the Hawk, and lament my own proceedings in depriving of life, without investigation, so dear a creature." The attendant said: "O King! this Hawk has warded off a great calamity from you, and conferred a deep obligation upon all the inhabitants of this kingdom; it would have been best had the King not hastened to kill him, but quenched the fire of rage with the water of compassion, and tightened the reins of the steed of natural propensity with the power of self-restraint, the words of the wise, who have said,

> 'Do not urge your steed so rapidly
> That you cannot curb his rein,'

not being departed from." The King replied: "I have repented this unbecoming action, at a time when regret is of no avail, and the wound of this reproach cannot be soothed with any salve. So long as I live I shall have the scar of this remorse on my bosom, and tear the face of my condition with the nail of reproach."

> How can I act? I did it myself; there is no device available for what one does one's-self.

"Now I have adduced this story for this—to show that many such occurrences as this have taken place, wherein persons, through the evils of haste, have fallen into the whirlpool of remorse, and having wandered from deliberation and consideration, have been drowned in the midst of the gulf of misfortune."

---

[1] That is, the tears rolled down his cheeks into his mouth.

Persons without weight lose themselves ;
Men's nature should be massive as stone ;
Swift-darting lightning does not last long ;
No souls are overturned save the contemptible.
Whenever any one stretches out his hands hastily,
The stone of violence will destroy the basis of his power.

The Devotee said : "O companion of my existence, and ornament of the days of my life! you have afforded me consolation with this anecdote, and placed salve upon the wound of my stricken heart. I am aware that in this crime and offence I have many partners, and just as their story is written upon the scroll of time, so will my case be inscribed ; so that, whoever is negligent in matters, and does not partake of the benefits of calmness and tranquillity, may find a warning in this story, and gain an example from this tale."

Such is the story of one who without reflection put into execution his designs in a certain respect, and without thought attempted a matter. Wise men must make experience their guide, and furbish [1] the mirror of their intellect with the warnings of the prudent and the advice of the learned, and at all times inclining towards consideration and deliberation, must keep apart from the way of haste and levity, till abundant prosperity and fortune may come in regular series to the shore of their happiness, and the assistance of goodness and benevolence be allied to excellence and nobleness.

Give over the reins of the heart to the hand of patience, if you would
Bear off the ball [2] of repose with the club of endeavour.
Gallop not the steed of negligence through the plain of precipitancy,
Since in the end it will throw you in disgrace on the ground.
Haste leads to danger, so that were you for a hundred years
To strain hand and foot, you would not emerge from that strait.
Be not precipitous, nor turn your face from the way of caution,
For want of patience and stability is not the way of the wise.

[1] See note 2, page 51.   [2] See note 1, page 138.

BOOK VII.

ON CAUTION AND DELIBERATION, AND FINDING ESCAPE, BY MEANS OF STRATAGEM, FROM THE WILES OF FOES.

INTRODUCTION.

THE King said: "I have heard the story of one who, without thought or deliberation, cast himself into the sea of regret and repentance, and without patience or resignation, became entangled in the net of remorse and torment; now, if it is expedient, describe the purport of the seventh precept, and narrate a tale of one who shall have been taken in the midst of enemies, and recite an account of one who shall have been surrounded right and left, before and behind, with powerful foes, while the antagonists, being numerous, overpowering him, took possession of all his beats and retreats: how, seeing himself in the clutch of death, and the grasp of destruction, he deems it advisable to strive to be courteous and conciliatory to one of them—nay, more, finds it necessary to enter into a bond and engagement, so as to escape in safety: how he sets about this matter, and after that, by the aid and assistance of an enemy, he has obtained deliverance from that calamity, in what way he discharges his promise to him: and after displaying kindness, with what stratagem he opens the way of expediency." The Brahman replied: "The majority of friendships and enmities are neither lasting nor permanent, since most of them are accidental, and what comes by chance soon vanishes; consequently some friendships are lost by lapse of time—nay, more, become, as it were, non-existent. In like manner, enmities too, being changed, are erased from the tablets of the bosom. The love and hatred of the inhabitants of the world are like the spring-clouds, which sometimes drop rain, and sometimes refrain, having no appearance of either permanence or stability.

As regards every one with whom my heart thought to be friends,
When I looked closely enmity was apparent;
Concerning the friendship or enmity of the people of the world,
I saw that no great reliance was to be placed.

" The affection and hatred of the people of the time, as regards instability bears
a resemblance to intercourse with kings, the charms of beauties, the voice of
striplings, the fidelity of women, the caressings of the distracted, the generosity
of intoxicated persons, the affection of the common people, or the allurements of
foes, since on none of them can reliance be placed, nor the heart be fixed on the
permanence thereof.

It is pleasant amongst friends to form engagements of intimacy;
Yet what advantage is it, since that agreement is not lasting ?

" Much friendship there is which reaches the extreme of affection, and the limit
of concord, the basis of sincerity and intimacy being thereby, in lapse of time,
extended to the summit of the spheres, but which suddenly is turned by the
effects of malignant[1] Fate from the purest affection to the deepest enmity, and
the freshness of which, owing to the blast of the cutting breeze of separation, is
annihilated. Again, ancient enmity and hereditary disagreement can be removed
by a little kindness, and the edifice of affection be rendered firm and secure, in
an excellent manner. Hence it is that wise men never omit to be considerate
towards foes, and never suddenly sever their desire after friendship : they
neither allow implicit confidence in every friend, nor do they depend or rely
upon his fidelity. Amongst the perfect speeches, the purport of this one, ' *Lore
thy friend moderately, not to the very extreme,*' which has come forth from the
reservoir of the Great Prophecy, has been honoured with manifestation.

Friendship must not be such,
That not a hair could find its way between you both.
Enmity, too, is not good of such a nature,
That there is not therein a taint of friendship.
Both extremes will be kept in view,
By him who is moderate in his nature.

" Since it is known that the friendship and enmity of men of the world are
not much to be relied on, it is necessary that a wise, foreseeing man should not
reject the request of a foe for peace and companionship, when it comprises the
warding off of troubles, and the attainment of benefits; but as regards everything
which may further the end of his own business, or which the requirements of
the time may demand, he should avail himself of it to gain his object; so that,
by the blessing of his foresight and prudence, the doors of prosperity may be
opened, and the morn of happiness may rise from the horizon of beneficence.
Illustrative of this state of things, which has been described, is the tale of the
Mouse and the Cat." The King said, "What was that ? "

---

[1] Literally, " wounding eye."

———0———

STORY I.

He said : It has been related that in the forest of Barda' was a tree surpassing all other shrubs in height, and standing forth in the midst of the plants in size and stability.

> From every tree which bears fruit,
> The garden derives strength and vigour.

Under that tree was the hole of a Mouse, of greedy disposition, subtle, quick-witted, and of sharp intellect ; with a single deliberation, he loosed a thousand difficult knots, and in half a moment a hundred kinds of devices passed through his mind.

> Wily and plotting was this Mouse,
> Who arranged schemes a hundred years in advance.

In the neighbourhood, too, of that tree, a Cat had made her abode, and Hunters used frequently to come there, and spread their nets in that part. One day a Hunter laid his net near that tree, and tied a little flesh upon the top of the snare. The greedy Cat, paying no heed to this, sniffing along, came towards the meat, and ere ever her teeth reached the flesh, her throat was seized in the noose of the net.

> It is greed which casts everything into the snare,
> And leads to the search after forbidden wealth.
> It is avarice by which all mankind
> Is deprived of ease, and constantly rendered miserable.

In short, the Mouse, also in search of food, came forth from his hole. By way of caution, he cast his eyes on every side, and directed his glance right and left, and above and below. Suddenly his glance alighted on the Cat. Though at the sight of her his eyes were darkened, and his hopes concerning the capital of life and existence became slender, he was not unsettled in his mind. Looking closely he saw that the Cat was bound in the meshes of misfortune. He inwardly blessed the Hunter, and returned thanks for the Cat's imprisonment. Suddenly on one side of the way he saw a Weasel, who was sitting in ambush for him, and having placed the arrow of Expectation in the bow of Design, was looking at the tree : he observed, too, a Crow on the top thereof intending to seize him. Fear and alarm overpowered the Mouse, and dread and horror came over him.

> Alas for this unlucky destiny, which, every day,
> Directs me to a spot, where calamity is rife !

The Mouse reflected : " If I advance the Cat will take me, and if I retreat the Weasel will seize me, while if I remain where I am the Crow will pounce upon me. What can I do in the midst of this misfortune, and with what stratagem can I ward off this difficulty ? To whom shall I tell my tale of woe, and from whom shall I seek a remedy for my incurable disease ?

> I know not a companion from whom to ask what is expedient for this busi-
> ness,
> Nor a comrade to whom to speak of the state of my desolate heart.

" Now the doors of calamity are open, and the way to the abode of safety is extremely far and long. Various misfortunes have arisen, and the path of flight is closed. In spite of all this I must keep my mind composed, and fix my eyes upon the highway of freedom; since the Cup-bearer of Fortune, if for a time she makes us taste the draught of the potion of desire, also mingles the poison of cruelty with the quaff of repose.

> Be not dejected, for the Cup-bearer of Power from the cup of Fate
> Gives sometimes the pure draught of pleasure; at others, the anguish of distress.

" A man of firm determination is he who neither smiles with his lips when putting on the robe of prosperity, nor drops tears of regret from his sorrowful eyes when drinking the draught of adversity.

> Vex not your heart, nor be glad at the world's sorrows or joys,
> Since the way of the world is sometimes one thing, sometimes another.

" Now in this whirlpool of misfortune there is no better protection for me than the shade of wisdom, nor any refuge more appropriate than the teacher of prudence. Whoever is endued with strong sense, in no case will allow dread to come upon him, nor admit fear or alarm to surround his heart. From the words of Philosophers it is understood that wise men must inwardly be like a sea, the extent of the depth of which cannot be fathomed, nor the bottom thereof reached, save by the diver of experience. Whatever falls therein of secrets and mysteries, does not reappear, and however great the torrent of misfortune and calamity which reaches it, its bulk contains it, nor are the traces of discoloration visible therein; since if adversity reach such a pitch that it conceals wisdom, and vexation finds a place in their mind that the intellect is overpowered, then deliberation is stifled, and the benefits of experience and penetration do not accrue to them.

> A man of firm determination is he who remains unmoved,
> Though he wander round the earth like the firmament.
> Like a phœnix, whom a tempest does not remove from his place;
> Not like a sparrow, which falls at the blast of a pea-shooter.

" Whenever any one allows himself to make various schemes, and commences to agitate his bosom with the temptation of ' would be ' and ' perhaps,' the edifice of his deliberations will be rendered worthless, and the market of his reflection and forethought be spoilt. Just as when he looks in the mirror of his mind, if it be clouded and darkened with the rust [1] of temptation, he will not see therein the face of his desire; and however much he may contemplate the tablets of device, if the eye of sight is darkened with the disease of foolish imaginations, he will not read thereon the inscription of his wishes. In this respect sages have said :

> ' Strive with resolution in your deliberations,
> Since from hesitation of purpose a hundred evils spring.
> Fixed determination plans a matter rightly ;
> In rippling water no true shapes appear.'

" No device is more suitable for me, than to make friends with the Cat, since being herself in the deepest misfortune, she is in need of my assistance; and just as by her help I may obtain escape from this calamity, so she, too, by my aid

---

[1] See note 2, page 51.

and friendship, may find delivery from that captivity. If the Cat, with ears of wisdom, listens to my words, and adopting a wise discretion, places confidence in the sincerity of what I say, and does not impute the same to hypocrisy and cunning, holding me clear of the rascality of treachery and imposture, and the crime of fraud and self-interest, we shall both, by the blessing of integrity and unanimity, acquire our freedom, and other enemies, having served their greed, will each of them pursue his own business."

When friends are with us, say to the enemy, " Mind your own business."

The Mouse, then, after these reflections, approached the Cat, and inquired, "What is the matter ?" The Cat, with a sad voice, replied :

> We are sad, it is indicative of our inward pangs ;
> Our mouth is dry, our lips parched, and our eyes moist.

" I have a body bound in the snares of distress, and a heart consumed with the fire of grief and anxiety." The Mouse said :

> " I have a secret matter for your mouth ; yes, indeed.
> Time is short, and I have not found a fitting opportunity."

The Cat, with the greatest condescension, said: " You must tell me, without ceremony, what occurs to your mind, nor must any delay be allowed by concealing it." The Mouse replied : " Never has any listener heard ought but truth on my part, nor are false words esteemed in men's hearts. You must know that I have always been glad at your woes, and have deemed your adversity the essence of delight. My ambition has always been confined to this, that misery and distress may befall you. However, this very day I am your companion in this misfortune, and I have planned my own escape by a means which will also embrace your delivery. For this reason I have entertained friendly feelings towards you, and raise the knocker of the door of companionship.

> This friendship embraces self-interest,
> But self-interest which comprises what is beneficial, not what is baneful.

" It does not remain concealed from your penetration and intelligence that I am speaking the truth, and in these words have no idea of treachery or malignity. Respecting the sincerity of my pretensions, too, I can call two witnesses—one a Weasel, who is waiting in ambush in the rear ; and another a Crow, who is perched watching on the top of the tree. Both of them are bent upon carrying off the breath from my body. When I am near you their hopes of me become deferred, and the desire of each of them entirely quenched. If you will render me secure, and enter into an agreement which shall be the cause of ease of mind, I will take refuge under the shade of your prosperity, both my object will be attained and also your bonds will be severed."

> From this procedure gain will accrue both to me and to you.

The Cat, after hearing these words, fell into a train of thought, and became immersed in a sea of reflection, desirous of measuring with the feet of deliberation the sides and regions of this story, and trying the genuineness of this device upon the touchstone of consideration. The Mouse, seeing that time much pressed, and the Cat was wrapt in meditation, cried out: " Listen to my words, and be assured of the honesty of my disposition and the purity of my nature, and having admitted my kindness, do not delay, since a wise man does not permit irresolution in his affairs, nor does he allow of procrastination in his arrangements.

Be not negligent in your affairs, since the opportunity is precious.

" Just as I gladden my heart with your fidelity, you also should take pleasure in my existence, since the escape of either one of us is linked with the life of the other. The case of you and me is just like that of the vessel and the captain, for the ship reaches the coast owing to the efforts of the commander, who in turn carries on his business by means of the vessel. My sincerity will be evidenced by trial, and my haste is on account of the opportunity being lost.

I fear lest life should not for another instant give quarter.

" I know that it is clear to your mind that my words are not wanting in practice, and that my actions are superior to my talk. Having taken a pledge of affection, I will discharge it with fidelity. Do you also in this respect nod your head, and say the word."

Give a token, for we have placed two eyes in expectation
In the corner of that arched eyebrow.

The Cat hearing the words of the Mouse, and seeing the beauty of rectitude upon the pages of his circumstances, was delighted, and said to the Mouse : " Your language appears honest, and the perfume of sincerity rises from the purport of your speech. I accept this truce, and willingly listen to the words of the Almighty, may His name be glorified, that ' *Peace is good;*' and from the purport of this saying—

'While peace can be concluded, do not knock at the door of war :
While you can free your name, do not follow the path of disgrace.
Open the door of humility to the creatures of the world :
Come forward, and strike not the ewer of affection upon a stone,'

" I will not deviate. I am in hopes that on both sides owing to the blessing of affection escape will appear, and I will make it incumbent upon me to requite and make returns for this favour, and will take upon myself, to all eternity, to be grateful for this bounty. I also in like manner, as you made a promise, will enter into an agreement; and my hope is that,

' I may carry out this agreement which I have made with you.'

" Now tell me what must I do, and how should I behave towards you ? " The Mouse said : " When I approach you, you must display the utmost kindness and befitting respect, so that the enemies on beholding the same, will be apprised of the confirming of the rites of our companionship and friendship, and will return unsuccessful and discomforted. I will then, in complete ease of mind, remove the cords from off your feet." The Cat deemed it incumbent to agree to this arrangement, while the Mouse, in the utmost expectation advanced, and the Cat paid him due respect and honour, warmly addressing him, and displaying towards him varied courtesy, attention, consideration, and kindness. When the Weasel and the Crow witnessed this proceeding, turning aside their minds from pursuing the Mouse they went back. As soon as the Mouse, owing to the aid of the Cat, was freed from two such calamities, he commenced to sever the cords, and fell reflecting as to how he should deliver himself from the meshes of another misfortune : he gently set about his task. The

Cat cleverly perceived that the Mouse was buried in deep and profound meditation; she became alarmed lest, ere the cords were severed, he should go his own way, and leave her bound by the foot. As is the way of friends she commenced to chide, saying: "You have soon tired, and my faith in the integrity of your promise, and the excellence of your generosity was quite different to this: when you have got what you wanted, and have gained a victory according to the desire of your heart, you are backward in discharging your engagement, and think as to how you can put off carrying out your promise. I know that fidelity is a medicine which is not found in the tray of the perfumer Fortune, and faithfulness is a gem which does not exist in the treasury of the world. Integrity is a second phœnix, which never appears save in name; and good faith resembles the Philosopher's stone, which no one can indicate what it really is."

Look not for fidelity, from none in the world will you hear of it.
Would you be a vain seeker of the phœnix, or the Philosopher's stone?

The Mouse rejoined: "God forbid that I should brand the countenance of my affairs with the scar of faithlessness, or enrol my good name, which for a long time I have been acquiring, on the scroll of those who do not perform their promises. I am aware that faithfulness is the lasso of desire, and a store for the way of happiness. It is the Philosopher's stone, which transmutes dark earth into gold; or a collyrium, which bestows sight upon the clouded eyes. The nostrils of every soul which has not inhaled the perfume of fidelity, have no portion of the fragrance of the sweet flowers of excellent dispositions; and the eyes of every heart which has not witnessed integrity, are destitute of the contemplation of the light of generous qualities."

O the earthiness of that head wherein is no marrow of fidelity!

The Cat said: "Since you are aware that integrity is the tire-woman of the bride of beauty, and the mole[1] on the cheek of excellence and perfection, it behoves you also to deck the face of your condition with this kind of ornament, since in the garden wherein the plant of uprightness does not grow, no bird of the heart will warble upon the branches of affection, and on no cheek, which is destitute of the mole of fidelity, will any one cast the glance of the light of regard: hence it has been said:

'She who follows not the path of fidelity, nor the way of integrity,
Though a húrí of Paradise, is not worthy of me.'

Whoever is destitute of the clothing of trustworthiness, and does not fulfil the promise he has made, will meet with that which befell the wife of the Rustic." The Mouse inquired, "What was that?"

STORY II.

The Cat said: It has been related that in one of the villages of Fárs was a Rustic of great experience, and unspeakable penetration, who had tasted deeply of the bitters and sweets of the cup of Fortune, and experienced many ups and downs in the tumults of Time.

[1] See note, p. 23.

> One who had travelled the world, knowing much,
> Of quick intelligence, and sweet-tongued.

This Rustic had a wife whose face was the taper of his bedchamber, and her sweet vermilion lips were mellifluous like sweetmeats placed before the worshippers of wine; she was tinted with a hundred colours like fresh spring, and darted amorous looks with a thousand charms, like Fortune.

> Maybe her body sprang from a holy spirit,
> Since such grace and beauty were not within the bounds of water and clay.

The old Rustic, in spite of the skill which he possessed, passed his time in poverty and distress, and sowed the seed of reliance on God in the field, " *Consign the affair to the Almighty.*" The proceedings of treacherous Fortune herself is to disappoint the worthy and men of ability, while elevating to the summit of prosperity and power those who are void of worth and talent.

> She gives a harvest to those who walk perversely,
> Often refusing a leaf to the upright.
> She gives sugar and sweets to flies,
> Presenting the phœnix with nought but bones.

The old Husbandman, though celebrated for his perfect skill in agriculture, since he had no implements to carry on the same, passed his life in idleness and penury. One day his wife, from excess of poverty, loosed the tongue of imprecation, saying : " Till when shall we pass our time in the corner of this small abode, and spend our precious life in need and want of food ? Anyhow, enterprise is advantageous ; and though from the store house of benevolence, the free pass, ' *Support is from God,*' has been written, the royal inscription, ' *The industrious is beloved of God,*' has also been affixed to the corner thereof : therefore employment must be considered as the means of sustenance, and the true Dispenser, the Almighty Lord, must be recognised.

> Occupation is indeed the means of support :
> Your Divine Dispenser is the Causer of causes.

" It seems to me expedient for you to set your feet in the way of employment, and, in whatever way you can, obtain means of support." The Rustic rejoined : " O dear life ! what you say is akin to truth, and apart from any degree of suspicion or interestedness ; but I have a long time been Lord of this village, and most of the rustics of these lands have been my hired labourers. Now that my fields are ruined, and the implements of agriculture have passed from my hands, there is no help but to work for hire. However, I cannot reconcile myself to the disgrace of doing the work of my labourers.

> I cannot bring myself to eat the scraps of my dependants,
> Nor can I bear the burden of my workmen.

" But if it is necessary for me to make choice of work, it is best to pack up my chattels from this locality.

> In a strange country there is no rejoicing of one's enemies.

" Come, let us migrate to another place, and there pass our time how we can." The wife being in distress through anguish of poverty and indigence, consented to the misfortune of removing, and joining in intention with her husband, they turned their faces from thence to the environs of Baghdád. One day in the midst of the way, bruised and weary, they had taken shelter under the shade of a tree, and with a view of removing *ennui* had engaged in every kind of talk. The Rustic said : " O dear friend ! having made choice of the distress of exile, we are bound for a country where no one knows us, nor are we acquainted with anybody : it may be that the men of that region are haughty and tyrannical, or knaves and rogues. Now the Most High and Holy God having adorned the tablets of your incomparable beauty with the inscription, ' *Formed in the very best mould,*' Heaven forefend that with treachery and deceit, or with force and violence, they should plot against you, or that you, through the allurements of youth, and the hope of prosperity, should conceive a liking for them, and turning your head from the society of this poor old man, consume my venerable brow with the scorching blaze of the fire of separation ! If, ' *God forbid,*' this state of things should come to pass, I could not possibly exist."

> I do not dread death, but I fear
> That I may die, and you be the beloved of others.

The wife replied : " What language is this which falls from your tongue, and what idea is this which enters your mind ?

> As long as I live I will wait on you ;
> If I die, I am also your servant.

" If I had such thoughts as these I would not have made choice of the difficulties of travelling, and would not have placed upon my distressed heart the scar of abandoning my native soil. I wish the promise concluded on the first night wherein I placed my foot in the cell of your company, to extend till the day of Judgment,

> I will keep till the day of Judgment the promise I made with you,
> So that you may not say that on that occasion I was unfaithful to you.

" If you desire it, I will again renew the compact, and promise that so long as the peacock of the soul shall be resplendent in the garden of the body, I shall not sweeten the palate of the parrot of my tongue save with the sugar of gratitude .towards you ; and so long as the phœnix of life shall cast its prosperous shade over my head, I will not ensnare the bird of my heart in the meshes of any person. If, as regards the way of the eternal journey, I should go before you, I shall have discharged my obligation ; while if for some days my fate is respited, my promise is the same, no less than my oath."

> If for two or three days I shall be secure of life,
> My promise towards you is the same, and will remain so.

The Rustic was happy at these words: and his wife having given her pledge in the way which has been described, confirmed it with an oath : while the old man, easy in his mind, placing his head upon the knee of his beloved friend, went to sleep. Concomitant with this proceeding a Horseman arrived there, sitting upon an Arab steed, and clad in kingly garments. The woman looked and saw a young man such, that if the pupil of the eye had seen his face in dark night, it would have fancied that possibly true morn had risen from the veil of the horizon of the east; and if the eyes of men, in the curtain of darkness, had cast their glance upon his beautiful cheeks, they would have thought that the world - illuminating sun had become manifest and refulgent from behind the screen. His cheeks were like a verdant rose, and his beard like the writhing hyacinth : you would say that the all-wise Designer, with the compasses of Creation, had drawn a circle of fresh amber upon the pages of his face ; or that by the nurture of the Rustic, Nature, a heart-entrancing verdure had sprung from the regions of the fountain of life.

> You laid a club of musk across the glittering moon,[1]
> And drew the moon like a ball into the hollow of the bat.
> The tender down which is called Khizr (Khazar)
> Grew up beautiful upon the brink of the fountain of your life.
> You formed of your black hairs a beautiful canopy,
> Which you drew across the face of the resplendent Sun.

When the woman's eyes alighted upon that Horseman's perfect beauty, the Sovereign of affection overpowered the kingdom of her heart with the dominion of love ; and reason, which is the lord of the home of the body, packed up the chattels of departure, and the tongue of circumstance began to chant this song :

> " A Horseman arrived, and ensnared me, both heart and body.
> He broke the reins of patience, and the bridle also of the steed of the soul."

On his part, too, the young man looked and saw a beautiful woman, whose heart-ravishing face had been adorned by the Almighty Tire-woman with the cosmetic of grace, and the mirror [2] of whose cheeks had been rendered radiant by the Polisher of Divine Power with the light of beauty : her face was such that the radiant sun was consumed through envy thereof ; and ringlets such that musk of Khatá was mortally jealous of them.

> Her bosom like silver, in stature like a fir,
> Every part of her better than the rest.
> Your soul, by reason of her two eyes, would have been transfixed with an
>   arrow ;
> You could have eaten sugar to repletion from her twin ruby lips.
> You would say that her mouth was sweet as sugar—
> Sugar so delicious as to resemble the water of immortality.

The neck of his soul, too, became a captive in the chains of affection, and the foot of his heart ensnared in the mesh of love.

> Love led its armies, and my heart took leave of life.
> Patience fleeing, turned its head in the world.

This young man was a son of one of the Kings of that country ; he had come forth with the intention of hunting, and had separated from his attendants. When his eyes alighted upon the two ensnaring deer of that disturber of the city, and from the bow of her eyebrows a heart-piercing arrow reached the target of his bosom, though designing to hunt game, he himself was overtaken in the net

---

[1] These are the most unmanageable lines in the whole work. Eastwick's explanation of them is as follows : " The round face of the youth is compared to the moon : and his black ringlets to a bat used at the game of *chaugán.* These bats have a hollow in them to catch the ball more readily : so the ringlets are said to have caught in the space between them, the moon of his face. The down on his beard is compared to herbage growing near the water of life ; and as Khizr or Elias is said to have drunk of the water of life, occasion is taken for an *équivoque* upon his name, and *Khazar,* ' verdure.' " Stewart simply says it is impossible to translate them literally, or to understand them without reference to a dictionary.

[2] See note 2, page 51.

of love. He inquired : "O envy of fairies! and O high altar of the idols of Ázur[1]! who are you, and how came you here?"

> O ripened fruit! from whose garden did you come?
> O new-appearing miracle! in respect of whom are you?

The woman drew a cold sigh from her heart filled with grief, and said: "O wakeful fortune! do you ask me concerning the condition of my drowsy fate, or do you inquire after the story of my sleepless eyes?

> I have a secret, which is boundless;
> My heart has an ailment, for which there is no remedy.

The companion of my time is this aged man, and my disconsolate heart is allied to sorrow and vexation. The basis of the garb[2] in which I appear is such as you see, and the end of my circumstances such as you behold. I pass my life in adversity, nor have I any pleasure in existence." The young man exclaimed : "O desire of the heart of the sad! and O friend of the soul of the desolate!

> 'Twere shame that a royal hawk like you should be confined in a cage!

"Is it allowable that with such an enchanting face you should elect to be the companion of a decrepit old man, and with such a capital of beauty and elegance should pass your life in poverty and destitution? Come, so that having seated you upon the throne of honour, I may make you Queen of this kingdom, and exalt the banner of your dignity and respect in the expanse of this empire."

> Whatever has occurred during your former life, say Begone!
> Now is a new day, and new Fate.
> Come, let us enter in at the door of prosperity;
> Since Fortune advances merry, let us be joyous too.
> You must be glad of heart, so that I may part with my soul;
> You must be the cup-bearer, so that I may drink the wine.

The woman hearing the good news of companionship, forgot about the promise which she had so recently made, and with the stone of infidelity and bad faith, broke the goblet of agreement. When the boy saw that she had a liking for him, he said : "O soul of the world! the opportunity is advantageous; rise and come to me, that I may cause you to mount, and ere the Rustic is awake, we may traverse a long distance on the road." The wife, removing the Rustic's head from her knee, placed it on the ground, and quickly and briskly mounting behind the young man, stretched out the hand of reliance towards the girdle of affection for him. While these proceedings were taking place, the Rustic awoke, and saw the young man riding on horseback, and the woman grasping the hand of intimacy round the waist of desire after him : grief issued[3] forth from his heart, and he said :

> My friend bore away her heart from her friends,
> And removed her former affection from the midst.

"Holloa! O faithless woman, what design is this which you have planned, and

---

[1] Name of seven celebrated fire-temples formerly standing in Persia.
[2] Literally, "of my garments."
[3] بِرآمَد in the Persian text is a misprint for بَرآمَد.

what deceitfulness is this which you have mingled with treachery?" The woman rejoined: "Utter not alluring words, nor breathe enticing sentences, since to expect beauties to keep their promise is much the same as joining Canopus with the Pleiades; and to look for fidelity from heartless charmers, is like planting a rose-tree in the fire of a furnace. Maybe you have not heard—

> "I said, 'Learn the way of fidelity from the affectionate;'
> She replied, 'This matter does not appertain to moon-faced beauties.'"

The old man said: "You have placed your feet beyond the region of what is right, and opened the door of cruelty with the key of anguish of the heart, take care lest you be overwhelmed by retaliation for breaking your promise, and the disgrace of failing your word befall you."

> Act not thus, for you will quickly repent, and it will be of no avail.

The woman paid no heed to his words, and said to the young man: "Make haste, so that having found escape from the violence of the desert of separation, we may convey ourselves to the abode of companionship." The Prince with his swift-going, plain-traversing, sea-crossing steed, which the fierce north wind was tired of accompanying, and the velocity of which swift-encircling imagination could not unravel—

> Rose-coloured, and of beautiful appearance, like the tears of lovers,
> Roaming the world more than the famous steed of Khusrau,[1]
> With one bound, like lightning, it would
> Have leapt from the regions of the west to those of the east—

began to gallop in that plain, and in the twinkling of an eye they were lost to the Rustic's sight. The helpless old man, notwithstanding the disgrace of exile, and the anguish of separation, proceeded after them.

> The desolate ask the way, and follow after.

He thought to himself: "The promises of women are faithless, and their sincerity is not lasting.

> *'Banish the recollection of them, for they are faithless.'*

"Having relied upon her words, I have abandoned my accustomed native land and my regular abode; now I have neither face to return, nor path to pursue: so how will my affair end, and where will this matter of mine terminate?"

> I go round the world in pursuit of a sweetheart, without strength or power.
> What can I do? My affairs do not appear to have either head or feet.[2]

But when they had gone upwards of three farsakhs of the way, they reached a fountain, and the shade of a tree. The Mistress being tired, and the young man also showing signs of fatigue, they said: "Let us rest here awhile, and after refreshing ourselves we will once more proceed on our way." Accordingly, dismounting from their steed, they sought refuge under the shade of the tree; and sitting for a time at the brink of the water, they conversed on all that had occurred. The young man opened his eyes at the delicious sight of the elegant face and musky ringlets of that enchantress; and contemplating the locks of the

---

[1] See note, page 153.
[2] The state of his helplessness is compared to a person without either head or feet.

curling scented hair round the region of his friend's rosy cheeks, like violet petals upon the surface of the jasmine, exclaimed :

"The musky ringlets of your tresses have been bound upon your fair face ;
I do not know how they have joined day and night together."

And that amorous-glancing beauty, casting her eyes upon the heart-ensnaring form of that youth, who was a shrub in the garden of elegance, more verdant than the bough of the Tree of Paradise, and scanning the uprightness of that charming cypress, and the allurements of that merry-looking branch, recited this verse :

"How beautiful, O God, has the tree of your stature been formed !
O how a hundred thousand delicacies have been joined together !"

In the midst of this conversation the rustic's wife wished to retire, as she was anxious to perform her ablutions afresh.[1] In order to remove from his sight, departing from beneath the tree, she betook herself to the edge of the desert, which was nigh to the spring. Scarce had she arrived at the margin of the waste, when a ferocious Lion, from dread of whom the Lion in the fields of Heaven could not move a step, nor the Bull in the pasture of the Spheres, from fear of his claws, draw a breath,

Came on, screaming and furious.
The Lion of the Spheres from dread of him took to flight.
The wound of his poisonous claws caused water to flow :
The sword of his teeth produced a torrent of blood.[2]

As soon as the eyes of the Lion alighted upon her, he carried her away, and bore her off within the desert. When the young man heard the roar of the Lion, and observed his mistress taken towards the waste, he immediately jumped upon the back of a swift steed, and set out for the desert.

He saw the misfortune, and turned his face away from his friend.

The Prince, in fear for his life, galloped his horse, and looked not behind. The woman being seized in the claws of the Lion, reaped the seed which she had sown in the field of faithlessness.

Every one at the end of the affair will reap what he has sown.

At this time the old Rustic, who was creeping and crawling after them, reached the brink of the spring ; seeing no trace of them, he uttered a cry, and said :

"Alas ! my friend departed, and left my heart uncured ;
She gave a hundred or more promises, and did not fulfil one."

After he had thought of the time of their intercourse, and the condition of their union had passed through his mind, he lamented, and tears of regret ran down his cheeks.

Happy the day when we were in the mansion of the garden of intercourse,
When rose and nightingale had an opportunity for smiling and converse!

---

[1] The translation of this passage is not quite literal, as an exact rendering of the original text could not with propriety be given.

[2] حون‌ناب is more commonly spelt خوناب .

"Alas that the splendours of the rays of companionship have been changed for the darkness of the signs of separation, and the spring of happiness and ease has passed away, through the attacks of the cold wind of the autumn of desolation and anguish!"

> Yesterday there was such soul-exhilarating union,
> To-day this world-consuming separation.
> Alas that time upon the scroll of my life,
> Should one day write such as this, such as that the next!

After much lamentation and endless wailings, he saw the foot-prints of his mistress which led towards the forest. Without further ceremony following after, he reached a place where the Lion had torn her limbs, and after eating somewhat thereof had departed. The old man was distressed at the sight of this state of things, and perceived that the evil result of want of faith had befallen her, and that she had been overtaken with the retribution of perfidy and the punishment of fickleness. For a while he looked thereon, and wept through affection for her, and at his own separation.

> From his lips his lament reached the Pleiades,
> From his eyelashes his tears joined the sea.

"The moral of this story is, that whoever lets the end of the thread of fidelity slip from his hand, will have placed the cords of punishment upon the feet of his heart, and thrown the collar of calamity round the neck of his soul."

> Wherever want of faith deposits its chattels,
> In the end it renders that place desolate.

The Mouse said: "I know that hypocrisy and stratagem have no connection with the friendship of the magnanimous, nor the ways of the great. The advantages of your affection and the benefits of your devotion having at this very time reached me, and the aims of my enemies having been crushed by the blessing of your friendship, it would be more consistent with generosity for me to deem it requisite to make returns for this, and to loose your bonds. But a thought has occurred to me, and an idea haunted me, and till the dust of this anxiety be removed from before the eyes of my deliberation, it is not possible that all your cords can be unfastened." The Cat said: "It appears that you are in dread of me, but as a matter of fact, I have made a treaty of friendship with you, and have read to you the scroll as to the disgrace of breaking faith; so deem it totally impossible for me to act contrary to my promises and pledges, and pass by the former enmity between us, seeing that the obligations of this new intimacy have removed the manner of previous hostility. As regards you, my expectations of fidelity and my anticipations of loyalty being confirmed, do not encompass yourself with the odiousness of treachery and deceit, and do not ruin or mar the beauty of your virtues, and the mirror of your good manners with the rust [1] of fraud and perfidy.

> Keep clear the mirror of the heart, for purity is always best;
> Do not violate your promise, for the habit of fidelity is in all cases preferable.

"A man of good disposition and kindly nature, by reason of a single glance of courtesy which he may behold on the part of any one, having placed his foot in

---

[1] See note 2, page 51.

the plain of affection, will push the edifice of his friendship and intercourse to the summit of the Spheres, and keep the tree of manliness verdant and luxurious with the dew of sincerity. If in his heart alarm and dread raise their heads, and the apprehension of suspicion occurs to his mind, having instantly eradicated all this, he will not any more allow the thought thereof to encircle the expanse of his imagination, more especially when a compact has been made, and confirmed with a solemn oath. You must consider, that the end of the faithless is despicable, and retribution rapidly alights upon the treacherous; while a false pledge renders desolate the fabric of life, and violation of promises in a little time overturns the basis of existence.

> Since man is a tree, and its root a promise,
> The root must be nurtured.
> A faithless pledge is a rotten root,
> Which should be cut off from the number of the sound.
> Breaking faith and word is the part of a fool;
> Fulfilling a promise, and fidelity, are the business of the pious.

" I am in hopes that, through the dues of faithfulness, you will pass over previous injuries, and not strive to violate the promise you have made." The Mouse replied :

> " Whoever, as regards being faithful to you, breaks his oath,
> May his heart and soul be afflicted with the wound of misfortune !

" But what I told you respecting my anxiety of mind keeps me hesitating and reflecting, otherwise, God forbid that I should not fulfil my pledge, or that I should not free you from these meshes ! " The Cat said : " Repeat to me the purport of your ideas, so that I too may scan it with the glance of deliberation, and discover the degree of your wisdom, and the measure of your knowledge. The Mouse rejoined : " My idea is this—friends are of two kinds: first, those who in perfect sincerity and entire devotion, and inclination of heart, are disposed towards affection and love, without admixture of self-interest or greed, and without the evil of hypocrisy or dissimulation; secondly, those who, through necessity, or by way of covetousness and avidity, adopt a course of friendship. The first set, who by the purity of their faith and the sincerity of their designs, open the doors of friendship, are in all cases worthy of confidence, and at all times one may live secure with them, and whatever delight they may exhibit, they will never swerve from the path of knowledge.

> A friend is an ease-giving salve ;
> In other case, quit the converse of the worthless.
> As regards your poison, will not your friend esteem it as sugar ?
> And will not your ally reckon your faults as merits ?

" But as concerns those who, of necessity, have made friendship a shield to ward off calamities, or have rendered it the medium of gaining and acquiring benefits, their condition will not be of a uniform tenor. Sometimes at the period of mirth they will spread the carpet of joy, and on other occasions in the dread spot of opposition they will look at a friend with a glance of unkindness.

> Sometimes they profess friendship, as it were milk and sugar ;
> Sometimes they display enmity more relentless than the arrow or axe.

" A wise man always defers some of such a person's needs, and does not all at once abandon the reins of his own power to the palm of his authority; nay, more, he seeks to hold back from finishing the matter by means of pleasant excuses, and proceeding by degrees, brings the case to an end. He looks also to himself, since self-protection is incumbent in every case. When he proceeds in this manner he both becomes celebrated for the glory of his generosity, and also is renowned for the abundance of his judgment and knowledge. I am behaving towards you in the manner indicated, and I will not by any means stay my hand from releasing you, as I have pledged myself. But as regards the preservation of my own soul, and the protection of my own person, I will also use my utmost endeavours, since my antipathy towards you is more than towards that set from whose designs I have found safety, owing to your protection. I considered it imperative to agree to terms of peace with you, with the view of thwarting them and keeping them off, and the courtesy also which was observable on your part was on the ground of temporary expediency, so as to ward off calamity. Now it is incumbent upon me to look to the end of the matter, and not all at once to abandon the way of caution and forethought, for it has been said :

> ' Labour to make your own matters sure :
> Forget not the canons of wisdom.
> Whoever places his affairs on a sound basis,
> Makes the edifice of wisdom flourish.' "

The Cat said : " O Mouse ! you are extremely clever and wise, and I did not know you were prudent to such a great degree as this, nor did I recognise to this extent the amount of your talent and merit. You have caused me benefit by these words, and given over to my hands the keys of the doors of experience and sagacity. Now I desire you to show me in what way both my cords may be loosed, and you may also remain in safety, and to describe in what manner this can be accomplished." The Mouse, smiling, said :

Wherever there is disease, there is an appointed remedy for the same.

" My idea is this, that I should sever your cords, but keep one knot, which is the foundation of the fabric, as a pledge for my own life, and should seek an opportunity when your own business is more pressing upon you than any designs against me, and you are unable to attend to me, and when there is no chance for you to molest me. I will then also loose that knot, so that you may find freedom from your meshes, and I, too, from any calamity." The Cat perceived that the Mouse was thoroughly master of his business, and would not be turned aside through treachery or fraud. Having no option, he agreed to that suggestion, and the Mouse severed the bonds, but left untouched one, which was the key to the rest. They passed the night in telling stories. As soon as the phœnix, Morn, came flying across the horizon of the east, and spread its light-giving wings over the regions of the world—

> The firmament drew from its sheath the sword—the sun ;
> Dark Night gathered up its skirt—

the Hunter appeared from afar. The Mouse said : " Now is the time for me to discharge my promise, and to thoroughly fulfil my engagements." When the eyes of the Cat fell upon the Hunter, deeming his own death certain, he expected to be killed. The Mouse then severing the remaining bond, the Cat, in fear of her life, forgot all about the Mouse, and, extending her feet, ran to the top of a tree, while the Mouse, escaping from such a whirlpool, crept into a hole. The

Hunter, seeing the cords of the net broken, and the knots severed, astonishment overpowered him; and bearing off the *débris*, he returned full of despair. A time elapsed, when the Mouse, putting his head out of the hole, saw the Cat afar off. He was frightened to go near her. The Cat cried out:

> Do not pretend not to see me, when you are looking at me.

"Why do you avoid me, and why do you think proper to shun me? Are you not aware that you have gained a dear friend, and obtained for your offspring, your relatives, your companions, and your friends a precious store. Come forward that I may make good returns to you by my own considerate treatment, and you may behold, in the most befitting way, the recompense of your manliness and generosity. I do not know with what words to express my apologies for your kindness, or with what explanation to return thanks for your goodness and favours."

> I am both open-faced and ashamed, both rejoiced and grieved,
> That I cannot discharge my obligation for this favour.

The Mouse, none the less, stood upon the edge of the carpet of separation, and remaining on the outskirts of the expanse of companionship, turned his face towards solitude and loneliness, and drew the inscription of this saying upon the volume of thought—"*This is an age of transgression, not a season of gratitude;*" and in tones of sadness exclaimed: "How beautifully has it been said:

> 'It is an age when, from the excess of injustice therein,
> It is not possible for any one to have life or property.
> How can we view with satisfaction the honour therein,
> When, if a person does no injury, it would be considered the excess of kindness?'

"It occurs to my mind, that it is a time for retirement and a season for repose. Henceforth I will not be friends with any one, and will abandon the habit of intercourse with the fellow-creatures of my day."

> If any one seeks me as a companion, let him be his own comrade.

The Cat rejoined: "Do not so, nor withhold your presence from me. Do not waste the rights of friendships, nor the honour of intimacy; since whoever, after acquiring an ally through much labour without cause readily allows him to pass from the circle of affection, will remain destitute of the results of friendship, and other companions, being hopeless of him, will abandon love for him.

> Deem him a bad man who has few friends,
> But worse is he who, having acquired them, has lost them.

"You have laid me under a vital obligation to you, and by your blessing I have acquired the boon of life. The promise of affection which I have made will be safe from the chance of alteration, and the compact of friendship to which I have agreed will be secure from the danger of decline.

> The breeze of fidelity and former promises can be inhaled,
> Till the day of Judgment, from every rose which grows in my composition.

"So long as my life lasts I will not forget your dues, and as regards the matter of requiting your actions, I will devote my efforts as much as possible to be kind and generous."

Thanks for your kindnesses, which are like roses around you:
Am not I a lily, proclaiming them with a hundred tongues?

Although the Cat uttered speeches in this manner, and adduced strong asseverations, desirous of removing the veil of separation from their midst, and opening the way of intercourse, assuredly it was of no avail, and the Mouse replied: "Whenever there is accidental animosity, it may be removed by mere sociability and courtesy appearing on both sides, and in such case cheerfulness and intercourse cannot be reckoned as defects; but when enmity is inherent, though to appearance the edifice of friendship is reared aloft, it cannot be relied upon, nor should a particle of care and caution be omitted, since the evils thereof are great and the end disastrous. It is therefore better that, since there is no connection of kinship, you should remove your heart from companionship with me; for I myself, in the depths of my soul, flee from your acquaintance, and whoever associates with an alien will meet with that which befell the Frog." The Cat inquired, "What was that?"

STORY III.

He said: It has been related that a Mouse had taken up his abode upon the brink of a spring, and had made his home at the foot of a tree. A Frog, too, lived in the midst of the water, and sometimes used to come to the edge of the fount to get air. One day, reaching the brink of the water, he croaked forth heart-piercing sounds, and making himself a thousand-trilled nightingale, with his unpleasant voice, freed the birds of the hearts from the cages of their bodies.

Though he had a heartrending unpleasant voice,
Yet his manner and performance were more truly hideous.

At the same time the Mouse was occupied singing in a corner of his abode. As soon as he heard the Frog's strife-exciting strains, he was perplexed, and came out with the intention of observing the singer. Busy hearing the Frog's cadences, he struck his hands together, and shook his head. The Frog was pleased with these proceedings, which appeared like expressing approbation, and he proposed to make friends with the Mouse. The tongue of wisdom forbade him to associate with one not akin, while the vanity of his disposition impelled him to be intimate with the Mouse. In short, having met in concord, they used constantly to associate together, and recite heart-entrancing tales and stories to one another.

With hearts as chessmen, they played together,
And cleared their breasts of apprehension;
The Frog used to come joyous of heart to the Mouse,
And recount the story of five years.
Readiness of speech is a sign of friendship in the heart,
But backwardness to talk shows want of affection.

The Mouse one day said to the Frog: "I have at times desired to tell you my secrets, and proclaim the griefs which I have in my mind, while you at that very period remain located under the water.

It is difficult for me to come where you are,
While here where I am a thousand troubles are in my mind.

"Though I shriek aloud, owing to the noise of the water you do not hear; and though I utter cries, by reason of the croaking of other frogs, they do not fall on your ears. A plan must be settled, so that when I come to the brink of the water you may be apprised thereof, and without my making any sound, you may learn of my approach." The Frog rejoined: "You say truly; and I, too, have often thought, that if my friend should come to the edge of the water, how could I, at the bottom of this spring, be aware thereof? and how discharge the obligation placed upon me through the anxiety he undergoes to see me? Sometimes, too, I also come to the door of my hole, while you have gone in another direction, and I am a while expecting you. I was desirous in this respect of introducing this matter in some degree to you; however, you yourself, with the kindness which you possess, have brought the case to notice, and with inward purity have made clear the secrets of my mind, now the deliberation respecting this affair appertains to you."

Your brilliant genius will devise all that is good.

The Mouse said: "The thread of a design has come to my hands, and so it appears expedient to me, that I should produce a long cord, one end of which I should fasten on your foot, and tie the other on my own leg, so that when I come to the edge of the water and shake the string, you may be apprised of my proceedings, while if you also arrive at the door of my cell, when you move the thread I may be informed thereof." It was arranged in this fashion on both sides, and the knot of affection was securely fastened by this cord; and they were always, too, aware of the state of affairs. One day the Mouse came to the brink of the water, so that having summoned the Frog he might lay the foundation of companionship. Suddenly a Crow, like an unexpected calamity, alighted from the air, and carrying off the Mouse, set out aloft: the thread which was on the Mouse's foot drew up the Frog from the bottom of the water, and since, moreover, the end of the cord was firmly fastened to his leg, he went into the air head downwards. The Crow proceeded with the Mouse in his beak, and lower down the Frog hanging head downwards. Some men saw this strange sight, and by way of taunt and gibe said: "What extraordinary affair is this? The Crow, contrary to his wont, has hunted a Frog! never was a Frog the prey of a Crow." The Frog cried out: "The fact is, the Frog is not the prey of the Crow, but rather, owing to the disgrace of keeping company with the Mouse, has been overtaken with this misfortune. And any one is deserving of a thousand times such as this who associates with those not of his own race."

O Alas! for the friend of dissimilar race, Ō alas!
Seek a good companion, O ye great men!

"The object of reciting this tale is this: that a person must not associate with those of a different kind, so that he may not, like the Frog, be suspended by the thread of misfortune. I myself have no intention of mixing with my own kith and kin, so what will occur as regards strangers?"

Seek retirement, and be far from this expanse;
Be yourself the comrade of your own people.
Through retirement the phœnix became the monarch of birds.
It is but a single bird, but is designated as if it were thirty.[1]

---

[1] The dissyllable سیمرغ if treated as two words would mean "thirty birds."

The Cat said : "Seeing that you have no idea of being intimate with me, why did you, at the commencement, display all that politeness ? By your show of love and deceptive manners, you have ensnared me, and now that my feet have been bound in the net of friendship, you sever the thread of intimacy, and keep apart."

> O cup-bearer! you opened the lid of the goblet in sincerity,
> When I became intoxicated you laid the vessel out of my hand.
> Seeing that you intended ultimately to present the anguish of separation,
> Why did you give me at first pure wine ?

The Mouse replied : "At that time I had need of you; and a wise man, if he meets with trouble—deliverance from which is to be anticipated through the efforts of an enemy—will assuredly resort to courtesy, and strive to make show of traces of affection ; but afterwards, if evil is to be apprehended, he will retire from companionship. This is not on account of enmity and obstinacy, nor by reason of disgust and haughtiness. Just as young animals who run after their mothers to get milk, when they have done drinking milk, without any former animosity withdraw from their mothers' society, and no wise man would impute this to enmity; but when benefit ceases it seems better to abandon a person's society.

> When a person occasions benefit,
> The sight of him affords delight of heart and soul :
> While if advantage cannot be derived from a man,
> His company will produce misery even in this world.

'Again, the origin of the enmity between you and me is through the enmity of our natures, and the report of our hostility has spread about, and is fixed in our dispositions. No great reliance can be placed upon a friendship which may have arisen through necessity, with the view of meeting a need, nor can any great weight be attached thereto ; since when the occasion passes from the midst, assuredly things will revert to their original state. Just as water, so long as you hold it over the fire becomes warm, but when taken off the flames it gets just as cold as it was before. Every one knows that a mouse has no more destructive enemy than a cat; and I have no other feeling regarding you, save that you are anxious to prepare for breakfast a potion from my blood, and make my flesh available for your early banquet. By no interpretation can it be fitting that I should be deceived by you, or that I should be aided and assisted by your friendship."

> When did a mouse have a maternal affection for a cat ?

The Cat said : "Do you speak these words in earnest, or in fact are you jesting and joking ? " The Mouse replied :

> In matters affecting one's life, what place is there for jest ?

" I speak these words in all seriousness, and am confident that it is safer for a powerless one like myself, to shun the society of a mighty being like you. A helpless man should avoid the company of strong enemies ; since, if the contrary to this takes place, a wound will befall him, which will not be healed with any salve.

> Whoever is inferior, and contends with his superior,
> Will so fall, that he will never rise up again.

"Now I deem it for the present expedient for me to be filled with suspicion of you, while you must be cautious of the Hunter, and henceforth between you and me the purity of faith will be respected, and the edifice of intercourse is best placed upon identity of spirit, and intimacy of soul.

> Since between you and me is community of soul,
> What difference does it make if we be physically separated?

"Matters must be confined to this, for intercourse is impossible, and the point of union is beyond the circle of talk or argument." The Cat began to be distressed, and made signs of lamentation, mingled with tears, and groans, combined with anguish of breast, and said:

> "If friends be severed with the sword of disappointment,
> Since such is the way of the spheres, what power have I?
> Look! how the soul is separated from the body!
> When a friend is the soul, the parting is a thousand times more harassing."

With these words they bid adieu to one another, and each one set out to his own abode. To a wise, enlightened-minded man the moral of the story is this: The opportunity of making terms with an enemy in time of need must not be lost, and after attaining one's object one must not be negligent in observing the way of circumspection. Thank God! the Mouse, notwithstanding his helplessness and weakness, when various calamities encircled him, and powerful enemies and strong foes gathered round him, holding his own by the minutiæ of subtlety, drew one of them into the net of companionship, and by means of that one's affection, became secure from the ruin of the torrent of misfortune: at a fitting time, too, he discharged his promise, and observed the way of caution and prudence. If men of wisdom and intelligence, and the possessors of understanding and ability, were to make these experiences the model for their own designs, and in the performance of their affairs were to set this example as their guide, assuredly the beginnings and endings of their proceedings would be joined to and linked with additional success, while happiness in this world, as well as honour in that to come, would attend and await their auspicious fate.

> Whoever make men of wisdom their guide,
> In no case will misfortune befall them.
> When the dust of calamity is laid with the water of experience,
> The grit of adversity will never settle on a person's beauty.
> If the edifice of eminence be based upon the foundation of caution
> No injury will reach the degree of its majesty and dignity.

BOOK VIII.

ON AVOIDING THE MALEVOLENT, AND NOT TRUSTING THEIR FLATTERY.

INTRODUCTION.

HE world-adorning King said to the radiant-minded Seer:

> O thou! like the latter Morn, from head to foot sincere and pure:
>
> O thou! like soundest Wisdom, from top to toe excellent and able.

"With description, exempt from the reproach of error, and narrative free from the quality of doubt or suspicion, you have given an account of one who was surrounded by overwhelming enemies and powerful foes, and who found in no direction a way of flight, nor was any passage of escape imaginable, yet he sought aid from one of them, and arranged a compact of peace, so that by the help of that person's assistance he delivered himself from the injuries of the rest, and became secure from danger, dread, alarm, and calamity: how in these circumstances he faithfully discharged his promise towards his enemy, by whom, also, his own soul was protected: and how, by the blessing of caution and the auspiciousness of wisdom, he reached the shore of success and victory from the whirlpool of misfortune. Now I request you to repeat a tale of the malevolent and quarrelsome, whether it is better to avoid and shun them, or more expedient to be merry and associate with them. If one of them makes display of kindness, and pretends to be courteous, must any regard be paid thereto, or must absolutely no place in the mind be given to the same?" The Brahman said:

> O thou! far seeing, from earliest experience, like intellect.
>
> O thou! subtle, from the commencement of creation, like wisdom.

"Whoever is aided by the grace of the Holy Spirit, and is beholden by the assistance of perfect wisdom, assuredly will deem the utmost circumspection necessary in his affairs, well recognising the places of good and ill, and the occasions of advantage and harm. It will not be concealed from him that to avoid vexed friends or incensed companions is nearer allied to safety, and to shun the treacherous ambuscades of the malignant, and the deceitful evils of those who sell barley and show wheat, is the cause of security from danger. Especially when he sees with the eye of wisdom internal changes and loss of confidence on their part, and observes with the glance of experience suspicions in their heart, and alarms in their mind.

> When your enemy is vexed, rest not secure;
> For he who is injured will strive to injure.
> Though at first he comes forward pleasantly and joyous,
> At last you will undergo much pain at his hands.

" Whenever any one recognises signs of enmity on the part of a foe, it is incumbent not to make him appear a recipient of confidence,[1] and not to be deceived with his smooth language and agreeable conversation. Nor must the way of wisdom, caution, and prudence be neglected, since if anything contrary to the above line of conduct proceeds from him, the soul will have been made the target for the arrow of misfortune, and the fire of calamity have been raised in the expanse of the breast.

> To rest secure from an enemy is fraught with much evil;
> He who sows the seeds of negligence will reap the fruit of anguish of heart.

" Of all the tales in this respect which have been inscribed upon the volume of the minds of those endowed with understanding, the story of Ibn-i-Madín and the Lark possesses the utmost beauty, and the greatest perfection." The King inquired, " How was that ? "

---o---

STORY I.

He said : It has been related that there was a King, by name Ibn-i-Madín, of exalted ambition, and enlightened judgment. By the efforts of the architect Dignity, he raised the lofty palace of sovereignty to the vault of the constellation Virgo and Arcturus ; and by the aid of the geometrician Majesty, he caused the capacious edifice of his greatness to pass beyond the summit of the sky of skies.

> A Monarch of the starry host, a King fortunate as Jamshíd ;[2]
> Exalted as the skies, the moon and sun being his throne.

He had a great affection for a bird called a Lark, who possessed the most perfect beauty, and a heart-enchanting song, combined with lovely appearance and exquisite form. The King used constantly to talk to her, and was charmed with her sweet responses and delightful warblings.

---

[1] I am rather doubtful as to the accuracy of this rendering.   [2] See note 1, page 12.

> Elegant soft words are pleasant,
> Sweet tales are very charming.
> Whoever is endowed with such,
> Is approved of great men and kings.

It chanced that the Lark laid her eggs in the King's palace, and produced a little one. The King, from excess of love, ordered that she should be carried to the women's apartments, and enjoined the attendants to use their best efforts to look after her and the young one. That very day there was born to the King a son, on whose brow the light of majesty shone forth, and on the page of whose condition the rays of happiness glistened.

> A moon risen in the summit of the sphere of perfection;
> No one during a thousand years ever saw such a moon.
> Happy-omened, enlightened-minded, of blessed steps,
> Of angelic appearance, prosperous fate, and auspicious destiny.
> From that rare form the rose-garden of the kingdom became verdant,
> Just as the rose-leaf is refreshed by the north wind.

In like manner as the Lark's little one grew up, the Prince also increased in strength and stature, and they conceived a great affection for one another. The King's son used constantly to play with that fledgling, and every day the Lark used to go to the hills and wastes, and bring two specimens of fruit with which men were unacquainted, or which they could not obtain even if they had known thereof. One of these she used to give to the Prince, and made her offspring eat the other. The little ones being delighted with this, used to devour them with joy and avidity; and the traces of this bounty· were quickly visible in their strength of person and vigour of body, so that in a little time they grew greatly.

> They raised their heads through growing and increasing,
> Like a verdant meadow from the effects of the new spring season.

By means of this service the Lark increased every day in dignity and advancement, and from hour to hour her near position and rank waxed greater. Some days elapsed in this manner, and time inscribed many white and black pages of night and day. One day, the Lark being absent, the little one jumped on the Prince's breast, and with the talon of severity scratched his hand. The fire of rage being aroused, cast the royal offspring into the whirlpool of hastiness and impetuosity, so as to throw dust into the eyes of his manliness and generosity, and give to the winds the dues of kindness and former intimacy. He seized the fledgling by the leg, and, twisting it round his head, struck it so hard upon the ground that it at once became as it were dust, and was annihilated on the rack of destruction.

> Alas that the stem of the fresh-bloomed rose,
> Should have drooped owing to the severe blast of autumn !

When the Lark returned, she saw her offspring slain. It was to be feared that the bird of her soul would fly from the cage of the body. From horror at this calamity, resembling that at the day of judgment, alarm overspread her soul; and from the occurrence of such a misfortune, the traces of distress took possession of her heart, indelible like inscriptions on stones. Raising her lamentations and cries to the mansion of the Moon and Mercury, she said :

" Alas that the collyrium of radiance no longer remains in my world-seeing
   eye ;
The leaf of delight and joy no longer continues in my sad heart ! "

After endless lamentations and countless groans, she thought to herself : " You
have raised the fire of this calamity, and you have sold the chattels of repose for
the uproar of adversity. You should have made your nest at the base of a thorn,
or on the top of a wall. What business had you to do with the Haram of a
Sultán ? and, occupied in rearing your own child, why did you busy yourself
with the care of the King's son ? Had you been content with your own nook
and provisions, you would not to-day have been overwhelmed with this misfortune. You should not be enraged at this circumstance. Sages have said,
' Helpless are the persons who remain in the company of the mighty, since the
reins of their honour are very loose, and the edifice of their fidelity extremely
weak : they always scratch the cheek of their generosity with the misfortune of
violence, and fill the fountain of magnanimity with the mire of faithlessness
and injustice : neither sincerity and friendship, as far as they are concerned, are
respected, nor have former service and the bonds of intimacy any weight or
worth.'

   In waiting on a person who does not recognise the dues of service,
   Waste not your time, for there is neither profit nor obligation.

" To ask pardon for offences, as is the nature of men of noble mind, is not considered allowable, and is prohibited, in the code of revenge ; while ingratitude,
which is the disposition of the wicked, is deemed permissible and lawful in
the canon of arrogance. Anyhow, what benefit can be derived from the society
of the mass, who are oblivious of former service on the part of friends, and what
profit can be procured from attendance on a set of persons who allow the ties of
disinterested affection to slip their memory ?

   'Twere a shame to include amongst the number of heroes his name,
   Who does not recognise the dues of intercourse on the part of friends.

" I have mingled with a body who, as regards their own affairs, deem as nought
the perpetration of great matters ; while, as concerns others, they think much
of the least negligence.

   They deem their own faults as virtues ; but none the less
   If you possess merit, they call it a great error.

" Anyhow, I will not lose the opportunity of retaliation, and the occasion of
retribution ; and till I wreak vengeance for my child on this pitiless, cruel,
bloodthirsty tyrant, who without cause slew his comrade, companion, associate,
and ally, and without reason caused the death of his playmate and intimate, I
will take no rest or repose."

   I will lay aside affection and pity,
   I will make my heated rage to boil.

She then ruthlessly darted at the face of the King's son, and dug out the world-
seeing eyes of that royal beloved object, and flying away, alighted upon a
battlement of the palace. The news reaching the King, he was grieved about
his son's eyes, and desired by stratagem to bring the bird within the snare of
Deceit, and confining it within the cage of Misfortune, to treat it in such way

as it deserved. Accordingly, coming beneath the battlement he stood opposite the Lark, and said: "O companion of my days! come down from aloft, for you are secure of life.

> If the hand of your musky ringlets did wrong, 'tis past.

"Now cease not converse with me, and do not cause the plant of my delight to wither." The Lark replied: "O King! compliance with your commands is imperative upon every one; but having a long while been wandering in the desert of consideration, I had arrived at this stage of thought, that the rest of my life I should not seek for the acme of my desires, and the summit of prosperity, save in the region of the King, and should not drive the steed of ambition save in the plain of attendance on his Majesty: and I had thought that, like the Pigeons of the temple of Makka, I might be happy and at ease under the shade of your favour, and labouring in the Holy Mountain of gene-rosity, might arrive at a degree of serenity. Now that they have allowed my son to be slain in the Sovereign's Haram, like a sacrifice for pilgrims, how can any desire to hover round this house remain to me? In spite of all this, did I know of any equivalent for sweet life, well and good; and I would enter the service of the women of the sacred Haram, but

> "When a bird has escaped from the net,
> Henceforth how will he be enticed with grain?

"Again, the tradition, ' *The believer shall not be stung from the one hole twice,*' is salutary: and it behoveth a wise man not to try the same thing two times, and not to be injured twice with the wound of the same animal.

> Have you not heard this proverb, which the wise have spoken?
> ' *He who tries what has been tried will repent.*'

"It is clear, also, to the enlightened mind of the King, that a criminal should not live in security, since if punishment in this life be deferred, yet eternal torment is to be expected; and if by the aid of good fortune he escape this, his children and grandchildren must taste the bitterness of the chastisement thereof, and experience the wretchedness of his degradation and crime: since the disposition of the world is surety for the quality of revenge, and the nature of Fortune embraces the attribute of retaliation. So the King's son conceived treachery towards my child, and from me unwittingly, nay, more, by way of revenge, ruin befell him. It is not possible for any one to drink a quaff from the cup of violence, and not be overwhelmed with the headache of misfortune; or to plant a tree of injustice in the expanse of practice, and not to reap the fruit of punishment and torture.

> The fool who sows the seed of the wild-gourd
> Must not expect the sugar-cane.

"Maybe the King has not heard the story of Dánádil [1] and the thieves, nor has it reached his ears how revenge overtook the robbers." The King inquired, "How was that?"

---

[1] Wise heart.

STORY II.

She said: It has been related that in the city of Rakkah was a Darwísh adorned with acceptable qualities and laudable disposition, and the plant of whose sayings and doings was decked with the flowers of excellent feelings, and charming manners. By reason that he had a heart wise in the subtleties of divine knowledge they called him Dánádil, and the inhabitants of that city liked him.

> He who has attained perfection in divine understanding,
> Is both a companion to the soul, and also a salve for the heart.

Once upon a time he set out on a journey to the temple of Makka and without companion or ally started on his way. A band of Thieves came up to him, and thinking he had much property with him, arranged to kill him. Dánádil said: " As regards the goods of this world, I have no more than provisions for my pilgrimage; if your desires are satisfied with such an amount, it is of no moment, take my property, and let me go, so that in reliance on God, and solitude, I may bring my travels to an end, and may apply the collyrium from the dust of the threshold of Makka to the extended eyes of expectation."

> I will go to its street, and bow my head at the threshold;
> I will make the dust of the earth before its door a collyrium for my eyes.

The pitiless Thieves paid no regard to these words, and drew their swords to slay him. The hapless wretch, in perplexity, looked in every direction, and, as is the way of the destitute, sought for a friend and helper: but in that horrible desert, and terrible and frightful waste, not a soul came into his sight, save only that a flock of Cranes flew over their heads. Dánádil cried out: " O Cranes! in this desolate spot I have been taken at the hands of tyrants, and save the Lord of the Invisible World, no one is aware of how I am circumstanced; seek vengeance for me from this body, and demand back my blood from them." The Thieves smiled, and said, " What name have you ? " He replied, " Dánádil." They rejoined: " Anyhow, your heart is unacquainted with wisdom; it is clear to us that you are an imbecile, and whoever is destitute of intellect it would be no great crime to kill him." Dánádil said: " ' You will see at the time the dust is cleared away.' In this respect I will whisper in your ears a little about revenge, and will bring to your gaze somewhat of retaliatory conduct. However, what idea of such matters have a band of whom the description, ' They are deaf, they are dumb, they are blind, and therefore will they not return,' is in accord with their natures ? "

> If a man of understanding has ears,
> These kind of words will fall pleasant on his ears.

Much as Dánádil spoke, the ear of their understanding was dull to listen to the words of justice, and the eyes of their experience did not contemplate the splendour of true beauty. They killed him, and bore off his property. When the news of his having been slain reached the people of the City, they were grieved, and mourned his death, and were perpetually anxious that haply they might find his murderers. At length after a while, at a religious festival, most of the people of the City on the day of the celebration assembled at the place for prayer, and the murderers of Dánádil also took up a corner in the assembly. In the midst of this an army of Cranes, rushing through the air, flew above the heads of the Thieves, and made such a noise that, owing to their cries and shrieks, the people desisted from their devotion and worship. One of those Thieves laughed, and by way of joke, said to his friend, "Assuredly they are seeking the blood of Dánádil." By chance one of the people of the City, who was near to them, heard these words, and giving information thereof to another, at that very hour the news was conveyed to the Magistrate. Being captured, after a little investigation, they confessed, and revenge for the blood of the innocent coming upon them, they were overtaken by retaliation.

> Who in all the world strung the bow of oppression,
> But himself became the target for the arrow of everlasting torment ?
> Who, in faithless times, planned the way of tyranny,
> But himself became a warning to the age ?

"Now I have adduced this story that the King may gather, that my offence in injuring the Prince, was in accordance with the demands of revenge, and the requirements of retaliation, otherwise how could a broken-winged bird have power for such a deed ? Since such conduct has been displayed by me, the decree of the ruler, wisdom, now is that I should not obey your command, and paying no regard thereto, should not go into the pit owing to the cord of deception and fraud."

> It is better for me to avoid the service of the King.

The King said : " What you have spoken is near akin to sincerity and rectitude, and replete with the benefits of wisdom, and the advantages of learning. I know that according to the decree, ' *The beginner is the most tyrannical*,' it was the fault of my son, in that he slew your child, without any previous offence on his part; so you by way of revenge, since ' *The retribution for an evil should be an evil alike thereto*,' made right requital. Indeed I am obliged that you did not proceed to kill him, but were satisfied with his loss of sight. Now neither are you inclined to feel aversion nor I to be cruel. At any rate rely upon my word, and do not vainly strive to keep distant, and avoid me. Know that I consider revenge amongst the defects of mankind, and deem forgiveness as one of the merits of the generous. I will never raise the hand of rejection against the brow of merit, nor will I turn the face of approbation towards crime. Nay, more, my wish is to requite evil with good, and if ill befall me at any one's hands, in return for the same I will confer benefits upon him."

> We will not make it our custom to seek pretences ;
> We will act in no way but as upright and honest.
> As regards those who behave wickedly towards us,
> Even if we have the opportunity, we will only behave kindly.

The Lark said : " For me to return will never be possible, since wise men keep aloof from the society of friends who have been distressed, and it is proclaimed amongst the observations of the learned, that however much men may deem it necessary to be kind and pleasant to those who have been hurt, and may consider it indispensable to be beneficent and conciliatory towards them, suspicion and aversion must be predominant ; and on this supposition it is necessary to avoid them."

My beloved ! when you have injured any one,
Do not display him kindness even if you can :
Since, however much show of service he may see on your part,
Suspicion will predominate in his mind.

The King said : "O Lark ! cease such talk, since you are to me in the place of
a son—nay, more, beloved ; and the affection which I have for you I do not feel
towards any of my own kith and kin, and dependants : no one plots evil against
his own people, nor does he feel enmity or revenge towards his own associates."
The Lark said : "The wise, as regards relations, have uttered some words, and
described the condition of each one, and have enjoined in this manner, to wit—
. father and mother are like friends, brothers resemble companions and comrades,
and maternal and paternal uncles are of the degree of acquaintances ; a wife in
the place of associates, daughters correspond with enemies, and the whole of
relatives are of the order of strangers ; but a son is desired to perpetuate one's
memory, and is deemed part and parcel of one's soul and body, others not being
allowed to share with him one's regard and affection. Now I can never be to
you in the place of a son, and on the supposition that you were to hold me as
such, at a time of the descent of misfortune, and the attack of calamity and
affliction, you would desert me ; since, however much any one may like another,
and may say, 'I esteem you before my own self, and deem my soul of no
account,'

What is the soul that it should not be sacrificed for you ?

"yet at a time when difficulty occurs, and the matter reaches such a pitch that
life must be abandoned, without doubt he will drag himself from the straits of
that danger to the region of security, and will in no way scatter the coin of
existence on account of another person.

A hero should not flee from misfortune,[1]
But should rise above considerations of life on a person's behalf.

"Maybe the king has not heard the story of the old woman and Mahustí, nor
been apprised of the circumstances of their case ?"   The King said, "Repeat to
me what that was."

STORY III.

She said : It has been related that a decrepit old woman, aged and broken
down in circumstances, had a daughter, by name Mahustí, from the radiance of
whose resplendent cheeks the full moon was envious, and the world-adorning
sun sat in the rugged mountain of shame owing to the representation of her
heart-ravishing face.

Pleasant-voiced, so as to take away the senses,
And bear off splendour from the sweet-seller.
Coquetting, she raised a thousand tumults in the world ;
Ogling, thousands were ruined in the city.

All at once the evil eye of cruel fortune alighted upon that rosy-cheeked cypress,

[1] As remarked by Eastwick this couplet is misplaced, the purport thereof not being in harmony
with what immediately precedes.

and laid her on the bed of sickness. In the garden of her beauty, in place of
the yellow rose the branch of the saffron shot forth; her tender jasmine from
the heat of burning disease lost all moisture, while the curling hyacinth through
raging fever became limp.

> Like her musky-perfumed ringlets,
> Her delicate body became attenuated.

The old woman wandered round and round the head of her daughter, and supplicating and lamenting with her eyes like spring clouds, cried out: "O soul
of your mother! may your mother's life be sacrificed for you, and this broken-
down head, desolate in the corner of adversity, be dust at your feet! I will
make myself an offering for you, and will give up the half remnant of my soul
which I possess to secure your life."

> If you have pain in the head, then do as you like [1] with me.

Every morning weeping and sighing, she exclaimed: "O God! pardon this young
inexperienced creature, and take this decrepit, satiated old woman in place of
her."

> Whatever there is of my life, at once
> Take, but prolong her existence.
> Though from grief I am become like a hair,
> May not a hair of her head be lost!

In short, the old woman, by reason that she had motherly affection and maternal
sympathy, day and night laboured in prayer and lamentation, and gave up her
own life for her beloved child. By chance, a Cow belonging to that old woman
had returned from the desert, and gone into the kitchen; from the odour of
some broth, she put her head into a pot, and ate what was therein; when she
wanted to pull her head out again she could not. The hapless Cow thus with
the pot on her head came out of the kitchen, and went from one corner to the
other. The old woman, at the time the Cow returned, was not in the house,
and knew nothing about this proceeding. When she entered her abode and saw
something in that form and shape wandering round the house, fancying it was
'Izráíl [2] come to take possession of the soul of Mahustí, she uttered a lamentation,
and, in the utmost distress, said:

> "O angel of death! I am not Mahustí,
> I am a decrepit, old, distressed woman;
> If you desire to take her soul,
> She is in the house, as you know;
> If you are concerned about Mahustí,
> Lo! take her, and leave me."

> When adversity was afar, she prized her as a beloved one;
> When she saw misfortune, she abandoned her.
> So you should know, that in danger there is not
> Any one more precious than one's own self.

"Now this day I am separated from all attachments, and am severed from
mankind. In your service I laid up so much provision, that the caravan of my
strength is loaded so as not to be able to endure any additional burden.

---

[1] Literally, "turn me about your head."   [2] The angel of death.

I fear that, as the frame is weak, it is not equal to this load.

"What animal can submit that the corner of his heart should be scorched with the fire of injustice, and the fruits of his soul given to the wind of destruction, or that the radiance of his eyes should be cast into the darkness of annihilation, and the delight of his existence removed? When I think of my dear son, who was the light of my tearful eyes, and the joy of my distressed bosom, the sea of regret, beating up into waves, casts the vessel of patience into the whirlpool of anguish, and the flame of the fire of perturbation, flaring up, all at once consumes the chattels of patience and restraint.

> I am one of those in the world who are surrounded with grief;
> No footing appears, how, too, can my feet reach the brink?
> I said: 'With patience the shore of the sea will appear:'
> But now, also, the vessel of patience and stability is wrecked.

"Added to all this, my life is not secure; and to be deceived with all this humility and soft flattery I consider to be removed from the way of wisdom. Consequently I recite the verse, '*Would that between me and thee there was the distance of the east from the west!*'"

> When intimacy embraces distress,
> Separation is better than such companionship.

The King said: "What proceeds from you, had it at the commencement been of a like nature, withdrawal and retirement from society would have appeared appropriate; but you now are acting by way of retaliation, and your conduct is due to revenge. The tongue of justice also enjoins the very same, and the ruler, Equity, in requital for such a deed as proceeded from my son, appoints just such a return. Therefore, what can be the cause of your withdrawal, and the reason of your aversion? At any rate call to mind that, before the birth of my child, you were the companion of my time, and the associate of my days; and when my son came from the secret recess of non-existence into the expanse of being, paternal affection demanded that at the sight of him cheerfulness should accrue to me. In these circumstances I made him your comrade, and by reason of your society and his company I passed my life in delight. Now that the malicious eye of fortune has brought ruin upon the pearl of his eyes, the pleasure which I had on seeing him is destroyed, but the happiness of your conversation, and the rapture of your voice and tones remain to me. Do not act so that all this too shall be entirely annihilated, and for the rest of my life I must retire to the house of the bereaved, and live in sorrow, vexation, anguish, and lassitude. The case of you and me is like that of the Minstrel and the King." The Lark inquired, "What was that?"

STORY IV.

The King said: It has been related that a King had a Minstrel of beautiful voice and sweet tones, who, by means of his heart-enchanting strains, brought the foot of wisdom out of its stirrup, and snatched the reins of self-possession from the hands of patience and restraint.

z

> One more melodious in voice and tones than him,
> This [1] crook-backed organ-player never saw.

The King was very fond of him, and was always charmed on hearing his heart-enchanting melodies [2] and joy-exciting strains.

> Listen to the sounds of the Minstrel, for his delight-increasing voice,
> With his tenor and base tones, like Venus, would have brought Saturn within
> the spheres.

This Minstrel used to teach a clever Slave, and kindly gave him instruction in playing and singing, till in a little while he surpassed his master, and his warblings and strains reached such a pitch, that the fame of his tones and songs passed the measure of imagination on the part of either understanding or fancy; and the ears of all, both mighty and humble, were filled with the sounds and tones of his performances and practice.

> With his heart-enchanting melodies,
> He rendered brisk the market of joy and delight.
> When he made the house resound with his lyre,
> Venus came back with both ears intent.

The King being apprised of the case of the Slave, generously patronised and assisted him, to a degree that he became an intimate companion and enrolled amongst his select courtiers; and the King was always fascinated with the Slave's charming songs, which were indicative of the miracles of the Messiah, and owing to the tones of his world-distracting lute, which raised fire within the hearts of lovers, conceived a hankering after the banquet of pleasure. A spirit of envy was aroused in the Minstrel's heart, and he slew the Slave, and conveyed the tidings to the King, who ordered the Minstrel to be summoned, and when he had been brought to the place of punishment, the Sovereign began in solemn awe to chide him, saying: " Did you not know that I am fond of pleasure? and my pleasures were of two kinds; first, in society with your playing—next, in private with the melodies of the Slave. What impelled you to kill the Slave and destroy half my joy? I decree that this very hour they shall cause you to drink also that very same potion which you made the Slave taste, so that no one again shall attempt such a rash act." The King's words brought to the Minstrel's memory a certain song,[3] and he said: " O King! I have done wrong, in that I have deprived the Sovereign of half his delight, but if his Majesty slays me, and destroys the whole of his joy, how will it be?" The King was pleased, and caressing him, delivered him from death.

" The object of reciting this tale is this: a portion of my joy and happiness of mind, owing to my child, has been lost; and you, too, are singing a melody of separation. It would seem as though the back of my hope had become bent, like the figure of the harp, and the bosom of my grief lacerated with the talon of remorse, as it were the soul of a lute. Ultimately separation between friends will of necessity occur; but, at any rate, do not now strive to bring about a parting, nor give from your hand the skirt of repose."

---

[1] Eastwick suggests that this alludes to the sky, but confesses his inability to understand the passage. I am, unfortunately, compelled to make a similar admission.

[2] دل آویز in the Persian text should be دل آویز و.

[3] Eastwick translates this " wit;" while not wishing to question the accuracy of such a rendering, I do not feel justified in adopting it.

> Do not estrange yourself, since you know that the Spheres
> Will themselves separate friends one from another.

The Lark said: " Enmity is concealed in the secret recess of the heart, and hatred remains hidden in the cloister of the bosom, and since it is not possible for any one to be apprised thereof, consequently what the tongue speaks is not worthy of credence, seeing that the tongue in this respect does not rightly express the purport of what is hidden in the mind, nor does explanation discharge the dues of integrity, as regards the meaning of what is hoarded in the soul. But hearts, in accordance with the saying, ' *Hearts are witness to each other,*' are just witnesses, and true testimony of one another.

> The heart alone knows the history of the heart's secret,
> But tongue and lips are not admitted into confidence.

" Your heart does not accord with what you say, nor does your language truly express what is in your soul.

> May a hundred lives be sacrificed for him whose tongue and heart are in
> unison !

" O King ! I thoroughly know the severity of your fury, and am well aware of the fearfulness of your punishment.

> You sometimes wound with the stirrups more severely than a mountain,
> And on some occasions you make an onslaught with your reins more furious
> than the wind.

" At no time could I remain secure from your might, nor for an instant could I find rest from the ruin of your power. I am not of that number to whom the Doctor said, ' Medicine for your eyes is more suitable for you than medicine for stomach-ache.'" The King inquired, " How was that ? "

STORY V.

The Lark said : A man came to a Doctor, and being distracted through pain in his stomach, rolled about on the ground, and, from the violence of agony uttered lamentations, and sought a cure.

O Doctor ! at any rate cure me, for the matter has gone beyond my hands.

The Doctor, as is usual amongst men of wisdom, who as a preliminary carry out the rules of the science of causes and symptoms, so that, after investigating the disease, a remedy may be propounded, which should be the occasion of a rapid cure, inquired of him, " What have you eaten to-day ? " The simple-minded man replied : " I have eaten some burnt bread, and with such food, which resembled a finger, the oven of my stomach has become inflamed." The Doctor commanded his servants : " Bring some medicine which will give brightness to the eyes, and increase the clearness of the sight, so that I may anoint this person's eyes." That individual cried out :

> Anyhow, is this a time for jest and sport ?
> It is a period of death, and loss of life.

" O Doctor ! put aside jest, and abandon raillery. I complain of pain in the stomach, while you would place a salve of gems on my eyes. What has an ointment for the eyes to do with a pain in the stomach?" The Doctor replied: "I wish to clear your eyes, so that you may distinguish between black and white, and may not again eat burnt bread. On this account the cure of your eyes is more necessary than any remedy for the stomach."

"My object in reciting this story is, that the King should not imagine that I am one of those who cannot distinguish between what is burnt[1] and what is fit, and cannot select what is raw from what is cooked."

> Thank God! as regards wisdom I am such,
> That I can discern between good and evil.

The King said: "Amongst friends many accidents occur of a kind such as has happened between you and me, and it is not possible that the road of strife between men should be completely barred, nor the way of contention and opposition closed. But whoever is adorned with the light of wisdom, and graced with the decoration of intelligence, will endeavour, according to his power, to quench the flame of discord, and, as far as he can, will cast the water of compassion upon the fire of rage, knowing that although it appears very bitter to drink the draught of pardon, yet the sweetness of delight is contained therein; and although it seems like poison to endure the distressing load of self-restraint, yet so doing comprises the antidote, joy."

> Give not vent to anger, since therein is misery.
> Quench your enmity, for therein is happiness.
> The splendour of lightning produces ruin,
> But the nature of the ocean is to swallow up.
> The bosom of the sea is never filled with dust,
> Though the rain makes it muddy.

The Lark rejoined: "This proverb is well-known, '*He who despises wrong-doing falls into mischief;*' whoever takes things easy falls into trouble. This arduous matter cannot be lightly undertaken, nor is it proper to treat contemptuously this important affair. I have spent my life in gazing on the jugglery of the deceitful spheres, and have wagered the moments of my time in contemplating the wonders of the treacherous globe. Assuredly from the stores of experience I have gained much benefit, and by the earnings of ingenuity, and the capital of intelligence and penetration, have acquired very great advantage. In truth, I have recognised that the sparks of choice and the flames of power burn up the edifice of promises and pledges, and the needle of the pride of prosperity sews up the eyes of modesty and fidelity with the thread of the pomp of tyranny; and when the Lion of royal might strikes the tail of revenge upon the ground, fawning and foxy cunning will avail nought. It is better that I should not indulge in a hare's[2] sleep, and dreading the nature of the leopard, like a deer, I should go towards the desert; since in no way can a weak antagonist contend with a powerful foe, just as that King in this matter recited a story about his enemy." The King inquired, "How was that?"

---

[1] The original text has a play upon sounds which cannot be preserved in English.
[2] See note 1, page 255.

STORY VI.

She (the Lark) said : In the kingdoms of Turkistán was a king, the phœnix of whose incomparable magnanimity spread upon the faces of mankind the shade of peace, and the wing of victory and success, and the fabulous bird of whose exalted standard extended the head of majesty beyond the nest of the peacock of the heavenly gardens. His perfect justice completely disposed of the affairs of state, and his universal diligence caused all matters of monarchy to be completely carried out.

> Khusrau,[1] crown-bestowing, throne-establishing !
> Scattering wealth over the top of diadems and thrones.
> As regards subduing worlds and protecting lands,
> The Solomon of his time, a second Alexander.

One of the Pillars of the State was overpowered with fear of mind, and turned his face from the King's sphere-like court, and using deceit towards one of the King's enemies induced him to declare war and hostilities. When the Sovereign discovered that the foe had turned aside the face of obedience from the holy place of submission, the temptation of rebels, and the wiles of the seditious, having found their way to the foundation of his confidence—and that with a head filled with rage, in the blackness of his lusts, he was raising ideas of sovereignty and power, and with a heart full of hatred, owing to former resentment, was seeking after dominion and advancement—he sent him a letter comprising kindly counsel, and an epistle embracing royal admonition. But the foe, inflated with excess of haughtiness and pride, paid no heed thereto, and, with the lasso of invitation, wherever he found a body of rebels to exist, drew them towards himself.

> He collected round him several scattered bands,
> Such as in the day of battle seek the fight.

In short, when the King saw that the medicinal draught of kindness could not cure their dense constitution, which, in truth, had entirely wandered from the highway of moderation, he sent a message to this effect : " You and I are like glass and stone ; whether you strike the stone upon the glass, or the glass upon the stone, in both cases the glass will be broken, and no harm will befall the stone."

" From the recital of this story the moral is this,—viz., it should become clear to the King's radiant mind, that I, too, am like the glass, and cannot meet the Sovereign's anger, which, like a stone, is firm and ruinous to his foes.

> O heart ! be not opposed to idols with iron hearts.
> You resemble glass, and are not a companion for an anvil.

" However much the King is disposed to be kind, and desires to console with the oxymel of apology the bile of alarm, yet in the code of wisdom it is forbidden to accept the excuses of the malevolent and envious, and it is an edict necessary to be obeyed, to reject and refuse the efforts for peace of men who are foes."

> From eloquent friends I have heard this advice :
> " Place no reliance upon the caresses of an enemy.

---

[1] See note, p. 153.

When your foe anticipates that he will ruin you,
Be not deceived, but do not shatter his expectations."

The King said: "It is not allowable, on mere suspicion, to sever intimacy or
overturn friendship, nor is it fitting through a whim, which is beyond comprehension, to overwhelm a companion with the flame of separation. It is not the
way of men of integrity to lay aside ancient acquaintance, and firm intercourse,
through a slight doubt, nor to let slip from the hand the cord of the promise of
friendship or the treaty of comradeship through a trifling alarm.

Such were your fidelity and promise; I knew it not.
Your vow of affection was hatred; how ignorant was I!
All the words you utter, like your own soul, are hard.
So harsh was your heart, but I was unaware thereof.

" Is not the quality of fidelity found in a dog, which is the most contemptible
in worth of all animals, and in station the most despicable? Why do you not
then draw back your feet from the expanse of faithlessness, and why do you not
discharge the engagement which you made at the time of our society and affection?"

Fidelity to your word is advantageous, if you could learn this.

The Lark said: "How can I lay the foundation of fidelity? In that direction
the pillars of loyalty are demolished, and the traces of good faith utterly annihilated. It is not possible for the King to smother the causes of alarm, nor to
avoid watching for an opportunity of revenge. So, now, when he cannot lay
hands on me by force and violence, he is desirous of drawing me by treachery
and stratagem into the grasp of retaliation. And the hatred which is implanted
in the minds of Kings is to be feared, since in the pride of sovereignty they are
addicted to revenge, and when they find an opportunity they will not on any supposition admit of palliation or excuse. Similar to hatred in the breast is dead
charcoal, though in that condition no effects are produced, yet when the sparks of
anger reach thereto, it flares up, and the flame of wrath springing up consumes the
world. The smoke of retaliation, which arises from the fire of the breast, has
dried up many brains and moistened many eyes. It is not possible, so long as
a spark of the charcoal of hatred remains in the grate of the bosom, for any one to
rest secure from the danger of the flame of rage."

When the flame of wrath is raised, it burns up both moist and dry.

The King said: "What a strange state of affairs! You in this matter incline to
one side, and desert the other direction. Why is it not fit that the preludes of
alarm should be exchanged for the auspiciousness of friendship, and the purity of
intimacy should appear after the foulness of enmity?" The Lark rejoined: " If
any one can completely discharge the observance of the directions of kindness,
and were to attempt to seek the satisfaction and repose of friends, deeming it
necessary to assist and help in procuring advantages for them, and to ward off
evils and misfortunes, it is possible that such alarm might be removed from the
midst: both serenity might be procured to the malignant, and also the timid
soul might be perfumed with the breeze of security. But I am too weak in this
respect to devise or make pass through my mind anything which shall cause the
natural feeling of malignity to lessen, or occasion the way of friendship and affection to increase. If I were to return to your service again, I should perpetually

be in alarm and dread, and every hour see death afresh. After this it is better to retire than to come back in such a manner, and preferable to exchange separation for return."

> When the roses of intercourse do not blossom upon the tree of Fortune,
> It is delightful in the desert of separation even for a thorn to pierce the foot.

The King replied: "No one has any power for good or for bad as regards another person without the will of God—may His name be glorified!—nor can anything, little or much, small or great, come to pass, save by the decree of Fate, and the previous eternal command. Just as the hand of the creature is powerless to create or reproduce, so also annihilation and destruction are denied him. The affair of my son and your retribution happened according to the Divine Mandate and the Eternal Will, and all this was but the means of causing that decree to be carried out. Do not call us to account for the decrees of Heaven, nor reproach us for the Divine Mandates, but be content with the Ordinances of God."

> Nought but submission to the Decrees of God is becoming.
> Nought but patience, at the time of misfortune, is suitable.
> Seeing that His Pen has flowed withdraw not your head; but otherwise, come,
> Go beyond His line, if you deem it fitting.

The Lark said: "The weakness of creatures in averting the decrees of the Creator is manifest and certain, and on the pages of imagination, amongst men of integrity, this thing is clear and plainly portrayed, that the varieties of good and evil, and the manifold sorts of advantages and disadvantages, are arranged according to the wish and the decree of the Almighty Will—may His name be glorified!—and it is not possible by any effort or endeavour on the part of the creature either to ward it off and repel it, or to hasten and delay it. '*There is no one who keeps off His decree, nor any one who retards His command.*'

> No one can breathe a word about 'why' and 'wherefore,'
> For the Designer of Circumstances is beyond 'why' and 'wherefore.'

"Notwithstanding that all sages are agreed upon this point, no one has said that the direction of caution and care should be neglected, or that the protection of one's soul from danger and misfortune should be delayed; nay, more, it has been declared that the causes of everything must be looked to, and the disposition of affairs left to the Causer of Causes.

> The Divine Decree enjoined that causes and ways,
> Should be incumbent upon those who toil under the sky.
> O thou! who art ensnared by causes fly not forth;
> Indeed, doubt not the Remover thereof is the Causer of Causes.
> Owing to causes, are you neglectful of the Causer?
> Can you turn aside your mind from the latter veiled mystery to the former?

"The proverb, '*Display wisdom, and trust in God,*' is an exemplification of this saying."

> Bind the camel's knee in reliance upon God.

The King rejoined: "The pith of this conversation is just this: I desire your society, and find in my mind a boundless hankering after your company; but in spite of all this eagerness which I display, nought can be understood on your part save tokens of vexation."

You are annoyed with me, while I hanker after you.
Hearts should yearn for hearts. What state of things, then, is this?

The Lark said : " Your desire is just this, to cure your own heart by killing me ; but the fact is, my soul at present has no inclination to drink the potion of death, nor any wish to put on the garments of destruction ; and so long as the reins of desire are in my hands, I refuse to accept all this, and it seems the essence of wisdom to avoid it.

The head will not again grow on the body, it is not like a cane.

" This very day from my own heart I can demonstrate as to the King's notions, since if I get the power and ability I shall not be content save with the death of the King's beloved one, so I know that my Sovereign also, owing to distress for his son, will seek nought but my destruction. Any one can understand the secrets of the mind of those overwhelmed with anguish, when he himself has been consumed with the fire of a similar grief, and swallowed the draught of bitterness on the same account. Easy-going adversaries are negligent of this state of things, and pampered persons, indulging in ease, are destitute of the trappings of grief.

O thou ! whose foot has not been pierced by a thorn, what do you know
As to the state of the Lion-hearted, whose head is struck with the sword of
misfortune ?

" With the eye of wisdom I perceive that whenever the King calls to mind his son's sight, and I think of the light of my own eyes, a difference will be manifested in our inward souls, and a change in our feelings will occur : it can be perceived what will proceed from this, and what matters will come to pass at this time. On this showing separation is more suitable than intercourse, and to keep at a distance more proper than to be near."

When intercourse is such, separation is better.

The King replied : " What good can there be in that person who cannot forgive the offences of friends, nor rise above ill-feeling and revenge ? A learned and truly wise man possesses power so to put aside retaliation for wrongs, as during the term of life not to refer thereto, no trace of their greatness or insignificancy being at any time found on the pages of his heart, while he accepts with the utmost joy the apologies of those who have done wrong, and the excuses of those who have acted improperly. ' *The worst of evil-doers is one who will not accept an excuse ;* ' that is, the worst of the bad is he who will not accept an excuse, and conceives dislike for him who tenders an apology.

An apology with me is the means of making amends for crimes.

" At any rate, as regards what I have said, I find my mind clear, nor do I perceive in my heart any traces of the violence of rage, the fury of anger, or the idea of revenge. I have always preferred pardon to punishment, knowing that however great an offence may have been, the quality of forgiveness will be greater."

If amongst the inferior crime is a great matter,
Amongst the noble, pardon is still greater.

The Lark said : " This is all very well, but I am an offender, and the person who has committed the crime is always in fear. My case is like that of a person who, having been wounded in the sole of his foot, if by strength of mind he evinces no alarm, and deems it permissible to go during the darkness of night in a stony place, yet it cannot be avoided that the wound is opened afresh, and his foot rendered helpless, so that he is unable to journey even on soft ground. My approach to the King's service bears the same aspect, and according to the rites of law and the canons of religion, it is an absolute duty for me to avoid this. ' *And cast not yourselves with your own hands into destruction.*' Sages have said three persons are removed from the path of wisdom, and apart from the highway of knowledge. 1st, Any one who relies upon his own personal strength; and assuredly such an one will cast himself to destruction, and his temerity will become his own ruin. 2d, He who does not recognise the measure of food and drink, and so gorges that the stomach is unable to digest it; such an individual is doubtless the enemy of his own soul. 3d, The man who is puffed up by the words of a foe, and is deceived by the talk of any person from whom he cannot be secure; and beyond dispute the case of such a party will terminate in ruin and remorse."

> Rest not secure from the stratagems of enemies,
> Reflect and turn your rein from such a quarter.

The King said: "O Lark! much as I enter in at the door of conciliation, and in a friendly way place before you the road of rectitude and expediency, you in like manner continue in your foolish ideas, and shake off the skirt of acceptance from hearing advice. Admonition as concerns any one who will not accept it, is without profit, just as the warning given by that Devotee to the Wolf." The Lark inquired, "How was that?"

STORY VII.

He said: It has been related that a Devotee of pious disposition, whose precious time after he had performed his daily devotions and prayers, was spent in nought save admonishing mankind, was passing through a solitary spot, and saw a Wolf with the mouth of greed and avidity extended, and the eyes of avarice placed on the road of search. All his ambition was fixed on injuring the innocent and depriving some animal of life, so as to bear off a portion thereof with the view of securing delight to his own refractory soul.

> If you regard that unjust tyrant, you will see that foolishly
> He inflicts a hundred miseries on a person, with a view to a single advantage
> to himself.

The Devotee who saw him in this condition, and observed on the page of his forehead the inscription of violence and oppression, out of natural kindness and innate compassion, began to counsel him, saying: "Beware not to circumvent men's sheep, and plot not against the oppressed and helpless, since in the end injustice is the cause of Divine retribution, and ultimately oppression draws down punishment and torture in the next world."

> He who indulges a habit of oppression,
> Places bonds upon his own hands and feet.
> Though for some days he may raise his head aloft,
> Fortune at length will overthrow him.

He spoke such words as these, and urged him to the utmost to abandon his cruel designs against men's sheep. The Wolf replied: "Cease your admonitions, for in the rear of this waste a herd are grazing, and I am afraid lest the opportunity of carrying off a sheep be lost, and then remorse will be of no avail."

"The object of adducing this story is, that much as I give you advice, you are intent on your purpose, and pay no heed to those words."

Hold! for the generous are ready listeners,
In an instant they pledge themselves for a thousand years.

The Lark exclaimed: "I have listened to your advice, and have paid heed to the monitor, Wisdom. I deem him wise who always opens the door of caution, and places the mirror of experience before him. I am come here through extreme fear and alarm, and wisely am standing at the end of the road of flight, and have got before my eyes a journey where no one will lay hands upon me, and for me to delay more than this would not be allowable, and to live in such anxiety and perturbation would be the cause of reproach. Since I know that the King deems my blood allowable, and that whatever is conceivable in the law of manliness he deems admissible, therefore for me to remain would be improper, and it is necessary for me to depart quickly."

I departed, for it is not good to be here longer.

The King said: "The means of support are ready for you here, and the doors of repose and ease opened to the face of your soul; to make choice of the anxieties of travel, and to be perplexed how to get food is not in any way desirable." The Lark replied: "He who makes five qualities a store for the road, and the capital of life, wherever he goes will gain his objects, and wherever he proceeds will obtain the benefit of acquaintances and companions. 1st, Putting away evil proceedings; 2d, Clothing himself in righteous dealing; 3d, Turning aside from the regions of suspicion; 4th, Sedulously striving to display a benevolent disposition; 5th, Observing at all times social manners. Whoever combines these qualities will nowhere be left a stranger, and the misery of his loneliness will be exchanged for the repose of intercourse.

A wise man is not a stranger in any city or kingdom.

"When a wise man cannot be safe in the city of his birth and native soil, and in the midst of his relations and kinsfolk, he must of necessity elect to separate from friends and connections; since for all these an equivalent is possible, but none conceivable as concerns his own self."

If in your native land matters are not in accordance with your wishes,
Be not, through folly, a captive in the house of negligence;
But travel, for you will not remain void of friends,
Wherever you go, and in whatever land you arrive.

The King said: "Till when will you go, and how long will you remain?" The Lark said: "O King! when I have departed, expect not that I shall come back, nor fancy that I shall return from this journey. This question and reply are very like the tale of the Arab and the Baker." The King asked, "What was that?"

STORY VIII.

She said: It has been related that an Arab of the Desert came to the City of Baghdád, and saw the shop of a Baker. Round cakes like the orb of the moon rose from the horizon of the shelves, and biscuits splendid as the constellation of Virgo and Arcturus placed their feet upon the top of the shop. The beauty of their golden appearance drew the claw of envy across the cheek of the sun, and anguish[1] at their crispness[2] rent the collar of the afflicted bread.

On the shelves of the Baker were warm orbs, such that you would have thought,
That it was the world-illuminating sun risen from the sky.
The oven of the Baker was like the fire in Abraham's case,[3]
Since thence every moment there came forth fresh bread like a rose.

In a word, the poor Arab, who at the odour of the bread found his soul revived, when he saw the face of the loaves rent the waistcoat of patience, and advancing to the Baker said: "O Sir! how much will you take to satisfy me with bread?" The Baker thought to himself, "This man will be filled with one man of bread, or at the utmost two mans, but certainly he cannot exceed three mans." He said: "Give me half a dínár, and eat as much bread as you can." The Arab gave the half-dínár, and sat down on the banks of the Tigris. The Baker brought some bread, and the Arab moistening it with water, ate till the value of the half-dínár was exceeded, and reached four dáng, and even that was passed, and a whole dínár was finished. The Baker could brook it no longer and said: '*O brother Arab!*' by that God who has endowed you with this miraculous power of eating bread, tell me till when will you go on eating the loaves?" The Arab replied: "O Sir! be not impatient; so long as this water flows, I, too, shall eat bread."

"The moral of this tale is, that the King should understand that so long as the water of life flows in the channel of the body, I cannot avoid eating the morsels of fear and dread, and I deem it impossible to derive benefit from the banquet-table of intimacy. Fortune casts separation between us, so that approach is not within the circuit of possibility, and time has caused the thread of our union to snap in such a manner, that the idea of intimacy is nought but a vain notion. Henceforth whenever desire impels me, I will ask news of the traces of the King's happiness from the morning breeze, and will see the Sovereign's perfect beauty in the mirror of imagination."

If intercourse produce no result, in imagination even I am happy;
There is no better taper than moonlight for the cell of the darwísh.

The King dropped tears of regret from the fountain of his eyes, knowing that this clever bird would not come to the net, nor would the intention of revenge strut forth from the secret recess of non-existence to the desert of being. Once again he commenced to scatter the grain of treachery, and put forward a variety of promises and engagements. The Lark said: "O King of happy fate,

---

[1] سور in the Persian text is a misprint for سوز.

[2] سنگبت means literally "cooked stone."

[3] Alluding to his being cast by Nimrúd into a fire, which was thereupon changed into a meadow.

who possesseth a glorious diadem and throne! however much you may prepare the edifice of beneficence, and offer various favours as regards security and safety, confirming the same with acceptable oaths and becoming attestations, it is not possible for me to place the ring of servitude in my ear, nor cast the covering of attendance over my shoulders."

Waste not your words any more, for they have no effect upon me.

The King perceived that he could not with the needle of treachery extract the thorn of alarm from the Lark's foot, nor with the strength of the arm of treachery could he bring to his hand the arrow which had left the bow-string. He exclaimed: "O Lark! I perceive that from the Rose-garden of intimacy nought but the perfume will reach the nostrils of desire, and the face of society will not display itself save in the mirror of hope.

> He has gone who was the very water composing the stream of joy,
> Or rather who shone forth radiant in the ringlet of desire.
> Alas that the time of delight, and the season of intercourse,
> Have gone, so that you would say it was but a dream!

"But I desire that by way of remembrance you will utter two or three sentences, the recital of which may cause traces of happiness to be visible on the leaves of time, and that you will with the furbisher of friendly advice remove the rust of negligence from the mirror [1] of my heart, which is darkened with the dust of distress."

> Say a few words to me as a remembrance of yourself,
> For no souvenir is better than suitable words.

The Lark rejoined: "O King! the affairs of mankind are arranged according to Fate, and no one has been given power to add thereto, or diminish therefrom, or to hasten or delay matters, nor can any one discover whether the royal superscription of happiness has been inscribed against his name, or whether he has been enrolled on the pages of the wretched. But it is necessary for every one to conduct his affairs according to the dictates of sound judgment, and to use his best efforts in observing the way of caution and circumspection. If his devices are in accordance with Fate, he will take his place upon the throne of prosperity, and the royal seat of dignity and majesty; while if the contrary should be the case, both friends will excuse him, and antagonists will find no opportunity for slander.

> The sage said: 'Fate is predetermined, it is true,
> Yet do not in any case omit your precautions,
> Since, if your plans accord with the decrees of Destiny,
> You will enjoy the result of your toils, according to the wish of your heart:
> While, if the contrary is the case, you will be excused
> By every one who is aided by the light of reason.'

"Again it must be known that the most useless of possessions are those from which no benefit is derived; the most careless of kings is he who takes no care to protect his kingdom and defend his subjects; the most despicable of friends is he who in times of distress and adversity quits the region of friendship; the most worthless of women is she who does not agree with her husband; the

---

[1] See note 2, page 51.

worst of children is he who refuses to obey his father and mother; the most desolate of cities is that wherein there is no security and safety; and the most disagreeable of friendships is that wherein the hearts of the associates are not in accord together. Since suspicion has occurred in the intimacy of myself and the King, it is fitting to abandon it, and akin to what is right to exchange the conversation of companionship for the discourse of departure."

> We departed ; with our hearts we must bid adieu,
> And with the water of our two eyes earth must be made clay.
> Have you experienced evil, yet you must say what is kind,
> And if your head aches it must be overlooked.

With these words the Lark terminated the discourse, and flying away from the projection of the palace hastened towards the desert. The King, biting the finger of remorse with the teeth of perplexity,[1] was somewhat sorrowed, and immeasurably vexed ; and, filled with anxiety and distress beyond the limits of comprehension, turned his face towards his palace, saying :

> "Where shall I proclaim it ? since with this heart-consuming pain,
> The physicians cannot cure my mind.
> How can I tell amongst my friends,
> That my companions so said, and acted thus ?"

Such is the story of shunning the treacherous ambuscades of the malignant, and avoiding giving any credence to their intercession and prayers; of not relying upon the hypocritical friendship of enemies, and of not being elate with the perfidy and deceit which they display with the view of seeking revenge. It will not remain concealed from a man of wisdom, that the object of reciting these speeches is just this, that a prudent person, as regards the accidents of the world, and the chances of time, considers every man as the guide of the path of salvation, and rears the edifice of his affairs upon the requirements of wisdom and deliberation, in no way trusting enemies, who have been injured, nor resting secure from the evils of their stratagem, and the dangers of their treachery.

> Would you desire not to be allied to grief and distress ?
> Then listen to words more pure than a precious pearl.
> "Be not indifferent as to an injured enemy.
> Nor rest secure from a haughty and malevolent person."

---

[1] See note, page 28.

BOOK IX.

———•———

ON THE EXCELLENCE OF PARDON, WHICH IS THE BEST ATTRIBUTE OF KINGS, AND THE MOST LAUDABLE TRAIT IN MEN OF HIGH DISTINCTION.

INTRODUCTION.

ÁBISHLÍM respectfully said to the perfect Sage, the pious Brahman: "We have heard the story of one whose heart would not be soothed by the coaxings of an injured antagonist, and who, when he saw the traces of enmity and signs of malignity remaining, though his foe strove to the utmost to be kind, would not deviate from the highway of caution. Now the fire of desire has been kindled within me, and till liquid from the spring of the ninth precept reaches my parched soul, the warmth of my heart will not be soothed. I have a firm hope that you will narrate a tale relative to kingly pardon and indulgence, and recite whether a monarch, when he observes on the part of those around him, after he has inflicted torture and punishment, evident traces of crime and iniquity, should once more caress them or not, and whether placing confidence on such a body, to restore them to their appointments would be in accordance with caution or not." Bídpáí, in heart-enchanting words, and soul-exciting terms, replied: "If kings close the door of pardon and compassion, and whenever they observe a slight offence, enjoin it to be punished, those round them will not have perfect confidence, nor again put faith in them. From this state of things two misfortunes will occur: 1st, Affairs will remain neglected, and in confusion; 2d, The offenders will have no share in the delights of pardon, or the favour of clemency. One of the great kings has said: 'If mankind knew what pleasure the palate of my soul finds in the taste of pardon, assuredly they would offer at my court nought but misdeeds and crime.'

Were the criminal to know this fact, that every moment
We are pleased in pardoning sinners,
Perpetually he would designedly set about attempting crimes,
Constantly he would seek pardon at our hands for his offence.

" There is no ornament more becoming the beauty of the condition of kings of
the world than pardon, and no clearer evidence of the perfect worth of the
mighty amongst the sons of Adam than lenity and compassion. The purport of
the miraculous speech of His Majesty, the Chief of Mankind—on Him be the
choicest salutations and greetings!—'*Ha! I will tell you who is the strongest
of you; it is he who subdues his spirit when in anger,*' pleasantly illustrates,
that a man's power may be known by his quenching the flame of wrath, and the
traces of manliness and heroism may be discovered by his drinking the distasteful potion of rage.

Think not that manliness consists in strength and valour;
If you overcome your wrath, I shall know you are perfect.

" The most excellent quality for kings is to make exalted wisdom their leader in
matters, at no time allowing their nature to be void of kindness, combined with
rigour. But compassion must be of a kind so as not to bear the impress of weakness,
while severity must be such as to be free from the blemish of oppression, so that
the affairs of sovereignty may be graced with the two characteristics of beauty
and pomp, and the centre of the kingdom may revolve upon the exercise of
dread and the glad tidings of hope, neither the sincere, through boundless favour
becoming in despair, nor the wicked, through fear of punishment, putting their
feet in the region of hardihood.

Jamshíd [1] kept his people
Perpetually in the midst of fear and hope.

" The sages of Islám—'*May God give them a good recompense!*'—have said:
'The Most High God has taught His people benevolent manners by the instruc-
tions of the Kurán and the admonitions of the Sacred Book, and inculcated
on them praiseworthy desires and acceptable qualities. Whoever are befriended
and aided by Divine happiness, and helped and assisted by Almighty Wisdom,
will make the decrees of His Kurán the temple of their hearts and the high altar
of their souls, and will constantly, with heart and soul, incline towards the sacred
sanctuary of that safe and sure precinct.' Of all the admonitions therein is a verse,
based upon the truths of the above-mentioned dictum (and its word is most high),
'*Who bridle their anger and forgive men, for God loveth those who do well:*' and
one of the chiefs of religion has elucidated the meaning of this verse as follows:
To stifle anger is not to punish with readiness, while pardon consists in the
traces of aversion being obliterated from the pages of the heart. Kindness is once
again to return to a friend who has done wrong but made amends. The substance of the verse is then just this: the edifice of men's proceedings should be
reared upon kindness and courtesy, humility and consideration being respected
in all matters; for it has passed into a true tradition that if clemency were to be
embodied in a form, the splendour of its beauty would shine and radiate in such
a manner that no eye would have power to look at it, and a more beautiful form
or more comely figure than it would never come into any one's sight. A wise
man, in one verse of this distich, has proclaimed this point.

[1] See note 1, page 12.

When God has given you power over a culprit,
Pardon him so that he may become your servant:
For a criminal is slain by his own deeds;
When he scents the perfume of pardon, he comes to life.
If the form of pardon were to assume a shape,
It would be resplendent like the Sun and Jupiter.

"Whenever this matter is properly cogitated, assuredly it will be ascertained that the dignity of mankind is increased by the virtue of pardon and condescension; accordingly, ambition must be confined to the diligent exercise of these two qualities. It is not hidden that a man cannot be free from negligence and carelessness, as well as crime and error: if in return for every offence punishment is inflicted, and in requital for every crime chastisement is administered, there will accrue therefrom complete ruin, which will overspread the affairs of State and Property.

Rashly to lay hand on the sword,
Will cause a man to bite the back of the hand of regret.[1]
The head which is void of reflection
Is deprived of having the Crown of Sovereignty.

"Again, it behoves a king to well recognise the extent of the sincerity, integrity, merit, and ability of any one who may happen to be accused, so that if he is of a class that the welfare of the kingdom may be advánced by him, or, in the occurrences of time, aid may be expected from his deliberations, the King should endeavour afresh to place confidence in him, and haste to patronise and advance him; deeming, too, that person's proceeding as free from defect and suspicion, he should restore the powers of such an one's heart to their accustomed composure by means of courtesy and conciliation. Since there is no end to matters of State, and the need, too, on the part of kings for able counsellors and reliable servants, who are worthy of being intrusted with secrets and deserving of full powers in emergencies, is assured, accordingly it is a condition of monarchy to nurture a body of persons who may be adorned with perfect wisdom, integrity, merit, and abstinence, and graced with rectitude, trustworthiness, piety, and uprightness, being distinguished amongst their fellows for loyalty, sincerity, affection, and veneration. The art of this is to ascertain of each one what business suits him, and of every one what is a fitting occupation, appointing to-morrow's business for to-morrow according to a person's ability, and the measure of his intellect and bravery, and the extent of his wisdom and understanding. If with any one defects are found together with merit, on this account indifference must not be displayed, since creatures cannot be without fault. It has been said:

'Seek not a friend free from error, lest you remain without a companion.'

"In this matter circumspection is necessary to such an extent that if any one should bring ruin on a matter with which he has been intrusted, he should be removed from the government; while if another by his cleverness should confuse affairs, he, too, must be avoided. And although it is an impossible state of affairs that ability should become the cause of harm in matters, yet this injunction has been issued, so that it might be known that to obtain an object men of merit and ability must be put aside. Accordingly, to keep at a distance stupid and mischievous persons is nearer akin to what is right. Therefore, after this matter

---

[1] See note, page 28.

is understood, and these details are recognised, it is incumbent upon the King himself to examine the circumstances and investigate the occupations which he intrusts to his agents and deputies, so that the details of the affairs of Property and State may not remain hidden from him. In this two full benefits are to be conceived: First, it will become known who amongst those employed are cherishers of the subjects, and who dispensers of tyranny. He who guards the populace should be caressed and confirmed in that employment, while he who has no sympathy for those beneath him should have his name erased from the scroll of occupation, and remain inscribed in the volume of dismissal.

> Appoint over your subjects a God-fearing man;
> A sober-minded person is the architect of the kingdom.
> He is evil-designed towards you, and bloodthirsty as regards the people,
> Who seeks to benefit you by injuring mankind.
> Dominion in the hands of such a person is wrong;
> For, owing to the work of his hands, men raise their palms to God.
> He who does well will never experience evil;
> When a man acts wrongly, he is the enemy of his own soul.

"Next, when this state of things is fixed in the minds of fellow-men—viz., that the King watches in the best way the fruit of the deeds of those who act well, and deems it incumbent to chide the faithless according to their crime, men of probity, being filled with hope, never omit or neglect to do what is right, while the wicked, inspired with alarm and dread, are not forward and daring in the way of sin and oppression. A story in harmony with these prefatory remarks is that of the Lion and the Jackal." The King inquired, "What was that?"

---o---

STORY I.

He said: It has been related that in the land of Hind was a Jackal, by name "Farísah,"[1] who had turned his face from the world, and his back from its unobtainable appurtenances. He lived in the midst of his likes and equals, but refrained from eating flesh, spilling blood, or afflicting animals.

> He did not stain his lips with the blood of any of them,
> And avoided what was wrong.

His friends began to quarrel with him, and commenced a dispute, which led to battle and conflict, saying: "We are not content with this disposition of yours, and we deem your ideas wrong in regard to these efforts; seeing you do not avoid our society, you must conform to our habits and nature, and since you do not fold up the skirt of concord from intercourse (with us), you should not[2] withdraw your head from the collar of unanimity. To pass your precious life, too, in divination, and to confine yourself in the prison of abstinence, will bring no great advantage. You must demand your share of the pleasures of the world, so that you may partake of the potion, '*And forget not thy portion in this world;*'

---

[1] The Lion's prey.
[2] The negative seems necessary to secure the sense of this passage, which in the original is in the affirmative.

2 A

and you should not be shy of eating and drinking, which are the support of the source of life, so that you may follow out the command, '*Eat and drink.*' The truth must be recognised that yesterday cannot be brought back, and it is not fit to determine upon finding to-morrow. What sense is there in wasting to-day and turning aside from enjoying pleasures?"

> Come! let us for a time, this very day be happy in private,
> For in the world no one knows the affairs of to-morrow.

The Jackal replied: "Since you know that yesterday goes and does not return, and that a wise man places no reliance on to-morrow, then to-day store up something which shall serve as provision for the road.

> Seek that to-day, in every corner,
> Which shall serve you as provision for to-morrow.

"The world although thoroughly defective, at any rate has this merit, that it has been proclaimed the field of eternity, and whatever seed you sow therein, you will reap the fruit thereof, in the Day of Judgment. '*To-day is thy sowing, to-morrow thy harvest.*'

> Labour to-day to scatter seed,
> Lest to-morrow you fall short of grain.
> If you do not sow the arable field,
> In the harvest thereof you will not be worth a half millet.

"A wise man should place his desires upon obtaining eternal rewards, which can be procured by the performance of good works and pious actions, and set his heart upon everlasting prosperity and perpetual bounties; this can be attained by abandoning the appurtenances of this treacherous world, and transitory home.

> Place not your heart on this fleeting threshold, for another place
> Has been appointed as a mansion, to secure you rest.

"To-day when you have the power, and are able, drive the steed of abstinence in the plain of holy endeavour, and from the fruits of health lay up a store for sickness; so, too, from the capital of youth acquire gain for the dull market of old age, and from the benefits of life, make ready subsistence for the journey through the desert of eternity and death. A wise man has said: 'To-day you are able, and know not how; to-morrow when you know how, you are not able.' *My sorrow is because I have been extremely negligent in my duty to God.*'

> When I could, I knew not what advantage there was;
> When I knew I could not.

"The world's pleasures are transient like a flash of lightning, and its distresses fleeting like a dark cloud; neither should affection be set on the benefits of its favours, nor should vexation arise from the annoyances of its troubles.

> If it grant your desires, it does not bring pleasure;
> While if they are disappointed it is not worth grieving about.

"To sum up,—for the heart to set its affection upon the cell of grief appears removed from exalted ambition, and to place an abode on the channel of the torrent of annihilation, is far from perfect intelligence, '*Pass over it, and do not repair it.*' As regards this deceptive home and abode which must be quitted,

> "Erect it not, but leave it till it perishes."

They replied: "O Farísah! you enjoin us to quit the bounties of the world; but the fact is, the luxuries of this sphere have been created so that we may reap the benefit of them, and derive pleasure therefrom. The saying, '*And we gave them as food things which were good*,' bears testimony to this pretention." Farísah rejoined: "Worldly luxuries are implements, by means of which a wise man obtains a good name and lasting reputation, and by help of which he acquires provision for the way to eternity. According to the saying, '*Righteous wealth is very good*,' wealth is the cause of his peaceful end, not the medium of his punishment and torture. If you seek happiness in both worlds, let these words sink into your ears, and on account of pleasurable food, the delight of which does not pass beyond the throat, do not permit yourself to destroy an animal, but be content with what, without violence or injury, comes to your hands, and do not exceed such an amount as is consistent with the support of your frame, and the existence of your body. But do not seek my assent to what is contrary to law and reason, since my intercourse with you is not the cause of evil, while to agree to improper deeds would occasion me torture. If you intend to worry me with these kind of annoyances, then give me leave to abandon your society, and betake myself to the corner of retirement."

I will go to the corner of solitude, and shut the door upon mankind.

When the friends saw that Farísah had firmly placed his feet upon the carpet of piety and religion, being converted, they repented having suggested such words, and loosened the tongue of apology, by way of excuse. Farísah in a little time gained a position, as regards piety and religion, such that the recluses of those countries used to ask a blessing from his spirit, and the anxious souls in the desert of holy endeavours used to implore favour from the guide of his glance. In a short interval the fame of his devotion and rectitude spread through the regions of that territory, and the renown of his worship and devotion arrived in the outskirts of that district. Near to the abode of Farísah was a waste, embracing rivers, fountains, and shrubs of various kinds. In its midst was a meadow, such that the Garden of Paradise from envy at the freshness thereof drew its face behind the screen of secrecy, and the aid of its northerly repose - producing breezes bestowed perpetual life on the withered heart.

> Its heart-enchanting plain enlivened the spirit,
> Its soul-enrapturing atmosphere captivated the heart.
> Luxuriant verdure grew upon the brink of its streams,
> Like down on the lips of ravishing beauties.

Many animals and beasts were congregated therein, and by reason of the extent of the plain, and the deliciousness of the climate, reptiles and insects rested in it. Their King was a Lion, awful and mighty, a monarch of the Beasts, excessively formidable, and extremely furious.

> His roar like the peals of mighty thunder,
> His eyes like fiery lightning.

All those who dwelt in that waste were enchained in servitude to him, and used to pass their time under the protection of his majesty, and the sanctuary of his might. He was named Kámjúí,[1] by which appellation his fame was spread

---

[1] Enjoyment-seeking.

throughout the regions of the land. One day Kámjúí was conversing on every subject with the officers of his government, and discoursing on every topic. In the midst of their talk the history of Farísah was introduced. So much on all sides and regions did they convey the nature of his perfect integrity and excellent life to the King's ears, that he most eagerly sought to be intimate with him.

> His cheeks, as yet unseen, as though they were the pupil of the eyes,
> Were at once allotted a place within their sockets.

In short, the desire of Kámjúí to meet Farísah passing all limit, he sent some one to inquire after him, while he, also, obeying the King's command, attended the Court of the protector of the world. The King observed the dues of respect, and bestowed on him the honour of a seat in the High Assembly, and tried his sincerity concerning various spiritual habits and knowledge. To sum up, he found Farísah a boundless sea in evidencing virtues and manners, and saw that he was a pearl-scattering treasury as regards his acquaintance with true wisdom. Once more he tested him again in the way of cleverness and ability, as well as eloquence of language and accuracy of deliberation. The coin of his condition proved of full value upon the touchstone of approbation.

> Gold which is pure, what fear has it of being tested ?

Kámjúí being delighted with his society, became intimate with him. After some days, being with him in private, the Lion said : " O Farísah ! my kingdom is extensive, and the affairs and arrangements thereof are numerous : the news of your devotion and piety has been conveyed to the royal ears, and I

" Not having (previously) beheld you, love you better than those I have seen ! [1]

" Now that I have beheld you, sight is superior to report, and hearsay inferior to ocular demonstration.

> I had heard that there was not a second like you in the world ;
> When I saw you, in truth this was the case a thousand times over.

" Now I will place confidence in you, and intrust the affairs of the State and Property to you, so that your dignity being exalted by my patronage, you shall be enrolled amongst the number of privy councillors and attendants, and by the blessing of my favour, and the beauty of my condescension, be distinguished above your relatives and brethren ; nay, more, above the men of your time, as regards the glory of being chosen, and the honour of being distinguished."

> Whoever places his head upon the threshold of my prosperity,
> Ere a week has passed will become the occupant of a throne.

Farísah replied : " It is incumbent on sovereigns as regards the conduct of State affairs to select worthy assistants and proper helpers, and added to this it is necessary that they should compel no one to accept any post; since when, with force, they place any business round a man's neck, and he is not able to perform it, nor fulfil what is requisite or incumbent, the evil effects thereof will fall upon the King, and the sin of such disobedience recoil upon the giver of the order. The object of these words is, that I dislike affairs of royalty, and am

---

[1] This passage might also be rendered—
"Not having (previously) beheld you, love you better than my own eyes."

unacquainted with them, and have no experience thereof; while you are a mighty Monarch, and a Sovereign of exalted dignity, in whose service are many animals, and numerous beasts, endowed with vigour and ability, and celebrated for their honest and upright qualities, and who are also in search of this very kind of position. If as regards them you are kind and condescending, they will cause the august mind to be at ease relative to the troubles of settling matters, while they will be joyous and aided by the presents and gifts which they obtain through taking office." Kámjúí said: "What advantage have you in thus refusing, or what benefit do you see in thus rejecting? Assuredly I will not excuse you, and, willingly or unwillingly, I will cast the collar of undertaking this matter round the neck of your care."

Whether you will or not, you are in my hands.

Farísah said: "Affairs of Sovereignty are suitable for two persons,—1st, The clever, austere man, who pertinaciously and ruthlessly gains his object, and with ability and stratagem carrying all before him, does not become the target for the arrow of reproach; 2d, The negligent, weak-minded person, who is habituated to undergo contempt, and who has no anxiety for want of reputation, or loss of name and honour. Such persons do not come to the region of envy, nor is any one opposed or antagonistic to them. But I am not of these two classes: I neither possess overpowering greed, that I should hatch plots, nor am I of an ignoble nature to bear the burden of disgrace.

By God, who created
The wise to restrain themselves,
In my estimation, the value
Of a kingdom in both worlds cannot be balanced against one mean act.

" The King must rise above this idea, and excuse me bearing the burden of distress, since a long time ago I sewed up the eyes of impudent-faced greed with the needle of contentment, and burnt with the flame of the fire of abstinence the faithless chattels of avarice which are full of necessities. If once again the King causes me to be defiled with the affections of the world, that will happen which befell those Flies which were sitting in the midst of a dish of honey." The Lion inquired, "What was that?"

STORY II.

He said: It has been related that one day a pure-souled religious mendicant, whose steps were firmly fixed on the way of piety, was passing the market. A poverty-stricken sweetmeat-seller, who had met with his share in tasting of want, requested this worthy person to take his place for a while at the door of his shop. The holy man, through condescension, seated himself there, and so remained. The sweetmeat-maker, by way of salutation, having clarified a dish full of honey, placed it before the Darwísh; and the flies, as it is their wont to settle upon sweets, not being restrained however much any one may attempt to keep them off—

Flies select no spot save the shop of the confectioner—

all at once swarmed round the dish of honey, some alighting on the edge of the vessel, others casting themselves into the midst thereof. The sweetmeat-maker, seeing that the attacks of the flies passed all bounds, switched a fan. Those who were upon the brink of the vessel easily flew up and went away, while the feet of those who had rested in the midst got stuck in the honey, and when they tried to fly, their wings being also smeared with honey, they fell into the snare of destruction. That worthy Darwísh was delighted, and commenced to utter frantic cries. After that the inward sea of the holy man was at rest, and the waves of the ocean of ecstasy and frenzy had subsided, the sweetmeat-maker said: "O my beloved! I have not grudged you material sweetmeats, do not, therefore, withhold from me anything spiritual which may now be revealed to you."

> Open your sweet lips and scatter sugar.

The Devotee said: "In this cup of honey are represented to me the contemptible world, and the greedy ones and aspirants therein. A secret inspiration said to me: 'Consider this cup the world, this honey the bounties thereof, and these flies the partakers of these luxuries. They who sit on the edge of the vessel are the contented poor, who are satisfied with a few morsels from the tables of the world; the others, inside the cup, are the avaricious and greedy, whose thoughts are that, as they are in the midst of the affair, their portion[1] will be greater, and they are neglectful of the saying, "*Food is apportioned;*" but when 'Izráíl[2] waves the fan of death, they who are on the brink easily fly away, and return to the nest—"*In the assembly of truth before a powerful king*"—while they who are resting in the midst, the more they move the deeper their feet sink, and they are overwhelmed in the straits—"*Then we rejected him as the lowest of the low*"—and the end of their state terminates in eternal misery and destruction.'"

> Why should one eat a solitary morsel,
> And henceforth undergo all this misery therefrom?
> Be disposed to be satisfied; lo! that is true capital.
> There is no wealth like contentment.

"The object of reciting this story is, that the King should not defile the wings and feathers of my property with the honey of worldly corruption. May be that when the time of returning the deposit of the spirit shall arrive, the road to eternity may be traversed in an easy way."

> So employ the time of your life,
> That if it be said, "Go," you depart.

Kámjúí said: "If a person keeps in view what is right, and being firm in the way of justice, does not omit any particle of rectitude, and wards off from the oppressed the ill effects of the misdeeds of tyrants, receiving with joyous heart and open countenance the representations of the distressed, assuredly in the world his fortune will procure the honour of being established, and in a future state he will attain an exalted position and dignity." Farísah said: "If, as regards working for kings, a person discharges his obligations, the perfume of the plants of eternity may be inhaled, but in the world the affairs of such an one do not appear permanent or settled, and the continuance of his occupation cannot possibly be certain or sure: since whenever any one is exalted by near approach to the King, both his friends join their heads together in opposing him, and also enemies make his soul the target of the arrow of calamity, and

---

[1] نصیت in the Persian text is a misprint for نصیب.
[2] The Angel of Death.

whenever a body are leagued together to contend with him, certainly he cannot be secure, nor live in joy of heart. Though he places his feet upon the brow of the planet Saturn, yet he will not secure his head in safety." The Lion exclaimed: " Since you have obtained my grace, do not cast yourself into the straits of distrust, seeing that the excellence of my sincerity is a screen against the malevolence of calumnious enemies. With one chastisement I will close the way of their deceits, and convey you to the extreme of favour, and the pinnacle of security."

> What harm is there from the wiles of foes, when there is a friend on our side.

Farísah said : " If the object of the King in this attention and patronage is a kindness which he bestows upon me, it would be more worthy the royal condescension and endless justice and equity, to leave me alone, so that I may rest secure and at ease in this waste, and, out of the bounties of the world, content with water and herbs, may remain apart from the evils of envy, and the enmity of friends and foes. It is certain that a short life in safety, ease, repose, and health is better than prolonged existence in fear, dread, anxiety of mind, and distress."

> A single moment of ease of mind is better, than that any one
> Should live a thousand years not in accordance with his desires.

Kámjúí said : " The worry of fear must be removed from your mind, and being near to me, you must take upon yourself, as a duty, the arrangement of affairs." Farísah exclaimed : " If this is the state of the case, and my aversion and refusal are without avail, I must have a pledge, that when those below me, in hope of getting my post, and those above me, through fear of the decline of their own dignity, plot against me, the King will not by reason of their clamour be changed towards me, but deem it incumbent to reflect and deliberate thereon, and as concerns my case and the intrigues of the malicious, will discharge to the utmost what is obligatory."

> At every accusation, the heart must not be annoyed with us ;
> It is easy, on the speech of enemies, to desert friends.

The King having made a compact with him, and concluded an engagement, intrusted to him his own property and treasury, and distinguished him above all the dependants and followers, as regards boundless grace, and taking no counsel about affairs save with him, disclosed the secrets of the kingdom to him alone. Every day the confidence of the Lion in him waxed greater, and his position and dignity increased in the King's estimation, till it reached a pitch of extreme intimacy, and ended in excessive friendship. Farísah was not a moment away from attendance on the Lion, nor used Kámjúí to rest without his company.

> When friendship reaches the utmost pitch, the case is such.

This state of things weighed heavily upon those around the Lion, and a body of the pillars of the State formed a league to oppose him, and entered into an agreement to defeat him. They passed days and nights in planning his overthrow, and spent nights and days in scheming how to hinder and thwart him. Ultimately they all arranged to accuse him of treachery, so that the feelings of Kámjúí, who never had any disposition to swerve from the highway of rectitude and integrity, might be changed towards him, and the faith of the Lion as regards his honesty, which his Majesty considered perfectly displayed in him, might be shaken. Then thorough breaches could be made, and they might strive to ruin and overthrow him.

> We will gain our object by degrees,
> For we will overturn his basis.

Accordingly they put one person forward to steal a little meat which had been set apart for the Lion's breakfast, and concealed it in Farísah's room.

> Next day when the golden-clawed Lion
> Went forth into the den of the spheres,

the chiefs and ministers arranged themselves in ranks to wait on him, and the nobles and senators attended the King's court, while Farísah had gone away with the view of properly settling a matter. The Lion was expecting his arrival, and not a word fell from his mouth save talk of his ability, and assertions in regard to his understanding and penetration.

> The name of a friend was perpetually on his tongue as the companion of his soul,
> Not a moment elapsed but what he repeated it.

The King's breakfast-time arrived, and his animal passions being aroused, the pangs of hunger overcame him. The more they searched for the King's daily portion of meat, the less did they find it, and the King was extremely annoyed. At this time Farísah was absent, and his enemies present. When they saw that the fire of hunger and the violence of fury were united, they commenced their wiles, and finding the oven of rage heated placed therein their dough. One of them said : " There is no help for us but to inform the King, and convey to the place of representation what we know respecting his Majesty's welfare or detriment, although it will not be pleasant to some." Kámjúí being on the alert said : " It becomes loyal servants and true dependants, at all times, not to neglect the dues of advice, and recognising the claims of gratitude, seasonably to disclose whatever they know, or is in their power.

> Those persons are loyal and grateful,
> Who conceal not matters from the King.

" Recount what you have heard, and tell what you have seen." One of the treacherous calumniators and weak-minded sycophants replied : " It has been explained to me, that Farísah bore away that flesh to his own house." Another one, by way of suspicion, raised misapprehensions, saying : " I do not believe this, for he is an animal free from oppression, and of honest disposition." Another commencing to indulge in deceit, exclaimed : " Caution must be observed in this matter, for every individual has friends and enemies, who may interestedly say what has not happened, nor can a person be quickly proved, or the secrets of mankind easily discovered." Another bolder, broke forth saying : " It is so ; information respecting secrets, and intelligence regarding men's minds, are not quickly gained : however, if the flesh is found in his abode, whatever regarding his treachery has passed on the mouths of high and low, and little and great, will be verified." In these circumstances the reins of power slipt from Kámjúí's hands, and he exclaimed : " What do men say regarding him ? and what proof do they adduce of his treachery ? " One of those present, who was in league with the opponents, said : " O King ! amongst the inhabitants of this waste, the news has spread of his perfidy and deceit ; if he be a traitor, he will never bear his soul in safety from this vortex, and the disgrace of treachery will soon over-take him." Another of the conspirators loosed the tongue of guile, exclaiming : " All the prefects are constantly conveying reports against him, and I hesitated to credit them ; now that I hear this verdict, it is probable that the darkness of my suspicion will be changed for the light of certainty." Another cried out : " His cheats and perfidy ere this, too, were not hidden from me, and I have taken such and such persons to witness, that the case of this hypocritical Devotee would end in disgrace, and a great crime and detestable sin come to light on his part. In this matter it has been said :

'He who has an impure heart will in the end be disgraced.'"

Another said : " It is strange that in spite of pretensions to piety, openness of disposition, religious habit, and good resolutions, a person should not be ashamed to behave with perfidy ; and marvellous is it if this verse, as applicable to his circumstances, is not inscribed upon the pages of language :

'My religious garb is not owing to excess of faith.
I place my mendicant's robe as a screen for a hundred secret faults.'"

Another entering the door of conversation said : " This pure abstinent person has been used for a long time to weep, to appearance considering the care of business of the State as a misfortune and calamity, a trouble and labour ; with all this, if his treachery is assured, it will be matter for astonishment." An-other said : " Seeing that he casts his evil eyes upon this trifle which forms the allowance for the King's breakfast, it can be imagined what bribes he must have taken in matters of importance, and what large sums he must have used from the King's property."

When a hunter cannot let a sparrow alone,
You may know what he will do when he sees a partridge or quail.

When the chiefs found the plain of impudence vacant, they brought the steed of evil-speaking into motion, and raised the dust of hesitation and suspicion in the expanse of Kámjúí's heart. The Ministers also turned the reins of explana-tion towards slander and infamy, and inscribed upon the scroll of the King's mind several inscriptions of every kind of nonsensical[1] stuff. One of them said : " If these words prove true, it will not be mere deceit and nothing beyond, nay, more, it will be a proof of ingratitude and unthankfulness, and assuredly by this effrontery he will have brought the King into contempt, and put aside the royal honour and dignity." Another, by way of admonition and exhortation, began to speak, saying : " O friends ! do not blacken the scroll of your proceedings with this kind of mad talk, and in accordance with the saying, '*Is there one of you who would like to eat the flesh of his own brother ?*' do not thrust the teeth of defect into the flesh of your own brother, since maybe the fact of his perfidy has not occurred, and all of you are in error and under a delusion. If the King will this hour issue the order that his house be searched, the dust of suspicion will be removed from the road of certainty, since if the flesh be in his home there will be a clear proof of these words, and the doubts of high and low will tend to certainty ; while if it is plainly only suspicion, and the flesh which is lost is not apparent in that cell, all must make apologies, and ask pardon of Farísah." Another said : " If caution is to be observed, haste must be made, for

---

[1] It is impossible to render this literally.

his spies are surrounding every locality, and any hour the news may reach him, and he will omit no necessary endeavour to remedy this matter." At the termination of the meeting, a confidant amongst the King's privy councillors, impudently stepping forward, said: "What is the benefit of investigating this matter, and what will accrue from examining this which has occurred ? since if the crime of this unrighteous villain is made clear, with hypocrisy and jugglery he will turn aside the King's mind from taking revenge, and display something wonderful, which will cause all to doubt, even though they are convinced."

> His mind is so potent to deceive,
> That he puts forward doubts, in the garb of certainty.

In short, in these circumstances, the Lion being hungry and defiled with rage, they uttered such speeches, that aversion towards Farísah found its way to the King's heart, and according to the purport, "*Whoever listens falls into doubt,*" a variety of ideas crossed his mind, and he ordered Farísah to be summoned to his presence. The poor wretch, unaware of the signs of treachery on the part of his enemies, set out on his way, and since the skirt of his integrity was clear of the disgrace of this calumny, he advanced boldly to Kámjúí, who asked: "What did you do with that flesh which yesterday I made over to you?" He replied: "I conveyed it to the kitchen, so that it might be brought at breakfast-time to the King." The Cook was also one of the conspirators; he advanced denying this, and eagerly said: "I have no news of this proceeding or circumstance, and you gave me no meat." The Lion sent a body of chiefs to look for the flesh in Farísah's house, as they had themselves concealed it, bringing it forth, they took it to the King. Farísah perceived that his enemies had accomplished their purpose, and had found an opportunity to complete the affair, the thread of the plan of which they had been a long time weaving: he said to himself:

> "The sun of my delight has reached the top of the wall,[1]
> For years I have dreaded this day."

Amongst the body of ministers was a Wolf, who till that hour had not spoken a word of reproach, and who deemed himself to be amongst the number of the just, and who so made it appear that he never placed his feet in a matter without investigation, and knowing for certain, nor till he was apprised of the ins and outs of an affair entered thereon; he boasted of being friends with Farísah, and made earnest show of protecting him. After learning the state of things he advanced, and disclosing what was in his mind, said: "O King! the crime of this vagabond is apparent, and the sin of this unmanly, mean fellow, has become evident; the proper course for the King is as quickly as possible to carry out the order for his punishment, since if this matter be neglected, without doubt other criminals will not fear to be disgraced, and from hour to hour will become more daring."

> If there be not punishment, matters will come to ruin.

The Lion commanded them to take away the Jackal, and fell into long and profound thought. A Lynx from amongst the King's attendants commenced saying: "I am amazed at the illumined mind of the King, from the light of which the sun gains radiance, and under the protection of the brilliancy of which the taper

---

[1] That is, the sun of my delight has sunk so low in the horizon as to cast a shade on the top of the wall.

of the chamber of the spheres illuminates its face, as to how the matter of this traitor and the treachery of this flimsy knave have been concealed from him, and as to why he has been neglectful of the baseness of this person's impure mind, and the deceit of his cunning nature, and why, in spite of this great offence and base deed he defers killing him, and renders turbid with the rubbish of reflection the potion of punishment, with the water of which the root of the tree of justice is rendered moist and succulent." Kámjúí, all attentive, exclaimed : "What are you saying ?" He replied : "O King! Sages have enjoined, '*He whose government is good, his rule will be lasting :*' to practise punishment causes perpetuity of government, and whoever does not draw the sword of chastisement from the sheath of revenge, will not be able to ward off the arrow of strife with the shield of defence, and he who does not overthrow the foundation of injustice with the axe of violence, will not plant the tree of desire in the rose-garden of Time.

> If the custom of punishment be laid aside,
> The foundation of security will be overthrown.
> That garden produces the fruit of safety,
> Wherein the fountain of chastisement takes its rise.

"Whoever seeks the welfare of the kingdom must punish criminals, and though they are the friends of his heart and the darlings of his soul, he must pay no regard to this. Just as the King of Baghdád, on account of the general welfare, punished his own specially beloved." Kámjúí said, "How was that ?"

STORY III.

He represented : It has been related that in the capital of China was a King, who like Jamshíd, as regards complying with the rules of justice, had made the world-depicting cup[1] of reason the mirror of his life, and who, in observing the regulations of government, like Alexander, sought the immortal waters of equity.

> By reason of his perfect justice oppression moved
> A hundred stages thence towards the desert of non-existence.

He had a son, beautiful-faced and of good disposition, who with the lasso of kindness ensnared the hearts of men, and with the grain of condescension and beneficence brought the bird of the souls of high and low within the net of affection.

> Mother World never gave birth to a person of such a pure disposition :
> The eyes of the Heavens never saw a perfect being like himself.

This boy was anxious to see the Holy Temple, which is indicated by the well-known extract, "*Of a truth it is the first home which has been arranged for men ;*" and a desire to journey round that sanctuary of excellences, which is emblematical of the house of peace, "*Whoever enters therein remains secure,*" appeared in the cell of his heart. Having replied with "I await your commands " to the summons of the Host, "*And announce to men,*" he conceived a settled intention of making a sacred journey to the holy precincts of the Temple at Makkah.

[1] See note, page 83.

The hope of journeying round the sanctuary of thy street, has cast
Into the desert of grief, crowds of desolate persons,[1]
Crying out, "Here I am;" on the top of the sacred mount of thy abode,
A hundred caravans of souls await the summons to enter.

After he had obtained permission from his father he set out by sea, together
with a body of attendants, upon ships such that the expanse of the Spheres,
side by side with the size of each of the vessels, seemed contemptible, and the
pages of the Heavens, in comparison with a single sail of each bark, were not
even a trifling shred. Setting in motion the footless, water-traversing steeds
they departed, and settling in those wooden houses, whereof the roof was below,
and the pillars above, they intrusted the reins of power to the hands of the
quick-racing wind.[2]

Like a moon they abode in the citadel of the water,
They urged the ship towards the coast.

In a little while, having traversed much of their journey, they reached the Holy
Makkah, and having performed the necessities and dues of the pilgrimage,
wended towards the kissing threshold of the sacred garden of his Majesty
the Sultán of the throne of Prophecy, and the King of the Court of honour and
might—

That hot-driving, high-soaring warrior,
Who made of the nine spheres a stirrup-leather.

"*May the benedictions of God be on Muhammad the chosen, and on his pure
family, and on his excellent companions!*" and by the good fortune of kissing
the exalted Royal Court of Prophecy they were rendered happy.

O 'tis the desire of every good man to kiss the dust of thy portals!
To drag this wish in the mire[3] is the trouble of all troubles.

Thence with a caravan of Khurásán they came to Baghdád, the King of
which, being apprised of the condition of the Prince, came out to meet him, and
observed the rules of politeness and courtesy in a fitting and proper manner,
and preparing him suitable food and provision, and a becoming and agreeable
abode, he begged him to stop there some days. When they had rested from
the fatigues of the road, and had resolved to return to their own native land,
the Prince tendered many apologies to the Sultán of Baghdád, and made
return for his service by offering thanks and praise, and by way of a present
and benediction sent a Chinese damsel to his Haram, and himself packing the
chattels of travel set out towards Khurásán. The Sultán, after the rite of
accompanying his guest, and the ceremony of bidding adieu, returned to his
Haram, and sought the damsel. He saw a form, such that the Divine Portrayer had never drawn upon the tablets of existence so beautiful a design, nor
the eyes of the Painter Imagination ever seen so delicate a shape in the scroll
of fancy. Her heart-ravishing ringlets enchained the earth with the lasso of
sedition, and the world-radiant moon, from its exalted position, had rubbed
its crown in the mire before her face: with one blandishment of her eyebrows,

---

[1] Literally, "crowds of persons without either heads or feet."
[2] The meaning of this high-flown passage is that the Prince and his attendants embarked in
ships, which are alternately compared to steeds and wooden houses; in the latter simile, the "roof
below" is the hull, and the "pillars above" are the masts.
[3] *i. e.,* To be disappointed in regard to this wish.

she placed the claims of arched-eyed beauties upon the shelf of oblivion, and with a wink of her half-drowsy eye, she consigned to the Winds of intoxication the claims to piety of recluses.

> Her cheeks were a taper for the bedchamber of lovers;
> Her lips, dainties and wine for the intoxicated.
> Her stature was lofty fortune to the upright,
> Her curling locks the sanctuary of those who watch at night,
> From envy at her voice, sugar remained in the bag;
> Cornelian from shame at her pearly lips turned to stone.

The feet of the heart of the King of Baghdád remained in the clay owing to the gait of that free Cypress,[1] and from tasting her wine-coloured lips, he became intoxicated and insensible without the use of wine.

> A person whose heart is bound to her form becomes miserable;
> Anyhow, what misfortune is this as regards my wretched soul?

Much as the dejected Sultán strove it was of no avail, and though powerful reason poured the water of admonition upon the fire of love, the flame thereof increased.

> The water of my eyes would not be stilled with talk,
> For this pain of a lover increases with reproach.

The King indulged in friendship with the damsel, and all at once drew back his hand from anxiety on account of the people's miseries, and from the management of the affairs of the kingdom. Whenever a King is occupied in ease and joy, and never inquires after the case of the oppressed, and abandoning his ears to the melodies of the harp and lute, does not attend to the sad laments of every desolate heart, in a little time ruin takes place, and strife and misery rising up, men's affairs end in trouble.

> Every king who devotes himself to sloth and luxury,
> You should know that his dignity will decline.
> The balance of Libra, which is the constellation of the stars of sloth and luxury,
> Is weighed down by the King of the Planets.

Several days elapsed in this manner; the pillars of the State, and nobles, through the King's neglect came to straits, and beheld the condition of the city and kingdom distressed. A band stretching forth the hand of supplication, turned their faces towards the recluses and men of piety, and begging benedictions from the souls of pure-minded darwíshes, made offerings for the King's welfare. Their disinterested prayers reaching the target of acceptance, at night the King saw in a dream a man coming towards him, and saying:

> O King! what will you say when you are questioned,
> In the place which you dread, but where none fear you?

"What matter is this that you have taken in hand, in that you have withdrawn yourself from the affairs of the oppressed? It has wellnigh come to pass that the case has gone beyond your control, and your government been overturned; arise, and take the head of your own affairs."

Otherwise all the evil you experience, will be entirely due to yourself.

[1] See note, p. 214.

The King in alarm at this circumstance awoke from his sleep. Having performed his ablutions, he loosed the tongue of apology and demanded pardon, and busied himself remedying what was past. He commanded that that damsel should not again come to him in private; and although he had no rest without her, and his heart without contemplating her beauty was not composed, yet from fear of the Almighty, and dread lest his monarchy should decline, he issued a decree to that effect. The damsel waited patiently for two or three days; one night the desire for the King's society having entered her head, she betook herself to the court, with a face like a fresh rose-leaf which had expanded in the morning breeze, and ringlets resembling a hyacinth full of twists, concealed in a bag of pure musk.

> Her twisting locks interwove the hyacinth and jessamine,
> Her curls formed a nosegay of violets.
> Her bewitching narcissus-like eyes were intoxicated and drowsy,
> The mole on her cheek like a hyacinth writhed in its blackness.

Once again on seeing her beauty the King lost his senses, and the hosts of love plundered the chattels of wisdom and understanding.

> Once more love advanced and madness returned;
> My heart was stung with the toying of this arch damsel.

For several days more being enamoured of her beauty, and ensnared with her ringlets and moles,[1] he passed his time in love, and once again the messengers of the invisible world, with unerring warnings, summoned him to the path of rectitude. The King came to himself and said: "There is no remedy for my ailment but to remove this cause of strife; and save this source of misfortune be banished, there is no hope of cure for me." Accordingly he commanded his Chamberlain: "Take away and cast into the Tigris this refractory damsel, who without permission has entered the court." The Chamberlain brought forth the girl, thinking to himself: "She is the beloved of the King, maybe to-morrow he will repent, and seek her at my hands; but when I have slain her, the hand of reflection will not reach the skirt of remedy." Accordingly he concealed her in his house. The King by reason of his proceeding was melancholy. When he had come back from the court into private, the desire to see his beloved again overtaking him, he became dejected, and once more reproaching himself he quenched the warnings of reason. At night, with the view of keeping away anxiety, he drank a cup of pure wine, and forgetting the dictates of reason and the admonitions of wisdom, the thought of his heart-enchanting friend rendered him beyond control, and summoning his private Chamberlain, he inquired after the condition of his beloved, and with the utmost vehemence said: "Unless you this night produce her, I will hand you over to be punished." Though the Chamberlain adduced apologies, it was fruitless, and seeing the rage of the King, and finding himself in the region of destruction, of necessity he conveyed the moon-faced girl to the King's court. Again the basis of joy was laid, and the materials for love were prepared.

> We are here, it is night, and our friend in our presence;
> The cup of pleasant wine also is at hand;
> The rose ready, and autumn passed,
> Winter gone, and bright spring before us.

---

[1] See note, p. 23.

To sum up, three times the King ordered her to be slain, and the Chamberlain, by way of circumspection, deferred doing so: at length the affairs of the State being altogether ruined, the King perceived that there was no remedy for this evil save at his own hands, and that this misfortune could not be removed by trusting to another;

> This matter will not be accomplished by the hand of another,

since whomsoever he ordered to kill the damsel, assuredly by way of circumspection, would delay. Accordingly the King himself contemplated removing her, but did not wish openly to slay any one who was without evident treachery. Ultimately one day standing upon the roof of his palace, he was looking towards the Tigris, while the damsel from afar, having girt the waist of attendance, was contemplating the King's beauty. The Sultán, fearing the future, and the evils of negligence, knew that this was the time. He said to himself: "Although I place round my neck the blood of an innocent person, yet a hundred thousand hearts, which owing to my want of care are immersed in blood, will be cured, and although this girl is as precious as my soul to me, yet to look after the state of my distressed subjects is more than this." Accordingly he said: "Come nearer, so as to enjoy the sight of this vessel." When the damsel arrived close, the King laid his hands upon her, and cast her into the Tigris, and displaying the utmost sorrow, made as though she herself had tumbled into the water. He then ordered her to be brought out from the stream and buried, and going into mourning, he fulfilled to the utmost all the obligations in that respect; and thus on account of the welfare of the kingdom, with his own hand he deprived his beloved object of life.

> Kings to insure a single advantage, slay a hundred persons.

"I have adduced this story so that the King may know that it is better to observe the interests of the State, than to associate with a base individual; and to remove one person, the evils of whom are universal, is more allied to what is expedient, than to abandon a thousand people." The fire of the King's rage was aroused by those deceitful words, and he sent a message to Farísah that, "If you have any excuse for this offence disclose it." Farísah being innocent, and since it has been said, "Whoever has short hands has a long tongue,"[1]—

> The innocent should be bold—

sent back a brusque answer. His violent words lent force to the seditious welcome of his opponents. The fire of Kámjúí's wrath rose up, and putting aside his promise and agreement, he gave an absolute order that Farísah should be put to death. This news was conveyed to the King's Mother, who perceived that there had been precipitancy, and the region of mildness and forbearance had been neglected, patience and firmness being changed for levity and want of stability. She thought to herself, "I must go at once and deliver my son from the temptations of the accursed Satan, since whenever rage overpowers kings, the devil, too, gets dominion over them, and enjoins whatever he wishes, and this same idea can be gathered from the purport of the true tradition, '*When the King is enraged, Satan overpowers him.*'"

> Rage is one of the flames of Satan,
> In the end it will cause regret.

---

[1] That is, as expressed in the following verse, "Whoever is innocent is bold."

She first of all sent some one to the Executioner saying: "Retard the destruction of the Jackal, till I have a conversation with the Lion." Coming herself to Kámjúí, she said: "O Son! I have heard that you have issued a decree for the death of Farísah. What has been his offence, and what wrong has proceeded from him?" The Lion repeated the circumstances of the case. The Lion's Mother said: "O Son! do not lose yourself in the desert of remorse, nor be destitute of the nature of justice and generosity. The wise have said: 'Eight things depend on eight others,—a woman's reputation on her husband; the glory of children on their father; the knowledge of a pupil on his master; the strength of an army on its leader; the dignity of a devotee on his piety; the security of subjects on their king; the conduct of the sovereign's affairs on equity; and the splendour of justice on wisdom and caution. Foremost in this respect are two things: 1st, To know your dependants and servants, and to bring down each of them to his station, patronising them according to the measure of their ability and merit; 2d, To be suspicious of them as regards one another, since there is a constant struggle amongst the attendants at the courts of kings, which cannot be settled save by extinction and death. Therefore if a king listens to the accusations of this one against that one, and accepts the information laid by this person against that person, no further trust will be placed in the sovereign or pillars of state, since whenever they wish they can cast a sincere friend into the region of accusation, and deck a traitor in the garb of rectitude: by this means the innocent are enthralled in the whirlpool of misfortune, and the guilty live on the shore of escape in safety and security.

> The innocent, broken-hearted, in prison;
> The guilty afar off, merry, and smiling.

"Doubtless the result of this affair will be, that those who are present will decline to accept office, while they who are absent will abstain from undertaking service, and the execution of the absolute decrees being delayed, a thousand evils will overtake the pillars of the state, and the troubles which will spring from this pass the limit of calculation, and are beyond the degree of measurement."

> Give no ear to the speech of the calumniators,
> For through them the kingdom and faith are overthrown.
> If the malignant get exalted at your hands,
> The basis of your worth and dignity will be destroyed.
> If you are fellow-travellers with the envious,
> You have given over the reins of wisdom from your hands.

The Lion said: "I have not issued this decree relative to Farísah owing to what any one has said; nay, more, till his treachery became clear to me my disposition was unaltered." The Lion's mother rejoined: "Change of feeling on the part of kings is not allowable, in the absence of manifest certainty, especially as regards confidants of the court; and as to what you said, that his perfidy was evident, as yet this speech is behind the veil of doubt, and when the curtain shall drop from the face of this matter, the truth thereof will be apparent. It was proper that this degree of crime which, on suspicion, they impute to Farísah, should have been contained in the expanse of your mercy, that his former service should have been kept before the eyes of your heart; neither should you have erased from the tablets of your mind the efforts and illustrious acts which proceeded from him at the door of this seat of government, nor have listened with the ear of approbation to the words of worthless, untried persons, concerning those who are truly deserving.

> The low person does not wish the success of another.[1]
> The miser will not leave a fly in the cup.
> The base introduce a hundred stratagems,
> So that the matter of the man of merit may not prosper.

"O Son! whatever circumstances may arise, and whatever occurrences may take place, far-seeing wisdom and world-adorning intellect must be considered just guides and sound judges, since the honour of a man's disposition is exalted by the purity of his ability.

> It is wisdom by which the edifice of honour is rendered secure,
> And by which the sons of Adam increase their reputation.

"Now Farísah, as regards your government, had reached a high station and exalted rank, and had attained great position and considerable dignity. In the assemblies you used to speak his praises, and in private you were wont to honour him by taking counsel with him. Now it is incumbent upon you to put aside your intention of breaking your word, and not to strive to level the basis of the edifice which you have reared with the hand of your own care; and also to preserve yourself and him from the exultation of foes and the rejoicing of the envious, so that in accordance with your firmness and majesty, deeming investigation and inquiry necessary, and taking every precaution, and making all research, you may be excused at the hands of reason, and in the sect of the learned may be free from the contamination of calumny. This offence which has been imputed to him is too conemptible for a wise man like him to darken with the dust thereof the mirror of his integrity, or stain the skirt of his uprightness with the impurity of such base deeds as these. I know that greed and avarice could not overpower his temperance and contentment, nor covetousness and avidity gallop the steed of hope in the plain of his vision and knowledge. During the time that Farísah has been in attendance at this threshold he has eaten no flesh, and before this his nature was known and proclaimed as such, and his reputation for abstaining from devouring animals had spread amongst all mouths and reached the ears of every one.

> Fruitless speeches would not be so lengthy.

"The most probable idea is that enemies have placed the meat in Farísah's house: and to go to this extent is not too much on the part of the treacheries of the wicked and the malice of the envious; since amongst the jealous are some who, in the idea that evil may befall another, will consent to destroy their own souls, just as that unhappy Merchant ordered the Slave to kill him?" The Lion demanded, "Narrate how that was."

---

[1] The text appears corrupt, and I have introduced the negative, otherwise the purport of the line would be that the mean person *does* wish for another to be successful.

STORY IV.

She said: It has been related that in Baghdád was an envious man, who had a neighbour, an honest, right-minded individual, who spent his days in crossing the valley of fasting with the steps of abstinence, and employed his nights in journeying the highway of worship by the way of religious endeavours and pious labours.

> He lit a taper of affection in his heart,
> And it consumed all save God.

The men of Baghdád used to turn the face of confidence towards that holy man, and in their assemblies and public gatherings the mention of his goodness was current; the great men of the city used to bear him in mind kindly, and by way of a present and a blessing scattered before him money and goods. For these reasons the envious neighbour was jealous of that excellent man, and in a variety of ways made plots against him; but every arrow of treachery which he shot from the bow of suspicion had no effect on the shield of that person's rectitude, and the armour of his piety, till he was miserable at this matter and extremely worried. He bought a Slave, and thought proper to bestow upon him the dues of kindness, as well as presents, and discharged the demands of courtesy and consideration. At times he used to say: "I am fostering you for an object, and am nurturing you for a certain matter; now I hope that you will relieve my heart of that burden, and set my desolate soul at ease in regard to that which occupies it."

> That my tears, which drop from my eyes through anguish of heart,
> May quench the flame—such is my hope.

When a time had elapsed, and the Slave had remained obedient and submissive, several times with the tongue of supplication he asked to commence the promised affair, and to undertake the task wherein the object of his master was included, and said: "The varied favours and kindnesses which you have lavished on this poor creature, are not to be explained by the power of expression; nor can the different courtesies and bounties, by which you have distinguished this lowly servant, be set forth in a clear manner by the aid of description.

> I, your servant, through your favour, am become like a lily;
> Each petal has a tongue, and of lilies there are a thousand.

"I desire in return for these favours to stake my life, and to perform the way of servitude in requital for these boons."

> I will scatter the coin of my life for you;
> I will devote to your business the soul of my existence.

The Master, when he saw that the Slave was filled with a desire to be grateful, and a longing to show his affection, removed the veil from before the matter, and said: "Learn and gather, that I am annoyed beyond measure at the hands of this neighbour, and am anxious in some way to injure him; but though I have laid snares and dug pits, the arrow of my deliberation has not reached the target of desire, and the fire of envy every hour raises a flame in my heart, and makes me disgusted with life. In rage against him I am disgusted with the pleasures of life, and am become wearied of my precious existence. For this reason have I fostered you all this time, in order that you may this night kill me on my neighbour's roof, and leaving me there depart, so that when in the morning they shall see me there lying slain, assuredly they will seize him on the charge of murdering me, and his property and life will come to the region of destruction; his reputation for integrity and uprightness will also be ruined, and the belief of mankind concerning him be falsified, nor will he be able again to vaunt his piety and integrity. Then, to the grief of mankind, the meaning of this verse concerning him will be verified, wherein it has been said,

'The Devotee, O Lord! soars beyond limit; cast away the curtain from before him,
So that mankind may see revealed his secret guilt.'"

The Slave replied: "O Master! cease such ideas, and devise some other plan for remedying this matter; if your ambition is to injure the Devotee, I will hurl him to destruction, and set your heart at rest concerning him." The Master said: "This is a deep and serious plan: maybe you cannot overpower him, nor manage to kill him so quickly; while I have no more strength or endurance. Arise! and perform this service, and make me pleased with myself. See, I make over to you your letter of freedom, and give you a purse of gold, which will afford you means of support for the rest of your life, so that you may quit this city and abide in another kingdom." The Slave said: "O Master! no intelligent man would conceive such an idea as you have planned, and he who has inhaled the fragrance of wisdom would not scheme such a notion as you have devised, since the ruin of an enemy should be sought during the time of life; but when you have gone beyond the pale of existence what pleasure will you have from his being slain, or what advantage from his tortures and imprisonment?"

When I am no longer in the pleasure-garden, say to the lily, "Cease growing."
When I am gone from the pasture, say to the box-tree, "No longer exist."

Much as he spoke in this way, it was of no avail. When the Slave saw that his Master could only be satisfied in that way, he cut off his head upon the top of the neighbour's roof, and left there his body, which was a disgrace to the expanse of existence, and carrying off his own letter of freedom and the purse of dínár, set out towards Isfahán, and deposited in that place of security the burden of residence. Next day, finding the evil-designed Master slain upon the roof of the good man, they captured the holy man and put him in prison. Seeing that the murder of the envious person was not legally proved against him, and many notables and men of Baghdád gave evidence as to his piety and innocence of mind, no one opposed him. But they did not remove his chains, and he remained some time thus imprisoned. By chance, after a while, one of the great merchants of Isfahán saw the Slave, who inquired about the affairs of this master's family and neighbours. In the midst of the proceeding, the conversation turned upon that good man and his imprisonment. The Slave said: "A strange injustice has befallen that innocent man; the fact is, this proceeding was done by me, at the command and by the orders of my Master, and that honest man is unaware of this matter." He then repeated in its entirety an account of the case. The master merchant brought a lot of people to testify to this that had occurred, and coming to Baghdád they narrated an account of what had happened, and the circumstances which had taken place. That true believer having obtained his liberation,[1] the envious man became the butt for the arrow of reproach, while the pious neighbour recited, as applicable to his case, the purport of these beautiful verses, which are the effusion of the mind of one of the excellent :

> "Through envy, one or two ignorant people, as regards me,
> Breathed (slander), and pierced the shell of falsehood.
> And in the night of error, by stringing the bow of fraud,
> Split the hair of selfishness with the arrow of treachery.
> From the occurrence of that affair complete good befell me,
> While they experienced the retribution of their own bad deed."

"I have adduced this story that the King may gather what kind of proceedings will issue from the envious; and seeing that they are such towards one another, how then can birds in the summit of the air, fish in the depths of the sea, or beasts in the expanse of the plain, live secure from the designs of the malicious? Amongst your servants, if those who are inferior to Farísah in station, but who previously had a higher reputation than him, plot designs against him, and stir up perfidy to lower his dignity, it is not to be wondered at.[2] Defer acting hastily and rashly, and practise the habit of compassion and sedateness, and in this matter using salutary reflection, remedy this in a way worthy of your greatness. Should you this day have pulled the reins of punishment, and to-morrow the truth of the affair become evident, and the particulars of the matter be known, there is no escaping from one of two things : if he was not deserving of death, you have been merciful to him, and have not fixed the blood of an innocent person upon the scroll of your life; while if truly he should be worthy of destruction, the power is left to you, and you are not precluded from slaying him."

> You may kill a man when alive, but
> You cannot restore to life one who has been slain.

The Lion listened to the words of his mother, and weighing them with the scales of wisdom, perceived that the advice was free from self-interest, and the admonition graced with loyalty. He deferred the period of punishment, and ordered Farísah to be brought to his presence, and summoning him to a private interview, said : "We have ere this tried you, and have seen and approved your disposition and qualities, and your words are more acceptable to us than the talk of your enemies and those who envy you. Again take charge of your affairs, and be not suspicious or filled with thought at the things which have been said or heard." Farísah replied : "Although the King has cast the shade of favour upon the brow of my condition, and displayed what proceeds from the kindness of monarchs, yet I shall not escape the annoyance of this accusation, till the time that the King devises a remedy and arranges a plan, so that the truth of the matter and exact details of the case may become recognised. Notwithstanding that I know for certain my own perfect integrity, and have complete reliance upon my own warrants of security, yet the more care is taken the more clear will become the fact of my sincerity and rectitude. I am convinced that the interest of my affairs and the wellbeing of my life is included in the folds of this matter."

---

[1] حلاص in the Persian text is a misprint for خلاص.
[2] Literally, "it is not far."

You must not be dejected, O my soul! at the taunts of the envious,
Maybe if you look closely, your own welfare is comprised therein.

Kámjúí said: "In what way can investigation be made, and with what device can the truth be ascertained?" Farísah replied: "The set who made the accusation must be summoned, and interrogated by way of inquiry as to what is the meaning of singling me out for this treachery, who have not for years eaten flesh, and passing by persons who consume meat, and cannot exist without it. Assuredly when the King eagerly presses his queries in this respect, they will tell the truth thereof. If they are fractious, the particulars of what has happened can be ascertained by the threat of punishment; while, if this should not be effectual, by the hope of mercy and the promise of favour, the veil of doubt can be removed from the face of certainty, so that the innocence of my hands and purity of my skirt may become clear to all the attendants and servants."

Every secret which is concealed in the veil of night,
When day arrives becomes clear to all.

Kámjúí said: "I will investigate the state of the case by threats of punishment, not by the good news of pardon and compassion, since forgiveness must not be expended on any one who confesses having plotted against, and having been envious of, one of my confidants and officers." Farísah said: "All clemency which is bestowed by one of absolute authority and power is quite proper. 'Pardon goes with power.' The mode of proceeding should be, that in spite of your enemy being in your power his offence should be overlooked, since to be superior to a foe is a boundless favour, gratitude for which boon cannot be shown save by pardon and clemency."

When you are superior to one who has done wrong,
Return thanks for this bounty by means of pardon.

When Kámjúí heard the words of Farísah, and observed the traces of sincerity and rectitude upon the pages of those utterances, he summoned separately each one of that body who had raised the dust of strife, and endeavoured to the utmost limit to investigate the secrets and extract the intricacies of that affair; and with the promise that if they should explain what had occurred, the pages of their offences should be washed with the water of pardon, and notwithstanding all this they should also be favoured with royal caresses and largesses, he laid severe injunctions upon them. At length some confessed, and others, too, of necessity avowed and stated with truth what had occurred. The sun of Farísah's rectitude came forth from beneath the cloud of suspicion, and the dust of doubt was removed from before the eyes of certainty.

We made investigations, and the case of every one was disclosed.

The Lion's mother said: "O Son! you have given security to this body, and it is not possible to withdraw therefrom, but in this respect you have gained experience from which warning must be taken, and henceforth the ear of attention must not be open to the calumnies of any low people. Till, too, open proof and extremely clear evidence, such as may keep you from irresolution, shall be visible, the idle stories of the malignant must not be listened to, and the words which they may speak relative to a person's crime, although they be but brief and short, must not be accepted. Since a trifling thing by degrees reaches such a pitch that the remedy thereof does not come within the pale of possibility, and the source of great streams like the Nile, Euphrates, Oxus, or Tigris is but a very little spring, but by the help of other waters they attain such a size that it is not feasible to cross them save in a ship; therefore, as regards the calumnies of persons, discrimination must be used between the importance and the unimportance of every word which they utter, and the path for further talk be closed, so that the termination of the matter may not end in evil."

> The fountain-head may be stopped with a needle;
> When it overflows it cannot be crossed by an elephant.

Kámjúí said: "I have accepted this advice, and am aware that it is not well without clear evidence to suspect any one." His mother replied: "O King! he who, without evident causes, injures his friends, is of the number of those eight classes, whose society the wise enjoin should be avoided." Kámjúí said, "Describe this briefly." The Lion's mother said: "Sages have inscribed upon the leaves of the pages of their admonitions, that it is necessary to avoid the company of eight classes of persons, and incumbent to associate and be intimate with eight other kinds. The eight individuals from associating with whom the skirt of consent must be folded up, are,—1st, He who does not recognise what is due to benefactors for their favours, and makes himself celebrated for ingratitude and unthankfulness; 2d, He who without cause takes offence, and his anger overpowers his pity; 3d, He who becomes elated with long life, and considers himself independent of observing what is due to the Creator and creature; 4th, He who bases his actions upon treachery and deceit, and deems this in his sight as of no importance; 5th, He who opens upon himself the way of falsehood and treachery, and keeps aloof from uprightness and integrity; 6th, He who, as regards lusts, elongates the thread of sensuality, and deems indulgence and frivolity the sanctuary of his desires, and the high altar of his ambition; 7th, He who is celebrated for want of shame, and lives on brazen-faced, and without manners; 8th, He who without reason becomes suspicious as regards men, and without evidence or proof suspects the wise. But the eight persons with whom one should associate, and deem their friendship a prize, are,—1st, He who considers gratitude for kindness an obligation, and takes care to perform the duties which are imposed upon him; 2d, He whose knot of affection and promises of friendship are not broken by the occurrences of life and the changes of the unstable heavens; 3d, He who deems it necessary to respect men of education and honour, and by word and deed is ready to recompense and requite them; 4th, He who abstains from treachery, deceit, pride, and arrogance; 5th, He who, at times of anger, possesses the power of restraining himself; 6th, He who raises the banner of generosity, and, in gratifying the desires of those who are hoping for something, labours to the utmost of his power; 7th, He who grasps the skirts of modesty and honesty, and never at any time deviates from the way of good manners; 8th, He who by nature is the friend of the upright and men of piety, and avoids the wicked and sceptical. He who is friends and allies with these last-mentioned sets, and avoids and shuns the kinds previously quoted, by the blessing of their society, the evil defects in his own disposition will diminish, and the complexion of his condition become more near true moderation; since vinegar, with all its sharpness and sourness, when mixed with honey, escaping from its mart of acidity, becomes the cause of removing a great many ills."

> Like vinegar, mix your sour face with honey,
> So that you may cure diseases, and give ease to the soul.

Be not dead at heart, but choose a dear comrade,
So that you may get life from the society of your intimate friend.
Be like a shadow, attending the righteous,
So that, like the sun, you may become renowned in the world.

When the Lion saw how suitably and carefully, with auspicious kindness, his mother settled this misfortune and remedied this calamity, after performing the demands of gratitude and thankfulness, he said: "O Queen of the time! by the blessing of your advice, and the kindness of your admonition,

"The road which was dark has been enlightened,
The matter which was troublesome has become easy!

"and an able servant and competent minister has come forth from the whirlpool of calumny, while I have gained information as to every one of my attendants; henceforth I know in what way each must be treated, and in what fashion to set about rejecting or accepting their words." Accordingly his confidence in Farísah's integrity increased, and offering various apologies and kindnesses, he summoned him to his presence, and said: "This calumny must be deemed the cause of increased confidence, and the reason of additional trust, and the management of affairs which was confided to you must be continued on the promised terms." Farísah said: "This is not right, and you do not unloose the knot from my affairs with these favours. The King has once before neglected his promises, and given the place of honour in his mind to the mighty efforts of my enemies."

O thou! who hast cleared thy heart of fidelity,
Thou hast leagued with my enemies.
If thou thus with all persons sportest in love,
Thou wilt never recognise what is due to any single person.

Kámjúí said: "You must not call to mind anything to this effect, since neither was anything wanting in your service nor was aught deficient in my favours; be of good cheer, and with the utmost confidence set about your affairs." Farísah replied:

"I have not a head and turban for every day.

"This once I have escaped, but the world is not free from the envious and calumniators, and so long as the King's favour rests upon me, jealousy on the part of the malevolent will occur. According to the measure of attention with which the King honoured the words of the mischief-makers, my enemies have discovered that his Majesty can easily be brought to their side; every moment they will devise some fresh wickedness, and each hour produce mischief. As regards every king who gives place in his ear to the words of a mischief-making tale-bearer, and pays regard to the hypocrisy and jugglery of a calumniator and informer, his service is perilous to the soul; and to risk life is not the way of the wise.

My soul does not spring up afresh every day.

"If the King's judgment sees fit, I will with a single word make clear my excuse for not accepting office." The King enjoined, "Say on." Farísah replied: "If the Sovereign in this misfortune has had pity on me, and placed fresh confidence and renewed trust in me, it was by reason of his kindness and condescension, and it must be considered the greatest favour and the utmost courtesy; but in that the King displayed haste, and [1] showed levity in punishing me without investigation, I have become suspicious of his royal virtues, and am not hopeful of his regal favours and endless compassion, since he has fruitlessly cast his previous patronage into the region of dissipation, and needlessly brought my past service into the area of destruction. He has allowed a severe punishment to befall me in respect of this contemptible accusation, which, if it were substantiated indeed, is of no great importance. It becomes a king that not even a great perfidy should darken the potion of his pardon. Just as the King of Yaman, in spite of a great offence, did not disgrace his Chamberlain, but drew the veil of mercy before the latter's wicked proceedings." Kámjúí inquired, "How was that?"

STORY V.

He said: It has been related that in the capital of Yaman was a King, the glorious morn of whose justice was evident on his illustrious brow, and the radiant light of his equity manifest on the face of his condition and the forehead of his circumstances—

> A King, in the way of whose court the Heavens
> Scattered coin from the Pleiades and Orion.
> He used to sit at the banquet of Cyrus and Kai,[2]
> Possessing the girdle of Farídún;[3] an auspicious-footed King.

One day he was vexed with his Chamberlain, and confined him to his house. The poor man no longer possessed the warmth of the King's glance, yet did not deem it expedient to depart from the city. Of necessity, sitting in the corner of his humble abode, he sometimes used to weep through distress at his affairs, and at others smile at the marvels of Fortune.

> Every night, from internal anguish at our wretched condition,
> We sometimes weep like a taper, and sometimes smile.

At length, from his want of means, the largeness of his family, and his distressed circumstances, he arrived at great straits, and thought that he must betake himself to the King's presence, whether his neck be given to the sword of punishment, or his head be decked with the crown of acceptance. One day, when the King had a distinguished company, and there was a general assembly, that Chamberlain sent to all his friends, and borrowing a horse and garments, mounted and came to the King's court. The doorkeepers and chamberlains, thinking that the King had relented towards him, and that the horse and clothes were given him by command of the Sovereign, no one stopped him. The Chamberlain boldly advanced towards the King's court, and rested at an eligible spot. The King was stting at a banquet of wine, and conversing merrily with the guests. When he saw the Chamberlain the fire of wrath began to raise its flame, and the executioner, rage, bethought himself of punishment. Again reflecting, he did not desire to upset the convivial assembly, and change the delight of pleasant wine to the sadness of injury and torture. His natural compassion sought to get the mastery by pardoning the offence, and the generosity of his disposition thought to overlook the fault.

---

[1] In the last line but one of the Persian text, و should be inserted after فرمود .

[2] Founder of the Kaiyúní dynasty in Persia.   [3] See note 1, page 12.

Drink wine, be generous, and leave the reward to God !

When the Chamberlain looked at the King's countenance, and discovered that his genial mirth and joyous face had returned to him, he warmly set about his business, and firmly binding the skirt of service upon the girdle of attendance, lent a hand in every direction, and laboured diligently at every duty, till, finding a seasonable opportunity, he concealed under his tunic a golden dish, the weight of which was a thousand miskál. The King, seeing this proceeding, knew that want of food and his distressed circumstances were the cause of this rashness : he made pity a screen over that offence. At the termination of the assembly, the attendants in charge of the dish were making search and suspecting the people, with the design of drawing a confession from them by violence and punishment. The King inquired from one of the deputies, "What has happened to this body that they are so disturbed ?" The deputy represented a description of the circumstances of the case. The King said : "Let these people go, for they have not got the dish ; he who has it will not return it, and he who saw it will not tell." The Chamberlain came forth, and for a year found means of support with the price of that dish. Next year at the same time there was a private banquet, and a public assembly. Again the Chamberlain betook himself to the midst of the throng. The King calling him, quietly said to him : "Is the dish all spent ?" The Chamberlain placed the face of intercession on the earth, and said :

O absolute Monarch ! may the evil eye be far from the moon of your dignity !
May the house of your life be firm till all eternity !

"What I did was deliberately, and I thought that might be either the King would see it, or some one else would become aware of it, and deliver [1] me to punishment, for through distress of hunger I had become satiated of life, while, if my proceeding remained in the veil of secrecy, at any rate food for some days would come to my hands. Such was my case, and I well know that the sincerity of my words will not be concealed from the mirror of your enlightened mind."

That heart-consuming taper is aware of my anguish,
And its pure mind internally testifies to my pretension.

The King said : "You say truly, and you are to be pitied." Accordingly he caressed him, and restored to him the position which he previously held.

"The object of reciting this story is, that the King's heart should be like the stormy ocean, so as not to become turbid with the rubbish of calumny ; and the centre of his compassion, like a majestic mountain, be fixed in a firm place, so that the severe blast of rage shall not move it."

Amongst true hearts anger has no friends ;
The cucumber will not be found in a warm locality.
Straws together with dust leave their place ;
But the mountain puts not its feet beyond its skirt.

The Lion said : "Your words are true and correct, but harsh and severe, and it is incumbent that the medicinal potion of advice should be pleasant to the taste, so as to be easy for the invalid to swallow ; and maybe the temperament

---

[1] زساند is a misprint for رساند.

of a sick person recoils from disagreeable drugs, although he knows that his recovery is comprised therein, and on this account he remains deprived of the bounty of health."

> When any one can with sweet smiles bear away our hearts,
> Why should bitter replies issue from such a mouth?

Farísah replied: "The King's heart is more in the wrong in having acted improperly than my words in stating what is right, and since he can readily listen to falsehood and calumny, it is better that it should not press heavy on him to hear what is sound and honest, and he should beware not to impute this proceeding to boldness and want of respect, for it comprises two distinct advantages. 1st, By calling out and clamouring, the oppressed obtain ease ; and by lamenting and complaining of injury, their minds are freed from the dust of sorrow. So, as well as I can, I proclaim to the utmost what is in my heart, in order that my presence or absence be one and the same with the King, and there may be nothing kept in the background which on a second occasion may become the cause of animosity. 2d, I was anxious that the judge in this case should be the King's penetrating reason and world-adorning justice, and that the decree should be put in force after hearing the words of the injured ; consequently it appeared necessary to explain the particulars of my pain to the physician of the court of justice."

> How can pain be concealed from one's own physician?

Kámjúí said: "So it is; but in extricating you from this whirlpool we showed great condescension, and our freeing you from the vortex of destruction, after your punishment had been ordered, may be considered a most profound kindness and perfect favour." Farísah replied: "I cannot during my life express my gratitude for the King's bounty, nor in centuries discharge the obligation due for the Royal benevolence. This pardon and compassion, after the command for retribution and punishment, is superior to all kindness, since most favours concern the care of the body, while this one caused rest to the soul.

> You have cast a glance of kindness upon my soul and heart;
> My soul is pledged to gratitude, my heart is abashed before you.

"Previous to this, I have always been sincere, obedient, honest, and loyal to the King, and have deemed my soul and spirit a sacrifice for his pleasure and commands; and what I now say is not with the view of imputing wrong to the King's judgment in this matter, or ascribing error as concerns his deliberations and reflections; yet for the ignorant to envy men of merit and intelligence is an invariable practice and habitual custom: and to close the way of jealousy respecting persons of worth, and those endowed with wisdom, appears impossible.

> The rose of merit and worth is never without the thorn of envy.

A great man has said, in this respect—

> If, through envy, some foolish person speaks ill of me,
> It is because he is sick at heart of me.
> They are jealous, but I fear not.
> He is without worth, who is not envied.

"From the sages' prayer, '*Return envied,*' the same idea may be gathered."

Kámjúí rejoined: "Of what consequence is the jealousy of enemies and the treacheries of the envious, since false words have no splendour, and the wiles of those destitute of merit, as regards the virtues of the worthy, are invisible like an obscure star, as compared with the glare of the sun? Falsehood is always defeated, and truth victorious. '*And the word of God is all superior.*' The splendour of the wise [1] is not broken by the opposition of the envious, nor does a man whose skirt is pure become blemished by the slander of the malevolent.

> If a base enemy speaks ill of you, it is of no consequence.
> Copper is not such that it can overthrow the dignity of gold.
> When did a bat's taunts affect the sun?
> When did a base-natured stone injure the worth of a pearl?

"Henceforth rest secure from the malevolence of the envious; for having become aware of the true state of their malicious words, we will not receive them with acceptance." Farísah said: "In spite of all this, I fear lest—*God forbid!*—my enemies once more, not by way of envy—nay, more, under the guise of advice, may interpose between us." The Lion inquired, "On what ground can they interfere?" He replied: "They will say, 'In the heart of such a one dread has occurred, because you ordered his punishment, and pride has found the way to his brain, seeing that you increased your favours to him: and he is nowadays both vexed with your Majesty and suspicious of you; he is not worthy of confidence, nor should he advance in your service.'

> Be not careless as regards those whose hearts you have injured.

"When by these wiles they affect the King's feelings, it is not improbable that suspicions on the part of his Majesty may arise. The truth of the matter is, kings should not rest secure from servants who have suffered violence, or have fallen from their posts, or been overwhelmed with dismissal, or over whom enemies whose rank was inferior to theirs have taken the lead." Kámjúí said: "How can such an occurrence be avoided, or how the doors of this way of access be closed?" Farísah replied: "Their words in this respect are extremely unprincipled, and nought but echoes and misrepresentations, since after such occurrences confidence on both sides will become firmer; because if in the mind of the master, by reason of some negligence which he has discovered on the part of his servant, there should be aversion, when he indulges his rage and punishes according to the case, without doubt the effects of his animosity will grow less, and no alarm, either much or little, will remain. Again, learning the untrustworthiness of the falsehoods of the messengers, he will no longer pay any regard to the idle talk of calumniators; and the excess of sincerity and penetration, and the perfection of merit and uprightness on the part of such a servant will become more assured. If in the heart of a dependant, too, there should be fear and alarm, when he has been punished he will become secure, and free from expectation of misfortune."

> I was in grief, but freed from the sorrow of additional trouble;
> I remained in misfortune, but was delivered from fear of further harm.

The Lion inquired, "From how many causes can suspicion fall upon a servant?" He replied: "From three causes: 1st, He may possess dignity, and ruin occur owing to the negligence of his master; 2d, Enemies may dart out upon him,

---

[1] حردمند in the Persian text is a misprint for خردمند.

and by reason of absence of the King's favour they may overpower him; 3d, The wealth and possessions which he may have accumulated may pass from his hands owing to want of kindness on the part of the Sovereign." Kámjúí said, " How can these be remedied?" He rejoined: " By one thing; that is, that he shall acquire the favour of his master, and the confidence of the King in him be renewed; then both the dignity which has passed from his hands will return, and also the enemies, who were victorious, will be punished. The property, too, which was scattered will be regained; since an equivalent for everything save the soul is possible, especially in the services of kings and great men. Seeing the King has remedied the condition of this servant, who has acquired perfect favour and complete satisfaction, in what way can injury remain? or how can enemies find an opportunity to speak? With all this, I hope that the King, having pardoned me, will not again cast me into the net of cálamity, but will leave me to wander in this desert, secure and quiet, and to offer up my daily allowance of praise and gratitude in sincerity of faith."

> By day I will repeat the lesson of your praise,
> By night I will perform the duty of eulogising you.

Kámjúí said : " Be assured, for you are not of those servants that such calumnies concerning you are heard, or that words tinged with malice, relative to you, reach the region of acceptance. We consider you faithful, and are aware that in adversity you are known to be patient, and in prosperity celebrated for expressing your gratitude, and whatever is contrary to generosity and integrity you ignore, deeming it an essential duty to observe liberality and faithfulness in your own decrees. Therefore rest secure as to protection and favour on our part, for my confidence in your penetration, uprightness, sagacity, and clemency is doubled, and in no way again will the words of an enemy find the place of hearing, and whatever imposture they may invent will be imputed to a clear plot."

> After this the strife-raising words of the envious,
> Concerning friends, shall receive no hearing from us.

Farísah said : " With all this favour what matter the wiles of enemies, and with the King's bounty what signifies the annoyance of foes ? "

> After this, what care I for the crooked-shot arrows of the envious,
> Now that I have met with the bow of my mistress's eyebrows ?

Accordingly he set about his affairs with most eager heart, and every day the degree of his power was augmented, and the rank of his preferment and patronage doubled, till, by the perfection of his integrity and the rectitude of his proceedings, complete confidence was restored, and he became intrusted with the secrets of Property and State.

> His tree was raised aloft to such a height,
> That it threw its shade higher than the heavens.

Such is the story of Kings, between whom and their followers and dependants something having occurred, after the display of severity and aversion, reconciliation and compassion returned. It is not concealed from the wise, what an amount of benefit is comprised in the compass of these stories and anecdotes. Whoever is distinguished, with the aid of heaven, and assisted by eternal happiness, will confine all his ambition to comprehend the warnings of the wise, and expend all his efforts upon penetrating the enigmas of the sages, making inquiries of the physicians of the hospital of piety, the invigorators of those borne down with the sorrows of truth, so that, by the blessing of the remedies of these spiritual doctors, he may be freed from the dangerous disease of ignorance and folly.

Seize the medicine of instruction from the Holy Father,
For a man can have no worse ailment than ignorance.
The face, however fairy-like and beautiful it may be,
Cannot be seen in a mirror which is not bright.
Darwíshes, devotees, and súfís [1] are all children on the road ;
If there be a true man it is nowhere save in the world of God.

[1] See note, p. 24.

BOOK X.

EXPLANATORY OF REQUITING DEEDS BY WAY OF RETALIATION.

INTRODUCTION.

ÁBISHLÍM, with respect, implored the Sage Bídpáí, saying: "I have heard the story of Farísah and Kámjúí, and it is a tale for wise men as to what happens between kings and their servants in regard to opposition and treachery, pardon and punishment, and a return to the renewal of favour and the increase of confidence in honest and able men, with the view of managing the country and arranging its affairs: as to how one must not be too eager in the direction of falsehood, but confess one's self wrong on (hearing) words of rectitude and integrity. The advantages of this story are beyond the limit of calculation. Now repeat an account of some one, who in self-defence and to protect his own soul, did not refrain from molesting others, and injuring animals, nor receive in his ears the advice of the wise, till, in consequence, he became overtaken by the like which proceeded from himself." The Sage said: "None but ignorant persons injure animals—persons such as cannot distinguish between the light of good and the darkness of evil, and the advantages of what is beneficial and the disadvantages of what is baneful; and who, by reason of their stupidity, wandering in the desert of error, are negligent as to the end of their proceedings, while the glance of their judgment, falling short of the termination of matters, is blind to the aspect of retribution. But he, the eyes of whose head are illumined with the jewelled collyrium of Divine grace, and the flower-garden of whose heart is perfumed with the odours of the sweet-scented herbs of Eternal favour, how can he permit towards those similar to him what he will not approve as regards himself?

Do not admit towards others what you do not approve concerning yourself.

" It must be known that for every deed a retribution is found, which assuredly will befall the authors thereof; nor must they be puffed up with any delay which may occur, since according to the decree—'*Of a truth God gives delay, but does not overlook*'—possibly there may be delay, yet there will be no overlooking. There may be an opportunity for two or three days' respite, but the idea of not meeting with punishment and retribution is an absurd notion. Every seed which is sown in the field of practice will bring forth abundance of fruit ere much time elapses; therefore, he who seeks for good, must sow nought but proper seed.

Do you wish that no evil may befall you?
Then, as far as you can, do no wrong, neither much nor little;
Since your righteous dealing and wickedness will both recoil on you,
As regards yourself, look how you act.

" If any one is anxious to conceal his evil conduct by treachery and fraud, and to deck his hypocrisy and dissimulation in the garments of good deeds, to such a degree that men may praise him, and the fame of his laudable qualities being prevalent throughout all districts and regions, may reach both far and near, the result of his improper deeds will never be changed by [1] this means, but the fruit of his internal malignity and impurity of mind will betide him; just as if a rustic, for example, were to sow seed of the gourd in the ground, and covering it over with earth, were to make it appear that he had planted sugar-cane in that soil, and every one were to believe that sugar-cane would sprout up in that field, without doubt by such stratagem his husbandry would not be altered, and those same gourd-seeds which he sowed therein would display their fruit.

When you act wrongly, beware! rest not secure,
Since there is the seed, and God will cause it to grow.
Oftentimes He conceals it, till
At length shame overtakes you from such deeds.
The Eternal God indicates as to retribution,
In that He says, " *If you return, we also will return.*"

" It may be that when any one discovers the truth as to retribution, and the meaning of the verse, ' *Therefore, whoever does good to the weight of an ant shall see the same, and whoever does evil to the weight of an ant shall behold the same,*' passes through his mind, avoiding what is wrong, he will turn towards what is good, and repenting of oppression and injury, will follow the way of kindness and compassion.

This, too, may spring from the Grace of God.

" Of the like of such speeches and illustrative of such sayings is the story of the Rank-breaking Lion and the Archer." The King inquired, " What was that?"

---

[1] It seems necessary to omit the ‌‌و after برسد .

STORY I.

He said: It has been related that in the kingdom of Aleppo was a waste, comprising many trees, and including gardens and rivulets.

> Rose, willow, the box-tree, and dart-like cypress,
> Locked together, bough with bough.

In that waste was a [1] Lion, a mighty beast, prepared for war and battle, with elephantine body, such that the planet Mars in the heavens, like a wild ass, became his prey; and, from the glory of his majesty, the Lion of the Spheres, as it were the energy [2] implanted by the Creator in the centre of the earth, fled beneath the ground.

> When at the time of anger he showed his teeth,
> An anvil from dread of him would have turned to water.
> His two eyes were like two grates of fire,
> His mouth resembled a cave full of daggers.

He was perpetually busied in shedding blood, and staining his claws and mouth with the gore of animals. A Jackal, who used to wait on him, seeing this state of things, became alarmed at the result of his violence and the fruits of his fury, and thinking of the threat—"*Whoever assists a tyrant, God gives the latter power over him*"—was anxious to quit his service.

> Dread the society of that person by whom people are oppressed;
> Whoever is near the fire runs the risk of being burnt.

With this idea he set his face towards the desert. On the edge of the waste he saw a Mouse biting the root of a tree with the utmost assiduity, and separating with its saw-like teeth the portions of the fibres. The Tree, in language applicable to the circumstances, said: "O heartless tyrant! why with the axe of oppression do you overthrow the edifice of my life, and with the sword of injustice sever the thread of my soul, which is indicated by my water-carrying roots, thereby depriving mankind of the rest of my shade and the benefits of my fruit?"

> Do not wrong, for evil is requited with evil;
> According to the creed of the generous wickedness is brutal.

The Mouse, paying no heed to his lamentations, continued to work in the same cruel fashion, when suddenly a Snake, with open mouth, came forth from ambush, and, planning the destruction of the Mouse, in an instant bore him off. The Jackal by this circumstance gained additional experience, and learnt that he who acts cruelly meets with nought but severity, and he who plants the thorn will not gather the rose of Desire.

> Act not wickedly, but remain honest-minded.
> The retribution of evil deeds will be nought but evil.

At the same time that the Snake, having finished eating the Mouse, had coiled

---

[1] A subsequent passage shows that the ordinary meaning of مادَه, "female," is not applicable. I have therefore omitted the word altogether as an unintelligible interpolation.

[2] This is the meaning given in Johnson's Dictionary, but the simile is not very comprehensible.

himself under the shade of the tree, a Porcupine arrived, and seizing in his mouth the tail of the Snake, drew back his head. The Snake, from excess of anguish, darted himself against the Porcupine till all his frame was pierced with the points of the quills, and he gave up his soul to the king of the infernal regions. The Jackal saw another inscription on the page of warning. When the Snake had finished his attempts, the Porcupine peeped out his head, and having eaten some of the Snake's entrails, which were fit food for him, again drew his head within the veil of concealment, and remained in the plain of the desert in the form of a ball. The Jackal was watching the proceeding of the Porcupine, when suddenly a hungry Fox arrived there, and saw in that expanse the Porcupine, who was a dainty morsel for him. He knew that in consequence of the sharpness of the quills he could not inhale the perfume of the rose of his desire, and that, save with the key of treachery and stratagem, he could not open the door of his wishes. Accordingly, turning the Porcupine on his back, he sprinkled some drops of saliva on his stomach, while the Porcupine, fancying that it was rain, drew forth his head from within the screen of concealment. The Fox, jumping up, seized his throat, and tearing off his head, with the utmost avidity ate the remaining portions, so that only his skin was left. Scarce had the Fox completely finished, when a Dog, bounding along like a tearing wolf, came forth from a corner, and tore the Fox to pieces, and with a portion thereof appeasing his dog-like appetite, hid himself in the wood. The Jackal saw these marvels, each of which was a clear proof of the truth of retribution, and remained expecting some other proceedings to come forth from the secret abode of Fate to the expanse of the plain of Destiny. Suddenly he saw a Leopard dart from a corner of the wood, and ere the Dog was aware thereof, with a soul-rending wound drew his heart from his breast. By chance the Leopard had jumped forth unaware of the ambush of a Hunter, who, having placed an arrow in the bow, was sitting waiting for him. When he saw the Leopard busy over the Dog, he shot a heart-piercing shaft at him, which, entering his right side, went out at the left.

> Heaven said, " Fortunate are that sword and shaft ; "
> The earth exclaimed, " Bravo ! that hand."

Scarce had the Leopard fallen utterly prostrate, when the Hunter with rapidity drew the skin from off its head. This done, a Horseman arrived at that spot, and coveted that Leopard skin, which was very speckled and tinted. The Hunter making a difficulty in this respect, the affair between them ended in strife and conflict. In the midst of the fight and onslaught, the Horseman drew a keen sword, and rushed at the Hunter's head, which, ere he could move it aside, the Horseman cast into the plain, and, carrying off the Leopard's skin from the ground, set out on his way. Ere he had gone upwards of a hundred steps, his horse fell on its head, and the Horseman, tumbling on the earth, broke his neck.

> Time did not give him quarter for two hours.

These experiences confirmed the Jackal's convictions, and, attending on the Lion, he sought permission to go from that waste. The Lion said : " You are at ease under the shade of my fortune ; while you share the tables of my kindness and the trencher-boards of my bounty, what can be the cause of your going from this abode, and your declaring that you will abandon my service ? " The Jackal replied : " O King ! an idea has occurred to me, and a thought from the depths of

2 c

my heart has struck me, to conceal which causes me to fear consuming away, and to proclaim which is to risk my life.

> To conceal from you the condition of my heart is difficult,
> From fear of God to proclaim it is hard.

"If the kingly magnanimity will make a promise which cannot in any way be broken, I will recount truly the state of the case." The Lion having given him security, entered into an agreement to this effect, and confirmed it with an oath, the Jackal said : "I see that the King's aim is set upon injuring creatures, and the reins of his power are turned towards molesting the innocent. Hearts are wounded with the claw of his violence, and bosoms rent through the scar [1] of his cruelty.

> Cease to oppress, and dread repentance ;
> View with fear the terrors of the Day of Judgment.

"I am extremely alarmed at this proceeding, and terrified at this matter." The Lion, since he had just made a promise, bore these harsh words, and said : "Since no oppression has overtaken you, nor any tyranny befallen you at my hands, for what cause should you turn away?" The Jackal rejoined : "For two reasons : 1st, No person of generous feelings can endure witnessing violence, nor has he power to hear the wails of the oppressed.

> Creatures are distressed at your existence ;
> I do not approve of the sufferings of the people.
> My face is half pale at my helplessness ;
> Grief for the destitute has made me sad.

"2d, Would that disgrace of such deeds may not overtake you ! and I, too, by reason of my association with you, may be consumed with the fire of punishment."

> When fire is lighted it consumes both moist and dry.

The Lion said : "Whence have you gathered as to the disgrace of evil deeds, and from whom have you learnt the blessings of good conduct?" The Jackal replied : "Whenever the nostrils of a person's heart have been perfumed with the sweet odours of the rose-garden of wisdom, he knows that he who sows the seed of violence will reap nought save the harvest of evil, while he who plants the tree of benefit will gather nought save the fruit of repose. The world, which is the house of retribution, has been compared to a hill, seeing that whatever you speak to it, whether good or bad, you hear the very same by way of echo.

> This world is a hill, and our deeds a voice,
> Of which the sounds echo back to us.
> Though a wall casts a long shadow,
> Yet that shade ultimately creeps back thereto. [2]

"This very day, with the eye of certainty, I have seen cases of retribution, and have witnessed the nature of requital." He then commenced to repeat the history of the Mouse, the Snake, the Porcupine, the Fox, the Dog, the Leopard,

---

[1] بداع in the Persian text is a misprint for بداغ .

[2] That is, says Eastwick, "as the shadow, though long, comes back to its original source, the wall ; so our cruelties, though it may be after a long interval, recoil on ourselves."

the Hunter, and the Horseman, just as he had witnessed it all, and by way of admonition, exclaimed : " O King ! the Mouse who bit the root of the tree became food for the Snake, who, having brought ruin on the former, was himself overtaken by the misfortune of the Porcupine ; and he having killed the Snake fell into the snare of the Fox's cunning, and the latter, who had spilt the blood of animals, was deprived of life by a hungry Dog ; who in turn, by reason of his want of justice, was racked to death in the claws of the Leopard ; and he, through the evil of violence and cruelty, became the target for the arrow of Fate. The Hunter, too, on account of his plots and want of compassion, gave his head to the winds ; while the Horseman, through his ruthlessness and base murder, remained desolate with his neck broken. The deeds of each, since they were based on evil, by way of retribution, became the cause of misfortune to themselves respectively. Consequently, to avoid evil and to depart from the wicked is necessary on the part of wise men, and to shape their conduct according to what is right, devoting their energies to good deeds, is incumbent and obligatory upon the prudent."

> The foremost sign of wisdom is this,
> To be in fear of evil all one's years.

The Lion was so elate with the might of his own strength, and so inflamed with the majesty of his power and prowess, that he deemed the words of the Jackal as mere fictions, and considered his admonitions as but jokes ; and the more talk the latter breathed forth in this respect, the more did the fire of greed and avidity increase on the Lion's part.

> O you who, through affection, give me advice,
> Say not so much, for you quicken my flame !

The Jackal saw that his advice had the same effect upon the Lion's heart as the foot-fall of an ant upon a rock or steel, and his admonitions a similar result in his bosom as the point of the spear of a thorn upon an armour of stone.

> Yes, when will the spear of a thorn be effective against adamant ?

He quitted the Lion, and retired to a corner. The Lion, enraged at the Jackal's words, went after him, whereupon he concealed himself in a thorny brake. The Lion passed him, and saw two Fawns grazing in the expanse of that plain, and their devoted mother, by way of protection, watching their proceedings. The Lion determined to slay them, while the Deer cried out : " O King ! what is the object of hunting two striplings, and what is the use[1] of eating them ? Do not make my eyes weep, through separation from my darling objects, nor burn up my heart with the fire of being severed from those who are the very flesh of my soul. Anyhow you have children ; think of that, lest the same happen to them as to my offspring.

Act the same towards me, as you would approve of, if done towards you.

By chance the Lion had two cubs, at the sight of whose faces the world became radiant before him, and to enjoy the spectacle of whose form he desired light to his eyes. At the time that he was there plotting the destruction of the Fawns, a Hunter had also busied himself in the desert capturing the young Lions.

---

[1] Literally, " what will be bound, what will be loosened ? "

There the Lion paying no heed to the Deer's lamentations, killed her offspring, while here the Hunter slew the Lion's two cubs, and tore off their skins.

> Maybe he is the enemy of his own family,
> Who approves of evil against other homes.

The Deer fleeing in terror from before the Lion, and lamenting for the loss of her children, ran distracted in every direction. Suddenly the Jackal met her, and inquired the particulars of the case; and when he had learnt the full details of the matter, his heart was consumed at the Deer's agonies, and he commenced to lament with her.

> Whenever my heart laments for the griefs of my beloved,
> Both doors and walls break forth, through the agony of its cries.

After endless crying, lamenting, sighing, complaining, and grieving, the Jackal consoled her, saying : "Be not [1] sad, for in a little time he will meet with punishment and retribution."

> True, the taper burns the moth,
> Yet it is soon consumed in its own oil.

But when in the other direction the Lion returned to the desert, and saw his cubs cast in the above manner on the ground, he raised a cry and shrill scream to the skies, exclaiming :

> "Pain entered my heart, for the delight of my soul has vanished ;
> My condition has come to this, that power and vigour have fled."

The Lion raised a cry, and commencing a grievous wail, lamented in such manner that the wild animals of that waste were distressed, through alarm at his grief, and complained in a fashion that the birds of the air broke into weeping through the agony of his distress.

> When a torrent of blood flows from my watery eyes,
> What place is there for a friend, since even an enemy would weep for my
>   distress ?

In the neighbourhood of the Lion was a Jackal, who had shaken worldly considerations from off his skirt, and had read the saying, " *Whoever is contented is full*," from the tablets of resignation in God, and trust in the Almighty.

> He rode the plain of resignation,
> He pitched his tent in the plain of contentment.

By way of condolence, he approached the Lion, saying, "What is the cause of all this lamentation and weeping?" The Lion repeated the circumstances of the case. The Jackal said : "Be patient, and wait, for no nostril has ever inhaled, from the rose-garden of the world, the perfume of fidelity; nor has any palate tasted, from the hand of the cup-bearer, Time, the potion of repose without the flavour of injury.

> In the cruel world, the quality of fidelity cannot be found,
> Nor can purity be traced, in the revolution of Time.
> For the wounds of the injured hearts of the distressed,
> There can be no more powerful medicine than patience.

---

[1] غفور in the Persian text is a misprint for غمخور.

" Restrain your feelings for a time, and open the ears of intelligence, till I read two or three sayings from the volume of wisdom, and explain to you the truth of the matter, and the burden of the perfidious world." The inward sea of the Lion calmed down from ebullition and lamentation, and, with the ear of acceptance, he set about listening to the Jackal's admonitions and precepts. When the latter saw that the Lion was disposed to hear his discourse, he commenced a pleasant harangue, saying: " O King ! for every beginning an ending is fixed, and a conclusion predetermined to every commencement. When the period of life is finished, and the time of death draws near, one moment's delay is not conceivable, ' *Therefore when their fate arrives they shall not delay it for an hour, neither shall they advance it.*' As a sequence of every sorrow, joy must be expected, and grief must be anticipated to follow every gladness.

> For years my heart, like a breeze, wandered round the garden of the Spheres,
> If it found in the expanse thereof a rose, it was not discovered without a thorn.

" In all cares one should be resigned to the decrees of God, and defer lamentations, which are of no avail."

> Give up your life, for the arrow of Fate
> Will not deviate one single hair's-breadth.

The Lion inquired, " Whence did this calamity befall my children ? " The Jackal replied : " This, too, happened to you at your own hands ; since, what the archer of Fate has done to you, you have done in a twofold degree to others, and this which has befallen you is retribution for your conduct, ' *As thou judgest, thou wilt be judged.*' Your case is very similar to that of the Seller of wood, who said, ' Whence came this fire to my sticks ? ' " The Lion said, " How was that ? "

STORY II.

He said : It has been related that in former times there was a tyrant who, violently and forcibly, used to purchase sticks of the poor, and making a great difficulty about the price thereof, used to give a lesser sum than the value. In winter time he acted in such a manner to the rich as to seize from them double their just price. Thus both the poor were in straits, through his violence, and also the rich were sad because of his tyranny.

> The bosoms of the distressed were consumed by him ;
> The cells of the oppressed were ruined by him.

One day he took by force some sticks from a poor man and gave no more than half the worth to that hapless destitute person. The Darwísh stretched the hands of prayer to Heaven, and raised the face of supplication to the high altar of submission and humility.

> O tyrant ! be not secure from imprecations, for at night,
> Lamenting they pray, that blood may flow owing to their intercessions.

At this time a pious man arrived, and being apprised of that circumstance, loosed the tongue of reproach against that tyrant, saying :

Beware of the arrow of the lowly man's tears in the ambush of night ;
For the more a person laments owing to his infirmity, the stronger is the
  wound of his spear.

"Do not act in this way to the helpless, who have no protection save the Court
of the Divine Majesty, nor allow yourself to oppress in this manner the distressed, who, all night, like a taper, drop tears from anguish of heart. Do not
render desolate the homes of the hearts of the poor with the calamity of injustice, nor pour the blood of orphans' hearts into the cup of revenge, in place of
ruby wine."

  Drink not this of this goblet, for to-morrow you will have a headache.

That Tyrant, full of pride, was vexed at the words of that Holy Man, and
through arrogance and the rage of folly, frowning, he said :

  Go ! O Shaikh ! and pain my head no more in this manner,
  For I would not purchase two hundred stacks of your tales for one grain.

The Darwísh turned his face from him, and hastened to the corner of his own
private apartment. By chance that very night a fire occurred in the piles of the
Tyrant's wood, and passing from thence to his house and home, burnt clean up
all the possessions which he had, and placed that unjust man from the bed of
softness upon hot ashes. It happened that in the morning that same Holy
Man, who the day previous had tendered his advice, reached the spot, and saw
the Tyrant, who was saying to his dependants, "I know not whence this fire fell
on my palace." The Holy Man said, "From the smoke of the hearts of the
poor, and the anguish of the breasts of the soul-stricken."

  Beware of the smoke from stricken hearts,
  For the inward wound will in the end overthrow you.

The Tyrant dropped his head and said to himself : "I must not wander from
the region of justice ; the seed which I have sown will yield no better fruit than
this."

  We have sown utterly bad seed,
  Behold what we have gathered in consequence !

  "I have adduced this story that you may know that what has befallen your
children is in return for what you have done to the offspring of others, who
have indulged in this same distress and anguish which you have exhibited : of
necessity they have all waited patiently, accordingly, just as others bided their
time, for you to be in distress, so have patience till harm befalls them." The
Lion said, "Confirm these words with proof and evidence, and thereby fix them
in my mind." The Jackal rejoined, "How long have you lived ?" He replied,
"Forty years." The Jackal said, "During this long time what has been
your food ?" He replied, "The flesh of beasts and men whom I have pursued."
The Jackal exclaimed : "Then may not those animals whose flesh you have
made food for so many years, have had fathers and mothers, and may not the
agonies of separation and the grief of parting have caused their children to
bewail and lament ? If on that day you had seen the end of this, and had
refrained from shedding blood, at the present time this occurrence would not
have appeared, nor in any case would such a calamity have happened.

Thou who hast never had pity on others,
Where wilt thou find rest for thyself?
When hearts cry out for the fear of thee,
Who will lay salve on thy wounded soul?

" If you continue pursuing this line of conduct, and remain just the same, blood-thirsty and tyrannical, be prepared yourself to experience as much. So long as people are afraid of you, you will not inhale the perfume of security and repose. Adorn your disposition with compassion and pity, and do not wander about injuring animals, and torturing this one and that one ; for the tyrant will never see the face of repose, nor will the unjust man ever attain his object or desire."

From such a bow no one ever hit the target with the arrow of desire.

When the Lion heard these words, and the truth of the matter was revealed to him, he perceived that the results of conduct, the edifice of which is reared upon cruelty, will be nought save disappointment and disaster. He thought to him-self : "The spring of life, which is the period of youth, is changed for the autumn of old age and helplessness, and any moment I may tread the way of Eternity, and take a far and long journey ; nought can be better than that I should make ready a store for the future life, and laying aside cruelty and oppression, be con-tent with but little food, and no longer sad as to more or less, abandon all ideas of what is or is not."

Vex not your mind as to what is or is not, but be happy,
Since all that is, excellent though it be, will come to nought.
Seeing that, of necessity, one must journey forth from this two-doored[1] inn,
What if the eaves and vault of the mansion of subsistence be high, what if
    they be low?

Accordingly he desisted from drinking blood or eating flesh, and being satisfied with fruits,[2] followed the path of contentment. When the Jackal saw that the Lion took to eating fruits, and that if he persisted in so doing, what would suffice a Jackal for a year would be consumed in ten days, vexation overcame him, and he again approached the Lion saying, "How is the King occupied?" The Lion replied, "I have turned aside from the world, and girt my loins with devotion and abstinence."

Since no one has drunk pleasant water from this azure ocean,
Our hearts have loathed the draught of the world.

The Jackal said : " It is not as the King says ; nay, more, greater misery than before arises to mankind at his hands." The Lion inquired : "In what way is any one injured by me, since I do not stain my mouth with blood, nor do I open my claws to injure any person?"

Were they to tear me in pieces with the dagger of injustice,
I would not molest any one in any way.

The Jackal said : "You have withdrawn your hand from your own portion, and

---

[1] Possibly meaning one door whereby to enter, another whereat to depart—in allusion to birth and death.
[2] The translator must not be held responsible for the absurdity that the Lion and Jackal, which are carnivorous animals, lived upon fruits.

eat the rations of other animals, to which you have no right; and the fruits of this plain will not suffice you for food for ten days, and those whose sustenance is comprised in those fruits, will quickly die, and the crime thereof will remain round your neck, and maybe, also, the retribution thereof will overtake you in this world. I fear your case may be like that of the Boar who plundered the fruits belonging to the Ape." The Lion said, " Explain how was that."

STORY III.

He said : It has been related that once upon a time an Ape found favour with God, and separating himself from his own kith and kin, took his abode in a corner of the desert wherein were many fig-trees. He thought to himself : " Animals cannot exist without food, and in this place nought can be found to eat but figs; if all of them are eaten fresh and green, in winter-time one must be without food or sustenance. Nought can be better than every day to shake one tree of figs, and consuming thereof what will suffice for my sustenance, to put the rest to dry, so that I may both pass the summer in pleasure, and also during the winter be at ease."

> During summer one must undergo fatigue on account of getting a store,
> If in winter one would be at ease.

In this manner he stripped several trees, and eating somewhat of the fruit thereof, stored up the remainder. One day, having gone to the top of a tree of figs, according to his daily wont he ate some thereof, and collected some to dry, when suddenly a Boar escaping from before a Hunter, cast himself into that desert. He saw no fruit on any tree at which he arrived, till he came to the foot of that one, on the top of which was the Ape collecting figs. When the Ape's eyes alighted upon the Boar, his heart recoiled, and he said :

> "Whence appeared this sudden calamity ?
> O God ! deliver me from this unexpected misfortune."

When the Boar saw the Ape, he saluted him, and performing the dues of congratulation, said, " Do you want a guest ? " The Ape, also, hypocritically replied in a friendly manner, saying :

> A graceful cypress entered the garden of my hope,—
> A guest from the Unseen World arrived at the cell of the Darwísh.

" May the arrival of your auspicious footsteps be blessed and fortunate ! Had you previously deigned to acquaint me with the arrival of your exalted steps, assuredly the dues of hospitality would have been discharged according to your condition : now the grief which I have is owing to the want of the means of entertaining you."

> The Darwísh is troubled when a guest suddenly arrives.

The Boar said, " We have now arrived from the road, and are anxious for anything at hand."

> Make no ceremony, but bring what you have.

The Ape shook the fig-tree, while the Boar, with the utmost avidity, went on eating, till nought remained either on the tree or the ground. He turned his face towards the Ape saying: "O dear host! the flame of appetite is still raging, and the lust of greed, through search of food, is distressed; shake another tree and place me under obligation to you." The Ape, *nolens volens*, shook another tree, and in a little time no trace of fruit also was left thereon. The Boar pointed out a further tree. The Ape said: "O dear guest! do not abandon the habit of generosity, what I have scattered for you was sufficient food for me for a month, and I have no more power to give you anything."

> I can no more be beneficent.

The Boar was enraged and said, "This desert has been for a long time in your possession, suppose now it belongs to me." The Ape replied: "To seize the kingdom of another is ominous, and the end of violence and oppression is unacceptable and discreditable; cease to practise cruelty, and restrain your hand from tyranny and persecution; for to injure the weak will produce no good results, and to molest the desolate will not yield proper fruit."

> If you bite his heart with your teeth you draw blood,
> Yet when you do so, you yourself will suffer toothache.

At these words the violence of the Boar's rage became greater, and he said, "I will now bring you down from this tree, and treat your bosom as it deserves." He then ascended the tree to throw the Ape down: scarce had he lodged himself upon the first branch ere the limb broke, and he fell headlong down, and fixed his face in the depths of the infernal regions.

"I have adduced this story seeing that you also seize the fruits of others, and make their sustenance food for yourself. When this mass die of hunger, enmity towards you will be fixed in the hearts of their children, and constantly busied in secret, not a single instant will they omit to imprecate you. If, previous to this, the traces of your oppression have been spread throughout the world, now the news of your piety is noised on the tongues of all: but in both cases it is not possible for animals to escape your violence, whether you be in the guise of tyranny and wickedness, or whether in the garment of rectitude and religion. What holy poverty is it, when you are just the same busied in self-gratification, and do not abandon the pleasures of bodily indulgences to acquire the delights of spiritual wisdom?"

> You remain a captive to the pleasures of the body, since indeed,
> What delights have you which are not centred in the kingdom of the soul?

When the Lion heard this discourse, he desisted also from eating fruit, and contenting himself with water and grass, increased his daily portion of worship and adoration, and at all times repeated to himself the purport of these verses, which bear the impress of truth:

> "O heart! abandon this cruel world,
> And leave behind the distress of the revolving Heavens.
> The affairs of the world are not worthy men of experience,
> Like a hero quit such business.
> While you can, reach the rose-garden of the Spiritual,
> Make the attempt, and abandon this path which abounds with thorns.
> In the ocean of grief, do not through greed, like a bold diver,
> Plunge, but let alone the royal pearls."

Such is the story of a violent tyrant, who overpowered mankind with his cruelty, not thinking of the evil termination thereof, till ultimately he was overwhelmed with the same misfortune which befell people at his hands ; he then recognised the road of piety and the way of salvation.　Like the Lion who, till he found his two dear children burnt with the fire of remorse, did not remove his heart from bloodthirstiness and violence, and when he had gained this experience, turning aside from the treacherous world, he did not again allow himself to pay any heed to its unstable charms, and would not in any way purchase the blandishments of this faithless sorceress.

It has been written upon the portico of the Palace of Eternity,
"Alas for him who purchases the caresses of the world ! "

Wise men ought properly to realise this warning, and make these experiences a store for Time and Eternity, rearing the edifice of their conduct in this world and the next upon this very point, that whatever is not liked as regards one's self, one's children and dependants, the same should not be allowed towards others, so that the commencement and termination of their affairs may be graced with fair name and good reputation, and they may be safe in the world and in eternity from the evil termination of wickedness, and the bad results of oppression.

The World is not worth that you should wound a heart ;
Take care, do not wrong, such as a wise man would not commit.
The World is like a deep Ocean, full of monsters ;
They are wise, and at ease, who betake themselves to the shore.

BOOK XI.

———

ON THE MISERY OF SEEKING TOO MUCH, AND BEING DISAPPOINTED IN ONE'S AFFAIRS.

INTRODUCTION.

THE world-subduing King, after hearing this pleasant story, said: "O true-saying, sound-deliberating Saint! with clear evidence and manifest proof, you have explained the case of a tyrant, who without thought as to the result, strove to inflict injuries and cruelties, and when overwhelmed with the like thereof, took shelter in repentance and devotion. Now I request you to tell a story founded upon the purport of the eleventh precept, and repeat the particulars of one inclined for a matter unbefitting his condition, and unsuitable to his circumstances." The perfect Sage, with description pure and elegant like the waters of immortality, and in sweetness and grace a twin-sister to the sharbat of sugar-candy—

> Words in purity better than a gem,
> In sweetness better than syrup of sugar.
> Any one into whose ears those sounds entered,
> Were he Plato he would have lost his senses—

said: "O King! protector of the world!

> May your desire be within the skirt of hope!
> May your kingdom, as well as your life, be perpetual!

"Ancient sages have said, '*For every action there are men, for every place a speech.*' In the wardrobe of the unseen world, the garments of one's particular proceedings have been sewn upon the mighty stature of every person, and from the treasury of Divine Power the dress of one's individual affairs has been arranged according to such man's shape. For every person there is a duty, and for every man a certain work is befitting.

Flies are not created for the peacock;
A locust is not given the glory of the phœnix.
One must not expect wine from vinegar;
The scented breeze of the rose does not proceed from the withered thorn.

"The cup-bearer of Divine Kindness, from the tavern '*Every party rejoiceth in that which is theirs,*' has given a bowl to every one, according to his circumstances, and deprived no one of the potion of bounty, and the fountain of his fostering care.

None are there, who do not partake of your benefits,
Either a quaff or a cupful, according to their capacity.

"Accordingly it behoves every one to busy himself in that occupation which the Divine Creator has assigned to him, and so to act as by degrees to bring the affair to perfection.

A man who makes pack-saddles, and is best in his line,
Is preferable to a bad hatter.[1]

"Whoever neglects his own occupation, and reverts to a thing which is not suitable for him, turning aside from that which, by way of hereditary succession or hard work, he had acquired, doubtless will be overwhelmed in the region of distress and vexation. Consequently, by the way which he is following he will not reach his destination, nor will he be able to return to the same path as before, and between the two he will remain confused and distracted.

Neither chance to go forward, nor means to return.

"Accordingly it behoves a man to advance firmly in the way of his own business, and not with greed to stretch his hand towards every branch of covetousness, but to lay aside the search after more, which commonly ends in ruin, and not quickly or lightly to abandon any affair from which advantage has been derived, and some results have accrued, so that he may act in accordance with the purport of the noble tradition, '*Whoever has obtained benefit from anything must attend thereto,*' and be freed from distress and anguish. And the words of His Excellency Maulawí,[2] who is a mine of spiritual pearls, are in allusion to this state of things, where he says—

'What is better than that a seller of figs
Should sell figs? O brother!',

"Of the tales which bear out these remarks, is the story of that Hebrew-speaking Devotee, and the ambitious Guest, who sought to learn that dialect." The King inquired, "How was that?"

---

[1] Eastwick says, with reference to these lines, "The oriental idea no doubt is, that he who makes gear for asses and other beasts, is below him who ornaments the noblest part of man, his head."

[2] A famous Persian poet.

———o———

STORY I.

He said: It has been related that in the land of Kinnauj was a pious, abstinent, pure, and holy man. He was assiduous, according to his duty, in his daily portion of worship, and performed in a sincere manner the rites of devotion; the purity of his heart removed the traces of foulness from his affections, and the integrity of his nature drew aside the dark veil of misfortune from before the sight of men of penetration. The hem of his prayer-carpet was the place of descent of the outpourings of the unseen Realm, and the threshold of his cell the abode of the infallible World's occurrences.

Upon his head was a crown composed of the letter, " shín," in the word
" shara' " (God's law).
His heart a throne, his prostrations a ladder.
He was honoured in the Courts of Paradise,
And a ruler in the Regions of Heaven.
Of angelic manners, Satan being under his control,
As he soared along, he trod down the air beneath him.

He expended his whole ambition in giving life to the rights of the law, and confined all his desires to performing the requirements of devotion. The bird of worldly affection found no nest in the expanse of his bosom, nor did the light of carnal lusts descend or shine upon the dark earth from the sun of his mind.

Happy are they who have lived pure as the sun,
Who have cast no shade towards this world.

Notwithstanding all this piety and devotion, he used to scatter amongst his guests whatever was allotted him from the treasury, ' *With God are the treasures of the heavens and earth ;*' and by reason of the power of his magnanimity, used to bestow upon deserving darwíshes the food intended for his breakfast and supper.

Bringing forth the stars of generosity, into the ethereal sky,
From the constellation of Liberality; for great is the effect of generosity.

One day a traveller alighted at his abode as a guest, and the Devotee, as is the custom of generous hosts (seeing that their tables appear free from the vinegar of frowns), coming before him, advanced with merry countenance and open brows, and displayed the utmost delight and joy at his arrival. After salutation, and partaking of food, they spread the carpet of conversation. The Devotee inquired, "Whence do you come, and to what country are you bound?" The guest replied: "My story is long and protracted, and my tale is composed of various divine truths and worldly mysteries; if your blessed heart is inclined to hear it, I will briefly narrate an outline thereof." The Devotee said: " Whoever opens the ears of understanding, can derive somewhat from every story, and, by the bridge of worldly considerations, can cross over to the highway of divine truths.

From every trifle a hint may be gained,
From every story, benefit may be derived.

"Without fear repeat your story, and narrate entirely what benefits and evils you experienced in this journey."

THE GUEST'S STORY.

The Guest said: O Devotee of the age, and O marvellous votary! you must know that my birthplace is Europe, where I was in business as a baker. I used perpetually to heat the oven of my bosom with the flame of the fire of greed, yet with a thousand anxieties obtained but a loaf or so from the tables of Fortune.

> My kidneys became blood, ere the loaf
> Was drawn by me from the oven of Good Fortune.

I was intimate with a Farmer, and constantly the way of companionship between us was followed, and the habit of comradeship observed. The Farmer, by way of friendship, and assistance, used to send to my shop corn, available for my business, and take the value thereof after a lapse of time; payment being deferred and delayed, used to fall easy upon me. One day he took me to a banquet at one of his gardens, and fulfilled the duties of host, as is the custom of high-minded men. After we had finished eating food, we engaged in conversation: he inquired, "What is the amount of profit of your trade, and what is the state of your capital and interest?" I repeated somewhat of my circumstances, saying: "My stock-in-trade at the shop is twenty ass-loads of wheat; and the interest which arises therefrom is just sufficient for the support of my wife and family—maybe somewhat about ten or twelve loads."

> Since I have no business more profitable than this,
> I pass my time in this manner.

The Farmer said: "O God! the profits of your business are not of a degree that one could build thereon. I used to think that your trade was very remunerative, and the gain countless."

> That was indeed wrong, which I thought.

I exclaimed: "O Sir! how about your business? what is the state of your interest and capital?" He replied: "In my trade there is but little stock-in-trade, but the profits are large; save the seed which I sow, all the produce comes to me, and in our business we are not very content with getting ten times our capital." I was astonished, and said, "How can this be?" The Farmer said: "Marvel not! for there are still more profits, too, than this. A single grain of poppy-seed, that being the smallest of plants, when it falls on good ground, and vegetates, sends forth upwards of twenty sprigs,[1] and it is possible even more than that: on the end of every sprig are pods of poppies, which cannot be counted. Hence you may guess that the profits of my business are beyond the pale of reckoning, and the returns of my husbandry more than can be imagined. The farmers of the fields of wisdom have said zara'[2] (planting) has three letters, of which the first two are zar (gold)—while the last, which is 'ain, is also a name for gold ; hence this business is gold upon gold."

---

[1] This happy rendering is borrowed from Eastwick.
[2] It must be borne in mind that in Persian the short vowel "a" is not written.

Two letters of zara' mean gold, and the one which remains
Also signifies gold, hence here is gold upon gold.

" According to the belief of alchemists, the workshop of husbandry is so understood that the Philosopher's Stone is indicative of the art of agriculture : as it
has been said :

' To seek the Philosopher's Stone is to waste life ;
Turn your face to the black earth, for it is the one secret of Alchemy.' "

When I heard these words from the Farmer, the desire for the gains of husbandry
entered my head, and closing the door of my shop, I busied myself getting ready
the implements for agriculture.   In my locality was a Darwísh, celebrated for
his perfect spirit, and renowned for his good qualities.

He had abandoned all ceremony, and retired to a corner ;
Of the things of this world he was content with necessaries.

When he learnt that I was about to abandon my own trade, and occupy myself
with another business, he sought me, and loosing the tongue of reproach said :
" O master ! be content with that which has been intrusted to you, nor seek for
more, for the quality of avarice is unlucky, and the end of the avaricious despicable.   He who has in his hands the coin of contentment is king of his own
time, while he who is overtaken with the baseness of greed, is on a par with
demons and brutes."

Break your cake of barley, and be patient,
Lest you eat wheat,[1] which deceived Adam.

I said : " O Shaikh ! from this business, which I have in hand, no great benefit
accrues to me, and I have learnt that the profits of agriculture are great.   I fancy
that possibly I may derive advantage from this occupation, and my ways of
support be gained with ease."   The old Devotee said : " For a long time your
means of livelihood have been procured by this employment, and the potion
of life cleared from the rubbish of trouble by reason of this occupation, while
this business which you now propose to undertake, is an affair replete with
toil ; maybe you will not be able to fulfil the requirements thereof, nor discharge properly the demands on you.   Not all that raises its head from the
secret chamber of desire, can be obtained according to one's wishes.

Your companions know that the way is far and long,
From the street of desire to the market of what is sought.

" Attempt not too much, nor withdraw your hand from your own business, since
he who neglects his own affairs and takes up with a matter for which he is not
fit, will meet with that which befell that Crane."   I inquired, " What was that ?"

STORY II.

He said : It has been related that a Bleacher used to pursue his business upon
the brink of a stream.   Every day he saw a Crane, who, sitting upon the edge
of the river, and catching the creatures which were in the mud, content therewith, returned to his nest.   One day, suddenly, a swift-flying Hawk appeared,

---

[1] Eastwick states, on the authority of Sale, that some Muhammadans suppose that wheat was the
forbidden fruit.

pursuing a fat Quail, part of which he ate, and leaving the remainder, went away. The Crane thought to himself: "This creature with so contemptible a body hunts large animals, while I with so great a frame am content with a trifle. Assuredly such a state of things is owing to meanness of ambition, and why should I not partake of a lofty spirit? It is expedient for me henceforth not to put up with trifles, but to cast the lasso of my desire on nought save the battlements of the highest heaven."

> Vapour, being thirsty, goes to the blue ocean;
> The cloud pays no regard to dew.
> The ambitious souls which rise aloft,
> Soar on high from the effects of their exalted spirit.

He then abandoned seeking after worms, and remained on the alert to pursue pigeons and quails. The Bleacher, from afar, contemplated the case of the Hawk and the Quail. When he observed the Crane's perturbation, and how he neglected his own occupation, he was amazed, and opened the eyes of amusement. By chance a Pigeon appeared in that expanse, and the Crane flying after it, tried to kill it. The Pigeon, selecting the brink of the water, outstript him in advance, while the Crane followed in the rear, and fell on the edge of the river, his feet remaining in the mud. The more he struggled to fly away, the more his feet stuck in the mire, and his feathers and wings became daubed with clay. The Bleacher coming up, captured him, and set out towards his own house. On the road a friend met him, and inquired, "What is this?" The Bleacher said: "'*This is a Crane that wanted to hunt;*' this is a Crane who wished to perform the duties of a Hawk, so he has given himself to the winds."

"I have adduced this story that you may gather that every one should attend to his own business, and let alone trades which are not suitable for him." When the old Devotee repeated this tale, my avaricious desires waxed stronger, and giving no place in the ear of my understanding to these words, which proceeded from the purest goodwill, I remained in the same mind, and quitting my bakery, converted the small capital which I possessed into implements of husbandry, and sowing a quantity of seed, set the eyes of expectation upon the road of acquiring a harvest. During this time, the means of support for myself and family became straitened, because in the baker's shop I used to recoup day by day what was spent, while now I had to wait for a whole year ere my profits were reaped. I said to myself: "You have acted foolishly in not hearing the words of the aged and wise; now you are in want of money for daily expenses, and in no way can it be acquired. Your best course is to get a sum by way of loan, and again opening your baker's shop, to return to your own business."

> He who has abandoned his own business,
> Cannot do better than return to his own occupation.

Accordingly I repaired to one of the lords of the city, and borrowing a sum, once again opened the shop, and leaving one of my servants at the head of the business, I myself went to and fro;[1] sometimes I used to repair to the plain to manage my farming, and sometimes came to market to grace my shop. When two or three months had passed in this manner, that servant, acting treacherously, left nothing in the shop, either of capital or interest; while a variety of evils befalling the crops, not a tenth of what was spent came back to me. I

---

[1] This might also be rendered, "I exerted myself."

returned to that neighbour, and telling my story, repeated to him an account of my undertaking two businesses, and suffering loss from both. The old Devotee smiled, and said, "How like your case is to that of the man with two colours of hair, who made over his beard to the care of his wives!" I inquired, "How was that?"

STORY III.

He said: It has been related that a certain man had two wives, one old, the other young; he also had two colours of hair. He liked both the women, and used to pass night and day alternately in the house of each, it being his custom when he entered the door to place his head on the woman's lap and go to sleep. One day he came to the old woman's home, and according to his wont, laying his head on her bosom, fell asleep. The old woman looked at his face and hair, and said to herself: "Nought can be better than to pick out several black hairs which are in the beard of this person, so that it shall appear altogether white, and that young woman will not care for him; when he, too, sees that she has no liking for him, and understands that she is averse to and annoyed with him, the fire of affection for her will then be quenched, and he will remove his heart from her, and devote himself entirely to me." She accordingly, as far as she could, picked out the black hairs from his beard.

'Twere better that the beard, which is in the hands of women, were plucked out.

Next day that person went to the young girl's house, and in his usual manner placed his head on her lap, and went to sleep. The young woman, seeing several white hairs in his beard, thought to herself: "I must pick out these white hairs, so that all his beard may appear black: when he sees himself dark-haired, assuredly, being disgusted with the company of the old woman, he will take a liking to me." Accordingly, she too plucked out as many of his white hairs as time demanded. When some period elapsed in this fashion, one day that person passed his hand over his beard, and found that not a hair was left therein, and the harvest thereof was utterly scattered to the winds. He uttered a cry, but it was of no effect.

"Your case is just similar. You have squandered some of your capital and interest in the baker's shop, and some you have wasted in husbandry; at the present time when you look you have not in the oven of sustenance a loaf cooked, nor in the field of existence have you collected a harvest."

> One day passed in that manner, another in this;
> Now on looking there is neither this nor that.

When I heard this story I perceived that what the old Devotee said had come to pass, and that I had procured from such proceeding nought but regret and remorse, and that all I had would not discharge the debt. It seemed to me expedient, according to the saying, "*Flight from that which is unbearable is according to the laws of the Apostles,*" at night to flee from that city: and I went from stage to stage in fear and dread, till I had traversed a long and far distance. After a while I heard news that my family were dead, and my creditors had disposed of my goods, according to the amount of my loan. Being in despair of returning to my native place, I am traversing stages and distances, and find a cure for my anguish of heart in meeting any pious persons, and place the salve of repose upon the wound of the anguish of travel, by encountering men of God, till at this very time the mirror of my heart is cleared from the rust[1] of anxiety with the polisher of your Excellency's society, and the potion of my delight is prepared with the sweetness of your Honour's sugar-producing conversation.

> Thanks to God, that though I have undergone troubles,
> I have seen you, owing to whom I have gained my object.

" This is the outline of my adventures, as I have related them."

---o---

The Devotee said : " From your words I have inhaled the perfume of sincerity, and my heart bears witness to the truth of what you have said : if for several days you have undergone the anxiety of flight, and the toils of travel, yet you have gained sound experience, and gathered reliable information as to the ways and manners of mankind ; henceforth you may live in peace of mind and ease of heart."

> The evening of grief has passed, and the morning of joy will appear.

The Guest was pleased at seeing his Host, while the latter, too, prizing the society of his friend, began to be cheerful. The Devotee was a man of the Children of Israel, well acquainted with the Hebrew tongue, and though he knew most dialects, and could speak various languages, yet, since Hebrew was his mother-tongue, his fluency in that was greater, and he used constantly to discourse in that language with his attendants. The European guest, although, to say the truth, he was not learned in the Hebrew dialect, yet was pleased with the talk of the Devotee in that tongue, and very frequently begged him to converse therein. The Devotee, also, in view of the other's satisfaction of mind and bent of disposition, loosed the tongue of eloquence, and in speaking Hebrew did justice to his oratorical powers. The Guest, becoming enamoured of that language, owing to the excessive sweetness of the Devotee's words, and the delicacy of his talk, was anxious to learn the Hebrew tongue from him.

> With his sweet-honeyed discourse, every instant,
> His sugared lips smiled sweetly.
> When the Guest saw the loads of sugar,
> Like a parrot he purchased the sweets.

Several days elapsed, and the veil of ceremony being raised from the midst, the feeling of strangeness became changed for that of affection, and the results of intimacy were obtained from the preludes of companionship.

> We can sit together according to the wish of our heart,
> When ceremony is put aside from between us.

The Guest boldly commenced to praise the Devotee, saying :

> O thou ! whose tones are the key of the secret recess of perfection,
> And thy talk the cause of increase of majesty.

[1] See note 2, p. 51.

" What kind of rhetoric and manner of oratory is this ? Indeed the eyes of the wisdom of men of sight have never contemplated more perfect eloquence, nor the ears of the understanding of orators heard more beautiful language.

> I know not the name of such a kind of talk,
> I can neither call it prophecy nor enchantment.

" I am anxious for you to teach me this language, and I request you not to withhold from me instruction in this tongue ; since without previous introduction you have performed the dues of kindness in honouring and esteeming me, and without the prelude of the bonds of friendship, have displayed a variety of courtesies in entertaining me, nowadays, when the chain of affection is strengthened by means of constant intimacy, I am in hopes you will be kind enough to grant my request, and with joy and delight draw the inscription of studentship upon the page of my condition, and that this becoming the cause of sincere affection, the daily portion of thankfulness, and the display of gratitude may be observed."

> In truth I can say nought but praise of you,
> Seeing that I am the slave nourished by your kindness.

The Devotee said : " In this respect why should I make any difficulty or trouble ? since I shall advance a person from the depths of ignorance to the summit of knowledge, and convey a student from the lowest abyss of want of understanding to the highest degree of perfection. But it occurs to my mind that between the Hebrew dialect and the European languages there is an immense barrier, and a great distinction. God forbid that in teaching it much anguish of heart should occur, or that the senses, by reason of the impossibility of comprehending or remembering it, should be in despair. On such a supposition both my life would be wasted, and also your time be lost." The Guest said : " Whoever sets out in pursuit of a matter, assuredly must bid himself attempt difficulties ; and he who turns his face to the High Altar of desire, must not fear the toils of the desert of distress.

> When, through anxiety after the temple of Makkah, you desire to set your
>   feet in the desert,
> Be not sad, if the Egyptian thorn [1] tears you.

" In this my design I am sincere to an extent, that were every hair in my head to become a sword, I would not turn my face from this affair, and were every eyelash in my eyes a spear, I would not cast my glance on another matter.

> Whoever wisheth for wealth must undergo toil.

" Every distress which is undergone in the pursuit after knowledge will in the end terminate in repose, nor will the toils of the student be in any way wasted ; just as the Hunter,[2] by reason of a little labour which he underwent to gain knowledge, and through a trifling service which he performed to some wise men, obtained a great benefit, and from the straits of want reached the expanse of affluence, and the area of repose." The Devotee inquired, " How was that ? "

---

[1] I do not know with certainty the allusion in this case, but fancy that the phrase rendered " Egyptian thorn," is intended to indicate the troubles of the world. See Johnson's Dictionary under the head of " Maghailán."

[2] I am not aware that there is any word in the English language applicable to a person who traps both birds and fish.

STORY IV.

He said : It has been related that a poor man used to hunt, and passed his life content with catching birds and fish. When angling after fish, his frame was all eyes, like a net, and when entrapping birds he made every hair on his body a noose.

Neither a bird escaped his meshes, nor a fish.

One day he had laid his net, and with a thousand labours had enticed three birds into the neighbourhood of his snare, while he himself was sitting in ambush watching, in expectation of bringing the necks of those luckless ones within the noose of the net. In the midst of this he heard the voice of tumult, and in fear lest all at once the birds should be frightened away by that sound, he issued forth from his ambuscade, and saw two students disputing about a proposition in law. Their words led to quarrel, and the Hunter implored them earnestly : " Do not cry out, lest these birds take fright, and my trouble be wasted."

He drew his breath, lest the game should be scared from his net.

They said : " If you let us share your prey, and give each of us a bird, we will ally with you, and no longer engage in strife and contest." The Hunter said : " O my friends ! I am a poor man with a family, and the food of several persons depends upon those birds. After you have taken away two of them, how can I return to my home, and in what way satisfy ten persons with one bird ? " They replied : " You follow this pursuit every day, while it is a long time since we have indulged in this sport. Anyhow, it is not possible for us to abandon these birds. We will either raise a cry so that the birds fly away, or you shall make a compact, that you will give a bird to each of us, in order that we may bring them into sight of the professor, and entertain the students of the college as guests." Much as the Hunter piteously vociferated—" Your professor did not net my snare, nor the hand of the students weave my cord. I have not set my traps in ground bequeathed for pious purposes, nor have I scattered a grain of corn belonging to the college. According to law it is not incumbent upon me to bestow my prey upon you by way of thirds and two-thirds "—it was of no avail. At length he promised them the birds, and, pulling the cord, entrapped the latter within the net. Once again he commenced to lament and complain, " Have pity upon me, and restrain the hand of greed from bearing away these birds." They said, " Cease such words, and fulfil the pledges which you have given." The Hunter saw no help for it, and gave each of them a bird, saying, " At any rate, since I have undergone this trouble at your hands, and have given you a present and offering, teach me the word about which you were wrangling, may be that some day it will be of advantage to me." They replied, " We were disputing about the word ' Hermaphrodite,' and were quarrelling about hereditary succession in such a case." The Hunter inquired, " What is the meaning of ' Hermaphrodite ? ' " They replied, " In truth the meaning is, one who is neither a male nor a female." The Hunter, bearing these words in mind, in much distress, came to his own house, and disclosed to his family the state of the case. They passed that night content with but little food. Next day, when the golden-winged bird, the Sun, came flying from the nest of the Horizon, and the silvery Fish, the Stars, from dread of the lines of its rays, took flight through the expanse of the Spheres—

> The Spheres, like a Hunter, with their golden threads,
> Snared the Sun as a Fish [1]—

the old Hunter, removing his net, set his face towards the edge of the sea, and in firm reliance upon God, let down the same into the ocean. By chance a fish fell into the net, of beautiful appearance and elegant shape, such that the maker of coats of mail, the water, had never constructed a suit of armour such as it, nor had the eyes of the denizens of the Deep ever seen a model like it in the expanse of the ocean. [2]

> Its pure breast like white silver,
> Its sparkling eyes resembling the fountain of the sun;
> Its back, like the garments of the chameleon,
> Possessing tints beyond conjecture.

The Hunter, being bewildered at its shape and form, thought to himself: " I have never in my life seen a fish of such a kind, nor beheld a prey of such beauty. My right course is to bring it alive to the King by way of an offering, and by such service to make my name exalted amongst my equals." Accordingly, casting that fish into a vessel of water, he set his face towards the King's Court. By chance the King had commanded them to make in his private garden in front of his Palace, where he used to take his seat, a fount of marble and alabaster, and to place therein fish of various colours.

> All silvery they sported therein,
> Their ears heavy with the rings of gold. [3]

A boat, of shape like a moon, had been moved forth upon the face of that heaven-like fount.

> Thereon was a ship, constructed of Aloe-wood,
> Like a new moon in the azure Heavens.

Every day the King used to resort to the edge of the fount for recreation, and to amuse himself with the gambols of the fish, and the motion of the boat. At the same time, too,

> He used to gaze within the fount,
> Enjoying the sight of the moon and planets.

When suddenly the Hunter made his appearance, and presented to the King's sight that beautiful-shaped, graceful fish, his Majesty was much pleased at seeing it, and ordered a thousand dínár to be given to the Hunter. One of the Ministers, who held a position of freedom, and a post of boldness, loosed the tongue of advice, and gently whispered to the King:

> May your enlightened mind be a fount of light !
> May your auspicious head be free from reproach !

" There are many fishermen, and the sea is full of fish. If the King is pleased to grant a thousand dínár for every fish, the money in the Treasury will not

---

[1] مهردرا in the Persian text is a misprint for مهررا.

[2] This extravagant metaphor simply means that no such beautiful fish had ever been produced in the ocean ; the "coats of mail" are the scales.

[3] Gold and silver fish.

suffice, nor will the revenues of the kingdom be ample enough. It is clear, too, how much the price of a fish should be, and to what extent a fisherman should be recompensed. A gift should be according to desert, and a return in proportion to the deed."

> Every fount which contains a hundred mans of water,
> When two hundred mans are poured therein will come to ruin.

The King said, " I have promised him a thousand dínár, how can I now allow myself to break my word ?" The Minister answered: " I have a device for this, so that you shall not violate your pledge, nor shall any more gold either pass your hands. The proper plan is for you to ask him the question whether this fish is male or female. If he says it is a male, we will tell him to bring its female, so that we may give the thousand dínár ; while if he proclaims it a female, we will bid him fetch its male, and take the gold. Assuredly he will be helpless in the matter ; then having pacified him with some little thing, we will get the better [1] of him." The King, then turning towards the Fisherman, said, " Is this fish male or female ?" The old fellow, who was a man of experience and penetration, discovering what design the King and Minister had in the purport of that question, sent down the diver of thought into the ocean of deliberation, as to how to obtain an answer which could be placed upon the tray of explanation. At length that word which the day before he had learned from the philosophers passed through his mind. He replied: " O King ! protector of the world ! this fish is a hermaphrodite—that is to say, neither male nor female." The Sultán was pleased, and, reproaching the Minister for that device, presented another thousand (dínár), and giving the Fisherman two thousand dínár, made him one of his select band and companions.

" The moral of this tale is, that the Hunter with a single word which he committed to memory, and with two birds which he presented to the philosophers, met with two thousand dínár, and, through the King's bounty, was exalted. Therefore, there can be no loss in the labour of learning, or the service of philosophers. Wise men have said :

> ' Learn wisdom, so that you may be beloved,
> For without knowledge man is not worth an atom.
> Through learning your dignity and position will be promoted,
> From the place where slippers [2] are left to the chief seat.' "

The Devotee said: " Now that you are so anxious, and with the feet of endeavour are traversing the path of search in the desert of exertion, I, too, will perform all that may be possible in teaching and instructing you, nor will I omit any particle in causing you to understand propositions, and making rules clear." The Guest set about that task, and spent a long time in studying the Hebrew tongue. His nature was in no way suited to that language, nor did the comprehension of its minutiæ accord with his intellect. The more instruction he received, the less clever was he in exercising it ; the more he planted the tree of learning in the garden of thought, the more the fruit of disappointment appeared on the branch of hope.

> If from the storehouse of grace a boon is not bestowed,
> It is vain to make any effort ; labour is wasted.

---

[1] Literally, "we will bring his heart to our hands."

[2] An allusion to the oriental practice of taking off the shoes on entering the presence of Royalty, or persons of rank.

One day the Devotee said to him : " You have undertaken a difficult matter, and have laid much anguish upon your soul. Your tongue will not flow in this language, nor is your nature in accord with this dialect. Abandon this task, and put not your feet in a plain in which it is not suitable for you to walk.

> As regards what cannot be accomplished,
> 'Twere shame to waste life on trifles.
> Listen to the advice of the wise, and enter not
> Upon a way, the end of which cannot be reached.

" To abandon the language of one's ancestors, and to attempt a tongue and dialect different from that of one's forefathers, is far from the highway of rectitude." The Guest said : " To copy those who have passed away, as regards their errors and ignorance, is the extreme of imitation and folly. In this respect I will not copy any one, nor will I deviate from the way of learning the truth, for imitation is the lasso of the wiles of demons, and verification the forerunner of the road of sincerity and certainty. The saying, '*Of a truth we found our fathers pursuing their creed*,' is a punishment to the children of the playground of imitation, so that they may come from the dreary abode of doubt to the safe dwelling of truth, and with the eyes of certainty may behold the radiance of the lights, '*God guides with His light whomsoever he pleases*.'"

> He who removes from the screen of imitation,
> Will see with the light of truth whatever exists.
> Between a person who states facts and one who merely represents what he
>   hears, there is a difference :
> The former is like David, and the other a mere echo.[1]
> Imitation scattered man's dignity to the winds.
> May two hundred curses rest upon such imitation !

The Devotee said : " I have discharged the dues of admonition, and I fear that the end of these efforts will lead to regret. At present you can discourse in the European dialect, and carry on conversation in the language of your tribe and race ; maybe when for the greater part of your time you have talked in the Hebrew idiom, the use of your own tongue will be hid from you, and neither will you acquire the other. Your condition would be like that of the Crow, who learned the strut of the Partridge, and forgot his own." The Guest inquired, " How was that ? "

STORY V.

He said : It has been related that one day a Crow was flying along, and saw a Partridge strutting over the surface of the ground, by which sweet gait and charming mode of walking the hearts of spectators were captured.

> When once you strutted towards me, you bore away my heart ;
> Again come and walk before me, so that I may scatter my soul.

The Crow was delighted with the motion of the Partridge, and amazed at his

---

[1] David is here used to symbolise the highest degree of perfection. Eastwick renders the passage as being a comparison between David and rust, on the ground that the former was, according to oriental tradition, supposed to have pursued the trade of an armourer. The passage may bear either meaning, both of which seem equally strained and unnatural.

graceful motion, activity, and agility.   A desire entered his own mind **to walk**
along in the same manner, and the ambition to strut in this fashion **appeared**
from the core of his heart.   Binding the loins of service in attending on the
Partridge, and abandoning sleep and food, he set about that attempt.   He constantly followed the Partridge's steps, and enjoyed the sight of his mincing step.

> O Partridge of graceful step! you pass by with elegant gait;
> I come in the rear limping along.

One day the Partridge said: "O ghostly-looking, dark-faced one! I see you are
always hovering around me, and whether walking or resting you watch me.
What is your object?"   The Crow rejoined: "O you of nice manners, and
merry face!

> Your gait bore away my heart, and now in your rear,
> Crying aloud, I am wandering in search of my soul.

"You must know that a desire to imitate your walk has entered my mind, and
I have for a long while followed your steps, desirous to learn that gait, and place
the foot of superiority upon the heads of my fellows."   The Partridge uttered
its cry, and said: "Alas! alas!

> Where are you, and where are we?

"My strut is a natural proceeding, and your gait is an innate habit.   Personal
habits cannot by any means be eradicated, nor can the requirements of instinct
be changed through any exertion.   My road lay in one mode of strut, and your
walk in another.

> Behold the difference in the road, whence it leads, and to where!

"Abandon this notion, and put aside this idea."

> Cease! for this bow is not for your arm.

The Crow replied: "'*The commencement is potent.*'   Since I have plunged into
the affair, I will not through deceits or tales abandon it, nor, till I have accomplished my object, will I turn back my feet from this road."

> We have launched the ship of patience in the sea of grief;
> We will either die therein, or get the jewel within our palm.

The poor wretch for a while followed after the Partridge, but did not learn his
gait, and also forgot his own walk, nor could he again in any way manage to
revert to it.
    "I have adduced this story, that you may know that you have given yourself
vain toil, and are making a fruitless effort: it has been said that the most ignorant of creatures is he who plunges himself into an affair which is not becoming
his skill, nor suitable to his race.   This story exactly resembles your leaving
the bakery and busying yourself with agriculture, and at the termination of the
affair the end of the thread of both affairs has gone from your hands, and you
have remained in the anguish of exile, and the calamity of loneliness."

> I said I would abandon my life, and attain his society.
> I gave up my life, but did not ultimately procure access to him.

The Guest did not receive the Devotee's advice with approbation, so in a little
time forgot the language of his fathers, and did not acquire the Hebrew dialect.

That slipped from his grasp, while this did not come to his hands.

Such is the story of one who neglected his own occupation, and undertook a business which was unsuited to him. This matter appertains to the caution and care of kings: every prince who is disposed to control his kingdom, to secure the welfare of his subjects, to favour friends, and exterminate enemies, should in this respect deem it incumbent to reflect and ponder seriously, not allowing himself to treat alike incapable and evil-disposed men, and the noble and pure-minded; since many mean wretches think they can grasp the reins with the heroes of the plain of generosity, and in the battle-field of struggle deem their own base carcasses as equal in speed with the lightning-darting charger of the magnanimity of such persons, whose very dust, in fact, they could not reach if they were to drive as hard as they could.

> How could an earthen vessel contend with Solomon's cup,[1]
> Even if it were decked with pearls and rubies?

Therefore to observe this distinction in the rules of government is of the highest consideration. If, God forbid! the differences of rank, as regards the regulations of men, are banished, and the mean and the mediocre sit together in a throng, and the latter boast equality with the noble, the majesty of monarchy will decline, and ruin and desolation overtake the affairs of the kingdom. For this reason former kings used to take care that the worthless and evil-disposed should learn knowledge and writing, and be acquainted with problems in figures and numbers; because when the custom is general, that men of business take the place of the illustrious, seeing that the latter cannot perform the duties of the former, assuredly the evil therefrom will become spread abroad and diffused, and the sources of support for both high and low will be utterly ruined; by such means matters would come to be neglected, and the traces of this, in lapse of time, would become evident. Accordingly, it behoves a man to deem it incumbent upon him to pay regard to the heads of admonition of the learned, and the advice of sages, so that deriving advantage therefrom, the fruit of experience may accrue to him in life, and his affairs remain protected and defended from the sin of defect, and the quality of negligence.

> Bid any one in the World, who is wise,
> To fix his mind on clever sayings, and lend his ear to advice.
> Words are pearls, the speaker the diver,
> With difficulty the precious gems come within the grasp.
> Concealed within these musky shells,
> You will find many spiritual gems.

[1] See note, p. 83.

BOOK XII.

ON THE EXCELLENCE OF CLEMENCY, SERENITY, QUIETNESS, AND FIRMNESS, PARTICULARLY AS REGARDS KINGS.

INTRODUCTION.

NCE again the Prosperous Monarch turned towards the famous sage, and with delicious phrases,

> Spoke his praises, " O rare sage !
> The eye of Time has never seen such as you."

" You have recited a story of one who abandoned his own profession and ancestral language, and took up with a thing which was unsuited to his condition, and not in harmony with his nature ; so his object being veiled from the eyes of his desire, it was impossible for him to revert to his original business.

He lets one thing go from his hand, and does not get possession of the other.

" Now repeat what quality is the more acceptable with kings, and most akin to the welfare of the country, the stability of government, the settlement of affairs, and the ease of persons' hearts. In the twelfth precept I observed, that it behoves sovereigns to make compassion the decoration of their life, and long-suffering the capital of their conduct. But a doubt has occurred to me, whether for kings pity is better, or generosity, or bravery ; do you with difficulty-solving deliberation, unloose the knot from the thread of this embarrassment, and with clear-discerning judgment explain in the best manner the state of this proposition."

> The wise man, on hearing these words,
> Opened the door of the treasury of language,
> Saying : " O Khasrau [1] of the land and the time !
> May this and that be under your sway."

---

[1] See note, page 153.

"Know that the most acceptable qualities, the most laudable attributes, by which both kings themselves will become majestic and revered, and also the army and subjects be thereby rendered content, are pity and good-nature. '*If thou hadst been harsh and cruel-hearted, assuredly they would have been separated from round about thee:*' and from the propitious-tending sayings of the Sovereign of the couch of prophecy, and the felicitous Lord of the kingdom of glory (on him be the choicest benedictions of those who pray!) it is understood that worldly happiness and eternal satisfaction are derived from pity and generosity; as he said, '*Amongst the lucky chances of men is a good disposition, therefore the person who is patient is wellnigh a prophet.*' As to these three qualities, regarding which the King is distraught, it is better that he should decidedly ascertain which of them is superior to the rest. All three are necessary to him, but bravery is not always available, and in some lives there is but once occasion for it, but liberality and pity are at all times of service: therefore beneficence and compassion are superior to bravery. Again, the advantages of courage are peculiar to one set of persons, and but a select body can share the benefits of the bounty of kings; but both little and great are in need of compassion, and the favourable results of good-nature extend to high and low, subject and soldier: therefore assuredly mildness is superior to the rest.

> Whoever possesses a good disposition
> Is a man amongst men.
> A person's goodness does not consist in beauty of face,
> A good disposition is the capital of worth.

"One of the wise has said, that if between me and all mankind there is but a single hair, and all agreed together to break it, it would not be possible to snap it; because if they loosed it, I would pull it, and if they dragged hard, I would let slack. That is to say, such is the extent of my perfect pity and great pardon, that I can live with mankind, and get along with the common people, and the learned, the innocent, and the guilty.

> I am within his noose, he is following his own ends;
> If he will not meet my wishes, I will fall in with his views.

"It should be known that firmness and constancy are the preferable ornaments for kings, and pity and patience the best adornment for the World's Lawgivers. Since their decrees as regards the lives, the property, and the land of mankind are current, and their commands and prohibitions universally prevalent, as concerns low and high, small and great, therefore if Monarchs do not grace their dispositions with compassion and uprightness,[1] it may be that, with a single harsh feeling, they will fill the inhabitants of a kingdom with alarm, and by levity and rashness, distress and afflict the world, and many souls and possessions will fall into the region of death and dispersion.

> Every decree which the King of the Age issues,
> Should be consequent on boundless deliberation:
> Since, if therein he does not use reflection,
> Perhaps from it endless miseries will ensue.

"If the King, with the water of generosity, washes the dust of necessity from off

---

[1] ديانت in the Persian text is a misprint for ديانت .

the face of time, or with the fire of bravery consumes the harvest of life, as regards the malevolent, when he is void of the capital of compassion, with a solitary display of violence, he darkens the spring of beneficence, and with a single harsh act raises up a thousand mortal enemies : but if as concerns generosity he is deficient, and in the plain of bravery he is wanting, by courtesy, affability, pity, and good-nature he may make both his subjects and his army grateful, and draw mankind within the chains of loyalty, and the bonds of servitude.

> It is better that, like a rose, your face should be radiant,
> So that your perfume may be charming in the universe.
> You will bring mankind to your service, at the time
> You grace the world by your disposition.

" In addition to compassion, it is incumbent to have a share of constancy and firmness, for gentleness without determination is not free from defect ; since, if any one bears the burden of much trouble, and endeavours to the utmost to display forbearance, when the termination of the matter concludes in hastiness, and the end thereof inclines to levity and frivolity, the whole bulk of such distresses will be wasted and fruitless.

> Be firm, in the way of forbearance, like a mountain ;
> Whoever displays most dignity possesses most majesty.

" It behoves a king at a period of compassion not to permit himself to be subservient to lust, and at a time of rage not to allow himself to obey Satan ; since anger is a flame from the fire of the devil, and a tree, the fruit of which is vexation and regret. It has been said that compassion is amongst the number of the qualities of the Prophets, while rage is natural to dogs, and a wile of Satan. Amongst men of truth, and persons of sincerity, it is agreed that till a person overcomes his rage he will not reach the rank of the righteous : and in the rare language of the Sages it is written, that a wise man was asked to describe in a single sentence the particulars of an excellent disposition, so that it might be easy to lay hold thereof; he replied, 'To abandon rage comprehends all fine qualities and good feelings, and to give way to anger embraces all shameful deeds and disgraceful actions.'

> Anger and hatred are qualities of beasts and animals ;
> Whoever indulges in rage and malignity is but a creature.
> Your spite proceeds from hell, so also your venom ;
> They are altogether a portion thereof, and a foe to your faith.
> Since you are a fragment of hell, then beware ;
> Atoms gravitate towards their whole.

" Again, it must be known that the need of a king for a minister, giving sound advice, and a wise, virtuous companion, is with the view that if the pride of despotic power, and the vanity of monarchy, should cause him to wander from the highway of compassion and forbearance, his right-deliberating minister, having by the way of counsel brought him to the road of rectitude, should cause him to set his feet in the path of constancy and stability, and by the sweet medicine of admonition, having put an end to the deflection of his nature from justice, should give him the quality of firmness in the way of safety; so that by the gifts of Omnipotent wisdom, and the blessings of compassion and constancy, coupled with the sincerity of the prosperous minister's advice, and the purity of his designs, the king may he victorious and triumphant in all his affairs, and in whatever direction he turns his face superiority and success may be his companions and allies, and prosperity and fortune aid and assist him. If sometimes in his affairs he should issue commands in accordance with his lusts, and in obedience to his evil passions, and should give orders without reflection or thought, not based on prudence and deliberation, the evils of the wrong he has committed will be averted by the clear judgment of such a sincere minister, and the remedy of the injury, and the amends for the ruin thereof, will not remain within the pale of impossibility. Just as was the case in the altercation of the King of Hind with his tribe." The world-adorning King inquired, " How was that ? "

---o---

STORY I.

The Brahman said : It has been related that in one of the cities of Hind was a King, by name Hílár, with endless treasures and hoards, and boundless possessions and stores.

> His wealth-protecting spear defended the kingdom and state ;
> His victory-spreading sword was surety for the faith and country.

He rose superior to all the sultáns of the time, by various deeds of prowess, and was distinguished above fortunate kings by numerous illustrious acts. He had two sons, such that the glittering sun borrowed splendour from their radiant faces, and the shining moon wandered desolate in the plain of the spheres, owing to the beauty of their cheeks, and the delicacy of their countenances. One, in stature like an arrow, drew to himself, as it were a bow, those who fast forty days in the corner of retirement; while the other with ringlets, like the chains of the enamoured, brought to the hospital of pain the thread of affection of those who tear their hair. On contemplating the uprightness of the heart-expanding stature of the one, the straight cypress, through jealousy, remained with its feet in the mire; while through envy at the soul-enchanting gait of the other, the sweet-voiced partridge forgot his own strut.

> One like a tulip, with radiant face ;
> Another like a rose, diffusing its beauty abroad.

In addition to their elegant appearance they were graced with a good disposition, and decked the plant of their beauty with the flowers of excellence and perfection; their form was extremely handsome, and their spiritual graces excessively enchanting.

> The eyes of the Spheres never saw such form or spirit ;
> All hail to such a spirit ! all honour to such form !

One was called Suhail-i-Yamaní,[1] and the other Máh-i-Khataní.[2] Their mother, Írán-dukht,[3] was very lovely : from envy at her delicate cheeks, the bride of the sun remained concealed behind the screen of vexation, and the locks of the hyacinth writhed from shame at her intertwining ringlets.

---

[1] Canopus of Yaman.   [2] Moon of Tartary.   [3] Daughter of Persia.

An idol, with radiant face and ringlets,
Such that desire with hundred ardours sought her.
Her cheeks mingled violets with roses,
And made the violet keep watch over the rose.
Her curling ringlets, in musky wreaths,
Cast a noose round the neck of the sun.

The King's heart was entirely wrapped up in affection for this rare pearl, and love for these two precious children, and he had no ease of soul nor repose of bosom in the absence of their beauty. Again, he had a minister called Balár, the meaning of which word in their dialect is " blessed face." He was a wise man, celebrated for the soundness of his wisdom, and renowned and famed for the accuracy of his judgment; the proofs of his intelligence and experience, and the evidences of his penetration and kindness, were manifest upon the face of his actions and the brow of his proceedings; while the traces of his sincerity and loyalty, no less than the auspicious results of his personal attachment and good intentions, were evident, and displayed in his gracious efforts and illustrious deeds. The tongue of time, in praising his perfection, chanted these words, and attempted to describe the points of his mighty and beautiful nature in these verses :—

O Ásaf !¹ such that the attendant on the skies,
In thy assembly would attain no lofty station ;
Wherever thy scribes send forth thy mandate,
The decrees of Fate will not reach the Lord of Orion.

His private secretary, who had the name of Kamál, was a scribe such that the Planet Mercury² in the skies could not draw the bow of his description, nor the Munshí of the Heavens be able with the foot of reflection to mount the steps of the creation of his fingers. You would say that the tongue of his graceful reed was a mine of the secrets of eloquence, and the scratching of his dexterous pen the horizon of the lights of perspicuity. Every pearl of signification which he pierced with the diamond of thought, the superintendent, his penetrating intellect, arranged on the thread of flowing words and beautiful sentences; and every coin of truth which he weighed in the balance of deliberation, his sound thought as it were a broker, submitted with perfect description and complete recommendation to the gaze of the purchasers in the market of subtleties.

The meanings of his descriptions were heart-enchanting ;
The edifices of his writings were entrancing ;
The reed of his pen caused the parrot of speech
To be ashamed at the melodies of its scratching.

Amongst his private animals the King had a White Elephant, who hastened to the plain of war like the world-striding wind, and with stone-splitting tusks rent the bosom of the flinty mountain. Generally iron is concealed in a mountain, but he, contrary to what is customary, was a mountain hidden in iron; and commonly a mountain remains fixed in one place, without pillars, while he, as opposed to what is usual, moved along on four pillars.³

---

¹ Supposed to have been Solomon's minister, and endued with miraculous powers.
² In the original there is a play upon words, which it is impossible to preserve in the translation.
³ That is, his four legs.

His vermilion-coloured head pierced to the skies,
The tints of twilight were reddened thereby.
His trunk curled up like a lasso,
As it were a dragon dropped from a high mountain.
From those terrible shield-impressing[1] hoofs,
The earth was trampled under foot.

There were also two Elephants,[2] extremely majestic, in largeness of limbs and frame equalling the Mountain Alwand; with trunks like clubs[3] they made the heads of rebels balls in the plain, and with their pillar-like feet trampled down the necks of the refractory; their crystal-appearing tusks brought forth sprigs of coral[4] from the breasts of foes, and with their ivory picks opened to light the mound of the rubies of Badakhshán from the mine of the enemies' bodies.

They were clouds, but in truth such as to drop daggers'-points,
They were towers, but their bastions indeed the ranks of war.
The tusks of one plunged into the heart of Mars,
The trunk of the other cast a lasso round the Pleiades.

Again, he had two Dromedaries, which travelled hills, mountains, and deserts, such that in one night they crossed kingdoms, nay, more, in an instant bestrode the world. As regards their neck and ears, they resembled a bow and arrow, while their feet and breast were formed like a battle-axe and shield. When they ran, they bent the surface of the earth like a shield; and when they moved along, they bore off with their feet, as it were a club in the game *chaugán*,[5] the ball of superiority from the swift-going messenger, the moon.

Traversing deserts as if they were themselves mountains, their heart was at ease under the load,
Carrying their burdens from night till day, and eating thorns from morn till night.

He had, too, a steed, swift-paced and rapid-going, with silvery hoofs and golden bridle, such as, if he were given the rein, would have outstript the world-encircling breeze, and the clime-traversing north wind would not have reached the dust around him. Ever since the bay horse of the skies had journeyed round the outskirts of the terrestrial globe, the equal of that steed had never been seen, and since piebald time had measured the expanse of the Heavens, the like of such a courser had never been heard of.

Heaven-encircling, world-traversing,
Drinking water from the fount of the sun;
Every time that he was bathed in perspiration,
It rained[6] and in the midst thundered.
Every time he went to battle,
He was encircled with a hundred morning breezes.

He had a sword, decked with jewels, and adorned with precious gems. You

---

[1] In allusion to his hoofs leaving a circular impress on the ground.

[2] I am not aware what sort of elephant is indicated by the epithet پیسرة. A native gentleman whom I consulted was equally at a loss to attach an intelligible meaning to this word, which signifies "the scale of a fish;" possibly, therefore, it is an interpolation. It has been suggested to me that it may perhaps mean "arrayed in armour."

[3] See note 1, p. 138.

[4] Jets of blood are compared to sprigs of coral.

[5] See note 1, p. 138.

[6] In allusion to his perspiring and snorting.

would say, maybe, the surface of the grass had been studded with drops of dew, or rather the expanse of the heavens had been dotted with the royal pearls of the stars. The jewels of its natural temper looked on its diamond-like sides as it were the feet of ants, and on its blue surface there appeared flies' wings. It was not a sword, nay, more, it was a cloud dropping blood, or lightning spreading fire.

> It was indeed green, like the stalk of a leek,
> But in the garden of battle it was like a bough of the arghawán.[1]
> Water-lilies are hidden in the stream, but, O strange!
> This was a water-lily with water concealed therein.

The King was much enamoured of all these which have been mentioned, and constantly used to boast himself over the sovereign of all the countries of Hind as regards this collection. In his kingdom were a number of Brahmans, who acknowledged allegiance to Brahmá, and confessed his Prophet: they used to turn aside from the true faith and the right way, and caused the people to wander in the desert of error, and the gulf of ignorance. Although King Hílár[2] prohibited them from leading astray and seducing the people, not accepting the rebuke, they did not abandon their base habits, and the matter ended in that the King through zeal for his faith, and in defence of his creed, slew upwards of twelve thousand persons amongst them, and plundering their homes, bore off their wives and children as captives. Amongst the number he made four hundred individuals who were graced with the arts of learning, and endued with varied knowledge, attendants at the foot of his exalted throne. *Nolens volens,* girding their loins in servitude, they travelled the road of attendance, and waited an opportunity for revenge, and an occasion for malignity, till one night the King was taking his ease on the couch of repose, and heard seven terrible voices: from dread thereof awakening up he became buried in thought and deliberation. In the midst of these proceedings, sleep once more overpowered him, and he saw in his dream two red Fish, whose splendour dazzled his eyes, standing upon their tails, and welcoming him. The King again awoke, and falling into a long and deep train of thought, dropped off asleep: a second time he saw two varied-coloured Ducks, and a large Goose flying after them; at length alighting before him, they commenced to pray to him. Once more he awoke from his dreams, and remaining astonished at what had occurred, a further time went to sleep, and saw a green-coloured Snake, with yellow and white spots, coiling round his feet; this hideous-looking viper was twining round a branch of sandal-wood. The King woke in alarm, and sad at those whims which he had observed in the veil of fancy. Once again the demon of Sleep gradually drew him to the land of dreams; this time he saw himself from hand to foot, like a sprig of coral, stained with blood, and decked as it were from his crown to his soles with pearls of Badakhshán, and red rubies. The King awakening, began to be distressed, and desired to summon one of the attendants of the Haram. Suddenly sleep again overpowered him, and he saw himself mounted upon a quick-going white mule, such that, like darting lightning, it crossed mountains, and passed along pleasantly like one's own dear life; and having turned the reins of the steed towards the east, he was riding on alone. Though he looked he could see no attendants save two messengers on foot. Again, in alarm at this circumstance, he jumped up from his dreams, and for the sixth time fell asleep,

---

[1] Name of a tree having a beautiful red fruit.
[2] The word in the Persian text is spelt differently in the two places.

and saw some fire burning round his head, the rays of which surrounded the regions and districts. On witnessing this state of things, he was filled with dread, and woke up, and for the seventh time fell senseless with the potion of sleep: he saw a Bird sitting above his head and pecking at his brow. This time the King cried out, so that the attendants in the confines of the court arrived on the alarm, and some betook themselves in perturbation to the exalted couch. The King having consoled them, sent them back. In alarm at these dreams, like a snake with his tail cut off, or a man bitten by a viper, he writhed about, and said to himself: "What varied phantoms are these which the Divine reed has created, and what armies of mischief are these which it has poured forth one after another?

> One tumult does not subside ere another trouble rises up;
> Scarce is one strife settled ere another calamity comes to pass.

"To whom can I describe the particulars of what has happened, or from what learned person demand a solution of this difficulty? whom can I make the confidant of these secrets, and with what individual can I hazard the dice of describing this affair?"

> To whom shall I tell this grief, and from whom seek a cure?

In short, he passed the rest of the night till morn in deep distress, and complained to dark night of its dreariness and length, saying—

> "O thou night! if thou art not the Day of Judgment,
> Why, at any rate, dost thou not more quickly disappear?
> O Morn! why dost thou so consume my heart?
> At any rate breathe[1] if thou hast a soul, O Morn!"—

till the time when the cheek of rosy Morn began to shine from the curls of the glistening ringlets of dark Night, and the pastile camphor ball (of the Sun) commenced to appear in the regions of the blue sky, in lieu of the ambergris-scented civet (of darkness).

> The brain of the earth, through the heat of the Sun,
> Awoke from sleep frenzied with madness.

As soon as the hand of Fate withdrew the veil of darkness from before the beauty of world-illumining Day, and the King of the Planets ascended the enamelled throne of the Heavens, and caused the report of his brilliant justice to reach the ears of mankind, the King arose and summoned the Brahmans, who could solve every difficulty, and were perfect in the science of divination. Without reflecting on the termination of the affair, he described to them all his dreams, just as he had seen them. Hearing the fearful occurrences, and seeing the traces of alarm and dread upon the King's brow, they said: "These are terrible dreams, and no one has ever witnessed a dream so awful, nor has the ear of any interpreter of dreams heard of events of this description; if the King will honour us with permission, we slaves will meet together, and have resort to the perusal of books which have been written regarding the art of divination, and will reflect thereon with the utmost anxiety, after which, representing the meaning of those dreams by the light of evidence, we will concoct a plan to ward off the evil and misfortune thereof."

---

[1] That is, indicate that you are in existence.

> An orator speaks with deliberation,
> Since speech without thought, is worthless.

The King gave them permission, and they went out from before him, and retired into private. In malignity of heart, and impurity of disposition, they put in motion the chain of revenge, saying to one another: "This cruel tyrant has lately slain several thousands of our tribe, and given our property and chattels to the wind of plunder; nowadays the end of the thread has fallen into our hands, so that by this means we can wreak our vengeance, and remedy, and set right our distressed circumstances; and since he has admitted us into his confidence in this contingency, and has placed trust in our interpretation and elucidation of his dream, the opportunity must not be lost, and we must hasten to vent our former hatred.

> The enemy, in anguish of heart, is overtaken by adversity;
> Crush [1] him, for the opportunity is favourable.

"Our proper course is to speak roughly on this matter, and frighten him with the greatest threats, saying: 'These dreams are an indication that seven terrible dangers will arise, each of which is fraught with fear for your life. These evils can be warded off in this way: let a body of the pillars of the State, the King's nobles, and his Majesty's private beasts of burden, be slain with the lustrous sword, and their blood poured out into a basin. The King then should sit therein a while, and we will breathe incantations upon him and rub his body with some of the blood. After which, having washed his skin with pure water, we will anoint him with oil, and return to the assembly happy and at ease.' After that we have by this device brought his attendants to destruction, in lapse of time, when he is alone, we can finish the matter with him; and although hitherto the foot of our heart has been wounded by the thorn of the injuries done by him, yet it is to be hoped that with the hand of desire we shall pluck the rose of gratification, and that the powerful enemy having alighted in the region of weakness, we shall gain our end."

> Though the heart has experienced the thorn of violence, there is hope that again
> The rose of gratification will be plucked in the garden of desire.

Accordingly, with such frauds and stratagems, they ungratefully leagued together, and went to the King's presence, saying:

> "O King! may your throne and dignity be perpetual!
> May your months and years be auspicious and happy!

"This fact is practically clear to the King's enlightened mind, that the interpretation of these dreams signifies nought save the attacks of misfortune, pain, distress, and adversity; but we have thought of a good means of averting the evils of these occurrences. If the King should hear with acceptance our words, which spring from the purest goodwill and most genuine desire for his happiness, assuredly the ruin which is connected with these dreams will be averted; while, if he rejects our injunctions, he must expect a great calamity, nay, more, the decline of his sovereignty, and loss of his life." The King was alarmed, and, falling into the pale of perturbation, his heart was upset. He exclaimed: "You must explain these words, so that by any means which may be within the circle of

---

[1] Literally, "bring forth smoke from him."

possibility one may endeavour to remedy this." Seeing the oven of treachery hot, they placed therein the dough of imposture, and in this fashion addressed him : " Those two Fish, which stood on their tails, are the King's children ; that Snake, which coiled round the King's foot, is Írán-dukht; those two Ducks of varied colours are the Elephants,[1] and the large Goose is the White Elephant; that swift Mule is the royal pleasant-paced Courser; the two attendants on foot are the Dromedaries ; that Fire which was alight on the King's brow is the Minister Balár; that Bird which stuck his claws on the King's head is the Secretary Kamál; and that Blood, with which the King's body was defiled, is the result of the lustrous sword, which was struck upon the King's head, his body being coloured thereby. We have settled a plan in regard to the evils of this dream as follows : let both two Sons, and their Mother, the Secretary, the Minister, the Elephants, the Horse, and the Camels be slain with that sword. A little of the blood of each being taken, let it be collected together, and the scimitar being broken, let it be buried under the ground with those who are killed. Having mixed that blood with some water from the sea, we will pour it into a basin, and having seated the King therein, will chant incantations and prayers, and with blood will again write on the King's forehead some cabalistic signs, and staining his shoulders and breast with that blood, we will wait three hours. Then, washing the King's head and body with water from a spring, and drying him, we will anoint him with pure olive-oil, so that the evil may be completely warded off. Save this scheme nothing will be effectual."

> To ward off misfortune (may it not be your portion !)
> The plan is this, which has just been described.

When the King heard these words, the fire of perplexity burnt up the chattels of his patience and tranquillity, and the wind of alarm gave the harvest of his long-suffering and compassion to destruction. He said : " O enemies, with faces like friends ! and O men, with dispositions like demons ! death is preferable to this plan of yours, and to drink the potion of annihilation is sweeter than this your device, which is fraught with evil. When I have slain this throng, some of whom are, as it were, my own soul, and the body of whom are the pivot of the State and Property, and the means of ornamenting my dignity and grandeur, what pleasure in life would there be to me, or what advantage in existence ?

> Life is necessary with the view of getting access to my dear friend ;
> If that good fortune be denied, what other advantage has life ?

" Maybe you have not heard the story of Sulaimán—on whom be peace !—and the Heron, nor have the details of their conversation reached you." The Brahmans demanded, " What was that ? "

STORY II.

He said : I have heard that Sulaimán—" *May the benediction of our God and His mercy be upon our Prophet and upon him !* "—was a King whose illustrious decrees were graced with the honour of being efficacious. Spirits, men, beasts, and birds bound on the loins of their soul the girdle of submission and obedience to him. The writer, Fate, adorned the scroll of his sovereignty with the royal signet—" *O God ! bestow upon me a monarchy which may not be suitable for any*

---

[1] See note 2, page 431.

one after me "—and the Divine Groom placed the saddle of his majesty upon the back of the steed of the breeze, of whose journeying the saying—"*In the morning a month, and in the evening a month* "—is indicative.

> The Spheres were his servant, and the sun his slave ;
> Time was obedient to him, and the world within his grasp.
> Men, no less than spirits, heartily served him ;
> While animals, as well as birds, arranged themselves round his doors.

One day one of the attendants in the heavenly cells came to see him, and presented to his Majesty a goblet filled with the water of life, saying: "'*The Creator of all—may His Majesty be glorified, and His dominion be exalted !*'—has given you your free choice, and has enjoined : 'If you desire, drain this cup, and till the end of time remain safe from tasting the potion—'*Every soul tastes death ;*' but if you prefer it, at once raise your feet, and set out from the prison of human life to the pure garden and capacious atmosphere of the plain of Divinity.'" Sulaimán—on him be peace!—thought to himself : "The coin of life is a capital wherewith in the market of the resurrection one can acquire boundless profit, and the expanse of existence a field wherein one can sow the seed of fortune in both worlds, and the tree of perpetual happiness.

> The hand of this world is powerless
> To reach to that good fortune.

"Accordingly, in any case, the odour of perpetual life must be preferred to the blandishments of annihilation and death ; so, for the two or three days during which the reins of respite are in the hands of my power, I must strive to attain the grace of the Omnipotent God." [1]

> Life is such that it is passed in anguish for our beloved ones.

Again he reflected : "The chiefs of the spirits and of men are present, and the leaders of the beasts and birds in sight. I must consult with them, and whatever they all agree upon in opinion, I must make my guide in this matter." Thereupon he took counsel with the body of fairies, of men, of birds, and of all the animals, as to drinking the water of life, and all recommended him to quaff it, and were holpen and glad at the perpetuity of his life, which comprised the wellbeing of the inhabitants of the world.

> Enjoy eternal life, and everlasting existence,
> Such are the evening and morning prayers of old and young.

Sulaimán inquired : "Is there an inhabitant of my kingdom who is not present in this assembly ?" They said : "Yes ; the Heron has not come to this meeting, and is not aware of this consultation." Sulaimán—may peace be upon him !— sent a horse in search of him. The Heron refused to come. A second time the King ordered a Dog to go, and bring him. The Dog went, and the Heron accepted his words and presented himself before Sulaimán, who said : "I have somewhat to consult with you ; but before I introduce the subject, solve a difficulty for me." The Heron, representing his weakness and inability, said :

> Who am I that I should occur to that noble mind ?

"Your slave has no power to solve a difficulty, or that a King like you should

---

[1] That is, having two or three days to deliberate on the matter, I must, during that time, seek the grace of God ; but Solomon's reasoning does not appear very intelligible.

honour him with consulting him; but for the great of exalted rank to inquire as to a matter from the lowest of his subjects, does it not appear strange?

> You are the sun, while I am a most contemptible atom;
> Is it not strange that a mite should be fostered by the sun?

" If his Majesty, glorious in prophecy, is pleased to disclose that difficulty, whatever occurs to my insignificant mind, shall be conveyed to the place of representation." Sulaimán—on him be peace!—said: "After man, the most noble of animals is the horse, and the lowest of creatures a dog. What is the wisdom of this, that you would not come on the words of the highest of animals, while you accepted the invitation of the meanest of creatures?" The Heron replied: "Though the horse appears in the beauty of honour, and the perfection of merit is visible and apparent in him, yet he has not grazed in the meadow of fidelity, nor tasted a drop from the spring of gratitude.

> Fidelity must not be expected from a horse,
> Since who has seen a faithful horse, or woman, or sword?

" Now, although the dog is known to be a mean creature, and celebrated for being impure, yet he has eaten the morsels of fidelity, and has made gratitude his custom.

> The dog places in his ear the ring of affection,
> And is never unmindful of a single morsel.

" In accepting the invitation of this your Majesty, who is the source of fidelity and the aggregate of sincerity and purity, I would not listen to the words of a faithless creature, but set out on the invitation of an honest one." Sulaimán— on him be peace!—approved, and disclosed to him the secret as to drinking the water of life. The Heron said: "Will you drink that water alone, or will you share it with your friends and dependants?" Sulaimán — on him be peace!—replied: "It was sent to me individually, and no portion or part thereof has been given to others." The Heron said: "O Prophet of God! how can it be that you should live, while each of your companions, friends, children, and loyal servants dies before you? I do not fancy any pleasure can be derived from such life, or that there can be any imaginable delight in an existence which is altogether passed in separation."

> Value the society of friends, since the coin of life
> Is enjoyable only when scattered in the company of comrades.
> It is delightful to enjoy the sight of the rose-garden of precious life,
> But the pleasure of that sight arises from the contemplation of friends.

Sulaimán—peace be upon him!—approving his speech, refused the deadly drink of separation, and, not tasting the water of life, sent it back to the same place whence it had been brought."

" I have adduced this story that you may know, that I do not desire life without this multitude, and do not recognise any difference between my death and their annihilation. Assuredly every kingdom tends to decay, and every sovereign is on the brink of departure and migration, and at the last this dreadful road has to be travelled, and one has to sleep in the awful house of the grave; why, with the view of two or three days of transitory life, should I set about so alarming a business, and with my own hand mar the foundation of my prosperity and the

basis of my delight ? If you are able, devise another plan, and settle a remedy
for this misfortune in some easier way than this,

> " For I cannot discharge this business."

The Brahmans said : " May the King live for ever ! true words are bitter, and
advice free from treachery appears harsh. It is strange, as regards the King's
world-adorning judgment, that he should consider others equal to his own soul
and person, and with the view of their continuing to exist, should abandon his
own precious life, and hereditary kingdom. He must listen to the advice of his
friends, and place confidence in the words of those who are disinterested, deeming
his dear soul and broad domains an exchange for all these deaths ; and in this
matter, which is the cause of universal joy, and the occasion of repose to high
and low, he should commence without hesitation or irresolution. Assuredly a
wise man desires all other people for his own ends, and it is not concealed from
the King that a man through much grief attains an eminent rank, and that the
key of the treasury of dominion comes to hand with countless labour. To bid
adieu to the dignity of life, and quit the throne of prosperity and good fortune,
appears far from the path of wisdom ; and so long as the King's own person
remains, there will be no lack of wives and children ; and so long as the country
is stable, there will be no scarcity, or want of the means of wealth and luxury,
nor of able, trustworthy servants."

> Though there be nought, since you live, that is everything.

The King, on hearing these remarks, and observing their boldness in saying
these words, became extremely sad, and retired from the court.to his private
chamber, and from the dais of his palace turned his face towards the corner of
the house of sorrow.

> Since I cannot repeat to any one the state of my grief,
> I will go to the abode of sorrow, and converse even with myself.

Accordingly, placing the face of supplication upon the earth, he dropped tears of
regret from his eyes, and his heart being consumed with the fire of despair, he
gave to the winds of destruction the harvest of his patience and endurance. He
said : " Whence appears this cloud of misfortune which pours down the rain of
calamity, and by what passage is the attack of this army of grief, which bears off
in plunder nought but the possessions of life ?

> There I was in my nook, with my friends, and full of song.
> Who gave my address to grief, and who conveyed the tidings to calamity ?

" Anyhow, in what way can I say that the death of my beloved ones is easy,
and what pleasure could I find in life and existence without the beauty of my
children and friends ? and deprived of my sons, who are the light of my eyes
and the fruit of my heart, in whom is my help in the present life, as well as my
hope after travelling the way of death, of what use will be sovereignty ?

> Of nought have fathers more need,
> Nought is more fitting than worthy children.

" As regards Írán-dukht, too, such that the fountain of the radiant sun is but
a drop from the well of her chin, and the rising light of the brilliant moon the
effulgence from the reflection of her pearl - scattering face ; whose cheeks are

blooming and merry like the days of prosperity, and her ringlets dark and inter-
twined like the nights of adversity—

> Her cheeks like the incomparable sun in the Heavens ;
> With arched eyebrows, she was as it were the new moon.
> From her face the light of the sun gained radiance ;
> From her pearly lips the ruby acquired lustre—

" whose society is enchanting, and her company enrapturing : without her, what
enjoyment shall I have in life ? Again, if Balár, the minister, whose brilliant
judgment in every night of accident is a light-spreading sun, and the radiance of
the taper of whose mind in the gloom of every occurrence is a darkness-dispelling
light—

> Without the aid of his restless pen,
> The throne of kings would not be stable—

" is not before my couch of glory, how could the kingdom endure, or the splendour of government, the repletion of the treasuries, and the attainment of wealth,
be brought about ? When the page of deliberation on the part of the secretary
Kamál, of whose fingers the painter of the lofty spheres is a pupil, and the
beautiful-talking Mercury the crumb-eater of the tables of his explanations ;
whose words are heart-enchanting, like a string of pearls, and his writing
resembles scattered joy-diffusing jewels—

> His pleasure-giving words caused water and fire to mix ;
> His charming writing made light and dark to mingle together—

" is not in my sight, how will the affairs of the outlying regions, and the occurrences of the neighbouring places be known, and by what device will intelligence
be gained as to the condition of enemies, and the designs of foes ? Whenever
the inscription of destruction shall be drawn across the volume of the life of
these two upright counsellors and honest officers, who are, as it were, helping
hands and bright eyes to the kingdom, assuredly the benefits of their advice and
the traces of their ability will be banished from the country. On this supposition, the splendour of affairs and the arrangement of matters will be amongst the
multitude of impossibilities. Without my White Elephant, whose frame shines
like the globe of the moon, and who is elegant and moving like the revolving
Heavens—

> His impregnable castle was bound with iron ;
> The wound of his tusks could overthrow ramparts—

" how could I face my enemies ? Without those two Elephants, who in the
ranks of battle like roaring torrents tread down the enemy, and who in the
midst of conflict, as it were a storm, bear away men—

> Twisting their trunks into lassoes,
> They ensnare the necks of heroes—

" in the day of warfare how shall I break the ranks of the enemy, and at the
time of contest in what way shall I defeat the attacks of my opponents ?
Without my quick-going Dromedaries, at the time of whose starting off the messenger of Morn could not see from afar their dust, nor the courier of the North
Wind ever think of keeping pace with the clouds on their road—

> Like fire, consuming thorns, laying low heads ;
> Ay ! like the wind pacing through the desert—

"how shall I gain intelligence of the outlying regions, and by what means convey my joyous despatches and exalted commands throughout the kingdom ? Without my coursing Steed, fleet, resembling the wind, and with nerves of steel, moving like lightning, and with dazzling speed, the effulgence of whose cheeks raised the fire of misfortune in the heart of Rustam's [1] courser (Rakhsh), and the celerity of whose movements caused a rosy tear to flow from the eyes of the horse Shabdíz, belonging to Khusrau [2]—

> A pacer, which, in one bound, would bestride
> The plain, were it as long as that of hope—

"how can I anticipate the carpet of pleasure, or in what way with the club [3] of joy bear off the ball of delight from the plain of satisfaction. Without the cutting Sword, which resembles water, since the flame of sedition is quenched through dread thereof, and is fiery in its actions, the reputation of the kingdom being maintained by its majesty—

> Your blue sword exhibited its qualities in its blade,
> Like the rain-drop upon the moist violet—

"what effect shall I produce in battle ? And whenever I am deprived of these weapons, and with my own hand render useless the multitude of my dependants, what advantage can I gain from my kingdom, and what pleasure can I derive from my life ? In truth,

> "Life passed in such a way is of no account."

To sum up, the King for a whole night and day immersed himself in a sea of thought, and did not find the pearl of deliberation, with which he could bring to his hand the thread of hope. The mention of the King's perplexity was spread amongst the nobles of the State, and the Sovereign's preoccupation of mind became clear to all the confidants of the Royal Sanctuary. The Minister, Balár, thought : "If I commence to clear up these words, and begin to inquire into the King's secrets before that a hint thereof has proceeded on the part of King, it will be far from the rights of respect and manners ; while if I delay, and adopt the way of reflection and procrastination, it will not be in accordance with sincerity and uprightness." He then repaired to Írán-dukht, and after the allowance of praise, commenced to intercede, saying :

> O thou ! who hast placed the veil of thy integrity on high,
> The Holy Spirit is holder of the curtain of the Haram of thy dignity.

"It is not hidden from your exalted intellect, that from the very day when I was honoured by being arranged in the string of attendants at this Court of the sphere of magnificence, till this hour, the King has not concealed anything from me, and has not allowed himself to enter upon any of the trifles or important affairs of government without consulting me. Yesterday, once or twice, he summoned the Brahmans, and had a conference with them ; and this day, also, he has retired into private, and sits contemplative and melancholy. Now you are the Queen of his Fortune, and the companion of the royal heart, while the subjects and army, after the King's favour, place their hopes in your grace, and

---

[1] The Hercules of the East.   [2] See note, page 153.   [3] See note 1, page 138.

consider your commands in settling affairs as second only to the decrees of the Sovereign. It seems advisable for you to go to his presence, and learning the state of what has occurred, to do us the honour of informing us, so that we may as quickly as possible set about remedying matters, for the Brahmans are treacherously disposed and malignant; God forbid that by means of fraud they should impel him to a business, the end of which will lead to remorse and repentance! for after a matter has occurred, regret and sorrow avail nought."

A matter must be remedied before it occurs.

Írán-dukht replied: " Reproaches have passed between me and the King, and several intimations and hints have been spoken. I am ashamed in such circumstances to approach the King, or to loose my tongue in inquiring into the matter." The Minister said: "O Queen of the World!—'*Reproof is the offering of friends*' —reproach is the cause of the stability of the edifice of affection, and the means of rendering firm the basis of friendship and intercourse.

Kindness is on your part, while I am reproachful;
Without tenderness and reproof, friendship cannot be carried on.

" At this time you must lay aside reproach, since when the King is engulfed in thought, and deep and long contemplation distresses his heart, his servants and attendants will not be audacious; and, save you, no one can open this door with the key of expediency. I have many times heard from the King, that ' Whenever Írán-dukht enters my presence, though I be sad I become merry, and through the auspicious sight of her I am freed from the snares of grief and distress.' Go and find out this matter, and confer a great favour upon all the servants and retinue." Írán-dukht, having approached the King, performed the dues of homage, saying:

May you be free from grief! may misfortune never befall you! and may you
    not be sorrowful!
For you are the ease of our heart, the rest of our soul, and the banisher of
    our distress.

" What is the cause of your perplexity, and the reason of your cogitation? If you have heard something from the Brahmans, you should acquaint your servants with it, so that, sympathising therein, they may discharge the dues of servitude." The King said: ' Questions must not be asked about ought, to which, if an answer were given, it would be of vexation of spirit. ' *Do not inquire about things which, if told you, would annoy you.*' " Írán-dukht rejoined : " If this grief is in regard to the mass of your dependants, be not dejected, since the welfare of your blessed person is a cure for all ills.

May a thousand precious lives be a sacrifice for your soul!

" If—God forbid!—it concerns the precious soul of his Majesty, also you must not be distressed thereat, nor in any way remain downcast; nay, more, manly determination, as indicated by the saying, ' *Steady purpose is of the purposes of kings,*' must be displayed by persevering in the qualities of patience and firmness; since to complain adds to grief, while want of resignation renders enemies delighted and merry, and grieves and distresses friends. As regards all that befalls mankind, when one clings to genuine patience, ultimately the face of gratification will come into sight, and the best of desires are those wherein divine rewards are not lost.

O heart! be patient regarding the calamities of the World;
Through resignation, the end of your case will be satisfactory.

"It is proper in regard to the King, that when an affair happens, and an occurrence comes to pass, the means of remedying, and the way of rectifying the same, according to the perfection of his ability and the abundance of his sagacity, should not remain hidden or concealed; especially when there is nothing wanting as regards the faculties of power and might, and the accessories for removing distress and obliterating grief and languor are ready and prepared."

You have both wealth and attendants; you possess kingdom, and also retinue.
Set your foot forth from retirement, and raise your standard upon the roof of
the World.
Turn your face towards your desire, banish grief;
Make your friends happy, and remove the load of sorrow from your soul.

The King said: "Of that which the Brahmans indicated, if but a syllable were to be whispered in the ear of the mountain, its sides, like the Mount of Glory, would have rent asunder, and the epithet, '*And the hills shall become broken to atoms*,' would be exemplified in regard to it; and if but a hint thereof were given to brilliant Day, from perturbation it would become the colour of black Night; and the sign, '*Shades, some of which are above others*,' would be displayed therein.

'Twere disgraceful did the moon not clothe herself in black at this grief;
'Twere shameful did not the cloud turn to blood at this calamity.

"Do not press your inquiries into this matter, nor endeavour to ascertain the truth thereof, since I have neither strength to tell, nor have you power to hear." Írán-dukht once again renewed her efforts, and the King, with the view of satisfying her mind, disclosed a portion of his inward secret, saying: "During the night I saw an occurrence, at the horror of which I was afraid, and with the view of its being interpreted and explained, I related it to the Brahmans, and those execrable wretches deemed it advisable that you, with both your fortunate and mighty Sons, the pure-minded Minister, the elegant-writing Secretary, the white hero-crushing Elephant, and the other mountain-formed, army-routing Elephants, the stony-crossing, thorn-eating Dromedaries, and the elegant-paced Steed, should be killed with the pearl-decked Sword, so that the evil results of that dream might be averted." When Írán-dukht heard these words, the smoke of grief came forth from the fire-temple of her heart to the aperture of her brain, and it wellnigh happened that tears of regret began to pour forth from the fountain of her eyes. However, being wise and sagacious, she smothered her soul-consuming distress, and did not show any perturbation, but said:

If I, through love for you, perish, may you live on!
May a thousand of my souls, and a hundred persons such as myself, be sacrificed for you!

"The King must not be distressed on account of this matter, since if the lives of your servants are not fit to be a sacrifice for the King's welfare, of what use are they? So that his august person remains lasting, and the degree of his power fixed, there will be no lack of wives and offspring, nor will there be any deficiency of servants, or the means of luxury. But when the evils of your dream are averted, and your blessed heart is at ease respecting this sorrow, no confidence must be placed in this treacherous multitude, and if they urge the King to slay a mass of people, he must not without reflection set about it; since to spill blood is a serious matter, and a grave thing to overturn the basis of a creature's life. If—God forbid!—innocent blood should be shed, the end thereof will be disastrous, and the punishment lasting torture, while regret, remorse, sorrow, and anguish will avail nought in regard thereto; for to bring back those who are slain, or to restore life to a man, is beyond the pale of human power.

> This matter is neither within my power nor yours.

"The King must know that the Brahmans have no affection for him, and although they have plunged into sciences, and, according to their opportunity, have learned several problems, yet the sages of religion are agreed in asserting, that a bad and base disposition will not be beautified with any adornment, nor will learning and riches grace it with the decoration of fidelity and benevolence; since if a jewelled collar be cast round the neck of a dog, his filthiness will not be changed, and a pig, if they gild his teeth, his impurity will not be altered into cleanliness. The saying, '*Like a donkey which carries books on its back,*' is confirmatory of this point.

> When knowledge touches the heart, it produces fruit.
> When knowledge touches the body, it is a serpent.[1]

"Knowledge is like a sword, by which all persons may be slain; they who are of pure disposition and honest nature, with that sword put to death the lusts and passions, than which a man has no worse enemies; while some, who are grovelling, and of impure feelings, with the same weapon oppress wisdom and justice, save with which mankind never attain noble stations. Thus the instrument for averting enemies is made the weapon for injuring friends. That perfect Philosopher indicates this meaning, where he says:

> To teach an evil-disposed person the arts and sciences,
> Is as it were putting a sword in the palm of a highway robber:
> To give a scimitar into the hands of a drunken Moor,
> Is better than that learning should be placed within the reach of the worthless.
> They who learn wiles, are inwardly consumed,
> And versed in evil deeds and perfidy.

"Their design in this interpretation is so as not to lose the opportunity of revenge; and by this treacherous proceeding, which they call a remedial arrangement, to find a salve for the wound, which is implanted in their hearts, owing to the royal chastisement. First of all they will remove your children, who are the like of your noble self, and the equivalent of the King's benevolent person, so that the Sovereign may remain without heirs: they will then ruin the great and true men, who are the pillars of the State, and on whose intelligence are dependent the welfare of the kingdom, and fulness of the treasuries, in order that the subjects may be emboldened, and the army become dispirited. Again, they would deprive the appurtenances of monarchy of Elephants, Camels, Horses, and Arms, with the view of the King remaining alone and friendless. I, your slave, am of no account,[2] and there are many like me in your service; but

---

[1] That is, knowledge which sinks into the heart, produces good fruit; while learning, which is but superficial, is pernicious.
[2] I have borrowed this suggestion from Eastwick.

when they find the King all solitary, in lapse of time, having manifested the design of revenge, whatever has lain quiet in their minds for years, they will put in practice. Till this period they have looked on, helpless and powerless; but when they find means of strength, and the reins of power fall into their hands, they will endeavour to bring tumult into the kingdom, and open the doors of strife; since in case the King should make away with his dependants, both the soldiers will be in despair, and suspicion, also, will occur amongst the subjects: and when the populace and troops become double-hearted[1] and ten-tongued, it will occasion triumph and exaltation amongst foes. On such a supposition kingdom and possessions would slip from your hands, and spirit and life be squandered. Now Kings should not be indifferent to the treachery and wiles of enemies.

> Rest not secure from dishonest acting foes,
> For they are treacherously disposed, and of wicked nature.
> To appearance they are friends,
> But inwardly, they are knocking at the door of faithlessness.

" In spite of all this, if as regards what the Brahmans deemed advisable, there is any joy or comfort, certainly no delay must occur; but if there be opportunity for deferring matters, there remains one other cautious mode of proceeding, and on the King's orders it can be revealed." The King gave the command, and said: "What you say, in my opinion, is free from the impurities of suspicion, and assuredly will be accepted and received." Írán-dukht rejoined: " Káridún, the Philosopher, who founded the edifice of virtuous attainments, and is the traveller on the road of noble qualities and talents, having a nature which is a storehouse of the precious things of mysteries and wisdom, and an understanding which is a mine of the private secrets of superiority and merit—

> His acute intellect is admitted within the veil of Fate,
> His pure soul is beautiful in the precious sight of God—

" at the present time has made choice of retiring to a cave in Mount Khazrá, and perpetually observes the way of belief in God, and austerity. Although, by birth, he is akin to the Brahmans, yet he is superior to them in sincerity integrity, fidelity, and uprightness: his sight with regard to the termination of matters is more perfect, and in warding off calamities and occurrences, his sound judgment is more comprehensive. If the King's mind demands it, he must deign to make this person a confidant, and disclose to him the circumstances of the dream, and the matter of the Brahmans' interpretation thereof, and doubtless he will announce to the King straightforwardly as to the truth of the same, and will not conceal an atom of the explanation of the purport of what has occurred. Should his interpretation accord with that spoken by the Brahmans doubt being banished, it will be necessary to put that very same design into execution; while if he indicates to the contrary, the King's illustrious mind will discern between right and wrong, and discriminate between honesty and perfidy." The King agreed with this speech, and at once mounting his horse went to the Philosopher Káridún, and having had the good fortune to see the Divine Sage, who was the aggregate of boundless graces, paid him the necessary respect. The Philosopher, too, having discharged the dues of regard, said:

> My cell is a Paradise, when the Lord of Heaven arrives;
> My eyes are enlightened, when the fragrance of Joseph of Canaan reaches me.

---

[1] That is, hypocritical and unreliable.

" What is the cause of the equipage of the fortune-resembling stirrup? Had the decree been issued, I would myself have repaired to Court, since it would be more proper for servants to do homage.

To perform the ceremony of homage, and the rite of attendance,
O my Lord, do thou intrust to me, and be yourself my Sovereign.

" Traces, too, of perturbation can be seen on the august brow, and signs of grief can be physiognomically traced on his auspicious countenance : he must represent the state of the case, and disclose the cause of his distress." The King repeated, by way of description, the circumstances of his dreams, and the interpretation of the Brahmans. Káridún shook his head in astonishment, and biting the finger of perturbation with his teeth, said : "The King has been remiss in this matter, for this secret should not have been proclaimed to such a multitude, nor this account repeated to that mass.

How should every ear be confided with the secrets ?

" It is not concealed from the King's world-adorning judgment, that these perfidious foes have no capability to interpret these occurrences, because they possess neither wisdom to direct them, nor integrity to keep them right. The King's joy should increase by reason of these dreams, and by way of gratitude he should bestow endless alms upon the deserving ; since proofs of happiness, and evidences of delight and greatness are manifest and clear on the pages of the interpretations of these occurrences. From moment to moment the course of events will be in accordance with his desires, and from hour to hour the concerns of prosperity and magnificence will be on the thread of arrangement.

The Spheres obedient to you, the Heavens your slave, and the Skies submissive :
Fate subject to you, Monarchy your devoted servant, and Time favourable to you.

" I will at this very time repeat the interpretation of all the numerous occurrences, and avert the arrow of the schemes of those opponents with the shield of wisdom.

If you possess an arrow, so have I a shield.

" First : those two red Fish, standing on their tails, are Ambassadors, who will come from the regions of Sarándíp, and who in homage will present before the King two strange-framed Elephants, with four hundred pounds of red rubies, from jealousy at the colour of which, the heart of the pomegranate would have been drenched with blood, and the globe of fire from vexation at their rays have remained concealed in the inner recess of stone. Those two Ducks and the Goose, which flew after the King, and alighted before his face, are two Horses and a Mule, which the Sovereign of Dihlí will send to your Majesty, by way of an offering. Those two Horses are such that they snort like thunder, and chafe like lightning, being of quick intelligence and indomitable pluck.

The earth's surface was marked with the circle of their hoofs,
Their ears were like spears in the air.
No languor befell their joints, from the violence of the stirrup,
Nor did fear overtake their nature from the fierceness of the rein.

" That Mule is a beast of burden, pacing like wind, violent as fire, passing like lightning over paths and gorges, and like a thunderbolt, with the blow of its hoofs raising fire from stone.

With silvery hoof and gilded bridle, quick-paced and swift-footed,
The Garden of the Spheres its abode, the fountain of the sun its drinking-
bowl.

" That Snake, which twisted round the King's feet, is a sword, fiery and re-splendent, which in the day of battle showers from its azure fount a torrent of liquid rubies, and scatters over the diamond-coloured surface particles of cornelian, and atoms of coral.

Victory and conquest await thy high-tempered sword,
No! no! thy scimitar is the embodiment of all triumph.

" That Blood, wherewith the King found himself stained, is a red dress, orna-mented with jewels, brought from the capital Ghiznah, by way of a present to the King's wardrobe. That white Mule, on which the King bestrode, is a white Elephant, which the Sovereign of Bíjánagar sent for the Monarch's service; and the King will enjoy riding on that Elephant, which is a creature shaped like a cloud, and which in the ranks of the army makes its emerald-coloured trunk like a lustrous pearl with the blood of the brave, while its dragon-attacking teeth, attached to a mountain of iron, in a moment annihilate the whole world.

Its form like a mountain filled the desert,
Though without pillars, yet moving on four legs.

" That which shone round the King's blessed head like fire, is a crown which the Sovereign of Ceylon will send as an offering. This Crown is such that the ornaments on its top join head to head with the azure Paradise of the skies, and by its profusion of pearls it will make every hair on the head of the royal Monarch a string of jewels.

The representation of that crown, decked with jewels, reached
The Orb of the Moon, like the Moon of Mukanna'.[1]

" As regards the Bird, which pecked at the King's head, from this some little unpleasantness must be anticipated, but no great effects or evil will arise therefrom, and the utmost of it is that for several days you will avoid a dear friend and kind companion, but the end will be advantageous and triumphant. Such is the account of the interpretation of the King's dreams; and in that you saw them seven times is a proof that the Ambassadors will come seven times with royal gifts to the King's auspicious Court, and his Majesty by acquiring those bounties, and the arrival of those gifts, will become delighted and merry of heart; he will also derive pleasure from the stability of his fortune and the prolongation of his life. It will behove the Monarch of the world, after this, not to admit worthless people as confidants of his secrets, and not to take counsel with a person till he shall have tried his wisdom.

Till a person has been tried a hundred times,
Admit him not to your presence as a confidant of your secrets.

" The essence of wisdom is this: to consider it an absolute duty altogether to

---

[1] A celebrated Magician, who produced a certain luminous appearance in the sky.

avoid impudent, impure, evil-disposed, bad-natured persons, and not to string the priceless pearl of one's precious soul on the thread of mean-natured, low-minded, and base-tempered individuals."

> See the water, how it complains[1]
> Every moment of rugged comrades !

When the King heard this harangue, he at once prostrated himself with grati-tude, and asked pardon of that old man of blessed spirit, who like Christ had given to the royal lifeless heart, joy without limit, and said : "The Almighty Grace has bestowed the aid of victory, and has shown me the way to this high personage, who is endued with wisdom and adorned with gladness, so that by the auspiciousness of his Excellency's blessed spirit, the severities of trouble have been exchanged for the benefits of repose."

> There was a burden of grief, which broke my heart—
> God sent the breath of Christ, and bore it away.

"*Praise be to God! praise continual and everlasting.*" Accordingly the King, with joyous heart, honoured the seat of government by alighting there. For seven successive days ambassadors arrived with presents and offerings, and in the way just as the perfect sage had spoken, conveyed the purport of their messages to the place of representation. The seventh day the King summoned his children, Balár the Minister, Írán-dukht, and the Secretary, in private, and said : "I have done a strange wrong, in that I repeated my dreams to my enemies ; and if Divine condescension had not become a screen against their wiles, and had not the advice of Írán-dukht opened the hand of remedy, in the end the suggestions of these cursed wretches would have accomplished the death of myself, and all my dependants and followers. But whoever is befriended by Divine happiness, and aided by Eternal wisdom, assuredly welcoming the advice of the sincere, will plunge into matters only after reflection and delib-eration, and cogitating in regard to the disastrous results, will not abandon the region of caution and the place of circumspection, for it has been said :

> ' He who acts without thought, will find no comfort.' "

He then commanded that, since the minds of his friends by reason of this occurrence were not free from anxiety, it was incumbent that these presents should be divided amongst them, more especially as regards Írán-dukht, who had enjoined the remedy for this calamity. The Minister Balár said : "Servants are of this use, that having made themselves, as regards what occurs, shields against misfortune, they may not withhold their souls and spirits.

> Whoever protects your life must not regard his own head.

"If any one, by the aid of fortune and the assistance of luck, renders service of this nature, and vital obligation of this kind, and places his property and exist-ence at the disposal of his benefactor, no reward or present can be looked for therefrom, nor can any recompense or return be expected ; but the Queen of the age laboured diligently for this purpose, and from these blessings the Crown decked with jewels, or the Red garment ornamented with gems, is fit for her ; whichever she may prefer the King must bestow upon her." The Monarch commanded both to be borne to a private chamber, and he himself entered

---

[1] In allusion, presumably, to the roar of a cataract.

therein with the Minister Balár. In the Haram was another damsel called Bazm[1] Afrúz, having a countenance such that the eastern sun, in shame thereat, hid its face behind the curtain, "*Concealed by a veil*," while the fresh rose-leaf, through bashfulness, concealed itself beneath the screen of emerald.

> Small mouth, round head, and large eyebrows,
> Her face like a red rose upon a green leaf,
> Her smile sweet, like sugar-cane;
> Pleasant, joyous, beautiful, charming, and delicate.
> Every smile which played round her lips,
> Scattered salt[2] upon desolate hearts.

The King was much enamoured of her, and notwithstanding that Írán-dukht as regards beauty and elegance was a strife in the world, and in respect to her charm and grace a sedition in the age, the Sovereign gave Bazm Afrúz a turn with her, and used to visit the former's house every alternate night. This day the King enjoined that Bazm Afrúz should be summoned, and the crown and clothes be fetched; he then ordered that Írán-dukht should select which she liked, and the other should be the portion of Bazm Afrúz. Írán-dukht was more inclined for the Crown, and that constellation, set with jewels like stars, appeared preferable in her sight. Having shown a hankering in that direction, she looked at the Minister Balár, as to whether what she had taken met with his approval. Balár signed with his eyes towards the garment. In the midst of these proceedings the King turned towards him. Írán-dukht saw that the Sovereign had observed that signal: she took the Crown, so that the King should not be apprised of the counsel, while Balár dropped his eyes so that his Majesty should not be aware of the suggestion; and after that, during the forty years which he attended the King, whenever he approached near the Sovereign he squinted, in order that the King's suspicions might not be verified; and had it not been for the wisdom of the Minister, and her own sharpness, both would have given their souls to the winds.

> Whoever makes wisdom the centre of his actions,
> Will, without doubt, be free from the bonds of misfortune.

Just as Írán-dukht was exalted[3] by accepting the Crown, so was Bazm Afrúz also honoured by choosing the Red garment. Accordingly, as has been described, the King passed one night till morn with Bazm Afrúz, and spent the next evening with Írán-dukht. By chance one evening when it was his turn to visit Írán-dukht's house, the King, according to his wont, went there merrily, while Írán-dukht, with enrapturing face and enchanting ringlets—

> She had washed with fresh musk each single hair,
> And sprinkled her face with the water of life—

placed the jewelled Crown upon her head, and taking in her hand a golden dish full of rice, stood before the King, who ate a morsel from off the platter, and indulging in her society, rendered the eyes of his heart radiant with the sight of her beauty. In the midst Bazm Afrúz, in the Red garment, passed by them,

---

[1] That is, "banquet-illuminating."
[2] That is, distracted them; the effect being compared to rubbing salt on a wound.
[3] There is a play upon words here which it is quite impossible to retain; the terms rendered "exalted" and "honoured," mean literally "head-raised" and "face-reddened," in allusion to the effects of wearing the crown and red cloak.

with cheeks like a Rose in blossom, and a countenance resembling the moon a fortnight old.

> A scarlet garment thrown over her bosom,
> You would say it was a wreath of cypress decked with tulips;
> Her two Turkish[1] eyes lying in wait for hearts.
> Two eyebrows casting arrows at the soul;
> Her cheeks shone radiant through her twining tresses,
> Like moonlight in the midst of dark night.

The King on seeing her, drew back his hand from the food; and an overpowering propensity towards her, and a sincere craving for her society, snatched the reins of self-possession from the grasp of the King's choice, and the bridle of restraint from the palm of his might. Departing after Bazm Afrúz, he loosed the tongue in commendation and congratulation :—

> "O graceful-walking cypress! O newly-opened rose!
> A narcissus, rose, or cypress such as you was never seen even in dreams.

"By your arrival you have opened to my bosom the doors of joy, and with this gait you have scattered to the winds the harvest of my patience and endurance."

> O excellent! by your arrival you have increased my fortune.

He then said to Írán-dukht: "This crown which you have borne away is fitting for the brow of Bazm Afrúz, and in selecting it you have inclined from the road of rectitude to the region of error." The jealousy of love seized the skirt of Írán-dukht, and the flame of the fire of envy fell on the grate of her breast. At these words she blushed, and beside herself, overturned the dish of rice on the King's head, and stained his face and hair therewith, so that the interpretation, by the occurrence which the sage had pointed out, became verified. The fire of the King's anger was raised, and he summoned the Minister Balár, and explained to him the insult which had proceeded from her, and said: "Remove this foolish person from my presence, and cut off her neck, that she may know that such as she are not of so great importance as to attempt such rash acts, and we overlook them." Balár brought forth the Queen, and thought to himself: "To hasten in this matter would not be proper, since this woman is without an equal as regards eloquence and powers of conversation, and without a compeer in intelligence and sagacity. The King will not remain patient without seeing her; and by the blessing of her pure spirit, and the felicity of her enlightened intellect, many persons have escaped from the whirlpool of death. Maybe the King will disavow this hasty proceeding; and even putting out of sight the King's reproach, it does not appear proper to proceed rashly in such matters as these. Nought is better than for me to base this affair upon reflection, that at the time of cross-examination I may not blush with shame.

> When the Judge with deliberation writes the decree,
> He will not be confounded by the learned.[2]

"I must delay for two or three days. If on the part of the King there appears regret, at any rate the opportunity of remedy will not have been lost, while if he is intent and determined upon killing her, to slay her will not be impossible.

---

[1] That is, dark eyes—a sign of beauty in the East.
[2] Literally, "wearers of turbans."

From such postponement three clear advantages will accrue: 1st, The reward of sparing a life; 2d, The acquisition of the King's favour, if he should repent of killing her; 3d, The gratitude of all the inhabitants of the kingdom, in that I have spared a Queen like her, whose good works extend to all, and the effects of whose pious deeds are general and universal." Accordingly, he took her to his own house, together with a throng of confidential persons, who were wont to perform the service of the King's Haram. He commanded that they should guard her with the utmost care, and treat her with becoming respect and kindness; while he himself with the sword smeared with blood, and his head downcast, like those overwhelmed with anxiety, repaired to the Court, and said: "I have performed the King's command, and conveyed to punishment and retribution that mannerless person, who placed her foot upon the carpet of rashness." The violence of the King's rage was entirely quenched, and the buffeting of the waves of the sea of his anger no longer continued. When he heard these words, and reflected on her beauty, perfection, wisdom, and integrity, he was extremely grieved, but ashamed to display traces of irresolution, and to combine with one another on his part flexibility and firm determination, which involve a mixture of contrarieties. He then began to reproach himself, saying: "You have done wrong in laying aside compassion and deliberation, and consigning your beloved to the region of destruction for a slight offence, which might have been overlooked at the time of its occurrence; I should not have issued such a command on account of such a degree of rashness, but should have quenched the fire of rage with the water of compassion."

> The person filled with violence, is like a piece of fire,
> Since with his breath he raises aloft the flame.
> The man is fiery beyond measure,
> From whose breath the smoke (of anguish) does not proceed.

But when the Minister saw traces of repentance upon the King's brow, he said: "The King must not be sorrowful, since the arrow which has left the bow-string cannot be brought back, nor can one slain be restored to life by might or gold: to indulge in profitless grief attenuates the body, and enfeebles the heart, the result of which will be nought but distress amongst friends and delight amongst enemies. Every one on hearing that the King makes a decree, and after that it is carried out at once repents, will become suspicious of the King's prudence and firmness. It would have behoved the King to have been gentle in this matter, and to have turned aside from harshness and severity, and, like the letter-possessing Monarch, to have subdued his rage, so that repentance should not arise. If he commands it, I will recount him the story." The King said, "Certainly you must repeat what it was."

STORY III.

The sound, deliberating Minister said: It has been related that in the capital of Yaman there was a King of enlightened spirit, and a Monarch with mature judgment and youthful fortune. The eyes of the quick-revolving Heavens had never in the course of their journey seen a Sun in the Spheres of Sovereignty like him, and the ear of man-testing Fortune had never in the expanse of time heard of a Sovereign endowed like him.

At the banquet, like the Sun, he enlightened the cheeks;
In battle, like dragons, he consumed the world.
He rendered the earth subservient by his distribution of justice;
Time was obedient to him, and the Spheres under his sway.

This King was fond of the chase. One day in the hunting-field he was galloping the steed of joy both left and right, and casting the glance of wonder in every direction, but saw in that proximity no game, either of beasts or birds, nor did an animal worthy of being the prey of a Monarch come into his sight. The King perplexed at. this circumstance looked about: by chance a wood-cutter from excess of want and poverty had put on garments made of skins of deer, and had cut down much bramble in that waste: from the labour of that occupation he became very tired, and rested on the side of a stone. The eyes of the King alighted on him from afar, and thinking it was a deer, he shot at him a heart-rending arrow.

The flame of the arrow which brought forth gore,
Darted like lightning upon that person, whose harvest was consumed.
Strife showed no respect for misfortune,
He did wrong, and yet he did not do wrong.[1]

In short when the King reached his prey, and found him wounded in the breast, with his heart suffused in blood, he himself became very sad and sorrowful, and commenced to tear the face of repentance with the nail of reproach, and was vexed in heart at that inconsiderate and precipitous action, which was the cause of regret and mortification. He expressed many apologies, and by way of a salve bestowed on the man the value of a thousand dínár of red-faced gold, and turning the reins of shame towards the capital, condescended to alight at the cell of a Devotee, who was famous in the city for his religion and piety —nay, more, renowned and celebrated throughout the expanse of the universe, for showing the right way, and pointing the true direction. From the holy man he demanded advice, such as should increase his dignity in this world, and smooth over his sins in that to come. The Devotee by way of explanation and beneficence said: "O King! the quality which comprises prosperity in this world, and happiness in the next, is to quench one's anger, and at a time when rage is predominant to show pity."

From him who raises the fire of anger,
Do not expect a display of manliness.
When rage inflames the steed of the passions,
Then hold in the reins till it is calmed.

The King said: "I am aware that the taste of the poison-mingled potion of long-suffering is very pleasurable to the palate of wisdom, but in the time of anger I cannot make compassion ruler over my passions, and on the occasion of the fire of wrath being raised, I cannot bring myself within the bonds of patience." The Devotee rejoined: "I will write three letters, which consign to the hands of a private servant and a trustworthy confident, so that when he witnesses signs of a change of temper on your brow, and sees the flame of your anger and hasti-

---

[1] I am rather at a loss as to the meaning of these two lines, but presume it to be that the act of transfixing the man with an arrow was due to the demon of strife, who paid no regard to the Spirit of Misfortune; while the King, though he did what was in itself wrong, yet, as he acted unwittingly, in that sense it was not a crime.

ness raised, he may recite one of them to you; maybe the benefit thereof becoming evident, your passions will be quieted. If he observes that the fire of wrath is not quenched by the pure stream of that admonition, he must bring the second letter to his aid; and if your refractory feelings do not become tractable by that also, he should show you the third letter. I am in hopes that the calamity of that fiery temper will be changed for gentleness and softness; and when the darkness of fury is repelled, assuredly the brilliancy of compassion and consideration will come in place thereof."

> When a demon departs an angel enters in.

The King was pleased with these words, and the Devotee wrote three letters and intrusted them to one of the King's servants. The substance of the first letter was this: "In time of power do not give the reins of dominion to the possession of lust, which will cast you into the whirlpool of eternal destruction." The purport of the second composition was as follows: "On the occasion of anger be considerate to those beneath you, so that at a period of retaliation your superiors may be kind to you." While the pith of the third epistle was to this effect: "In issuing decrees, do not deviate from the limit of the law, and in no case depart from what is equitable."

> Though your decree is potent, as regards your sovereignty,
> Do no violence, since tyranny is not effectual:
> Assume not haughty airs, though your lips are smiling like a rose-bud;
> For the eyes of the oppressed are March clouds.
> Be not puffed up with the rose-garden of the palace of your prosperity,
> Since you will soon leave it, and yourself pass away.

The King bidding the Devotee adieu, returned to his capital, and constantly in the assembly of justice, especially in times of rage, these three letters used to be read to him, and owing to his confidence in these epistles, they gave him the name of the "Letter-possessing King." This Monarch had a damsel, handsome-faced, pure-minded, with stature like the cypress, and cheeks like the moon, with ruby lips, silvery dewlaps, with gait like a partridge, and speech like a parrot.

> Moon-faced, perfumed like musk, heart-enchanting,
> Soul-delighting, heart-ensnaring and moon-like.

The intoxicated narcissus was enamoured of her languishing eyes, and the cornelian of Yaman drenched its heart in blood at her sugar-bearing pearly lips. The beauties of the land of Khatá were captive in the snares of the folds of her ringlets; and the blandishers of Kashmír, through affection for her chains of twisting and curling locks, had the feet of the soul in bonds.

> O idol! what beauty is there which your cheeks do not possess?
> In the art of ravishing hearts, what is there with which you are unacquainted?

The beauty of her condition gained grace from the mole[1] of purity, and the bride-chamber of her charms was decked with the ornament of chastity and modesty. The King's heart was so infatuated with her good qualities, that he withdrew his presence from the society of his own particular wife, and from companionship with other loves. The King's consort, through jealousy of her

---

[1] See note, p. 23.

lord, was always shedding tears of regret, and with the view of removing the other girl, in envy and malice, used to invent every kind of device. In short, she repeated her story to the Tire-woman of the palace Haram, and sought help from her as to killing the King and putting away the damsel. The Tire-woman said: "Inform me what in the maid does the King like, and on which part does he most fix his glance." The Lady replied: "I noticed that in private he plants many kisses upon her apple-like chin, which, through excessive purity, you would say was a grape remaining suspended near the fountain of Immortality, or a delicate quince, which the hand of Omnipotence had placed on the fold of her dewlap, and in explanation of his case says :—

> ' O Devotee ! invite me not to Paradise,
> For the apple of her chin is better than ought from that Garden.' "

The Tire-woman said : " I have found an easy way by which the King can be quickly removed. The proper course is for you to give me a little deadly poison, so that I may mix it with indigo, and going to the damsel's chamber, place a mole thereof near her chin and dewlap : when the King, in a state of intoxication, places his lips there, he will at once expire, and you will find rest from this anxiety." The lady was delighted at this device, and got ready what the Tire-woman wanted ; while the latter, in the manner which has been described, prepared a compound of treacherous mixtures, and placing it in a casket of imposture, repaired to the damsel's chamber, and with black action placed a mole upon the chin of that Moon, and made the evil-faced angel Hárút[1] take up his abode upon the wall of Bábal.

> That mole is placed upon the chin, as a bait,
> O Lord ! keep him from the misfortunes of the world.

The King had a Slave, who had the right of admission[2] into the palace Haram. By chance from behind a screen he heard the conversation of the Lady and the Tire-woman, and witnessed how the latter went to the damsel's abode, and placed the mole upon her chin. His pretensions to fidelity and loyalty impelled him to inform the damsel of that treachery, but he could in no way find an opportunity, and the King, too, was in a state of intoxication, and it was not possible by any means to reveal that secret to him. At length the King, according to his usual wont and habit, came to the girl's chamber, and through excess of inebriety fell asleep. Kind gratitude having seized the Slave by the skirt, he went gently to the damsel's pillow, and with the corner of his sleeve cleaned away the traces of indigo from her chin. In the midst the King awoke, and saw the Slave with his hand extended towards the damsel's chin. The heat of extreme rage placed him upon the top of the fire of wrath ;· with a sword, like water,[3] he endeavoured to slay the Slave, who ran forth from the private room, while the King, following behind him with drawn sword, rushed to the door. The private confidential servant stood, and taking the letters in his hand, when he saw the King distracted, advanced, and showed him one epistle. The billows of the sea of his wrath did not subside. Again he made a representation to him,

---

[1] Name of an angel who, having censured mankind before the throne of God, was sent down to earth in human shape to judge the temptations to which man is subject. He could not resist the seductions of the world, and committed every kind of wickedness : as a punishment he was suspended by the feet in a well in Babylon, where he is to remain in great torment till the day of judgment.

[2] Literally, " the mark of intimacy."

[3] As we say in English, " of pure water."

but the fire of his malignity was not quenched; but on showing the third composition, the King allowed himself to become somewhat pacified and tranquil, and quaffing the unpleasant potion of rage, he soothingly sent for the Slave, and said, "Why have you acted so rashly?" The Slave accurately recounted what had occurred. The King addressing his wife, used his best endeavours to investigate that treachery, and to inquire into that perfidy. The wife denied the matter, saying: "The Slave speaks falsely, and I have often observed that this discreditable rascal has carried on his proceedings like this with this damsel, but I was ashamed on the King's account to proclaim this boldness; and it might have been imputed to me, that this charge had originated by reason of jealousy. Thank God! the King has seen it with his own eyes; now if the King allows the death of this villain to be deferred, it will lower the King's authority, and when anger properly arises, it will be more dignified than compassion.

> The thorn, which is fit to be burnt,
> If you place it round your neck, it is not becoming.

The King looked towards the Slave, who said: "O august King! the source of the security of the age! it is possible that the remainder of this indigo may still be in the Tire-woman's casket. If the august mandate should be issued to summon her, may be that this uncertainty will be entirely removed." The King commanded the Tire-woman, together with the casket, to be brought before him, and made her eat some of the indigo. As soon as she tasted it, she expired. When the truth was revealed to the King, having bound his wife, he gave his Slave a letter of liberation, and intrusted to him the government of some of the countries of that kingdom. Since that King, the Protector of the World, decked the face of his affairs with the ornament of compassion, misfortune did not befall him at the hands of the Tire-woman; and by the blessing of self-restraint, he remained secure from the ills of that black deed. The secret, too, of so great danger was disclosed to him, and he discovered the true state as to his friends and enemies.

"I have adduced this story that in the mirror of the King's enlightened mind this beautiful picture may appear—viz., that in no case should kings display haste, nor, without reflection and deliberation, should they put their decrees into execution.

> The decrees of a king, like fire and water,
> In a moment will ruin the world.
> Therefore, as regards such a mandate, it is not allowable,
> That the King should issue it through vexation.

The King said: "As regards this decree I have done wrong, and my words fell from my lips in a state of rage. At any rate, it is fit that, as becomes the condition of counsellors, you should have used reflection, and it appears strange on your part that you should have been so remiss as to cause the death of this incomparable one." The Minister replied: "The King must not allow so much anxiety to enter his august mind in regard to one solitary woman, so that he may not be deprived of enjoying the society of other servants who are in the Haram."

> Though the cypress has vanished, the cherry-tree remains;
> Though the tulip is not left, there is still the jessamine.

The King understood from the purport of the Minister's speech that Írán-dukht had been slain. A sigh came forth from his frame, and falling into the whirl-pool of sorrow, he said to himself:—

> Gladly consume with grief for her, O my bosom! for see my heart, too,
> Is girded up, and ready to do the same.

"Alas for that splendour of the pleasure-garden of youth, which, like the time of the rose, has but a short existence! and ah for that plant in the parterre of prosperity, which has become leafless and desolate through the misfortune of the autumn of separation!"

> Thy cypress form is in the dust, alas! alas!
> Thy pure spirit is under the soil, alas! alas!
> There was a spot—a place, indeed—for you, my eyes;
> But you took up your abode in the dust, alas! alas!

He then turned towards the Minister, saying: "I am grieved at the death of Írán-dukht." The Minister replied: "Three persons are always captives to grief, and ensnared in the meshes of sorrow: 1st, He who expends his ambition on acting wrongly; 2d, He who at a time when he has the power does not do good; 3d, He who acts without thinking, and in the end repents thereof." The King said: "O Balár! you did not put off executing Írán-dukht, and by your foolish efforts she met her death." The Minister rejoined: "The labours of three individuals are futile: the person who puts on white garments and carries on glass-blowing; a bleacher who stands in the water with his dress tidily arranged and washes clothes; and a merchant who gets possession of a beautiful woman, and leaving her in her native country, elects to go on a far journey. I did not strive to kill her—nay, more, I carried out the King's in-junctions. In this matter the reproach appertains to his Majesty, seeing that though his deliberation regarding the issue of matters is not deficient, and the glance of his experience extends to the termination of affairs, in this mandate he deprived his sound judgment of reflection, and denied consideration to his right understanding."

> The mandate of a King must be dictated by wisdom;
> If it be prompted by judgment, such things will not appear.

The King rejoined: "Cease such words, and reflect over this matter, for the desire to see her makes me very sad, and I know no help for this affair, as to how it can be accomplished." The Minister said: "The hand of remedy will not reach the skirt of this business, and in this case regret will not avail. Whoever, without thought, plunges into an affair, and conducts a matter wherein remorse avails nought, will meet with that which befell that Pigeon." The King inquired, "What was that?"

STORY IV.

He said: It has been related that a couple of Pigeons in early summer had collected together some grain, which they placed in a corner as a store for the winter. This grain was damp, and when summer was ended, the heat of the atmosphere having taken effect upon it, dried it up, and it appeared less than it was before. During this time the male Pigeon was away from home. When he returned and saw that the grain was less, he began to reproach his mate, saying: "We had placed this grain as food for winter, so that when the severity of the cold arrives, and from the abundance of snow not a seed remains in the waste, we might live thereon; but in these days, when in mountain and plain grain is procurable, why have you eaten the store, and deviated from the direction of prudence? Anyhow, have you not heard that wise men have said—

'Labour now when there are leaves and seeds,
Lay up a store against your poverty'?

The female Pigeon replied: "I have not eaten of that grain, nor in any way consumed any thereof." When the male Pigeon saw that the seed was lessened, he did not believe her denial, and pecked her till she was dead. Then in the winter season, when the rain followed consecutively, and traces of moisture were visible on door and wall, the grain, becoming damp, returned to its original condition. The male bird discovered what was the cause of the deficiency, and began to lament, and commenced to sorrow at separation from his dear friend. Weeping with grief, he said: "To be severed from one's friend is hard; but harder still, regret will avail nought."

Reflect over what you do, since owing to rashness
You will suffer injury, and there is no remedy to a person for such misfortune.

"The moral of this story is, that it behoveth a wise man not to be hasty to punish, lest, like the Pigeon, he be overwhelmed with the agony of separation." The King said: "If I have spoken hastily, you, too, have acted precipitately, and have cast me into this distress." The Minister rejoined: "Three persons bring trouble upon themselves: 1st, He who in the ranks of war is careless of himself, so that he meets with a severe wound; 2d, He who has no heir, and amasses property by unlawful means, so that it is swept away by the plunder of misfortunes, and calamity overwhelms it; and 3d, An old man who takes in marriage a bad young woman, and places his affections upon her, while she every day prays God that he may die, and does not consort with him." The King said, "By this proceeding a proof of your precipitancy can be gathered." He replied: "Precipitancy is evident in the actions and postures of two persons: 1st, He who confides his property to a stranger; 2d, He who makes a fool judge between himself and an enemy. But I have not acted hastily in this matter; the very most is that I have sought to obey the King's command." The King replied, "I am very grieved about Írán-dukht." The Minister retorted: "It is allowable to be sad on account of five kinds of women: 1st, She who has a gentle nature, a noble soul, charming beauty, and perfect purity; 2d, She who is wise, patient, sincere, and affectionate; 3d, She who, in all matters, strives to do what is right, and is kind in your presence as well as your absence; 4th, She who through good and bad, and well and ill, clothes and arrays herself in courtesy and submission; 5th, She who is of good omen and august spirit, and the felicity of whose step is evidenced to her husband. Now Írán-dukht was graced with all those qualities, and if the King manifests distress concerning her, it verifies this, since without a faithful friend there is neither pleasure in life nor comfort in existence."

Life has no great pleasure without a friend;
Existence does not possess much delight in the absence of a companion.

The King said: "O Balár! you speak boldly, and exceed the limit of good manners. I am of opinion that I had better leave you." The Minister exclaimed: "To remove from two persons is commendable: 1st, From him who deems good and ill as alike, and imagines that there are neither future rewards nor punishments; 2d, From him who outwardly does not keep himself pure from what is prohibited, and inwardly from amusements interdicted by law." The King rejoined, "Do we appear contemptible in your eyes, seeing that you deem it right to talk so boldly as this?" The Minister said: "The great appear despicable to the eyes of three classes: 1st, The impudent servant, who, whether opportunely or inopportunely, whether sitting down or rising up, whether at supper or breakfast, joins on an equality with his master, who in turn jests with him, and admires his ribaldry; 2d, The mean servant, who, getting the control of his master's property, opens the hand of possession thereon, so that in a little time his wealth exceeds that of his master, and he deems himself superior to his benefactor; 3d, A servant who, without merit, becomes trusted, and being apprised of his master's secrets, is elated with such dignity." The King exclaimed, "I have tried you, and it were better I had not tried you." The Minister replied: "Eight persons cannot be tested save on eight occasions: a warrior in war, a farmer in agriculture, wise men in the time of anger, merchants at a period of casting accounts, a friend in the occasion of need, a true man in the days of adversity, a devotee when obtaining his eternal reward, and the learned in the time of conversation and debate." In short, however much the King spoke to the Minister in terms expressive of his disgust, the latter gave replies keener than the point of a spear bathed in poison, and breathed forth words in sharpness like a diamond sword, while the King bore[1] it all patiently, and drank down that unpleasant-flavoured potion.

> He who is wise bears patiently,
> Since with wisdom he brings his anger under his control.
> Patience at first seems to you like poison,
> Yet it becomes honey when settled in your nature.

At length he loosed the tongue of praise, saying: "May the shade of prosperity, the shadow of God, illumine the brows of mankind, and the sun of his magnificence shine forth from the summit of his glory and the pinnacle of his greatness! I, your slave, who have traversed with bold steps the expanse of rashness, and have been eager to trouble your exalted Majesty with my excessive importunities, did so, with the view of trying your noble disposition, but— thanks to the Most High God!—if any one seeks the like of the King, and searches for one his equal,

> His compeer could not be found save in the mirror,[2] or the water.

"What a noble disposition is his, graced with the beauty of compassion and virtue! And what a precious spirit is his, adorned with the ornament of patience, sedateness, and good-nature! Assuredly greatness has been intrusted to such a person, and the name of magnificence appertains solely to the like of so famous a being."

> Greatness consists not in reputation or hearsay,
> Nor mightiness in pretension or conceit.
> Seek not for any one more worthy of renown,
> Than him whom men call good-natured.

---

[1] عمل in the Persian text is a misprint for حمل .
[2] That is, the reflection of the King himself.

The King said : "O Balár! you well know that I have reared the edifice of my administration upon compassion and kindness, and have laid the foundation of my sovereignty upon gentleness and non-oppression; and if sometimes, in correcting a set of persons who, through pride, make a display of obstinacy, or manifestly and clearly enter into battle and contest, warnings have been given, it was with the view of protecting the courtesy due to sovereignty, and defending the rules of royalty; were it otherwise, the ocean of my exalted magnanimity is not of such a nature, that the billows of rage should arise by the medium of the like of these words.

> I am not a willow, that my leaves should shake to and fro with every wind;
> Nor am I a straw, whose body is consumed with the flame of fire :
> I am not a mountain, which reverberates at every sound of men;
> Nor am I a cloud, which weeps a hundred times owing to the influence of the
>   atmosphere.

"As regards the command for killing Írán-dukht, I was powerless, for it has been said, ' *The giver, too, is empty-handed* '—that is to say,

> The pleasant-paced horse, too, sometimes stumbles."

The Minister said : "That kind of command is rare; ' *The rare is like the non-existent ;* ' but compassion has this very day been a set-off to it, since at no date has it been indicated, that a fortunate king and powerful monarch, with a cutting sword and potent decree, has sat upon the throne of majesty, while an offending servant has stood at his feet in a state of humility, and spoken disrespectful words, and placing his feet beyond his proper limit, uttered whatever he would. What could restrain the carrying out of the way of punishment, save great compassion, and perfect pardon ? "

> The more I offend, the more is your magnanimity.

The King said : "When a servant confesses his fault, and sees the traces of offence on the pages of his condition, assuredly he will be on the road to obtain pardon; for a beneficent man cannot refuse to accept an excuse."

> ' *An excuse amongst men of liberality is accepted.* '

The Minister replied : "O King! I acknowledge my sin, and my crime is this, that I have allowed the execution of the King's command to be delayed, and have deferred killing Írán-dukht; from fear of your terror-exciting words, and dread of your reproachful remarks, I have not hastened to destroy her. Now the decree and command rest with the King."

> Whether you show mercy, or whether you strike with the sword,
> Like a captive I have placed my neck in your grasp.

As soon as the King heard these words, the tokens of joy and gladness, and the signs of delight and pleasure, were evident on his august brow, and he hoisted to the highest summits the banner of reciting the praises of God; performing the adoration of gratitude to the Almighty, and raising a cry of joy beyond the pinnacle of the ethereal Spheres, he said :—

> "Good news, O Fortune! for my desire has entered in at the door;
> Another soul has come to the bodies of these broken-hearted persons.

She who, like a rosebud, with her fragrance caused the lips of the soul to
    smile,
And whose auspicious cheeks were more brilliant than the rose, has returned."

He then added: "I was very astonished that you spoke in a way that it might
be understood that Írán-dukht was dead, for I was aware of the soundness of
your sincerity and uprightness, and knew that you would defer carrying out
such a thing." The Minister replied: "My conversation was with the object of
ascertaining truly the King's intention, and seeing whether or no he repented of
that decree. If I had found you in the same idea of killing her, I should have
secretly hastened so to do; but since your mind is more disposed that she
should live, I have declared my fault, and offered apologies for the delay." The
King said: "Your caution and sagacity in this matter have become more than
ever clear to me, and my trust in your intelligence and ability is increased;
the service, too, which you have performed is accepted, and the rewards thereof
will reach you as quickly as possible. This very hour, with the utmost alac-
rity, you must go to Írán-dukht, and conveying to her endless apologies, as
gently as possible request her to repair here, as such would be the key of the
doors of the attainment of security, and the capital of the acquisition of joy and
delight."

Come! for I will ask from God that you may approach;
Come! for my ears are listening for your sound, and my eyes intent on your
    arrival.

Balár went forth from the King, and conveyed to Írán-dukht intelligence of her
deliverance, and the good news of her reunion.

O heart! do not, like a rosebud, complain that the matter is impossible,
Since the morning wind will bring a breeze such as will open the knot.

Írán-dukht, having obeyed the command to be present, hastened to do homage,
and performing the dues of servitude, loosened the tongue of gratitude and
thankfulness. The King said, "You must impute this favour to Balár, in that
he discharged the obligations of sincerity, and deferred carrying out this intention." Balár said: "I had the most entire confidence in the perfection of the
royal compassion and condescension, and the abundance of your endless benevolence and kindness. My pensiveness arose from this, otherwise how could
it have been allowable for your servant to defer the King's command?" The
King said: "O Balár! rest assured, for your hand stretches over my kingdom,
and your decree is potent equally as are my injunctions; as regards what you
say or do concerning loosening and fastening, or commanding and prohibiting, no
opposition shall occur." Balár rejoined: "Former favours and auspicious kindnesses on the part of the King surpass any service of your slave, and if I were
to live for a thousand years, I could not express my gratitude for one in a thousand thereof.

Though the lily were to speak with a hundred tongues,
How could it express its thanks to Spring?

"But it is needful for your servants, that henceforth you should not display haste
in your affairs, so that the purity of the end thereof may be void of the foulness
of repentance." The King said, "We have listened to this advice with the ear
of acceptance, and in future we will issue no decree without counsel and per-

mission." He then bestowed dresses of honour upon the Minister and Irán-dukht, and walking forth from the cell of separation to the bridal chamber of intercourse, graced the assembly of joy.

> They decked an honoured feast,
> They adorned the rose-garden of delight.

The graceful cup-bearer poured forth from the silvery cup pure wine into the mouths of the companions, and the pleasant-tasted liquid moistened the plant of joy in the stream of their breasts.

> O excellent! the joy-producing wine,
> Has made brisk the market of merriment and joy.

Pleasant - voiced minstrels, performing on every kind of instrument, both stringed and percussion, brought forth the bird of the heart into ecstacies, and the melodies of songs invited to the feast of delight and joy. The pleasant strains of the harp emulated the tones of the thousand-voiced (nightingale), while the heart-enchanting plaint of the lute removed the rust [1] from the mirror of the heart of the frantic ones.

> Singers with voices like Venus,
> Goblets glittering like the planet Jupiter.
> The tones of joy are accurate according to harmony,
> In a way just as ravishing feelings would wish.

They passed the remainder of the day, and all the night, in merriment and joy.

> When, next day, world-illumining morn
> Victoriously ended night in day,

the King having held a levee, took his seat upon the throne of justice, and Balár the Minister, having performed the dues of homage on his own account, as well as being the substitute of the wife and children, demanded justice on the Brahmans, and recounted the interpretation they had made of the dreams in the way above-mentioned; on which account the King's decree obtained the honour of being issued, to the effect that Káridún the sage should be summoned: he then intrusted the public punishment of the Brahmans to the seer's discretion. Káridún deemed it expedient that they should hang [2] some of them, and that, casting a mass of them under the feet of elephants, they should render them as it were part of the dust of the highroad. He said, "Such is the punishment of traitors, and the retribution of the perfidious."

> He who draws his dagger to oppress,
> The Heavens will also strike off his head with that same sword.
> No one can harden his face like an anvil,
> But what the hammer of correction will crush his head.

After repelling his enemies, the King gave over to the Minister the command of the kingdom, and spending his time with Irán-dukht, he abandoned himself to a full measure of happiness.

> Prize the night of delight, and seize the measure of happiness;
> For in this world, no one knows what will occur to-morrow.

---

[1] See note 2, page 51.   [2] Eastwick renders this "impale."

Such is the story of the excellence of compassion and firmness, and of the superiority thereof over other qualities and attributes in kings and sovereigns. It is not concealed from the wise that the advantage of recounting this story is to afford warning to readers, and put hearers on their guard, so that making the experiences of their predecessors, and the suggestions of the wise, an example for their own case, they may place the affairs of religion and the world, and the edifice of their proceedings, both as regards to-day and to-morrow, upon the foundation of wisdom, and the basis of intelligence, and turn from rashness and precipitancy towards sedateness and self-restraint. Whoever is distinguished by the Divine favour, assuredly the brow of his ambition will be decked with the crown of humility, and the shoulders of his glory graced with the cloak of compassion; since gentleness and pity make enemies friends, and place friends in the dignity of relations.

If you are the associate of compassion and humility,
Your rivals will become faithful, like your dearest allies.[1]
Do not make enemies with any being in the world,
So that your fortune may turn out according to the desires of your friends.

[1] Literally, "friends of the cave"—see note 1, page 25.

BOOK XIII.

———◆———

HOW THAT KINGS SHOULD AVOID THE SPEECH OF THE TREACHEROUS AND MALIGNANT.

INTRODUCTION.

THE ancient and experienced Philosopher
Spoke these words, which drew aside the veil.

When King Dábishlím heard these tales from the Sage Bídpáí, he offered praise, by the import of which the sweet odours of affection reached the nostrils of the holy, and the purport of which brought tidings of the royal mandates of the dawn of happiness; he said—

O thou! by whose intellect problems have become clear to wisdom;
O thou! by whose understanding all difficulties have been solved for imagination—

"I have heard a description of the advantages of compassion and self-restraint, and the evils of rashness and precipitancy, and have recognised the superiority of firmness and pity over other kingly virtues and regal qualities, now repeat a tale of kings as to their possessing trustworthy and reliable servants, and explain what class best consider the worth of patronage, and are most grateful for favours." The Brahman, in return for the King's praise, prepared an offering of salutation, saying: "May every gift of prosperity which puts forth its face from the workshop, '*Assistance from God and victory is nigh*,' and every present of happiness which shines resplendent-in the marriage-chamber of '*There is no help save on the part of God*,' to the fullest extent and utmost degree, solely appertain to his Majesty, the Lion of Sovereignty.

May the nurse of the meadow, with the hand of the zephyr, remove
The dust from the brows of the tulip and the cheeks of the arghawán![1]
May the rose-garden of your prosperity, over which blow the breezes of
  Paradise,
Be preserved from the effects of the ravages of autumn!

"The most powerful aid as regards what the King has said, is to recognise the place for favour; and it behoves a king to try the coin of his servants with a variety of tests upon the touchstone of proof, and ascertaining the purity of the judgment, knowledge, sincerity, and uprightness of each of them, to place reliance in their caution, honesty, trustworthiness, and integrity. For the capital (required in) the service of kings is rectitude, which cannot exist without fear of God and piety; and the root of all knowledge is fear and dread. *'Assuredly amongst His servants God makes those who are wise to fear Him.'* Whenever any servant of the king fears God, both the sovereign will more readily have recourse to his assistance, and also a pillar of hope to the subjects will arise by his means.

Appoint over thy subjects a man who fears God,
For the upright man is the architect of the kingdom.
It behoves a minister to fear the Lord,
But not to dread the King, or quail at death.

"Assuredly it is not proper that the false-speaker and untruthful man should be admitted to the region of confidence, or find an opportunity of intermeddling with the king's secrets, since ruin will proceed therefrom, and traces of evil appear for a lengthened time." The King said: "This matter needs explanation, for ignoble and worthless men may be adorned with good qualities, while ultimately their condition having relapsed, will cause shame to their patron."

An essentially bad person, though at first he may act faithfully,
In the end he will turn therefrom, and be disposed to wickedness.

The Brahman said: "The explanation of these words is this. The servants of a king should possess three qualities: 1st, Trustworthiness in their conduct, since an upright man is approved of both the Creator and the creature, and fit and worthy to be admitted into the secrets of kings, and to be intrusted with the affairs of the State; 2d, Truthfulness in speech, since the crime of falsehood is a great offence, and it is absolutely incumbent on kings to avoid persons who do not speak the truth—and if any one were to combine every virtue, and be renowned for loyalty and fidelity, if he be a liar he is not worthy of confidence; 3d, Pure disposition and exalted ambition, for the base and ignoble do not properly recognise the worth of bounty and favour, and their inclinations are manifested in whatever direction the wind comes.

In whatever direction the wind blows he in like manner turns.

"As regards the unfaithful it has been said—

'In the way of friendship stand firm like the earth;
How many are like the wind which, every moment, blows in another street?'

"It behoves a king to regard the virtuous dispositions of his servants, not their dress or pretensions; since wisdom and ability are the ornaments of the attend-

---

[1] Name of a tree whose fruit and flower are a beautiful red.

ants on monarchs, and knowledge and intelligence their boast. When any one happens to be graced with the decoration of virtue, and to be free from base habits, combining together hereditary purity and acquired probity, and coming forth clear and unblemished from the crucible of trial, in the manner which has been described, it is incumbent upon the king to carry out right arrangements in patronising him, and gently and by degrees to advance him to the rank of favour and the dignity of authority, so that his reputation may be fixed in persons' eyes, and dread of him in their hearts. Sages have said, that kings in dispensing favour to their servants, must be like a skilful physician, who, till at first he has thoroughly inquired and investigated respecting the condition of the invalid, the time of his ailment, the particulars and nature of his disease, and the causes and diagnosis thereof, and till he has gained complete information, and is perfectly apprised respecting general matters as well as minute details, no less than regarding the condition of the pulse and state of the stomach, will not commence a cure, nor set about administering remedies. Just so it behoves a king to learn the state of his servants, fully and minutely, and recognise the measure of the action, the extent of the speech, and the mode of conduct of each of them: then he should commence to favour and assist them, and should not, easy-going, place confidence in any one, lest so doing become the cause of repentance and remorse. The pith of the matter is, that attendants on kings must be trustworthy and reliable, so that both the secrets of property and state may remain guarded from the knowledge of rivals, and also the army and subjects be protected from evil and harm: since if, God forbid! one of the courtiers should be endowed with a treacherous nature, and his words attain the dignity of acceptance at the king's hands, maybe he will cast the innocent into the region of destruction, and this will cause the sovereign to be dishonoured, and in the end will bring ruin on him. As illustrative of these words is the story of the Goldsmith and the Traveller." The King inquired, "What was that?"

---o---

STORY I.

He said: It has been related that in the capital Aleppo was a famous King and prosperous Monarch, in obedience to whom most of the sovereigns of the world had placed the ring in the ear of their soul, and the greater portion of the mighty emperors thrown the cloak of submission to him on the shoulders of their heart.

> A Sovereign, by the splendour of whose justice the ways of the world were regulated;
> An Emperor, by the light of whose judgment the arrangements of the age were settled;
> Wherever his world-subduing intention pressed the stirrup,
> In that direction victory and triumph loosed the rein.

This King had a daughter, in form like the sun, and moon-faced, the light of whose cheeks lent radiance to the face of the sun, and the perfume of whose musk-laden ringlets scented the nostrils of Time.

Her pearly lips were the device in the seal of Solomon;[1]
Her mouth was smaller than a finger-ring.
From the tints on her cheeks the face of the air was reddened ;
Her flowing curls caused [2] the utmost perturbation.
Her cheeks were the high altar of the Fire-worshippers ;
Her mouth was the object of desire with the distressed.

The King kept this rare gem concealed from the sight of rivals, and, like a royal pearl, preserved her within the shell of secrecy and purity.   One day they were making ready an ornament for this girl, and there occurred a need for the skill of a goldsmith, who should be perfect in his craft.   Now in that city there was a Goldsmith such that the heated furnace of the sun was fit for smelting his gold, and the radiant crucible of the moon appeared a suitable workshop for his silver-refining.   He was a judge of gems to a degree, that on merely seeing the shell, he knew the value of the pearl which was contained therein, and in making assays, to a point that without trying on the touchstone, he discovered base metal from pure gold.

> Day and night he laboured at his trade,
> By his skill in his business all things turned to gold ;
> Whatever could be made of silver and gold,
> He shaped like none other could accomplish.

The King had heard of his fame, and seen some of his beautiful productions, and best works: at this juncture he summoned him to the Haram, and discussed with him the preparation of the ornament.   The Goldsmith was a young man of elegant face and sweet discourse : the King in the midst of the conversation became disposed for his talk, and his Majesty's auspicious mind inclined perpetually to meet him; while day by day, by strange tricks, and marvellous words, he distracted the King, and from hour to hour the Sovereign lavished more and more patronage and favour upon him, till he became the confidant of the Royal Haram, and the King's daughter, upon whom the Sun and Moon had not cast a shade, admitted him behind the screen.[3]

> He who is the confidant of the heart, will remain in his friend's Haram.

This King had a Minister famous for the strength of his intellect, and celebrated and well-known for the accuracy of his judgment.   The inscription from his world-subduing pen was the victorious scroll of triumph, and the results of his clime-adorning deliberation the fringe of the garments of majesty.   Men of piety and prosperity used to place confidence in his clear judgment, and the Lords of the Kingdom and faith added to the store of life, by reason of his pen endowed with the qualities of Khizr.[4]

> Thy pen, good God ! opened its nibs for country and religion ;
> A hundred springs of the water of life flowed from a single drop of ink.[5]

When the Minister saw that the King, in patronising the Goldsmith, passed the limits of moderation, and pushed to an excess his efforts to honour and exalt

---

[1] The Muhammadans attribute wonderful qualities to the seal of Solomon.
[2] Literally, " placed a hundred horse-shoes in the fire."   The same expression occurs at page 129, verse i.
[3] In allusion to the oriental custom of keeping women in seclusion.
[4] See note 4, page 158.   [5] Literally, " drop of blackness."

him—from the purest sincerity and loyalty, at a fitting time, and suitable occasion, on a pretence which was not beyond the pale of propriety, he turned the reins of the courser of speech in the direction of the matter of the Goldsmith, and said: "O King! former rulers did not place men of business on the chief seat of persons of authority, but aggrandised them amongst their own equals and companions: yet the King has now made this person the confidential attendant on the Haram, not having previously ascertained, as was befitting and proper, as to his merits. It occurs to my mind, that this individual does not possess a beneficent nature, or pure disposition, since his talk is confined to oppressing and torturing mankind, and his ambition expended upon executing commands and prohibitions, such as are unsuitable and out of place. From such a person, the habit of fidelity and the custom of gratitude are not to be expected.

> He who expects fidelity from a base-natured person,
> Is, as it were, seeking fruit from the willow-tree.

"I have observed that whenever the King is disposed to be bountiful and kind towards any one, that mean wretch, from excess of vexation is content not to exist; and sages have said that the indications of the low, are not to possess the power of seeing one man kind towards another.

> A mean wretch does not wish another to be gratified,
> A low person will not leave a fly in the bowl.
> When you invite to your tables one who is untrue to his salt,
> He will eat more than bread, to whet the anguish of bread.[1]

"More befitting the society of the King are the set of persons who combine natural nobility with honourable virtues; and it is incumbent to shun the company of evil-natured ignorant individuals, since from intimacy with this class of men various troubles arise, and they who are inherently low and inwardly base will not observe rectitude, nor pay any respect to integrity. When these qualities are removed from the midst, every vice which enters the region of possibility is to be expected from such despicable beings."

> He who has no share of uprightness,
> If he does wickedly, it is not strange on his part.
> Perfidy is the worst of all bad deeds,
> Every evil is embraced therein.

The King rejoined: "This young man has a beautiful form, and elegance of shape is a proof of spiritual grace, since '*The external is the frontispiece of the internal*,' and the wise have said, that the chasteness of the frontispiece is indicative of the beauty of the contents of a book.

> Whoever is wise, knows from the beauty of the frontispiece,
> That pretty things will be found in that volume.

"Again, when the Lord of Prophetic dignity—upon him be the best and most perfect blessings!—said, 'Read the letter of necessity to one, the pages of whose cheeks are graced with the verses of beauty and elegance; and look for good from one of an open countenance, the face of whose condition is adorned with

---

[1] Presumably this means that when a mean wretch eats bread at your table, at every turn he is filled with anguish on seeing you and other guests eating bread likewise. See note, page 385.

the mole of comeliness, '*Seek good from the fair-faced,*' it was an indication that a charming form betokens spiritual grace."

> Whenever externally the nature of a man
> Seems to you good, suspect him not of evil.

The Minister said : "In the school[1] of wisdom men do not read the chapter of beautiful appearance, nor do they consider the verse of elegance, in fact, as ought save acceptable qualities ; since there are many persons who, with comely form, carry off the hearts of mankind, and when the coin of such a person's spirituality is struck on the touchstone of trial it is worthless. It has passed into a saying of the wise, that a Sage saw a young handsome man, and conceived in his heart a desire for his society. Advancing, he tested the coin of the young man's true condition, but it possessed no sterling weight, such as could be mentioned. The Sage passed on and said, ' It is a beautiful house, were there any one therein.'"

> Conduct yourself spiritually, since to appearance two reeds may grow together,
> Yet one of them produces sugar, and the other is only fit for mats.

The King said : "From elegance of appearance one may deduce equality of temperament, and a man of even disposition is worthy of encouragement. Since during all this time he has not had a patron, maybe some of his qualities may have deviated from the highway of moderation, but now we will fix the glance of favour upon him, so that having acquired praiseworthy feelings, he may attain to a degree of perfection. For the result of attention makes a hard stone become a joy-giving ruby, and a gleaming heart-ravishing pearl ; so, by the blessing of art, dark blood becomes beautiful-scented, fragrant musk, and a drop of rain a royal unique jewel."

> It is by culture that water becomes a gem,
> And blood in the midst of the bladder becomes the purest musk.
> So also, that black-faced valueless iron,
> When fostered by alchemy turns to gold.

The Minister replied : "O King ! it is not fitting to encourage that person who has not natural worth, since every stone does not become a pearl, nor all blood most perfect musk, and if a worthless individual were to be patronised for a thousand years, no good could be expected from him.

> If a willow be nurtured like an aloe,
> The fragrance of the aloe would not proceed from the willow.

"And if a base person is changed and altered a hundred times, his personal nature would not become different. A holy man in this respect has well said :—

> ' Whoever happens to be ignoble by nature,
> Will not become noble through the changes of the Heavens.
> If the word sag-magas (dog-fly) be inverted,
> The transmutation is nought but sag-magas.'[2]

"Seeing that this point is established, it behoveth one not to associate with such

---

[1] دردِ is printed as one word, whereas the last letter belongs to the commencement of the following word.

[2] Here again it must be recollected that in Persian the short vowels are not written.

a mean wretch, so that one may not be captured in the whirlpool of disgrace: just as that Prince, owing to keeping company with a Shoemaker, fell into the opprobrium of servitude, and from being intimate with a Jeweller, reached the extreme limits of the desert of destruction." The King inquired, "How was that?"

STORY II.

He said: It has been related that in the regions of Fárs there was a King, of good disposition and pure nature, who based his monarchy upon gaining favour by fostering his subjects, and who, on the couch of royalty, meted the measure of dispensing clemency.

> His dignity opened the hand of justice to the world;
> His awe enchained the foot of oppression.

A son was born to him, upon whose brows were evident the traces of discretion and generosity, and the signs of worldly power visible in his beautiful countenance.

> When the planet Jupiter saw the day of his birth,
> He justly admitted, 'This is the most fortunate of all the stars.'

Upon the shoulders of this boy was a black mole the size of the palm of the hand. The King was distracted at beholding it, and inquired from the sages of the age the peculiarity of that token. They said: "We have seen in the books of the ancients, that whoever has this mark will meet with dangers, but in the end will become a conqueror of kingdoms, and a subduer of worlds." The King was delighted at this good news, and darted upon his condition the glance of general culture. In the King's neighbourhood was a Shoemaker, shameless and naturally impure. The King, having performed the dues of neighbourly consideration, bestowed upon him a fixed allowance, and a stated salary: so he used perpetually to pass his time comfortably and at ease, under the shade of the King's kindness. When the Prince attained the age of four[1] years, and his disposition was inclined to be full of fun, he used constantly to come to the cell of the Shoemaker, and engage himself in play. The Minister being apprised of the circumstances of the case, endeavoured to stop and put an end to it, and said: "The plant of young persons' nature is very tender, and it will assuredly turn in any direction to which it is given an inclination, and remain in that fashion.

> The bough which, when tender, is crooked,
> If you bend it will become straight;
> But if two or three years elapse,
> In no way will its wryness become rectified.

"It is expedient that the King should restrain the Prince from the company of the Shoemaker, so that all at once the blameable qualities of the latter may not infect the disposition of the royal youth, nor cast the incomparable ambition of that Star of the Sphere of Sovereignity into the abyss of disgrace, whereby again a variety of dangers are to be imagined."

> Since from a man of base spirit all you say will occur.

---

[1] The sequel clearly shows, as suggested by Eastwick, that the age of the boy was four, not fourteen. See p. 472.

The King said : " He is young, and has taken a fancy [1] to the Shoemaker. He is, too, very dear to me ; maybe if I prohibit him from the other's society he will be grieved, and his anguish of heart will become the means of torture of soul on my part. I will be somewhat patient till he gets bigger, and distinguishes good from bad ; then, by advice, we will rectify his disposition." The Minister was silent, while the King, having summoned the Shoemaker, lavished a variety of kindnesses upon him, and filling him with hope through regal promises, said : " You are my neighbour, and this precious darling of mine has conceived an affection for you, and is very anxious that you should be his companion and protector, and guard him from water and fire." The Shoemaker kissed the ground in submission, saying :—

> May the rose in the King's garden illumine the world !
> May the lamp of his night be the lantern of day !

" I, your servant, do not behold that I am fit for this exalted station, nor see that I am deserving of such a dignity, which may be termed the greatest thing one can desire, but the royal glance is an alchemy, which will turn dark earth into pure gold, and cause a worthless stone to become a perfect gem.

> He would give life to the very ground over which you pass ;
> The stones on which you look would become gold.

" I am hopeful, that by the regal auspiciousness, the dues of service will be observed in such a manner that they may attain the honour of approbation." In short, he agreed to accept service with the Prince, and fearlessly carrying him off, used to bring him to his own quarters, and take him back to the King's Court. Sometimes, too, the Prince used to pass the night in his cell, and the King showed delight at his intimacy with the Shoemaker, who discharged his duties to the Prince in such a manner, that from day to day his familiarity with the King's Majesty waxed greater, till he became altogether a confidential attendant, and by means of service, bore off the ball [2] of honour from his equals.

> By means of the club of service, the ball may be borne off.

Some days he used to take the Prince roaming the flower-gardens, and engage him till evening in pleasure and frolic ; and some nights, too, he used to pass in the gardens and places of amusement. Once upon a time a necessary journey befell the King, and he fixed his determination on starting, together with a body of his private servants. Summoning the Shoemaker, and intrusting to him afresh the Prince, he enjoined upon him a variety of precautions as to protecting the latter. The Shoemaker, having readily acquiesced in the King's commands, girt afresh the loins of servitude. Now the King had a garden in the outskirts of the city, like the glorious garden of Paradise, and a resemblance of the exalted realms above. The breeze from the intertwining ringlets of the violets therein, opened bags of pure musk, while the perfumer of the northern gales bore off sweet ambergris from its tangling musky curls. The sweet-scented plants of Paradise sought to gain freshness from the perfume of its dew-clad roses, and the flowers of the trees of Sidrah [3] and Túba borrowed splendour from the radiance of its heart-enrapturing trees.

---

[1] This rendering, which is very happy, is taken from Eastwick.
[2] See note 1, page 138. [3] Trees in Paradise.

In beauty the garden was like the Paradise above;
In that glorious Eden the roses were the eyes of nymphs.
The jessamine was Cup-bearer, the narcissus took the bowl in its hands;
The violet languished, and the red rose was mad with raptures.
The delicate hyacinth cast its ringlets o'er its shoulders;
The wind opened the lobe of its ears to the wild rose.
The strains of the nightingale and the sound of the partridge,
Plundered lovers of their patience.

The Prince most generally used to have a liking for the pleasures of this garden.
At the time when the King elected travel, the royal youth, as was his wont, had
desired to go into the garden, whence he set out, together with several of his
servants and dependants, who used always to attend on him. The Shoemaker
saw that this day the Prince had a jewelled crown upon his head, and on his
bosom a garment set with gems. His mean nature and low disposition inflamed
him with treachery and deceit, and he thought to himself: "This garment and
crown are capital for a hundred merchants; nay, more, the stock of a thousand
oceans and mines. At present his father happens to be away from the capital,
and his mother, together with all the people of the Haram, are at ease concerning
me. It seems expedient that I should carry off this boy, and having borne him
to a far city, should sell his ornaments and clothes for a high price, and pass
the rest of my life in ease and comfort."

Having found an opportunity arise, esteem it a chance:
Fortune turns her face to you; let not go her hand.

Ultimately that inconsiderate wretch, from the lust of his treacherous soul, raised
the fire of evil, and spilling the reputation of integrity upon the ground of
cruelty, schemed against his own lord's son. He revealed this secret to a discreet slave, who was in his confidence, and with a kind of medicine he caused
each of the attendants to drink of insensibility. The Prince, too, being bereft of
consciousness, he put him to sleep in a large box, and when night arrived, tied
the same upon the back of a quick-going she-camel, whose rapid pace was
applauded by the quick-revolving moon, and whose nimble footsteps were
recognised by the world-bestriding Spheres.

In swiftness outstripping the Spheres;
In speed equalling the moon herself.
Sometimes preferring to descend like a torrent;
At others, disposed to ascend in the air like vapour.

He himself mounted on a dun-coloured steed, which rushed along like the life
of the prosperous, and arrived, as it were sudden death. In its flight it kept
pace with an arrow, and made lightning furious with its cantering. If the reins
had been intrusted to it, it would have carried off the ball[1] of superiority from
imagination; while if they had shown it the whip, it would have leapt from the
terrestrial globe to the vault of the Heavens.

From the ruin following on its footsteps and hoofs where it paced,
A mark was placed upon the cheeks of the moon, and the back of Pisces.
In rapidity of pace it was not inferior to the Heavens;
The breeze was no antagonist for it.

[1] See note 1, page 138.

He mounted, too, the slave upon another horse, journeying like the wind, iron-biting, lightning-resembling, thunder-sounding, and world-bestriding.

> Earth-encompassing, like hope; wide-stepping, as it were pride;
> Quick-paced, like youth; and precious as the soul.

Having made ready two other spare horses, and taken provisions and food, they set out on their way, and ere day was resplendent had traversed a long and far distance. At dawn resting a little while, they again mounted, and, like lightning, commenced eagerly to traverse the road, and passing a long way beyond the limits of the King's dominions, reached another kingdom. On the other hand, the attendants and slaves remained senseless, and did not awake till mid-day. Ultimately, the gardener being apprised of their condition, poured in the brains of each oil of almonds with vinegar which had been kept a long time, till they recovered consciousness. When they saw no trace of either the Prince or the Shoemaker, they set out towards the city, and disclosed the matter to the boy's mother. The Queen, having mounted, came to the garden, but no perfume of that beautiful Rose reached her nostrils.

> I went to the garden, but my graceful cypress was not there;
> Nor was there that smiling, new-blossomed rose-bud of mine.
> Like a spring cloud, I wept on every side,
> Since that cypress did not appear before my tearful eyes.

But when the mother found no tidings of the Light of her eyes, she drew a cry of lamentation, and raised to the Heavens her note of sorrow, and enjoined that all day they should traverse with the foot of quest the sides and regions of the garden, and search the outskirts and environs of the city and kingdom. When, after boundless investigation and endless inquiry, the way to the abode of their desire was not by any means reached, the scouts returned in despair, and represented the condition of affairs. The Queen's tender, delicate disposition melted from the fire of separation, and, taper-like, she was consumed with the flame of his absence. From the state of her condition the purport of this verse was understood:

> "I am this night so distracted in my head, that I will not sit down from off
>   my feet,
> Till I have thoroughly consumed my existence like a taper."

All night long she passed in anguish of heart till morn arrived, and her distress of mind having reached a climax, she heaved a cold sigh from her bosom, filled with grief, and said :—

> "I am like morn—one breath is left with which to see my friend;
> If my beloved does not display his face, I will waste my soul like a taper."

At length the mandate,[1] "_Return to thy God_," having arrived, the taper of her life was quenched with the blast, "_Whatever is therein must pass away._"

> He went from this rose-garden, and the thorn of regret for him remained in
>   my foot.

The attendants on the Haram represented to the King the state of thing which had occurred, and his Majesty having returned to his capital, rested there his

---

[1] I expect there is a play upon words intended, as the term rendered "mandate" also means "moth."

dignity, and grieved and lamented to the utmost extent possible the loss of his wife and child. At length, having placed his head upon the line of resignation, he assumed a habit of patience.

> In such a state, when I referred to wisdom, my guide,
> He said: "There is no refuge, save indeed we return to him."

But the Shoemaker having borne the Prince to the kingdom of Damascus, after seizing his jewels, sold him to a merchant, in whose company for ten years he grew and increased, till by his beauty he ruined the market of Egyptian Joseph.

> What was Joseph? Yet they bought him for a like weight of musk.
> You are worthy to be purchased with souls.

Whenever that delicately-nurtured Cypress used to go forth from his house, a thousand hapless wretches scattered their souls on the highway of supplication, and in every nook and corner raised the hand of prayer for the long life of that erect form.

> Whatever road he traversed, in order to avert the malevolent eye,
> A thousand hands were raised in prayer from their sleeves.

The Merchant was a discriminating and able man, possessing profound sagacity and judgment. He said to himself: "The company of this slave henceforth will neither be beneficial nor advantageous to me, since if I keep him concealed at home his existence is much the same as if he had no being, while if he issues forth from my house the fire of evil is raised, and no one has power to look on that face.

> My beloved has arrived. Beware, O spectator!
> Close your eyes, if your soul be of service to you.

"It is expedient for me to take this slave as a present to the King of Fárs, for he is a beneficent sovereign, who will assuredly present me with twice the value of the Slave." Thereupon the Merchant, bringing him to Fárs, left him as an offering to the King. After he had been separated from his father's bosom for ten years, and, like a full moon, had reached his fourteenth[1] stage—

> I have a beautiful and sweet idol fourteen years old,
> For whom the full moon has willingly placed the ring in its ear—

he once again reached the capital of Fárs. The King, unconscious as to its being his son, agreed to honour the Merchant's gift with acceptance, and sent the boy to the circle of his private slaves, and day by day bestowed on him increased favour, till in a little while he was distinguished above all his fellows. He formed an intimacy with a Jeweller, who was always in attendance in the Treasury, and to whom were intrusted valuable gems and ornaments. To this Jeweller he always paid regard, and sent to him a portion of any present which the King gave him. But when the Jeweller saw how thorough a confidant the Slave had become, his mean nature conceived a crude desire, and he said to himself: "I will delude this Slave to bring me the King's private seal, by the aid of which signet I will plunder the Treasury, and extract from thence an abundant store, and precious valuables." Accordingly, he said to the Slave: "O beloved! every day you expend varied kindnesses upon this humble servant;

---

[1] See note, page 468.

now I am desirous by some acceptable service to requite some of them. The King has on his auspicious seal a signet, such that he into whose hands this engraving on the seal falls attains absolute sway, and the kingdoms of the world are insured to him.

> You would say the engraving on his seal was the signet of Sulaimán.
> Whoever possesses it, the kingdoms of Jam[1] come within the ring of his sway.

"If you will give yourself this trouble, and at a time when the King is indulging in the delightful sleep of repose, take that ring off his finger, and bring it to me, so that I may, on your behalf, remove that engraving, soon the couch of sovereignty will be adorned with the glory of your beauty; but on the condition that you allot to me the duties of Minister."

> Bestow upon me a morsel from the tables of your bounty.

The Jeweller by these representations deceived the Prince, so that at night-time he went into the King's bed-chamber, and extended the hand of audacity towards the King's finger, and gently removed the ring. The King awoke, and said to the Slave, "Why are you thus rash, and of what use is this seal to you?" The Prince was powerless to explain, and the fire of the King's wrath being aroused, he summoned an executioner, and ordered the boy to be killed. The executioner first of all stripped the clothes from his bosom, when that black mole appeared on his shoulder. The Monarch, on seeing that spot, became senseless, while the executioner withdrew his hand from punishment. When the King recovered his senses, he kissed the head and eyes of his child, saying: "O light of my eyes! the company of that hypocritical Shoemaker has brought me into the flames of separation." The son, too, asked pardon, exclaiming, "The friendship of a Jeweller has impelled me to this impropriety." The King severely reproved the Jeweller, and advised the Prince for the future to fold up his skirt from associating with worthless people, so as not to be overtaken with the like of such circumstances.

"The moral of this story is, that it may become evident to the King's illustrious mind that the company of evil-dispositioned persons will make the King a slave, and his servants desolate. Now the Goldsmith is of the class of those whose society must be avoided. The fact is, the King has favoured him to a degree of excess, and it is expedient that he should observe moderation in promoting him and giving him authority, lest a fearful misfortune thence arise, to remedy which will be beyond the limit of possibility." The King paid no regard to the Minister's words, but said: "Sovereigns, without the instruction of Fortune, do not commence an affair, nor without the assistance of inspiration do they plunge into dangerous undertakings. In what way do lofty connections and ancient lineage concern a man's personal honour and perfect disposition? Indications of virtue and courtesy, not the vain glories of descent and family, are the cause of respect, and the ground of reverence and veneration.

> Let thy bosom glory in thine own merit;
> Lay no store on thine ancient lineage.
> Seek not lustre in ancient jewels;
> When a pearl is old it becomes yellow-faced.

"That person may be considered noble and great whom the King of the time selects;

---

[1] Solomon.

and one of the mighty monarchs has said: '*We are fortune: whomsoever we have raised has been exalted, and whomsoever we have overthrown has been laid low.*' Whomsoever we advance, his exalted head is raised beyond the brow of the Lesser Bear; and whomsoever we debase, the star of his fortune tumbles into the abyss of contempt. If the breeze of our kindness blows upon a marsh, it becomes the envy of the rose-garden of Paradise; and when the lightning of our anger scatters its fire, it consumes a thousand harvests of esteem.

> Whomsoever kings drive from before them,
> Are dashed from the summit of the Spheres to the Earth.
> When they cast the eye of morn upon any one,
> They remove from him the coarse garment of severity.

" We have advanced this youth, and have exalted the brow of his dignity to the pinnacle of honour, and it is to be hoped that our expectations concerning him will not be falsified." The Minister, seeing that the King was determined to favour him, held his breath, and did not again oppose what he said. But when several days had elapsed, the Goldsmith, seeing the hand of power opened, placed his feet beyond the circle of moderation, and with hopes and fears, with promises and threats, commenced to take possession of men's property. One day, with the view of decking the King's daughter, some jewels were needed, but the kind desired could neither be found in the Royal Treasury, nor procured in the Jeweller's mart. The Goldsmith, busying himself searching, ascertained that a Merchant's daughter possessed precious gems of this nature. He despatched a person to her in quest of the jewels; but she put forward a refusal, and though they pressed her to the utmost it was of no avail. In short, they summoned her, and the Goldsmith said to the King's daughter: "I have heard that this Merchant's child has some royal pearls, such that since the Jeweller of the Spheres arrayed in splendour the glittering pearly grains of the stars in the emerald dome of the Skies, no jewel of such pure and brilliant water has been seen, and since the nurse of the Ocean nourished a rare pearl in the cradle of the shell, the diver of sight has not beheld the like of those unique gems.

> Like Venus in beauty and brilliance,
> It carried off the prize from the moon in splendour.

" And in her possession are some rubies of beautiful water, which the shining sun, like a mother, has cherished with a hundred pains in the womb of the mine, and which the flinty hill, in spite of all its hardness, has guarded in the hollow of its bosom with a thousand favours.

> Like [1] drops of wine which in time of winter
> Become congealed on the pearly glasses.

" And she possesses several pieces of delicate green emerald, such that the eyes of the spectator, in enjoying the sight thereof, are dazzled, and the pupils of the eye, on beholding that charming green, are filled with splendour.

> The light of the eyes is increased thereby, and I am sure,
> That from its delicate green the eye gains lustre.

" In her jewel-casket, too, are several red-coloured rubies, which, like the pomegranate of Persia, sparkle in the sight of the beholder; and several turquoise of

---

[1] For مانل in the Persian text I read مانند.

beautiful colour and purity, such that the Spheres acquired their delicate hues from the complexion thereof.

> Her rubies were indicative of cornelian-coloured Canopus;
> Her turquoise were typical of the azure [1] Heavens.

" The Queen must command this girl to bring those jewels, and sell them to us at the price of the day. If she will not willingly and readily assent, they must be obtained from her by harshness and severity." The Queen enjoined on the Merchant's daughter to bring her jewels. The girl took an oath——"I have not got such gems;" and produced a few pieces which she possessed. The Goldsmith did not approve of them, and impelled the Queen to punish her. The King's daughter was intoxicated, and bereft of sense by the cup of folly—'*They are deficient in intellect*'—and the wiles of the Devil befriending her, and the pride of sovereignty and prosperity, as well as the instigations of the passions, aiding the adoption of violent measures, she gave the order for the Merchant's daughter to be put upon the rack, and, in a short time, that helpless miserable wretch, by the wound of the eagle claw of punishment, fell into the clutches of death. The relations of the Merchant's daughter raised a cry and plaint to the summit of the ethereal skies. The pure-hearted Minister represented this circumstance upon the tablets of the King's mind. From the smoke of infamy which issued from the window of the Haram, the cell of the King's bosom became darkened, and by way of conciliation he caressed the heirs of the Merchant's daughter, and giving them much wealth satisfied them, and casting his daughter from his kindly regards, abandoned patronising the Goldsmith. By the disgrace of keeping company with that base tyrant, the famous Princess fell from the rank of trust; while the Goldsmith, fearing the King's revenge, fled. The girl's mother deemed it expedient that the child should go away for some days from the city, and remain in the King's Pleasure-garden; [2] and when the lightnings of the storms of the regal anger should subside, and the flames of the royal world-consuming rage be quenched, she should, on the intercession of some of the favourites, come to the Haram. The girl went forth to the Garden, [2] while the Goldsmith, being apprised thereof, came to attend on the royal maid. When the Princess saw the Goldsmith, she commenced to be distressed, and said: "O ill-starred, evil-visaged wretch!

> 'Twere shame were one to look on a wall,
> Whereon your effigy had been drawn.

" Have you returned so as to raise another sedition? and will you employ some stratagem by way of greed and self-interest? Go! for to meet you again is painful to me, and for me to carry on conversation with you is out of the region of possibility." The Goldsmith, having no hopes as regards the Princess, departed, and setting out towards the desert, went along perplexed and distressed. Night came on, and a dark cloud placed its black curtain over the expanse of the air, and quenched the lamps of the stars. The hapless Goldsmith, at this time when the dust of indigo was sifted over the expanse of the earth, and the dark-coloured ink was poured on the waters—

---

[1] سبر in the Persian text is a misprint for سبز .

[2] It is clear, as suggested by Eastwick, that چارباغ in the Persian is intended for چارباغ, the name of a celebrated royal garden in the environs of Ispahán. A few lines lower down it is again spelt differently.

> A night black like the face of an Ethiop;
> The rays of night reached the back of the moon—

moved along distracted. By chance, in that plain a pit had been dug with the view of catching beasts of prey, and a Tiger, an Ape, and a Snake had fallen therein. The Goldsmith, who had dug a pit of violence for men, having arrived in that direction, fell into the hole at the animals' heels.

> O thou! who by oppression diggest a pit,
> Thou makest a hole for thyself.
> Do not encoil [1] thyself like a silk-worm;
> Reckon what thou art doing as regards thyself.

The throng which were at the bottom of the hole, through their own distress, did not injure one another, but remained some time in the same condition at the depths of the pit, till one day a Traveller, from amongst the inhabitants of the city, having determined to make a journey, passed by them, and witnessing those circumstances, became distressed in his mind. He thought to himself: "Anyhow this man is a son of Adam, who has been overtaken in this calamitous misfortune, and is in nearer proximity to the desert of death than the abode of life. Manliness demands that, in whatever way is possible, I should release him, and as a reward of such proceeding, lay up a store on account of '*The Day in which neither wealth profits nor children.*'" Thereupon he let down a cord. The Ape clinging thereto reached the top of the pit; on the next occasion the Snake got the precedence; the third time the Tiger struck his claws into the cord. When these three reached level ground, they implored a blessing on the Traveller, saying:—

> It is the act of Fortune, not our own endeavour, if sometimes
> Such as you gratify your desires by aiding us suppliants.

"You must know that you have placed and laid upon each one of us a great obligation and immense favour, and it is not possible for us at the present time to make return or requital for the same." The Ape exclaimed: "I live at the skirt of that hill which is nigh the city; if you will be good enough to honour my home with your auspicious footsteps, the way of gratitude will have been observed." The Tiger said: "I, too, have taken up my abode in the neighbourhood of a town, in such and such a plain; maybe, if you pass that locality, according to my power I will perform the rights of service." The Snake added: "I have made choice of a habitation in the walls of a city; when you honour me with a visit, and Fortune aids me, I will, to such degree as may be possible, make amends for this kindness: and now we give you advice, to listen to which is obligatory upon you—viz, do not bring that man out of the pit, for he is a faithless person, and deems it incumbent to recompense good with bad. You must not be deceived with his external beauty, nor rest secure from his inward malignity and the impurity of his disposition.

> Abandon appearance, cling to purity of nature; since
> Man is a figure in reality worse than beasts.

"Most persons of the age busy themselves decking their exterior, to the neglect of their inward grace; therefore,

---

[1] That is, "do not wind round thyself the cords of thine own treachery."

To the eye they are like Joseph, but at heart wolves;

"more especially this man, who has been our companion, for some days, and whose character and disposition we have well gathered. Assuredly we have not seen on his brow the signs of generosity, nor have we inhaled from the rose-garden of his nature the perfume of fidelity.

Seek not fidelity from beauties, since no one ever inhaled,
In any way, the perfume of fidelity from the rose-garden of the Heavens.

"If you do not avail yourself of what we say, it will one day happen that you will repent what you have done." The Traveller paid no heed to their words, and let down the rope, and not listening with the ear of acceptance to disinterested advice, brought the Goldsmith to the top of the pit. The Goldsmith expressed his apologies to the Traveller, and repeated somewhat of the King's unkindness, and his own distress. At the same time he requested that he would pass one day with him, might be he could make some return. The Traveller said: "I have now placed down the foot of reliance upon God in the way of intention, and purpose journeying about the world for two or three days; but I make a pledge that, if Fate spare me, and the decree of Destiny be issued, I will again honour myself with your society."

If life permits, I will again place myself at your service.

With this promise they bade adieu to one another, and each betook himself to his own way. The Traveller set out on the road, while the Goldsmith returned to the city, and concealed himself in a nook. The King, regretting his having patronised the Goldsmith, and ashamed that he had not listened to the advice of his Minister, paid no regard to his daughter, and much as the great men endeavoured to intercede and made their requests, they did not reach the place of acceptance. So a year elapsed from these occurrences, and the Traveller, having visited some of the countries and kingdoms, and acquired three hundred golden coins, at length a longing after his native soil came over him. He thought to himself: "Although in my wanderings matters have answered my expectations, and from hour to hour my prosperity in this world, and my happiness in the next, are on the increase, yet the atmosphere of my native soil is more in harmony with my feelings, and the water of the springs of my birthplace more agreeable to the palate of my soul."

Though cases for narcissus are made of silver and gold,
Yet for a narcissus its native soil is best.

Accordingly, he turned his face from exile towards his own abode, and at night-time, arriving at the skirt of the mountain where the Ape dwelt, he alighted. The night was a little spent, when two murderous, mischief-making thieves, such that the dagger-brandishing Mars avoided their bosom-piercing arrows, and spear-lifting Arcturus, through dread of their soul-destroying sword, drew across his face the shield of fear—

Like the eyes of beauties, full of malignity and slaughter;
Their swords sharpened to slay mankind—

arrived at his pillow, and taking possession of the money and chattels which he possessed, tied his feet firmly with the folds of a lasso, and thus bound, cast him in a fearful gully apart from the highway. The hapless wretch said to himself:

" As yet when you have still the breath of life, and can read an inscription from the pages of existence,

" It is no place for complaining, but rather for giving thanks."

All night long the Traveller lay bound, and bowed his neck to the decrees of Fate, and the Divine mandates.　At time of morn he became powerless, owing to the agonies of his hands and feet, and commenced crying:

> " If my heart make a complaint, I give it vent,[1]
> But I do not see any one to help me."

He dropped tears of sorrow from his eyes, and with anguish of his distressed heart he lamented, saying: " Alas! I am annihilated in this whirlpool of affliction, and no one is aware of my condition; and in addition to all this soul-consuming anguish, I have fallen into the vortex of destruction, and no perfume of remedy reaches the nostrils of hope."

> In this distress, whose heart burns for me, consumed in soul?
> Save my own heart, there is not any one at my side to burn in sympathy
> 　　for me.

At this time the Ape came forth in search of food, and passed in the neighbourhood of that gully.　He heard a dreadful noise, and perceiving from that sound the perfume of acquaintance, he went into the gully, and came across the Traveller.　When he saw his friend bound in the meshes of calamity, he poured blood-stained torrents from the fountain of his eyes, and said: " O beloved friend! how have you fallen into this place, and what is the state of your case?"　The Traveller said: " O dear comrade! in the mansion of worldly adversity no favour of delight arrives without the anguish of pain, and in the ruins of treacherous Fortune no wealth of pleasure is procured without the deadly[2] wound of grief and misfortune.

> No one in this shop enjoys honey without the sting;
> No one plucks fresh flowers without the thorn in this rose-garden.

" Whenever any one is aware of this point, and the truth of this state of things is disclosed to him, he must not, like an autumn cloud, drop tears of distress at the anguish of the thorn of the world's injuries, nor, like the season of spring, break forth in joy by reason of the splendour of its fresh rosy cheeks, since neither is its grief fixed, nor its joy certain."

> In this existence, which quickly decays,
> One must not be enchanted either with life or death.
> It makes us taste water, and seats us on fire;
> It bestows somewhat, and snatches it back.
> It gives, it takes away, and has no shame:
> Its sole occupation is giving and taking.

He then fully related the matter of the thieves, and how they had snatched off his money, and cast him there bound.　The Ape said: " Rest assured; since,

> ' There is much hope even in despair;
> The end of dark night is bright.'

---

[1] Literally, " it arrives."　　　　　　　　　　　　　　[2] Literally, " dragon."

" I will endeavour to the extent of my power to remedy this misfortune; but the most important matter is securing your release." Thereupon he tore the Traveller's bonds, and conveying him to the home which he himself had made of sticks and straws, produced fresh and dried fruits, and requested : " Do not to-day issue forth from this abode, but, with mind at rest, lay your head upon the bed of repose till I return." Having quitted the presence of the Traveller, he tracked the thieves' footsteps, and followed after them ; while they, having borne off the goods and money, journeyed all night long, and at morn, wearied and fatigued, reached a spring ; sleep overpowering them, they removed from their backs the Traveller's chattels, and fell asleep, dozing with hearts secure and minds at ease. At breakfast-time the Ape came up with them, and finding them off their guard, availed himself of the opportunity,[1] and tore open the load of clothes. First of all carrying away the bag of gold, he removed it to a corner, and, concealing it in the earth, returned. They were not as yet awake from their sleep, so he bore away another portion of the Traveller's garments, and hid them in a certain locality. Ultimately carrying off all the Traveller's chattels, together with some of the thieves' goods, which were within his power, he put them in a certain place, and afar off betook himself to the top of a tree to watch their proceedings. When a time had elapsed the thieves awoke from sleep, and not seeing any indication of either gold or chattels, perplexed and astonished, commenced to run in every direction. One of them, who in excellence of judgment was superior to the other, said : " O brother ! this spring is not a thoroughfare for mankind—moreover, no traces of persons' footsteps appear on the outskirts of the spring : this state of things can in no way proceed from a human being. I am strongly of opinion that this fountain is the resort of demons and fairies, and we having imprudently come here, and, stretching our hands and feet, having fallen asleep, this proceeding has occurred on the part of their tribe : there is even ground for gratitude, that they did not arrange to destroy us, and it is expedient for us as quickly as possible to take to flight, and running along, to bear away the half life which remains to us."

> There is in this waste a region of demons ;
> The house of the heart is narrow, but the soul's grief extensive.
> Whoever is disposed to remain in this desert,
> Sometimes his soul will freeze, at others his spirit will melt.
> Whoever reposes in this path,
> Will either lose his head or his cap.

The thieves then, with hearts full of fear, betook themselves to flight; while the Ape, being easy in his mind at their departure, returned to his own house, and related to the Traveller the state of affairs. That night he watched over the Traveller, and at morn, when the thief of night clad in darkness took to flight, owing to the fountain of the radiant Orb, and the traveller of the world-encircling Sun, escaping from the snares of obscurity, set out on its destination—

> When there was displayed in the expanse of the Heavens,
> A clear ball of gold from beneath a mass of earth—

the Ape led the Traveller to that spring, and brought forth the money, clothes, and what he had seized from the thieves. The Traveller was content with his own share, and would not take their goods ; but, bidding adieu to the Ape, set

---

[1] عنيمت in the Persian text is a misprint for غنيمت.

out towards the city. By chance his path lay in that waste wherein was the abode of the Tiger, who appeared from afar raging like a ferocious Lion. The Traveller, dreading him, was anxious to avoid him, but the Tiger exclaimed, Rest secure."

I still remember to be grateful for your bounties.

He then advanced, and made most earnest apologies to him, and requested that he would halt an hour. The Traveller, according to the desire of the Tiger's heart, stayed; while the latter wandered in every direction in search of an offering worthy of his guest, till he arrived at the palace in the King's Pleasure-garden,[1] and entering, saw a damsel, who, sitting upon the edge of a fount, had priceless ornaments round her neck. The Tiger with one blow of his talons deprived her of life, and bringing the decorations to the Traveller, apologised to him. The Traveller, too, returning courtesies for his kindness, set out towards the city, and thinking over the affair of his acquaintance with the Goldsmith, it occurred to his mind : " I have observed the fidelity of beasts and animals, and their acquaintance bears this much fruit : if the Goldsmith gains intelligence of my arrival, assuredly he will display varied exultation when I appear, and will deem it incumbent to take much pains in discharging the dues of hospitality. By his aid and assistance these genuine gold coins can be sold at their full value. And this ornament, which is a magazine of gems, will pass for a good price, since his experience in this matter, and his knowledge of the value of each of them, is greater than that of other persons." It was morn when the Traveller arrived at the city. At that time the tidings of the death of the King's daughter had reached the town, and the populace, filled with alarm, went towards the King's court. The Goldsmith, too, with the view of investigating the matter, came forth from the corner of his retirement, desirous of seeing one of his friends, and inquiring the circumstances of the case. Suddenly he observed the Traveller, and rejoicing to the utmost, brought him with reverence and honour to his own home. After the customary inquiries, he once again repeated in detail what had befallen him, as to his being banished from the King's service, and the decline which had occurred in his dignity, and the amount of money and possessions which had gone from his hands. The Traveller consoled him, saying : " O brother ! if as regards your means of support some deficiency has appeared, and the pillars of your prosperity are shattered with the blast of adversity, grieve not, for I have several gold coins, and possess, too, some ornaments comprised of many jewels ; now you are a man of experience as regards judging of gold and pearls ; be good enough carefully and considerately to sell them, and take whatever you will, for it will be of no consequence." The Goldsmith sent for the ornaments, and when he looked, beheld the decorations of the King's daughter. Putting on an open face, he said to the Traveller : " The value of these jewels is more than the arithmetician, reason, can manage to reckon. Be of good cheer, for this very hour I will set your heart at rest : remain here at ease till I return." The Goldsmith then thought to himself : " I have found a fine opportunity, and obtained a rare chance ;[2] if I act carelessly I shall spoil matters, and remain deprived of the benefit of caution and wisdom. Hitherto the King's disposition towards me has been changed, and at this time, when the news of his daughter's murder has been conveyed to him, assuredly he is distressed and sad, and in quest

---

[1] See note 2, page 475.　　　[2] عنیمی in the Persian text is a misprint for غَنیمی.

of the girl's destroyer. No means is better, than for me to make over the Traveller to the King's hands, so that he may retaliate on him : perhaps the King, being satisfied with me, I shall again advance to my (former) dignity." He then determined upon perfidy ; and going to the court, proclaimed, "I have caught the girl's murderer, together with the ornaments." The King having summoned him, and seen the decorations, sent some one to fetch to his presence the Traveller, who, hapless, when he saw the course the affair had taken, said to the Goldsmith :—

> Thou hast slain me in friendship, but no one has destroyed,
> At any time, in enmity, any person more piteously.

"This is my condign punishment, and my retribution a thousand times such." The King thought that he was the culprit, and spoke these words to compensate for his misconduct ; and the ornaments, too, verified that suspicion. He ordered that he should be led round the city, and after being confined, next day, when they had finished the dues of torture, he should be delivered over to death. At the time that he was being conducted round the town, the Snake from the top of the walls opened the eyes of contemplation. When he saw his friend in that plight, he followed behind ; and after that they had thrown him into prison he approached him, and learning the state of affairs, cried out saying : "Did I not tell you that a bad-natured man has no fidelity, and in return for kindness and friendship indulges in insincerity and cruelty ? You would not listen, and the very day that you turned aside your face from the words of your comrades, and paid no heed to advice which was free from the suspicion of self-interest, I perceived that the termination of your case would end in regret."

> I severed my desire from Farhád[1] that very day
> When he gave to the palm of Shírín[1] the reins of his distracted heart.

The Traveller said : "O dear friend ! at present nought but anguish of heart and distress of mind will arise from the salt of reproach, which you scatter on my wound, and it is sufficient grief to me that from not listening to that advice,

> "I have became a reproach to the city, and a disgrace also to mankind.

"Now devise a remedy which may ward off this misfortune and cure this calamity." The Snake said : "Yesterday I inflicted a sting on the King's mother, and all the city are powerless to heal it : keep this grass, and at early morn, when they come to you, and seek a cure, go and wait on the King, and after that you have repeated the particulars of your case, give her this grass, that she may eat it and be healed. Perhaps in this way freedom and delivery may come to pass." The Traveller expressed his acknowledgments, while the Snake returned to his hole, and at morn coming to the roof of the King's palace, cried out from a window, "The cure for her who is bitten by the Snake is with the innocent Traveller, whom yesterday the King put in prison." At this time the Monarch was sitting at the pillow of his mother, and grief for the death of his daughter was added to sorrow for the wound of his mother : he was taking counsel with the physicians, in regard to the cure for the Snake's poison, and though they used as remedies antidotes and banes for the poison, it was of no avail. When the sound reached the King's ear, he said, "See what person is on the roof, and whence he speaks these words." Much as

---

[1] A celebrated Persian statuary, who, to please his mistress, Shírín, dug through an immense mountain.

the doorkeepers searched they saw no man on the roof, and it was imputed to this, that a voice from the Invisible World had given forth that sound. They brought forth the Traveller from prison, and bearing him to the King, busied themselves verifying the matter of the remedy. The Traveller said: "O King!

> May perpetually your Court of Justice, and excellent Majesty,
> Be the High Altar of the necessitous desires of the World's inhabitants.

"The cure for this poison is in my possession, and this very moment the Queen of the World will get perfect health. I desire first of all to convey to your Majesty's ears somewhat of my distressed condition, and it becomes the King's justice for an instant to open the ears of intelligence to listen to the state of the oppressed."

> So sleep, that a lament will reach your ears,
> If the suppliant for justice raises his cry.
> In this abode whoever is not awake,
> Is not worthy to govern the world.

The King's heart was alive to the correctness of the Traveller's words, and he kindly said, "Repeat your case from beginning to end, and without fear tell your whole story." The Traveller, by reason of the boldness appertaining to those who speak the truth, bravely narrated his history, and his certificate of innocence respecting that crime was established in the King's illustrious mind. Having then added that grass to some milk, they gave to the Queen to drink, and immediately traces of recovery appeared; the King clad him in a robe of honour such as became the royal condescension. The Goldsmith underneath the gallows, was expecting that the Traveller would be immediately put to death, and the gold coins remain with himself, while he would attain with the King the same rank and dignity which he formerly possessed. All of a sudden the King's mandate was issued, to the effect that the Goldsmith should be led to the gallows in the place of the Traveller. Now the result at that time of unjust imputations was simply this—after that a calumniator overwhelmed a certain person with misfortune, when the falsehood thereof became clear, and the malignity hid under cover of such a proceeding evident, there was inflicted on that lying traitor the very same punishment which he desired in regard to the suspected injured individual. In like manner they led to the gallows that ungrateful, faithless wretch, who had neither seen the face of generosity, nor inhaled the perfume of magnanimity, and cleared the expanse of existence of the disgrace of his impure person, which was an aggregate of treachery and wickedness, and the source of cruelty and injury, and he met with the retribution of his deeds, and the punishment of his actions.

> In this house of retribution, whoever does wrong,
> Affects his own soul, not those of other persons.
> If you wish for prosperity, be upright;
> Always, too, act rightly, and be honest-minded.

Such is the story of Kings, as regards the selection of intimates, and the investigation of the circumstances of those appertaining to them. If the Sovereign of Aleppo had not patronised that bad-dispositioned, mannerless person, his daughter would not have overwhelmed an innocent party in destruction, nor by way of retribution, have been herself slain with the tiger's claw; while if he had not opened his ears to listen to the words of the oppressed sufferers, he would not have distinguished right from wrong, nor truth from falsehood. It behoves kings not without circumspection to patronise any one, nor inconsiderately to issue a decree of punishment against any person; but they must know of a certainty that righteous conduct is never wasted, while the punishment of evil-doers is in no case entirely deferred : therefore, at the time when the Chamberlain, Fate, has exalted the court of their fortune, and the Divine Monarch has left with them the chance of prosperity and sovereignty, they should strive that conduct should proceed from them such as may be the cause of worldly reputation, and the means of everlasting dignity and salvation.

The Heavens are every instant looking down upon some particular person,[1]
And Time gives at every turn the earth to some one.
Since perpetual prosperity is not to be conceived,
Happy is he whose name endures for ever.

[1] That is, first on one person then another, never continually on one individual.

BOOK XIV.

ON THE WANT OF KINDNESS IN THE REVOLUTIONS OF TIME, AND ON BASING ONE'S AFFAIRS ON FATE AND DESTINY.

INTRODUCTION.

HEN the Clime-adorning King heard this story replete with benefits, which was a store filled with the jewels of wisdom, and a treasury charged with the coin of admonition, he was heart and soul obliged to the perfect and able sage, and said :—

> O thou ! such that the thirsty souls in the desert of desire
>   have found,
> In the Ocean of thine enlightened nature, the pure water of
>   wisdom ;
> With the hand of thought thy radiant mind has removed,
> To-day, for the thousandth time, the veil from the beauty of
>   knowledge.

"The trouble that your Excellency, possessed of wisdom, has had in my service,[1] has passed all limit, and the excess of my importunities has reached the bounds of want of manners, and it has wellnigh come to pass that the tent-ropes of your sublime language have been severed. Since you have been good enough to apprise me of the purport of the thirteenth precept, and I have heard a story regarding kings and their patronage of companions and dependants, and have been informed of the evils springing from the society of the low and mean, now you must be kind enough to repeat the pith of the last precept. On this point you must recount why a learned, beneficent sage, and thoroughly wise man, should be bound in the snares of calamity, and broken down with the wound of

---

[1] I am somewhat doubtful as to the accuracy of this translation.

misfortune; while a base, ignorant person, and careless fool, passes his life in ease and comfort,—neither wisdom and ability aiding the former, nor folly and ignorance overthrowing the latter. Again, tell me by means of what stratagem advantage is attained and misfortune warded off: by what device one can be blessed by the auspiciousness of happiness, and by what remedies the road to the abode of one's desires can be traversed." The Brahman replied: "O King! there are preludes and means of prosperity, which when any one procures, he becomes worthy of dignity and might, and deserving of honour and majesty; but the results and fruits thereof are dependent on Divine Power, and the Almighty decree and Royal command are the origin of all. According to the exigencies of Destiny and Fate, means and ways may be vain and fruitless, since many wise men, though worthy of fortune, have been deprived of food sufficient for a day, while numerous ignorant persons, without the aid of dignity or might, have sat on the couch of chiefship.

> The treasure of royalty is given to the mean,
> While men of merit do not receive even half a loaf.
> The base get the chief seats, while men of wisdom,
> Even by mistake, are not allowed a place at the threshold.

"Assuredly this state of things is dependent on nought save Divine decree and the Almighty command. Though any one may be possessed of sound wisdom, by aid of which he can provide himself with support, or has a business wherewith he can procure means of existence, or is extremely handsome, so that ensnaring people's hearts, he can obtain advantages for himself, when Divine Fate is not in harmony therewith, he will reap no reward, nor experience much results from these forerunners of merit, beauty, wisdom, or perfection. A royal Prince wrote upon the gates of the city of Nustúr a certain proposition, the memory of which is held in remembrance: and as regards those words there is an elegant story and sweet tale." The King inquired, "What was that?"

---o---

STORY I.

He said: It has been related that in one of the regions of Rúm, there was a prosperous King, and a Monarch of exalted power.

> Great in wisdom,—of lofty ambition;
> Mighty in arm,—of intelligent mind.

He had two sons adorned with varied charms, and graced with different virtues.

> One by his gentleness caused hearts to rejoice,
> Another by his justice made souls flourish.

When the King accepted the invitation of the Almighty (and said) "I wait your commands," the elder brother seized the treasury of his father with the hand of might, and with the noose of courtesy and attention, bringing within the snare of his possession the hearts of the Pillars of the State, and the Nobles of the Court, and capturing them with perfect dissimulation and blandishment, sat in the place of his father.

> At a fortunate time, the happy-fated king,
> Like as his father, sat on the throne.

When the younger brother saw that the Phœnix[1] of Sovereignty had cast its shade upon the head of his elder brother, which reached the stars of Heaven, and that the leader, Fortune, had intrusted the reins of the steed of Time to the grasp of his power and might, through fear lest he should raise treachery in regard to him, placing the chattels of travel upon the Camel of flight, he accepted the anguish of exile and the dangers of travel, and bearing off a provision of grief and lamentation, set out on his road.

> I am sick of my own city, and intend to set out on travel;
> Save grief for you, I am not aware what provision I have.

The Prince alone pursued his way for long and far, and at the end of the day, having arrived at a stage, lamenting and bewailing his solitude and exile, he exclaimed :—

> "Every two strides have caused my eyes to become a fount of trickling blood;
> In what manner shall I proceed, if such be my first stage?"

In short, he passed that night in solitariness. Next day, when the exquisite charmer, the Sun, showed its beauty from the curtain of the horizon, and the Mistress of the West blazed forth upon mankind, from the veil of blue, her shining cheeks and resplendent face—

> The wheel of the Heavens opened the door on the Sun,
> And adorned the face of the earth with radiance—

the Prince determined to start. A Youth, sweet - faced, with curling locks extremely fresh, and excessively comely, joined him. The Prince looked and saw a lovely boy, upon whose form, you would say, the garment of elegance had been sewn, the heart of the moon being consumed from sparks of envy at his beauty. The down on his chin sprouted like fresh violets upon the edge of a delicate rose-leaf, or a circle of moist ambergris drawn upon the page of a dewy tulip.

> His beard was like ants round a rose,
> Which gathered portions of ambergris from the hyacinth.
> The down on his chin cast a chain round the moon;
> Wisdom itself lost its head by reason of his beard.

When the Prince beheld that heart-ravishing chin, and those lustrous cheeks—

> The down grew marvellously; his cheeks were resplendent,
> Like the verdure of Abraham[2] which sprang from the fire—

he said to himself: "Perhaps by the aid of the company of this young man I can bear the burden of the distress of separation, and under the shade of this rosy-cheeked cypress may find security from the glare of this fiery desert."

> Wandering is pleasant for him who has such a companion.

Accordingly those two jessamines of the expanse of youth, and those two plants on the rivulets of existence, were delighted with each other's company, and

---

[1] See note, page 159. [2] See note 3, page 363.

imagined the desert filled with anguish to be the Garden of Paradise, and fancied that the thorny spot of distress was the pleasure-affording region of Elysium.

Though when your ringlets come within my grasp there be pain and anguish,
Still I would disdain the condition of the Nymphs of Paradise;
And without you, were I summoned to the expanse of Heaven,
The abode of the blessed would cause distress to my heart.

At another stage, a Merchant's Son, clever, experienced, of sound judgment, far-seeing, and truly wise, such that at the fitting time, with his perfect wisdom, he used to bind the thread of Night upon the neck of Day, and at a period of negotiation, by his penetration and ability, obtain the true coin of the Sun from the four-sided market of the Spheres—

A clever companion, and sweet-tongued;
Endowed with talent, able, and skilled—

joined them, and the resemblance of happiness came to pass on the appearance of that trio. The third day a Rustic's Son, powerful and vigorous, who possessed universal experience in matters of husbandry, and perfect skill in details of agriculture, the happiness of whose art in farming reached such a pitch, that every dry stick which he planted in the ground arrived at perfection like a plant, and yielded fresh fruit, and whose auspicious steps in rustic labour arrived at a point, that when he put his foot on any spot, it yielded produce without his placing seed therein—

The garden, owing to him, became fresh and verdant;
The field, through his means, was decked—

became their companion. By these four pillars, which joined together, the house of association was completed, and the saying—"*Four friends are good*"—was evidenced. The sympathising friends, through joy of one another's companionship, forgot their grief for beloved ones and native country, and journeyed stages and distances; with the sight of one another, also, they were comforted, and quiet at heart.

Whoever associates with friends,
Is in the midst of a rose-garden even when in a furnace.
Whatever you seek is secured by companionship;
Neither your tongue will avail, nor your hand.
The heart derives nourishment from every friend,
The soul gains purity·from every creature.
By intercourse with every one you derive advantage,
And from sociality with each individual you reap benefit.
When star is linked with star,
Behold how the traces of both increase in glory.

After traversing a far distance, they arrived at the city of Nustúr, and selected a good halting-place in the outskirts thereof, to rest and ease themselves. None of them had any provisions or food remaining, nor possessed either a diram or dínár. One of the companions said: "It is now expedient for each of us to display his skill and ability, and by labour and effort obtain a feast and bounty, so that we may live in comfort for some days in this city." The Prince said: "Matters depend upon the Divine decrees, and a man by toil and endeavour will not occasion any variation therein. Therefore, they who are wiser amongst mankind, assuredly will not plunge in search of ought, nor sacrifice their precious life for filthy trash, which, notwithstanding its transitoriness, has many enemies.

> This world is like carrion,
> Round which are thousands of vultures :
> This one strikes that one with its claws,
> That one darts at this one with its beak ;
> Till at length they all fly away,
> And all that remains is this carcass.

"The provision which is allotted in the workshop—'*We divided amongst them their means of support*'—will not be increased by means of greed and avarice; the result, too, of the proceedings of the covetous is nought but misery and exposure."

> Though we obtain possession of many dainties,
> How can we enjoy more than what is allotted to us ?
> Therefore, in pursuit after that which is not destined for us,
> Why undergo all this anxiety ?
> Follow the path of contentment, and be satisfied ;
> Lay aside greed, and be happy.

The handsome-faced Youth said: "Beauty is a reliable adjunct in attaining bounties, and elegance is a powerful means of acquiring property and possessions. Whenever the letter Jím (J) in the word Jamál (beauty) shines forth, Mál (property) follows thereon; and whenever Zá (Z) in the word Zaráfat (elegance) is displayed, Ráfat (grace) and kindness will be added thereto."

> Though a man be destitute, if he possesses a handsome face,
> Wherever he passes all eyes will be upon him.

The Merchant's Son, too, read an inscription from the pages of his condition, and said: "The capital of beauty at the market of business is a fleeting coin, and in a short time nought of capital or interest will remain in one's possession. The advantages of right judgment, and the benefits of sound deliberation, experience, and commercial industry, are preferable to all means; and whoever knocks the foot of sustenance against the stone of poverty, no remedy thereof will avail save the results of wisdom; and whoever has no capital of subsistence remaining, no help will be of any assistance save skill in transacting business."

> If your proceedings be based upon wisdom,
> The door of ease of mind may be opened upon your chattels.

The Rustic's Son said: "Wisdom and deliberation will not avail on every occasion, nor will benefit be derived therefrom at all times. If knowledge entered into the acquirement of wealth, it must needs be that they who are superior to the rest in learning, and surpass others in judgment and wisdom, would raise the standard of prosperity in the expanse of sovereignty, and would plant the tree of their happiness upon the brink of the rivulet of monarchy. But we have seen many wise men confined in the prison of want, and observed many who, not having inhaled the perfume of the rose-garden of ability and skill, yet disport themselves in the pleasure-grounds of wealth and luxury. Hence it has been said :—

'The Heavens intrust to a foolish man the reins of desire.
Are you a man of wisdom and merit ?   This is merely your fault !'

" Therefore the blessings of occupation, and the auspiciousness of enterprise, render men prosperous and happy, and a person, by means of merit, and the advantages of skill, becomes adorned with the ornament of pleasure and delight."

> Labour, so that you may gain money,
> Since by wisdom you will acquire nought.
> The King, notwithstanding he possesses a throne and crown
> Yet has need of the money of artisans.

When the Prince's turn came to reply, they requested : " Do you, also, once again explain somewhat of this matter, and dilate to some extent on the purport of this conversation which has passed between us."   The Prince said :—

> We will not mar the reputation of poverty and contentment.
> Say to the King, that his daily portion is predetermined.

" I am of the same idea as previous to this I have sketched to you the details thereof ; yet I do not dispute the words of my companions, in that they say that a thing can be obtained with the ornament of beauty, the capital of wisdom, or adequate occupation ; yet I maintain that if the beauty of the decrees of Fate do not shine forth from behind the screen, the light-diffusing star of elegance will not rise from the horizon of prosperity; and till the Curator of Omnipotence opens the door of the shop of destiny, the chattels of knowledge and ability cannot pass current in the bázár of acceptance.   The advantage of the tables of occupation is a mouthful which, according to the charge of Divine Providence, is apportioned to the meritorious; and the benefit of occupation and agriculture is a cluster of provisions, which accrues to the labourers in the field of skill from the harvest of Omnipotent desire.   Save it be in accordance with the Almighty will, every inscription, which colour-mingling thought draws upon the tablet of imagination, will at the last be marked with ruin ; and every device, which the exerciser of deliberation puts forth, in the end will be tinged with fiction.

> Oh ! the many images which I have raised ! but it was of no avail ;
> My devices turned out mere fictions.

" Therefore it is certain that if the Most High God wishes it, the desire of every person will be gratified, without any toil or trouble; while if the Divine will is not in accordance with its attainment, endeavour and enterprise will avail nought.   Therefore the decree of the Almighty must be twined round the neck, and the head of resignation placed upon the line of Fate.

> The medicine for us is simply to rest content with the decrees of Fate.

" Just as that old Rustic who intrusted his affairs to Divine grace, in a little time attaining his object, was freed from the confinement of distress."   The companions inquired, " How was that ? "

STORY II.

He said: It has been related that in the city of Andalus was a Rustic, open-handed and hearted, whose agricultural proceedings were successful. Once upon a time his receipts were greater than his expenses, and he collected together three hundred dínár of money, with which capital of gold he was highly pleased, nor did he in any way spend an atom thereof even in necessary disbursements. Every day he used to bring forth the purse of money and count it, and by such joy-exciting yellow (coin) he used to make the lips of delight to smile.

> Yellow fruit was showered down thence,
> Which, like saffron,[1] was the source of joy.

One day, according to his usual custom, having reckoned the money, he placed it in the purse, intending to put it in a secure spot. A dear friend came to the door of the house, and called out. The Rustic, from fear lest he should come in, and become apprised of that resplendent-faced bride, which, according to the decree, "*Conceal thy gold*," it was incumbent to keep within the veil of concealment, did not properly take possession thereof, but, removing it, threw it into a water-ewer, and together with his friend, on account of some important business, set out towards the village. At the time of departure, he earnestly impressed upon his wife to prepare some food. When the Rustic had gone, the woman was anxious to make some soup. Seeing the ewer empty of water, she removed it, and coming to the door of the house, stood looking out for an acquaintance to pass. By chance the village Butcher, having come to the city with the view of purchasing an ox, arrived there. The Rustic's wife seeing he was a friend, inquired of him: "Will you give yourself the trouble to bring me a little water, and thereby discharge the obligations of neighbourship, and reap the reward of assisting one in distress?" The villager consented, and the woman gave him that ewer, wherein was that purse of gold. The Butcher, placing the ewer on his back, went to seek for water. On the road, finding that there was something moving inside the ewer, he made a search, and saw the purse of gold. With the utmost joy he drew it within the sleeve of possession, and said:—

> This is a prize which, without any anxiety of mind, comes to my embrace;
> Indeed the garden of Paradise is of no great account when obtained by manual labour.

"Praise and thanks to His Glorious Majesty! may his dignity be exalted! who, without the distress of toil, and the anxiety of trouble and worry, has bestowed upon me an abundant favour and bounteous reward. Now I must deem it incumbent to return my gratitude for this unexpected fortune, but, not neglecting my trade, I must store up this money for a day of necessity. Thereupon the villager, through delight at the money, forgot about the water and the ewer, and having with the gold which he had with him bought a young fat ox, set out for his house. When he came forth from the city, he reflected: "If I keep to myself this purse, I cannot remain safe from fear of thieves; while if I bury it somewhere in the city, owing to anxiety of mind and suspicious ideas I cannot remain happy, and I have no sufficient confidence in any one to intrust him with this as a deposit.

---

[1] Orientals, according to Eastwick, are much addicted to the use of saffron.

Seek not fidelity in this age, for it does not exist.

"My best course is to place this purse in the throat of an Ox, and so arrange that it shall go down his gullet. After that I have slain him, I will safely extract the purse of gold." He thereupon overwhelmed the hapless Ox with that torture, and, like the brazen calf, filled it with treasures of gold. He then returned to his own place. By chance, on the road, his son came to him, and recounted several other matters which had happened in the village, and which it behoved the Butcher to put to rights. The Butcher, with the view of performing the business, returned to the city, and intrusted the Ox to his son. At this time, the Rustic, together with his friend, had returned from the village. Some while previous he had vowed that he would sacrifice a fat ox; so when he saw so plump a calf, he took steps to buy it, and giving somewhat more profit than the Butcher's Son expected, he made a bargain, and bringing the Ox to his home, proceeded to sacrifice it. At this juncture the matter of the money reverting to his memory, he arranged to remove the coin from that place, and bury it in a secure spot. The more he searched for the ewer, the less could he find it. He inquired of his wife, "Where is the pitcher?" The woman repeated the circumstances of the case. Grief arose in the Rustic's heart, and the eyes of his cupidity wept through regret for his money, while far-seeing wisdom smiled at his ignominious condition.

The throng who weep on account of property and possessions,
Know thou, for certain, that they make themselves laughing-stocks.

The Rustic, for a while distracted, fell into the vortex of perplexity, and for a season was overwhelmed in the whirlpool of anxiety. At length he became resigned and consoled, saying—

We have let be, as to what his beneficence will do.

He then commanded that the Ox should be sacrificed. When the entrails came to be cleansed, his eyes alighted upon the purse of gold. He was distracted with joy, and when he returned to his senses, removed the purse, and cleaning it from filth, extracted the money. Every moment he took a coin, and kissing it, rubbed it upon his eyes, and returned it to its place, saying—

"May ruin never befall thy fortune!"

He then reflected within himself: "On this occasion, by happy coincidence, owing to this strange affair and curious marvel, which no eye has ever seen, nor ear heard, this gold has come to my hands. Henceforth the locality of this purse of money shall be nought save my girdle, and it shall not be conceivable for me to be without it for an instant."

I cannot imagine it possible to separate from you.
Why should any one part from his precious soul?

Henceforth that Rustic always carried that purse with him, for which his wife used to reproach him (saying): "This proceeding is far from the way of confidence in God, since to lay up a store is not to place any trust upon the Almighty Provider, and seeing that, according to the decree, '*Therefore seek your provision from God,*' daily food must be sought from the treasury of His beneficence; for he is truly wise who does not display avarice in the accumulation of property, but opens to the bounty of the Almighty the eyes of trust in God, of the tables of whose kindness no individual is without a share; knowing for certain that as regards his daily portion, whatever is allotted him by Fate, and the Divine decree has determined, will suffer neither addition nor diminution."

Since in the Cup of Fate neither more nor less is contained.

The Rustic said: " O wife ! in the world of causes there is no help but to contemplate means; externally, causes must be observed, while inwardly the wine of resignation must be tasted from the cup of confidence in God."

Do not disregard that it is a world of causes;
Contemplate these means, and place your trust in the Almighty.

The wife ceased her talk, and the Rustic, having bound the purse of gold round his waist, occupied himself at his business. One day he was performing his ablutions in a spring; and having loosed the purse of money from his loins, he placed it on the brink of the fountain. When he had done, having put on his clothes, forgetting the money which was there, he departed on his way. After him there arrived there a Shepherd to water his sheep, and seeing the purse of money upon the brink of the spring, he at once bore it off, and returned with the utmost joy and delight. Coming to his own home he counted it: there were three hundred dínár. He said to himself: " This money is just even; whatever I take therefrom will diminish the number, and perhaps again it will not reach the same amount. Of necessity I must exercise patience, and store this sum against the day of want." Accordingly that simple-hearted person, fixing his mind thereon, placed the money under his arm, and rubbing the dust of silence upon his lips, pursued his ordinary avocation as shepherd. But when the Rustic bethought himself of his gold, with a heart full of alarm, he began to drop tears of regret from his eyes, and with a hundred laments and anxieties, commenced to run from right to left.

Much he searched, but attained not his object.

Ultimately he returned to the house annoyed and grieved, and repeated the state of the case to his wife. The woman's heart was brimful of anger at her husband's story, and when she heard the particulars of what had occurred, she loosed the tongue of reproach, saying: " O imprudent man ! you guarded that money with the utmost diligence, and withholding the necessary expenditure, deprived your family of the means of support. Now lament and be sad with remorse for the same." The Rustic said : " You speak truly.

If we are overwhelmed with the pain of separation, we deserve it,
Since in the day of approach we did not express our gratitude for the boon.

" It was a pure mistake, and an absolute error, for me to have striven to acquire a hoard, and withholding it from my wife and family, to have laboured to the utmost to preserve it. No wise man acts like this, in binding a purse of money round his waist, and passing night and day in anxiety; while, on account of repose on credit, he is overtaken with the hard cash of grief, and suddenly from the workshop of Fate, a representation appears which was never on the tablets of imagination, and like myself, having fallen into the whirlpool of perturbation, he remains far away from the coast of deliverance."

He who has jewels, and yet continues to mine,
Risks his life for others.

> Often through riches your grief increases.
> Seeing you have milk and wine, why are you distressed ? [1]
> How long will you suffer misery in search after riches ?
> Strive to be content, and become distinguished.

Accordingly the Rustic indulged in repentance and remorse, and vowed that he would not again hoard money, but that whatever came to his hand, he would without loss of time, expend. Thereupon seeking acceptance with God by reliance on His will, he committed his affairs to the Almighty, and acquiescing in the decrees of Omnipotence, placed the head of submission upon the line of resignation.

> Remain quiet, and rely on the beneficence of the Creator.

On the other hand, the Shepherd, with the purse of gold under his arm, grazed his sheep. One day he was pursuing this very avocation on the brink of a pit, when suddenly a troop of horsemen appeared from afar. The Shepherd, in fear lest they should take the money from him, threw the purse of gold into that pit, and it being late in the day, made his sheep move homewards. After he had left, the Rustic was proceeding to a certain place. The wind began to blow hard, and sweeping off his turban, cast it into that very pit. The Rustic quickly descended therein in search of his turban, when all at once the purse of gold came to his hands.

> He sought for amber and found a ruby.

Having returned thanks to God, he went back, and narrated the history of that money to his wife. When the Rustic had counted it, and found just the three hundred dínár, he exclaimed : " Lo ! the Most High God has returned to me from the Invisible World the very amount which He hid from me." Thereupon, in discharge of the vow which he had made, he commenced to expend the money. Some he spent upon his family, and some he disbursed on behalf of God, till two hundred dínár were lavished away. But after the Rustic had departed, the Shepherd, having set his mind at ease regarding the sheep, at night came to the pit's mouth, but did not see his radiant-faced Joseph therein. Jacob-like, he raised a cry,[2] " *Ah, Joseph !* " and said : " After this loss, what profit is there to me from the capital of life ? and in remorse for this precious-loved object, what delight or pleasure do I derive from existence or being ? "

> I do not desire that henceforth the blessing of sight should remain to me,
> When my eyes are deprived of the grace of such a contemplation.

The Shepherd then wandered days and nights distracted and unhappy. After a while having come to the city, his path lay towards the Rustic's abode ; the latter, according to the wont of his benevolent nature, entertained the Shepherd as a guest. After eating food, they discoursed on every topic. The Shepherd recited a story, but traces of the utmost anguish were displayed in his words, and sometimes in the midst of his speaking, involuntarily tears of regret dropped from his eyes. The Rustic inquired the cause of his lamentation and anxiety of mind. The Shepherd said, " Why should I not be broken-hearted, and agitated in my soul ?

---

[1] Literally, "drink blood."   [2] نقیر in the Persian should be, I think, نفیر .

> Had Sulaimán lost what has passed away from me,
> Both fairies and demons would have bewailed for Sulaimán.

"You must know that I possessed three hundred dínár of gold, which were the support of my mind, the ease of my soul, the light of my eyes, and the joy of my breast. On such a day, through dread of several tyrants, I cast them into such and such a pit, and did not again find any trace thereof." The Rustic, on hearing these words, being distracted, jumped up, and going to his wife, said: "This wealth which we thought our lawful portion, and which, having extended thereon the hand of prodigality and dissipation, we have been spending without stint, was the property of this guest, and by reason of our negligence we have fallen into the whirlpool of sin and error. Now we must make over to him, by way of an offering, the little which remains; and be cautious not to disclose this secret, otherwise he will demand all the money, and we shall be powerless to pay it." The wife agreed with him in this view, and said: "What is due must be given back to the person entitled thereto; and we must be satisfied to be content, and rely upon Providence, till the Most High God shall give us something in place thereof."

> He who rests his convictions upon reliance on God,
> Will quickly see the face of his desire.

The Rustic, by way of a present, placed before the Shepherd the hundred dínár which remained. The Shepherd was obliged, and carrying off the money, counted it: there was just a hundred dínár. He said to himself: "This is the prelude to fortune, and I am in hopes that the remainder will likewise come to hand. I must now well protect this, so that it shall not again fall into such peril." Thereupon, having a stout crook, with which he used to tend the sheep when grazing, he hollowed out a portion thereof, and placed the money therein, so that no one should be apprised thereof. One day he was standing on the brink of a large river, when the crook fell into the stream from his hand: much as he sought to snatch it, he was unable. Now the current of that water went along by the gates of the city. The Rustic, who was performing his ablutions on the brink of the river, saw a staff which the water carried towards him; seizing it, he took it to his house. His wife was cooking, and had no sticks left; the Rustic commenced to break the staff so as to finish the cooking, when all of a sudden his skirt, like the dish of the heavens, became filled with fiery gold. He removed the money, and, counting it, there were a hundred dínár complete. He prostrated himself in gratitude, and once more opened the hand of prodigality and lavishness. Two or three days elapsed, and the Shepherd again arrived at the abode of the Rustic, and, more distressed than on the first occasion, repeated the matter of the staff and the hundred dínár. The Rustic inquired: "Say truly, whence did you obtain that gold which first of all was lost to you, and in what manner did you amass it?" The Shepherd recounted the circumstances accurately. "At such a time, at such a spring, I found a purse wherein were three hundred dínár of gold, and cast the same into a pit; then you yourself gave me as an offering this hundred dínár. The Rustic smiled, saying: "Praise and glory to God! who fixed what is right in its own circle! You must know that I myself forgot the purse at the spring, and also found it in the pit: the hundred dínár which I gave you were the balance thereof. Again, the staff came to my hands, and with it the hundred dínár which we have been spending."

The Shepherd remained perplexed, and said, " From the marvels of this story it is clear that no one can consume the portion of another."

" The moral from the recital of this story is, that you friends should not let the abode of contentment slip your hands, nor place your feet outside the circle of reliance on God ; you should not, too, be indifferent to the marvels of time, which result from Fate and Providence, but, prizing the opportunity of life, should place no trust in wealth and beauty, since the true state of matters is hidden and concealed behind the veil of Destiny."

No one is aware what the end of the affair will be.

In short, with this conversation they brought the day to a close. Next morn, when the divine Rustic displayed the hundred-leaved rose, the Sun, in the expanse of the horizon, with a hundred lustres and tints, and the musk-laden haycinth, dark Night, in the violet bed of the Spheres, drew the curtain of concealment across its face—

> Like a tulip, the face of the Sun shone from the Heavens ;
> The blossoms of the Stars were hidden from sight—

the Farmer's Son rose up, and said : " Remain quiet till I bring to your sight, this day, some of the fruits of my labour ; and to-morrow, when we shall be less tired, let each of you, according to his own plan, procure the means of support." The friends were agreeable to these words, and the young Rustic having come to the gate of the city, inquired, " In this town what occupation is best ? " They said, " At present sticks are valuable, and are bought for a high price." The young man at once went to a hill, and, taking a heavy load of dry wood, conveyed it to the city, and sold it for ten diram. After buying some pleasant food, he turned his face towards his companions. When he came forth from the city, he wrote on the gateway, " The result of one day's labour is ten diram." In short, the companions that day ate from the tables of the young Rustic some morsels of food. Next day, when the world-adorning beauty of the radiant Sun perfectly illuminated the dark Earth with the brilliance of its splendour—

> The world-adorning Sun, with open face,
> Pushed forth its head from the chamber of day—

they said to the beautiful-faced Youth : " To-day, by your beauty, contrive some plan which may be the means of repose, and the occasion of comfort to us friends." The young man arose, and, full of thought, went towards the city, saying to himself : " Nought will proceed from me, yet I cannot return without accomplishing my object : I am in great straits, I have neither face to conceal, nor courage to speak."

> My business was upset owing to your ringlets, and my difficulty is,
> That I cannot disclose to another my perplexity.

In such thoughts he entered the city, and, sad and anxious, sat down at the corner of a street. Suddenly a pure-faced woman, with dishevelled hair, who possessed abundance of wealth and boundless riches, passed by him, and seeing that enchanting face and captivating chin, gave the chattels of patience and restraint to the winds of love.

> Her heart became enamoured in a way
> That every hair broke forth into clamour.

She wrung her hands, and, dragging the veil from her moon-face,
Cast her heart-ravishing snares in his way.

She said to her damsel: "Look at this elegant-faced beauty, from shame at the freshness of whom the petals of the rose are abashed like a yellow jessamine, and enjoy the sight[1] of this charming form, from anguish at whose brightness and elegance the erect cypress remains with its hand on its head, and its feet in the mire.

My Cypress has come forth from the expanse of my soul and heart;
There is not the equal of that Cypress made of water and clay.

"If I were to describe that lip, it is a pearl mingled with sugar; and if I were to read the inscription of that chin, it is calamitous misfortune.

Good God! what face is this, and what chin?
Rose and verdure produced by the mercy of the Almighty.

"And in any case, '*This is not a human being; nay, more, he is a beneficent angel.*'

This beauty is not within the pale of mortal man.

"O damsel! devise some scheme whereby this august bird may fall into the net, and concoct a stratagem by which this delicate idol may come to my hands." The damsel consented, and approaching the young man, said:—

O light of my eyes, desire of my soul, who art thou?
Sweet-lipped, who? and sugar-like, who art thou?
From thy lips distraction has befallen the market of the Universe.
Anyhow, say of whose table art thou the salt?

"O charmer! my mistress has sent an intercessory message to you, saying: 'You appear lonely in this city, and persons who are desolate may be broken-hearted. I have a nice, pleasant spot, and a delightful abode; if you would honour me, and for a while regale me with your beauty, I shall find perpetual life, and you will suffer no loss.'" The young man replied, "I obey the command, and no apologies are necessary." He then went as the woman's guest, and spent the rest of the day with her.

The desires of his heart seized imagination by the rein;
Patience leapt from his bosom, like an arrow.
He saw a beautiful bride, and his heart was enamoured of her;
The oven being in a state of warmth, he shut in the bread.

In the evening he departed for his companions. The lady placing before him a hundred diram, made her apologies; and the young man, having got provisions for his comrades, wrote upon the gate of the city, "The value of one day's beauty is a hundred diram." Next day, when the merchant of Wisdom opened the mart of the crystalline Spheres, and revealed the gold-work brocade of the Sun, from the shop of the exalted Heavens, to the men of business of the World's market—

The jewel-scatterer of the Spheres poured down gold;
From the mart of the Heavens there issued a din—

---

[1] تماشا in the Persian text is a misprint for تماشا.

they said to the Merchant's Son, "To-day we will be the guests of your wisdom and ability." The Merchant's Son agreed, and repaired to the entrance of the city. All at once a vessel freighted with a variety of valuables came by water to the gateway, and the people of the city hesitated purchasing thereof, till the goods should become cheaper. The Merchant's Son bought the same at a fair price, and having sold them the same day for cash, gained a thousand dínár, and having prepared the wherewithal for his friends, inscribed on the gate of the city, "The profit of one day's wisdom and ability is a thousand dínár." Next day, when the king of the Stars ascended the throne of the fourth Heaven, and raised the ensign of sovereignty over the capital of the Skies—

> Morn, with silver garments and golden crown,
> Put on a diadem of gold, its throne being ivory—

they said to the royal Prince: "You are perpetually boasting of your reliance on God, and describing your resignation and submission. Now, if there be any reward to you from these qualities, you must make ready for us." The Prince met their words with acceptance; and with lofty ambition, and intention free from the suspicion of irresolution, set out towards the city. Through Fate, death had overtaken the king of the city, and men were engaged in lamenting for him. The Prince, by way of looking on, went to the King's palace, and sitting apart, remained still. The porter, seeing that all people were occupied with lamentation and crying, while one individual was seated silent in a corner, and not joining with them in their distress, conceived the idea that he might be a spy, and was harsh to him. The royal Prince, quenching the fire of anger with the water of meekness, was saying,

> " If a fool, through pride, acts harshly,
> Nought but gentleness will be displayed by me;
> And if, through displeasure, he raises a hundred cries,
> Such unkindness on his part will fall pleasant on my ears "—

when they brought forth the corpse, and the palace was deserted. The royal Prince remained in the same spot, and looked round the sides and quarters of the palace. The porter once again increased his insolence, and removed the Prince to prison. Night came on, and no tidings or signs of him reached the friends. They said to one another: "This hapless youth has raised the edifice of his affairs on reliance upon God, and since he has found no advantage from such a state of things, he has turned aside his face from our company; would that we had not imposed this task upon him, and had not distressed his blessed soul!" In this place they loosed the tongue of reproach, while in that the Prince, bound in fetters and in prison, was sending a message to his friends by the hands of fancy—

> "Convey tidings of me by the birds of the plain,
> Yet your voices, too, are encaged."

Next day the Chiefs and Nobles of the city, and the Supports and Pillars of the State, having come together, were desirous of allotting to some one the affairs of government, their King not having any heir. After consulting over this matter, they were deliberating on every point. The porter said to them: "Keep this matter secret, for I have captured a spy, and maybe he has also some companion: God forbid that they should be apprised of your dispute, and mischief hence ensue!" He then gave an account of the Prince, as to his being present,

and how he himself had treated him harshly. It seemed expedient to them to
send for him, and investigate the circumstances. A person went and brought
the royal Prince from prison to their presence. When their glance alighted upon
his kingdom-adorning beauty, they perceived that his face had no resemblance
to that of a spy, and that an act of such a nature would not proceed from such a
beneficent individual and noble personage. Having observed the dues of respect,
they inquired, "What is the cause of your advent, and of what city are you
born and bred?"

> With this form and elegance, whence come you?
> Sit down, if you arrive on account of our hearts.

The Prince gave them a reply in a befitting manner, and informed them of
his birth and family, and narrated the particulars of his father's death, and his
brother's usurpation. By chance, a body of great men happened to have been
in the service of his father, and to have seen this pearl of the royal shell in
a corner of the kingly throne: they at once recognised him, and recounted to
all the Pillars of the State the condition of his ancestors' sovereignty, and the
extent of their dominions. All the great men of that kingdom were delighted
with the sight of him, and charmed at his august appearance. They were
unanimous in saying: "He is worthy of the government of this country, seeing
that he has a pure disposition and unsullied descent, and without doubt in opening the doors of justice and benevolence on the subjects, he will follow after his
illustrious progenitors, and imitating their praiseworthy traditions and laudable
habits, and combining hereditary virtues with acquired endowments, he will
keep people at ease under the shade of his protection. The ray of Divine
splendour, which shines from his propitious brows, is a decisive proof and
clear indication of his merits for sovereignty, and his fitness to subdue kingdoms; and the signs of his monarchy, and the tokens of his fame, will not
be concealed from any man of judgment."

> If a person entertain any doubts as to the majesty of Sulaimán,
> Birds and beasts will smile at his wisdom and knowledge.[1]

They then, at that very time, inaugurated him; so the kingdom in this easy
manner came to his hands, and from the auspicious results of reliance upon God
he attained such good results. Whoever firmly treads the path of trust in the
Almighty, and unites sincerity of purpose with integrity of thought, having
obtained the results thereof in religion and worldly matters, will be gratified in
both palaces.

> If the key of reliance upon God comes to your hands,
> The door of the treasury of prosperity can be opened.
> With the club[2] of sincerity, in this court,
> The ball of fortune can be borne from the plain.

In that city there was a custom that kings, the first day, seated upon a white
elephant, should be carried round the city. In his case the same practice was
observed, and the Prince arrived at a spot where was a gateway, and seeing the
writing that the friends had inscribed upon the entrance to the city, ordered
that there should be added thereto: "Toil, beauty, wisdom, and skill yield fruit,

---

[1] See note 1, page 185.   [2] See note 1, page 138.

when Divine fate issues a decree in accordance therewith, and the case of one who at the first was fettered in the prison of adversity, and in the end sat in the palace of sovereignty, upon a golden throne, is sufficient as an example." He then came to the royal palace, and sitting upon the throne, the kingdom was confirmed to him.

When Fortune saw him on the throne, she offered her congratulations, saying :
" O thou ! who knowest how to sit upon the throne [1] of monarchy,
Like kings gird thy loins, and conquer the world,
The time of action has arrived, thou canst no longer remain doing nothing."

He then summoned his friends, and made the man of wisdom and ability copartner with the Minister of State, and appointed the Farmer's Son at the head of the estates and private possessions, while he bestowed upon the beautiful Youth a precious robe and endless wealth, and said : " Although it is arduous to separate from a dear friend, yet it is not expedient for you to be in this country, lest women be led astray by your heart-ensnaring beauty, and thence wickedness and mischief be produced." He then turned to the grandees of the assembly, saying : "Amongst you there are many superior to me in wisdom, bravery, merit, and ability, but a kingdom can be obtained by Divine favour and the assistance of the Almighty, as is understood from the saying, ' *Thou givest the kingdom unto whom Thou wilt.*'

O aim of the spirit of the great !
Desire of the heart of the suppliants !
By Fate comes servitude and royalty :
You give fortune to whomsoever you will.
If your grace does not show the way,
How can this road be opened by wisdom ?

" My companions have toiled at work, and have each acquired a small return, while I placed no reliance upon my own wisdom and strength, and did not seek aid from the help or assistance of any one ; nay, more, I reared the edifice of my proceedings upon reliance on God, and resigned myself to the Divine Fate and Almighty Power, and said :—

' The head of acceptance must be bowed, and the neck bent in obedience,
Since whatever the Just Judge does is pure equity.' "

From amongst those present an eloquent man jumped on his feet, and said : " The words which have proceeded from the King are pearls pierced with the diamond of wisdom, and gold tested upon the touchstone of learning, and there is nothing so befitting monarchy as wisdom and ability. Now, according to this showing, the merits of the King shine on all his servants like the Sun, and the Creator of the world Himself knows in what kind of manner a man's abilities should be encouraged. ' *God well knows whither He appoints His messenger.*'

From the tables of his unstinted bounty, every one,
According to his capacity, obtains a morsel.

" The happy fortune of the men of this country brought you to this station, and the potent destiny of the inhabitants of this region spread the propitious

---

[1] برغت in the Persian text is a misprint for برتخت .

shade of a Phœnix [1] like you on the heads of the broken-winged birds, your subjects."

> Blest abode! since such a Moon alights there;
> Auspicious spot! since the cheek of such a King comes in that direction.

Another got up, and graced his talk with praise of the King, whose fortune was in the ascendant, and his throne in the Heavens, and placing the pearls of these verses upon the platter of explanation, scattered them upon the royal brow.

> "O King! whose prosperous gold-bestowing palm,
> Cast a lasso round the bosom of the spheres of Fortune.
> There is security, as in Heaven, from the advent of calamity,
> To that country where your tent has cast its shade."

Thus each of the grandees spoke according to his station, and read a portion from the pages of kingly virtues. At length an old man, pure-minded and pleasant-speaking, rose on his feet, and after discharging the dues of praise and laudation, said: "O King! as regards the matter of Fate and Destiny, respecting which the pearl-scattering tongue of the King has described somewhat to the minds of the assembly, your servant has had experience: if the mandate, which all obey, should be honoured by being issued, I will repeat and recount it." The King said, "Disclose what you possess, and as to what this was."

STORY III.

The old man said: I used to be in the service of one of the nobles; when I recognised the inconstancy of the world, and was apprised of the treachery of this deceitful old woman, and perceived that the husband-slaying bride—the World—rendered many persons who were distracted with affection for her, in despair of gaining their desire, and that this perfidious wretched mistress overthrew numbers of foolhardy lovers, I said to myself: "O idiot! you are binding your heart in affection for one who has placed the hand of rejection upon the bosom of hundreds of thousands of prosperous monarchs, and given to the winds of annihilation the harvest of repose of so many famous sovereigns. Abandon this affair, and place not your house upon a highway, where any instant one must make ready to depart.

> Whoever well considers the ways and habits of the world,
> Will not erect therein a house for occupation.
> Why should you inhabit this old edifice,
> When at last you must leave it for another?

"Awake from the sleep of negligence, for time is short, and the steed of work lame. Take from short life some provisions, since the way is far and long, and the heat of the glare of the desert heart-melting."

> Seek that to-day in every corner,
> From which to-morrow you will derive sustenance.
> Your path will be afar, and the stages long;
> Make ready stores for the way, and provisions for the journey.

[1] See note, page 159.

Ultimately, on these thoughts, in which I indulged, my refractory feelings were subdued, and with the utmost joy and purity of intention, I betook myself to the matters of eternity, and turned my heels on the service of the world, and on the company of its inhabitants. One day in the market I saw a Fowler selling two doves, which, in language applicable to their case, were desponding together, and, distressed at being captured, were seeking of God the joy of freedom. I had compassion on them, and became desirous of buying them, with a view to my eternal salvation, and so that, delivering them from that snare, I might expect the fortune of escape from the confinement of Divine wrath. The Fowler priced them at two diram, which exactly I had in my possession. I was irresolute, and my feelings would not give me permission to spend those two diram. Yet my mind was intent on freeing the birds. At length I resigned myself to God, and buying both of them, bore them out of the city, and let them loose. Going upon the top of a wall they addressed me, and as is the way of the grateful, expressed their acknowledgments, saying: "At present our hand cannot manage to requite and recompense you, but underneath this wall is a small box filled with precious pearls. Dig away, and carry it off." I was astonished at what they said, and exclaimed: "It is a wonderful state of things that you see a box of pearls below the ground, and overlook a snare underneath a clod." They replied: "When Fate descends, the eyes of wisdom are darkened, and the day of minute-seeing intelligence becomes clouded. The requirements of Destiny cannot in any way be repelled, and at such time neither experience remains to a man of prudence, nor does sight advantage the wise. All this was because the execution of the Divine decree was included therein."

"This story is sound testimony to the words which the King spoke in regard to Fate and Destiny; and wise men, in confirmation of this point, have said—

' If your affairs are prosperous, it is not by reason of your deliberation;
If, also, they go wrong, it is not your fault.
Assume a habit of resignation and submission, and live happy,
Since the good and ill in the world are not ordained by you.' "

He then said: "O King! I searched under that wall, and obtained possession of a box of gems. I disclose this, so that the King may issue his august mandate, that it be conveyed to the royal treasury." The Prince said: "You have sown the seed, and reaped the fruit thereof. For any one to share with you in this matter is not fitting, and these pearls of wisdom which in this assembly you have strung on the cord of description are sufficient for me, since no gem can be better than charming discourse, and by the alchemy of conversation the copper of counterfeit coin can be rendered pure gold."

Say, O converse! whence is your alchemy?
Who is the Alchemist who produces your pure coin?
Whence proceed from you such images?
None, as yet, have exhausted your discourse.
I know not what bird is so beautiful as you;
Should a memorial of us remain, it would be yourself.

The attendants congratulated the Prince on his intelligence, and all at once bound their hearts in alliance with him, and placing their heads on the line of his commands, intrusted the reins of choice to the grasp of his power, and passed their time under the shade of his fortune,

> Until the time when their career was finished.

Such is the story of the advantages of reliance in God and resignation, and the results of Fate and Destiny. No wise man can escape from recognising this Power, since if he intrusts the reins of choice to the hands of Providence, he will obtain all that is good, for no affair of his will occur contrary to his desires, but in fact,

> Time displayed a thousand images, and there was not
> One, such as was in the mirror of our imagination.

And in the opening of this poem, how beautifully has it been said,

> " If Fate do not direct the affairs of mankind,
> Why do affairs prove contrary to our desires ? "

When the Brahman terminated this discourse, and with the recital of this story finished describing the precepts of Húshang, King Dábishlím, having performed the dues of thanks, said : " By the felicity of the spirit of the sage of exalted rank, the veil of secrecy has fallen from the face of my desire, and the object which I possessed has been attained, by the blessing of the society of this teacher of lofty station.

> Thanks to God that at any rate our efforts have not failed.

" Now I make a request, that the enlightened-minded Sage should accept an offering from me, and not refuse a present, which I have brought by way of sincerity." The Brahman said : " O King ! apart from the house of the World, I rest content with a nook and food, and have washed the skirt of my heart from the contamination of its affairs ; it is not possible that I should, in any way, once again be defiled with the impurities of its concerns.

> So long as I can be at rest from the World,
> God forbid that I should be defiled therewith !

" But if the King is anxious to do me a service, and place the collar of obligation round my neck, I hope that, having strung these wisdom-combining words on the thread of compilation, he will consider them his guide on the road of salvation, and his leader on the path of perfection, so that by this means constantly passing me through his lofty mind, he will not refrain his prayers ; since according to the saying, ' *The prayer of the just priest will not be rejected,*' the invitation of just monarch's prayers attain the honour of acceptance." The King agreed, and bidding adieu to the Brahman returned to his own capital, and stringing on the thread of composition the pearls of wisdom which he had obtained, he arranged them, and invariably in the occurrences of affairs used to appeal to the admonitions thereof, and in matters of importance to seek the aid of those precepts.

> He who follows the advice of the wise,
> Will ultimately reach the abode of his desires ;
> But he who turns aside from the path of those who act rightly,
> Will lose his way, and fail to find a trace of his object.

When Khujistah Rái had recited these pleasant stories, and incomparable tales, from beginning to end, Hamáiyún Fál, like a verdant rose, began to blossom on the carpet of joy, and the plant of his condition commenced to raise its head in the expanse of prosperity. By means of regal presents he infused hope into the Minister, the eyes of whose heart he enlightened by the attainment of its desires. He said :—

> O excellent are thy heart-enrapturing tales, the seat of delight for the soul !
> Thy salutary discourse increases the pleasure of the human heart.

"By the recital of these sweet stories you have afforded pleasure to the palate of my soul, and by recounting these speeches, which conduce to wisdom, you have sown the seed of eternal happiness in the soil of my heart, and henceforth the foundation of my sway will be nought save these perfect admonitions, nor will I recognise ought but these honest precepts as the basis of the house of my proceedings. These words have made a marvellous effect on my heart, and this is owing to nought save your abundant sincerity and rectitude ; since words, however radically good they may be, owing to the contamination of the speaker, lead to no beneficial result ; and exhortations, in spite of their springing from soundest wisdom, by reason of the foulness of him who utters them, produce no effect."

> If a man, with impure skirt, utters all that is proper,
> The bad through his beautiful language will not become better ;
> While he who is pure-minded, though he remains silent,
> Every one will gather advice from the honesty of his nature.

The Minister praised the King, saying : "What has flowed from the wise tongue of the Sovereign is the essence of sincerity, and the purest expediency ; since the words of men of hypocrisy and dissimulation have a false splendour, and in a little time die out, like the sparks of wormwood ; while honest and upright speeches, like the streaks of dawn, every moment increase in brilliance, and, as it were, the lantern of the sun, from hour to hour grow more brilliant."

> The words which flow from passion will not affect the soul,
> But if they proceed from the heart they take up their abode in the soul.

Once again Hamáiyún Fál caressed the Minister, and raised the standard of his Fortune to the pinnacle of the exalted Spheres ; while the Minister, seeing the traces of the King's worthy qualities, and the lights of the Sovereign's laudable disposition, reared the edifice of praise and thanksgiving in the following way :—

> "Thou, O King ! by the excellence of thy disposition,
> Hast taken the precedence over former monarchs.
> All hail to your faith and knowledge ! all hail to your justice and equity !
> All hail to your kingdom and fortune ! may they be enduring ! "

On these words the assembly ended. Hamáiyún Fál, too, following the example of Dábishlím, inscribed these pleasant stories upon the pages of his proceedings, and in erecting the edifices of benevolence observed what was equitable, and left upon the scroll of time the remembrance of a good name, and fair reputation.

> The sum of life is two things,—honest repute and good name ;
> When you proceed beyond these two, there is but ' *Whatever is therein is perishable.*'
> Follow not in the track of oppression, but gratify the wishes of mankind,
> For by these two actions you will attain happiness in both worlds.

Such were the several speeches which, according to the requirements of the time, the tongue of the pen has carelessly composed, and which in the way that the nature of the fare[1] demanded, were inscribed by the reed of explanation. My hopes in the benevolent disposition of the most excellent of mankind, and the fine qualities of the exalted chief,[2] are such that with the train of indulgence he will conceal the unweighed expressions and unacceptable phrases of this his abject slave, and that by reason of cherishing this atom, and fostering this poor wretch,

> Notwithstanding it is full of faults from head to foot,

he will view it with the eye of satisfaction.

> The pearls which I concealed in this bosom,
> One by one from my heart I placed on my tongue.
> Be they bad or be they good which I adduce,
> Conceal them under the skirt through thy beneficence.
> Since I have carried my speech to such a point,
> It is better that I should make an end of talking, and say farewell.

---

[1] Sir F. Goldsmid suggests that as the word in the original text means "a table upon which provisions are placed," it may be supposed to indicate in this place intellectual fare.

[2] His patron.

PRINTED BY WILLIAM BLACKWOOD AND SONS, EDINBURGH.

CPSIA information can be obtained at www.ICGtesting.com
Printed in the USA
BVOW08s0036110215

387247BV00018B/263/P